PRIMO LEVI

Born in 1961, Ian Thomson was one of the last to interview Primo Levi, and the first to journey in his tracks as a biographer. He is an expert on Italian literature and has translated the Sicilian crime writer Leonardo Sciascia into English. Thomson's account of Haiti, *Bonjour Blanc*, was highly praised in Britain and America. He is a freelance writer and journalist living in London with his wife and children.

Also by Ian Thomson

Southern Italy
Bonjour Blanc: A Journey through Haiti

Ian Thomson

Primo Levi

VINTAGE

Published by Vintage 2003

2 4 6 8 10 9 7 5 3 1

Copyright © Ian Thomson 2002

Ian Thomson has asserted his right under the Copyright, Designs
and Patents Act 1988 to be identified as the author of this work

First published in Great Britain in 2002 by Hutchinson

Vintage
Random House, 20 Vauxhall Bridge Road,
London SW1V 2SA

Random House Australia (Pty) Limited
20 Alfred Street, Milsons Point, Sydney,
New South Wales 2061, Australia

Random House New Zealand Limited
18 Poland Road, Glenfield,
Auckland 10, New Zealand

Random House (Pty) Limited
Endulini, 5A Jubilee Road, Parktown 2193, South Africa

The Random House Group Limited Reg. No. 954009

www.randomhouse.co.uk

A CIP catalogue record for this book
is available from the British Library

ISBN 0 09 9515210

Papers used by Random House are natural, recyclable products made from wood
grown in sustainable forests. The manufacturing processes conform to the
environmental regulations of the country of origin

Typeset by MATS, Southend-on-Sea, Essex
Printed and bound in Great Britain by
Cox & Wyman Ltd, Reading, Berkshire

For
Laura in London,
and
Laura in Rome

Over the hospital grey clouds move slowly northward,
And, inside, the nurses chart the human world's defeat.

Alan Ross, 'German Military Hospital',
The Derelict Day: Poems in Germany, 1945–1946

CONTENTS

ILLUSTRATIONS

PREFACE

When I arrived in Turin in early 1991 to start work on this biography, I had few contacts and was unsure how to begin. It is fantastically difficult to fashion a narrative out of the inchoate facts of someone's life. I knew, however, that Primo Levi had been an enthusiastic mountaineer. So my first move in Turin was to visit the National Museum of the Mountains. Unsurprisingly, there was little information of use there beyond some Fascist-era alpenstocks, plus-fours, and a stuffed ibex. Levi's widow, Lucia, had made it plain to me that she was unavailable for interview. I met her son, Renzo, for aperitifs in Turin. Like his mother and sister, Renzo was not prepared to be questioned about Levi. However, he wanted to confirm that while the family would not help, neither would they hinder my research.

From the start, I was determined to construct a life of Primo Levi not found in his books. It seemed to me dishonest, as well as dangerous, to recast Levi's printed words in a biography. Levi contrived some elaborate autobiographical fictions, and that is partly why he is such a difficult subject for a biographer. So I set out to interview as many people as possible; under no circumstances would I take Levi's own words as gospel.

Turin is a small city, and soon word got round. I was considered diligent (some reportedly said 'obsessive') and Levi's friends began to speak to me. Until then, my knowledge of Levi was confined largely to the interview I had conducted with him shortly before he died. Few biographers get to meet their subjects. The interview had provided me with an enduring image of Levi, and much of my research was informed by it.

Primo Levi was in shirtsleeves for our appointment, and the tattoo '174517' was visible on his left forearm. ('A typical German talent for classification,' he tartly observed.) It was a summer's afternoon in July 1986. Levi was then almost sixty-eight, but he still had a sprightliness about him. I had seen him earlier that year at the Italian Cultural Institute in London, where he gave a talk. Afterwards I contacted him for an interview, which I hoped to publish somewhere. I had already printed in the *London Magazine* several interviews with Italian writers, among them Italo Calvino, Natalia Ginzburg, Leonardo Sciascia and Alberto Moravia. Levi was to be part of a set. Throughout our conversation he sat in a worn chintz armchair, smoking the occasional 'Alaska' menthol cigarette. His beard was neatly clipped and he wore metal-rimmed glasses. The study, sparsely furnished, contained an anglepoise lamp, a word-processor and some other basic necessities for writing. Books lined the walls, a few in English. There were framed certificates from Levi's former profession as a chemist and, suspended above a glass-fronted bookcase, an owl, a penguin and a giant butterfly modelled by Levi out of industrial copper wire. For thirty years he had been the manager of a paint and varnish factory outside Turin. The only other ornament in the room that I could see was a sketch of a half-destroyed wire fence: Auschwitz.

In Italy, Levi is a national monument. I was twenty-four and nervous of meeting him. The Turinese, moreover, are considered by other Italians to be two-faced and frosty (*falso e cortese*, they say: 'false and courteous'). Yet the Levi I met was warm and engaging, a mixture of seriousness and sweetness. The afternoon was full of unexpected laughter, and there were moments when Levi became animated, for instance when the talk came round to mountaineering. I had decided to leave the question of Auschwitz until later, unsure how to approach it. Absurdly, I was fearful that it might distress Levi. I asked him instead about his science fiction and chemistry. Listening to the tapes of the conversation today, I am struck by how stock Levi's answers seem. Levi was a practised interviewee by the time I met him; he could professionally field questions on the Nazi scourge. The second half of the conversation centred on *If This is a Man*, which is now a set text in Italian schools. No other work conveys the unique horror of the Nazi genocide more directly and profoundly, or interrogates our recent moral history so incisively. For its quiet testimony of man's inhumanity to man, it remains one of the essential books of our age.

On my way out, I noticed a horseshoe nailed to the wall by the front door. An uncle had found it in the street, 'but I don't know if it's brought me any luck,' Levi commented wryly. I was thrilled when he added that the interview had given him 'much pleasure'. Nine months later, Levi was dead.

This book has been under way for some time. In the course of the five years of my research in Italy, Germany, Poland, America and the United Kingdom, I interviewed more than 300 people, and corresponded with half that number again. I had six long interviews with Levi's sister, Anna Maria. She is an attractive, unconventional woman with a sharp sense of humour. When she learned that I had met her brother, she seemed both moved and delighted. During our final conversation she announced, quite unexpectedly, that Aldous Huxley's second wife had not only been to the same school as Levi, but had lived in the same block of flats where he was born. I pursued the connection and found Mrs Laura Archera Huxley living in a Hollywood villa. She was able to tell me about the pre-war Turin that Levi had known as a boy.

In the hope of tracking down others who knew Levi, I placed advertisements in *Scientific American* and *Chemistry and Industry*. The response was good. A Jungian analyst in London contacted me, as did a biophysicist in Atlanta, and a Polish-born survivor in New Mexico. They had all known Levi, and all had interesting things to say about him. The biographer is also a sleuth, piecing together information, and attempting to trace witnesses. An Italian ex-deportee, Elena Simion, had been repatriated to Venice in late 1945 from the Soviet transfer camp of Katowice in Poland. She had briefly known Levi in Katowice. For the statutory fee of 30,000 lire, a clerk in the Venice births-and-deaths register was able to inform me that, while Simion herself was dead, her daughter Nadia was still living in the Veneto area. Nadia Hamilton had been born in Poland on 25 May 1945. Her father, Robert Hamilton, was a Scottish POW, who had also been repatriated from Katowice. I very much wanted to track him down, not just for his memories of post-war Poland (which I hoped might complement those of Levi in *The Truce*), but for his daughter's sake. Nadia had never met her father. I got as far as Woking, Surrey, before reaching a dead end.

Other quarry proved less elusive. The late Fulvio Tomizza was a gifted writer from Istria, the border region between Italy and the former Yugoslavia. My letters to his publisher had gone unanswered and he was not on the phone. So I went to Croatia on the off-chance of finding him. Arriving by taxi at the village of Materada, I asked where Tomizza lived and was given directions. He was raking leaves into a bonfire when I found him. 'You've come from *London*?' Over a bottle of local wine, Tomizza spoke to me of Levi and the difficulties I would surely encounter in writing about him. 'Primo's is not an easy life to enter,' he warned. Levi was noted for his determination to protect his privacy and for keeping secret what he wished to keep secret. He often surrounded himself with people who were not well known: they were factory-hands, wine producers, metalworkers. Most of them would enthusiastically respond to my requests for information. But in a few cases their memories of Levi proved to be uncertain, tainted by third-party reminiscences or just dimmed with the years. Unreliable sources were one of many pitfalls that awaited me as Levi's biographer.

One episode in my investigations stands out. I was scrolling through a collection of old newspapers on microfilm in Turin when I chanced upon an item that described the violent death of Levi's grandfather. This was a revelation. Engineer Michele Levi had been rushed to Turin's general hospital, San Giovanni Battista, in the summer of 1888. In its vastness and melancholy the hospital still resembles a military garrison, and is about as welcoming. It was a surprise for me to find that the admission registers for 1888 still existed; conserved in a dank wing of the building, they were freckled brown with age. Other lucky moments followed. When I originally contacted the Italian survivor Italo Tibaldo, who had known Levi, I was quite unaware that he had laboriously composed a transport list of the Jews who had been deported with Levi to Auschwitz. The list provided me with the dates of birth and nationalities of all the known deportees and allowed me to imagine something of that cattle-train's doomed cargo.

Inevitably, much of the material I gathered is of tremendous significance to the Jewish people. I am not Jewish, and perhaps this fact gave me a useful objectivity in writing this book. Levi hesitated to call himself a 'Jewish writer', and wrote of Auschwitz not from a religious standpoint, but from the broader perspective of a secular humanist. For all that Levi wrote of other subjects, it was the Nazi camps, and the moral and material ruins of post-Nazi Europe, that provided him with his enduring subject matter. There have been other massacres in recent times, but none so ferocious, so 'total in intention and effect', observed Levi, as that willed by Hitler's Germans in the heart of Europe. Even Levi's adored H. G. Wells, with his uncanny gift of scientific foresight, could not have predicted the industrialised killing of Treblinka or Auschwitz. We are still learning to understand the catastrophe to which Levi was witness. His life and work mirrored his time, and this biography places him within the larger frame of the twentieth century.

With Levi's death, European literature was deprived of one of its most humane and civil voices. His fame has grown subsequently, and now he is one of the most respected writers in the world. It was not long after he died that Levi was making an impact on other people's work. Philip Roth's novel *Operation Shylock* pays anguished, if comic, tribute to Levi's memory. Arnold Wesker, the East End London playwright, sent me a copy of his television play, *Breakfast,* in which he quotes from *If This is a Man* (it has never been performed). And Woody Allen surely had Levi in mind when he made his film *Crimes and Misdemeanours*: a philosopher named Louis Levy kills himself by leaping from a high place. 'I've gone out the window,' his note reads. Since adolescence Primo Levi had suffered from low spirits which later developed into a depressive illness. He was a difficult and complicated man. Yet he was loved by a multitude; I hope this book conveys some of the reasons why.

ONE

11 April 1987

THE ITALIAN WRITER PRIMO LEVI DIED TODAY FROM
A FALL DOWN THE STAIRWELL OF HIS TURIN RESI-
DENCE. POLICE SAID THEY WERE TREATING HIS DEATH
AS SUICIDE. HE WAS 68.*

Turin, Italy, Reuters

Some time between 10:00 am and 10:15 am on the morning of 11 April 1987 the commissariat at 73 Via Massena in Turin received a telephone call. It had been relayed from the police emergency number 113: there had been an accident. An ambulance accompanied by the police flying-squad proceeded to 75 Corso Re Umberto. This was a block of flats in a residential area of the city; the main doors were already open to let the police inside. In their first report to the Public Prosecutor's Office, dated that same Saturday 11 April, the police noted: '. . . Corpse found in vicinity of lift . . . Identified as Primo Levi.' The body had fallen fifteen metres head-first down the stairwell of the building and struck the marble floor at the foot of the lift shaft. Death was instantaneous.

Preliminary investigations ruled out the possibility of third-party involvement. However, there had been no witness to the last moments of Primo Levi's life. According to the police reconstruction, Levi opened the door to his third-floor flat,† stepped out unseen on to the landing and pitched himself over the railings. He fell in silence. The time of death was approximately 10:05 am (and not, as the Italian newspapers reported, 10:20 am or 10:30 am). This would have been about ten minutes before the police arrived on the scene. One of the last to have seen Levi alive was Jolanda Gasperi, the concierge.

---

*He was actually three months short of his sixty-eighth birthday.
†This corresponds to the fourth floor in United States convention.

I

Nineteen days after the incident, on 30 April 1987, she was questioned at the Via Massena commissariat. A small grey-haired woman, her recorded testimony is unnaturally stilted, owing to police formality: 'I confirm that I perform the duties of concierge at 75 Corso Re Umberto.' So begins the transcript. 'At about 10:00 am, after sorting out the post, I went to the residence of LEVI the writer, which is situated on the third floor of the aforesaid address, and personally delivered his post. I then went to the main entrance hall of the building to do some work. I was about to start sweeping when I heard a thud from the small lobby by the stairs. I went in there at once and saw the body of LEVI on the ground, adjacent to the base of the lift.' Jolanda Gasperi tried to telephone the Red Cross for an ambulance, but her call went unanswered. At that point a man entered ('the owner of the cleaning company, I don't know his name') and dialled 113 for the Police Central Operator. After the police and ambulance arrived, the concierge called Primo Levi's son, Renzo, on the intercom and told him what had happened.

Renzo Levi, twenty-nine, a biophysicist, was living in the flat next to his parents. In spite of the proximity he had heard nothing of the commotion downstairs. Levi's daughter Lisa, thirty-eight, a biology teacher, lived nearby in the same neighbourhood: she arrived soon afterwards. The speed with which the flying-squad reached 75 Corso Re Umberto was due to the absence of traffic that morning; many had left Turin for the long Easter weekend. Everyone agreed that 11 April 1987 was an unusually bright day; after months of rain the horse-chestnuts along Corso Re Umberto were showing the first spring buds.

According to one journalist's report, Jolanda Gasperi had said to Primo Levi that morning: 'Have you seen what sunshine there is today, professor!' Many people addressed Levi as *professore* (he held no such title; it was a mark of deference). Gasperi was just ten days younger than Primo Levi; born on 10 August 1919 in the nothern Italian province of Trentino, she had worked at 75 Corso Re Umberto for the last twelve years.

That Saturday, as was her custom every morning at ten o'clock, Signora Gasperi had left the porter's lodge with a bundle of post for any occupants who were still in. Milan's *Il Giorno* says she took the wide granite stairs by the lift; making her way past the brass name plates and double wooden doors, she routinely delivered parcels and envelopes. Presently she reached the third floor and rang the bell to flat 3A. Primo Levi opened the door and extended a hand for the correspondence. 'No, there was nothing in particular,' Gasperi told the Rome daily *La Repubblica*. 'Some publicity leaflets, a book, a magazine. Nothing, I mean, that could have upset him.'

In her long years as concierge, Jolanda Gasperi had got to know Levi well.

A week earlier he had signed her copy of his latest book: 'With friendship and esteem'. As far as she could remember, there was nothing untoward in Levi's behaviour that spring morning. 'He greeted me as he had always done. A smile, a thank you.' *La Repubblica* also quotes Gasperi as saying: 'I knew that he had been depressed for some time. But he never betrayed his condition – his sadness – to me.' From *Il Giorno* we know what Levi was wearing that morning: a white short-sleeved shirt, grey trousers, black shoes.

Jolanda Gasperi had returned downstairs when, scarcely five minutes later, she heard '*un tonfo*', a thud. At that moment only Primo Levi's mother, Ester, and a nurse, Elena Giordanino, were in the flat. 'I wasn't aware that anything had happened,' the nurse told a regional newspaper. 'I was busy looking after the elderly lady.' In fact the two women were in the room furthest from the entrance; no sound would have reached them from the third floor landing of the stairwell. Giordanino was also questioned at the Via Massena commissariat. Born in Turin on 26 October 1930, she opens her testimony in the usual formal way: 'I confirm that I am a nurse and that, from the month of August 1986, I have carried out my duties at the residence of PRIMO Levi* the writer, where I assist his mother, Ester, aged ninety-two.'

The transcript continues: 'The writer PRIMO Levi, after having been discharged from hospital where he had undergone a prostate operation, was extremely disturbed. In fact he sometimes asked if he would ever be entirely cured, as he found it difficult whenever he had to receive visitors. On 11/4/87, as I had always done at about 8:00 am, I gave him his usual injection, then I continued my work. At approximately 10:00 am Levi called me; he asked me if I would stand by the telephone as he had to go downstairs to the porter's lodge.' It would appear that Levi had wanted to ensure that the only mobile person in the flat at that time – nurse Giordanino – could not accidentally distract him from his awful task. 'From that moment I never saw Levi again,' the nurse went on. 'I only became aware of what had happened when LEVI Renzo, his son, arrived at the residence accompanied by police officers.' Prompted by another question, the nurse repeats herself: 'I confirm that the writer LEVI Primo was very disturbed. In fact sometimes I would see him sitting with his head in his hands, thinking.'

So it seems likely that the nurse, and not the concierge Jolanda Gasperi (as the Italian newspapers claimed), was the last person to see Primo Levi alive. Levi's wife of forty years, Lucia, had gone out shopping that morning at

---

* Sometimes the police transcript records 'LEVI Primo', and at others 'PRIMO Levi'.

about 9:30 am. She had not yet returned when Gasperi's cry for help alerted Francesco Quaglia, seventy-two, a dentist who had known Levi since school and had an office in the same building. (Whether Quaglia is the owner of the 'cleaning company' mentioned earlier by Gasperi to the police is not clear; he was responsible for administering the condominium.) 'It was a terrible sight,' Quaglia told *La Repubblica*. 'One look was enough: there was no hope.' Levi's wife came back laden with groceries. Reportedly both Quaglia and the concierge tried to hold her back. 'We didn't have time to shield her from the spectacle,' explained Quaglia. Lucia embraced Quaglia. 'Primo was depressed,' she repeated to him. 'You knew it, too, didn't you?'

All the Italian newspapers allude to Primo Levi's depression, or to some sort of mood disorder, in his last months. One of them quotes his wife as saying: 'I feared it, everybody feared it. Primo was tired of life . . . We did our best never to leave him alone, ever. Just one moment was enough.' *I feared it, everybody feared it.* Allegedly those were Lucia Levi's first words as (according to the august Milan newspaper *Corriere della Sera*) she 'flung herself down beside her husband and tried to lift his head'. Presently the police were joined by forensic detectives; someone had thrown sawdust on the marble floor by the lift, where a small pool of blood had gathered. Levi's mother apparently had intuited a calamity. The Turin daily *La Stampa* claims she cried out: 'What's all this coming and going . . . this disturbance . . . has something happened? . . . Primo . . . has something happened to him?' She was told that her son had been taken to hospital following a heart attack.

There is a brief, hand-written note from the doctor called in by the police to the scene of the accident: 'Confirmed hereby the decease of Primo Levi as the likely result of suicide. Faithfully, Dr Roberto Mandas. 11/4/87.' Signed on-site at 75 Corso Re Umberto, this is the first mention in any official report of a self-inflicted death.

Well-wishers, friends and relatives gathered outside the apartment building. Some placed orchids and forget-me-nots where Levi had fallen; there were so many floral tributes that Jolanda Gasperi had to remove them to the porter's lodge. The Italian Communist newspaper *L'Unità* tried to capture the sense of shock and bereavement. 'Just as the concierge is closing the main doors half-way as a sign of mourning, a girl arrives on a bicycle. The woman says a couple of words to her and the smile vanishes from the young face. "Primo Levi *dead*?"'

As ordered by Turin's Assistant Public Prosecutor, Dr Loreto, the body was taken to the University's Institute of Forensic Medicine; it was deposited there at 11:45 am, less than two hours after the incident. Two days later, on Monday 13 April, a post-mortem examination was performed on behalf of the police by Professor Mario Portigliatti. Although there was no doubt that Primo Levi's death had been self-inflicted, the autopsy was carried out in accordance with the Italian penal code Article 365, which obliges a pathologist to report his findings to the Public Prosecutor. It notes: 'Rigor present. On the extensor surface of left upper forearm is the tattooed number 374572 (the numerals are scarcely legible). Bilateral haemorrhage from ears and right nostril . . .' The pathologist, a personal friend of the deceased, might not have known that the concentration-camp tattoo was clearly visible in life as 174517, not the numerals quoted in the autopsy.

The cause of death is summarised: 'Cerebral crushing with multiple fracture of cranium. Severe traumatic lacerations of heart, lungs, liver, spleen . . . Multiple fracture of vertebral column, sternum, of all ribs, clavicles, pelvis, right femur, right wrist.' The physical act that led to death is recorded as '*precipitazione dall'alto*', a 'fall from a great height'.

This sad chronicle was closed on 5 June 1987 when a Turin law court officially declared that Primo Levi had died by his own hand. There would be no penal proceedings, therefore, and 'all papers relative to the suicide' were consigned to the tribunal archive.

TWO

The Family Before Levi
1819–1919

Primo Levi liked to portray his ancestors as unworldly, scholarly characters lost in idle speculation. They appear in his work under heavy disguise, a mixture of fictional elaboration and gossip. He wrote almost nothing of his immediate family, however: nowhere does one learn of the circumstances of his marriage, his wife's name, even if he has children. He came from a family that guarded its secrets: a scandal in the previous generation had been suppressed. It had undermined the family's position in Italian society. The Levis were bankers, and much envied as successful, newly emancipated Jews.

Like most northern Italian Jews, the Levis claimed descent from the Sephardim (after *Sefarad*, Hebrew for 'Spain') who had fled anti-Semitic Castile in the fifteenth century. In about 1500 they settled in Piedmont, 'at the foot of the mountains', a region later ruled by the House of Savoy. The earliest records link the Levis to the Piedmont town of Mondovì. Giuseppe Levi, the writer's great-grandfather, was born in the town ghetto in about 1819. Later he showed a cautious dislike of the clergy and suffered a misfortune in business matters that echoed down the generations. The Levi bank was established in Mondovì a year after his birth; business, however, was restricted by the ghetto.

Ghettos as punitive institutions were first established on the Italian peninsula in 1555. Mondovì did not institute one until 1725, and even then it was not typical of others along the peninsula, which witnessed poverty, malnutrition and disease. According to the available accounts, there was no overcrowding there, and the gates remained unlocked at night. In 1796, seventy years after the ghetto was erected, Mondovì's Jews were liberated by Napoleon when the armies of the new French Republic invaded from across the Alps. A tree of liberty was planted in the main square, and some of the town's 200 Jews named their newborn sons 'Bonaparte' in honour of the emancipation. However, civil liberty for Piedmont's Jews lasted scarcely twenty years until the end of the revolutionary era when, in 1815, the House of Savoy reinstated the ghettos, and purged their kingdom of Jacobins.

The Levis had to wait a quarter of a century until they were liberated again. In 1848 the ruling Savoy King, Charles Albert, proclaimed the epochal Edict of Emancipation, which granted undreamed-of rights to the Jews in his dominions. The ghettos of northern Italy were dismantled once more and assimilation spread across Piedmont. Emancipation allowed Giuseppe Levi to leave Mondovì, and within twelve months of the proclamation he and his wife Enrichetta had moved eighty kilometres south to the smaller town of Bene Vagienna, where they established a branch of the family bank. Their son Michele, Primo Levi's grandfather, was born in Bene Vagienna on 13 May 1849.

The Levis, a household of six people, were then the only Jews among Bene Vagienna's 6,039 inhabitants. Though the town occupied the site of the Roman colony *Augusta Bagiennorum*, it was not in any way remarkable – the streets arcaded with low ochre-coloured vaults are to be found in all Piedmont villages. Adjacent to the Town Hall was the nondescript baroque church of San Francesco; in the distance the rolling plains were furrowed with mulberry trees and vineyards. The Levi bank was situated in a large house off the town's main square, Piazza Botero. A contemporary engraving shows stables for horse and carriage opposite the cash tills, and balconies trailing wisteria. Giuseppe Levi negotiated deals in property and gold, but the most profitable branch of his Bene Vagienna operations was banking. His family was considered ostentatious. At a time when there were no pavements in Bene Vagienna, they laid flagstones along the verge outside their home. The locals would tut-tut in Piedmontese: '*Trope pere 'n tsa ca!*', 'Too many stones in that house!'

Michele Levi was ten years old when, in 1859, the Savoy King Victor Emanuel II led the patriotic unification movement in Italy known as the Risorgimento. Unification was proclaimed in 1861: Italy was officially a single kingdom under the House of Savoy and, except in papal Rome, discrimination against Jews was definitively abolished. Prior to their emancipation, the only careers open to Italian Jews would have been finance or the rabbinate. Now they could take their place as equal citizens with the Catholic majority, and follow a profession. Michele Levi was among the first generation of northern Italian Jews to relinquish the traditional ghetto trades of money-lending and goldsmithery. It seems he did not want to go into his father's business, and graduated instead from Turin in civil-engineering. No one in his family had lived in the Piedmont capital before.

Michele was considered a cultivated man by provincial standards. His doctoral thesis on the French engineer Camille Polonceau, completed in 1873, was dedicated to 'My Dearest Parents'.

Little is known of Primo Levi's grandfather. By all accounts he was frail, prone to melancholy, and not very tall ('1 metre 67 centimetres'). He failed his army medical owing to a 'hernia on the right side of the groin'. While he was studying in Turin, he met his future wife Adele Sinigaglia, a Turin-born sophisticate five years younger than he. On her father's side, Adele came from a family of wealthy Piedmont silk traders. Records show that she was *benestante*, 'well-to-do'; everyone assumed that Michele had made an advantageous match. The families of Michele and Adele approved of the marriage, and cooperated over the dowry and wedding expenses. Michele brought his new wife back to Bene Vagienna, where he became an associate of the family firm. At first the marriage went well; Michele was twenty-eight when their first son, Cesare (Primo Levi's father), was born in 1878. Another two sons were to follow.

The Levi family business had profited greatly by the secular liberalism that followed the Savoy edict. A legal document dated 3 November 1863 discloses that a property in the hamlet of Narzole was sold for 600 lire by a 'Signor Giuseppe Levi late of Salvador, native of Mondovì and resident in this town of Bene Vagienna.' Jews were now able to trade with the Church, and in 1875 the bishop of Mondovì negotiated a loan of 5,300 lire – then a substantial sum – from 'Levi & Sons'. The Levis took advantage of the new laws that abolished clerical immunities and allowed Jews to purchase ecclesiastical estates. Records at Bene Vagienna indicate that Giuseppe Levi owned at least fourteen properties, many of them formerly church lands. In today's terms his 500,000 lire of property would amount to more than one million pounds sterling. According to a local newspaper, 'The firm owned over half a million lire in real estate and was the town's lifeblood. Everyone from wealthy landowners to tradesmen down to servants and country labourers entrusted their savings, great and small, to the LEVI COMPANY. One could almost say that the Levi bank was the National Bank of these lands.'

Primo Levi's father was the scion of an extremely wealthy family; Giuseppe and his son were among the town notables. But, having left Turin to live in the provinces, Adele Sinigaglia was not happy in her marriage. By the time of her third pregnancy in 1881, she was conducting an affair with the town physician, Dr Felice Rebaudengo. This man is remembered today as a tall Freemason with a long black beard. Not only was he five years younger than the vampish Adele, but he was baptised a Catholic. While the

8

doctor flirted with Adele, the Levis were about to lose their family business as well as much of their wealth and social position.

If asked today, the elderly inhabitants of Bene Vagienna speak fondly and quixotically of '*i Levi dei tulipani*', 'the Levis of the tulips'. The epithet refers to a flower-strewn *cascina* or 'farmhouse' outside Bene Vagienna that now stands semi-dilapidated by a chalk stream. For miles around it was the only place where wild tulips grew; tulip bulbs were eminently portable and ripples of tulip-growing in Piedmont indicated where persecuted Jews had settled. At some stage, however, the affectionate nickname 'the Levis of the tulips' was replaced by the Piedmontese for a 'soft touch'. ('You're a right tulip', the locals say of a naive person). Villagers gossiped about that foolish 'old tulip' Giuseppe Levi and his wife Enrichetta, who were too rich and were later devastated by the scandal that was to involve their son Michele.

In the summer of 1888 a rumour (of unknown origin) spread that 'Levi & Sons' had run out of credit. Angry creditors descended on the family bank in Piazza Botero; they intended to lynch Michele Levi and his father Giuseppe. So 'Levi & Sons', once respected financiers, were now seen as despised Jewish money-lenders. One of the mob, a local tax-collector known as 'Cedularius' (*cedola* is Italianised Latin for 'receipt'), was also a priest. He was Canon Pietro Dompè. Dompè had savings with the Levi bank of 11,000 lire and raised such an outcry as he tried to recover them that 200 peasants assembled in the street outside the bank. The mob was easily swayed by the Church, and Canon Dompè had no difficulty in whipping up anti-Jewish passions among them. In post-Risorgimento Italy, half-educated country priests had reason to fear the Liberal new age. One of the Levi properties, on what is now Via XX Settembre, was formerly a Francisan priory. No doubt Dompè resented the family's appropriation of a church domain.

The crowd had to be pushed back by *carabinieri* and the Levi house cordoned off to avoid 'further troubles'. Two days later, on Tuesday 24 July 1888, Michele Levi fled to Turin with his servants. It is not known if he was accompanied by his parents Giuseppe and Enrichetta. According to a newspaper, the 'frightened' engineer stayed in Turin's former ghetto with 'relatives of his wife'. Almost certainly these were Adele's brother Moise, a lawyer, and his daughter Celeste. Under the bleak headline 'Suicide of an Engineer' the Turin *Gazzetta del Popolo* reported in its weekend edition of 26–7 July: 'Last night at 2:00 am Engineer Michele Levi of Bene Vagienna, aged 40, threw himself out of a window from the second floor* of a residence

*Third floor, in American usage.

at 18 Via San Francesco da Paola into the courtyard below, where he was severely concussed. The concierge and Engineer Levi's servants rushed to the scene and carried the man to bed. Having promptly called for a doctor, the servants advised Levi's family to take the unfortunate man to San Giovanni Battista Hospital. This prudent advice was taken, but Levi died before arriving there.' The report added that news of the suicide had 'provoked very great surprise and remorse' in Bene Vagienna, as well as in Turin.

Primo Levi's grandfather was hurried to the hospital at 3:00 am, one hour after he had pitched himself out of the window. The admission registers for 1888 state that on Thursday 26 July Engineer Michele Levi was declared 'dead on arrival'. He was thirty-nine, not forty as the local newspapers stated. The physical cause of his death is recorded as *precipitazione dall'alto*', a 'fall from a great height' – exactly the same words would appear on Primo Levi's autopsy ninety-nine years later.

A special newspaper report from Bene Vagienna, dated 1 August 1888 and published in the *Gazzetta del Popolo* of Turin, corrected a previous news item about the suicide: 'In announcing the death of Engineer Michele Levi of Bene Vagienna, who took his life in Turin last week, this newspaper said the reasons for the unhappy man's desperate act were a mystery. Unfortunately here in Bene Vagienna those reasons were well known even before the suicide occurred. They are directly related to the catastrophic failure of GIUSEPPE LEVI AND SONS, of which Engineer Michele was an associate'. The paper speculated that Michele Levi had killed himself in desperation over the family's alleged insolvency; it makes no mention of his spouse's infidelities.

On Friday 3 August, another of the newspapers that covered the suicide and the financial collapse, *La Sentinella delle Alpi* (The Sentinel of the Alps), reported that 'a well-known Israelite', Giuseppe Levi, had once again narrowly escaped a mob lynching. This second assault occurred just four days after Michele Levi's suicide. Again the violence was most likely orchestrated by Canon Dompè, alias 'Cedularius'. A group of peasants had 'discovered' that Giuseppe Levi was hiding in his shooting lodge. 'The Paradise' stood on the crest of a steeply sloping vineyard in Lequio Tanaro, and must have been hard to besiege. Nevertheless the mob climbed up through the vines and, 'certainly not intending to hug the bankrupt fellow', broke down the door. Giuseppe Levi was nowhere to be found. The paper does not say what happened to him next, but after his son Michele's suicide he sold 'The Paradise' to the Colombo family from Fossano, a town nearby. Dr Cristofero Colombo, an elderly descendant, told me in 1995 that the Levi company was never actually bankrupt. Instead, it had been forced to close down by the efforts of an 'anti-Jewish priest'. In fact, a newspaper report of 4 August 1888 demonstrated that the bank's liabilities exceeded their assets by only 81,277 lire (£17,000 in today's terms). So 'Levi & Sons' were not seriously in debt. If there had been less 'raving madness' on the part of its creditors, the journalist concluded, the bank 'might still be going'. Soon after the Levis were hounded out of Bene Vagienna, Canon Dompè founded a replacement bank in the town.

2

On 18 August 1888 the civil court of Mondovì declared that 'a committee of inspection', which was to include Adele Sinigaglia's lover, Dr Felice Rebaudengo, would look into the bank's collapse. This egregious body was made up of directors from the Bank of Fossano, the Bank of Alessandria and the Savings Bank of Mondovì: all the esteemed financiers ranged against 'Levi & Sons'. In the minutes to the bankruptcy proceedings we can also make out the name of 'Adele Sinigaglia, widow of the late Michele Levi'. She had filed a claim (it does not say what sort) against the Levi bank.

On 17 November the Mondovì court adjourned to pass final sentence on 'Levi & Sons'. The judge was not impressed by the bank's state of affairs and, in summing up, condemned the Levi family to bankruptcy. 'They can do business only by ever more ruinous operations.' The minutes to the trial are stamped '*GRATUITO PATROCINIO*' (free legal aid). Giuseppe Levi, sixty-nine, once a pillar of the community, could not afford to pay for his own lawyer.

All the newspapers agreed that 1888 was a terrible year for the inhabitants of Bene Vagienna, the *benesi*. Following the Levi bank's collapse 'there had been a fever and indescribable commotion in the region'. First the *benesi* were stricken by a cholera epidemic. Then, on the evening of 4 September, two months after Michele Levi's suicide, a storm devastated the grape-harvest. 'The horizon blackened and hailstones rained down with such violence that in less than 10 minutes they were an inch thick on the ground . . . Decidedly 1888 is the year of *jattura* [the evil eye].' The New Year opened with a solar eclipse; earthquake tremors were registered in Turin.

In this wretched story, Giuseppe and Enrichetta Levi are not heard of again; presumably they left Bene Vagienna after liquidating their assets. Today their properties are ruined and filled with scaffolding holes. It is not known what sort of financial settlement Adele Sinigaglia and Dr Felice Rebaudengo obtained in court, though it was probably substantial. In Turin they bought an apartment on Via Po, one of the city's most elegant streets. Michele Levi's three sons, Cesare, Enrico and Mario, aged ten, nine and seven, moved to the city with them. In Turin's old Jewish cemetery there is an isolated section for suicides. Broken and overgrown with weeds, a headstone marks the grave of Primo Levi's grandfather:

> To the dear memory of
> Engineer Michele Levi
> Snatched from the affection of his
> Loved ones on 26 July 1888
> His wife and sons pray for his
> Eternal peace.

3

The move from Bene Vagienna to Turin, which took place probably in 1888 or 1889, must have been difficult for Primo Levi's father, Cesare, and his two brothers. The family had lost its pre-eminent social position. Cesare had been removed from his birthplace and grandparents to come and live in the Piedmont capital with his bereaved family. As soon as propriety allowed, his mother would have to remarry: gossip about Adele Sinigaglia and her sweetheart Dr Rebaudengo spread quickly in Turin. At ten, Cesare Levi was not too young to understand the awful nature of his father's death or to feel responsible for his younger brothers Enrico and Mario.

In about 1890 Dr Felice Rebaudengo married widow Sinigaglia and became the Levi boys' stepfather. His surgery was at 24 Via Po, the family's new address in Turin, and consultation hours were in the afternoon between 1:00 pm and 3:00 pm. The doctor spent much of his free time in good works; a city guide lists him as 'Honorary Health Inspector' of an orphanage. His charity was typical of Turin's moderately progressive bourgeoisie. No doubt it also helped to remove the doctor from his three Levi stepsons, who had not favoured his marriage to their mother Adele and grew to dislike him intensely.

By marrying a Gentile, Adele had shown a willingness to assimilate into Catholic Italian society. Her grasp of the finer points of synagogue ritual was reportedly shaky, but she remained Jewish in her regard for education. At a time when Italy's population was largely illiterate, most Italian Jews were able to read or write. Adele insisted that Cesare went to a technical school that taught him the rudiments of mathematics, design and geography. Later he read Applied Mathematics at Turin University. Cesare could have gone to a rabbinical college, but Adele wanted her oldest son to follow in her late engineer husband's secular and scientific footsteps. Cesare's younger brothers also attended technical institutes. Mario later graduated in medicine from Turin University; Enrico followed his grandfather Giuseppe Levi into finance.

4

In November 1898, aged twenty, Cesare Levi enrolled in Turin's Royal School of Applied Engineering. Thirty years earlier his father had done the same. Unlike Michele, however, Cesare was declared fit for military service and in 1900 was conscripted into the Army Engineer Corps as a mature student; his regiment was stationed in Turin. Times were changing and Turin was among the most flourishing of European cities. In their Frenchified dialect the inhabitants said: '*Turin ca bougia*', 'Turin really moves'. And in a few years the city would be the industrial dynamo of Italy. On the streets, in the cafés, everywhere there was talk of enterprise, credit, publicity and the new business of travelling salesmen. Turin had money and entertainment. Cesare Levi, a *bon vivant* and the son of a wealthy woman, liked to mingle in the city's Valentino Park with the fashionable *belle époque* loungers and their courtesans. Cafés under the plane trees dispensed beer, while a military brass band played on the banks of the River Po. The engineering school, its green lawns sloping down to the river, resembled a Loire château, and Turin would never again be so elegant. 'You'd think you were in a drawing room!' marvelled the philosopher Friedrich Nietzsche, who in 1888 had finished his crowning opus *Ecce Homo* in Turin.

For his two-year engineering course, Primo Levi's father had to sit fourteen exams ranging from hydraulics to practical geometry. That was gruelling but Cesare, an ambitious young man, wanted to specialise in electrical engineering. Six months earlier, he had seen the electrified festivities that marked the fiftieth anniversary of the Savoy Edict of Emancipation. The Turinese had never seen such dazzling artificial light: 'Nobody wanted to stay at home, everyone was as if tipsy on bottles of Asti Spumante wine'. Turin was now an innovative, technological city that looked eagerly to the future. In 1900 a small car factory opened on Corso Dante. It was called Fiat (Fabbrica italiana automobili torino); and as the first motor cars chugged through the streets of Turin, horses whinnied in fear.

But Turin had more to offer than automobiles and factories. The city's *belle époque* poet, Guido Gozzano, described a place 'favourable to pleasures'. By the time Primo Levi's father was a student, Turin was capital of Italy's cinema industry, a small Hollywood on the banks of the Po, as well

13

as of *la moda italiana*. The city set the fashion for swirling art-nouveau (Liberty-style) patterns and the 'S' line in dresses, which daringly accentuated body curves. And, to judge by the myriad theatres, cinemas and cafés, cultural life in turn-of-the-century Turin was much more lively than it is today. In the Caffè Nazionale, a gilded octagonal saloon with a palm-court orchestra, Cesare liked to indulge his boisterous side and flirt with the *chanteuses*. A fashionable man, he subscribed to Turin's gossipy dialect paper, *Birichin* (Cheeky Rascal), and prided himself on knowing every shop and housekeeper on Via Po. He had an enduring love of the theatre. Directly beneath the family apartment stood the Teatro Rossini. Cesare must have been a regular here if an actor on stage could call out *'Salut, ingegné!'*, 'Bless you, Engineer!', on hearing him sneeze.

As well as being a hive of film and fashion, Turin in Cesare Levi's day was a noted pocket of the paranormal (and still is). Spiritualism, the first modern heresy, appealed to emancipated Jews and other free-thinking rationalists. Cesare liked to experiment with table-turning, wall-rapping and other fogbound marvels, as these appealed to the superstitious in him. (On one occasion, he had dashed off to fetch another dinner guest to ensure that fourteen were seated at table; throughout the year 1913 he would write '1912+1' on his correspondence).

By the end of 1900, Primo's father had begun to investigate the latest in positivist thinking. He was absorbed by this philosophy, which held that only 'positive' facts (demonstrable as opposed to merely theoretical ones) constituted true knowledge. In 1876 the self-styled 'craniometrist' Cesare Lombroso had founded in Turin the new discipline of criminal anthropology. He and his circle called themselves 'positivists' not because they were certain (though they were), but in reference to their objective and empirical methods. With the aid of callipers and craniometry charts they tried to define the existence of a 'delinquent type' according to physical characteristics. Handle-shaped ears, prehensile feet and other apish stigmata were all considered telltale atavisms.

Primo Levi's father knew Lombroso well and was familiar with his disciples in Turin.* Each Sunday he frequented the salon that convened at Lombroso's house on Via Legnano. This was then the only intellectual

---

*Though Lombroso was Jewish, his book *Anti-Semitism and the Modern Science* scorned the singular appearance and pathology of Jews, who were deemed unattractive and more prone to suicide than Catholics. The book was extremely influential. Bram Stoker, in giving a Semitic curve to the vampire's nose in his Victorian novel *Dracula*, not only betrayed his xenophobia towards the East European Jews who had flooded into Britain since the late 1880s, but borrowed directly from Lombroso's biological approach to criminality.

meeting-place in Turin and many distinguished guests – among them perhaps Nietzsche – attended. One habitué, Dr Giacinto Pacchiotti, was the physician who had confirmed Michele Levi's suicide in 1888; believing that public hygiene was essential to a progressive society, Pacchiotti went on to found Turin's first Public Health Office.

Lombroso is now justly discredited. The Museum of Criminal Anthropology in Turin is full of boxed precision instruments and daguerreotypes of handcuffed 'delinquents'. Moreover, Lombroso's head is gruesomely preserved in formaldehyde (students say its cranial bumps betray a strong criminal tendency). Yet the misguidedness of Lombroso's theory – that born criminals shall be known by their anatomy – in no way diminishes the value of the positivist method. This was very exacting and recognised the sensory limits of knowledge (never believe anything until it is proved true). Cesare Levi, in spite of his spiritualist dabbling, understood these qualities; he would pass them on to his son Primo, whose mature writing is suffused with the positivist spirit of his birthplace.

5

At the end of December 1901 Cesare graduated in civil engineering. He had been a bright student, with his highest marks in technical physics. Two years later, in about 1903, he began work as an engineer. His first job was to siphon water from a lake bed in southern Italy. In about 1911 he moved to Budapest, where he was promoted to specialist designer for the Hungarian engineering company Ganz-Danubius. The firm was based on Csepel Island south of Budapest and was a bastion of Germanic Jewish culture; almost one in four of Budapest's 30,000 inhabitants was Jewish. Cesare rapidly became friends with the most gifted Jewish engineers at Ganz. In Budapest he liked to socialise, and consumed vast plates of goulash with beer. He honed his chessboard skills in Budapest's glittering coffee-houses. And at Christmas the Ganz chairman sent him chess problems on the back of a postcard. These were happy bachelor years for Cesare.

After four years, his Hungarian idyll ended abruptly when, in May 1915, Italy joined the Allies in the Great War against Austro-Hungary. Cesare was now an alien in enemy territory. The Hungarian government expelled him, along with all other foreign nationals, paying for his rail trip home. On his return to Italy, Cesare met the dark-haired daughter of a fabrics merchant who owned a textile shop in Turin. Ester Luzzati was good-looking, and had great resources of patience and loyalty. She liked Cesare's dash and wit, and her parents encouraged the match. The engagement of 'Engineer Francesco [sic] Levi and Ester Luzzati' was announced in the social columns of Turin's *La Stampa,* and the marriage took place in the synagogue on 7 October 1918. Europe was about to be devastated by the Spanish influenza and public-health notices in Turin warned against taking trams and moving in crowded places; as a result, the newly weds stayed at home for their honeymoon. One of the most severe outbreaks of disease ever, *la spagnola* would kill more than twenty million people before it had run its course by the spring of 1919.

The Great War over, Cesare was re-employed by Ganz. But he did not like what he found in Budapest. The city was swarming with ragged Ashkenazim made homeless by war. As an emancipated Jew from the West, Cesare recoiled from the sight of these Eastern Jews whose sidelocks, kaftans and Yiddish he considered backward tribal marks and customs. The Hungarian capital was now known as 'Judapest' for its swelling East European refugee population. However, it was not the Ashkenazim that most concerned Cesare, but the spectacle of Hungarian Bolshevism. When revolution occurred in Budapest in March 1919, Cesare's wife Ester was five months pregnant. Alone in Turin, she must have feared for her husband's safety as the Italian papers reported a Red takeover in Hungary. In Budapest statues, bridges and balconies were draped in red banners; the opulent Hotel Hungaria, where Cesare had liked to play chess, became the new Communist headquarters. Budapest was now the *voros varos,* 'Red city'. Ganz, like all Hungarian industries, was commandeered by the Bolsheviks. Spies were everywhere. By April 1919 the rioting had spread to neighbouring Bosnia, Croatia and Slovenia, as Hungary allied itself to Soviet Russia.

Once again, Cesare Levi was to be repatriated. On 10 June 1919, under police escort, a train left Budapest for the Adriatic port of Trieste in Italy. As Cesare's transport steamed westwards, workers in Turin occupied factories in protest at poor wages. The newly formed Hungarian soviet was an inspiration to them. By the time Cesare returned, the 'Red scare' had spread across Italy. A new anti-Liberal epoch had opened in Europe. During Cesare's absence in Hungary, an obscure former socialist, Benito Mussolini, had gathered a ragbag of Futurists, anarchists, Communists and Liberals into a Milan town hall and launched the movement that was to become, two years later, the National Fascist Party. That same year the National Socialist German Workers' Party – soon to be named the Nazi Party – was founded. Ester Levi, now twenty-four, was about to give birth to her first child.

THREE

A Blackshirt Childhood
1919–27

I

Primo Michele Levi was to spend most of his life in Turin, living and dying in the house where he was born. In many ways Turin is a most un-Italian city, providing a gateway to the Italian peninsula. After Italy's unification in 1861, when Turin was briefly the nation's capital, the Turinese would ask if the 'post had arrived from Italy'. Because of the city's proximity to France, Levi's parents, like many bourgeois Piedmontese, would dot their conversation with French or almost-French words: *Monsù*, 'Mister'; *bon-a neuit*, 'good night'.

Turin is a famously symmetrical city of straight avenues and grandly arcaded piazzas. French architects laid down the grid-plan in the sixteenth century, and their mathematical design created 10,000 metres of interlinked sheltering colonnades, 'useful when it rains', Primo Levi observed. He was profoundly attached to Piedmont and proud of his Turin roots. Turin was 'logical', 'spacious', 'self-controlled', he said. He believed that the city's orderly layout is mirrored in the restrained character of the Turinese. In their dialect they like to say: '*Esageroma nen*', 'Let's not exaggerate'. Levi would uphold this virtue of concision in his writing, just as much as in his life.

By the time Levi was born, Turin had acquired a stolid bourgeois air. This was reflected in the clockwork eating habits of the Turinese, with supper taken at precisely 8:00 pm followed by a routine digestive. Recreations and the cultural life of the city were increasingly mindful of middle-class propriety, and the high bourgeois tradition is still maintained in Piazza San Carlo. Known as the 'parlour' of Turin, this grand airy square has many elegant cafés with dark-panelled walls and marble-topped tables. Here the city's old guard sip coffee over slices of *gianduiotti*, hazelnut-studded chocolate cakes. Turin is an innately conservative city of protocols,

17

etiquette and due proportions. There are few modern structures here (a six-storey building is ambitiously referred to by locals as a *grattacielo*, a 'skyscraper'). And, as with all cities built to a grid, it can be difficult to know where you are. From Turin's disorientating design comes a vague melancholy. In the evenings, when the sun casts shadows across the angular arcades and porticoed squares, the city appears unreal. The painter Giorgio de Chirico was moved by this ghostliness; his lunar cityscapes with their broken statues and endless colonnades are really portraits of Turin.

The city's renown as a supernatural centre hints at a darker undertow. Nietzsche reputedly went mad in Turin (the philosopher was seen to embrace a carthorse off Via Po) and occultists claim the city as part of a magic triangle with Lyons and Prague. The mountains that encircle Turin provide an escape from the city's confinement. In the summer this alpine backdrop looks cool and inviting, and the city's one extravagant landmark, the Mole Antonelliana, or 'Antonelli's Pile', seems to rise above the peaks. With its knitting-needle spire, the Mole was commissioned in 1863 as a synagogue. In the post-Risorgimento Turin of that time a mere 1,500 Jews lived in the city. They had wanted to commemorate their new-found emancipation with a grandiose temple, but for lack of funds the synagogue was never finished. The Mole (which still gets a capital M in Turin) is now a museum, and a failed monument to the aspirations of enfranchised Jewry.

2

Primo Levi was delivered at home on the morning of 31 July 1919, the year the Great War formally ended. He was one of twelve babies born in Turin that summer's day: 'Nine males, 3 females', according to the local newspaper. His parents named him Primo, not a common name in Italy, after *primogenito*, 'first-born'. In keeping with Jewish custom, the baby was circumcised on the eighth day of his life, and a drop of wine placed on his lips in blessing. They gave him the middle name Michele after his paternal grandfather. As time went on, Ester preferred to call her boy 'Mino' from the affectionate diminutive *Primino*, 'Little Primo'. A studio portrait taken in 1920 shows Ester cradling 'Mino' at about eight months: a Botticellian angel, according to one family friend. He wears a teething necklace of amber beads and a lace pinafore. Ester's devotion to her son was complicated by anxiety. A sickly baby who suffered from croup and whooping-cough, Primo was soothed by Ester with Piedmontese lullabies. As a first-born Jewish son, he bore a heavy burden of parental hopes.

When Primo was born, the Levis were living in Turin at 75 Corso Re Umberto. Ester Luzzati's parents had given the newly weds the flat as part of their marriage dowry. The property, in a fashionable neighbourhood, had been in Ester's family since 1909. It was a five-storey apartment block, built to the west of the city in the first flush of *belle époque* prosperity. The couple's new home was huge but rather dark, with not much sunlight. The high frescoed ceilings were slightly domed, the parquet floors beeswaxed. Two north-facing balconies overlooked the elegant Via Vico, with a rear balcony above a courtyard a giddy three flights below. Genteel standards and conditions prevailed in the Levi household and Primo was raised on a mixture of coddling and bourgeois stiffness. In the main entrance hall the concierge had put up the polite notice which is still on display: 'BEGGING IS NOT ALLOWED'.

After the Great War this part of Turin had lost its leafy exclusivity when it attracted the nouveaux riches grown wealthy on munitions. Known as *pescecani* (sharks), they flaunted their war-wealth by building stolidly outsize new tenements with fairy-book turrets. Many of them affected the airs of the Savoy nobility and even named their children after royalty. Primo's new home was in a district of Turin known as the Crocetta, or 'Little Cross', after a church nearby. With its wide airy avenues the Crocetta is effectively a city within Turin, its inhabitants known as *crocettari*. Middle-class Jews were especially keen to settle there. The Jewish population of Turin had almost doubled in size since the Emancipation Edict of 1848 and by 1919, when Primo was born, the figure stood at 2,500. With the city's crumbling ghetto a half-hour's walk away, the Crocetta had become a desirable new suburb for enfranchised Jewry.

Over half a million Italian troops had perished in the 1914–18 conflict, and a further million wounded. In Turin, as elsewhere in northern Italy, discontent was high as demobbed soldiers roamed the Crocetta in search of a livelihood. They were attracted to the city's metalworks and Fiat automobile plants. A lucky few found work in the Crocetta repairing umbrellas or windows. All post-war Italy was in economic chaos and vulnerable to revolution. Each day housewives haggled over tins of American corned beef. And as the bread-lines grew, so the shop-floor grievances multiplied. Strikes and illegal occupations were to reach a peak in Turin between 1919 and 1920, the turbulent *biennio rosso* ('two Red years') when the city seemed to tumble into chaos as workers took over the postal and telegraphic services. Levi's father, in his middle-class enclave of the Crocetta, shuddered at the thought of a domestic revolution. His son was not yet born when he had witnessed the violent Red uprising in Budapest.

*

Béla Kun's Hungarian soviet had no sooner collapsed when Liberal Europe was under threat again, this time by an Italian. In September 1919 the poet-aviator Gabriele D'Annunzio seized the Adriatic port of Fiume, in the newly formed Kingdom of Serbs, Croats and Slovenes, and reclaimed it as Italian territory. In doing so D'Annunzio hoped to restore Italy's national pride after the Great War. Though prematurely bald with crooked teeth and blind in one eye, D'Annunzio was a legendary lover. Cesare Levi disliked his extremist balcony-ranting and feared that Fiume would unleash a new intolerance in Europe. A tinpot Caesar, D'Annunzio rehearsed in Fiume many of the future forms of Mussolini's dictatorship. His nationalist irregulars were dubbed 'legionaries' to recall ancient Roman greatness, and they wore black shirts long before the word *fascismo* was current. Fiume operated for a little over a year as an independent quasi-Fascist republic. Its existence was a turning-point for the twentieth century; with it, the die was cast for a totalitarian Europe.

Meanwhile Primo Levi was growing into a well-behaved, slim little boy, with a pale face and pale blue eyes. Like most Crocetta children he was beautifully dressed, often in a smart blue sailor suit with a starched white collar. By any standards, his was a comfortable childhood, and his early years unfolded happily. On the same floor as the Levis lived another small boy, Franco Archera, Primo's playmate. Primo was to lose Franco early, however, when he died of meningitis at the age of three. He was the younger brother of Laura, a prodigy on the violin, who later became Mrs Aldous Huxley. One day Laura Archera saw Primo fall from his tall baby carriage head-first on to the pavement. Primo seemed to recover from the fall, though it gave Laura nightmares for some time.

3

Primo's reign as the adored only child lasted just eighteen months. Early in the morning of 27 January 1921, Ester Levi gave birth to a daughter, Anna Maria. The baby girl was given the middle name Fortunata after her great-grandmother. No self-respecting Jewish family in the Crocetta was without a Catholic domestic, as they could work on the Sabbath when Jews are not supposed to cook or clean. And by now Ester had a nanny to help her with the children. Born in 1867, Silvia Meneghelli had been employed by the Levis long before Primo was conceived. In her early fifties, she wore her long silver hair in a bun and sometimes she sold her combings to the wig-makers who went about the Crocetta. Sober, honest and obliging, she came from Emilia-Romagna at the gastronomic heart of Italy, and knew how to cook a rich pasta. In deference to the nanny's religion, the Levis ate fish on Fridays. Silvia ate alone most nights in the kitchen; familiarity with servants was disapproved of in those days, and Silvia 'knew her place'. Like many Turin children of their social class, Primo and his sister grew deeply attached to Silvia, whom Primo called 'Cia', his first word. She was the sure centre of his world.

According to those who knew her, Ester was happy and fulfilled in motherhood, and early on gave something of her own tastes and style to the family. Among friends and relatives she was known as Esterina – 'Little Ester' – which was often abbreviated to Rina. Her long dark hair was held in a chignon with tortoiseshell combs. Of medium height, she never wore makeup and smelt faintly of chemists' eucalyptus. Outwardly she was shy, with a quiet, peaceable nature. Friends recall a 'sober-minded', 'thrifty homemaker' who put her duties as a parent before all else. Cesare seems to have been indifferent to the chores of fatherhood, and it was she who attended to the routine side of the household, including the children's school bills. Though not an intellectual, and lacking Cesare's bookish knowledge, she was much sharper than he. In adulthood Primo's relationship with his mother would go beyond filial devotion: he respected her intellectual judgment, and liked her to sift through the many books he was sent to review.

In later years, however, Levi told a journalist that he could not remember a 'single kiss or caress' from his mother. This is a rather hostile overstatement (and perhaps characteristic of men who are overly attached to their mothers). Levi was unquestionably devoted to Ester, and it is inconceivable that she did not kiss or caress him. As a typically bourgeois matriarch, it is true, she was not a demonstrative woman. She herself was the first-born – the *primogenita* – of a family of six. Many have remarked on the temperamental similarities between her and Primo. Ester had a slightly old-fashioned formal manner, which she passed on to her son. Prudish and cautious of revealing her feelings, she was a stickler for decorum and had strict standards of behaviour, a fastidious dislike of animals and at all times laid great stress on cleanliness at home. Outwardly serene, Ester always seemed to be smiling.

Born on 29 June 1895, in Turin, Primo's mother was seventeen years younger than her husband. Like most Jewish matches in those days, their marriage had been arranged by the couples' parents. The four Luzzati girls – Ester, Ida, Nella and Jole – had been educated privately at the Magda de Lazzari finishing school in Turin. Like all middle-class women in those prefeminist times, the Luzzati sisters were expected to be dutifully demure and feminine. Yet they were accomplished (Ester obtained a diploma in French, while her sisters studied dressmaking, watercolour painting and the piano-forte) and were far from subservient to their husbands. Their playboy brothers, Gustavo and Corrado, had rejected a university education for a life of fast cars and pleasure. They were teased by their practically minded sisters as *fagneans*, or 'lazybones' (from the Italian *far niente*) – spoiled young men lacking direction.

By contrast, Primo's paternal uncles Enrico and Mario Levi were bookish sorts, not unlike their older brother Cesare. In their devotion to reading they routinely stole from each other's libraries, though none of them really minded. All three Levi brothers had inherited the quick-witted discernment of their mother, Adele Sinigaglia. Mario, the youngest, lived with his wife Agostina Emma Coen on Turin's old ghetto street of Via Maria Vittoria. Their son, Roberto, was considered a cry-baby and a bore, but Primo tolerated him as a playmate. The wealthiest of the brothers, Enrico, ran a bank in Genoa and had his own chauffeur. Primo loved to visit Uncle Enrico, his wife Luisa and two sons at their home in the seaport's Salita Santanna neighbourhood. A fanciful character, Enrico kept a pet monkey and dabbled amateurishly in oil painting. He had copies of Marcel Proust in the first French Gallimard editions, which Primo grandly determined to read one day. Enrico's antiquarian three-volume Dante, complete with God-fearing illustrations by Gustave Doré, was later inherited by him.

4

By the early 1920s Primo's father was Ganz sales representative for Piedmont and the neighbouring region of Liguria. Now that Béla Kun's revolution had failed, Budapest was free to trade again with capitalist Italy, and Cesare sold Hungarian Ganz machinery to Italian engineering firms. His office was situated close to home on Corso San Martino, where a Ganz company calendar showed the blue Danube. As Cesare did not own a car (automobiles being a luxury few could afford), he walked to work. It was the same route each morning for eighteen years: down Corso Re Umberto, a quick coffee at his parents-in-law on Corso Vittorio, then a brief stroll on to the Ganz office adjacent to Porta Susa railway station. Puffing a cigar, short and squat with florid sausage-eater cheeks, Primo's father was a reassuringly portly figure in his peregrinations round the city. He was thought to resemble the cartoon character Arcibaldo in the *Corriere dei piccoli* children's comic; in the original US strip, *Bringing up Father*, Arcibaldo is the podgy Irish immigrant Jiggs in spats and top hat, with a gluttonous craving for corned beef. Cesare was a hale, full-blooded man, unlike the man Primo was to become.

Though Levi's father was not conventionally handsome, he was attractive to women, and chaperoned them with ease. Charming and flirtatious, he was a connoisseur of claret and cigars, and while shaving he liked to hum arias from Offenbach's *Orpheus in the Underworld*. A man about town, he did not make Ester a very constant husband, and by the mid-1920s was conducting an affair with his Ganz company secretary, Signorina Gribaudo, a prim Piedmontese half his age. A family cousin recalled Cesare at this time: 'His arms were too long for his body, but he was so full of enthusiasm and bookish charm that you didn't notice how ugly he was.' In photographs Cesare has the air of a dignified paterfamilias: here is a man, you feel, who was served the best cuts of meat at table and who smoked a good cheroot. Yet his stateliness was undermined by something.

Though Cesare liked to think of himself as a cosmopolitan, he was an autodidact, a skimmer rather than a scholar, with a touch of bumpkin gaucheness. He never lost an opportunity to flaunt his cleverness. In the cheese shops where he was known, he ostentatiously computed grocery bills on his engineer's logarithmic slide-rule. Primo would inherit something of this tendency to swank. On his way home after work Cesare browsed among the second-hand bookstalls on Via Cernaia and haggled over prices. In order to accommodate the many bargain books that he found, he had pockets stitched into the lining of his jacket (so Primo later claimed).

From his earliest days, Primo grew up in a household saturated with printed matter. His father collected the pink-coloured paperbacks in the German Tauchnitz fiction series and subscribed to the Turin spiritualists' journal *Gnosi* (published from the same address at Via San Francesco da Paola where his father had taken his life in 1888). Cesare also haunted the patrician bookseller 'Pregliasco & Sons' at 51 Via Principe Amedeo. The owner, a friend, allowed him to borrow books on the understanding that he returned them in mint condition. Consequently Cesare was often to be found stretched out on a sofa with one eye squinting between a book's uncut pages.

Sometimes Primo's father had as many as three books on the go. He tried to read Kant and Schopenhauer in the original German and even mastered some Hungarian, a maddeningly difficult tongue. Strangely, for a polygot, he was quite unable to get to grips with English. Not to be dashed, he put key verbs in his pockets after the Berlitz method: but it was no use. As the 1920s advanced, Engineer Levi acquired a stockpile of books for his children when they were older. The gruesome German story *Max and Moritz*, in which a pair of trouble-makers fall into a flour mill and their remains are fed to the ducks, was to be a favourite with Primo. Other early reading included Giovanni Bertinetti's *Meo's Ears*, about a lazy boy who sprouts donkey's ears every time he lies. (Eventually Meo turns into an honest son, embodying those vaunted Piedmontese virtues of tenacity, self-conviction and knowhow – *saper fare*.)

From an early age, Primo liked to look at his father's books, especially the African big-game texts with their coloured plates of Kaffirs and meat-eating cats. There were also handbooks on bees and ants by the French naturalist Jean Henri Fabre, dubbed the 'Insects' Homer', as well as spiritualist studies. One of these, Lombroso's treatise *After Life – What?* contained photographs of crystal-gazing hypnotists and clouds of white ectoplasm. Spiritualism had flourished mightily following the bereavements of the Great War, and Ouija boards were still all the rage in genteel Crocetta.

5

Ester's parents had a holiday villa in Piossasco, a half-hour's drive from Turin. Primo spent his early childhood summers there, often staying with his mother until the September grape-harvest. He would look back on those torpid, shimmering autumn days as among the happiest of his childhood. Most of the Luzzati clan descended on the villa at 26 Via Montegrappa; it had wrought-iron gates and stone-carved pineapple motifs. Inside, the house was cool and reposeful with whitewashed walls. Ester's father had bought it in 1912, when she was a girl, and she remained passionately attached to the villa all her life, taking her children there for the green fields and clean air. Primo and his sister loved the place as intensely as their mother had done as a child. They went beetle-hunting, or made wigs of crinkly maize-cob hair. And the garden was wonderful, teeming with animal life. In the Rio Sangonetto at one end of the orchard Primo fished for tadpoles. On washing day he watched the peasant women washing laundry in the stream; later it would arrive crisply starched at 75 Corso Re Umberto and other Crocetta households.

The villa's Catholic caretaker, Clemènt Bruno, was invited with his family to join the Levis and the Luzzatis for the Jewish New Year at the summer's end. The Hebrew words *Shana Tova*, Happy Year, would be traced with apple pips on the farmhouse linen. The only time Clemènt was said to have left Piossasco was during the Great War when, to his distress, he had been called to arms. Any journey outside his birthplace (even if it was only to Turin) was for Clemènt a journey to 'Italy' and a wrenching inconvenience. Whenever Levi thought of Piossasco he thought of Clemènt, and the sound of his rake on the villa gravel in the early morning. Clemènt's daughter, Maria, looked after Primo and his sister in Turin when their nanny Silvia was away. She was a country girl who felt nervous in the

24

city; once, she sat through an entire Jewish banquet cradling a pet goose in her lap.

Primo as a child was awed by his maternal grandfather, Cesare Luzzati. As an army conscript he had helped to shift 84,000 corpses from the rubble of Sicily's cataclysmic earthquake of 1908. He had fought in the Great War, and it was from him that Primo knew about such things as shell-shock and trench fever. In his black Homburg, Luzzati was a man of some style and presence. His main interest was food, yet he paid dearly for his sweet tooth: diabetes eventually killed him. A weighing machine stood by his bed, but, away from his wife, he binged lavishly. Not a tall man, he weighed 102 kilograms and was only just able to squeeze behind the wheel of his motor car. Aside from his bulk, what distinguished Grandpa Luzzati was his wonderfully stubborn character. Here was a man who knew his own mind and stood by it immovably: in Piedmontese he was a *bougianen*, 'one who never moves'. Primo would acquire something of his grandfather's inflexible streak. (Grandpa Luzzati would say: 'Better to be a mule than a weathercock.') A taciturn man, he hardly ever read books and had never been heard to utter a sentence of more than six words.

If Primo and his sister grew up amid affluence and comfort, it was partly due to Cesare Luzzati. His textile store was reckoned to be the best in Turin and sold decorative knicknacks as well as tartan for every Scottish clan. The weekly visit to the store was an important part of Primo's early life. It was situated at 37 Via Roma in a row of wedding-dress showrooms and *pasticcerie*. To enter grandpa's shop was to stray into a dark cave; at one end was a single opaque window for customers to inspect their fabrics. Levi loved to watch the staff bustle among their ledgers and pencils; one of them, a man nicknamed 'Ghiandone' (Big Acorn), wore an ill-fitting red wig that Primo found particularly sinister. He was also fascinated by Signorina Savina, the cashier, who had a spectacularly large bosom. As a special treat, Grandpa Luzzati would take Primo and his sister Anna Maria to the café-bar next door to buy them sugar-sticks or coloured marzipan confections. The counter was covered in tiny pieces of coloured glass, so that when Primo looked down, his legs were reflected a hundredfold.

An inventive man, Grandpa Luzzati had coined some bizarre family sayings for use in his Via Roma store. A shop assistant called Emilio, in rented accommodation upstairs, refused to hear whenever Luzzati called for him. 'Emilio's upstairs!' became Luzzati-speak for anyone who was hard of hearing. Another coinage, 'thirteen-one' (*tërdesun*), meant 'nuisance customer'. It was applied to the non-Jewish client who came into the store on the 13 January, having spent all his money at Christmas. (Typically the client pulled down every bolt of fabric, only to leave without buying anything.) The store was one of the few places in Turin, moreover, where Judaeo-Piedmontese could still be heard. This strange dialect was used by staff whenever they did not want to be understood by Catholic clients. A tiresome *tërdesun* might be sold a bolt of *stofa hasirud*, 'rubbishy fabric', for example. Just occasionally these discourtesies were mistakenly used in the presence of a Jewish customer; then Grandpa Luzzati was embarrassed.

Primo's grandfather was a shrewd businessman, yet his real love was not for textiles or money, but for the rural Piedmont of his childhood. In provincial Casale where Luzzati was born in 1869, his family were humble Jews who measured life by the seasons and harvests. The only man Grandpa Luzzati really trusted was the Piossasco caretaker, Clemènt Bruno. Together they made wooden rat-traps and demijohns for wine, and blew pipe smoke over the grapes to kill greenflies.

Grandpa Luzzati's wife, Adelina, was a sharp-tongued, sour-faced woman who did not suffer fools. She controlled all aspects of her husband's life, down to the insulin injections she administered for his diabetes. Of Adelina one relative said: 'She was a wise old bird who could be quite aggressive at times; she was the real brains behind the fabric store.' When she got angry (which was often) Adelina's voice rose to a bird-like shrillness, and her husband wisely fell silent. Adelina was born Adele Della Torre in 1867, one of an astonishing twenty-one offspring, few of whom survived beyond a day. Her father owned a tannery in Alessandria, Piedmont. Her eldest brother, Natale, was a revolutionary who was said to have met the Russian anarchist Mikhail Bakunin.

Relations between Adelina and the family's other Adele, Primo's paternal grandmother Adele Sinigaglia, were not good. If Sinigaglia considered the Luzzatis socially beneath her, Adelina Della Torre disapproved of Adele's second marriage. ('Whoever trusts a goy eats forbidden pork,' she would say.) Sometimes, in a fine show of tact, Adelina was heard to gossip that Adele had pushed her husband out of that second-floor window. So Adele Sinigaglia was not welcomed into the pious, convention-bound Luzzati household; a scorned relative, she lived her last days in Turin amid a decay of stuffed hummingbirds and ill-fitting wigs.

6

Primo Levi was three years old when, between 26–28 October 1922 an obscure political agitator, Benito Mussolini, staged a dramatic assault on Italy's ailing Liberal government. During the so-called March on Rome, Fascists took over the city's public offices and telephone exchange. King Victor Emanuel III, the last Savoy monarch, failed to impose martial law and, in a panic, installed Mussolini as Italy's new prime minister. (Mussolini's participation in the March on Rome was later dramatised in monuments of the Duce striding purposefully towards the Eternal City; in fact he arrived hours later in the luxury of a *wagon-lit*.) At just thirty-nine, Mussolini had succeeded in ousting Italy's despised ruling caste. The crisis had been simmering for some time. A year earlier, in May 1921, Fascist deputies had been elected to the Rome parliament for the first time. Parts of Italy were subsequently put under the control of Blackshirt militiamen known as *ras* (Ethiopian for 'chieftain'). These *ras* were among the dishevelled mob who had converged round Mussolini in the wake of D'Annunzio's dictatorial activities in Fiume. Though as a young man Mussolini had been attracted to Socialism, by 1921 he had shifted to the right, and he exploited the *terrore rosso* in order to take power. Any doubts about his greed for power had vanished by November 1921 when he formally proclaimed his movement the Partito Nazionale Fascista (PNF). The party's name was taken from the ancient Roman symbol of authority – an axe bound in rods, or *fasces*. Mussolini dreamed of a second Roman empire for Italy and, as in the days of Emperor Augustus, dominion over the Mediterranean.

Predictably, the March on Rome unleashed a flood of violence across Italy. Punitive Fascist expeditions ransacked opposition offices and brutalised enemies with the *santo manganello*, 'holy cudgel'. In Turin the most horrific violence occurred on the night of 18 December 1922 when Mussolini's execution squads went out of control and massacred twenty-two people. In Crocetta households the word was of a bloodbath. Half a century later Levi spoke of the rationale behind the violence: 'The Blackshirts had not just killed Turin's trade unionists, Communists and Socialists. First they made them drink half a kilo of castor oil. In this way a man is reduced to tatters, is no longer human; he has intestinal cramps and has to run to the lavatory every five minutes. There's a direct connection between the Turin massacres of 1922 and the entry ceremony in the Nazi camps, where they stripped you, destroyed your personal photographs, shaved your head, tattooed you on the arm. This was the demolition of man; this is Fascism.'

In a riot of cudgels and castor oil, all opposition to Fascism was expelled from parliament. Then corruption set in. The spring 1924 elections were so shamelessly gerrymandered that the Socialist leader Giacomo Matteotti declared them 'invalid'. Matteotti was bundled into a car and murdered. Primo's father muttered darkly that Italy had become a 'Prussian barracks'. Having witnessed Béla Kun's Hungarian dictatorship, he was wary of the extremist cult of *mussolinismo*, with its veneer of respectability.

*

That same year of 1924 Primo Levi joined the Fascist youth movement, Figli della Lupa. The 'children of the wolf' were Romulus and Remus in Roman legend, and the organisation aimed to instil a nationwide conformism in Italy's children. In some ways it resembled the British Boy Scouts, with a more military cut. Amid a roar of hand-clapping, *Vivas* and flag-waving, the five-year-old Primo was publicly inducted into a Wolf detachment. Later he joined the uniformed juveniles on guard duty outside school: politics now intruded unavoidably on his life. Yet any open discussion of the new Fascist state was actively discouraged by his parents, who preferred not to be involved in politics. Cesare Levi was not anti-Fascist, or even a mild dissenter. At most he dismissed Mussolini (in private) as a *mamzer,* 'bastard' in Hebrew.

Nevertheless, Levi's father became a *Fascista,* a party member, if grudgingly. Like many Italians he regarded his Fascist badge as a convenience only: without it, his tenure with Ganz would be threatened. Now forty-six, Cesare was what Italians call a 'last hour' Fascist. If he secretly objected to Mussolini it was on aesthetic as much as on political grounds. The dictator provided vulgar theatre for the masses, and his bellicose posturing got on Cesare's nerves. Cesare hated to wear the Fascist black shirt for business conventions (it was too itchy), but that was as far as his resistance went. Much of Turin was slow to endorse the new dictatorship based in Rome. Fascist police informers reported that the Piedmontese were 'hidebound' and 'slow in making up their minds' – in a word: *bougianen.* Hostility to Rome went back at least to the Risorgimento, when Turin had gained then lost its capital-city status.

As the 1920s progressed, however, everyone in Italy was Fascist, including Jews. An estimated 130,000 Jews lived in Mussolini's Italy (today they number barely 50,000) and by the mid-1920s they proudly backed the dictator. They saw Fascism as the legitimate heir of the Risorgimento, which had instituted national unity. 'Italians all and only Italians!' Mussolini liked to say. Moreover, the Fascist Party seemed to endorse the Jews' patriotic, middle-class aspirations. Eucardio Momigliano, a lawyer and Primo Levi's first cousin once removed, had helped to found the Fascist Party in 1919.

7

Now that Fascism was established, Turin was a well-ordered city. Streets were clean, crime was rare: people were too frightened to break the law. 'YOU CAN SLEEP WITH YOUR DOORS OPEN', the Fascist slogan promised. From the third floor of 75 Corso Re Umberto, Primo and his sister threw money wrapped in sweet papers to the travelling musicians; one serenaded them on milk bottles played like a xylophone. Primo himself was learning to play the piano, but he was not a diligent pupil, and complained that his hands hurt. After two teachers he was exempted from further lessons.

Between tea and supper the Levi children were free to play. As they got older Primo and Anna Maria grew very close. They spoke with such rapidity – rattling out ten words to everybody else's one – that they were not always understood. Moreover, they invented a private coded language, which was indecipherable even to their parents. By temperament Primo was the ringleader in the children's games. But he was not a *bambino prodigio*, a child wonder, warned his sister Anna Maria. 'My brother was fun to have around – certainly no anxious tagger-along'. Levi's sister was nicknamed 'Evelina' by other *crocettari*. She wore her hair in plaits and was pale, with a quick nervous manner.

Corso Re Umberto was lined with magnificent horse-chestnut trees, and in autumn the children held competitions to gather the most chestnuts. (Primo became a champion conker-fighter.) Street games among the *crocettari* required only a skipping rope and knowledge of every cul-de-sac and lamp-post in the area. Primo regarded hopscotch as 'cissy' and preferred the scary excitement of hide-and-seek and 'off-ground-he'. Best of all was an unfrequented patch of Crocetta wasteland known as 'The Lung'. With Leo Avigdor, a local Jewish boy living a few doors away, Levi dug for treasure in 'The Lung' while nanny Silvia supervised them. The Crocetta was a reassuring and intimate world.

Before he went to school, Primo was given a Meccano set with which he built cranes that could lift up toy bricks. For his fifth birthday his father made him a present of a junior carpenter's kit. So Primo could build wooden furniture for his sister's doll's house. Right from the start, he was a resourceful boy. In Piossasco he made a vehicle from a penny-farthing bicycle, a four-wheeled dogcart and a table on castor wheels. On this nine-wheeled charabanc he whizzed down Via Montegrappa. Precociously he baptised his invention an *enne-ciclo* ('n' being Greek mathematical shorthand for 'nine'). Other children were unable to pronounce the word, however, and instead abbreviated it awkwardly to '*menne*'. The term was perilously close to the Piedmontese *menno*, 'pussy cat' (and by extension, the pudenda); so the children's parents banned it.

According to his sister, Primo had learned to read and write before his fourth birthday, 'and he was in a hurry to teach me to read too', she recalled. At Grandpa Luzzati's, Primo put low wooden tables together to make a desk for Anna Maria and his cousin Giulia Colombo (daughter of Aunt Ida

Luzzati), who lived nearby in the Crocetta on Via Lamarmora. He gave the girls paper and pencils and began to teach them the alphabet. Clearly Primo had a gift for teaching; when he helped Anna Maria with her sums 'everything became crystal clear to me: my brother simplified mathematics for me'. Once he had learned to read, Primo's favourite book was the English classic, Arthur Mee's *Children's Encyclopaedia*. The Italian edition, the *Enciclopedia dei Ragazzi*, was edited by Paola Lombroso Carrara, daughter of the Turin criminologist Cesare Lombroso. The volumes were individually bound in leather, and on the cover of each was a picture of apple-cheeked Italian children in white frocks. Published bi-monthly between 1922 and 1925, a complete set cost 170 lire – a fortune in those days. Levi 'positively devoured' the volumes, recalled his sister. From an early age he liked to impart knowledge to others. In later years Levi's own teacherly essays might explain (among other things) how a flea is able to leap one hundred times its own height, or why we have a biological need to yawn.

8

In the autumn of 1925 Primo Levi entered the 'Felice Rignon' state primary school in Turin. Founded in 1879, it catered for well-bred *crocettari*. At 39 Via Massena the school was a short walk from home; the six-year-old was accompanied there by his nanny or mother. He wore a black smock over grey shorts; class began at 8:00 am and was single-sex, with forty-five pupils.

Primary schools were the regime's most important agency in moulding obedient young Fascists. Mussolini was mired in a drawn-out battle to build a Fascist Empire in East Africa, and Primo was required to chant the regime's bellicose youth anthem, 'Giovinezza', during his weekly singing lessons. Slogans in the corridors reassuringly proclaimed that 'MUSSOLINI IS ALWAYS RIGHT' (item eight of the Fascist Decalogue). Most school hours were devoted to Italian grammar and *bella scrittura*, 'fine writing'. History lessons were essentially propaganda, which Primo found oppressively boring. Geography appealed to him only 'slightly more'. At all times, great emphasis was placed on so-called Hygiene classes, where pupils were upbraided for nail-biting and failure to wash behind their ears. Levi took a keen interest in most school activities except sport, which had become a vital focus of Fascist propaganda. The school's gym instructor, Signor Cassinelli, was so zealous in his desire to turn out little 'new men' (as he called his six-year-olds) that he taught them his own complicated version of the stiff-armed Fascist salute. 'Forward march!' was his favourite watchword.

There was one member of staff, Emilia Glauda, whom Levi never forgot. When she died long afterwards at a hundred, he sweetly apostrophised 'my virginal mistress of primary school'. Glauda had immense clarity, and her early influence went very deep. She was forty-seven and a spinster by the time she taught Levi. A tall woman with a slight stoop, she wore a long, high-collared black silk dress and the children feared and respected her. Like all those who worked in the public sector, Mistress Glauda was a Fascista, but not doggedly in thrall to Mussolini. The regime's populist stories of hearty children overcoming Communists, Africans and (before long) Jews were to be avoided if possible. Salvatore Gotta's *The Little Alpine Soldier*, the most widely read children's novel at this time, was in Glauda's eyes ludicrous. The book's inflated rhetoric offended her sense of decorum, and she banned it from the classroom. Instead she had her boys read Edmondo De Amicis's edifying novel of post-Risorgimento Turin, *Heart*. De Amicis had served Mistress Glauda well enough for generations of pupils and she did not intend to change now.

For the three years that Emilia Glauda taught Levi, she was concerned that he appreciate the virtue of concision and due proportion in prose. The notion that literary style is a decoration – something you can apply to your subject – never appealed to Levi; indeed a concise use of vocabulary would be the hallmark of his mature prose. But even then, at the age of six, he was far from what Italians call *pressappochista*, 'slapdash'.

Levi had been at school for a year when, in 1926, he was dragooned into the Fascist Balilla organisation for boys up to the age of fourteen. Submerging himself in the Balilla for a few hours each week fostered a feeling of belonging and national unity in Levi that he found not altogether unpleasant. Yet on the whole he did not appreciate the button-cleaning and shoe-polishing – few seven-year-olds would. School Balilla activity was supervised by the gym instructor Cassinelli, blown out with rank and self-importance. A parade was held every Saturday afternoon in the Valentino Park, and might involve up to three hours of group exercise. In the course of these Levi would be sternly reminded by Cassinelli that more was required of him than a perfunctory drill attendance. He had to have some basic knowledge of rifle parts and how to form fours and slope arms. On each 28 October, to commemorate Mussolini's March on Rome, Cassinelli frogmarched his boys to Turin's football stadium for a dazzling tournament known as the *grosso saggio*, 'grand show'. Adolescent ski corps and crack horse divisions moved in formation across the pitch with regiments of older children, Centurions, trooping behind. Levi's sister was in the Piccole Italiane for girls, and she also had to attend Saturday-morning manoeuvres. The girls wore ill-fitting uniforms and carried bows and arrows instead of the boys' rifles. It was clear to Anna Maria, even then, that they were marching to the orders of 'pretty stupid men'.

9

Meanwhile Levi was top of his class and was routinely awarded a 'First' for Behaviour, Hygiene and Reading Comprehension. '*Primo Levi Primo!*' said his classmates. Levi found it easy to learn, and had a marvellously retentive memory. In 1927 he was a prizeman, winning the 'First Degree Grade', yet he did not boast about his achievement; instead, he seemed more embarrassed by it. Though he was a model pupil, Levi managed to be popular. 'He was everybody's friend,' recalled his classmate Sergio Valvassori. 'He didn't come across as a swot, but in a quiet way he preferred to share what he knew with others, even to help us lesser mortals with our homework.' When Ignazio Filogamo first met the seven-year-old Primo in the autumn of 1927, he recalled, Levi asked to be taken to the Filogamo Automobile Showroom run by Ignazio's father. There Levi recounted out-of-the-way-facts about car engines gleaned from Arthur Mee's encyclopaedia. 'Levi was an industrious ant, not an eager beaver,' judged Filogamo later.

Levi was also rather clever with his hands. Another classmate, Leo Avigdor, was awed by his 'envious ability' to reproduce electrical phenomena with a tiny transformer given to him by his engineer father: 'I tried to do the same with an expensive kit called *The Little Engineer,* but the results were abysmal and I soon gave up.' Levi left a mark on Avigdor's life, as he did on most boys who knew him at this time, though not because he was brilliant. 'Primo was very modest and sweet, if perhaps easily hurt and introverted. He was decidedly the best of our bunch at school.' No one I spoke to had a bad word for the schoolboy. Unanimously he was described as somehow more gifted than others.

Levi's subsequent literary brilliance may have coloured the memories of his schoolmates. A picture emerges of an unobtrusively quiet child of above-average intelligence, certainly well behaved, but in all likelihood not manifestly 'exceptional'. In fact, it is likely that Levi did not stand out in his class. An unassuming boy, he developed a habit of watchful observation; this was to avoid drawing attention to himself, but later on it could give an impression of aloofness. From Levi's own later remarks it is clear that at some stage he began to feel different from his peers. This unease would increase as he approached puberty. By then he was more aware of being Jewish; he became delicate and was often ill.

FOUR

An Anxious Boyhood
1927–34

I

Uniquely for Fascist Italy, the 'Felice Rignon' offered Jewish lessons. Under Mussolini, only Catholic instruction was permitted in state schools, but it was suspected that the deputy mayor of Turin, himself a Jew, had been able to sway the Rignon governors. The class convened for twelve months only, every Monday during the academic year 1927–8, and had a family-like atmosphere. Ida Fubini was an ironical, self-contained Jewish teacher who instructed her pupils in Old Testament doctrine. According to one classmate, Levi was unusually stirred by the fierce moral parables of deliverance and survival. In spite of his later claims to be just 'five per cent Jewish', Levi was unavoidably shaped by Judaism and exposed to its cultural traditions from an early age.

At 75 Corso Re Umberto, it is true, the family's Jewish identity was not strong. Ester and Cesare Levi were so integrated within Gentile society that they were virtually indistinguishable from the Catholic majority. Even on the pious Luzzati side of the family, Jewish ritual was not as impeccably observed as it might have been. Adelina Luzzati had a special brass name-plate in the synagogue, but she practised a highly idiosyncratic Judaism. On the Sabbath she allowed any kind of work at home, so long as it was not sewing. On the Day of Atonement (Yom Kippur) Jews are not supposed to eat or cook, but Adelina sacrilegiously broke the mood of rue and penitence by making vast quantities of tomato sauce.

The Luzzatis, a close-knit family, ensured that the most important Jewish festivals were celebrated by the Levis. This was done less to worship God than to gather relatives for food and entertainment. At Passover, unleavened bread was broken and, in an Ashkenazi custom adopted by Sephardi Jews, a goblet of wine was poured for the Prophet Elijah. But the important thing was to eat: turkey galantine with parsley was a favourite. At the Jewish carnival known as Purim, the Levi children were dressed in sparkling harlequin rags, and ate sweet ravioli filled with marmalade. (These were quite unlike the prescribed orthodox pastries, which were thought not to taste very pleasant, so the Levis concocted their own approximation.) Often the ritual food was not even Jewish. The Yom Kippur fast was broken with a non-kosher macaroon called *bruscadela*, soaked in wine. One evening Primo's father arrived late for the Passover meal with his brother-in-law Oreste Colombo. Fed-up and hungry, the men began to skip pages in the prayer-book in order to get to the goose salami. Grandpa Luzzati grumbled irritably: 'I must be getting old because I don't understand these prayers any more.'

Levi's father felt the odd twinge of remorse for his wavering faith. He suspected that God might exist and obediently shunned pork. At the same time he delighted in prosciutto, and had even been known to enjoy a nice bit of gammon. Pulling a guilty face to his children, he would tell them: 'If I sin it's because the flesh is weak – but you must behave yourselves!' The prevailing tone in the Levi family was one of irreligion. Cesare's was a respectably bourgeois family, though, and the idea of *not* calling on one's Jewish relatives was unthinkable. So it was that every Sunday Primo and his sister were taken to see their paternal grandmother, who was still living at 24 Via Po with her second husband Dr Rebaudengo. Forty years had elapsed since Adele Sinigaglia fled Bene Vagienna with her goy lover, but an air of scandal clung to her like camphor. Visits were dutiful occasions marked by fear. In Levi's childish imagination Dr Rebaudengo was the Scissor Man of *Struwwelpeter*, who snips off children's sucked thumbs. Adele, now in her early seventies and losing her sight, wore frayed velvet skirts and jewelled slippers. Primo could hardly believe that she was papà's mother. She would offer the boy chocolates, the foil wrappings of which she sent to Catholic missionaries in the Fascist Africa colonies; at one time she had thought of becoming a nun.

Afterwards Cesare would take his children downstairs to the gilt and red-plush Teatro Rossini. There they would have to sit through entire performances of Piedmontese-dialect plays without understanding a word. Primo and his sister squirmed at the sight of Cesare roaring in the aisles: the Rossini theatre was not a hit. In other areas Cesare was more successful with his children. Primo developed a lifelong love of chess from his father, who liked to re-enact the legendary games played by Alexander Alekhin and other grandmasters, and many of his best moves were learned from Cesare. Chess was to play an increasingly important part in Primo's life, appearing several times in his mature writing. As well as chess, Cesare taught his son to play cards – this, at a time when cards were considered socially demeaning by bourgeois Turinese. And in the winter he took his children off to see the flea-circus at the Turin Carnival. The floats were decorated as Moorish seraglios, and veiled concubines shivered in the February cold. In 1928 a troupe of black dancers came from Fascist Africa; for days afterwards Primo enthused at the 'amazing' discs he had seen in their lips.

Engineer Levi tried hard to convey his love of Turin to his son, by taking him to see the city's monuments and museums. On Via Po with Primo he stopped to stroke passing cats (so long as they were not black) and pointed out where Nietzsche once lived, where Montesquieu walked, and Count Cavour (the artificer of Italian unification) had eaten his suppers. None of these names meant anything to the nine-year-old, and Primo would later observe that 'real dialogue did not exist between me and my father'. There was a forty-year difference between Cesare and his son and already they were quite unalike. Primo had become rather serious and did not always approve of his father's bluff jokiness. At the age of five he had asked Cesare what it meant to be 'Jewish', but got a very vague and unsatisfactory response. Try as he might, Primo was unable to come to an easy intimacy with his father. Even at this early age he suspected that he was not the son that his father would have liked. Partly this was a first-born son's resentment of the male authority figure in the family. However, Levi also resented Cesare's undisguised preference for Anna Maria. While Ester's central passion would always be for Primo, Cesare Levi adored his daughter. After supper, he loved to read to her from a French edition of Dickens, without Primo.

Undoubtedly Primo felt anxiety over his father's closeness to Anna Maria, which was intensified by his sister's more sprightly and outgoing nature. Like her father, Anna Maria was sociable and she already showed signs of the charm and generosity that were to characterise her life; Primo was similar to his mother in his gentle shyness, and was more serious and pacific. From the start, he was a mother's boy, and remained so all his life. To add to his anxieties, Anna Maria was 'filling out splendidly' and 'shooting up no end', according to Crocetta relatives, while Levi remained small and fragile-looking. A photograph of the boy at the age of nine shows him half a head shorter than his sister, who was two years younger than he.

Much of Levi's mature testimony about his father suggests unresolved resentments. Levi planned to write a novel, so he later said, about an extrovert Italian engineer who married a textile merchant's daughter. Their son was girlish and frail; their daughter was a tomboy. Thus the father's expectations were fulfilled by his daughter, but not by his son, who was a disappointment. (The novel was never written.) In various interviews Levi made ungenerous and grudging remarks about his father. Cesare's attempts to seduce women by 'trying to tell them about Schopenhauer' were roundly scorned. So were his clanking piano recitals. 'I didn't like the way my father played. He was a mediocre musician, extremely *fragoroso* [noisy] and repetitive. He played for his own pleasure rather than anyone else's.' Cesare hammered his way through Beethoven, playing a battery of base notes for the loud bits and treble arpeggios for the bits he did not know (or were too difficult). This was done with tremendous brio, but it offended Primo's sense of propriety; there was something rather priggish about the boy.

2

Primo was off sick for eighty days during his first school year and a doctor's certificate often had to exempt him from Balilla assemblies. When he could, Levi tended to avoid organised sports and games, a non-conformity regarded as eccentric at a time when team spirit was the key to Fascist manliness. Levi was a frail boy prone to sickness. A popular Italian book at the turn of the century, *Mens sana in corpore sano,* by the positivist doctor Angelo Mosso, recommended the newfangled 'Swedish Gymnastics System' to build a child's strength and promote a 'zingy, full-blooded tingling in the joints'. Levi's mother approved of exercise (she alone of the six Luzzati siblings rode a bike), and when a new gym opened in Turin offering 'Hygienic Swedish Drill' she entered Primo for classes. Situated at 25–7 Corso Oporto (now Corso Matteotti), the gym had Swedish ropes, rings, beams, springboards and pommel horses. After a few lessons, Levi enjoyed the exercise so much that his mother took him there twice a week, if possible, for the next three years. The gym's clientele was mainly from the Crocetta and quite upper-crust (among them was Fiat's future chairman Gianni Agnelli). A photograph labelled 'Children's Warm-Up' shows twenty-six juvenile 'Swedish' gymnasts, Primo holding one foot forward like a ballet dancer's. He has an epicene air.

The family paediatrician, Professor Giovanni Allaria, also recommended boxing as formative for the character. So Levi was given a leather punch ball which he looped round a plaster cornice above one of the doors at 75 Corso Re Umberto. Apparently he hit the ball once too often and the top of the door 'splintered clean off'. As he grew older, Levi displayed a fierce determination to overcome his frailty. Believing that his slight frame was cruelly obvious to others, as soon as he had mastered ball-punching he began to hoist himself up and down from the ceiling by means of specially fitted rings. Primo was also keen to try ice-skating. A rink on Corso Monte Cucco, on the city outskirts, was frequented by Italy's Olympic figure-skating champion Dina Kind. Levi loved to watch her spin on the tips of her blades, tracing shapes across the ice. Primo's skates clattered loudly, but he attempted the odd pirouette. And it was about this time that he was also introduced to the mountains. His uncle Oreste Colombo, an outdoor type, began by taking Primo on strawberry-picking expeditions in the hills above Turin. 'Walk in my footsteps!' he would say. Before long, Levi accompanied Oreste to more ambitious altitudes. These excursions greatly improved the boy's physical confidence: one day he would approach mountaineering with the seriousness of a vocation.

3

In August 1928 Primo's mother rented a holiday farmhouse in the Waldensian valleys south-west of Turin. The Protestant Waldensians had occupied the valleys for more than six centuries, and Ester Levi had a number of relatives there. The local basketball champion, Giovanni Turìn, was married to Ester's cousin Elda Calderoni, an Argentine Jew: theirs was just one of many successful Jewish-Waldensian marriages. The Waldensians, not unlike the Jews, saw themselves as a persecuted elect and their puritan tendency to thrift and moderation was admired by the practically-minded Ester. The Levi farmhouse was in the hamlet of Baussan; it had leather cooking utensils and stone floors. Dragonflies skimmed the Angrogna stream, where Ester sat knitting in the shade while her children explored the shallows. To his cousin Giulia Colombo in Turin, Primo sent letters with sketches that explained the tadpole's evolution into a frog. In spite of his naturalist curiosity, however, he developed a lifelong fear of spiders. One night in Baussan he was startled from semi-sleep by a black Tegenaria crawling towards him. Alerted by his screams, Ester disposed of the creature. Hearing of the incident, Cesare gave Primo a copy of Fabre's classic *Life of the Spider*, in the hope that he would overcome his arachnophobia. He did not.

Usually Ester and her children travelled on their own to Baussan, leaving Cesare in Turin. Her husband was uncomfortable in the country and said he felt 'out of it' among rural folk. The heat and dust, the noise the grasshoppers made, depressed him. And he had bad memories of childhood holidays in his grandfather's shooting lodge, 'The Paradise', where he was made to eat horse chestnuts. On the rare occasions when Cesare went for walks in Baussan, he took books along, which he read sitting on a newspaper mat so as not to dirty his suit. One weekend he turned up with a French copy of *Lady Chatterley's Lover*; the scabrous pages marked with a thumbnail crease were inspected by Primo when his father was not looking. Now fifty, Cesare had soft paunchy features and was to some degree a comic

37

figure. To avoid confusion with his father-in-law Cesare Luzzati, he was known as Cesarino, 'Little Caesar'.

Another reason for Cesare's absence at Baussan was his mistress in Turin. One weekend, Signorina Gribaudo came to Baussan ostensibly to help with domestic arrangements. It is impossible to know Ester's thoughts on the state of her marriage, which, based as much on habit as affection, endured. But somehow news of the affair reached the children. Perhaps Cesare was behaving with the suspect attentiveness of a guilty husband. The matter came to a crisis when Anna Maria Levi (according to cousin Anna Yona in Boston) caught Cesare *in flagrante delicto* at home in 75 Corso Re Umberto. It is not known whether the discovery led to an abrupt termination of the misbegotten affair, but it must have undermined the marriage. According to Anna Yona, Cesare's ill-treatment of Ester explains why Primo grew to be so overattached to his mother. 'In a way, Primo felt he had to provide Ester with the love she didn't have as a wife.' Whatever the plausibility of this claim (and it does not sound very plausible), certainly Levi was angry with his father and looked elsewhere for a more straightforward and affectionate male role-model. He found this in his mother's brother Corrado Luzzati.

Born in 1900 on the cusp of the machine age, and never solemn or pompous, Uncle Corrado had the Futurist's passion for speed and technology. He drove fast in winter for the thrill of skidding on ice; the dashboard's trembling needle seemed to measure not his speed but his very modern soul. Uncle Corrado had a string of sporty models (including the Fiat 508 Balilla) and kept a silver powder horn on the back seat as a talisman against crashing. Aside from cars, Corrado's other great enthusiasm was for film. At Grandpa Luzzati's he arranged private screenings of Tom Mix westerns, featuring Cherokee chases and Buffalo Bill punch-ups. He even made a film, *La Zingaresca* (Gypsy Music), with a Pathé Baby cine-camera, starring Primo in a Mardi Gras Purim costume. Evidently Corrado liked to exaggerate, as he told Primo he had been assistant to the legendary Turin director Giovanni Pastrone, whose 1914 epic slave extravaganza, *Cabiria*, had been a box-office hit worldwide. Yet Corrado would have been barely fourteen at the time the movie was made.

Levi worshipped his uncle. While Cesare provided a more cerebral stimulus, Corrado enthused Primo with a love of modern gadgetry. This gave him a technical know-how and a manual resourcefulness that would later serve him well. In addition to film and automobiles, Uncle Corrado had one other consuming passion: the wireless. One of the earliest radio pioneers in Turin, Corrado made valve radios inside cigar boxes and rigged up an aerial mast on his Crocetta balcony with complicated clamps and guy wires. Domestic radios were expensive in the late 1920s, but Primo's uncle had contacts in the 'Magnadina' factory of Turin, which produced crystal sets. With a heavy headset on his ears the boy heard, through the squeaks of radio static, the disembodied voices of a new age. During the summer of 1928 he was held spellbound by radio bulletins of Umberto Nobile's doomed polar expedition. Six men died when Nobile's airship plummeted into pack-ice; news of the catastrophe sent Fascist Italy into collective mourning, while for Primo the polar calamity illustrated a new epoch in human progress, and human failure.

On 17 April 1928 Adele Sinigaglia became a widow for the second time. Her husband's cremation in Turin was attended by his stepsons Enrico, Mario and Cesare Levi, who preserved his ashes in a black marble urn. After the funeral no one was surprised when Masonic capes and swords were discovered among Dr Rebaudengo's personal effects: the doctor had always had a confidential, furtive air. Meanwhile Adele, having exchanged her Bene Vagienna diamonds for imitation paste, began to gamble secretly on the Turin stock exchange.

4

Primo was ten when his health seriously deteriorated. What began as a hacking cough developed into pleurisy which required medical attention. His sickness was aggravated by the worst cold spell in European memory. During the winter of 1928–9 palm trees froze on the Italian Riviera and Turin was deep in snow. Ester remained at her son's bedside, ministering pectoral syrups and cough pastilles. For Primo this was an enchanting period of succour and love, when he strengthened his ties to his mother. After a long spell recuperating at home, he was taken out of school and for a year tutored privately. This solitary interlude must have sharpened the boy's sense of being different. At the same time Levi had the luxury of a room where he might study, and his appetite for knowledge had space to grow. He had two tutors. The first was Emilia Glauda, his primary-school teacher, who agreed to coach him in mathematics. The second was Marisa Zini, the twenty-two-year-old daughter of Turin's anti-Fascist philosopher Zino Zini. Marisa had known Primo since he was a baby in petticoats: she was to coach him in Italian and Latin. Together Glauda and Zini would prepare the boy for *ginnasio* or Gymnasium, the equivalent of high school for thirteen- to fifteen-year-olds. Already an able student, Levi flourished under individual attention. His later excellence as a classicist was thanks first of all to Zini, and soon he was correcting his sister's Latin homework.

Indeed, Levi did so well academically that he was able to condense two school years into one. And this would have dramatic significance for him later on.

He read voraciously during this period, and ransacked his father's library, revelling in the unknown foreign fiction to be discovered there. He tried Hungarian writers (in translation) whom his father had enjoyed in Budapest. His favourite Hungarian discovery, according to his sister, was Kálmán Mikszáth's folk novel, *St Peter's Umbrella* (1895), in which Slovak peasants find a baby abandoned under a giant red umbrella believed to belong to St Peter. Levi also tried to read that most Byronic of Magyar poets, Sándor Petöfi, and thrilled to his lyrics of peasant life.

To help with his French, Levi was given Alphonse Daudet's 1872 adventure story, *Tartarin of Tarascon.* The big-game-hunting Tartarin, with his knuckle-dusters and sword-sticks, is a prototype Blackshirt who scorns Arabs, blacks and 'the filthy Jews'. (When Levi reread this novel forty years later he found it in dubious taste.) Other staples were James Curwood's American tales of Hudson Bay fur-trappers and Wild West shoot-outs. With such titles as *The Grizzly King* and *The Last Frontier*, these schoolboy yarns satisfied Primo's craving for rough adventure. However, Cesare prohibited Emilio Salgari, Italy's first *Boy's Own* writer, who had committed suicide in Turin in 1911. Salgari's high-sea tales of cannibals and filibusters were slices of pernicious exotica, said Cesare. Adventure was all very well, but it had to have some grounding in scientific plausibility. Middle-class Italian children could then be divided into the *salgariani* and those who read Jules Verne, the *verniani*. Primo was put firmly in the Verne camp. The engineer's literary monitoring was not confined to his son. Anna Maria was banned from reading *libri rosa*, 'pink books'. The bulk of these girls' romances, with their distorted rosy view of the world, were written by the Marquess Amalia Negretti ('Liala'), Italy's own Barbara Cartland. They were 'trash and nonsense', Cesare informed his daughter; he disliked their ardent, treacle prose.

5

In September 1930 Primo, his pleurisy now behind him, entered Turin's premier classical school, the 'M. D'Azeglio' Royal Gymnasium. Academically he was accelerated by a year and, at eleven, almost two years younger than some of the entrants for Gymnasium. Having been the centre of such loving attention under Marisa Zini and Emilia Glauda, Gymnasium was a rude awakening. His class, Course II A, was a mixed group of eight girls and sixteen boys. The school, known as 'The Ancient One', was situated on the outskirts of the Crocetta at 8 Via Giuseppe Parini. It had a high academic reputation with a vaguely Liberal and reputedly anti-Fascist inclination. Some of its teachers had been disciples of the austere Turin moralist Piero Gobetti, founder of Italy's first anti-Fascist weekly, *Rivoluzione liberale*. But they had been silenced or expelled by the time Levi arrived, and Fascist censorship ensured that he was kept ignorant of these disgraced intransigents. Spies stalked the corridors. And the headmaster, Giovanni Marchesa Rossi, was rumoured to eavesdrop on lessons in specially padded overshoes, like a sneak-thief. The beadle, Signor Caruso, was an ex-policeman and a suspect Fascist informer: 'Out, idiot! Other door!' he would yell at boys who tried to enter through the girls' doorway.

The hinged desks were screwed fast to the floorboards, and the sexes strictly segregated. A few of the pupils came from bookish Crocetta homes, but most had parents in business. Sleek-haired hearties, the boys wore Norfolk jackets and double-breasted suits, while the girls were fitted decorously with black pinafores. One of them, Fernanda Pivano (later the consort and confidante of Ernest Hemingway), was in many ways typical of the privileged *dazegline,* or D'Azeglio girls. 'We thought we were the *crème de la crème*,' she said. 'My parents had nine maids, and I suppose many of us were just plain spoiled, waited on hand and foot.'

Not only was Levi the youngest in class, he was also the smallest, the shortest and, by a long chalk, the most clever. The older boys adopted a sneering contempt for cleverness, and Levi was made to feel their contempt. His situation was made worse by the fact that he was also the only Jew in the form. 'Classmates began to look at me as if I was a strange tiny animal' (or at any rate a *strayed* animal – one not quite of the fold).

The Fascist school reforms of 1923 had ensured that the Classics provided the core curriculum, not science. The more children knew about the ancient world, the better they were able to command their own: such was the theory. Technical colleges of the sort that Levi's father had attended still existed in Italy, but Fascism had dealt a blow to science. Blackshirt ideologues scorned laboratory disciplines as grossly materialist and vulgar. Today familiarity with Latin and Greek is still considered a mark of breeding in Italy. Most of those at the top of Italian society have been to a classical school such as the 'M. D'Azeglio'.

School hours were from 8:00 am to 3:00 pm, six days a week, from late September until May. Thanks to his private Classics tutor Marisa Zini, Levi could already read some Xenophon in the original Greek. But now he would have to submit to a more rigorous classical drill. Each morning he had to decline Latin verbs in chorus. Soon he would be expected to make deft and mellifluous translations from Greek directly into Latin. Children of Levi's generation were given a classical education that has never been equalled in Italy for its depth and thoroughness.

His class teacher was Anna Borgogno, an attractive thirty-two-year-old with a reserved, intelligent expression. Most boys were blushingly enamoured of her. She taught Latin, history and Italian; for his grades Levi rarely scored lower than eight out of ten. To make a shining example of Levi, Borgogno sat him next to Course II A's most disruptive and lazy boy. She joked that a plaque would go up in the classroom: 'PRIMO LEVI STUDIED HERE'. According to her sister-in-law, Emma Andriani, Borgogno had a 'mischievous, unconventional intelligence' that could be caustic but always remained good-natured. One boy had poliomyelitis and she routinely helped him negotiate the corridors. She kept her eye on Levi, too, as it must have been obvious that he was not happy. In every Gymnasium photograph he stands apart from his peers, with an anxious, diffident gaze.

Assigned the class topic 'Avarice', a boy at the back shouted out 'Jewishness!' Borgogno was indignant and scolded him. The boy was one of two teenagers who bullied Levi during his time at the 'M. D'Azeglio'. Though not 'particularly stupid' or even 'unpleasant', recalled Levi, they mocked his Jewishness. Circumcision was tantamount to castration, and they viewed Levi as somehow unmanly. They tormented him in the playground and routinely called on him to copy his homework (which he let them do). Levi hated the boys for the misery they caused. And he hated the weakness in himself that allowed them to abuse him. In old age he could not remember his wretched self-subjection without astonishment.

Life had turned its cruel side to Levi; it began to affect his health and he was frequently off sick with chest infections. One spring he missed two full weeks of lessons. Levi began to believe he possessed repulsive traits, an imagined runtiness, and was easily upset by remarks about his 'Jewish' appearance. He learned to hide his feelings, though. And in later years Levi dramatised his early shame in a science fantasy, 'The Synthetic Ones', in which the schoolboy Mario has no navel (for which we read he is 'circumcised'). Finding his otherness unbearable, we see him huddled alone in the school gym, weeping.

With some pain, Levi recalled the jibes of his tormentors in a late interview. The worst offender (though Levi did not name him) was Rodolfo Villa; with the help of his accomplice Salvatore Roggero, he turned Levi's life into a hopeless misery. Villa had a sly quality, while Roggero radiated a rough bonhomie – the bossy type. Interestingly, most of Levi's contemporaries cannot clearly recall either boy. Like many bullies they were conventional types and left the 'M. D'Azeglio' with no great distinction. When I corresponded with Roggero in 1998 he would not comment to me on the humiliation he had caused Levi, but revealingly described Levi as '*un israelita*'. This too-polite Italian term often carries an undertone of prejudice, if only because it is used to avoid the connotations of the more direct word *ebreo*, 'Jew'.

Levi looked elsewhere for friends. Mario Piacenza joined Levi's class late in 1932. A blithe, round-faced boy, he was at ease with himself, and in him Levi found an emotional mooring. Levi saw himself as the more clever boy and let Piacenza know it. 'Yes, Primo was my brainy maestro,' recalled Piacenza, 'but I think he rather relished the teacher–pupil imbalance.' Another sympathetic friend at this time was Giorgio Lattes, a Jewish boy at another school in Turin. Levi called him 'Giorgione', Big George, for his broad, big-boned appearance. Phlegmatic, lazy, sensitive and generous, he was one of two brothers who lived just outside the Crocetta on Via Duchessa Jolanda. Later Lattes would fall passionately in love with Levi's sister (only to be rebuffed). If Piacenza was meekly admiring of Levi, Lattes's role was to puncture his pretensions. 'Giorgio undermined Primo's intellectual flights with a slow, dogged sort of irony,' recalled his widow Giuliana Lattes. Yet it was Lattes to whom Levi felt he could confess his failures and secret humiliations.

Levi was tremendously loyal to his friends, and he and Lattes acquired a mutual friend in Piacenza. They made an inseparable trio. On their way home after school the boys stopped at the Caffè Platti (where in 1897 the Juventus football team had been founded by a group of athletic *dazeglini*) to buy slices of the café speciality 'Russian bread', made from bakery leftovers and candied peel. The Crocetta, with its middle-class intimacies, encouraged these sorts of diversions.

6

In the summer of 1932, at the end of his second year at the 'M. D'Azeglio', Levi went for the first time with his family to Bardonecchia. Due east of Turin, Bardonecchia is an old-fashioned holiday resort hemmed in by steeply sloping woods where deer and foxes roam; further out are the Alps with their leftover summer snow. Levi's parents had rented a house off Piazza Carlo Suspize in the heart of the old town. Here Cesare felt more at home than in an old Waldensian farmhouse. Just one factor spoiled the idyll. At weekends Bardonecchia was flooded with day-trippers from the Fascist After-Work Leisure Organisation. They would gather noisily beneath Primo's bedroom window to read the Latin motto painted above a sundial on the wall: 'I, THE SHADOW, AM THE SUN'S DAUGHTER' (which is still there). Levi scoffed at the hoi polloi's attempts to translate the Latin.

He joined the Bardonecchia tennis club, where he dabbed his tennis balls with silver nitrate to identify them from the others, and balanced arms akimbo on a high wall round the court. One day he caught sight of Mimi and Pupi Kind, sons of the ice-skating champion Dina Kind whom he had admired in Turin. The brothers' Swiss grandfather Adolfo Kind had introduced Italy to winter sports in 1896 and earned himself the title 'Apostle of Italian Skiing'. Mimi and Pupi were two or three years older than Levi and exuded a freckle-faced athleticism and manliness that powerfully attracted the pubescent Primo, who was not quite thirteen. Neither of the brothers belonged to a Fascist youth movement, which to Levi's unsophisticated eye lent them a daring, rebel edge. He admired the brothers from a distance as they practised rowing, archery, skiing; a Dobermann retrieved their javelins, and they were rumoured to build igloos on mountain tops. Tennis was a 'namby-pamby' pastime, according to Mimi Kind, who wrote to me in 1995: 'Who wants to move about like caged animals inside a fence?' Levi's diffident, feminine nature yearned to be noticed by them. Anna Maria said: 'My brother idolised the Kinds as Greek gods.' They lived with their parents in Turin in a big, German-style chalet on Via Vincenzo Monti: Primo longed to visit them. Perhaps it is merely romantic to suggest that the attraction he felt for Mimi and Pupi had a kind of homoerotic component; certainly this was the first of many such fixations that Levi was to have for more physically robust boys and men.

On the first Saturday after his thirteenth birthday Levi had to sing in synagogue for his Bar Mitzvah. The ceremony fell on a swelteringly hot day in August 1932; dry-mouthed with nerves, the thirteen-year-old made his way to the altar to sing from the Book of Isaiah. For the past two years Levi had attended the Talmud-Torah (Hebrew School) in Turin for lessons in Jewish doctrine. From his teacher, Rabbi Bolaffio, he had digested a mass of lore and culture. Half a century later he could still remember 200 Hebrew words, but had little idea what they meant. The sole aim of the Talmud-Torah, it seemed to Levi, was to teach boys how to read their prayer-books so fluently that their grandparents could reap honours with them in temple on Bar Mitzvah day. Now Primo was officially counted a man. Half his family were away for the August holidays, however, but at the depleted reception Primo was presented with a gold watch, gold cufflinks, a set of fountain pens and a leather *nécessaire* with brushes and combs. His maternal grandmother Adele Sinigaglia was absent, having died four months earlier on 23 April 1932. Each of her three sons had been been left a diamond ring that turned out to be fake.

At first Levi took his religious obligations seriously. He prayed intermittently, professed to believe in God and laboured to achieve a pious virtue. His brief religious conversion was motivated chiefly by fear – 'fear of being judged by an ever-watchful Holy Father' – and Levi later said he felt guilty whenever he broke one of the 613 sacred commandments (no ham rolls, no tram-riding on Saturdays: these shalt-nots are a mix of the positive as well as proscriptive). In the hope of winning a bicycle from his grandparents, he vowed to wear the ritual praying bands, or *Tefillin*, at morning orations. Once Levi had obtained his bicycle, however, he became indifferent to God. And, as his attachment to religion tottered, so a counter-process began: Levi became interested in science. He began to investigate the godless evolutionary theories of Charles Darwin. In Baussan one day Levi had seen a tadpole wriggling unhappily on the ground, when a robin swooped down and swallowed it; within seconds the adored farmhouse cat pounced on the robin and ran off with it in its jaws. Here was an early lesson in nature's cruelty. In Darwin's *The Origin of Species* Levi found an alternative theology that recognised no God. And as Levi moved a step closer to his eventual atheism, so he told his classmate Mario Piacenza that evolution theory was the 'most portentous natural truth that science had discovered'. (Piacenza recalled that Levi was a 'magnificent philosophy companion'.) Levi's period of piety was done with, and he was on the edge of an intellectual blossoming.

On his father's recommendation, Levi read Flammarion's classic 1884 guide to astronomy, *Territories of the Sky*. Armed with Flammarion's star charts, he began to explore the marvels of the night sky. He spoke to his sister of the 'geography' of the skies and the 'grandeur' of the night-time firmament. Whenever he thought about the cosmos he wondered about the 'driver' behind the enormous machine of the universe. But if this 'driver' exists, as Levi declared conclusively many years afterwards, 'he is not someone worth praying to'.

7

Political developments, meanwhile, were whirling darkly in the world outside. On 30 January 1933 Hitler was made Reich Chancellor of Germany. Immediately his razor-and-cosh gangs went to work on German Jews. On 4 April Storm-Troopers raided the Berlin ghetto, beating the inhabitants. Three days later, on 7 April, the first in a raft of anti-Jewish laws was promulgated. All 'non-Aryans' were eliminated from government posts; soon Germany's Jews would be excluded outright from citizenship.

The Levis, like most Italian Jews, felt under no direct threat of such violence. They could not believe they were at the same risk as their co-religionists elsewhere in Europe. Polish or Russian orthodox Jews with their Hasidic kaftans and curls might arouse Jew-hatred, but not assimilated Italian Jews. Their integration into Italian society was a guarantee of safety. Bad things were happening in Germany, but to the Levis the persecutions were a remote rumour, irrelevant to them.

Mussolini greeted Hitler's rise to power with mixed emotions. A racial dogma that glorified blond-haired northerners conflicted somewhat with the Fascist cult of ancient Rome. In fact, Mussolini did not approve of Hitler's biological anti-Semitism. His mistress, Margherita Sarfatti, was Jewish, and her influence on the dictator was stronger than is generally realised. She was the mastermind behind Mussolini's pompous celebration of ancient Rome: the eagle motifs and suckling she-wolves seen on Fascist buildings in Italy today are partly her legacy. With publicists like Sarfatti on his side, Mussolini could ill afford to alienate Italy's Jewish lobby. Moreover, Italian Jewish writers and artists still unapologetically supported the regime. The Piedmontese poet Arturo Foà, a Jew, wrote a bestselling epic of Fascism, *Italy on the Move*, which championed Mussolini as a hybrid of Jesus Christ and Garibaldi. If this was hero-worship, Mussolini was happy to encourage it.

But with Hitler as Reich Chancellor, Mussolini had pragmatic reasons for closer ties with anti-Semitic Germany. Hitler, with his superior armies, might help Mussolini realise his dream of a revived Roman empire in the Mediterranean and East Africa. The Italian dictator knew that an anti-Semitic campaign would greatly please Hitler. If it was diplomatically advantageous for him to persecute Jews, then he would do so. And with Machiavellian adroitness, he tried to win Hitler's approval by allowing a small but insistent anti-Semitic campaign to flare up in Italy's extremist Fascist press. The campaign did not last long, petering out in mid-1933, but its effects were clamorous and a first step towards official persecution of Italy's Jews. Initially the campaign unfolded in the form of a Fascist debate on Jews and Zionism, but it quickly assumed anti-Semitic overtones. The unofficial Fascist newspaper of Rome, *Il Tevere,* complained of 'unpatriotic' Italian Zionists who dream ungratefully of a Jewish homeland in Palestine; their new Zion was not in the Middle East, but here in Fascist Italy, the 'country that had given them prosperity and citizenship'. Beneath *Il Tevere*'s ostensibly anti-Zionist stance lay the usual anti-Semitism; the paper even lambasted an Italian shipping company for renaming its vessel the *Tel Aviv*. Meanwhile as the Zionist debate sputtered in the maverick Fascist press, Mussolini stood by.

In retrospect it is clear that a latent tension had always existed between Fascism and Italy's Jews. Mussolini was wary of those who appeared cosmopolitan or who transcended the confines of the nation. Zionists, especially, were seen as a self-regarding, supranational sect inimical to the sturdy Blackshirt bond of race and nation. If any Italian Jews understood the menace, the evil and the spread of Nazism, they were the Zionists. Ever since the Savoy Edict of Emancipation in 1848, assimilated Italian Jewry had argued that medieval Jew-hatred would evaporate with the inevitable progress of mankind. But Hitler was proving them wrong. The year 1933 was a turning-point in the fortunes of Italy's Jews.

8

In 1933, as usual, the Levis took their summer holiday in Bardonecchia. Levi was now fourteen and he embarked on what turned out to be a foolhardy mountain expedition. Mountaineering was a maverick, risk-taking sport, but Levi wanted desperately to be like Mimi and Pupi Kind, and needed to test his physical limits. So one hot summer's day in early July he set out from Bardonecchia to scale an Alp. He was accompanied by the sixteen-year-old future historian Luigi Firpo, who declared himself in charge, and another boy his own age, Giorgio Diena. They planned to cross the Catena dei Magi range and descend the other side into the Valle Stretta. This was a punishing day-long hike from Bardonecchia: had they known, Levi's parents would never have allowed such a risky venture. Still, the boys felt elated with freedom: their guide-book calculated a three-hour climb to King Melchior's peak, but Levi reckoned he could do it under two, easily, and return home in time for supper.

By the time the three boys reached Melchior's summit it was almost dark, and they were close to exhaustion. With no food or warm clothing, it was too dangerous to head for the mountain shelter in the distance; 3,000 metres below them lay the plains of Bardonecchia, an impossible descent. Levi and his companions were now at risk of hypothermia. They began to scream for help and eventually were heard. At 2:00 am a rescue team arrived. 'Who've you got up there?' echoed a question from below. 'Ah, just three cry-babies [*gagno brodos*]!' replied the advance party, with all the valley-dweller's contempt for townsfolk. Tied together like salamis the boys were lowered over the rock face by lantern-light. Such were the follies of Alpinism.

News of the mishap spread quickly through Bardonecchia. It would take Levi many years to live down the disgrace. Nevertheless, his night on the bare mountain had been a vitally maturing experience. Years later in a short story, 'Bear Meat', Levi recalled the adventure, and attached importance to

47

learning from one's mistakes. His hike into high Bardonecchia had been his real initiation into adulthood, not his Bar Mitzvah.

Closer to home, more pressing concerns weighed down on the Levis. The textile store at 37 Via Roma was to be bulldozed as part of a massive public-works programme to generate employment: 8,000 Turinese had been drafted in to demolish the shops and houses of Via Roma to make way for 'Mussolini modern' buildings with stone eagle motifs and *fasces*. On 28 October 1933 the first section of the pseudo-imperial Via Roma was opened; Blackshirts marched triumphantly down the flower-strewn street. The Luzzati store was moved to nearby Via Santa Teresa, but the new premises, surrounded by Fascist insignia of shields and naked torsos, lacked the charm of the old. Grandpa Luzzati was never the same again and was demoralised and unhappy until his death eight years later.

During the subsequent years of the decade Mussolini's cult of imperial Rome was to reach lunatic proportions. The dictator assumed the title Duce after the Latin *Dux*, 'leader', and a stern new Fascist morality was abroad. Thomas Mann had been fined fifty lire for allowing his baby daughter to paddle naked in Italian waters. The high priests of Fascism began to hail Mussolini as 'Divine Caesar'. They called for an embargo on all foreign words and non-Latin terms. The handshake was scorned as fey and unhygienic. And, in a publicity coup for geese, the goose was eulogised as the bird that had saved ancient Rome (after its loud honking had warned of impending attack by the barbarian Gauls). The Italian army adopted the *passo romano,* the Latin goose-step copied from Hitler. And Primo was expected to live in the most Latin-Italian way possible, by speaking in Latin to friends at school and refraining from the use of French and English words. He could no longer take a ferry-boat and had to travel instead by *pontone*, just as Julius Caesar had done (when he invented mobile bridges). The word 'cocktail' was Latinised, absurdly if imaginatively, to *coda di gallo*.

9

At the end of 1933 Levi graduated from the Balilla Fascist youth group into the Avanguardia movement for older boys. Avanguardia leaders were often the worst sort of reactionaries, demanding absolute discipline. Fortunately, Levi managed to escape weekend rifle drill by joining the Avanguardia ski division. Each Saturday, at the unearthly hour of 5:30 am, a coach left Turin's Via Sacchi for the mountains; on board were thirty male Avanguardisti skiers, all itching to gain the slopes. Skiing offered them glamorous escape. Yet the sport had also become a measure of physical daring – *ardimento* – and the manful Fascist soul. 'If we truly want our future generations to be as rock-like and robust as the great Mussolini commands, we must call an end to all frolicking and cuddling!' Thus Angelo Manaresi, in his delirious 1932 guide to winter sports, *A Word to Alpinists*. The mixture of fear and contempt for girls implicit in Manaresi's book (which Levi had read with interest) was reinforced by Fascist propaganda films, which showed bare-chested, lantern-jawed sportsmen flying down the snow slopes or laughing heartily *après ski*.

Levi's new passion for skiing satisfied, no doubt, some need for reassurance about his virility. As the youngest in his class, there must have been some relief when his voice finally broke. He had no girlfriend, and his classmates were so much more knowing about relationships, the girls maturer than he by more than just their years. Luckily at this time Levi found another male hero to look up to, Roberto Perdomi. A sturdy Catholic boy his own age, Perdomi became his companion on the ski slopes. After school hours Levi's social life, apart from visits to Giorgio Lattes and Mario Piacenza, centred increasingly on the Perdomi family at 63 Corso Re Umberto. They kept open house at the weekends and encouraged Roberto to invite Primo, whom they reckoned good for their non-bookish son. Perdomi had a taste for athletic competition and had won a variety of cups for his prowess in slalom races. For Levi, he was a paragon of sophistication and ruggedness. Perdomi, for his part, was delighted to bask in Levi's unqualified admiration.

He reckoned that Levi looked 'slovenly' on the slopes in his baggy Avanguardia plus-fours and primitive skis made of hickory planks. He had no style and tended to 'wobble' downhill, taking many croppers. Perdomi's tutoring was done in a spirit of rough but good-natured ragging. In time, however, skiing usefully encouraged Levi to think with his body instead of just his head, and the boys set out on longer trips together. The Susa hamlet of Sauze d'Oulx was a favourite destination. There, a peasant family cooked the boys potato dumplings with braised meat, alpine-style, and prepared them a bed for the night. Early next morning, strapped and buckled, they set out for the forests. The Adolfo Kind Shelter above Sauze d'Oulx resembled a Klondike log cabin with a cast-iron stove and swinging shutters. Fired up with the pioneer spirit of sleds and ice-picks, the boys felt like Jack London heroes, and returned to Turin stronger men, they believed.

By spring 1934, Levi was ill again with a chest infection. He spent two weeks in bed, enjoying the luxury of books and chocolates brought by Perdomi and other friends. He then convalesced in Bardonecchia. Levi was susceptible to bronchial disorders, but his sickness had one obvious cause. The previous autumn his adored teacher Anna Borgogno had been replaced by a doughty Fascist patriot, Professor F. Taverna, who was an unrepentant anti-Semite. 'He was extremely unpleasant, and very strict. He had no love for us children,' recalled Levi. Under the repressive Taverna, boys were forbidden to stay too long in the lavatory, or to look at girls in class; there were prohibitions against 'touching oneself' and keeping one's hands in one's pockets.

About this time Levi read Alberto Moravia's extraordinary novel of sexual domination and alienation in Fascist Italy, *The Time of Indifference*. Moravia, the son of a Venetian Jew, had written his novel in 1925 when he was sixteen (two years older than Levi was now) and recovering from tuberculosis. His portrayal of double-dealing, intrigue and violence in Mussolini's Italy outraged the Fascists, who publically condemned Moravia as a 'destroyer of every human value'. No other Italian book was so revealing or disconcerting of its time, and *for* its time. Levi's father warned Primo that he was reading a dangerous novel; nevertheless Moravia's cynicism and brutally frank attitude to sex aroused the teenager. Levi began to ask himself which writers had truthfully sounded the depths of their nature. He coined the bizzare term *pancia-sentito-o-no?* ('gut-stirring-or-not?') as a point of literary discrimination. Jack London's *The Call of the Wild* was supremely 'gut-stirring'. The novel's canine hero (half St Bernard, half sheepdog) must adapt to his brutal new life as a sled-dog or die. Another significant novel at this time of sexual awakening was Lajos Zilahy's Hungarian epic of love and war, *Two Prisoners*, which went well beyond the normal schoolboy range of reading. Set in Austro-Hungarian Budapest, the novel contained a peeping-tom fantasy as well as a pre-marital sex scene. For Levi, sunk in his turbid and troubled adolescence, Zilahy intensified his confused longings. 'Once Primo finished the novel he read it all over again, reading it through from start to finish,' remembered his sister. Zilahy wrote of adult relations more explicitly than most Italian writers under Fascism (except perhaps Moravia).

Meanwhile, the fifteen-year-old Levi had become infatuated with a girl in the Crocetta. Vera Gay, a Protestant, was a bright and popular recruit to the neighbourhood gang. She lived with her parents at 30 Corso Re Umberto, and the mere mention of her name was enough to make Levi flush deep red. Seeing this, other Crocetta girls chanted teasingly in chorus: '*Arrossisce Primo!*', 'Primo's blushing!' In the crushingly self-centred embarrassment of puberty, Levi was mortified.

On 31 March 1934 more bad news came for Italy's Jews with reports of a 'Jewish plot' to overthrow Fascism. The ringleaders were all based in Turin, and panic descended on the city's Jewish community. The Fascist national press emphasised the Jewish background of the 'subversives', where previously their religion would not have been mentioned. While Mussolini's secret police cracked down on the instigators, Levi's family realised that the arrested were all known to them; a few were even relatives. News of the conspiracy was deliberately leaked to the press on the Jewish Passover, a full two weeks after the police had uncovered it. Anti-Semitism was palpable in this gesture, designed to cause maximum damage to Jews.

On 11 March 1934 Sion Segre Amar, a wealthy Turin Jew, had been arrested while smuggling anti-government propaganda into Switzerland. He belonged to Italy's 'Justice and Liberty' anti-Fascist group, then the largest organised political opposition in the country. Members were known as *giellisti* after the movement's initials 'g' and 'l' (Giustizia e Libertà). A high proportion were Jewish, though overall the organisation recruited from Catholics. Affiliates upheld the Liberal spirit of the Risorgimento and aimed to overthrow the Savoy monarchy (now pro-Fascist), as well as the Duce.

Perhaps a more experienced intriguer might not have bungled. Sion Segre, a gentle, indolent character, had fitted out his American sports car with removable panels to conceal anti-Fascist propaganda. He was accompanied on the smuggling mission by Mario Levi (no relation), who was an Olivetti office-machines director and frustrated adventurer. Italian border police stopped the pair at the Swiss frontier. Mario Levi managed to escape to neutral territory across Lake Lugano, but Segre was arrested. Though Segre viewed Zionism with distaste, the Fascists believed they had uncovered the core of a nationwide Zionist conspiracy to topple the Duce, as Segre's first name, Sion, is Italian for 'Zion'. So a second anti-Jewish campaign was allowed to take hold in Italy. Again it was agitated by a minority of obscure pro-German Italian extremists. But this time it led to the publication of crude anti-Jewish cartoons in satirical Italian magazines and papers, and revealed unexpected depths of prejudice in ordinary Italians. For Levi's family the campaign must have evoked memories of the mob violence that had hounded them out of Bene Vagienna in 1888. Indeed, as Primo Levi saw it later, there was a premonition of violence in this early Fascist anti-Semitism: the Nazis' *Kristallnacht*, when the shattered plate glass of Jewish properties littered German streets, was just four years away.

Seventeen suspected *giellisti* were detained in Turin for questioning. One of them, the painter and doctor Carlo Levi, was later famous as the author of *Christ Stopped at Eboli,* and was related to the Levis by marriage. Other friends and relatives were bound to be implicated as Turin's Jewish community was so small. Vittorio Foa, chief of the Turin branch of 'Justice and Liberty', was related to Grandma Adelina Luzzati. (Foa's maternal grandfather was Adelina's brother.) Foa lived at 64 Corso Re Umberto, rather close for comfort. Professor Giuseppe Levi, the father of the escaped Mario and of the future novelist Natalia Ginzburg, was a friend and neighbour on Corso Re Umberto. He too was arrested. The youngest detainee, Ennio Artom, was at Primo's school.

In the event, only three of those arrested were tried and convicted. These were Sion Segre, Leone Ginzburg (later Natalia Ginzburg's husband) and, *in absentia,* Mario Levi. To their relief, Primo's family were not compromised in any way for knowing the conspirators. Nevertheless, Ester and Cesare were shaken and angry by what had happened. Two wayward young men had by their incompetent smuggling jeopardised the safety of Italian Jews everywhere. But above this and more dangerous still, the 1934 scandal threatened to weaken and divide Italian Jewry at a time when they faced the common threat of Hitler.

Turin's Jewish community was split into two factions: those Jewish anti-Fascists who approved of the 'Justice and Liberty' subversives, and those who opposed them. A group of Fascist Jews in Turin now launched a pro-Mussolini weekly, *La Nostra Bandiera* (Our Flag). The paper's inaugural edition of 1 May 1934 was a strident call to arms, which urged Italian Jews to unite in their duties to the Fatherland. Cesare Levi, who was politically the Italian equivalent of a Gladstonian Liberal, strongly disapproved of the *Bandiera*'s brand of Jewish para-Fascism, and spoke of the paper as a 'betrayal'. He and the *Bandiera*'s editor Ettore Ovazza had rubbed along together for years, but now they looked the other way when they passed on the street.

It was suspected that the arrests were the result of a Jewish spy who had infiltrated the ranks of 'Justice and Liberty', and in the event that suspicion proved to be squalidly true. After the war the spy was identified as Sion Segre's cousin, Dino Segre. Codenamed Réné Odin (an artful anagram of his name), Segre was not only Jewish, but lived in the Crocetta. He wrote awful erotic novels (*The Chastity Belt, Luxurious Beasts*) under the pseudonym 'Pitigrilli'; Primo often saw him walking his dog down Corso Re Umberto. (The imposter was related by marriage to the Levis, as he was the husband of Celeste Sinigaglia, daughter of Adele's brother Moise.) After the war Segre-Pitigrilli fled to Argentina, where he allegedly became Eva Perón's ghost-writer.

*

52

Four months after the arrests, in July 1934, Levi sat his entrance exams for the 'M. D'Azeglio' *liceo* or Lyceum (sixth form), and was admitted the following autumn. By then Italy's anti-Semitic campaign had lost its momentum, as the prospect of a Fascist alliance with anti-Semitic Germany aroused little enthusiasm. Hitler's designs on Austria and the threat this might pose to Italy's northern borders alarmed many Italians. Anyway, they thought Hitler looked unappealingly furtive and rat-like beside their grandly uniformed Duce. Mussolini began to seek improved diplomatic relations with Britain and France. Ever the opportunist, he judged that a domestic anti-Jewish campaign was no longer expedient. Few could see it now, but the Duce's wavering attitude towards Hitler was to be the downfall of Italy's Jews. No matter how brutal the Fascist persecutions became, Italian Jews could always cling to a last hope of reprieve: Mussolini had vacillated so many times, surely he would not go as far as Hitler? When the deportations finally began in Occupied Italy, it was too late for the Jews to leave.

FIVE

Chemistry and Adolescence

1934–7

I

In September 1934 Primo Levi was in a new, all-male class of thirty-seven older boys. The pupils included some boys Levi had known before, among them the sympathetic Giorgio Lattes, who had moved to the 'M. D'Azeglio' from a minor school in Turin, and Mario Piacenza. Levi's sister was already much in evidence in Gymnasium, the winner of prizes and praise for her art. Yet against her brother's ink-stained tormentors she was powerless to act. The bullies Rodolfo Villa and Salvatore Roggero were among the five classmates who stayed on with Levi to Lyceum. So he could expect more provocations from them. Now fifteen, Levi began to see himself as a '*complessato*', he said in later years, 'a neurotic', and attributed his perceived inadequacies to his being Jewish. A caricature of Levi at this time, done by Lattes, shows him with an anxious expression, a fine sensitive nose and a studious, vulnerable air. The school magazine unkindly named Levi as author of a book called *Lo sviluppo* (Physical Development) published by Mingherlini (The Puny Ones); Levi must have found this teasing hurtful.

Moving up to Lyceum was a watershed for Levi. From his earlier position of unqualified favourite under Anna Borgogno, he was now just one of many bright contemporaries, and his work suffered for it. According to most old boys, Levi was not exceptional in his new class. 'I don't remember that he shined at all. There were many other prodigies,' recalled Bruno Foa. Levi's new class, Course B, contained a variety of human types. Scions of Turin's bourgeoisie, the boys had brilliantined hair and incipient moustaches. Mostly they were 'scoundrels', Levi would remember. In a class photograph of 1934 we can make out the debonair one in his pin-striped suit, the philanderer with his gold watch-chain, and the sportsman standing four-square. A slice of classical school excellence, these young men were also unrepentantly snobbish. The one token proletarian in class, Paolo

Perosino, was booed by the proverbial *figli di papà* (spoiled brats) on his first appearance in the classroom. Yet it was Levi, not Perosino, who was conspicuously the misfit in all group photographs. His awkward expression and posture make him look like a child among adults, which in a sense he was.

Victims of bullying tend to stand out from the crowd. And Jews, as a minority, might have been especially vulnerable. A high proportion of Course B were Jews – seven in all – yet there is no evidence to suggest that they suffered. The intellectually bumptious Ennio Artom, who had been one of the eleven Jews detained in Turin after the spring 1934 'Zionist conspiracy', was a sure candidate for bullying. The school's iconoclast, Ennio was already distinguished for his advanced literary tastes and somewhat bizarre manner and appearance. (He wore an intellectual's thick pebble-lens glasses and comical plus-fours.) Yet he was not bullied at all. It was only Primo.

Tellingly, Levi was teased even by the Jews in his class. Bruno Foa, a good-looking Juventus football fan, reckoned Levi was a 'shrimp' and 'physical lightweight' who deserved to be made a butt of. 'Levi was a bit of a joke, frankly, something of a prig – his name was a byword for sexual backwardness.' The fierce-browed Foa would never have invited, still less allowed, anti-Semitic slights. Yet for Levi the bullying and derision he endured at Lyceum were later interpreted as uniquely anti-Semitic. How far this impression was coloured by Levi's eventual persecution is hard to tell.

Levi's shyness could come across as standoffish and no doubt he was snobbish regarding non-bookish boys. Pupils like Bruno Foa, with their off-colour talk about girls and their four-letter bravado, incurred his disapproval. Two years older than Levi, his peers were physically more mature, and took an interest in girls while Levi remained in an agony of embarrassment and self-scrutiny. Course A was brimful of attractive *dazegline* but, tormented by the notion that he was ugly, Levi never dared approach them. Nevertheless he conceived an intense passion for one girl, Lidia Carbonatto. When Levi met Lidia at a classical concert in Turin forty years later, she had become *La Stampa*'s music critic Lidia Palomba. In the concert's interval he decided to confess his old teenage infatuation. 'It doesn't really matter now that I've nothing to hide,' he blushingly owned up. Levi admitted that he had followed three steps behind Lidia in the school corridor just to see her walk. She had queened his imagination in a way she could not have believed. 'Primo Levi! You never told me!' she exclaimed.

Levi began to envy his father's reputation as a great flirt. Cesare loved to tell risqué jokes to women and thought of himself as a *conquistadore di dame*. He advised Primo (without success) to buy girls drinks and flowers. But Levi remained awkward with women all his life, and at the age of sixty-three was still deeply embarrassed by the subject of sex. When asked by a journalist about his 'first crush', he side-stepped the issue by joking: 'It was when I was thirteen – for astronomy!'

2

Frustrated by girls, Levi strengthened his friendship with boys, chiefly Mario Piacenza. On the top floor of the Piacenza home – 18 Via Giuseppe Galliano – was a makeshift laboratory. Chemistry was to be a powerful magnet for the inadequate teenager looking for a focus to his life. The lab belonged to Piacenza's older brother Gino, who was at university. For Levi the room was imbued with alchemical, magical properties: like Faust in his apothecary's den, he was awed by the test tube's bubbling contents. The boys took rough notes as they went along and wrote them up later in special exercise books. For reagents they went to a pharmacist on Corso Re Umberto, who was faintly amused by (and later interested in) their experiments. The more dangerous substances he put up in dark-blue poison bottles, and quoted the boys special prices for such things as filter papers and the pieces of lab glassware they could not make for themselves. After a while Levi tried rudimentary glass-blowing; he singed himself on the blow-pipe's flame, but 'developed a pretty good craftsman's ability,' recalled Piacenza. Nitrous oxide – laughing gas – intoxicated the concierge, and neighbours complained of light-headedness.

It was at about this time that Levi decided to become a chemist. One book clinched his decision. *Concerning the Nature of Things* by the British Nobel physicist Sir William Bragg contained photographs of ball-bearings floating on mercury, as well as instructions on how to make atomic-structure models from dentist's wax and wooden balls. Levi sent off to a special address in England for these, and advised Piacenza to do the same. Though the boys were on the same journey of exploration, it was Levi who chalked the chemical equations on the blackboard, and who initiated water electrolysis with the aid of a battery and old jam jars. Piacenza remained happy to be the lesser partner in the relationship as he admired Levi's wide-ranging scientific knowledge. Long after the war, when Piacenza had moved to Peru, the men made a point of keeping in touch; in 1981 Levi saluted 'this curious friendship of ours – transatlantic, intermittent – but with very deep roots'.

The year was still 1934. One day, Cesare Levi gave his son a slim, leather-bound microscope manual he had found. Published in London in 1846, *Thoughts on Animalcules* was by the Victorian naturalist Dr Gideon Algernon Mantell, best known for his 'Mantellian Museum' of prehistoric bone fragments. There were no ugly natural objects in the magical world of Mantell. Leech-like animalcules with their hairy bodies, the greenish jelly on pond twigs, were all part of what the author called the 'Invisible World of Being'. *Animalcules*, a 140-page manual, encouraged Levi to explore the natural world through practical experiment. It contained coloured plates of water polyps and other aquatic insects, but Levi needed a microscope to appreciate the creatures' delicate waving fibres. Despite Cesare's belief that microscopy was a lonely, closet activity, he bought his son a Zeiss. A microscope would teach him the cardinal positivist virtues of accuracy, experimental verification and observation. So, using the bicycle he had wangled two years earlier for his Bar Mitzvah, Levi pedalled off into the woods in search of flies' wings, bees' stings, spiders' mandibles. He scraped his teeth for plaque samples and pricked his sister's thumb for red blood cells. More confident now, he arranged microscope shows for friends and family. Slides of evaporated alum solution were placed into a low-gauge Pathé Baby cine-projector: instead of flickering film, giant crystals were screened directly on to the wall, and you could actually see the crystals grow.

3

At school, science tuition was meagre, and Levi resented it. Under 'Natural Sciences' were lumped human anatomy, botany, zoology, chemistry, mineralogy and astronomy. This motley reflected the Fascist demotion of science in favour of the humanities. The school's single ill-equipped laboratory was too small for anything other than the most elementary teaching. And the regime's anti-modern bias seemed incarnate in the school's decrepit Science beadle, Signor Mulassano, who was said to reek of embalming fluids. In this antediluvian atmosphere pupils were not encouraged to venture beyond their set books. *The Origin of Species* was something only a few students read at home, if at all.

The Divinity and Philosophy teacher, Father Alberto Pagani, was a staunch creationist who could not accept the biological fact of our descent from the animal world. Neither could the Natural Science teacher, Giorgina Pangella, a tiny silver-haired woman who lived near the Levis on Via Vespucci. The adult Levi spoke of Pangella, without ever mentioning her name, with a kind of tolerant disrespect. He doubted if she had ever seen a crystal, let alone evaporated a solution, and complained that all she ever taught him were 'pages in a book'. Once a week Pangella sent her pupils out into the parks of Turin to gather nature samples in a dustpan: seemingly that was the extent of her practical science lessons.

But, in spite of Levi's later objections, the 'M. D'Azeglio' was not an egregious example of anti-science prejudice in Fascist Italy. Though much had become automatic and sterile in Giorgina Pangella's teaching, she had the merit of perceiving Levi's interest in science, and of encouraging him. Her tuition, far from being deficient, was merely limited by the Fascist educational guidelines, which had effectively shut the laboratory door. Back in their ramshackle lab the budding Darwinists, Levi and Piacenza, tried the experiments recommended a century earlier by Dr Mantell. Into a glass containing water polyps they dropped a microscopic worm; the worm was drawn into a polyp's wafting mouth, and devoured. Under Levi's Zeiss, these polyps were transformed into monster killers. The cruel discipline of natural selection extended even to the tiniest living entities.

4

Primo Levi did not shine in the academic year 1934–5. He had interests beyond his courses – the Via Galliano chemistry lab – and merely coasted along at school. Latin was the only subject in which his marks denoted a growing interest, going from seven in the first form to eight in the second and third. He had a cautious admiration for his Classics master, don Lorenzo Coccolo, a pear-shaped Catholic priest who was known to be sympathetic to the Jews in his class. He would arrive late to lessons in a black soutane, fling down the sack that he carried over his shoulder and extract from it a battered copy of Homer or Virgil. He had a weakness for drink, and frequently slurred from a lunchtime tipple. Sometimes he slipped into vulgar Piedmontese, and during one prolonged bout of ragging he turned round to blurt out: '*Chi ch'a l'è col rompabale?*', 'Who's that breaking my balls?' Don Coccolo later apologised. The boys tried to undermine the priest with their collective baiting; Levi devised a limerick in which he was made to dance the carioca with the school's obese female cook. Levi's excellence as a classicist made itself obvious to don Coccolo, who nicknamed his pupil '*Gramaticus*' for the interest he showed in Latin etymology and grammar. Even if Levi did not yet imagine writing as a career for himself, don Coccolo made him aware of the fitting use of words, and therefore how *not* to write. As Raymond Chandler said: 'A Classical education helps you from being fooled by pretentiousness.'

Don Coccolo's was not the only Lyceum class that provoked flamboyant misbehaviour. Levi's maths teacher Maria Mascalchi was made the butt of ribald jokes involving chamber-pots and umbrellas. A proud Fascist, personal charm was not Mascalchi's strong point, and Levi styled her '*Saltante-Tram-in-Corso*' ('She-who-Jumps-off-the-Moving-Tram') after her habit of leaping off trams in between stops. Another teacher who incurred Levi's displeasure was Diana Reduzzi, a glossy forty-five-year-old with a large hooked nose, who taught history of art. 'Pure affliction' was Levi's assessment of her lessons.

5

Despite his ill health and frailty, Levi wanted to develop a robust physique. And in 1935 he found another sporting idol to add to the Kind brothers. Luigi Beccali, Italy's champion middle-distance sprinter, had the looks of a matinée idol. Levi helped to set up a Beccali fan club at school, which included his ski companion Roberto Perdomi, his primary-school mate Sergio Valvassori, and the Crocetta toughs Guido Bonfiglioli and Luigi Firpo (who was known to be don Coccolo's chief tormentor). Misogynist behaviour was required of all members; girls could be discussed only in the crudest terms. Hoping to appear manly, Levi made worried, self-conscious jokes about sex, observing that the Venetian dramatist Goldoni's name sounded like the Piedmontese for 'condom', *goldon*.

The *beccalisti* indulged their physical fantasies in a disused Crocetta sports stadium. Opened at the turn of the century by Princess Laetitia of Savoy, the stadium had not been used since 1932 when Beccali shot home a winner in Los Angeles. Valvassori would pick Levi up outside his house after school. 'Practising pseudo-Olympics in the stadium was our way of compensating for fear of girls,' Valvassori later judged. A year younger than Levi, today Valvassori is a gentle, blue-eyed man whose engineer father, like Levi's, had been a hale and extrovert character. The pair wore Avanguardia plus-fours and string vests. For high-jump poles they used bamboo tent-poles that bowed dangerously. Levi took his pole-vaulting 'extremely seriously', according to Valvassori, and practised for up to three hours daily in all weathers. Word got round the Crocetta that Primo was an accomplished athlete and this bolstered his self-esteem. Levi was still not interested in team sport; what he wanted was the lonesome thrill of solitary competition. In his mind he began to see himself as an athlete in *The Iliad*, flying down the track in a whirl of dust, outhurling his javelin opponents. A volunteer timed him with a stopwatch as he hared round the track with other *beccalisti*.

Towards the end of the summer term of 1935 Levi surprised those who knew him by participating in a sexually charged striptease. A newcomer to the Beccali club, **Mario Losano**, was very successful with girls. Levi knew him from junior school, where he had been held back in class by laziness and truancy. One day Losano had invited two girls to the sports stadium. They arrived in a chauffered car ('But I won't tell you their names because they're still alive in Turin,' said Guido Bonfiglioli.) And, as the *beccalisti* began to take off their clothes, the girls exchanged mock-scandalised glances. Levi's face was stiff with excitement. He wanted to look at the girls, but his eyes shied guiltily away. 'I don't believe he removed a stitch of clothing,' recalled Bonfiglioli (who is now an assistant physics professor in Sardinia). 'Primo had this terrible *pudore*, you know; his sexual education was slow.'

Years later, Levi gave a highly coloured account of his pseudo-Olympic escapades in his autobiographical reminiscence 'A Long Duel'. Though the piece is largely a fabrication, nevertheless it is revealing. A handsome boy called Guido aggressively challenges Levi to strip off his clothes during a Natural Science lesson. (Needless to say, the very thought of Levi attempting a striptease in class is preposterous.) Drawn to sturdy older boys, Levi admires Guido's 'sculptural body' and wayward 'sexual lusts'. Indeed, his virility seems to awaken in Levi a vague physical attraction. (Guido is 'provocative, Dionysiac', full of a 'terrestrial vigour'.) Levi describes a solitary stadium race with Guido, when in reality six *beccalisti* habitually ran round the track with him. 'A Long Duel' touches on an adolescent anxiety that seems to have lingered in Levi for an extraordinarily long time; he was still troubled by his sexual confusion and imagined physical shortcomings. Laura Firpo, who later married one of the *beccalisti* (Luigi Firpo), told me in 1995: 'All his life Primo was terrified of us women, he feared us.'

6

By now, Levi knew that he wanted to be a chemist. Chemistry was a reassuringly earth-bound science, which 'smelled good'. Its clean, distilled quality was an antidote to the regime's harping on the Glory that was Rome and its florid propaganda. He chose his sixteenth birthday – 31 July 1935 – to announce his decision to his father. Cesare was now in hospital with stomach cancer. The tumour had been removed by Italy's premier gastro-surgeon, Luigi Stropeni, but it came back. Seven more operations were to follow, each bringing a period of respite, but in the end it was a losing battle. In San Giovanni Battista Hospital, where the engineer lay recuperating, he tried to be his old affectionate self. His son had shown a rare independence of mind in choosing chemistry when the regime was biased so strongly towards the humanities. However, both Primo's father and paternal grandfather had been engineers. The fifty-seven-year-old Cesare was cheered by Primo's news. If there was a lack of intimacy between father and son, it resulted more from differences in personality than from lack of common interests.

7

The teenager had little notion of the storm that was gathering in Europe. In Levi's ten months at Lyceum the political situation in Italy had deteriorated. On 15 May 1935 the Fascist police struck again in Turin. On the basis of information supplied by the spy 'Pitigrilli', more than 200 'Justice and Liberty' suspects were arrested on subversion charges. The novelist and poet Cesare Pavese, a supply teacher at Levi's school, was among the detainees.* Carlo Levi was 'confined' for two years to southern Italy. In the Fascist punishment of *confino*, political offenders languished and occasionally died in remote Italian villages. Aliano, where Carlo Levi was exiled (disguised in his book *Christ Stopped at Eboli* as 'Gagliano'), was a desert settlement with scarred hillsides. Once again, a high proportion of the arrested *giellisti* were Jews, sparking further fears of persecution.

The tide was turning against Italy's Jews, there was no doubt. Two months after Primo's sixteenth birthday, in September 1935, Hitler issued the most murderous legislative document known to European history: the Nuremberg Laws. German Jews were to be denied German citizenship and forbidden to marry 'Aryan' Germans. German Jewish children, turned overnight into biological heretics, were not allowed to sit on the same school benches as non-Jews; their parents were hounded from their professions. In Italy it did not seem possible that such horrors could be so near: *La Stampa* devoted more column space to Mussolini's impending invasion of Ethiopia than to the Nuremberg Laws. The newspaper reassured its Turin readers that Mussolini would be in Addis Ababa 'before next year'; but the Duce was to be quicker than that.

On 2 October, a clouded autumn day, Italians were summoned by bells

*Here we must dispel one of the more curious myths about Levi's schooldays. In spite of articles and literary papers to the contrary, Levi was not taught Italian by Cesare Pavese. During his brief seven months at Levi's school (October 1934–May 1935), Pavese only taught the girls' Course A. Consequently, his signature does not appear on any of Levi's school reports. One could ignore such false accounts, were it not for the tendency of academics (and in a highly fanciful newspaper memoir by Fernanda Pivano) to repeat them, so that they are widely accepted as the truth.

and factory sirens to the squares of their towns and cities, where loud-speakers broadcast Mussolini's message to the nation that Ethiopia had been invaded. The dictator promised to combine Ethiopia with Italy's existing colonies of Eritrea and Somaliland to create a great new empire in East Africa. Now that he had the hypnotised consent of the majority, a new mood of jingoist triumphalism swept Italy. In Levi's classroom an oilcloth map with red arrows showed Mussolini's rapid Africa conquests. Levi eagerly absorbed the optimistic newspaper reports of Italian victories. Only the most perceptive Italian Jews could see that the Ethiopia war presaged the gravest danger to them. By attacking Ethiopia, Mussolini had pitted Italy against the League of Nations (of which Ethiopia was a member) and alienated his citizens from the western democracies. Britain was to impose unexpectedly harsh sanctions on Italy for its aggression, which pushed Mussolini closer into the arms of his future accomplice and master, Hitler. Mussolini's reputation had stood high with King George V; now Britain was *La Perfida Albione*, a sworn enemy. Any hope of a united front against Nazi imperialism was destroyed.

Increasingly, Mussolini blamed setbacks in the Ethiopia campaign on the twin ogres, Jews and Bolsheviks. Hitler prophesied ominously that Italians 'will recognise at the end of this struggle [in Ethiopia] that there is a Jewish question'. Indeed, if there was an obvious link between Mussolini's Africa war and European anti-Semitism, it was racialism. Racialism had always been a part of Fascist doctrine. In conquered Ethiopia, laws were soon introduced to separate whites from black people. Ethiopians were not even considered worthy of Fascist castor-oil treatment; they were half human; they ate their babies. This was propaganda: to have disbelieved it would have been unpatriotic. From this unpleasantness in Africa it was a short step to advocating racial supremacy at home.

After the excitement of the Ethiopia invasion had died down, the Levis carried on with their daily lives. Their legal position in Italy as Jews was still unaffected, and their place in the national life not greatly changed. Very few Italian Jews sensed the uncertainty and gathering emergency. One exception was Levi's classmate Ennio Artom, who said: 'It's all over for us Jews.' The boy's political maturity seems astonishing now; Ennio had been arrested in the first crackdown on *giellisti* in 1934. Another Jew who feared the consequences of Mussolini's ambitions in Ethiopia was the Levi family doctor, Giuseppe Diena. Talking in private of the catastrophe that impended, he told his pro-Fascist brother Clement, 'Can't you see we Jews are finished?' In 1944 the Nazis eliminated Giuseppe at Flossenburg camp.

*

Within seven months Ethiopia was conquered, and Italian joy was unconfined. The Duce appeared on his balcony in Rome to herald the annexation of the promised African land, the founding of the third Rome, the triumph of civilisation. He seemed transfigured, messianic. 'He is like a god,' said one Fascist. 'Like a god? No, no,' said another, 'He *is* a god.' But, as Mussolini consolidated power in Ethiopia, so Levi's school became more repressive. In the summer term of 1936 the school magazine which Primo helped to edit was censored. A 'Special Issue' had been cobbled together by the pupils, *D'Azeglio sotto spirito* ('D'Azeglio in Formaldehyde', with the punning sense of 'pickled' or 'drunk'). It was a hotch-potch of schoolboy foolery and ripe-flavoured jokes. The editor, Franco Fini, asked Levi to contribute, and Levi provided him with some indifferent cartoons (one of them, interestingly, was of the bully Salvatore Roggero). In recent months the school had appointed a new pro-Fascist headmaster, Natale Grimaldi, who declared the issue 'inimical' to the spirit of Fascism. He took exception to the editorial which described D'Azeglio pupils as 'trembling' while they awaited the outcome of the Ethiopian war, and referred the matter to the Fascist political police. When Fini put his case that nothing subversive was intended by 'tremble', the Blackshirt accepted it with an air of bored weariness.

Eventually the magazine was distributed with black censor bars across the offending cartoons and text. Levi's most important contribution was a pretty dreadful poem, 'You Don't Know How to Study!' This is his first-known published writing and it groaned with mock-heroic doggerel and highfalutin allusions to botany. Levi sends himself up as a buffoonish, accident-prone 'swot' on a bicycle, his head in the clouds. The poem provides a spoof of Petrarch's famous love sonnet VII, as well as the work of the eighteenth-century Swedish naturalist Linnaeus. Undistinguished though it was, 'You Don't Know How to Study!' expressed a love of literary pastiche that proved to be lifelong in Levi.

8

Levi was among the last generation of Italians to be educated in large measure by rote. Huge gobbets of literature had to be memorised. His classroom memory of Italian literature was on the whole one of 'great boredom'. Poetry seemed to him not only an irrelevance, but a purgatory to recite in class; consequently his Italian essays were uninspired. Throughout his first school year Levi was saturated in the medieval canon of Petrarch and Boccaccio, as well as Dante's *Inferno*. His second and third years were dominated by Dante's *Purgatory* and *Paradise*, with excursions into

Shakespeare and classical French prose. This cramming was as unlike the civilised literary discussions with his private tutor Marisa Zini as anything could be. Not only was Levi required to read all of Dante; entire cantos of the *Divine Comedy* had to be learned by heart. Small wonder he was drawn to chemistry: compared to this dreary rote memorisation, science was truly creative. Outside the classroom Levi's extra-curricular reading was more adventurous. In the winter of 1935, during the Easter half at school, he had ploughed his way through Victor Hugo's *Les Misérables,* finding Hugo's high-flown prose like a great 'muddy river in spate'. He also read a popular gloss on Einstein and embarked on a reading course of Freud.

Levi's Italian teacher, Azelia Arici, was vital to his unconscious formation as a writer. Born in Turin in 1895, Arici was 'jowly and masculine-looking', recalled Fiat's Gianni Agnelli. Another contemporary, Luisa Monti, remembered that Arici refused to be photographed. Course B's thirty-eight unruly boys teased her mercilessly, but Arici used her heavy physical presence as a deterrent against the worst misbehaviour. Nevertheless she was admired for her sensitivity and warmth, and her literature classes were of a high order. Arici looked for originality in her pupils rather than conformity. Each new generation that came into her hands presented her with a challenge: she wanted to make her boys think and read, and make judgments for themselves. Vacant or woolly prose, what she termed 'vapourings', was to be discouraged. And it was at about this time that Levi coined the term *greco applicato* ('applied Greek') for anything wilfully obscure.

As a Classicist, Arici believed that the monuments of human achievement worthy of study were Athens, Rome and Dante. Dante, for her, was the highest expression of European civilisation and the first step from Gothic darkness to the Renaissance. In a favourite classroom performance, she would recite from the *Inferno*'s fifth canto, where the lovers Paolo and Francesca are twisting in a black whirlpool without hope. 'Arici ground her teeth, and totally bewitched us,' recalled one pupil. Excited as Levi was by these brimstone recitals, he later admitted that he was also 'embarrassed' by them. Arici was one of two sisters descended from the Virgil translator and minor Lombard poet Cesare Arici. She spoke in the cultivated, faintly nasal voice of upper-class Turinese and wrote florid verses on pastoral themes. Many pupils only valued her legacy once they had left school – Levi among them. Later he praised her humanist teaching which instilled in her pupils a 'diligent critical awareness' and 'never once surrendered' to Fascist rhetoric. This was not quite accurate: Azelia Arici was tempted by Fascism. In fact, she was amorously entangled with the school's pro-Fascist Philosophy teacher, Samuele Gerbaz, and was said to admire the Fascist regime's philosopher-in-residence and education minister, Giovanni Gentile. Moreover, she endorsed Mussolini's buffoonish cult of *la maglia carne* ('the undershirt of flesh') by which young men were encouraged to climb mountains half-naked in homage to the manful Duce.

Arici's harping on aesthetic matters, together with her conviction that scientists were mere lowly creatures of the laboratory, irritated Levi. In Arici's view, chemistry was 'stinks', and here, too, she was Fascist. Very few voices, among them a harmless crew of crypto-positivists and evolutionists, dared to argue that science had been undermined by the Fascist education reforms of 1923, or that it even mattered. The regime's prominent ideologues, Benedetto Croce (until he became vehemently anti-Fascist) and Giovanni Gentile himself, regarded science as dangerous and feared that boys would be corrupted by studying it. Croce's angry onslaught on scientific materialism and positivism helped pave the way for Fascist neo-idealism and the Fascist values of the so-called Spirit. Levi never forgave him his dictum that 'scientific problems are not real ones'.

9

On the morning of 3 July 1936 a Viennese Jew, Stefan Lux, shot himself at the League of Nations in protest at the Nuremberg Laws. A letter found on the dead man explained: 'I can find no other way to reach the hearts of men.' A month later, to show his solidarity with Hitler in the Spanish Civil War, Mussolini sent aircraft and *matériel* to Franco in Spain. The fate of Italy's Jews was sealed. However, Primo was more concerned with news that the champion athlete Beccali had been defeated at the Berlin Olympics in August; his toe spiked by a runner's shoe, Beccali had limped home to Italy with a bronze.

Months of uncertainty followed and ever worse news for Italy's Jews. On 15 November, Giuseppe Bottai replaced Giovanni Gentile as Fascist education minister. A former *squadrista* (Fascist action squad member), Bottai was to be the strongest supporter of Mussolini's anti-Jewish measures that were just two years away. His intolerant, bull-headed politics percolated down to every aspect of Italian schooling and beyond. Mussolini, with his characteristic opportunist diplomacy, had ordered a pro-German stance in the mainstream Italian press. So the evil now hatching in Europe had begun to intrude, though marginally, on Levi's life. He began to reassure himself that 'Nuremberg can't happen here'. Other anxieties and upsets settled on him. His nanny Silvia Meneghelli died. She was buried where she was born, in Emilia-Romagna, on 30 November 1936, aged sixty-nine.

As the New Year – 1937 – progressed, Levi had to face a new worry. In May he began to revise for his school-leaving exams, or *maturità*. Pupils who failed their summer matriculation could not go on to further education. Over a period of three weeks they were to be grilled in ten subjects, ranging from Greek to the sinister-sounding Military Culture. Each of these subjects required four separate written papers and as many *viva voce* inquisitions. In later years, Levi confessed to an 'intense feeling of dizziness' whenever he looked at his own children's essay themes. Fear spread through the school as pupils settled down to revision.

In July 1937, as Levi was due to begin the *maturità* marathon, a summons arrived from the Fascist War Ministry in Rome ordering him to present himself at a designated location for 'urgent communications'. Levi was led to understand that if he did not comply with the order, he would find himself in deep trouble. On 4 July, a Sunday, he reported to Turin's seaplane port where he and another boy (also called Levi) were accused of ignoring a navy call-up notice. The Fascist who confronted the two Levis threatened punishment for draft-evasion. Clearly there had been some bureaucratic foul-up. 'Maybe my brother's name *was* on a Fascist National Service list, but he never received an Italian Royal Navy summons,' said Anna Maria Levi. Today War Ministry documentation regarding this episode no longer exists.

There was nothing the Fascist press enjoyed so much as a minor Jewish scandal, and Levi was in a state of near-panic at the consequences of desertion. A family conference was convened, the first of many in these increasingly difficult months. If Levi was to join the navy, he ought at least learn how to swim. Cesare Levi, though seriously ill, began to plead with the relevant Turin authorities to see what could be done to exempt his son from service. The Army Recruiting Office said they were sorry: orders were orders. The Fascist Federation likewise said they could not help. The deadlock was unresolved until a paradoxical solution was arrived at: Primo Levi would be exempted from the navy if he enrolled in the Fascist University Militia – the MVSN – the following autumn. (Assuming, that is, he obtained a place at university.) The MVSN, an organisation for officers-to-be, was hardly Levi's idea of a bright future. 'I was certainly not destined to become a good soldier, and in fact I never did become one,' he recalled.

The weather had been hot for more than a fortnight, a torrid stifling heat, and on the Monday morning of 5 July Levi sat the first of four Italian exams. The timing could not have been worse: the Fascist threats of the day before, combined with the unexpected death of a Jewish school friend, brought Levi down with a 'very high fever', recalled his sister. The deputy president of the examination panel, Carlo Pasero, read out the Italian essay theme that morning to the fearful candidates. Italy's recent entry into the Spanish Civil War had to be discussed with reference to words by the classical Greek historian Thucydides: 'We have the singular merit of being brave to the utmost degree.' Levi was still traumatised by the previous day's Fascist encounter and wrote a 'stunted and deranged' essay, handing in a virtually blank sheet of paper.

In the interval before his Natural Science exams, Levi set out for the mountains. The bracing air might help him forget his humiliation in Italian, and on 20 July he was in Sauze d'Oulx with his cousin Giulia Colombo. While taking a path uphill towards the Adolfo Kind Shelter, for no apparent reason Levi carved Guglielmo Marconi's name on a rock. Later that day Marconi died. While Levi's rational mind dismissed this as coincidence, he was only half joking when he told Cousin Giulia that he had the power to kill 'important people' at a distance of 650 kilometres.

On 30 July, the day before his eighteenth birthday, Levi jostled with other pupils round the noticeboard to see his *maturità* grades. Next to 'Italian' he saw the awful word in red ink: 'RETAKE'. The examiner Carlo Pasero had awarded Levi a meagre three out of ten for his Spanish Civil War essay. That year Pasero failed six other candidates in written Italian. One of them was the future friend and Italian translator of Ernest Hemingway, Fernanda Pivano. Levi and Pivano stood glued in abasement to the noticeboard. When Pivano asked Levi if he had written an anti-Fascist essay, he replied: 'I'd never be such a fool. And you?'

'Me? I wrote an *anti-war* essay!'

'Then you're an even bigger idiot than I am.'

Levi's later verdict – 'I made a hash of my *maturità*' – now seems like a cheery version of the event. He was devastated. All his life, Levi had set himself the highest standards, and for much of his boyhood he had excelled. But this humiliation made him feel worthless. Some sort of nervous breakdown seems to have followed. Levi's failure in Italian was considered a 'family tragedy', his sister told me. A late autobiographical story by Levi, 'Decodification', suggests that the author feared failure to quite an irrational degree. A 'thin, timid' schoolboy is crushed by 'a whole chain of failures', not just one, after failing his summer matriculation.

A bleak summer lay ahead revising for the autumn resits. Levi's failure in Italian meant that the entire set of exams had to be taken again. He must have worried whether he would attain the same marks, but to ensure success he was coached privately in Italian by the Dante expert Umberto Cosmo. Cosmo, well known in Turin as an anti-Fascist, planted a seed of resistance in Levi. 'It wasn't from what Cosmo told me but from what he *didn't* tell me that I learned of an alternative to Fascism.' In the event, Levi obtained seven out of ten for Italian; he had done well enough to pass, though not to excel. His other matriculation grades were respectable, if middling. Surprisingly, given Diana Reduzzi's reportedly deficient tuition, Levi got his highest mark in history of art: eight. Otherwise he did poorly, scraping a disappointing six for Latin, supposedly his best subject. He had to admit that his results were not up to his old reputation, but at least he had come through. His school-leaving diploma, issued two months later on 20 December 1937, stated that Primo Levi was now *maturo*, had graduated. The diploma was stamped with a medallion portrait of Dante; the year, it stated, was Anno XVI of the Fascist Era.

After five years of Greek, and eight of Latin, Primo Levi left the 'M. D'Azeglio' Royal Gymnasium-Lyceum saturated in the Classics. He knew he could disregard the school's scientific teachings, but in many other ways it had done him well, giving him an excellent training in Italian literature, for example, and at least one foreign language, French. Most teachers at the school had treated him with understanding, and on the whole he had been a diligent and well-behaved pupil. Yet Levi's main effort had been outside the school – the Via Galliano lab – and it was chemistry that beckoned now.

SIX

University and Persecution
1937–8

At the end of October 1937 Primo Levi registered for a chemistry degree course at Turin University. After three months of textbook theory, an exam would select which undergraduates could complete their studies in the laboratory. Until then Levi was just one of eighty hopeful freshmen. The full four-year course would involve a taxing twenty-two exams, from maths to metallurgy; chemistry was to be a long trial of nerves for the eighteen-year-old. During this time, Levi lived with his family at home in the Crocetta, while his sister, Anna Maria, finished school.

For the next three autumn months Levi arrived at the Chemistry Institute at 8:00 am sharp on his way to the lecture hall. The Institute had seen better days, as indicated by the crumbling splendour of its ventilation tower (built in 1906 to resemble an exotic minaret). It was dominated by the lofty eminence of Professor Giacomo Ponzio. A short, po-faced man with an uncompromising expression, he had been the Institute's director for the last twenty-two years. Ponzio crammed each year's intake for their February exam, expecting little from them.

Levi regarded his new professor as the classic *burbero*, 'grump', though he approved of Ponzio's remark to the freshmen: 'Chemistry is a bricks-and-mortar trade and you lot are brick-layers. Don't expect to discover the meaning of life round here.' This bluff streak ran in the family. The professor's radiologist brother had famously refused anaesthetic during the amputation of his little finger. In similar fashion, Ponzio boasted he could hold in his bare hands (without flinching) a crucible heated to seventy degrees. His idiosyncrasies amused Levi. In conformist Fascist Italy, Ponzio's public persona was somewhat unusual; outside the laboratory he liked to wear a fez.

Prior to the Great War, Ponzio was professor of pharmacology at Sassari University in Sardinia, where he had researched an obscure organic compound called the oxime. Students were a distraction, and Ponzio was patently bored with them. He had been known to fail ten 'nuisance pupils' in a row with a trick question on atomic weight; the discomfiture that first one and then another pupil suffered was a pleasure for him to behold. That the professor was a misogynist was also generally recognised. If they had no gift for chemistry, women were told to go off and darn stockings, while the laziest of his male pupils were advised to take up cycling. '*Signori, datevi al ciclismo!*' he would say, his thin lips pursed in disapproval.

Born in Turin in 1870, Professor Ponzio was sixty-seven by the time Levi knew him, and approaching retirement. As a young man he had made a discreet name for himself in carbo-chemistry (for which he gets a brief mention in Volume XXVII of the *Enciclopedia Italiana* of 1935), but that scarcely put him in the vanguard of contemporary science. His contempt for Rome – in many ways, a classically Piedmontese contempt – unfortunately distanced the Chemistry Institute from the most exciting developments in science. It was in Rome that the future Nobel Laureate Enrico Fermi was leading a circle of world-class physicists and chemists, but Ponzio would have none of them. Rome and the Vatican were a 'viper's nest', he said. In 1939 when Ponzio was told that Pope Pius XI had died, a look of amusement came over him as he replied: '*E chi se ne frega?*', 'And who gives a toss?'

If Professor Ponzio was conservative, the Science Faculty's younger assistants would introduce Levi to the cutting-edge of chemistry. Until such time he was under Ponzio's efficient, if determinedly Old School, instruction. This prickly character was to be a tremendously important influence on Levi. In my interview with him, Levi complimented Ponzio as 'my first and best science teacher' and 'the man who showed me how to love chemistry'. He compared Ponzio to a hunter, who relied more on instinct and a keen sense of smell than on textbook theory to track down his chemical quarry. As a teacher Ponzio tended to the Gradgrindian (facts, not the imagination, were his forte), but his exactitude would be mirrored years later in Levi's clear, essential prose. Ponzio's organic and inorganic chemistry primers were considered models of precise exposition; while other first-year primers weighed in at more than 1,000 pages, the professor's were a quarter that length. 'If something could be said with three words the professor always preferred to say it with two – and never with a redundant three and a half,' said one of his students.

2

The freshmen were all nervous as the day approached for their *colloquio*, 'oral exam'. Their number would be whittled down from eighty to twenty, the maximum that the Institute's laboratory could hold. With the recent disaster of his *maturità*, Levi did not want to fail again. So he thoroughly digested the required rudimentary mineralogy, botany, physics and inorganic chemistry. By early February he was fully prepared in all subjects, and knew Ponzio's *Chimicia Inorganica* by heart. Some students reckoned they could survive the interrogation by digesting the Professor's books at home, and had not bothered to attend lectures. Ponzio knew exactly who they were; he would choose to test them on information that came, not at the beginning of a chapter, but somewhere in the middle. (On one famous occasion he had failed a pupil for not knowing the difference between Arabian and Romanian petroleum, which was explained in a footnote.) In alphabetical order the aspiring chemists were summoned to the blackboard, where they were fired a question; if they responded correctly, Ponzio handed them a piece of chalk to write some formula. Edith Weisz, an Italian-born Czechoslovak Jew, remembers that she had to write up the equation for potassium permanganate. She had to score the minimum pass (eighteen out of thirty), but Ponzio could easily prevent her. Earlier that day he had quizzed a candidate on the colour of calomel, a white powder then used as a children's laxative. A friend in the front row helpfully tapped her teeth to indicate white; but the candidate incorrectly suggested yellow after glancing at Ponzio's nicotine-stained dentures. '*Bocciata, si accomodi*,' the Professor had told her with relish. 'You've failed, do sit down.' This was Ponzio's stock remark to unsuccessful candidates. University records show that Levi easily obtained his attendance certificate, and was selected for higher studies.

3

Fortified by his success, Levi was now a full-time student on the chemistry degree course. This first academic year, 1937–8, was the crucial one in his studies. During this time he would have to sit four key exams which he needed to pass before progressing to a second year of analytic chemistry. Morning lectures were followed by an exhausting five hours in the laboratory. That was a giddy commitment for Levi as he cut and scalded himself at the workbench, cooking and filtering. Everything was clean and ordered – racks, stop-cocks, retorts, neatly arrayed. Kidney-shaped porcelain sinks screwed to the end of tables were for rinsing glassware.

The first-year lab work for inorganic chemistry preparation was very basic. The aim was to teach students to filter, crystallise and distil, how to handle test tubes and the nuts and bolts of their 'brick-laying' trade. Sights and smells were considered important and students were expected to recognise the garlic odour released by incinerating arsenic. Levi was a diligent student and enjoyed himself in Ponzio's laboratory-cum-kitchen. Most important, the laboratory was a social facilitator where the boys mixed with girls. At 5:00 pm the students paused in their practical experiments to brew tea in chemistry glassware; biscuits fried over a Bunsen were passed round. The more adventurous attempted mayonnaise. One day Professor Ponzio questioned a terrified student about her beakerful of improvised zabaione pudding. 'Most interesting. Is it a pharmaceutical soap?' he asked, though his chemist's nose knew better.

Maths and physics were compulsory for chemistry students. Levi's maths professor was Maria Cibrario, a Piedmontese countess in English tweeds, a gifted teacher. Less impressive, and enfeebled by boredom, was his physics professor, the fifty-year-old Alfredo Pochettino. Pochettino shuddered at the mere mention of post-Einsteinian physics: his chief interest was in meteorology and he pored over atmospheric pressure charts in a dingy room in the Physics Institute. When not teaching he wove giant Gobelin-like tapestries, which were much admired. Botanists, medics and chemists squeezed into the lecture hall to hear Pochettino talk.

Levi also studied physics for a time with Professor Enrico Persico, a more modern soul whose primers on atomic physics are still highly regarded in Italy. 'Physics goes much deeper than chemistry into the riddle of existence,' said Persico. Indeed, the laws of physics – gravity, energy, motion, time – underpin those of all other sciences, but this revelation only dawned on Levi halfway through his course, by which time it was too late for him to change to physics. (Although later he wished he had done so.)

The day-to-day running of the lab was left to Ponzio's faithful technician, Domenico Caselli, and to the professor's twenty-four-year-old assistant, Guido Tappi. At fifty-two, Caselli had learned a fantastic amount of chemistry during his years at the Institute. In 1935 Ponzio had asked the University rector to award Caselli 700 lire for 'services rendered well beyond the call of reasonable duty'. Caselli was adored by the students, unlike Tappi, who had a fastidious manner. Levi considered him a *barone*, a 'career academic', who harassed female undergraduates. Yet despite this unsavoury trait, Tappi was an extremely able chemist, and Levi profited from his practical advice as surely as he did from Ponzio's. His first task under Tappi was to obtain silver nitrate by dissolving five-lire coins in acid, corroding the King's face clean away. By the end of the afternoon the lab would be thick with semi-toxic nitrous-oxide fumes.

Each evening at 7:00 pm after laboratory practicals Levi walked home with his friend Mario Piacenza, who was also in Ponzio's class. Piacenza had recently moved to 87 Corso Re Umberto, a few doors from Primo, and this bought the young men closer together. If they had money they stopped at the scruffy Café Elena for mugs of *bicerin*, hot chocolate fortified with coffee. Here, 'sometimes long after midnight', Piacenza recalled, they tried to grapple with relativity and evolution theory. That Charles Darwin had been discredited by Fascist ideologues as a 'materialist' made reading him faintly subversive. The deeper Levi read into *The Origin of Species*, however, the more he was awed by the work's dark grandeur. It was a secular Genesis that linked the animal kingdom from man-o'-war jelly fish to man. What Levi caught from Darwin was a 'grand design' for the universe and a sober delight in extracting order from chaos. And this was the attraction, too, of chemistry – chaos giving way to order in the periodic table.

Like Piacenza, Levi joined the University Fascist Group, or GUF. This was the one social club on campus where students could meet and relax away from their studies, and Levi participated actively during his first university year. He had been enlisted in Fascist youth movements since the age of five, so he took the club in his stride. The regime controlled most student organisations, and GUF was no exception. Its bellicose slogan on the club wall announced: 'BOOK AND MUSKET MAKE A GOOD FASCIST', and the Turin branch had its own weekly magazine, *Il Lambello* (The Label), which glorified war and the fighting spirit. Yet politics was not the point for most *gufini* and Levi was unaware of any serious indoctrination. For poorer students, GUF was a boon as it allowed them to ski, or go to the cinema, at a members' discount. The club garden had a splashing fountain and a bar where undergraduates could eat brioche or play ping-pong. Levi was often there after lectures, waiting for friends or drinking coffee. A noticeboard advertised cut-price ballroom dancing, plays or films.

Two new cinemas – the Ideal and the Eliseo – had opened on the new-look Via Roma among the triumphal Fascist shop fronts. Mussolini was soon to launch his anti-Hollywood campaign, but that spring of 1938 the Ideal was showing Jean Harlow in her latest film, *Personal Property*. With his GUF discount card, Levi went to the pictures most weekends to see romantic films starring Myrna Loy, *Pépé le Moko*, and Fred Astaire musicals. But the most popular GUF activity was sport. And here the club was supremely Fascist. Each April it arranged cultural and athletic competitions known as Littoriali. Students were bused for these to Rome or Naples where they met athletes from across Italy, even Masai tribespeople from the Fascist Africa colonies. These were exciting times and most *gufini* wished Fascism well. One boy in Levi's class, Giorgio Burla, was a national champion backstroke swimmer; another, a record sprinter. Many of these aspiring young men would die in the coming conflict; Burla drowned when his submarine was torpedoed by the British.

As well as sports, GUF organised propaganda lectures and rallies, which Levi was expected to attend. There was also a ridiculous uniform, with a green tricorne hat and a toggled blue kerchief, that *gufini* had to wear for exams: the dress was roundly despised. At this time it was still reasonably safe to poke fun at the regime. The National Fascist Party acronym, PNF, became known in class as *Per Necessità Familiare*, 'Out of Family Necessity'. (You could lose your job if you were not a paid-up Fascist.)

By now, Levi was still rather slight and not very tall, but he had lost much of his teenage gangliness. His hair was thick and tightly waved; photographs show a smiling, healthy young man. And, as Levi caught up with his peers physically, so his sense of inadequacy faded. He was not concerned what religion his friends were, though he still was rather anxious with girls. Edith Weisz was dark-eyed, tall and statuesque. She remembered Levi as 'a shy small boy' hidden in the corner of the lab. He was always better one-to-one. Another girl in Ponzio's course, Giovanna Balzaretti, was a 'fashion plate with a figure to match', according to Weisz. She found Levi embarrassed in her glamorous company. Most male chemists sniggered when they spoke of sex, but Levi was still very prudish. Women, however, rather liked him for it.

Levi was attracted to Edith; she was warm-hearted and clever, and had a healthy disregard for GUF propaganda. He had first met her during a university maths *colloquio*. Engineer Levi had come to see his son examined – and Primo had passed 'with merit'. After the exam Levi introduced Edith to his father at the back of the lecture hall. Edith noted Primo's devotion to Cesare. Despite his declining health, the engineer remained a ladies' man and for Levi, who was still so shy, it must have been uncomfortable to see his father flirt with a new friend.

4

Whether Levi liked it or not, he was one of Professor Ponzio's favoured few, a bright student with an enquiring, independent mind. For his first-year exams, according to his mark sheet, he never scored lower than twenty-eight out of thirty. Levi had a scientific idealism that set him apart; he dug deep into science with a seriousness that eluded his peers. Even at school, he had tackled difficult books on human biochemistry, such as *Man the Unknown* by Alexis Carrel. According to Piacenza, Levi was also reading Paul De Kruif's history of the world's legendary bacteriologists, *Microbe Hunters*. When this book was first published in 1927 the world's scientific community was still small enough for every schoolboy to dream of scientific stardom. Levi was inspired by the heroics of Louis Pasteur, and by the Berlin scientist Robert Koch, who discovered the bacillus that caused tuberculosis. Chemistry seemed then to promise glory and the thrill of the chase.

By the mid-1930s it was already known that a certain substance – DNA – played a central role in our biology. Levi was aware of these developments and loved any opportunity to discuss them. However, many students had embarked on chemistry with an eye to employment, a careerism that Levi considered a 'heresy'. His high moral seriousness was not so unusual among young Turin intellectuals in the 1930s, though it had its gaucheries and priggishness. While it was not in Levi's nature to be unfriendly, in the lab he could appear detached or haughty. Vittorio Satta, a Sardinian, was paired with Levi at the workbench and later claimed that 'you couldn't ask him the time of day!' Another chemistry classmate, Liborio Casale, recalled that while Levi was 'attentive and kind and cordial and all the rest of it, he was absolutely not *modest*'. Rather, implied Casale, Levi was sanctimonious. When Professor Pochettino's physics primer was reissued in contraband précis-form, and sold in class as an exam crib, Levi was disapproving. 'He told me I was harming sales of Pochettino's book,' recalled Sidney Calvi, the guilty party.

Levi was the only first-year student who knew how to blow, bend and mould glass, and his craftsman-like ability was much admired. He also had the reputation of being a library cormorant. While most students were impatient to go home in the lunch break, he hurried upstairs to the Institute's *biblioteca* with a packet of sandwiches. He loved this library with its glass-fronted bookcases and view of the engineering school from which his grandfather Michele had graduated sixty years earlier. Like his polyglot father, Levi was not put off by foreign languages and he tried to fathom the daunting *Chemisches Zentralblatt* periodicals, which gave a résumé in German of the world's most recent and important chemistry experiments. Most chemistry texts were then in German, as pre-war Germany claimed all the outstanding scientific developments. Indeed, students could be forgiven for thinking, as some of them did, that chemistry was a German science. They used F. W. Küster's celebrated *Logarithmic Tables*, and a rumour spread that the German publisher was offering a cash prize to any student who discovered so much as a misplaced decimal place. Such was the Teutonic reputation for accuracy.

Though the students' first-year inorganic chemistry primer, Dr Rüst's *Anorganischer Präparate*, was available in Italian, Levi bought his in the original as he said he wanted to learn German. And so Levi absorbed the language of the Jews' oppressors from a well-thumbed textbook published thirty-five years earlier (1903) in Stuttgart. For those pupils who were interested, Professor Ponzio arranged German lessons. These began in Levi's second year and took place once a week, late in the afternoon. Frau Henke came from an upper-class Berlin family and liked to be addressed as 'madam'. During the Great War she had married an Italian army officer, but was now widowed and stranded in the Crocetta. A glance at Madam Henke's carbon-copied grammar sheets shows what a thorough teacher she must have been. Words like *Ofen* (oven), *Säure* (acid) and *Wasser* (water) would prove useful to Levi in the dark times ahead.

In spite of his aspirations and intellectual flair, Levi did not see himself in competition with his fellows. Rather, he was happy to help them with their chemistry preparations and homework, earning himself the nickname 'Mini Encyclopaedia'. Nereo Pezza was one of the weakest students in physics, but Levi guided him through Professor Pochettino's ponderous texts. 'Primo was a wonderful teacher – patient, enthusiastic – he had a mind like a computer and a public reference library rolled into one. Without his help I'd never have graduated.' Pezza was not a classical school *privilegiato*, but a poor boy from the orphans' seminary of San Guiseppe in Turin. The Catechism was more familiar to him than problems of viscosity and surface tension. So Levi agreed to coach him privately. Typically, the pity he felt for Pezza contained a sense of superiority and patronage, but Pezza was happy to take on the role of the tutored one and Levi the role of tutor.

Inevitably, Levi had a rival in his chemistry class. Maurizio Panetti was the son of a well-known Polytechnic professor and had a family reputation to live up to. Panetti worked ferociously hard and studied in the GUF club while other students dabbled at cards. He was, as the Italians say, a *violino*, 'swot'. Students wagered among themselves: who's the brightest? A few answered Panetti, but most insisted: 'No, it's Levi who's the more *brillante* [sparkling], the more *estroso* [gifted], the more *geniale* [clever].' Levi was considered naturally bright while Panetti slogged for his grades.

On a Fascist skiing trip back in 1936, a young man was belting out mountain ballads in the coach going home. His name was Alberto Salmoni, and he had a ready sympathy and sense of fun that Levi found exciting. When Salmoni joined the first-year chemistry students, Levi was glad of the chance to get to know him better. He was one of eight Jews in Professor Ponzio's class and, exotically, his Jewish background owed something to the Levant and the souks of the Middle East. Salmoni's Italian father, Augusto, was born in the Egyptian port of Alexandria and, with his bushy white moustache, was said to resemble Lord Kitchener. The Salmoni home in Turin was an Aladdin's cave of illuminated Korans and yellowed piles of Arabic newspapers. Nothing could be more different from the bourgeois orderliness of 75 Corso Re Umberto.

Alberto, the youngest of three brothers, was born in cosmopolitan Heliopolis (just outside what is today Cairo airport), in August 1918. He was an easy-going, unconventional character who had inherited his father's eccentricity and self-assurance. After the Great War the Salmonis had moved from Cairo to Naples, where one of the family ran a timber yard. As well as shark-hunting, Augusto liked to take his three sons rowing off the Naples coast in a long-boat called *The Nile*; one day they got drenched and Augusto wore his suit inside-out to dry the lining, but was taken for a tramp and refused a place in a restaurant. After a madcap timber-business venture in Bosnia, Augusto's long-suffering wife Dora despaired: 'This is not the life for me!' So in 1936 the Salmonis moved to Turin, where they remained. In Turin, Augusto's most outlandish business developed from the monopoly he obtained of the blood of cattle slaughtered at the Municipal Abattoir on Corso Inghilterra. He named the business 'EMA' after the ancient Greek for blood, *hæma*, but nobody understood the allusion. In stainless-steel cauldrons, blood was boiled to the consistency of glue, then turned into polishing paste, sausages, even buttons. Giant rats infested EMA's processing plant.

Young Alberto was a tall, handsome Italian with an imperturbable manner quite unlike Primo's anxious, retiring personality. By the time Levi met him, Salmoni had been living in Turin for just two years and spoke Italian with a marked Neapolitan accent. As with many of Levi's important relationships, this one was based on an attraction of opposites. Salmoni was as confident, slapdash and outgoing as Levi was hesitant, precise and solitary; he had a good mind for chemistry but did not train it, being too lazy, and was famous for getting lost in the mountains. In spite of these differences, their friendship was to last a lifetime.

5

In early 1938 Levi's life at the Chemistry Institute was exciting. University gave him a new sense of intellectual calling, ideas, freedoms and time – time seemingly inexhaustible before him. He met his friends daily in the lecture halls, the lab or in the Valentino Park, where they picnicked under the chestnut trees or went punting on the Po. Inevitably Levi associated with Jews from other faculties, but only later would their shared religion prove any kind of significant bond. A Biella textile-merchant's daughter, Luciana

Nissim, was a medical student. Elfin-faced and with an air of detached curiosity, she came from a similarly assimilated background to Levi's. In the winter of 1944 she was deported with Levi to Auschwitz. Levi's life would cross with that of another Jewish student at Turin University. Vanda Maestro was a frail-boned Turinese girl with green eyes, who was reading industrial chemistry in the year above. Often in the evenings she would wait with Levi for the tram on Corso Massimo D'Azeglio while Luciana Nissim and another medic, Franco Operti, chattered behind. University brought old acquaintances together, for Operti had been at primary school with Levi twelve years earlier. None of these students could have envisioned the catastrophe ahead, or imagined the future war. Vanda Maestro was also deported with Levi to Auschwitz.

In early 1938 many Italian Jews were still convinced Fascists. Franco Operti recalled his furious row with Nissim over Hitler. 'German Jews were being hunted down like rats, but Luciana didn't want to know.' She believed that Hitler was Mussolini's rightful ally, and was unrepentantly Fascist then. Another of Levi's laboratory colleagues, Emma Vita-Levi, was the best athlete in class: she swam, high-jumped and ran the 100 metres, outstripping all competition at the 1938 Littoriale in Naples. Emma had personally collected a gold letter M from Mussolini, and was thrilled. Yet her joy was short-lived. Though she was a general's daughter, soon she would be banned from all national sports and branded an alien within Italian society. Having destroyed liberalism, democracy and human rights, Mussolini was now poised to strengthen his ties with Hitler and become a declared anti-Semite. Italian Jews were to be branded as second-class citizens and in just a few months the Duce would succeed in destroying all that they had achieved in ninety years outside the ghetto.

6

The Fascists had been monitoring the growth of Nazism with interest. In the five years since Hitler had become Reich Chancellor the climate in Germany had changed utterly; anti-Semitism had become an indispensable part of the Nazi regime. News of Hitler's persecutions was censored by Mussolini as he did not want to be associated with Nazi brutality, but word had begun to leak into Italy of German brutalities against Jews. Until then, Mussolini had arrogantly disdained Hitler and the German 'barbarians' north of the Alps, but intervention in the Spanish War had cemented Italy's lethal alliance with the Führer, as the dictators joined forces in the anti-Communist crusade. Now Mussolini was indisputably the lesser figure in a fatal new relationship. In the words of the Italian novelist Elsa Morante, the

Duce had 'irrevocably yoked his carnival chariot to the other's funeral hearse'. Levi's parents surveyed the international scene with growing despair. The Fascist participation in the Spanish Civil War must have brought them a step nearer to a bleak realisation of what was in store for them. The situation was irremediable, like Cesare's cancer, but they cultivated a disregard for it.

Since Levi's entrance to Turin University in October 1937, Mussolini had begun to prepare for anti-Jewish legislation. Earlier that year Italian Jews had come under serious attack when an incendiary publication, *Gli ebrei in Italia* (The Jews in Italy), had flooded the bookshops. The author, Paolo Orano, was a Fascist publicist whose book helped to harden Italian public sensibility against the Jews and pave the way for their eventual persecution. Beneath the text's academic veneer lurked the usual prejudices. Orano called on *all* Italian Jews, whatever their politics, to abandon their cultural heritage and participate gratefully in the glorious Fascist state which had done so much for them. The book quickly became the talk of the Italian press and a basis for the various media to discuss the so-called Jewish Question. The most virulently anti-Semitic notices appeared in Turin's now sycophantic *La Stampa*. 'If the Fascist state is totalitarian,' the newspaper lectured, 'then it cannot allow Italian culture to be polluted by Judaism.' This word 'polluted' was something new and sinister in Italy.

However, anti-Semitism had been evident in Italy long before 1937. The Fascist novelist Giovanni Papini had published a widely circulated pamphlet in 1930, which accused Schoenberg, Freud, Einstein, Marx and other Jewish hate-figures of 'destroying western morality'. Levi had read the diatribe with astonishment. Jews were beyond civilisation because civilisation was based on Christianity; Jews were dragging a trail of slime and the ten plagues of Egypt through the Christian world.

Throughout early 1938 the Fascist press had become increasingly shrill in its condemnation of Jews. It railed against the presence in Italian universities of foreign Jews, and denigrated all Jewish contributions to the cultural and intellectual life of Italy. Alberto Moravia, whose landmark novel *The Time of Indifference* had criticised bourgeois Fascist society, was singled out for abuse. Moravia, born Pincherle, was Jewish only on his father's side; nevertheless the Fascist journal *Il Tevere* gloatingly referred to 'that Jew Pincherle'.

By March–April 1938 Italy's media had united into an all-out onslaught of racial abuse. Mussolini knew that an anti-Semitic policy would delight Hitler, as it signalled Italy's further distancing from Britain and the now impotent League of Nations. And so, that troubled spring, while Mussolini whipped up anti-Jewish prejudice, the Fascist radio bulletins dominated the rooms at 75 Corso Re Umberto. Levi's mother, her brothers and sisters listened fearfully as the 'Jewish Question' was discussed in endless broadcasts on the wireless. Levi's father meanwhile had undergone a third operation for intestinal cancer. Broken in health, the sixty-year-old engineer began to criticise East Europe's Ashkenazim, who with their stubborn piety and backward-looking rites were making life difficult for Jews everywhere. Like most Italian Jews, he just hoped that Mussolini's anti-Semitic propaganda would 'blow over'. He could not imagine how much worse was to come.

7

On 7 July 1938 Levi took his end-of-term chemistry exam. A week later he was on holiday with his family in the Piedmont resort of Cogne, near France. In spite of many warning signs over the past months, the news on the bright summer morning of 14 July came as a shock to most Italians, Jews and non-Jews alike. Splashed on the front page of Italian newspapers was 'The Manifesto of Racial Scientists'. Commissioned by Mussolini and signed by a group of so-called 'racial experts' at the Ministry of Popular Culture in Rome, the Manifesto announced the discovery of an Italian race. For 2000 years the Italians had been 'Aryans', and since Jews were not members of that race, therefore they could not be a part of the Italian nation. According to this pseudo-biology, the Italian Jew was a contaminant akin to the Nazis' *Fremdkörper*, an alien within the state.

At first the Levis reacted to the Racial Manifesto with shock. Jews had enjoyed assimilation and relative acceptance within Italian society for almost a century. They took great pride in their contribution to the unified Italian state, and were virtually indistinguishable from the Catholic majority. Agata Pèlerin, Ester Levi's new cleaning woman, was flabbergasted to learn that her employers were Jewish. 'What? You don't look it!' But overnight it seemed that Italian Jews were beyond the pale. More than 10,000 of them – one-third of Italy's Jewish adults – were still Fascist Party members. After seventeen years of Blackshirt rule, Mussolini had betrayed his own most loyal subjects. Nazi-inspired biological anti-Semitism was deeply offensive to the Levis, who retreated into an anxious, if dignified, silence. Fortunately they were consoled by other Jewish families on holiday in Cogne that July. Together, they could only hope that the Racial Manifesto marked an end to their official persecution. Instead it signalled a second, violent press campaign later that year.

Throughout the summer of 1938 the pressure continued as the Fascist government announced its intention to enact laws 'in defence' of the so-called Italian race. First, articles began to appear in Turin's *La Stampa* and other newspapers condemning 'pietism', the crime of sympathising with Jews. These articles, written by the wretchedly anti-Semitic journalist Concetto Pettinato, caused the Levis great distress. Primo's cousin Giulia Colombo was staying with relatives in Oulx, near Turin, as the persecutions were stepped up. The Colombos were the only Jews in town. Giulia, knowing that 'pietism' could put her Catholic friends in jail, was afraid to ask them for her usual game of tennis. However, while the new anti-Semitic propaganda was endorsed by the Fascist Party and the muzzled Italian press, it was not taken seriously by the larger public: to most Italians the Racial Manifesto seemed an unnatural Teutonic import. So it was Giulia's Catholic friends who came to ask for her company on the tennis courts. They said they were 'disgusted' to be Italian. In Turin, Levi's old literature teacher Azelia Arici said to one of her pupils: 'Shame on Italy!' Most Turinese were slow to attend to the details of persecution. Therefore the German consul in Turin, Dr Dirk von Langen, agitated for stricter anti-Semitic measures. He operated from 77 Corso Galileo Ferraris in the heart of the Crocetta.

8

On 31 July 1938 Primo Levi celebrated (if that is the right word) his nineteenth birthday. His father was terminally ill, his family stressed by events that raised ancient fears of the ghetto. Levi was still studying hard; he hoped to finish his chemistry degree and maybe find work in a laboratory. Yet the Fascist regime was making life increasingly difficult for him. Non-Jewish chemistry colleagues noted that Levi had become more withdrawn. 'Before the persecutions we didn't even know who the Jews in class *were*,' recalled Giovanna Balzaretti. Now it was glaringly obvious who the Jews in Professor Ponzio's class were. Edith Weisz was known to have roots somewhere in Eastern Europe, but now she was conspicuously an *israelita*. Even without the imposition of a yellow star, the regime had its ways of making those differences obvious. While Catholic students had to wear Fascist tweed jackets to exams (with special pockets for grenades), Jews could only wear mufti. Emma Vita-Levi in her glowing silk suits was much envied by her Catholic female peers as they sat, uncomfortably warm, in their Sardinian black tweeds.

A few days after Levi's birthday the Bureau for Demography and Race Protection was set up in Rome. Its express task was to conduct a census of all Jews resident in Italy. However, this was not before a new popular Fascist review, *La Difesa della Razza* (The Defence of the Race), began to appear on the news-stands on 5 August. The journal championed the Italians as a breed of Mediterranean supermen, though these home-grown attempts at racial anti-Semitism were often slipshod. One edition of the review carried a photograph of a blue-eyed baby boy above the caption: 'A typical example of the Aryan race', but the infant turned out to be Jewish. Another issue, more unpleasantly, showed a sculpture by the Jewish artist Jacob Epstein of a woman shaped like a monkey. Here, according to the learned review, was evidence of the 'simian degeneration of Semitic peoples'.

Though the 1938 census was carried out dispassionately, like any routine survey, it had the underhand violence of a police operation. Data were gathered on every living Jew in Italy – name, address, profession – and set down with lapidary coldness in official communiqués. There was a luminous Indian summer that year. The Levis were still on holiday in Cogne when warrant officers went about their business in Turin. Equipped with rubber stamps and dockets, they interrogated the concierge at 75 Corso Re Umberto: how many Jews live in this apartment block? And what do they do for a living? There would be other, more humiliating interrogations. In late August the results of the Turin census were dispatched to the Ministry of the Interior in Rome. The number of Jews resident in the Piedmont capital was calculated at 4,057. This was a much more accurate figure than the overenthusiastic estimate of 24,637 arrived at earlier in July through a hit-and-miss trawl of presumed Jewish surnames. Even after the census was officially closed, the police dossiers continued to swell, creating a climate of suspicion in the city. Fearing guilt by association, 'Aryans' dragged into the racial investigations distanced themselves completely from Jewish acquaintances.

The census was only the beginning. Early that September came the first anti-Jewish legislation. No 'persons of Jewish race' were to be admitted to Italian state schools or universities. Jewish teachers were forbidden to teach in public institutions. In addition, Jews could neither begin nor continue their studies at university. Now Mussolini's intentions for the Jews of Italy were clear, and the impact on Levi's life was direct and shocking. The nineteen-year-old was to be thrown out of the Chemistry Institute. Edith Weisz's brother, Rodolfo, thought of transferring to Prague to complete his medical studies. Fortunately he stayed where he was: Prague was soon to be invaded by the Nazis. Levi, still with his parents in Cogne, also chose to bide his time.

A week later, on 7 September, a second Fascist law ordered that all Jews of foreign birth, including those who had acquired Italian citizenship since 1 January 1919, leave Italian territories within six months. For the purposes of the law, Jews were defined as persons having two Jewish parents, 'even if they profess a religion other than the Jewish'. This sinister clause was copied from Hitler's Nuremberg Laws and intended to send a strong signal to Italian Jews who contemplated religious conversion.

The bulk of Fascist racial legislation was made official two months later on 17 November. An earlier government decree was clarified when all citizens judged to be of the 'Jewish race' were prohibited from marrying 'Aryans'. A host of other severe restrictions ensured that Italy's Jews were now reduced to pariahs. Expelled from state jobs, sometimes forced to sell their property, Jews were also banned from Fascist Party membership or joining the army. However, one important concession was made: Jews currently in their second year at university could complete their studies. Levi now had good reason to be grateful to his old private tutor Marisa Zini, who nine years earlier had coached him through two years of secondary school in twelve months. Without Zini, Levi would now be studying first-year chemistry and thus disqualified from his course. University records show that Primo Levi successfully renewed his registration on 31 October 1938, but his sister Anna Maria was not so lucky; she could only go to university at the war's end, having lost five years of schooling through state persecution.

9

Incredibly, the first bureaucratic effect of the persecutions on Levi's life was positive. Every Saturday afternoon throughout his first year in the laboratory he had had to attend the University Militia (MVSN) as punishment for neglecting his call-up papers for the navy. He did not enjoy marching the *passo romano* in closed ranks to a military band and his training was virtually useless. Most days his cartridge-case contained an afternoon snack of bread and salami instead of bullets; he never learned how to load a rifle: he was not the military-minded type. Levi's fellow recruits were just as green and unenthusiastic. Bored, they gave each other idiot nicknames – 'I Too Am Disgusting', 'Cravero the Bastard', 'Simoncelli the Turd' – and assigned jovially obscene names to dismantled rifle parts, such as 'grained knob', 'tube with nib'. Levi joined wholeheartedly in these japes. To help take the tedium off the manoeuvres, Sidney Calvi concealed a medallion of Trotsky in his MVSN jacket pocket (there was a frisson in carrying the forbidden image). For the most part the recruits stood in silence while their superior, Major Pipino, bawled incomprehensibly over their heads. Levi's stint in the University Militia had been as ridiculous as it was brief, and that autumn of 1938 he surrendered his kit-bag without regrets.

The all-pervasive disorder and corruption of Fascist bureaucracy meant that months, sometimes years, passed before anti-Semitic decrees were made law. Though Levi left the University Militia immediately, some official roadblock meant that he was not officially thrown out until a year later, on 2 September 1939. His Conscription Register from this period is a chaos of crossings-out and deferred legislation. The only clearly legible words are '*APPARTIENE ALLA RAZZA EBRAICA*' (MEMBER OF THE JEWISH RACE). This classification, rubber-stamped on to a document, was all it took to seal a man's fate.

10

In the autumn of 1938 Levi's sister was expelled from her state school, along with all Jewish children. A marble plaque commemorating the Jewish history teacher Arturo Segre was ceremonially thrown out with the rubbish, along with banned Jewish school texts such as Paolo D'Ancona's three-volume *L'Arte Italiana* (from which Levi had acquired his meagre knowledge of Italian art). Not to be defeated, all over Italy Jewish communities set up schools to educate their children. By early November Turin had its own Jewish School. Situated near the synagogue on Via Sant' Anselmo, its teaching staff were excellent: many were university professors who had lost their jobs following the racial laws. Anna Maria Levi found a highly 'cultivated environment' there. Her Classics master was the great Arnaldo Momigliano, later professor of ancient history at University College, London. A well-known literature teacher, Giuseppe Morpurgo, was appointed headmaster and his daughter Lucia was in Anna Maria's class. After the war Lucia was to become Anna Maria's sister-in-law. Naturally no photograph of Mussolini hung in the classrooms; instead the school instilled a greater pride in being Jewish. Asked how long his family had lived in Italy, one Jewish pupil answered: 'Since 1516'. Actually Jews had been present in Italy since before the destruction of the Second Temple in AD 70.

Though the Nazis welcomed Mussolini's Racial Manifesto, they were not at all satisfied with the actual racial laws, which Hitler's propagandists sneeringly called 'Kosher Fascism'. Mussolini had failed to strip Jews of their citizenship. Rather, he had fudged the issue by creating a new category of 'Italian citizens of the Jewish race', now sometimes politely referred to as 'Italians of Mosaic persuasion'. In Germany anyone with just one Jewish grandparent was classified as a Jew; Hitler had cast them out from society. Levi was a year and a half into his chemistry course when, on the night of 9–10 November 1938, 191 synagogues across Germany were set ablaze.

Many Jews were murdered, thousands carried off to camps, their houses, shops and other properties destroyed. The resulting devastation inspired the Nazis to name that night *Kristallnacht*, or 'night of the broken glass'. These words were deliberately chosen to belittle the damage done and mock the victims. *La Stampa*, while it scarcely covered the event, informed its Piedmontese readers of the 'exemplary lesson' meted out to 'international Jewish crime'. A turning-point had been reached in the fortunes of European Jewry.

II

Levi's sister was in an improvised school; news from abroad was bad; Cesare was dying. The Levis had to consider their options. The laws had taken the family by surprise. For Jews all over Italy it was the same. The social fabric had been torn apart by the anti-Semitic measures just as surely as if the ghettos had been reconstructed across the land. Perhaps assimilation did not after all eliminate discrimination; maybe it had made the Levis more vulnerable to the persecution ahead. For years they had believed they were untouched by Jew-hatred. Now the unthinkable had happened.

Of course the family was unaware of the mortal danger they were in from Mussolini's German ally. Their first thought was to go abroad and wait for things to calm down. On 19 December, one week after *Kristallnacht*, Levi's uncle Oreste Colombo went to the French consulate in Turin hoping to emigrate to a still-civilised country. Only the day before, however, the consul had ceased to issue visas to Jews. Oreste would not have been helped by a visa anyway: a year and a half later the Nazis would march into Paris. On Christmas Day the moribund Cesare Levi and his brother Enrico held an emergency family conference with a wealthy Catholic, Signora Giaccone, who had a ranch for sale in Brazil. The meeting had been arranged through Signora Giaccone's sister, the Levi family's greengrocer. Instead of attending the family meeting, Levi went with his cousin Giulia Colombo to see *The Good Earth* starring Luise Rainer – one of the last American movies to be released in Italy before Mussolini's Hollywood embargo. The other film showing in Turin that dreadful Christmas was the new Disney animation, *Snow White*.

After a long family consultation, the Brazilian property was bought jointly by the three Levi brothers – Cesare, Mario, Enrico – and by Oreste Colombo. So for a while it looked as though Primo might live in Brazil if the situation at home deteriorated. The ranch was in Santa Catarina province on the border with Uruguay, a huge estate apparently, with cattle and forest. Mussolini's persecution had forced the Levis to consider emigrating, but Fascist Treasury regulations made it illegal for them to take more than 2,500 lire out of the country. This pitifully small sum would only allow for a few weeks' living. The Levis paid for the ranch in hard cash. Now, illegally, the money left the country for Brazil in suitcases carried by Signora Giaccone and by Enrico Levi's two sons Paolo and Franco. On arrival in Brazil, however, the family realised that the contract was dubious and that criminals had a vested interest in the property. '*El Ramundo*' was resold after the war; Levi never went there.

Within eighteen months of the racial laws, some 5,500 Jews had left Italy – over one-tenth of the country's Jewish population. Among them were Elda Calderoni, a first cousin of Levi's mother, who fled to Buenos Aires with her Protestant husband Giovanni Turìn. Slowly the Levi family was breaking up. In January 1939 one of the four Luzzati sisters, Nella, left Turin for São Paolo, accompanied by her two children. The family would not return to Italy until after the war. Nella's husband was travelling to Brazil separately on a false work contract: otherwise he would not have been able to get a visa. Corruption was so widespread within Fascist bureaucracy that easy money was to be made in forged passports and 'Aryanisation' certificates. Indeed, bribery would soon become the main determinant of non-Jewish status; if you had money you could change your religion by the stroke of a notary's pen. Some applicants even claimed eligibility on the grounds that their parents had had sexual relations with 'Aryans'. It was all starkly symptomatic of Fascist opportunism. Mussolini made no clear attempt to justify his about-turn regarding the Jews.

12

In Turin the police continued to investigate citizens of suspect Jewish birth. One of Cesare Levi's two surgeons, Cristofero Colombo, was a family relative. But did the regime consider him a Jew? Colombo had an 'Aryan' mother; now the race officers were not so sure. A bureaucrat in the Turin *municipio* recommended an investigation in the city cemetery 'to ascertain whether Signora Carola Spagnoli [Cristofero Colombo's mother] had been interred in the Jewish section'. Here was officialdom gone mad: the Duce's faceless inquisitors were making trips to the local graveyard. If Colombo was proved to be Jewish, he would lose his job.

Uncle Oreste Colombo, having failed to emigrate with his wife and daughter to France, tried one last bureaucratic loophole to safeguard himself and his family. The November regulations had stipulated an exemption for Italian Jews who had shown 'great service' to the nation. If they had seen combat in the Great War, in Libya, Abyssinia or Spain, they might be spared discrimination. Oreste had fought in the front-line trenches for three years against the Austrians and had nearly died of his wounds. Surely he was eligible for exemption status? The authorities wanted proof that Oreste had been a lieutenant, but he had mislaid his military papers. Where were his medals, then? For months Levi's uncle waited anxiously for his application to be processed at the Office of Demography and Race in Turin. He bribed officials – only to be refused exemption. Even if he had been one of the lucky *discriminati*, the racial laws had destroyed his career. Oreste was thrown out of the Turin bank where he had worked faithfully as a manager for twenty years. Then he became depressed and was nicknamed *L'Uomo Nero*, the Gloomy Man, of the family. Italy would soon go to war, Oreste predicted with his Tarot deck, and the mass destruction would continue until the spring of 1945.

Levi's father briefly sought salvation in the possibility of baptism. Someone had suggested that he procure antedated baptismal certificates for his children. In Italy there was a long – and for most Jews, vile – tradition of converts. Baptism would mean abandoning the family and Judaism to embrace the Catholic Church. Levi and his sister decided it was best not to consider baptism at all; but other Jews felt differently. Levi's university colleague Emma Vita-Levi was hurriedly baptised on 29 November 1938. Her mother, Fanny Gaudoglia, was a Catholic. Unfortunately, children of mixed marriages could obtain 'Aryan' standing *only* if they were baptised before 1 October 1938. So, by just one month, Emma Vita-Levi, who had won the gold M medal from Mussolini, had missed her chance of salvation. Her older sister Olga had been a proud *dama del fascio* (Fascist Woman), but now she was ejected from the movement. The irony is that neither Emma nor her sister had any clear notion who or what Jews even were; it was Mussolini's racial decrees that had irremediably stigmatised the women as *israeliti*.

Levi's father blamed his misfortunes on imaginary 'enemies', and turned in on himself. Fortunately he was allowed a Ganz company silver handshake and an adequate pension, so the family kept financially buoyant. After Ganz, Cesare was expelled from the Fascist Party, not that he cared. Like many Italian Jews at this difficult hour he tried to hide his worst fears behind platitudes that were now meaningless, as the poison of Jew-hatred seeped down from Hitler's Europe. 'Ah, but we're in Italy,' Cesare would say hopefully, 'the Church and the Vatican are right here – they wouldn't dare do anything to us.'

Years later, Primo Levi compared the sense of resignation that prevailed among Italy's persecuted Jews after 1938 to a peasant's on the eve of an earthquake: 'The catastrophe has to happen, but we hope to be able to save ourselves when it does.' This fatalism was shared by Cesare's father-in-law, the increasingly dour and diabetic Signor Luzzati. After the racial laws his textile store had gone downhill as Catholic clients, fearing the stigma of 'pietism', discreetly withdrew their custom. The Luzzatis accepted the state of poverty without ever accepting the word. Sometimes Luzzati's playboy sons Gustavo and Corrado were asked to help in the store. Neither of them had a head for business and made such a hash of the accounts that the ex-banker Oreste Colombo had to come in to set the records straight. Only thirty-eight years old, Primo's adored Uncle Corrado was sunk in despair. As Jews could no longer even own a radio, the Fascist police had confiscated his beloved equipment, dismantling a lifetime's passion in one night of vandalism.

As the persecutions became ever more constricting, so it was a serious offence for Jews to employ an 'Aryan' domestic. Agata Pèlerin nevertheless crept into 75 Corso Re Umberto under cover of dark to help with the cleaning when she could. Many domestics wept at having to leave Jewish families whom they had served faithfully for years. Uncle Mario Levi was allowed to keep his maid, Maria Rinaldi, on 'compassionate grounds' because, said a police spy's report, she was 'almost blind' and had nowhere to go.

Somehow, in spite of all they had suffered, the Jews of Turin pulled together. The initials of a Jewish textile shop in the city – S.A.N.E.T – became secret code for *Siamo Ancora Noi Ebrei Torinesi*, 'We Are Still Turinese Jews'. Life had been made difficult for the Levis by the race legislation; nevertheless these were *Italian*-style laws and Italians reputedly have a flair for disregarding laws. The future was still uncertain, but Primo adjusted to his new, enforced identity: he was now not an Italian, but a Jew. This adjustment was hardest for those Jews who had felt the most assimilated. On 29 November 1938 the Jewish publisher Angelo Formiggini, an associate of James Joyce, threw himself from the bell tower of Modena cathedral. He had wanted to draw the world's attention to the persecutions. News of his suicide was suppressed (during Fascism all suicide cases were considered a crime against the state – tainted with dishonour – and therefore not reported). Yet news of Formiggini's suicide spread quickly on the Jewish grapevine, and the Jews were shocked.

13

Branded an outcast, thrown out of GUF, it is a wonder that Levi kept his equilibrium. Catholic colleagues began to speak of the 'Primo Levi Who Never Gets Angry'. Occasionally he was reproached for his lack of fierce response to the new Fascist laws. A Jewish veteran of the Fascist Ethiopia campaigns, Bruno Jesi, had gone about Turin in a fury smashing up anti-Semitic shopfronts. Surely that was the way to behave? Levi's equanimity led many to believe that he was complacent or even forgiving of the regime. In fact he was fiercely indignant and resentful. Levi was a Jew writ large in a country that had turned anti-Semitic – in legislation if not in practice – overnight. A minority of Christian acquaintances had even started to keep their distance; one schoolmate tried to avoid Levi on the street. 'I think we should stop meeting,' he said. Thirteen years later, when this same man asked Levi if he would like to renew their friendship, Levi told him: 'No – not with you.'

At university, by necessity, Jews continued to associate with non-Jews, but Levi now had to think twice before telephoning Christian acquaintances, as he could implicate them in 'pietism'. Jews were supposed to be conspicuously different. Yet Vanna Rava, a Catholic, insisted: 'We never for one moment believed that just because Primo was Jewish he was "dirty" and "greasy" as the regime wanted us to think.' Many Fascists flinched at the persecution of their Jewish friends and neighbours. If the Germans had departed from the community of civilised peoples, then the Italians had their saving humanity. Even the most zealous Blackshirt in Levi's class, Emilio Lagostena, tried to help Edith Weisz, now officially declared 'stateless' as a Slovak Jew. A gentle soul, Lagostena was a genuinely earnest disciple of *ducismo* and the one pupil in Professor Ponzio's course noted for his Fascist idealism. What little money Lagostena had he spent on Blackshirt uniforms for himself and his Fascist associates in Torre Pellice, where he lived with his mother and two sisters. Yet he was deeply ashamed of the racial laws. And, as if to make amends for the persecutions, he went out of his way to procure Edith a *tessera del dopolavoro* (after-work pass), which entitled her to discounted cinema or theatre tickets that as a Jew she could no longer have.

Naturally there were government stooges and *gerarchi* (Fascist functionaries) who zealously persecuted Jews. In one brutal episode, Fascist police tried to bully Alberto Salmoni's father into quitting his blood-processing business in Turin. When he refused, they trumped up a charge of treason: the Jew Salmoni had insulted king and country. Salmoni was not the sort to be easily cowed. (In Port Said he had defended a Jew from a Greek mob after a rumour spread that Christian blood was used in Passover bread.) But when the Fascist police came back to threaten him with *confino* – internal exile – he caved in, and lost his business. Augusto Salmoni had not even thought of himself as a Jew. He had named his son 'Alberto' after the secular King Albert I of Belgium. Now the entire Salmoni family was forced to acknowledge the stigma of their racial origin and their glaring 'difference' from other Italians. They learned that Jews were different not only because they were Jews, but because they were *non-Aryans*. And who exactly were the *Aryans*? Nobody in Italy seemed to know. Meanwhile a café on Turin's Via Roma put up the notice: 'JEWS ARE NOT WELCOME HERE.'

SEVEN

University and War
1939–41

I

On 11 January 1939, six months after the promulgation of the Fascist racial laws, one of Professor Ponzio's students committed suicide. No one understood why Agostino Neri had crept unseen into the lab to swallow hydrocyanic acid. He was not Jewish. To those who knew him, Neri was a good-natured if dreamy youth. His father was the distinguished literary critic, Ferdinando Neri, so the suicide made headline news in *La Stampa*. Two days after the incident, on Friday 13 January, Ponzio's chemistry class filed past Neri's corpse, which was laid out at the Molinette Hospital in Turin. Primo Levi, like everyone else, was deeply disturbed by Neri's death, a uniquely incoherent event.

2

The weather in Turin that winter was very cold (the newspapers report sub-zero temperatures). During these freezing months Fascist officials continued their investigations into 'suspect Jewish' families. Those previously unaware that they had Jewish blood were forced to confront upsetting revelations. Marisa Zini, Levi's childhood tutor, was summoned by the Fascist mayor of Turin to provide evidence of 'Aryan' blood. (It had been discovered that her mother's maiden name was Terracini, a Jewish surname.) Diana Reduzzi, who had taught Primo history of art, was required to explain why her mother was called Eugenia Levi.

All 'non-Aryans' resident in Turin now had to register themselves officially as Jews. And they had to do this before 3 March or face jail. Mass registration was the quickest way to update the regime's census of the previous summer. A declaration by the head of the family sufficed for all; each Jew was then allocated a 'Jewish dossier' number. Levi's family was

91

slow to comply. It was a humiliation for Jews to have to confirm their pariah status on a city register. Levi's uncle Mario had 'denounced' (*denunciato*) his family on 7 February 1939. Nine days later, with just two weeks until the deadline, Levi's father added his kin to the register. In the bitter cold he walked to the city offices on Via Bellezia carrying his birth certificate as well as those of his children and his parents, Adele Sinigaglia and Michele Levi (fortunately not alive to witness this indignity).

3

At about this time Levi developed a breathless interest in a thin, serious chemistry student. Clara Moschino had white skin and a bony face, and a melancholy that appealed to Levi. Moschino was very different from the middle-class *crocettari* who had marked his social world. Fiercely motivated and bright, she had applied for a maths degree but switched to chemistry, she said, after realising it could make her more money. Her stepfather was a book-binder with a workshop near Turin's synagogue. Her family were poor Catholics. Moschino was aware of the risk she ran of committing the crime of 'pietism'. Soon an unspoken 'feeling', as Moschino called it, developed between her and Levi. It was a shy, platonic romance (what in those days was called an 'understanding'), and the first of several asexual relations Levi was to have with women.

Once he had overcome his shyness, he surprised Moschino by his lively manner and wry humour. She understood Levi better than most with her suggestion that he was a 'melancholic' or 'vulnerable' person who seemed to have no obvious natural sufficiency. 'Primo was looking for a shoulder to lean on, and maybe I gave him the impression of strength.' Moschino was famous in the lab for not breaking glassware (that was Emma Vita-Levi's speciality), and this lent her an air of cautious judgment and dedication. In reality she was far more gregarious than her fictional counterpart 'Rita' in *The Periodic Table* (who is 'nobody's friend'). On weekends she went dancing with her sister Gigi on the banks of the Po. After chemistry class Levi took her to classical concerts and accompanied her home.

It is difficult to gauge how unhappy Levi was made to feel by these frustrations in love. The anti-Jewish legislations did not help his feelings of awkwardness. Yet even without the burden of racial persecution, university can be a deeply unhappy time, and though he may not have understood it in any utterable way, Levi was sometimes low-spirited and significantly depressed. Alberto Salmoni was shocked to hear from Levi – in his second year at university – that he had contemplated suicide. Today Salmoni does not recall if Levi had said this in a moment of despair, or if it was actually an admission of something long brooded on. One might note that Levi's long-term tendency to depression started in his teenage years; his comment to Salmoni is indicative of the severity of the depression that killed him.

4

Levi found a distraction from these anxieties in the mountains. Like many Turinese he enjoyed the fatigue – *la grande fatica* – attendant on a strenuous mountain hike. For his nineteenth birthday his sister had given him a pair of springhooks, three nails and a hammer for rock-face assault. With these Levi planned to prove himself equal to his persecutors: the racial laws had branded him as 'inferior', but he would show that he was made of sterner stuff. But now he had an ally. Sandro (Alessandro) Delmastro was a rock of a man with dark, intelligent eyes, who in 1939 flared brightly into Levi's life; Delmastro introduced him to dizzy mountain heights, and taught him to endure physical labour and to push himself to the limit.

Born in 1917, Delmastro was twenty-two to Levi's twenty, one of the oldest in the chemistry class, and a cryptic character. His strong black hair, parted to one side when he bothered to comb it, gave him a stubborn look. He was excited by danger and went out of his way to scale virgin ice-cliffs, climbing the great peaks of the Val di Lanzo in gung-ho style. 'Sandro wasn't interested in gentle sunset rambles,' said his fiancée Ester Valabrega, 'he was a wild man.' His bible was Eugen Lammer's *The Fountain of Youth*. First published in Italy in 1933, this Nietzschean hymn to the mountains glorified rock-climbing without the use of maps and guides. On Friday nights Delmastro would disappear with a chunk of bread and some artichokes, and return two days later without a word to anyone. The hungrier and more exhausted he was 'up there', the happier he became. Delmastro had resigned in disgust from the Fascist-infiltrated Italian Alpine Club (CAI), though his mountain-worship was quite in keeping with the Fascist cult of *arditismo*, which celebrated a bare-chested toughness. When he had nonchalantly eaten a sandwich at a 3,000-metre altitude in mid-winter, his breast manfully exposed to the sleet, it had not occurred to him that this was a rather Fascist thing to do.

Delmastro was born in middle-class Turin to a Catholic master mason, though the family's wealth came from textiles. They had made enough money to build themselves a smart modern house (still standing) on the corner of Turin's Via Foscolo, and were very much a part of the city's *Torino-bene*, the well-heeled bourgeoisie. The racial laws had prevented him from marrying Ester Valabrega, who was half-Jewish; Delmastro's liberal Catholic spirit flinched at the outrage. He told Levi that Italy's Jews

93

were trapped in a sluggish, fearful pacifism; it was time they looked the future in the face. Hitler had already invaded Czechoslovakia and entered Prague. Now he was starting to move in on Poland. Where next? If Delmastro was unkind to Levi's innocence, under his influence Levi became gradually less naive. Delmastro was a lone wolf, with a wolf's snarl for the coming danger.

Levi was attracted by Delmastro's maverick character as much as his prowess and political convictions. He kept a cocker-spaniel named Flush, after Virginia Woolf's eponymous canine hero. Not only could Flush walk along a rock ledge attached to a rope, she could jump on to Delmastro's lavatory and pee. Delmastro had a taste for frolics and foolery. He became a university hero when he flooded the lab with nitric acid, and his mother was confronted with a hefty end-of-term bill. Alberto Salmoni was another who idolized Delmastro. They had been at school together in Turin, but Salmoni was a very different character, more woolly-headed, though he could be equally clumsy; but vague, charming and attractive to women. The three friends formed a tight clique that was considered 'almost misogynist', recalled Emma Vita-Levi. Delmastro, in his old-fashioned way, reckoned the mountains were too dangerous for women. They were places where men alone could rediscover their spiritual values, which were repressed by the smoke and grime of the city. In this romantic vision, mountaineering was less a sport than a way of life, and one more honest than the orthodoxy and political expediency of Fascism. 'Up there, when a rock falls and wants to hit you, at least it warns you first, by the noise it makes,' Delmastro wrote.

The divinity of the mountains was all-important. Prompted by Delmastro, Levi had begun to read books by the intrepid English mountaineers Edward Whymper and Alfred Mummery. These were available in Italy's excellent 'Ice-Pick and Pen' series. Whymper's *Scrambles Amongst the Alps* seemed to Levi to capture the pioneering quality of the Victorian climbers and gave a sense of dangerous remoteness to the mountains near Turin. Mummery had climbed the most daunting Piedmont peaks with a bottle of champagne in his rucksack and, in homage to Mummery's magnum, Levi took a battered aluminium thermos with him. Instead of champagne it contained egg yolks and milk; shaken with a scoop of mountain snow and a pebble, it made a crude if fortifying zabaione. Levi called his shaker '*Lo Sbatti-Uovo*', 'The Egg-Buster'.

Before taking Levi and Salmoni up into dangerous altitudes, Delmastro trained them on a rock gymnasium near Turin. The Sbarüa is a vertiginous heap of granite named after the Piedmontese verb 'to terrify', *sbarüé*. To reach it the three men took the bus to Pinerolo and from there climbed uphill to the Melano Shelter. Levi came prepared with a sixty-metre coil of rope, crampons and slings to protect him against a fall. After the Bardonecchia fiasco he did not want to come dangerously unstuck again. Being roped to these male friends made for an extraordinary sense of inter-independence. 'We were *physically* bound in every sense – a triplet – and it made for a very powerful camaraderie,' explained Salmoni. One by one the three inched over the crest of the Sbarüa. France was just fifty kilometres away across the Val Sestrière. This proximity to a nation where the Jews still had their liberty gave Levi a feeling of hope. In a real sense mountaineering became synonymous for him with freedom; it was a form of *antifascismo alpinistico*. After a pause of breathless silence Delmastro exclaimed to his charges: 'Just look around you!' In a few days Levi had promoted himself to *capocordata*, 'lead rope-climber'. This early training on the snow peaks was to prove extraordinarily important to him over the coming years; as Levi became physically more resilient, so he could better withstand the hardships ahead. 'Perhaps, in some obscure way, we felt the need to prepare ourselves for future events.' For the moment, Levi felt proud to have conquered the Sbarüa, and brave in measuring up to its heights.

Throughout the spring Levi's tenacious mountaineering life continued. He was in training on the Alps when, on 7 April 1939 – Good Friday – Mussolini invaded Albania. With this cynical smash-and-grab raid the Duce had struck another blow against the sanctity of international law. But worse was to come. On 22 May, Mussolini forged 'The Pact of Steel', a military alliance with Nazi Germany. Previous pacts between Hitler and Mussolini had been fairly meaningless, but this was the signal that a general European war was about to start, and very soon. Moreover, it committed Italy to come to Germany's aid when the war started.

Delmastro stepped up training sessions for Levi and Salmoni. This time his plan was to traverse the Valle d'Aosta at 3,000 metres, and descend with his disciples through pack-ice on crampons into the Gran Paradiso. As they trudged up from the medieval fortress town of Bard towards the shimmering glacier heights, they used seal-strips to stop their skis from sliding backwards. The men got lost, and emerged ravenous and swaying with exhaustion on the crest of a wrong peak. The way down looked treacherous – one slip and they would all fall – so the trio spent the night in a bivouac on an overhanging cliff-face. 'How do we get down?' Levi asked Delmastro. 'We'll think about getting down when the time comes. The worst that can happen to us is that we'll have to eat bear meat.' An uneasy night was spent as the men lay pressed together for warmth. They returned to the lowlands with three-day stubble, their eyes dazzled by the bright snow. In memory of that time Levi later wrote a short story, 'Bear Meat', a compilation of mountain experiences, in which his wrist-watch unaccountably stops as he lies shivering by Delmastro's side: 'as though time itself had frozen'.

5

Of Levi's ten Science Faculty teachers, only one that we know of was a dyed-in-the-wool Fascist. Massimo Fenoglio, his mineralogy professor, was a proud ex-serviceman with a metal plate in his skull from a Great War shrapnel-wound. Years later Levi would comment on Fenoglio: 'I found him unpleasant, and his lectures stupid, I couldn't take them seriously.' Behind this verdict lay an unpleasant memory. On 30 June 1939, the day after his mother's forty-fourth birthday, Levi was humiliated at a *viva voce*. He was one of three Jews waiting to be examined by Professor Fenoglio. The others were Emma Vita-Levi and Guido Bonfiglioli. All three took their places alphabetically in a queue of twenty or so 'Aryan' students, just as they had always done for exams. When Bonfiglioli's turn came to be examined, Fenoglio told him that Jews had to wait last in line. It was the new regulation. Vita-Levi burst into tears, while Levi remained immobile and speechless. Bonfiglioli started shouting at Fenoglio that the 'regulation' was just another attempt to dress-down and shame Italy's Jews. The professor's face was congested with embarrassment and he turned a deep red. Levi was indignant at the discrimination, and did not do well in the mineralogy exam, obtaining a low (for him) twenty-six out of thirty. Half a century later Bonfiglioli conceded that Professor Fenoglio probably 'felt offended by this business of Jews having to go last in line; it was an affront to his profession'.

Levi concentrated on studying for his other second-year exams. Physics revision took place at Vanna Rava's house on Via Silvio Pellico. Evenings there often ended with Levi, Rava and Vita-Levi sitting up until late. Rava recalled that Levi had repeatedly spoken of switching to physics. 'Chemistry is superficial,' he told her. 'It's limited to problems to do with the *transformation* of matter, but it doesn't go *inside* the atom like physics.' Levi was moving closer to a realisation that physics, not chemistry, was his vocation. Disappointingly, chemistry had not provided him with the key to life's mysteries as he had hoped: it seemed to him to be the baser, messier science of bad smells and explosions, though chemistry satisfied his practical bent in a way that physics never could.

In spite of the Fascist racial laws, Italy was still a country where Jews felt safe. In fact Jewish refugees from Occupied Europe were flooding into the country. On their arrival in Turin they were often met at the station by Giorgio Segre, a medical student who was known to be sympathetic to Zionism. Though Segre was not strictly speaking Jewish (his mother being a Catholic), he gave the refugees what little money or kosher food he could. He was pious – far more pious than Levi – as he demonstrated by his familiarity with Hebrew. He had even compiled a Hebrew dictionary for Italian Jews hoping to emigrate to Palestine. Levi showed little interest in helping these East European transients; indeed, he kept a conscious distance from them. Segre explained: 'To most assimilated Jews these low-class ragged Ashkenazim were unsavoury – no anti-Semitism is more corrosive than Jewish anti-Semitism.' Levi did not want to believe their accounts of Nazi atrocities: Piedmont was his true home, and things did not look so disastrous from where he stood.

Yet the long summer that led up to the fatal last days of August 1939 – the vigil of the Nazi invasion of Poland and the so-called Phoney War – Levi was to remember personally as a progressive political awakening. During this time his life revolved increasingly round Turin's Jewish School in Via Sant' Anselmo where a Jewish study group held twice-weekly meetings on cultural and political themes. The force behind these meetings were the brothers Ennio and Emanuele Artom. A remarkable pair, they perceived in Judaism not so much a religion as a morality and a weapon against oppression. As Hitler menaced Poland, and Europe was on edge, Jewish culture offered a civilised alternative to war and the soon-to-be-tested Nazi science of massacre.

It is difficult to imagine how culturally sterile Turin had become by the late 1930s. Piero Gobetti, the inspiring editor of the city's short-lived anti-Fascist journal, *Rivoluzione liberale,* had been dead for thirteen years, and most political opposition had died with him. 'Justice and Liberty' had been silenced, and all Turin lay under the dull hand of Fascist respectability and propriety. Into this cultural vacuum came the Artom brothers, and for the next two years Levi attended their study group regularly, eager to learn more. For Levi, as for many Italian Jews, the racial laws had provoked an unprecedented interest in Jewish culture. So he scoured the Torah, the Pentateuch and the Talmud, which he had not read since his Bar Mitzvah, for signs that Jews were a peaceable and devoutly moral people. Old Testament tales carried considerable symbolic weight for Europe's Jews in the late 1930s. Even without making the obvious comparison, it was easy to identify Mussolini with the tyrant King Haman who had wanted to kill all the Jews. Ennio Artom, known as 'Knickerbockers' at Levi's school for his plus-fours, was the younger brother and the more gifted. Levi compared him to the Jewish Jesuit Leo Naphta in Thomas Mann's *The Magic Mountain*: like Naphta, Ennio spent his days in restless searchings of the conscience ('What does it mean to be Jewish?') and impressed friends with his elegant intellectual arguments. Emanuele, a much more reserved character, was a frail twenty-four-year-old with a pallid, pious demeanour. He could see that Mussolini had established a juridical, if not a physical, ghetto and that the time had come for action.

Aside from the study group, the Artom house at 58 Via Sacchi (a now legendary Turin address) provided a cultivated environment for many of the city's non-conformists and free-thinkers. Though they were non-Jews, Zino Zini, Umberto Cosmo and other 'Gobettian' intellectuals were frequent guests. They associated Mussolini's racial persecution with the old reactionary elements that had opposed the Risorgimento and the Liberal principles on which the Kingdom of Italy was founded in 1861. Levi often visited 58 Via Sacchi, as well as the Artom country house at the foot of Mont Blanc in Courmayeur. Crocetta highbrows and Risorgimentists gathered at the Artoms to discuss literature, science and the burning issues of the day. A frequent guest was Livio Norzi. Levi had first met Norzi in 1935; he was a skinny, cerebral boy with a laconic wit and a shared passion for the mountains. 'Are you the famous Primo Levi?' Norzi had asked, and Levi had held out his hand: 'Are you the famous Livio Norzi?' In the Crocetta's close-knit Jewish community everyone had heard of everyone else. Levi grew to know the Artoms more intimately, now in 1939, when they moved to 36 Corso Re Umberto nearby.

The brothers' father, Emilio Artom, was the mathematician son of a rabbi and one of the few university professors in Italy brave enough to renounce Fascist Party membership. It took exceptional courage to reject the regime so blatantly. Non-conformism did not come naturally to Levi; until the racial laws of 1938 it had been routine for him to accept Fascism, but now he was changing. The Artom meetings in the Jewish school were supervised by a Fascist policeman, who was quickly bored by the cerebral discussion and fell asleep at the back of the hall with a pipe in his mouth. Much later, Levi claimed the Artom meetings were vital to Turin's fledgling Resistance. Even the mildest dissent counted for so much during that climate of repression. No other anti-regime group in Turin was allowed to meet at this time.

Talks were given on any suitable Jewish subject for discussion. A fortnight before his twentieth birthday, in July 1939, Levi was asked to deliver a paper on the proposition that 'Anti-Semitism in the Last Decade has Reached a Low Ebb'. He put together his thoughts with great care, and discussed the argument step by step with his sister. He had to give the paper in the library of the Jewish School and the room was packed. Many in the audience were non-Jews (it was considered important to show goys how Jewish culture was apparently suffused with elements of liberty, dignity and justice) and they hushed considerably as Levi began to read aloud. But he was so nervous and awkward that he mumbled incoherently. It was a mediocre performance and, for Levi, a traumatic one. He vowed never again to speak in public and for the next sixteen years he kept his word.

7

On 1 September 1939 German troops invaded Poland; two days later Britain and France declared war on Hitler. While Italy could not possibly be 'neutral' in a war that involved its German ally, for the moment it would not engage in hostilities. In the first fifty-five days of the German invasion, an estimated 5,000 Jews were murdered behind the Polish lines. The apprehension of massacre came slowly to the Levis, like bulletins of a sickness. Italian newspapers began to give vague and partial accounts of how Jews had been *übertragen* – 'transferred' – to certain 'zones'. Meanwhile Polish Jews continued to arrive in Turin, telling of relatives who had been dragged from their homes and hiding places. During this time Levi, like most Italian Jews, was uncertain what to believe. The terrible events developing in Poland took their place in the rumour-ridden politics of the moment.

On the Jewish New Year of 1939 – Thursday 14 September – the Levis and Luzzatis gathered for the usual family banquet. But the future was murky; as the family dipped bread and apple in honey to symbolise the hoped-for sweetness in the year ahead, the Second World War was under way. What would become of the Levis if Mussolini decided to fight alongside Hitler in Poland? In Stalin's Russia, now opportunistically allied with Hitler's Germany, Jews were not safe, either. Béla Kun, who had sparked the Hungarian revolution of 1919, was stripped of his post in the Comintern and executed.

Jewish families in Turin began to prepare their children for an uncertain future. Some Jews took boxing lessons from Kid Anderson, an American with cauliflower ears and a broken nose who ran a gym down by the gasworks. Others took English lessons. English was the language of the Allies, and Levi had not learned it at school. Now that Hitler's goal of Teutonic domination over Poland was virtually accomplished, the Levis had no idea where they might end up as a result of war – it might even be in England.

Levi was assigned an English teacher, Gladys Melrose, who was a Londoner born in 1901 to a music-hall actress, Zina Melrose, and an Indian army sergeant. She had green cat-like eyes and was stately. In these months before the European war, Gladys was to exert a vital influence on Levi. She was the last in a series of exceptional women teachers – Emilia Glauda, Marisa Zini, Anna Borgogno, Azelia Arici – who moulded Levi intellectually. Gladys had three children to support as well as an alcoholic Italian husband. (Her youngest child became the Italian film star Marina Berti, who starred in *Quo Vadis* alongside Robert Taylor.) The Melrose family saga was not a happy one. Gladys had lived contentedly with her husband in London until 1936 when Mussolini invaded Ethiopia. Then sanctions were imposed on Italy for its Africa aggression, and Italians and Anglo–Italians in London suffered from gangs yelling 'Wop' and 'Aye-tie'. Some were later sent to internment camps on the Isle of Man, in Canada or Australia. Gladys fled with her family to Turin, where she taught at the Berlitz School of Languages. Money was tight, and she was often to be seen trawling the fish stalls at closing time for cheaper scraps. Levi affectionately nicknamed her 'Gladys Snores' as she always looked so tired and worn out. But despite her circumstances, living on skimpy pittances, Gladys retained an Edwardian sense of propriety.

Though she was not Jewish, most of her pupils came from the Artom circle. She encouraged Levi to read her favourite English authors and introduced him to Aldous Huxley, whose mordant, subversively libidinous novels of the Twenties and Thirties she saw as an antidote to Fascist lies and obfuscation. Huxley had understood the power of hidden persuasion and the techniques of mass suggestion better than any tyrant. Moreover, his habit of examining humanity under a microscope – his anthropological detachment – appealed to the scientist in Levi, and would later powerfully influence *If This is a Man*. Gladys closely followed Levi's literary career until she died in Rome in 1980.

November 1939: Poland was conquered – starvation had begun to haunt the Jews of occupied Warsaw – and the Jewish position in Italy deteriorated. In a flush of paranoia the Fascist Party in Turin began to investigate even its own members. On 6 October 'racial details' were requested of Aldous Huxley's future father-in-law, Felice Archera, whose family had been neighbours of the Levis. For years Signor Archera had lived like an 'Aryan' among other 'Aryans' in the Crocetta. On those rare occasions when he had had to show his documents (for example, at the Turin Stock Exchange where he worked), his mother's name had gone unnoticed. But his mother was called Lina Segre: and Segre is a Jewish surname. Investigations into

Archera were conducted in a haphazard fashion. One communiqué lists the family address as 71 Corso Vinzaglio; another, 71 Corso Duca degli Abruzzi. (Actually the Archeras had moved to 31 Corso Duca degli Abruzzi.) In Nazi Germany, where the anti-Semitic bureaucracy was both *pünktlich* and *akkurat*, one cannot imagine this sort of carelessness. By the time Felice Archera's name appeared on a government list of persons who are 'Not to Be Considered of the Jewish Race', his daughter Laura had fled to the United States to become a violinist in the Los Angeles Philharmonic, and later married Aldous Huxley.

Now Italians were told to expect air raids. It seemed ridiculous to be issued with gas capes and blackout material when as yet there was no sign of war. For these were the months of the Phoney War when nothing seemed to happen but the passage of time. Yet the prospect of having to 'live with bombs' became frighteningly real for Levi and his family when on 9 November 1939 the Turin municipality began to prepare for bomb attack. It was the day after Levi's Pharmaceutical Chemistry exam. Body bags, coffins, buckets of fire-fighting sand, standby generators and water-purification plants were ordered, as Turin braced itself for an apocalyptic Armageddon in the style of H. G. Wells. Bicycle lights had to be painted blue so that they were less easily seen from the air at night. Street lamps, even cemetery candles, were ordered to be extinguished. During the first trial blackouts, the colour of the sky took on an unreal depth of blue. Meanwhile at 75 Corso Re Umberto the concierge lugged sandbags and barrels of drinking water down into the cellar. Levi's life was soon to change from that of a disinterested spectator to a protagonist in a European war.

8

Levi spent the New Year – 1940 – under a snowfall in the Dolomites, the mountain range stretching across the Austrian and Italian border. A Zionist youth group had offered cut-price winter camping holidays at the foot of the Marmolada peak, and Levi wanted to go. Jews were banned from Fascist youth activities, and here was an opportunity to meet other persecuted Italians. Levi was not interested in Zionism for religious reasons. In many ways Zionism was a consciously secular movement; early champions had been known to picnic on ham sandwiches in their disregard for ritual. Only in extreme circumstances would Levi have considered Palestine as an alternative to Turin. Though persecuted, he was too assimilated an Italian to want to settle among the dunes and palm trees of the Middle East. And yet intellectually, Zionism fascinated Levi, and he was far more closely involved in the movement than he admitted in later years. Probably on the suggestion of Gladys Melrose, he translated the controversial British government White Paper of 1939, known to Zionists as the 'Black Paper', which had drastically restricted the number of Jewish refugees into Palestine.

Levi had also attended talks at the Jewish School on the Zionist thinker Theodor Herzl. A Hungarian, Herzl had founded the Zionist movement in 1896 with the publication of his book *The Jewish State,* which Levi had read. According to Herzl, Jews were not merely a religious group, but a nation waiting to be born. Some foreign Jewish Zionists sheltering in Turin talked passionately of Herzl's dreamed-of *Juden-Staat* in British-ruled Palestine. Levi's sister remembered one of them in particular. Max Varady was a young Hungarian newspaper editor who had made his way to the sanctuary of the Jewish School in Turin. Having escaped the Gestapo, and the ever-increasing numbers of Hungarians who supported Hitler, he saw Palestine as the Jews' only hope. According to Anna Maria, Varady gave a very rosy picture of Zionism as an innocent, agrarian form of Socialism. But the Levis could not be persuaded to leave Turin: they were 95 per cent Italian, they said, and 5 per cent Jewish.

From Turin it was six hours by train to the Dolomites. Levi went with a familiar group from the Artom circle, but there was one new face. Eugenio Gentili was a most fascinating man, a beaming, good-natured architecture graduate. It was from Gentili that Levi first came to know of the struggle against the Fascists and learned of the existence of other political parties, in particular the Socialists and Communists. Born in 1916, three years Levi's senior, Gentili was far more worldly-wise and politically mature than Levi. Through his old history teacher, Piero Operti, he had known an older generation of anti-Fascists in Turin. Operti was a Great War *grand mutilé* who spoke with disarming candour of the evil of Nazism. Levi had never known such non-conformists at his school; his teachers were cowed by the regime. Though Gentili was Jewish, he had a much wider circle of friends than Levi, including the legendary anti-Fascist schoolboy Renzo Giua, who had fought on the Republican side in the Spanish War and been killed in 1938.

From the Fedaia Shelter at the foot the Marmolada, the Zionist holiday-makers spent ten days skiing and hiking on the snow-covered peaks. Few persons of sense could have thought that a general war could be postponed indefinitely. Yet almost everyone, even the bitterest of refugees here in the Marmolada shelter, pretended to hope. They sang the Zionist anthem, the 'Hattikvà', and danced a whirling tarantella. Before returning to Turin, Levi set off on a horse-drawn sled for the Marmolada's glacier. As the sun went down over the Alto Adige, hillsides of dripping fir trees floated in a landscape of fog. Everyone agreed that it was like a scene from *The Magic Mountain*, a book then all the rage in the Jewish Crocetta.

9

On 9 April 1940, Hitler occupied Denmark and the principal ports of Norway. A month later, on 10 May, the invasion of the Low Countries began. Within weeks the German armies had overrun Holland and Belgium, forcing the British to evacuate Dunkirk. Then the Germans were marching through France, and a final escape route for Piedmont's Jews was cut off. Hitler's success in France, which Mussolini had not expected, convinced the Italian dictator that he must enter the war now, before it ended in a German victory, for the Duce wanted a share of the spoils.

Two weeks before Ester Levi's forty-fifth birthday, the inevitable happened. At 6:00 pm on the evening of 10 June 1940, under pressure from Hitler, Mussolini declared war on Britain and France. The Duce's speech, transmitted nationwide by wireless, boomed into the Levis' rented holiday villa in Lanzo, near Turin. 'People of Italy, to arms, and show your tenacity, your courage and your valour!' Mussolini yelled from his balcony in Rome, pounding his brow. The family decided to leave immediately for Turin to seek out friends and relatives. Primo, rather than wait for the next train home, cycled all the way to 75 Corso Re Umberto. Swooping downhill on his bike, he sensed the 'planet's imminent fall'. Within a week of Mussolini's declaration the Nazis were marching down the Champs-Elysées. To show solidarity with the Führer, Mussolini ordered Jewish Italian street names to be changed. Turin's Via Cesare Lombroso became Via Padre Reginaldo Giuliani. Just who Reginaldo Giuliani was, nobody knew; but he was not Jewish.

The Levis could only hope that the conflict would be as short as Mussolini had promised. 'WE WILL WIN!' boasted *La Stampa*. The British air attacks began immediately: in the early hours of 12 June, just two days after Mussolini's war-cry, Levi was awoken by air-raid sirens. The bombardment of Turin continued uninterrupted for two hours until 3:30 am. By the time the sirens wailed the All Clear, thirty bombs had fallen on the Piedmont capital, killing fourteen civilians in Via Priocca and wounding as many again. The following day Levi sat his Industrial Chemistry exam. On his way to the Institute that morning he saw collapsed masonry and homeless families camped out on the pavements: a vision of rubble and fear.

Throughout the summer the bombardments of Turin continued; the sirens sounded as smoke and dust rolled over the city. Levi's father, bedridden with cancer, had to be abandoned upstairs during the air raids as he was too heavy to carry down the cellar steps. The family's only hope was that 75 Corso Re Umberto would not be hit. During lulls in the attack, recalled Anna Maria, she and her brother slipped out to nearby cellars to join Jewish friends. Down in the unventilated shelters the acetylene lamp's glow created a neighbourly atmosphere. Levi and his sister found it hard to disguise their joy at the bombardments: the bigger the bombs, the sooner Italy's Jews would be liberated from Mussolini and Hitler. Each Crocetta cellar was supervised by a *capo fabbricato*, 'building warden', who was required to report on anti-Fascist activity. These officials had the power to make an individual's life a misery, so the Levis had to be careful about what they said.

As the raids continued, it became more dangerous to stay in the city. On 13 July, Levi's sister was lucky to escape with her life when the artist's studio where she worked took a direct hit. Undaunted, she continued to frequent the studio in Piazza Fontanesi. Prior to the racial laws, sculpture would have been considered a frivolous pastime for middle-class Jewish girls, but the persecutions had forced them to look elsewhere for employment. Anna Maria was one of four assistants working for the Jewish sculptor Roberto Terracini, known as the artist of 'Sadness and Death', who as a Jew was now banned from exhibiting his work in Italy. (Today most municipal cemeteries and remembrance gardens in Italy have a Terracini sculpture: in Verona his statue of Cesare Lombroso is still standing.) A shy forty-year-old when Levi's sister knew him, Terracini had also taken on Lucia Morpurgo as his assistant, who was later to be Primo's wife. Anna Maria recalled that Lucia positively 'shone' in the studio and was a 'superb' sculptor. A gypsy encampment nearby provided the girls with live horses for models. There is some dispute as to whether Levi knew Lucia at this time, though his cousin Giulia has a firm memory of an encounter. One can only speculate whether he was attracted to Lucia. A graceful girl, she seemed to conform to Terracini's old-fashioned ideal of waifish femininity.

To escape the air raids later that summer, Levi set off with Alberto Salmoni on an 800-kilometre cycling holiday. They aimed to reach the Slovenian town of Postumia (now Postojna) while visiting the Italian lakes en route. The friends left Turin at four in the morning with camping pots and pans clanking on their handlebars. Alberto had been cycling for two hours when he noticed that his pans had fallen off. Cycling on through Brescia, the French Alps shimmering behind them, the two pushed on north-east towards the casino-town of Maggiore, with its lakeside tearooms, and up towards the Dolomite resort of Cortina d'Ampezzo. Alberto's girlfriend was staying there with her aunt, and the men stopped off to visit her. Bianca Guidetti Serra was an energetic, high-spirited trainee lawyer and a lapsed Catholic. Her love for Alberto had strengthened after the 1938 racial laws; before that, she had been indifferent towards Mussolini, but the persecutions had shown her the illiberal face of Fascism, and Bianca's options had become clear: she would resist.

By 1940 Bianca had ceased bothering to disguise her contempt for Fascism. Among the many Blackshirt prohibitions she objected to was the substitution of the pseudo ancient Roman *voi* for the polite form of address, *lei* (you). Fascist shopkeepers in Turin informed their customers on notices: 'WE ONLY USE *VOI* HERE.' Many other absurdities followed. Women were forbidden to wear trousers under Fascism as they were considered insufficiently feminine. Bianca wore shorts all the same. ('If this is Fascism,' she thought, 'they can keep it.') She was to become one of Levi's most intimate lifelong friends: 'Bianca's an extraordinary woman,' he said of her. What Bianca admired in Levi was his infectious curiosity and desire to communicate his knowledge of the world to others. 'Primo had a gift for observation and an almost religious sense of wonder at the world.' That summer in Cortina they talked of many things, but above all the hoped-for end to the Axis pact, or at least the fall of Mussolini. The first cracks in Mussolini's popularity were beginning to show. The Spanish Civil War was supposed to provide glory for the Fascist cause, but instead of swift victory the conflict was dragging on interminably.

By the time Levi and Salmoni had reached Postumia in early August, Primo had celebrated his twenty-first birthday. During their absence a tragedy had occurred. On 29 July Ennio Artom had been climbing in Courmayeur when he slipped down a ravine and died. Still only twenty, he was the first of several friends whom Levi would lose to the mountains. When the swastika had been raised earlier that year by Fascists at Turin University, Ennio had shouted at them indignantly: 'We're in Italy, not Germany!'

10

By November 1940, as Levi embarked on his fourth and final year at the University, Mussolini was leading Italy to ruin. The Duce's ill-advised invasion of Greece in October 1940, announced as 'an easy stroll', had ended in disaster when the Italians retreated in a disorderly rout across the Epirus mountains. Badly as the dictator had fared in Greece, in North

Africa he fared even more disastrously. In another heavy blow to national morale, Britain's desert army roundly trounced the Italians at Tobruk and Benghazi. Meanwhile the sky over Turin filled nightly with the drone of bombers as the British continued their air raids. The ground-floor windows of the Chemistry Institute had been sandbagged; the homeless slept in the empty lecture halls for warmth. These were the months of coupons and rationing and increasingly desperate Fascist clichés. To feed a nation at war, the Valentino Park had been planted with maize and potatoes. Jews, cruelly denied ration cards, began to improvise foodstuffs; Alberto Salmoni convinced his mother that a rat was an edible guinea pig. 'It tasted really quite good,' he recalled mildly.

Meanwhile at the Chemistry Institute, Levi was working on a number of projects. In his second year he had discovered the work of the Latvian-born chemist Paul Walden and his theory of 1892, 'Walden's Inversion', which looked at molecules in three dimensions. Walden had revolutionised classical organic chemistry, and was still alive in 1939 when Levi applied his 'inversion theory' to soap molecules (more specifically, oleic-acid molecules) as part of his second-year chemistry course. Experiments were conducted in the freezing Physics Institute lab known as 'The Siberia'. Within days the workplace was awash with white soapy foam. 'We could have shaved on the stuff,' recalled the physics student Guido Bonfiglioli, who worked with Levi. Levi's research into Walden further convinced him that physics was the purer, sublimer science. The Latvian had encroached on the physics of matter and what would later be termed quantum chemistry – the point where chemistry ended and physics began.

Levi chose 'Walden's Inversion' as the subject of his main graduation thesis. This was a highly unusual choice for a chemistry student and it says much for Levi's adventurous, questing mind. In his dissertation he insisted that Walden should take his place among the scientific thinkers of his time. For Walden had demonstrated that chemistry's most common form of asymmetry is the carbon atom. Therefore it followed that all the living world is asymmetrical, as carbon is the quintessential element of life. Half a century later, in his 1984 article 'Asymmetry and Life', Levi returned to his youthful doctoral argument, and asked why it was that all the vital single-celled protagonists of life – DNA, protein, cellulose – are asymmetric. The essay provided a wonderfully clear development of his notion, first mooted at university, that biological problems boil down to a question of asymmetry.

But now Levi faced a new dilemma in his academic life. While the Fascist racial laws had allowed him to complete his degree course, he was not permitted to pursue further avenues of study. He wanted to be taken on as a university assistant or *interno,* as the best students always were, but he needed help in order to achieve this. If anyone had the power to override the Fascist injunction preventing Jews from becoming *interni,* it was Professor Ponzio; Levi believed Ponzio would be sympathetic to his cause, as he was supposed to be a 'notorious anti-Fascist'. But Levi was wrong. Ponzio was frightened of showing favouritism to Jews, and refused to take Levi on as an *interno.* Levi was not the only Jew to be thus snubbed by the Chemistry Institute's *gran capo.* Emma Vita–Levi was also denied interneeship by Ponzio. 'For me this was a clear sign that he was not the great anti-Fascist he liked us to think he was. Ponzio was at the top of his career by 1941 and had nothing to lose by taking on a Jew as his assistant.' Evidently Ponzio was not of the same dissenting mettle as Professor Artom; on two occasions – in 1926 and 1931 – he had sworn loyalty to the Fascist regime. He also attended chemistry conferences in Nazi Germany, including a 'Week of High Culture' in Frankfurt, during which he must have wondered at the absence of his Jewish chemistry colleagues. In Levi's attempted palliation, Ponzio was a 'Liberal' who made a concerted show of being anti-Fascist. Yet Levi was always forgiving of those who had taught him well; he was similarly indulgent of Azelia Arici.

Disappointed, Levi knocked on other doors. Guido Tappi, Ponzio's deputy, also said no. (Tappi was a frightful conformist.) But another tutor was not so fearful. Dr Nicolò Dallaporta was a tall, pale astrophysicist with an easy charm. Born in the future Italian port of Trieste in 1910, he had worked in Turin's Experimental Physics Institute for four years. The inter-racial mix of his birthplace, Trieste, essentially a Central European city of Italians, Slovenians, Croats, Greeks, Serbs and other minorities, had made for a cosmopolitan and tolerant man. Highly civilised (no one else in the Science Faculty had read Joyce's *Ulysses* in the original), he provided an unusual example for Levi. A staunch believer in individual freedom, neither a Fascist nor a Communist, Dallaporta was opposed to any kind of narrow nationalism. He ignored the convention that segregated professors and students, and liked to invite pupils round to tea, while his wife Gabriella Merlin played Cole Porter tunes on the baby-grand. Handsome in a patrician way, on his mother's side 'Nicò' (as Levi called him) was Greek; indeed his full name was Nicolò Luciano Dallaporta-Xydias. Partly because he was in a minority himself – Greek-orthodox Triestino – it made no difference to him that Levi was Jewish. So he did not hesitate to take Levi on as his assistant, though he did so at great risk to his career. 'If Primo was Jewish or Hindu, I couldn't give two figs, I was delighted to have such a top-notch student,' he told me in his antiquated English.

I met Dallaporta in September 1993: he was then an eighty-three-year-old who had survived near-fatal kidney tuberculosis in the early 1940s. We met in Padua, where he lived. Having spent a lifetime wrestling with the secrets of the physical universe, there was something unworldly about him. Nicò was one of the first Italian physicists to research what became known as Big Bang theory, and had spoken excitedly to Levi of the collision of alpha particles and the sun's energy production. 'I also tried to explain to Primo my attempts to reconcile Catholicism with Hinduism – though I think these struck Primo as exercises in pure and applied pointlessness!' (Dallaporta found a more sympathetic audience for his religious theories in Professor Iganzio De Paolini, the emotionally unstable supremo of analytic chemistry who, for much of his time, struggled with religious crises. His early death after the war, apparently from suicide, shocked Levi.) In spite of their differences, Levi not only admired and respected Dallaporta, but kept in touch with him all his life. There was a connection, too, with mountaineering, as Dallaporta's daredevil rock-climbing brother Spiro Xydias had written books on the subject that Levi had enjoyed.

Levi was one of just two Jewish *interni* taken on by Dallaporta in the Experimental Physics Institute that summer. The other was Guido Bonfiglioli, with whom Levi had practised pseudo-Olympics five years earlier. Dallaporta asked them to assess recent research conducted into electrostatic energy by the Norwegian scientist Lars Onsager. Their findings could be written up as one of two sub-theses that students were expected to submit in addition to their main dissertation. Levi produced an extremely able paper on Onsager, for which he was applauded by Dallaporta. For reasons that would only become clear to Levi in Nazi captivity, Onsager was his 'true thesis', not 'Walden's Inversion'. Inspired by Nicò's mandarin example, the *interni* Levi and Bonfiglioli discussed the troubling uncertainties of relativity and other physical exotica. Ultimately Dallaporta's astrophysical abstractions, much as they intrigued Levi, exasperated him. Only later in his depressed years would he become interested in Dallaporta's black holes and other tentative physics; for the moment he flinched from his tutor's belief that the world might ultimately be inexplicable and beyond our grasp.

Nevertheless, Levi drew strength from Dallaporta's anti-Fascism. In the physicist's poky lab on Via Pietro Giuria was a highly sensitive radio receiver, the heterodyne. Radio London had announced the number of German planes shot down, as Dallaporta followed news of the Battle of Britain on the heterodyne in 1940. The radio bulletins, read by Colonel Harold Stevens in a most plummy Italian, had been transmitted to Italy illegally since January 1940. Levi joined Dallaporta in listening to the outlawed bulletins, but he had to be careful of the physics beadle Giovanni Giacosa, who kept his ears open in the corridor while pretending to water plants.

II

With the summer came Levi's finals. The pressure was intense as he hurried to complete his dissertations. As well as investigating Lars Onsager, Levi was also working on a sub-thesis, 'Electronic Rays', supervised by Professor Mario Milone, who had studied X-rays at Cambridge under Sir William Bragg. Levi's interest in the subject may have been sparked by *The Magic Mountain*, which describes in detail pulmonary-consumption X-rays and electronic radiation clinics.

On Thursday 12 June 1941 – Anno XIX of the Fascist Era – Levi sat his finals. The eleven examining professors summoned him for a *viva voce* on his three dissertations – Walden, Onsager, X-rays – as well as on much of what he had learned in his four years as a chemistry student. Each examinee was dressed in Fascist black to mourn the first Allied bombing of Turin exactly a year before (12 June 1940). Opposite Levi sat the president of the Science Faculty, Professor Alceste, a lofty, intimidating eminence. Professor Ignazio De Paolini, with his chalk-white face and forked beard, asked Levi questions on analytic chemistry. A professorial whim could make or break a Jewish candidate; but instead of subjecting Levi to scrutiny, the umpires spent the time complimenting him.

Primo Michele Levi ('Matriculation No. 808 of the Jewish Race') was awarded a first-class honours with merit: *summa cum laude*. The eleven examiners had each lavished him with ten votes out of ten: 110 out of 110, 100 per cent. *And* merit. In all his twenty-five years as the Chemistry Institute director, Giacomo Ponzio had dispensed only one other first-class honours degree. Now Levi was a *dottore*, the envied title conferred on Italians after obtaining a degree. Yet no fellowship had been offered him, and as a Jew he had no career prospects. Dr Primo Levi had to confront the wider world outside.

EIGHT

Life During Wartime
1941–3

I

By the summer of 1941 three-quarters of Italy's Jews – 42,000 citizens – were without work. The racial laws had destroyed their careers. Primo Levi's graduation diploma, stamped 'Member of the Jewish Race', deterred potential employers. Anyway he suspected that his first-class honours was a professorial protest vote against the government persecutions, and therefore of doubtful value. Yet it was expected as a matter of course that he would earn a living. And earn it at once, what is more, as his father – the family's sole bread-winner – was dying. A minimal pension accrued to Cesare from Budapest, but the stomach cancer had attacked his liver and he had not long to live. Levi wrote to everyone he knew: could they get him 'some small job', 'a livelihood of a few lire a day?' Nobody took him on. He looked for a university job, and asked Professor Ponzio about the possibility of a chemistry studentship. Ponzio did not reply. Then Grandpa Luzzati died, unexpectedly, on 26 June at the age of sixty-two, leaving the family financially straitened.

Work, or lack of it, was not the only difficulty on the horizon. Levi wanted to escape the sickroom hush of 75 Corso Re Umberto, but his father's impending death held him there. In melancholy mood he feared for the future. The only friend he saw regularly over the summer was his chemistry sweetheart Clara Moschino. To her consternation, each time they met Levi would cry. At home Levi did not want to reveal his anxiety to his mother and sister – but once he was in Moschino's company he would begin to cry again. Levi was essentially alone with his despondency, and his mood did not improve.

His efforts to find work continued throughout 1941 as more horrors accumulated on the eastern front. On 22 June, in an abrupt betrayal, Hitler attacked his unsuspecting ally Stalin. This was the decisive moment in the

Second World War. The Russians and Germans, briefly non-aggressors, were again ideological enemies. By early July German troops were advancing across the Stalin Line. And with the Vatican's blessing, 230,000 Italian troops went to join Hitler in the Soviet blitzkrieg. Levi was banned from conscription as a Jew, and watched hopelessly as his chemistry companions were called to arms. Nereo Pezza was sent to Russia on 26 June; two days later Sidney Calvi was drafted to fight in Montenegro. In August, Sandro Delmastro was conscripted into the navy at La Spezia, a town by the sea on Shelley's coast near Livorno.

Russia was a severe trauma for the Italian soldiers. Temperatures dropped to fifty degrees below zero. There were atrocities perpetrated against Jews as Nazi plans for the Final Solution were crystallised on the Russian front. One of the first Italians to witness anti-Semitic brutality in the east was Lieutenant Nuto Revelli, a Piedmontese, and later one of Levi's closest friends. In the summer of 1942 Revelli's rail transport stopped near Brest-Litovsk for victualling. From the train window Revelli saw ragged civilians with yellow stars clearing rubbish at gunpoint from the rails. Further down the line he watched in mounting disbelief as SS troops hurled stones at Jewish children who were also sweeping the tracks. A sickly smell hung on the air. 'It was then I understood the true nature of the war I was fighting.'

By late June 1941, Italian police had begun to arrest foreign Jews in Turin. The purpose of these round-ups was allegedly not to persecute the Jews, but to intern them as anti-Axis refugees. Levi knew many of them from University. Janek Trachman (misspelled 'Jakub Trackan' by an ignorant Fascist spy) was a Polish graduate engineer. Rodolfo Weisz, a Slovak-born medical student, was Edith Weisz's brother. On 27 June Weisz and Trachman found themselves with murderers and other criminals in the Turin city jail, 'Carceri Nuove'. Conditions were appalling, lavatory facilities virtually non-existent and the overcrowding compounded the filth. Beppe Rosenthal, an architecture student from Lodz, and Salamone Brawer, a physicist (provenance unknown), were among the other interned non-Italian Jews. Most of these men, in manacles, were later sent by train to internment camps in central and southern Italy. Rosenthal and Weisz survived; what happened to the others is uncertain.

Italy was now little more than a Nazi satellite. On 30 September, the eve of the Jewish Day of Atonement (Yom Kippur), the German Consulate in Turin distributed the anti-Semitic propaganda film *Jud Süss*, much admired (perhaps to his later shame) by the Italian film director Michelangelo Antonioni. Other abuses followed. In the early hours of 15 October petrol was poured over the steps of the Turin synagogue; the flames were extinguished, but the Jewish community understandably was alarmed. Next day anti-Semitic posters were found pasted to walls around the Jewish School. Though the slogans were in Italian, the posters bore the hallmark of a Nazi defamation campaign and were probably the work of the German Consulate. Indeed, Italian authorities were later seen tearing the posters down, perhaps an indication that the biological anti-Semitism at the heart of Nazism was distasteful to most Fascists. As Levi noted later: 'A Turin *Kristallnacht* was clearly a long way off'. Nevertheless, as a precaution the Jewish community posted sentries round the synagogue. Levi volunteered for at least one of these lookouts – a prelude to his imminent involvement in the Resistance.

During this period of uncertainty Levi began to remove valuable items from 75 Corso Re Umberto and put them into safekeeping. Nothing was safe in the bomb-threatened city. Paintings, carpets, silver candelabra were loaded on to an oxcart and taken to an eighteenth-century villa in the hills called 'The Saccarello'. Grandpa Luzzati had bought the property in 1935; its top-floor windows gave a fabulous view of the city below and, close by, of the twin-towered Savoy mausoleum known as the 'Superga'. Farmland behind the villa was tilled by *mezzadri* – tenant farmers – who provided the Levi family with a few precious vegetables. The ox lived in the villa cellars, and neighbours gossiped enviously that the Levis were keeping a milk cow.

2

In December 1941 after six months without work, Levi was offered a job. There was a vacancy in an asbestos mine for a chemist to extract nickel from the quarry's fibrous spoil. Lieutenant Ennio Mariotti, a chemist and army bomb-disposal expert, was looking for someone to replace him in the mine as he was needed on bomb alert. Mariotti, a tall moustachioed Florentine, twenty-seven years old, had a darting, kingfisher curiosity in books and science. He oversaw Levi in his new post, and Primo grew to adore him. After graduating in biochemistry in 1937, Mariotti had worked at the Hydrobiology Institute in Rome, where he conducted esoteric zoological research into the sex-cycle of the rainbow trout. (The research was sponsored by the *Curia*, who considered the fish a delicacy.) Aside from biochemistry, Mariotti's great enthusiasm was cooking. In his Turin laboratory he grilled T-bone steaks, Tuscan-style, over a blazing gas flame, and synthesised artificial lemon to help with the war shortages. When he was not gourmandising, Mariotti was disposing of bombs. One time he managed to defuse a British device that had crashed unexploded through the roof of a stationer's on Via Lagrange. 'Just don't blow up my shop, Dr Mariotti,' implored the owner.

Levi could only work in the mine illegally, under a false non-Jewish surname. But Mariotti, the son of a Tuscan Socialist, was well disposed to help 'enemies of Fascism'. He gave money and food to a Jewish family from Florence, who were sheltering beneath his lab on Via San Secondo. His mother was the minor Tuscan poet Margherita Lollio, and Mariotti shared her dislike of mob rule and her sympathy for the oppressed. Levi began work in the asbestos mine on 7 December, just as news came through that the Japanese air force had bombed Pearl Harbor and sunk part of the American navy at its base. The Second World War now dramatically altered course as the United States entered the war and the conflict became worldwide.

The mine, known as San Vittore, was situated in brooding mountaineer country, 800 metres above the town of Balangero. It was one of the largest asbestos quarries in Europe: ear-splitting detonations yielded a lucrative 500 tonnes of asbestos daily; sometimes the dust was so thick that staff could write their names on the furniture. Some of them later contracted asbestosis. Levi lodged in San Vittore on a weekly basis, returning home at the weekend. The Crocetta, with its middle-class composure, was far removed from the draft-dodgers, petty vineyard proprietors, small-time Fascists and other chancers who operated in the San Vittore community. Jobs there were jealously coveted: the alternative, military conscription, meant likely death on the eastern front.

The mining community welcomed the newcomer and Levi quickly found a place for himself within the workforce. Today only one staff member survives, Libero Vernoli, formerly the head foreman; he recalled that Levi was a 'perfect gentleman, without pretensions'. No one seemed to care that Levi was Jewish. The general disrespect for the Fascist state made disobedience a point of pride among many Italians. Levi boarded with the Matrells, who ran a staff pension at San Vittore. The Matrells' other boarders included Angelo Battiston ('Bartolasso' in *The Periodic Table*), who ogled women with sad, hangdog eyes; his wife in Personnel apparently was determined to remain a virgin, and so to let off steam he blasted out Fascist anthems on his trombone. Signora Battiston apparently did not share the sexual mores of San Vittore's other eighteen families. 'We all knew each other intimately and we all shared each other's beds,' confessed Vernoli.

Engineer Giorgio Marchioli, the mine's youthful director, was the son of Russian-Italian aristocrats from Kiev. He lived on site with his mother Olga Kumilowski, from St Petersburg. Levi's enduring affection for Russia and

Russian culture began at this time when he heard Olga play Rachmaninov concertos on her pianoforte. Levi was stimulated by the strangeness of this place. Each morning the miners in their black boots and balaclavas like the fur-trappers in a Jack London novel, trudged to work by lantern-light along the snow-bound paths. The deputy foreman, Luigi Macario, had become a hero in 1939 when San Vittore's crater had flooded with rain; machinery, locomotives and huts would have been swept away if he had not dynamited a rock face to create a dam. This was just the sort of heroic story Levi loved, and years later he embroidered it for the 'Nickel' chapter of *The Periodic Table*, where Macario is disguised as the 'obese giant' Antaeus.

Over Christmas Levi spent a week in Turin; after which he retreated to San Vittore. Possibly he began to write at this time. Years later he claimed to have composed the allegorical fantasies 'Lead' and 'Mercury' in *The Periodic Table* while at Balangero. He was then reading Joseph-Henri Rosny's 1916 Stone Age extravaganza, *Quest for Fire*, which was a clear influence on 'Lead'. (Just as Rosny's prehistoric man is locked in a Darwinian struggle of survival against his predators, so Levi's tribespeople are beset by dogs and other primordial threats in their hunt for precious metals.)

Meanwhile more anti-Semitic posters had gone up in Turin, this time on the busy Via Roma. Some friends of Levi decided to storm the street in daylight and tear them down. Among the saboteurs were Guido Foa, Eugenio Gentili, Alberto Salmoni and his brother Bruno, Bruno's wife Lilla and Bianca Guidetti Serra, both these women 'Aryan'. The action went on for several evenings under the public's astonished gaze. Most passersby expressed concern for the saboteurs. 'Don't you know it's dangerous?' When the police finally arrived, the two-metre-tall Foa, who had a 'marvellous charmer's smile', caused pandemonium when he pretended to be a plainclothes agent and demanded to see their *carabinieri* documents. (Later he died in a Nazi camp.) Levi was unable to take part in the Via Roma sabotage as he was engaged in the mine, but it left a deep impression on him: it was the first anti-Nazi action taken by his circle.

3

Levi was quite busy that winter. Keen to do well in his first job as a working chemist, sometimes he stayed in the laboratory long after the 5:00 pm siren had sounded. His assistant was Novella Maffei (the green-eyed 'Alida' of *The Periodic Table*), a flirtatious girl who rather intimidated Levi. Novella had slept with several of the mine workers and was known as 'Novella,

Everyone's Friend'. She had a raucous laugh with a leer in it that made Levi blush. Novella made Levi feel inadequate: her father, a self-important Tuscan businessman, was a Fascist bigwig in Balangero. Her jealous boyfriend, Signor Gremigni, worked in the Technical Office.

Working steadily in the lab, Levi first made mistakes and roused vain hopes, but in the end his fingers were sure. He succeeded in extracting a uselessly small amount of nickel from the asbestos spoil. For this intensely satisfying, if pyrrhic, victory he was congratulated by Lieutenant Mariotti. Just what purpose the nickel was to serve, nobody knew; Levi suspected (rightly) that it was destined for use in the Fascist aircraft industry.

Early one Monday morning at the mine, 23 March 1942, Levi was telephoned that his father was dying. It was a miserably wet day as he rushed back to Turin. The little train was agonisingly slow and Levi was filled with helpless terror that Cesare would die before he reached his destination. At Turin's Porta Susa station he was met by Giorgio Lattes, 'Big George'. Blackshirt bunting hung forlorn and soggy in the streets: celebrations for the twenty-third anniversary of the Fascist Party had been washed out by the 'grey incessant rain'. Lattes accompanied Levi home where he found his mother and sister in a state of extreme distress; Cesare was dead. Levi, silent and grief-stricken, felt overwhelmed by remorse. His father had suffered appallingly during his last weeks. The doctor tending him, Giuseppe Diena, had been jailed on anti-Fascist charges at the beginning of January, and since then Cesare had insufficient medical attention. He had been denied morphine and the family watched helpless as he was consumed by pain.

Though Italian Jews were no longer allowed the dignity of newspaper death-notices, *La Stampa* printed in its social column: 'LEVI CESARE, of Bene Vagienna, died at the age of 63 at home at 75 Corso Re Umberto.' Rabbi Disegni of Turin, a sombre bearded presence, officiated at his funeral two days later, on Wednesday 25 March. Primo, as the family's first-born son, had to recite at the graveside the Jewish prayer for the dead. In future years he would say that his father was fortunate to die before the Occupation of Italy, which he could not have survived. The day after Cesare's funeral saw the arrival of the first trains at Auschwitz. The destruction of European Jewry had begun in earnest. On Cesare's tomb were hewn the Hebrew words, 'May his soul be bound up in the bundle of life.'

Today the metal 'A' in Cesare's name has fallen from the tombstone; it now reads 'CES RE', 'Ces the King'. At a time when fathers could be very authoritarian with their children, Cesare had ruled over Primo and Anna Maria genially, and showed them a natural warmth and sweetness of temperament. A lively, inquisitive man who was excited by much of human concern, interest and puzzlement, Cesare had influenced Primo in many ways, encouraging in him an empirical habit of mind. But, now that he was gone, Levi was acutely conscious of his new responsibility as head of the household. His relationship with his mother was changed. Anti-Semitic Europe placed Ester in danger, and it was Levi's duty to watch over her.

A month later, relatives gathered at 75 Corso Re Umberto for the memorial service. Cesare's younger brothers Mario and Enrico, the Luzzati uncles Gustavo and Corrado, stood along the wall of the dining room, hats on their heads, prayer-books in their hands. On a sofa against the wall sat Adelina Luzzati, herself a widow. 'Ces the King' was dead but not forgotten, and for the rest of his life Levi paid for the upkeep of his father's gravestone.

4

Six weeks after Cesare's death, on 6 May 1942, a Fascist decree announced that all Italian Jews were to be mobilised for forced labour. With this decree, Hitler's war came another step closer to home: in Nazi Vienna Jews had been made to scrub pavements. All able-bodied Jews had to register at the Turin Prefecture by 15 June or face a military tribunal. An initial registration of 476 Jewish males in the city included: 'No. 253: Levi Primo – employee'. Though Levi was still working at the asbestos mine, he was eligible for labour duty on weekends, and was assigned to a roadworks corvée in Piazza Sofia. He was shunted to the site in a bus: no talking was allowed. Work began at 8:00 am and continued until 6:00 pm, with a two-hour lunch break. Anna Maria Levi's artist boyfriend, Franco Tedeschi, as well as Emanuele Artom and Alberto Salmoni, were there. Educated middle-class Jews were not used to shifting sacks of concrete, and they were treated with open contempt by the Fascist foremen. Salmoni nicknamed them *bastipi*: bastards ('*bastardi*') from the Town Hall ('*municipio*'). They resented the bourgeois Jews' presumed superior intellect and privilege, and gleefully forced them on the treadmill. Levi's cousin Giulia cycled each day to Piazza Sofia with drink and sandwiches for the Jews. The forced-labour scheme was not without its absurdities, like everything else under Fascism. One Saturday Levi was forced to unload timber from Porta Susa station, but for some reason the wood caught fire and work had to be halted. Not all the Jews eligible for *lavori forzati* in Turin were conscripted and the project was conducted with the usual Fascist flare for inaccuracy. Thus Levi's university friend Vanda Maestro was registered in the Fascist files as 'Mestro Xanda', while Primo's sister was apparently a '*scuttrice*' (sculptress), the Italian misspelled.

During Levi's five months at the asbestos mine, Turin had become an intolerably claustrophobic and distasteful city: rationing of food and clothes, shortages of drink. Bread was kneaded from potato peelings or sorghum mixed with sawdust, coffee made from chicory (it tasted like gall) or astragalus plant substitute, and soap from pulverised horse chestnuts. 'It's impossible to stay in Turin,' Levi declared, and in June 1942 he decided to leave the asbestos mine. A Swiss pharmaceutical company in Milan, A. Wander Ltd, was offering a generous 2,000 lire a month (£500 at today's rate) for a chemist to work on a diabetes project. A friend of Levi's from Professor Ponzio's class, Gabriella Garda, had been toiling ineffectually on the project when she remembered Primo. 'I told my boss of this genius I knew in Turin who was bound to crack the diabetes business.' Garda, a Catholic, was aware of how difficult life was for Jews in small-city Turin. Milan by contrast was a bustling metropolis where the forced-labour scheme had not adhered well. (Hamburg, another mercantile city, had been similarly slow to succumb to anti-Semitic measures.) Moreover, Italian race laws did not apply to a Swiss company; in Milan, Levi could be just another young man with no past.

The Milan company director, a worrisome Milanese named Dr Mario Molina ('Dr Martini' in *The Periodic Table*), agreed to take on Garda's friend so long as his Jewish identity was concealed. The presence of a known Jew in the Milan laboratory could blemish the Swiss company's high standing with Fascist Italy. A brisk, self-made man with the Milanese passion for *la ricchezza*, Dr Molina wished to go down in history as the one who discovered a diabetes cure. Records at A.Wander Ltd show that Levi was taken on under the anodyne name 'Dr Primo'. He began work on 1 July 1942, just four weeks short of his twenty-third birthday.

Milan is as extrovert, genial and open as Turin is steadfast, introverted and cautious. In this metropolis of trade and capital, everything is a vivacious, outgoing bustle, and the people chatter with an exaggerated expansiveness. On the crowded trams Levi felt inhibited by the Milanese and found he could not even talk to friends. This shyness was partly a bourgeois Turin-Jewish trait, partly the result of snobbery. Milan, with its well-fed merchant class, is supremely a city of *bottegai*, 'shopkeepers'; money-making and enterprise are its hallmarks, just as surely as the House of Savoy and the intellectual life are Turin's. Levi found the mercantile racket of the place off-putting. But one thing that is never lacking in Milan is *denaro;* before long Levi had made enough money to spend on himself and others.

He went to La Scala opera house, listened to banned Louis Armstrong records, and watched the Rogers and Astaire classic *Top Hat.* Plenty of American films prohibited in Fascist Italy were shown illegally in Milan, and Westerns were the most popular. (To Levi the taciturn cowboys who rode off into the sunset seemed ruggedly free: they made no florid balcony speeches, like the Duce, but saddled up.) The other sensation in wartime Milan was the Irish-American playwright Eugene O'Neill, whose dramas opened a window on to a world untouched by the moral stagnation of Fascism. At the Teatro Nuovo Levi saw O'Neill's *Beyond the Horizon* three times, and the more he saw of O'Neill, the more his appetite for Americana grew. Renato Cialente and Elsa Merlini, then two of Italy's greatest actors, starred in Thornton Wilder's play *Our Town,* which Levi also adored. If the Fascists and anti-Semites failed to censor *Our Town,* it was because they did not understand the play's brazen American avant-garderie. Milan had one other great advantage over Turin: it did not lack for food. Black marketeers cycled by night into the rich Lombard plains and returned with eggs, poultry, creamy blue-veined cheeses. Rice was scarce in virtually all of Italy but in Milan one could always find a good risotto or some other filling rice dish.

Levi found a furnished room at a relative's, Ada Della Torre. A pert-faced, bright woman with poise and worldly grace, Ada was five years older than Levi, and had an impressive two degrees from Milan Univeristy, one in law, the other in literature. As the sister of Uncle Corrado Luzzati's wife Irene, she was Levi's second aunt. But there was another family link: Ada's father, a wealthy factory owner, had sold 'The Saccarello' villa to Grandpa Luzzati in 1935.

Ada's ground-floor flat was situated at 7 Via San Martino in a leafy quarter of Milan. Above the porter's lodge was a stone plaque with the beguiling Latin inscription: 'KNOW THAT THERE ARE FOOTSTEPS IN THE GARDEN.' Wrought-iron gates opened on to a maze-like garden with marble niches, fountains and, set back in an alcove with rhododendrons, a baroque statue of the Greek philosopher Diogenes. The aristocratic owners – Milan's powerful Pellegrini-Cislaghi family – charged Ada minimal rent. Because her flat was spacious and comfortable, other Turin Jews routinely gathered there for food and chat. Eugenio Gentili, whom Levi had first met in the Dolomites in 1940, worked for Milan's legendary architect Giò Ponti (later founder of *Domus* magazine). Ada's boyfriend, Silvio Ortona, was a tall beanpole of a man employed by the Milan shipping company Allianza. Born in 1916, and three years older than Levi, Ortona's extra years counted for a good deal at this time of historic upheaval. He spoke fluent English and had a reputation as a *bastiàn contraire,* a 'contrary Joe', who took a proud, irascible line with authority. Indeed, Ortona's name was on a list of Jews wanted for forced-labour evasion back in Turin. Vanda Maestro, alone among Levi's Turin friends, was without a job in Milan. To earn a crust she and her Zionist boyfriend Giorgio Segre translated a German natural-science book by Bernhard Bavink. But because Jews were not acknowledged as translators, their names were pointedly omitted from the Einaudi publisher catalogue (they are still omitted). Another of Ada's visitors was the Turin engineer Emilio Diena, who was much prized for his ability to procure contraband cigarettes. Diena had been a childhood friend of Levi's and, like Primo, had been born at 75 Corso Re Umberto.

Though Jews were not allowed to work in publishing, Ada Della Torre was employed clandestinely by the anti-Fascist Milan publisher Corbaccio ('The Bad Raven'). Ada's Milan circle was scarcely typical of the social life of Jews elsewhere in Italy; not only had they absconded from forced labour, they had illegal jobs within non-Jewish companies. Among this group of vivacious young people were Catholic and Protestant friends, including the good-looking Carla Consonni, who was loved for her charm, generosity and wit. Carla was sleeping with Eugenio Gentili and was employed at the 'Furlotti' art gallery on Milan's Via Borgo Nuovo. Paintings were a good investment in wartime, being both portable and easy to hide. Another guest at Ada's was the Sardinian artist, Abele Saba, who was thought to resemble Joseph Stalin. He was famous for flooding Ada's bathroom and drinking her *grappa* brandy. Ada's was an open house and, under the stimulus of her colourful friends, Levi flourished.

7

By July Levi was settled at A. Wander Ltd. His task was supposedly to synthesise an anti-diabetic from burdock juice. A certain cock-eyed logic adhered to the project, as burdock stimulates the pancreas to produce insulin, and diabetes is caused by insulin deficiency. For three months Gabriella Garda had inconclusively tested the purple-coloured sap on rabbits. She was quick to see the futility of her research and grumbled to Levi that it was like 'drawing blood from a turnip'. Levi also considered the work purposeless and doomed to fail. Not that he minded. He had a good salary, and was busy and contented. The Swiss company was situated in the industrial sumplands of Crescenzago north of Milan. The tram there was known as the 'Crescenzago Express' for its near-biblical slowness: it took a good hour to reach the sluggish River Lambro. The factory at 39 Via

Meucci was built in the 1920s to produce Ovomaltina malt-extract and throat tinctures like Formitrol. ('The wise smoker never forgets FORMITROL!') Levi filched powdered Nestogen baby food for Ada, who blended it with milk and crushed ice for an improbably delicious ice-cream.

Seven months older than Levi, Gabriella had dark curly hair, expressive eyes and a knowing smile. As the result of childhood poliomyelitis, she wore a metal leg brace. Some hoped that Garda might marry Levi. She understood his withdrawn, shy temperament. Now in her eighties, Gabriella Garda Aliverti admitted that she was '*maliziosa*' – 'mischievous' – with Levi, leading him on. In their lunch breaks she would balance on the crossbar of his bicycle and wobble round Crescenzago with him, visiting the Romanesque church down by the canal, cycling on past the ditch where people made love on Saturday nights. Levi was overwhelmed and fell for Gabriella. Yet she was not a girl whom he could have married without incurring much danger: Gabriella was Catholic, Primo was not. Anyway she was already engaged. In *The Periodic Table* Garda is transformed into the coquettish and predatory 'Giulia Vineis', while Levi mock-heroically compares himself to the lovelorn Greek god Hercules (tellingly, Garda's real-life fiancé was called Ercole – Hercules). At the time, Levi wrote her (unpublished) poems, which suggest the melancholy of the lover who anticipates his own failure. Verse such as 'The First Time' and 'All That Can Be Called Love' are syrupy and could have been dreamed up by greetings-card versifiers.

The two friends enjoyed themselves in the laboratory, however. Gabriella liked to bring in chocolates and other treats. One day she obtained a bag of peas – a luxury in these straitened times – and cooked them in a chemistry beaker. They were dreadful; Garda said she only learned to cook once she married Hercules. Another time, on Levi's advice, she cooked spaghetti at below boiling-point and again the result was inedible. ('Call yourself a chemist, Primo?') At lunchtime the lab filled with the distracting aroma of contraband risotto, which the pair ate off evaporating dishes. They poured themselves Pyrex beakerfuls of wine. After the war, though it remained an 'affair of the eyes rather than of the hearts', as Italians say, Levi's friendship with Garda developed into one of extraordinary affection.

8

Meanwhile, throughout that summer of 1942 the pace of deportation and murder of Jews in Occupied territories accelerated. Between 22 July and 12 September a total of 265,000 Warsaw Jews were gassed at Treblinka. It was the largest slaughter of a single community – Jewish or non-Jewish – in the Second World War. Apart from Occupied Denmark, the only Axis country where Jews were not yet deported was Italy. Few Fascist officials wanted to go *beyond* the call of duty in pressing for anti-Semitic measures. Yet there were exceptions, as Levi discovered one Saturday in July.

He had set out from Milan with Silvio Ortona to climb the 3,680-metre Monte della Disgrazia peak south of the Bregaglia mountains. Laden with equipment, they travelled by train across the Lombardy plain passing Lake Como with its pergolas and Edwardian casinos, to Sondrio station. From here they trudged uphill to Chiesa, their starting-point. Lombard peasants shouted in dialect, '*Müdand!*' – 'Underpants!' – at the sight of Levi and Ortona in their white climbing shorts. Having arrived at Chiesa, they left their documents at the Hotel Amilcar opposite the parish church. Trouble came soon after supper at 10:00 pm when a girl knocked on the door to say that a Blackshirt functionary was waiting downstairs. Pompously the Fascist explained that Jews were not allowed near a frontier locality: did they not know that Chiesa was just across the border from Switzerland? They would have to return home at once. 'Return home how?' Ortona reasonably objected: it was night-time and there was nowhere to go except jail. Eventually a compromise was reached. The Jews could stay the night in the hotel, but under house arrest. This was done, and the next morning they were put on the first bus back to Milan, their hike aborted.

9

On 20 October the Fascist forced-labour scheme caught up with Ada Della Torre in Milan, and she had to give up her publishing job. Was her flat under surveillance? Levi feared that Gabriella Garda might also get sucked into a pressgang as her surname, unusually, was Jewish. He asked her to stop visiting Ada's. There could be a Fascist *rastrellamento* – 'mopping-up operation' – at 7 Via San Martino, and then what? Ada's cruel persecution concentrated her thoughts on Fascism. During the early morning shift in a freezing shack she had to stitch canvas covers on to water bottles for Italian troops in Africa. During her four-month slavery her hands got calloused and raw, and winter chilblains made it hard for her to hold a needle. The overseer, Galliano Vecchi (or *Gallina Vecchia*, 'Old Hen', when his back was turned), was a fool whose shrewish wife called Ada a 'jumped-up Jew'. Ada never got used to the squalid factory; each dawn, tired, she caught the 5:30 am tram, with a mess-tin of turkey scraps on her lap. A thug was hired to speed up bottle-cover production, which he did by yelling at the Jews: 'Off to the concentration camps!' One day Ada threatened him with the sharp edge of a water bottle: he shut up.

*

Meanwhile, the nights in Milan rumbled with British bombers, sirens and cries for help. There was growing disillusionment generally with Fascism, and Levi's own anti-Fascism was increasingly more determined. He wrote slogans – 'LONG LIVE PEACE' – on ten-lire notes and put them into circulation. It was a start at least. Ada and her friends filled exercise books with satirical anti-Fascist rhymes and lampoons, for circulation among acquaintances. These scurrilous texts, known as *I libri segreti* (The Secret Books), were hatched in a spirit of mischief over alcohol and pasta at 7 Via San Martino, and if found by the authorities could be damning. Eugenio Gentili, with his architect's flair for design, provided the illustrations, while Primo, Ortona and Ada wrote the words. The results were cheerfully provocative, if seditious and potentially incriminating. Mussolini was caricatured variously as a plumed death's head, a Mardi Gras buffoon or an obese wetnurse pushing the Italian king in a baby's pram, as Hitler traipses unpleasantly behind. Whatever their artistic merit, *I libri segreti* provide a stylish chronicle of the times, with Thurber-like cartoons of Chiang Kai-shek, Roosevelt and the pro-German wartime Pope Pius XII spouting pontifical greetings from the balcony of St Peter's.

On 24 October 1942, at 6:00 am, Milan was bombed nineteen times in the space of half an hour. It was the first time that a northern Italian city had been raided in daylight. Fire engines tore past Ada's house, ringing their bells. Blackouts were imposed from 9:00 pm to 5:30 am in readiness for more raids and the streets now swarmed with the homeless trundling their valuables on bicycles, and anything else with wheels. At the Teatro Nuovo a false air-raid alarm sent the audience screaming from a performance of *The Iceman Cometh*. As winter approached, the air attacks on Milan multiplied, becoming gradually more ferocious. One night, Levi found himself with Vanda Maestro and Carla Consonni in the city's industrial zone of Sesto San Giovanni, where the airport was inevitably a target. As the three pedalled furiously back home they could hear above them the low hum of the Allied bombers. Next day, the Milan newspapers gave a long roll-call of the night's fatalities.

Three weeks later, it was Turin's turn. On the night of 18 November three consecutive bombardments cut off the city's electricity and water supplies. The RAF dropped leaflets warning in bad Italian of a worse attack for the night of Friday the 20th. Levi rushed back to be with his mother during the promised fire-storm. He took the funicular railway up to the 'The Saccarello', where his mother had evacuated with five families and their worldly possessions. On arrival he saw that the villa's skylight, which should have been concreted over, had collapsed: had Ester or Grandma

Adelina been standing underneath they would have been cut to ribbons. Factories were targeted near the property and sometimes during bombardments the air inside the villa seemed to whistle. Turin had been bombed a total of fourteen times and worse was promised.

The roar of the Allied air fleet on 20 November was accompanied by flashes and explosions. In Turin families hurriedly dragged suitcases down into shelters. From the woods above 'The Saccarello' Levi was able to watch the bombardment. First the planes illuminated the targeted area with flares; then came a bang like enormous thunder, a blaze of red fire, and a black layer of dust descended slowly. The thuds reached Ester in 'The Saccarello' cellars, as big four-engined Lancasters, 250 of them, created a formidable fireworks display. This was the most violent air attack so far on any Italian city: 1,000 incendiary bombs – 'carpet bombing', the RAF called it – fell on the Piedmont capital. Driven by the wind, flames roared against the twin onion domes of the synagogue, reducing to ash a century of Jewish birth and death certificates.

Hatred of Fascism was so widespread now that some Italians had turned to the monarchy again for leadership. During the 20 November night-attack on Turin a slogan had been daubed on an equestrian statue of a Savoy king: 'WHEN YOU SEE THE LIGHT OF DAWN THE DUCE WILL BE NO MORE.' In the single worst night of the Fascist war, the riverside capital of the Savoys had fiercely burned. From the rubble of Via Principe Tommaso firemen pulled out a sequined music-hall dancer, just breathing, her hair white with plaster dust. In the working-class San Paolo district the Lancia and Fiat automobile plants were flattened. Cousin Giulia Colombo's house on Via Lamarmora was destroyed; Bianca Guidetti Serra's was made un-inhabitable. Within ten days 30,000 people had abandoned Turin. This was a time of ever-growing casualty lists and bad news every day.

Levi managed to celebrate the New Year – 1943 – at 'The Saccarello', whose twenty spacious rooms could accommodate his friends from Milan. Alberto Salmoni turned up with some dubious pizzas garnished with (unidentified) meat and cheese. Where he managed to come up with the ingredients in these times of critical shortages was a mystery, but the party guests agreed that the result was excellent.

10

On 2 February Stalingrad was reclaimed by the Red Army. Hitler's defeat was only a question of time. His winning war was over; his losing war had begun. Italian soldiers, stranded in Russia without leadership, began to die during the chaotic retreat, left unburied on the frozen steppe. At the retreat's end an estimated 43,580 Italians had perished: entire Piedmont villages were bereft of male citizens. Returning on occasion to Turin, Levi found a ghost city where no one wanted to live, the stations abandoned and unearthly, the shops emptying fast. During these winter months of horror and uncertainty, Levi began to write poetry. 'Crescenzago', set amid the belching smoke-stacks of his Milan workplace, is dated 'February 1943', two months after Gabriella Garda had left the Swiss factory to marry her Hercules. It is a poem of loneliness and lost love. And it is echoed thirty-five years later in the 'Phosphorus' chapter of *The Periodic Table*, where Garda ('Giulia Vineis') darns stockings as she waits to clock-off work. In 1942 Levi made this same, bored *tricoteuse* the unnamed subject of his poem:

> At Crescenzago there's a window
> Behind which a girl is fading.
> Needle and thread always in her right hand
> She sews and mends, never stops looking at the clock.
> When closing-time sounds
> She sighs and weeps; this is the pattern of her life.

Northern Italy that spring of 1943 was dangerously unstable, and each morning Italians got up a little more tired and demoralised. Industrial strikes, the first of their kind in Fascist Europe, disrupted Turin on 5 March as Fiat workers protested at the ravages of bombardments and the soaring cost of living. Implacably opposed to Mussolini, they championed the cause of the Communist *agitatore* Antonio Gramsci, who had died at the hands of Fascists in 1937. The Turin strikes marked the beginning of the end for the Duce. By late March industrial action had spread to the Piedmont towns of Asti, Biella, Vercelli and Aosta. By the time it reached Milan, the mood in the flat at 7 Via San Martino was sombre.

Amid the general shambles, some of Levi's circle became Communists. Levi might have become one himself, had it not been for the 1939 Molotov-Ribbentrop pact. He could not accept that Comrade Stalin, architect of the brave new Soviet Russia, had shaken hands with a Nazi and even seemed to admire Hitler's ruthlessness. For a while Levi did listen to Communist propaganda. Camillo Treves, known as 'Old Sickle-tongue', was a Communist Jew and chemist who often visited from Turin. For hours he discoursed on the proletariat's plight. Levi thought him a frightful bore, rattling out dull, patronising information. What Levi craved was action.

Ada was in contact with Italy's underground anti–Fascist Action Party (so named after the Risorgimento patriot Giuseppe Mazzini's *Partito d'Azione*). Founded in July 1942, the Action Party was not Communist, but its Members were committed to proto-Socialist liberties, and the secular trinity of *liberté, égalité, fraternité* preached by Napoleon as he liberated the Piedmontese ghettos in 1796. Many *Azionisti* had belonged to the now outlawed 'Justice and Liberty' movement, whose founders Carlo and Nello Rosselli had been murdered by Mussolini's agents in 1937.

As the industrial dispute spread further into northern Italy, so Ada strengthened her Action Party ties. She was instructed to infiltrate factories with anti-Fascist propaganda and listen to workers' grievances. She was becoming, as she later put it, less '*borghesuccia*' ('finicky-bourgeois'), a prerequisite for the coming armed Resistance. Her underground activity had begun casually when Milan's *Azionista* chief Dino Luzzatto had asked her to type out an anti-Fascist manifesto signed by Riccardo Levi (brother of the Carlo who later wrote *Christ Stopped at Eboli*). Luzzatto, a thin serious man, had been jailed for protesting against the violent Fascist beating of the Socialist conductor Arturo Toscanini in 1931. After the Fascist racial laws, he lost his job as a lawyer because he was Jewish. He was ten years older than Levi, and Ada now introduced him to Primo. The Action Party's intellectual integrity and cautious Liberal Socialism appealed to Levi, and he asked Luzzatto to induct him into its ranks.

Levi's first task was to smuggle clandestine propaganda – newspapers, leaflets – to Action Party nerve centres outside the Lombard capital. He did this under cover of dark, on one occasion travelling by train 130 kilometres east to Cremona. It was dangerous work and his nerves were strung-out. Police randomly searched civilians, and harsh penalities awaited black marketeers. But carrying anti-government propaganda was a far graver offence. At this stage Levi's anti-Fascism was rather more adventurous than earnest.

11

There was much rain that spring of 1943; according to his cousin Giulia, Levi was plagued by colds and pleurisy. He still had to complete his diabetic research at the Swiss factory, but he missed Gabriella, and wondered if the war would be over in time for his twenty-fourth birthday in July. Meanwhile Silvio Ortona had discovered a black-market trattoria, 'The Piantanida', on Via Moscova opposite the *Corriere della Sera* newspaper. Elsewhere in Italy meat was available only on coupons, but 'The Piantanida' served veal shanks and other illegal cuts artfully concealed beneath rice and peas. Diners sat at long refectory tables and Levi often ate opposite the

Corriere's foppish theatre critic Eligio Possenti, with his ruby tie-pin, or the paper's film critic Filippo Sacchi. Sacchi was well-known for his disdainful reviews of Fascist 'White Telephone' films with their ermine-clad countesses and bearskin rugs. These *Corriere* journalists were privy to news of what was happening to Jews in eastern territories. The paper's Russia correspondent, Curzio Malaparte, had visited the Warsaw ghetto in the winter of 1942 and seen corpses in the snow and the frightful overcrowding. Though he could only publish his uncensored impressions after the war (in his gruesome masterpiece *Kaputt*), Malaparte's circle in Milan knew very well what was happening; the truth casually leaked out into 'The Piantanida', where the word 'pogrom' was on everyone's lips, but no one dared pronounce it. Rumours of the atrocities in the East reached Levi from several other sources.

At the Swiss factory he had access to copies of the *Gazzette de Lausanne*, which carried quite precise news of Germany's war against the Jews. In addition, Levi listened to Allied wireless services, chiefly Radio London, which in November 1942 had broadcast news of the Warsaw ghetto deportations and the gassing of 'whole groups of children'. Levi also had chance conversations with repatriated Italian soldiers who had witnessed the mistreatment, killing and deportation of Jews by Germans in Russia, Croatia and Greece. Then, on the 'Crescenzago Express', he had met a young Jewish refugee from the Nazi protectorate of Bohemia (formerly part of Czechoslovakia). A friendship developed, and for two months Levi took German lessons from him. It is unthinkable that his Bohemian tutor did not mention the pogroms in his own country; from 1939 onwards, tens of thousands of Jews had been deported from Bohemia to Theresienstadt ghetto, where they were deliberately starved. The greatest mass-killing in recent history was going on daily, and yet Levi concentrated on not knowing, on looking the other way. 'Our ignorance allowed us to live,' he later wrote of this period.

In 1943 the Jewish Passover fell on 19 April. This was a special day in the 'Goebbels calendar' as the Warsaw ghetto was to be annihilated that night. Most of Ada's friends had turned up to celebrate at Via San Martino, among them Sandro Delmastro's fiancée Ester Valabrega. Ada, in high spirits, prepared an unleavened bread pudding with candied peel and cream cheese. Instead of the customary bitter herbs to mark the bitterness of slavery in Egypt, guests swallowed a spoonful of vinegar-soaked oregano. Steaming gold broth was served while Ada dished out ritual bright-orange sticks of jellied carrot, matzo balls and gefilte fish wangled on Milan's black market. Meanwhile the Warsaw ghetto was going down in gunfire and flames.

Everywhere the bodies of children and women lay with burned hair and rifle-shot wounds. The SS pulled back in disarray as the survivors put up an heroic struggle. The unequal combat lasted a month, until 16 May, when the ghetto surrendered and the Nazis razed the quarter. The Jewish revolt would have astonished the world, if the world had known about it.

12

By early June Italy was on its knees. In Milan the trams no longer ran, there were hardly any trains: civil life seemed to have collapsed. Amid this chaos there was a certain amount of drunkenness at 7 Via San Martino, yet Ada in her firm but tactful way tried to keep order. On 16 June Levi wrote to Alberto Salmoni in Turin: 'It's 1:20 am at night and we're still drinking.' His handwriting, usually neat, was a tipsy scrawl. 'And this Silvio fellow is flat out on his bed. He really should write to you but he can't be bothered to get up. He wants you to buy him a big mountain rucksack.' Levi recommended a sports shop on Corso Re Umberto. 'If you happen to go to "Ravelli's" could you ask if they've got any size 12 crampons? Here in Milan they cost 700 (!) lire.' This postcard shows how determined Levi was to enjoy life in the face of an uncertain future.

Levi was asleep in Ada's flat when, on the night of 9–10 July, American and British troops landed on Sicily and began a steady advance up the Italian peninsula. In a panic Fascists burned their Party cards. Three days later, on 13 July, Turin was pulverised in an American air-raid that killed 792 inhabitants and wounded 914 others. The Flying Fortresses flew in close to 'The Saccarello', bombing the green hills above the Po. Then came the final straw. On Monday 19 July, for the first time in the war, Rome was bombed. Fire engines loaded with soldiers and coffins sped to shattered parts of the capital. Thousands of Romans now suffered the fate of their northern brethren. The Germanophile Pius XII offered his sympathies to the families of the bombed-out San Lorenzo district, but it was insulting to see the Holy Father dispensing 1,000-lire notes from his black Mercedes. Crowds threw rubbish at the pontifical limousine.

Mussolini was now the most hated man in Italy; he had lost the war, and King Victor Emanuel III plotted his removal. This was carried out within the week. The incredible news that the Duce had been deposed came on Sunday 25 July, at 10:45 pm, a hot, muggy night. Levi was sleeping when the announcement was broadcast to the nation. The next morning he woke up to learn that Italy had a new, non-Fascist government. Field Marshal Badoglio, a seventy-two-year-old career officer with a weakness for champagne, had assumed premiership of the country. Twenty-one years after his March on Rome in 1922, Benito Mussolini had fallen to the very king who had first summoned him to power.

NINE

Resistance and Betrayal
1943

I

On Monday 26 July 1943 jubilant crowds surged on to the streets of Milan cheering: '*Viva l'Italia! Viva Badoglio!*' A butcher put up the ghoulish advert: '*DUCE: ENTRAILS*'. As in Sicily, so now in northern Italy: Fascists were in a frantic anti-Fascist zeal, whispering denunciations, throwing away their Blackshirt badges. Every vestige of the regime was attacked with chisels, fire and spit. The *fasces* insignia were machine-gunned from the front of buildings. In Turin the Fascist Party headquarters were set ablaze and angry crowds prevented firemen from reaching the cathartic pyre. One unrepentant Fascist was thrown from a window, many others lynched. The worst offenders had fled into hiding: because it was their turn to be hunted.

In some way Primo Levi wished for Italy's destruction by the Allies: Italy had banished Jews from society, let Italy hang. Still, he celebrated Mussolini's fall, crashing out on Eugenio Gentili's sofa at dawn. Italians were overwhelmed by the belief that there would be no more war; Levi, like most Jews, was willing to wait patiently for Field Marshal Badoglio to end the racial persecution. With a thrill of happiness and expectation, synagogues across Italy began to display the Italian flag above Badoglio's portrait. The desire for a new society burned bright.

But Levi's rejoicings were brief. Now began the tragic story of modern Italy at its saddest hour. In the confused and increasingly dramatic forty-five days (the famous '*I 45 Giorni*') until Italy surrendered to the Allies, the king and Badoglio dithered fatally. They wanted peace but they were paralysed by fear of Germany. The Führer would gladly obliterate a nation that joined the Allies and reneged on the Axis. Badoglio played for time where none existed, negotiating secretly with the Allies while assuring Hitler that Italy would not desert him. Mussolini was no sooner jailed than Hitler began to pour troops over the Brenner Pass into northern Italy. A few German soldiers were seen on the streets of Turin, their helmets painted provocatively '*Viva il Duce*'. Levi's mother was terrified to see a German anti-aircraft Flak gun in a sandbag emplacement beneath 'The Saccarello'. Italy might yet become a battleground. Meanwhile, in a naval barracks high above the Ligurian Sea, Sandro Delmastro prepared to arm himself against the enemy.

Badoglio's forty-five-day rule proved a disaster for Italy's Jews. Forced labour was not officially ended under his premiership, nor was the Office of Demography and Race dissolved. Blindly loyal to the monarchy and to its conservative values, Badoglio proved to be a man of straw: though he aped the style of the officer caste, at heart he remained a Piedmontese peasant, earthy, primitive, brutal. Some Italian Jews saw what was coming. Guido Bonfiglioli, who had worked alongside Levi in the Physics Institute, vowed to escape to Fiery high in the Valle d'Aosta if the Germans came. Levi had no such contingency plan. He wished to stay on in Milan, at least until the August holidays when he could distribute *Italia Libera* ('Free Italy') leaflets for the Action Party. It was not an unreasonable plan, considering the difficulties of travel to Turin – the trains delayed by strikes and breakdowns.

On 10 August Levi got the order from the *Azionista* Dino Luzzatto to tear down Fascist posters in Via Vincenzo Monti intended to welcome the last of Italy's troops home from Russia. He was accompanied on the mission by Eugenio Gentili, Silvio Ortona and Camillo Treves. It did not occur to Levi that these returning Italian soldiers were surely sick of the war, and in need of consolation. In later years he bitterly regretted the action. ('It was not a nice thing to do. Those expeditionary corps were coming home half dead and demoralised. Poor souls – they were our *colleagues*.') As matters turned out, the four subversives were stopped in their task by plainclothes police. 'Idiots, go back to bed!' they yelled. It could have been nasty.

2

Italian cities continued to be bombed by the Allies for as long as Field Marshal Badoglio showed no sign of surrendering. On the night of 12–13 August Milan suffered its worst raid yet. The next day the Public Gardens were a ruin of bomb-torn trees and up-turned flower beds. Monkeys, escaped from the zoo, chattered terrified in the burned trees, while in Piazza del Duomo marble statues had been blown out of the Cathedral niches. The only signs of life were the prostitutes picking their way through the rubble: 'Christ Almighty, are there no more men?' a newspaper reported. As Milan smouldered, Levi went on his last holiday of the war. He and a group of friends put in at the Hotel Miramonte in the Piedmont resort of Cogne: Levi's sister, her fiancé Franco Tedeschi, cousin Giulia Colombo, Silvio Ortona and Bianca Guidetti Serra. Five summers ago in Cogne, Levi had first read the awful 'Racial Manifesto'. It was galling to think that Italy was still officially a Nazi ally.

One morning the friends, having spent the night in an abandoned mountain hut, heard a knock at the door. Germans? They made no answer and remained quite still, but the knocking grew louder. In mooched a cow followed by a cowherd who had warm milk for sale. So it was breakfast in bed for all. As they drank, the British planes echoed round the mountains. They were so close, Carla Consonni remembered, that you could smell their fuel on the summer air. Slowly the murmur faded over the Gran Paradiso in the direction of Turin. Within minutes anti-aircraft shells would burst high above 'The Saccarello'.

The brief holiday almost ended in catastrophe when Silvio Ortona slipped down a snowfield in the Vallone di Money, and would have plummeted clean into a glacier had he not landed on a plateau and come to rest with his legs dangling over the ledge. His front teeth were knocked out and he cut his tongue; Levi sustained a few bruises in the attempt to rescue his friend.

Returning to Milan a week later, on around 20 August, Levi found that 7 Via San Martino had been hit by bombs. Ada Della Torre, luckily, had left some weeks earlier to work in the Piedmont town of Ivrea for Olivetti. Outside the house smouldered the remains of a couple of bombed Italian staff-cars. Levi was now without a home and for the next fortnight he slept on friends' floors. Anna Cases gave him a bed at her parents' house at 12 Via Pisacane; she had known Levi in Turin, and now found him in a state of nerves as Italy headed for an uncertain future. On 8 September, a Wednesday, Levi met Eugenio Gentili, Vanda Maestro and the (now gap-toothed) Silvio Ortona for lunch at 'The Piantanida'. As usual the diners ate at long wooden tables, passing wine and breadsticks: it was a day like any other. Gentili recalled: 'At two o'clock we all said *ciao* – "See you tomorrow" – but I didn't see Primo again until after the war.'

Later that evening at 7:45 pm Field Marshal Badoglio announced an Armistice with the Allies. Officially, at least, Hitler's war was over; Italians were liberated from the Nazi-Fascist war machine. Now there really would be no more bombing, no more humiliation for the Jews. Italy's surrender filled Levi with 'a stupid joy', he recalled. There was a sensation of something momentous in the air; whatever happened now, life could not carry on in the way it had. Fascism apparently was finished. Yet the jollifications of the first days of peace died rapidly. While the British and Americans moved fast to send in troops, they were not fast enough. With ruthless speed the Germans occupied key points in the north. Within two days, 10–11 September, Italy was effectively cut in two: south of Naples, under the Allies; north of Naples, under the Germans.

Levi's first thoughts were for his mother and sister in 'The Saccarello'. Without collecting his wages he left A. Wander Ltd on Armistice Day – 8 September – and hurriedly made his way to Turin. He found the city surprisingly calm. A few German soldiers milled round the Hotel Astoria on Via XX Settembre where the Nazi high command was billeted; there was no sign of the *furor teutonicus* to come.

3

In the confusion of the Armistice Levi's friends fled to wherever they had contacts. Dino Luzzatto made it to Switzerland, where he was joined by the *Corriere*'s ex-film critic Filippo Sacchi. Other of Levi's Jewish acquaintances hurried to the Protestant valleys near Turin, which had traditionally sympathised with Jews as a 'People of the Book'. Sandro Delmastro, hoping to catch up with the Allies in southern Italy, had abandoned his naval barracks at Acqui Terme. Too late: the fleet had already left for Sicily. Losing no time, he scrambled into the mountains to prepare himself against the invader. For Delmastro, with his cast-iron morality, the decision to fight the occupying Nazis had not been difficult. He was joined in the Waldensian valleys by Bianca Guidetti Serra, now a Communist *compagna*, and her boyfriend Alberto Salmoni.

Communist formations, known as Garibaldi Brigades, were by far the strongest anti-Fascist influence at this stage. Silvio Ortona joined a Garibaldi unit in Biella, near Turin, where his uncle ran a timber business. He had been a reserve officer in the Italian army and at least knew how to dismantle a rifle. Levi had no such military training. He had left Milan without any clear idea of the armed struggle ahead and certainly did not intend to take up arms against the Germans. 'I was a young bourgeois pacifist and I'd rather have died than shoot anyone.' For the moment all Levi felt he could do was bide his time and dream hopefully of an Allied liberation. This *attendismo* – 'wait-and-see attitude' – was typical of most Italian Jews at the Armistice hour.

Levi's one concern was to save himself and his mother and sister from the Nazis. As soon as he joined them in 'The Saccarello' on 8 or 9 September he told them to pack their bags for a small spa town, St Vincent, in the Valle d'Aosta. A Jewish family there in rented accommodation, the Segres, could shelter them. Wealthy evacuees who hoped to reach Switzerland, the Segres had been neighbours in 75 Corso Re Umberto. Levi assumed that St Vincent would be a safe place to hide from the Nazi dragnets. He went on ahead, arriving there on the evening of 9 September 1943, with a little money and clothes in a suitcase. St Vincent is situated almost 100 kilometres north of Turin, not far from the Matterhorn. With its thermal springs and antiseptic Swiss-style hotels, the impression the town gave was of discreet wealth. Having made contact with the Segres, Levi waited anxiously for his mother and sister to arrive. Anna Maria later summed up the difficult situation: 'September was a month of planning, manoeuvring and great uncertainty for us Italian Jews. During my brother's absence in St Vincent I was frantically running round Turin trying to contact friends and find alternative places to stay in case St Vincent fell through: the chaos was unbelievable.'

There were no more certainties, no more guarantees: all the Levis knew was that Italy was half German, half Anglo-American; and that there was no longer an Italian army. In the days immediately following the Armistice it became increasingly apparent that Jews, should they be found by Germans in the Occupied half of Italy, were in mortal danger. And not only Jews. In the hills round 'The Saccarello' swarmed Italy's disbanded troops returning from France and Liguria. Tattered and filthy, without leadership or discipline, they were fleeing the slaughter and despair of a lost war. 'We gave them what civilian clothing and food we could,' recalled Giulia Colombo. 'Most of them were fleeing conscription into the German army, without knowing where they were going.'

The German occupation of Turin unfolded as if in slow-motion. On 10 September, at 6:30 am, the SS requisitioned the Hotel Nazionale off Via Roma. Armoured cars, the cavalry divisions, poured into the city from the north. Scuffles at Porta Nuova station left a couple of Germans wounded. Otherwise Turin acquiesced to Occupation in gloomy silence. In no time at all posters began to appear calling on the able-bodied to fight 'the traitor Badoglio'. Streets were blocked off as telephone exchanges, bus stations, newspaper offices were taken over. Italian soldiers who refused to fight on Hitler's side were shot as deserters; or, branded with fine Teutonic irony as *volontari*, they were deported to Germany for slave labour. Trucks lurched through Turin loaded with handcuffed men. Cousin Giulia's father Oreste Colombo came running up to 'The Saccarello' at about 9:00 pm: 'The Germans are at the railway station.' His voice was thick with fear and disgust.

The city's new masters meant business. Clocks were brought forward by one hour to correspond with German Reich Time, so darkness fell one hour earlier than usual. A delirium of vetoes followed. A curfew was imposed from 9:00 pm. At any time of the day it was forbidden to circulate publicly in groups of more than three. Public transport, already bombed by the Allies to a virtual standstill, was to cease running from 6:00 pm. Any citizen found in possession of arms after 10:00 pm on 12 September – the deadline for surrendering them – would be executed.

Levi's mother and sister, after hours of slow travel on a crowded train, reached St Vincent on the morning of Friday 12 September. Guido Bonfiglioli, hoping to reach his hideout in Fiery, left Turin the same day; he had with him his skis, ice-pick and mountaineer's rope. Outside Porta Nuova station he encountered Anna Maria's boyfriend, Franco Tedeschi, and his father Gualtiero. They said they were not going to leave Turin. Bonfiglioli remonstrated: 'Don't you know the danger you're in?' The Tedeschis were not the only Jews who stayed on to the last. Giulia Colombo, her parents Ida and Oreste, Grandma Adelina Luzzati, Ester's sister Jole and her two baby boys Luciano and Bruno, remained at 'The Saccarello' for another four weeks. Only when an Action Party activist yelled at them 'Are you insane?' did they abandon the villa. Before they left they put away the family silver and covered the furniture with sheets. Peasants then set about taking everything from 'The Saccarello' they could lay hands on. Electric flexes were ripped out for copper wire, walls knocked down in the hope they concealed treasure. Cousin Giulia's piano, too heavy to steal, was abandoned midway in the garden where it remained until the war's end, cultivating mould.

On 13 September came news that Mussolini had been rescued from his jail in the Apennines by German parachutists, and was about to be installed as head of Italy's new Nazi-Fascist Republic. From now until the end of the war the Duce was to be the Führer's lapdog, and a brutal new 'Italian' government was set up at Salò on the shores of Lake Garda.

4

Half of Italy had surrendered to the western Allies; Hitler was in charge of the other half. Mussolini's resurgence had laid the choices starkly before Levi: either he was with the Fascists or against the Fascists. 'After Salò it was no longer possible for anyone with a conscience *not* to fight the Nazis,' recalled Bianca Guidetti Serra. Levi chose to fight. Any lingering doubts he may have had about the necessity for armed resistance evaporated with news of Italy's first pogrom since the ghettos. On 15 September the SS Panzer Division *Leibstandarte Adolf Hitler* arrived at the small town of San Giulio on Lake Orta near Switzerland. They were looking for Jews. Primo's uncle Mario Levi was hidden there with his wife Emma Agostina Coen, their son Roberto and his wife Elena Bachi. Someone, probably an Italian, must have informed on the Levis, because Roberto, aged twenty-three, and his father, sixty-two, were herded by the SS on to a truck and drowned with other Jews in nearby Lake Maggiore. Inexplicably, that Wednesday the Germans spared Elena and Emma. Three days later, more atrocities followed at the Maggiore village of Meina; three children under fifteen from the Diaz family were bound together with wire and held down in the lake with oars.

On 18 September a notice went up in St Vincent, where Levi was now hiding with his mother and sister. All 'foreigners' (Jews, in other words) were to present themselves to the SS by 6:00 pm that day on pain of death. The Nazis were offering a 5,000-lire reward (about £2,000 in today's terms) for information leading to the arrest of Italian Jews. For Italians motivated by greed, envy or just vindictiveness, that was a tempting sum. Giulia Colombo's family, having vacated 'The Saccarello', received an anonymous blackmail letter at their hideout near Turin. The pompous circumlocutions and pidgin Italian make this an especially sinister document. Addressed to 'The Occupants of the Saccarello', it was probably the work of the thieving tenant farmers who had already burgled the premises. 'A number of Authorities in this land know that you belong to the Jewish race so you will be stripped of everything and finish in a concentration camp. But this will not happen if you agree to our invitation.' A sum of 50,000 lire was to be deposited at an agreed place and time. 'Otherwise we will do our duty as Fascists and report you as property-hoarding Jews. Investigations will be done and it will be your ruin. I believe that you will not fail in this invitation or else we will do our duty as Fascists and see to the suitable cleansing of your race.' Those last words – '*pulizia competente per la vostra razza*' – betray the Nazis' efficient influence in Occupied Italy. Nothing happened, fortunately, when Giulia's father bravely decided to ignore the letter.

With the Germans advancing rapidly up the valley from Turin, it was too dangerous now for the Levis to stay in St Vincent. On 17 September they moved uphill to the hamlet of Amay in the Colle di Joux. It seemed a sensible move. The couple who ran the inn there were said to hate the Nazi intruder. The Germans had yet to take 'rebel' activity seriously in the mountains, concentrating their round-ups instead in towns and villages. Studded with medieval castles, hemmed in by some of Europe's highest mountains, the valleys were admirably suited to guerrilla combat. All round Amay was a dark and disorientating world of mule paths, mossy wayside shrines and dense chestnut forest. If Nazi-Fascists came to take away cattle, homes, or crops, the inhabitants would fight with their lives.

The Albergo Ristoro looked more like an alpine barn than an inn. Outside were piles of firewood, a chopping block, a water trough. Eleuterio and Tina Page, the proprietors, had just finished stacking the last hay crop when the Levis arrived. The Pages kept a shotgun under their bed and served wayfarers coarse *vino da pasto*, cheese, bread, eggs and polenta. They charged little rent and lodgers could make a down-payment with jewellery if they wished. Ester Levi, now forty-eight, felt comfortable here; the inn was clean and there was running water. From the top floor the Levis could make out the 'snowy dells' of Monte Rosa celebrated by Tennyson. St Vincent, 1,500 metres below, could be surveyed for enemy activity. A forest path led to Brusson town, where Vanda Maestro and Luciana Nissim had been concealed, frightened and confused, since the Armistice.

With its meagre chalets, cowsheds and single stone chapel, Amay is a remote village. No more than a hundred people have ever lived here; the village faces dandelion meadows on a ridge between two valleys – the Val d'Ayas and the Val Tournanche – into either of which, theoretically, it was possible to escape in the event of attack. Or so Levi believed. In fact there were two obvious ways into Amay from St Vincent. One was up the mountain path through Moron Trueil; the other was up through moss and streams to the hamlet of Petit-Rhun. From either place Amay was vulnerable to attack.

By early September Guido Bonfiglioli had reached Fiery hamlet thirteen kilometres north of Amay. Unlike Amay, Fiery was inaccessible from St Vincent; the last three kilometres were along a narrow rain-rutted ditch. 'Amay was a trap,' Bonfiglioli judged fifty years later, 'and to this day I can't understand why Primo ran such a risk of discovery.' Levi's sister conceded that Amay probably *was* within dangerous reach of St Vincent, but in the confusion after the Armistice, mistakes were made.

Amay's isolation was soon undermined by the hordes of Allied POWs, Jewish refugees and Italian soldiers fleeing the Germans. Each day they tried to get through the frontier wires into Switzerland. A few of these tatterdemalions stopped by the Albergo Ristoro for a bowl of polenta before moving on ('like a flock without a shepherd', recalled Levi) towards the hoped-for safety of neutral Europe. The tatters of Italy's army swarming across the mountain peaks were a wretched and unforgettable sight for Levi: some soldiers were prepared to trudge the mountain passes as far as

Bergamo 320 kilometres east, to find a haven. At all costs they had to avoid the roads and railways on the valley floors controlled by Italian Fascists in German uniform; these Blackshirts were often more fanatical than they had been in their glory days.

In late September three disbanded soldiers made their way up to Amay seeking sanctuary. By chance one of them happened to know Levi's sister from school. Aldo Piacenza was a former law student and survivor of Mussolini's Russia campaign. He was accompanied by his Sicilian commander, Captain Lo Bue, and a third man, Lieutenant Rota. Lo Bue had heard of a small *albergo* in Amay where they could take stock and recover. In St Vincent a column of Germans passed the men but luckily did not stop to ask them questions. Even though the trio were not Jewish, they had no delusions about Nazi brutality. Piacenza had fought alongside the Germans in Russia, and knew what they were capable of.

At first Anna Maria did not recognise Piacenza in the thin, ragged soldier standing before her. It mattered greatly to Levi that his sister had been at school with Aldo. In a civil war, where there was a risk of betrayal, a sense of trust and fellowship was vital. Not that Piacenza was any better prepared, psychologically, for the coming Resistance than Primo and Anna Maria. He was a mild-mannered, peaceable man. Nevertheless Piacenza's military experience was an asset to Amay's slowly evolving band, now made up of Italian army stragglers and Jews who lacked funds, weapons and contacts. Piacenza had 5,000 lire left from his army wages, and while this was not enough to buy an arsenal, it was sufficient for a couple of months' food stocks. Piacenza's first-hand account of Nazi atrocities in Russia must have further convinced Levi of the rightness of armed revolt. In the summer of 1941 Piacenza had been in Dnepropetrovsk when he passed by a long column of Jews under SS escort. 'The machine-gunning went on for three days,' he recalled, 'we heard the Jews were dumped in lime pits.'

Quite soon Levi felt confident enough to reconnoitre the territory. He had learned of Guido Bonfiglioli's whereabouts in nearby Fiery and of the other Jews hiding there with him. These were the Turin physicist Vittorio Finzi, his three cousins Aldo, Achille and Alberto, and a young Yugoslav named Bier. None of the Finzi family was interested in armed resistance; they planned to escape to Switzerland over the Monte Rosa glacier. But time was running out: the Jews were not the only ones hiding in the mountains. The Germans were burning enemy houses and villages in a punitive expedition against *banditen*, as they called Resistance members. Vittorio Finzi wrote in his (unpublished) diary for mid-September: 'This evening our mood is even more black. Bonfiglioli and Bier have created an atmosphere of doom with their talk of Nazi reprisals. What's to be done?'

Finzi's diary tells us much about Levi's movements in the Valle d'Aosta that autumn. On 19 September – the day the Germans burned to death twenty-two people in the Piedmont town of Boves – Levi was in Fiery for the grand-sounding 'Council of Twelve'. This was Finzi's mock-heroic name for an emergency gathering of Jewish friends and families. They were undecided what course of action to take. Some wanted to flee to Switzerland. Others, like Levi, planned to resist. In his diary Finzi noted: 'Primo Levi, who goes by the name of "Dr Michele", has come down from the Collè di Joux to help us decide what to do.' Levi's *nom de guerre* of Michele (his middle name and that of his unfortunate grandfather) was a clear indication that he was now part of a partisan band, as a false identitiy was a prerequisite for clandestine activity. At the meeting Levi declared that he was firmly against the idea of fleeing to Switzerland and even said it was 'cowardly' to do so. As matters turned out, Finzi failed to get there; the Swiss frontier guards accepted his bribe, only to turn him away. Instead, under the false name 'Vittorio Rossi', he joined the *ribelli* (as the Fascists called the partisans) and did not see Levi again until 1947.

According to his post-war military papers, Primo Levi joined the Italian Resistance on 1 October 1943. He was assigned to a 'Free Italy' band affiliated to the Action Party. Actually the word *banda* confers a spurious martial status on Levi's ragtag outfit, making it sound more organised than it was. The term 'Resistance' did not yet exist in Italy. No one quite knew what the partisans stood for. Those who had seen them spoke of rough, unshaven types in filthy Fascist or German tunics with the badges and pips ripped off. Some of them wore hobnail boots and green alpine hats stuck with feathers. At this early stage the Italian Resistance was extremely chaotic and disorganised. 'We more or less had to *invent* the Resistance,' Levi recalled.

As the Nazis took control in the north of Italy, so, slowly, the anti-German underground took root in towns and cities, involving the mass participation and collusion of priests, factory and office workers, peasants, housewives and intellectuals. Italian Jews joined the Resistance for obvious reasons. By the war's end some 1,000 of them were partisans, almost one in thirty of the population of Jews under Occupation. Many of them propagated the idea of the Resistance as a 'second Risorgimento' which, like the first Risorgimento prior to unification in 1861, sought to rid the country of a foreign power.

In Amay the band was ill-equipped and underfinanced. Traditional forms of military order and hierarchy now inspired nothing but contempt in Captain Lo Bue, Lieutenant Rota and Second Lieutenant Piacenza. And in early November, to nobody's surprise, Lo Bue left Amay to join his brother in Florence. He was followed soon after by Rota. Much later Levi confessed that his partisan days were among 'the most obscure' of his life and 'best forgotten'. Speaking today with former Amay band members, one's impression is of overwhelming remorse. They share painful memories of naive trust placed in informers, and shifting allegiances. Aldo Piacenza, now a lawyer in Turin, sighed: 'We were foolish kids. Well-intentioned ones, all right, but still kids.' Carla Consonni was less forgiving: 'How can I put this? Primo and his comrades *played* at being partisans. Oh, they did some brave things, but they were *so* inexperienced. It's easy to say this now, in hindsight, but they really were childish.' Levi was unlucky to join the underground battle at a time when it lacked central organisation or a military structure. Later, when the Occupation became more entrenched in Italy, the Resistance operated more effectively. Nevertheless, Consonni reflects the view of many Italians on the young people involved in the early stage of the Resistance. Consonni lost a sister-in-law to the partisan struggle.

If Amay was dangerous, Brusson – where Vanda Maestro and Luciana Nissim were trying to operate as partisans – was even more so. A small town of some 2,000 inhabitants, Brusson crawled with Fascist spies. Eugenio Gentili, on a brief visit there from his secure hideout in Morgex near France, warned Maestro of the danger she was in. 'Get out of Brusson. Tell Primo to leave Amay. Go where there's a *minimum* of contact with the locals.' Vanda would not listen; she said the mayor of Brusson was her 'friend', and his wife 'a good woman'.

5

Vanda was a delicate-boned woman, whose eyebrows arched darkly over a pale face. Some said she resembled the youthful Edith Piaf. She was two months older than Levi, but seemed considerably more mature; vivacious, she gave the impression of a capable and poised young woman. Vanda had studied chemistry in Turin for a year, but graduated from Genoa University. She had the rare medical condition of *inversa viscera* – her heart on the right side, her liver on the left – and was likely to have had other congenital abnormalities (such as heart problems) that may significantly have reduced her life expectancy. This may have accounted for the impression of frailty she gave others. She was the eldest child of Cesare Maestro and Clelia Colombo, with whom she had lived in substantial bourgeois comfort in the Crocetta. The Maestros were prosperous tradespeople who owned a textile shop on Turin's Via Lagrange. Vanda's mother had died young, leaving her in the hands of an authoritarian father. Levi was attracted to Vanda, even though she already had a boyfriend, the Zionist sympathiser Giorgio Segre.

Today there are conflicting impressions of Vanda among the surviving partisans. Piacenza claimed that she went on 'risky' reconnaissance missions to gather information on a hydroelectric dam 'bristling' with Nazi gun emplacements. Luciana Nissim, who knew Vanda intimately, was greatly surprised by Piacenza's view. 'Vanda was bright and sweet, but courageous? Hardly. In Piedmontese we'd call her a *frisinin*, a 'waif'. She was a sparrow. She tagged along meekly in the Resistance, just as we all did.'

Levi did not blow up any bridges, derail locomotives or kill Germans. Most of his time was spent hustling to survive. Often hungry, he ate whatever the innkeepers brought his way: hot chestnuts, lamb if he was lucky. The Amay group numbered no more than eight – nine, if we count Levi's mother – and was accident-prone. One day Piacenza miscalculated the time it would take him and Levi to reach a village twenty-four kilometres away to pick up ammunitions. Night fell before they were even halfway. 'We had to sleep together huddled for warmth on a bed of maize leaves with our feet tucked into our rucksacks.' During the trudge, Levi had shown a keen interest in all manner of alpine phenomena, from glaciers to marmots. The sight of Aldo's Russian service revolver frightened him. 'Primo kept asking me why men had to kill each other, he seemed astounded by the world's malignancy,' remembered Piacenza.

Through the cold autumn nights in Amay, vehicles were routinely stopped and searched in St Vincent. Ignoring the danger, on 23 October Levi ventured down to the Hôtel de Ville to act as witness to his friend Lia Segre's marriage. Jewish friends and relatives, among them Livio Norzi, were attending the ceremony that morning at 10:00 am; Levi's signature on the marriage certificate was a deliberately unintelligible scrawl. An SS van pulled up outside as the couple were about to exchange vows, but it seems the SS did not wish to disturb the occasion. 'If just *one* registry official had betrayed us as Jews I wouldn't be here talking to you today,' said Lia Segre. She and her husband, an Olivetti engineer, escaped to Switzerland.

6

With the onset of winter, Anna Maria Levi decided to leave Amay to join the Resistance in Turin. The band was now in desperate need of morale and solidarity. The late Guido Bachi, a Jewish Action Party chief code-named

'Giulio Bartoli', was dug in with his brother Emilio on the other side of the Colle di Joux. Born in Turin ten years before Levi, he was a reserved, orderly man who in 1939 had fought with the French Foreign Legion in Occupied Norway. Bachi's dry, analytic mind made him an ideal *capobanda* – 'band chief' – and he set about welding the Amay group into a fighting force, renaming it the '7th Justice and Liberty Division, 1st Brigade'. Bachi urged Levi to obtain a false ID in Turin, which he did. 'It was *so* false it looked genuine.' Levi's fictitious birthplace was either Eboli or Battipaglia (Levi was not clear after the war which it was) in southern Italy. Birth registers in the Mezzogiorno could not be checked by the Germans, as they were in Allied hands.

Levi now had reason to be very concerned for his mother. On 1 December 1943 the Salò puppet Fascist state decreed that all Jews, 'no matter their nationality', were to be arrested and their properties sequestrated by the state. With this decree Mussolini sanctioned the Final Solution in Italy; Jews were to be placed in 'specially fitted-out' (*attrezzati*) camps. Now it was not merely dangerous, but fatal, for them to live openly in Italy. No sensible Jew wanted to run the risk of being visible in the new Nazi-Fascist state; there was no option but for them to go into hiding. Anna Maria's first instinct was to hide her mother in a big city. While Ester hesitated about where to go, Anna Maria decided on her behalf. Ignoring her brother's pleas for his mother to stay with him in the inn, on 1 December Anna Maria sent a young *Azionista* ('whom my mother did not know') to fetch her back to Turin. One may imagine Primo's distress: deeply attached to Ester, from now on his mother was no longer under his protection. Yet had Ester stayed on at Amay, she might well have been deported. There began a nerve-racking peregrination from house to house in Turin as Levi's sister looked for suitable shelter for their mother.

That night, after the 1 December decree, any Jews left hiding in St Vincent scrambled desperately uphill to the Amay area. Italo Diena and his pregnant wife Pia Astrologo had known Levi in Milan through Ada Della Torre. By lantern-light the couple trudged up through the forests in the snow. 'All we could hear in the dark were the voices and the footsteps of other Jews – Yugoslav? French? – on the run from that decree,' recalled Pia Astrologo. On reaching Brusson, she was reunited with Vanda Maestro and was shocked by her fragile appearance. Vanda was pale, cast-down and frightened. After eleven months in Brusson, the days were getting shorter, and morale was sinking. In mid-December the SS installed the XIX Blackshirt Brigade at nearby Aosta. They were answerable to the newly appointed prefect of Aosta province, Cesare Augusto Carnazzi, a Nazi lackey and lawyer who had a legal practice in Bergamo, not far from Milan.

Carnazzi's agents were aware of an unusual amount of to-ing and fro-ing in Amay. Why was the Albergo Ristoro open in winter? On 10 or 11 December, Carnazzi gave orders for a spy to infiltrate the area. He wanted to destroy two self-proclaimed Communist partisan bands camped beneath Amay; for all their revolutionary militancy, they indulged in robbery, rape and reprisal. In later years Levi described these bands as 'one of the *macchie nere* – black stains – of the Resistance and very dubious'. It was his misfortune to be caught up in Prefect Carnazzi's retaliatory espionage operation. 'Otherwise I probably would not have been deported.' What follows is a reconstruction of events based on records (held in the Aosta Tribunal archives) of a post-war spy trial.

7

The infiltrator, Edilio Cagni, went by the false name of Lieutenant 'Renato Redi'. Born in Genoa on 29 June 1917, Cagni was an architecture graduate, and no unlettered thug. Unscrupulous and slyly watchful, he was (according to his police files) a 'worthy imitator and disciple of Gestapo methods'. His chief pleasure was to coax the truth out of prisoners by means of a hammer. Handcuffed, a partisan (Giuseppe Barbesino) was led to a chamber beneath Prefect Carnazzi's office, where Cagni and 'two other accomplices' broke his feet with a hammer. Laden with military honours, Cagni had valiantly fought in France with Italy's 5th 'Pasteria' alpine division, yet he was a sadist. Guido Bachi, head of the little Amay band, in his statement at the spy's post-war trial, referred to Cagni as one of the 'most dangerous elements of the Salò Fascist Republic' and a criminal in the 'gravest sense of the word'.

We can identify Cagni's two assistants as Domenico De Ceglie and Alberto Bianchi. They were constantly bickering, and by artfully exploiting their disagreements Cagni was able to bend them to his will (divide and rule was Cagni's way). With their fawning, unpleasantly conspirant manner, all three men represented a final stage of Italy's degradation: their allegiance, like that of the Italian SS, was to Adolf Hitler.

On the evening of 5 December the infiltrations began. Posing as an anti-Fascist, Cagni chatted with a barmaid at the Caffè dello Sport in Verrès, where it was believed one of the two rogue Communist bands was based. The barmaid told him: 'If you want to join the partisans, go to Brusson and get yourself informed.' Brusson was where Luciana Nissim and Vanda Maestro were hiding. Cagni hurried back to Prefect Carnazzi to tell him what he had gathered. Meanwhile the more brutal of his underlings,

Domenico De Ceglie, drove to Verrès in a preposterously small Fiat Topolino (Little Mouse) piled high with weapons and 'leaflets of a Bolshevik nature'. All this was to win the partisans' trust and greater admiration. Having deposited the Red propaganda at Verrès, De Ceglie drove to the medieval fortress town of Arcesaz, where it was now known that seventy Communist partisans and twenty-three escaped British POWs were hiding. At Arcesaz, Cagni was waiting for him. This was on the afternoon of 9 December.

At first De Ceglie did not recognise his superior, Cagni, who had managed to appoint himself leader of the Arcesaz band. De Ceglie very publicly handed 'Commander Redi' (Cagni) a stash of guns and Communist propaganda, a piece of theatre that hoodwinked everyone including Aldo Piacenza, who had come down from Amay. Cagni then held endless firing practice; the more gullible of his dupes threw grenades into the river. In this way he destroyed the Arcesaz band's ammunition. Meanwhile De Ceglie prepared to penetrate Levi's band, which was ripe for exploitation. Levi and his comrades had been devastated by events the night before in the nearby village of Frumy.

On the night of 8 December, two Frumy partisans, who had been on a drunken rampage down in St Vincent, were disciplined by their Sergeant-Major, Berto. Berto forced them outside into the snow 'and from a distance of between 100–150 metres shot them dead with a Beretta machine-gun'. Berto removed documents from the dead men (one of whom was a demobbed soldier, Giovanni Bertolino) to send to their kin. Today people are understandably reluctant to discuss this obscure imbroglio, which hints so strongly at Cagni's destabilising influence. 'Look, it was wartime – drastic situations impel people to drastic acts,' said Aldo Piacenza. 'Those lads had taken the law into their hands and could no longer be trusted.' Partisan justice was undeniably rough justice, and Piacenza's apologia for the 'necessary murder' is quite commonly heard today among ex-partisans.

This was the dark side of the partisan war. All the books Levi had read on the glorious Risorgimento, the fine ideas in his head, were meaningless in the light of this appalling incident. Two band members had been executed by a *fellow partisan*. Where was the glory in that? The killings had robbed the Resistance of its slender romantic allure.

8

On 10 December, a Friday, Edilio Cagni and his subaltern Domenico De Ceglie turned up at an important partisan conference in Brusson. This was the first time that Guido Bachi had set eyes on the undercover agents. Cagni looked innocuous enough: not very tall, pallid, with a 'rather closed expression', Bachi recalled. If anything he came across as cultured and rather serious – 'the sort of person who encourages confidence in others'. De Ceglie's was a sweet, oddly pleasing presence, blond and trim. 'I was so fooled by De Ceglie that I gave him my brand-new pair of mountain boots!' Not only that. In a state of shock from the executions two nights before, Bachi personally asked De Ceglie to take his place as leader of the Amay band. Today Bachi feels 'gnawed inside' by remorse that he allowed himself to be fooled by this infiltrator. 'Maybe it was my fault that we were captured. We weren't really partisans. We were refugees – Jews on the run.' By now Carnazzi's agents had all the information they needed for the destruction of the bands in Amay, Arcesaz and Verrès. Cagni and his henchmen had infiltrated so swiftly and efficiently that today Aldo Piacenza admits to a sneaking admiration for them. 'They penetrated very ably among us and, I must say, with a certain courage.'

With the unsuspecting Piacenza leading the way, De Ceglie reached Amay by 2:00 pm on that same Friday. Later that evening the spy was able to report to Prefect Carnazzi in Aosta: 'Piacenza introduced me to Signorina Nissim (Jew), Signorina Maestro (Jew), Signor Levi (Jew).' He noted the group's meagre ammunition supplies, the precise location of the Albergo Ristoro, and the presence in the inn of two other Jews: Signor Scavarda, and another 'who turned out to be Bachi's cousin' (actually his brother Emilio). Scavarda was in fact the key Action Party link between Turin and Amay. Needless to say, De Ceglie went under a false identity (Mario Meoli).

De Ceglie did not stay long at Amay; with less than three days to go until the planned round-up he drove like the wind back to Prefect Carnazzi in Aosta, to whom 'I referred and consigned my ample and very detailed reports.' Meanwhile, at a partisan base nearby, in a cunningly arranged night's entertainment, De Ceglie's accomplice Alberto Bianchi poured the rebels so much *grappa* that they were unable to walk, let alone resist attack. On 11 December, in another part of Piedmont, Primo's uncle Enrico Levi had his sixty-fourth birthday. The last one of the three Bene Vagienna brothers still alive, he was hiding with his family in Alessandria under the protection of priests. Levi's uncles Corrado and Gustavo Luzzati, having been forewarned by sympathetic Italian police of their imminent arrest, had fled with their families into the Monferrato hills near Turin, where they remained until the war's end.

Late in the afternoon of Sunday 12 December, Vanda Maestro stopped at Pia Astrologo's hut for roast chestnuts and a chat. Since it was getting dark, 'and Vanda looked so tired and pale', Pia insisted that she stay the night. But Vanda went instead to join Luciana Nissim, who by chance was in Amay. 'Maybe if Vanda had remained with me she would have been saved.' (This sad, tangled story is littered with 'if's'.) When Vanda reached the Albergo Ristoro she found Levi, Nissim and Aldo Piacenza seated round the fire in the presence of a man she did not recognise. The man had just returned from a 'knuckle-whitening' partisan mission to Switzerland. During the trial after the war he was revealed as the Fiat director and Action Party activist Aurelio Peccei (later a world-famous environmentalist). 'But, being a sensible man, Peccei did not stay with us long,' recalled Levi. He hurriedly abandoned the inn, leaving behind his bags.

On his last night as a free man, Levi engaged Luciana Nissim in one of those animated and wide-ranging conversations he so enjoyed. The subject was the famous 'talking Lippizaner horses' of Vienna, which are able to spell out words with their hooves and 'read' numbers. 'Primo was interested in everything.' The night waned, and he was still talking.

Monday 13 December, 4:00 am: a total of 297 Fascists, bristling with arms, set out from Aosta to arrest eighty-odd partisans. Taking no chances, Prefect Carnazzi had dispatched a veritable war machine made up of legionaries from the XII 'Monte Bianco' Republican National Guard, the XIX Blackshirt Brigade, a handful of Centurions and German personnel, among them a Colonel Schmidt. One part of the posse, the larger, headed for Arcesaz, the other for Amay. It was still snowing softly as dawn broke over the Albergo Ristoro to a distant crackle of automatic fire: Arcesaz was under attack.

At some time between 5:30 am and 6:00 am, the little inn at Amay was surrounded. Fifty Fascists, their boots bound in cloth to make no sound in the snow, had crept uphill unheard. Shouts went up: 'Nobody move!' Aldo Piacenza stumbled out of bed, bleary-eyed, to look through a rear window, where a machine-gun was pointing at him. The Fascists had the inn covered front and back. Fifteen of them entered and rounded up the *ribelli*. They meant business, and Levi was punched in the face during the scuffle. 'Call yourselves Italians!' their leader sneered. '*We're* the ones to liberate Italy. *We're* the ones full of bullets from Ethiopia!' Rooms were in chaos. Luciana Nissim was found with anti-Fascist leaflets torn and strewn across the bathroom floor. Levi hurriedly threw his and Aldo Piacenza's revolver into the stove: Aldo's dangerously contained six bullets. ('I just hoped the damned thing wouldn't go off in the embers.') The innkeeper Eleuterio Page refused to get out of bed, claiming that a mule had kicked him the night before. The Fascists jabbed at him with their guns; his wife Tina lashed out at them.

Levi's false papers identified him as 'Signor Ferrero' from southern Italy.

He was unlucky: a militiaman from the Mezzogiorno was able to expose that imposture. How many rebels were hiding here? Whose luggage was that in the corner? Levi claimed the bags were his; he did not want to incriminate Aurelio Peccei. Later Levi said that Peccei must have known something was going to happen, but Peccei may just have been lucky.

TEN

Into Captivity

1943–4

1

Trudging in snow, the prisoners were escorted out of the Albergo Ristoro downhill to Brusson. Weighed down by Peccei's bags, Levi had no hope of escape. During the descent Vanda Maestro considered running, but the ex-soldier Aldo Piacenza warned her: 'Ten feet in this snow and it's ten bullets in your back.' Instead, if she was tortured, Vanda planned to cut her wrists with Piacenza's safety razor. Aware that he was carrying potentially incriminating names and addresses, on the pretext of relieving himself, Levi managed to hide his notebook of partisan contacts in the snow. In Brusson the handcuffed *ribelli* were displayed to gawping villagers, then shoved on to a lorry for Aosta thirty-two kilometres away. Prisoners from Arcesaz were already loaded on other trucks. Full of bravado, the captors lobbed grenades out of the speeding lorry and sang Blackshirt anthems. Theirs was a pathetic haul: two frail girls, a skinny chemist and an orphan, Aldo Piacenza, who wanted only to spend Christmas with his aunts. The pro-Nazi prefect of Aosta, Cesare Carnazzi, had overestimated the strength of Levi's band.

The innkeepers Eleuterio and Tina Page were still allowed to run the Albergo Ristoro, but in partisan slang their hotel was now *bruciato*, 'burned': it was unsafe. Any Jews left hiding in the area got out if they could. Six months pregnant, Pia Astrologo waited anxiously for nightfall before fleeing with her husband to Turin. Luciana Nissim's parents, Davide and Cesira, were smuggled out to Switzerland with the help of a local priest, Don Giuseppe Péaquin.

2

Edilio Cagni, the infiltrator, could be proud of his good day's work. This was the first anti-Fascist round-up in Occupied Italy and it had been a success. A month later, on 11 January 1944, Prefect Carnazzi dispatched a self-congratulatory report to Mussolini's secretary Giovanni Dolfin: Amay had been 'burned down' and 'six rebels' killed; two other *ribelli* had allegedly fallen into a (non-existent) ravine. The communiqué contained many other self-aggrandising untruths. 'We now have in our hands the bedrock of organised political subversion in Piedmont.' After two months of further arrests and extorted confessions, Prefect Carnazzi was able to denounce forty-five more 'anti-Italians' to the occupying Nazis. Meanwhile Cagni penetrated a wide network of suspects in Turin. Posing as a partisan he tried to entrap the Action Party commander Camille Reynaud, but Reynaud escaped over the icy rooftops.

3

Aosta, a grey, alpine city of amphitheatres and triumphal arches, had been built by the Romans. Two stone eagles glowered from the entrance of the 'Cesare Battisti' barracks on Corso San Martin de Corléans. Here Levi was held prisoner under his false name 'Signor Ferrero'. Alone in his cell he planned to plead all ignorance of the Resistance. On the orders of the newborn Salò republic, any captured *ribelli* were to be shot. Levi awaited his fate in a stark room with a wooden cot and palliasse, a sanitary pail and bed table. The interrogations began within twenty-four hours. A Gestapo officer interviewed the partisans individually, with an Italian SS acting as his interpreter. The German was looking for Jews and other so-called 'Reich enemies'. Much unlocking and locking of doors followed as Levi was ushered into the interview-room, where the Gestapo questioned his protested innocence. What business did Levi have in remote Amay? Surely he was not just escaping the bombardments? Levi continued to deny all involvement with the *banditen;* he said he was in Amay to ski and hunt with friends.

The interrogations resumed the morning after, swift and fruitful. This time they were conducted by Centurion Ferro, the Blackshirt leader who had led the attack on the inn. Ferro was not taken in by Levi's denials, and began to bargain with him: 'If you're a rebel we'll put you up against the wall – if you're a Jew we'll send you to a camp here in Italy.' He tried to reassure Levi: 'Nothing will happen to you.' Reportedly a humane man, Ferro had said this in good faith. After some days the false-named 'Signor Ferrero' relented and declared himself a Jew called Primo Levi. To Levi, this proud admission of Jewishness might have recalled the Prophet Jonah's revelation: 'I am a Hebrew.' Physically exhausted, unable to face further inquisitions, Luciana Nissim and Vanda Maestro also confessed to Jewish birth.

*

The comrades could associate only during the hour-long daily exercise. None of them could leave their cell after five o'clock. Pen and ink were banned. After two days Aldo Piacenza managed to remove the screws from the top hinge of his cell door with a razor. He communicated his progress to Levi in a coded book (certain letters underlined in pencil formed key words), and by tapping the pipes with a spoon. For a while Levi considered sawing through his iron bars with a nailfile, a *Boy's Own* fantasy of escape. During the hour's exercise Levi encountered fugitives from the Salò government call-up and petty criminals arrested for infringements of wartime restrictions. Many had been beaten; some had bruises from third-degree interrogations.

Now that Levi had preferred to declare himself a Jew rather than risk execution as a partisan, the inquisitions were continued under the Nazi operative Edilio Cagni, who was now based in the Aosta barracks. In the interview-room 'Lieutenant Redi' revealed to Levi his true identity as a spy. This gave Cagni the upper hand and a frightening control over Levi. He was just two years older than Primo. He threatened him with the *bastonatura in stile* – a 'beating in style' – using a rubber truncheon. Then he placed a pistol on the table and began to circle Levi in a menacing display of power. At times Cagni, after yelling abuse at his terrified captive, would suddenly revert to a gentle tone, speaking reasonably to him. Far from seeking to moderate Gestapo methods, the Italian zealously imitated them. Cagni knew there was little more information to extract from Levi; he was aware of how ill-equipped his band was, how few partisans it contained: he enjoyed the taste of power.

Levi was to be sent to a camp in northern Italy called Fossoli. The two other Jews arrested with him in the Albergo Ristoro – Luciana Nissim and Vanda Maestro – were also destined there. Aldo Piacenza (a non-Jew) was charged with 'political subversion', as was the (Jewish) partisan leader Guido Bachi. Bachi had been arrested in Frumy on the same morning as Levi. Furious that seven other 'rebels' had managed to escape Frumy, the Blackshirts pushed Bachi up against a wall in a mock-execution. It was an unlucky morning for Bachi when a gun was found on him. This offence carried the automatic death penalty. Referred to the Special Tribunal for the Defence of the State in Turin, Bachi and Piacenza prepared to face the firing squad. As it turned out, they were able to corrupt the judiciary through influential friends, and spent the rest of the war in Aosta as prison-clerks.

News of the arrests reached various of Levi's friends. Vanda Maestro's brother Aldo was in Milan when a Fascist radio broadcast announced a round-up of 'Jewish anti-Italians' in the Aosta valleys. Though no names were given, Aldo knew that Vanda was implicated as a quantity of 'pounds sterling' – the bulletin stated – had been found on one of the arrested. Aldo had recently given his sister some English cash. What to do? Under a false name he went to visit Vanda in the 'Cesare Battisti' barracks. Hoping that Vanda would not give the game away, he pre-emptively addressed her: 'Good morning, Signorina, I come from your brother.' Aldo found matters more simple, but more terrible, than he had dreamed: his sister was to be transferred to a concentration camp. Vanda's health had been seriously affected since her confinement; shattered by fatigue, malnutrition and diarrhoea, she had grown much thinner. For an hour the siblings spoke in the corridor in the presence of a prison warden: nothing could be done to release Vanda.

Anna Maria Levi was in Turin the day her brother was arrested. She contacted Ada Gobetti, the widow of the legendary anti-Fascist activist Piero Gobetti, who might be able to secure Primo's release. The Nazi-Fascists never suspected Ada's Turin address – the now-famous 6 Via Fabro – as an Action Party nerve centre. From here this courageous woman ran a network of safe homes for anti-Fascists in need of refuge. She offered Anna Maria comfort and a bed; yet her brother's rescue seemed impossible. Contemplating Primo's likely death, Anna Maria became a fiercely motivated partisan, smuggling clandestine literature past German blockades.

Ada Della Torre, Levi's cousin, was at the Olivetti headquarters in Ivrea when she heard of the round-ups. Losing no time she contacted her fiancé, Silvio Ortona, who was in nearby Biella with a Garibaldi partisan brigade. Ortona was not much help; his suggestion was to kidnap a local Fascist dignitary to offer in exchange for Levi. Nothing came of the plan.

When Luciana Nissim's teenage sister, Dindi, tried to visit her sibling in the Aosta barracks she was shouted at by Centurion Ferro: 'Get out of here!' By rights, Ferro should have arrested Dindi as a Jew and found out where her parents were hiding. But he was protecting Luciana, whom he liked; on the lorry to Aosta from Brusson he had advised her to lie about the anti-Fascist propaganda he had confiscated from her in the Albergo Ristoro. 'Just say they're pharmaceutical leaflets.' Later, in an amorous outburst, Ferro asked Nissim to elope with him from the barracks. 'With a Fascist? Never!' Nissim did not hear until after the war the distressing news that Ferro had been executed by partisans.

On 17 January 1944, day thirty-six of their captivity, Levi, Maestro and Nissim were transferred to a smaller barracks, 'The Mottina', adjacent to the main Aosta caserne. Here they were held for three days prior to their transfer to Fossoli. All the prisoners were Jews: for the first time in his life Levi was physically segregated from 'Aryan' society. It was here that Nissim first learned of the Nazi exterminations. A group of Yugoslav women told her how Jews in Occupied Croatia had been asphyxiated in closed vans with carbon monoxide. Nissim recalled that neither she nor Levi was alarmed by the news: 'Unable to believe the atrocity, we shrugged it off as far-fetched.' Among the jailed Yugoslavs were Slava and Gugliemo Lausch, and their thirty-year-old daughter Olga; all were to be gassed.

After their three-day sequestration in 'The Mottina', on 20 January Levi and his companions were handed over to the *carabinieri*, who showed them every courtesy. The police accompanied them to an ordinary third-class Pullman train waiting at Aosta station for the long journey east to Fossoli. By the afternoon, when the transport arrived at Chivasso, a few kilometres outside Turin, the sky was overcast and stormy: away in the January sunset Levi could make out the knitting-needle spire of Antonelli's failed synagogue. The sight tugged nostalgically at his heart: 'That was the moment I said goodbye to my past for ever.' From Chivasso it was another 400 kilometres to Fossoli. Several times when the transport slowed down, Levi and Nissim thought of jumping off: all that stood between them and freedom was a flimsy grille. But they could not abandon Vanda, who was now emotionally and physically very fragile. Nissim explained this decision to me: 'Under the Nazis it would be different. Where we were destined the Good Samaritan ethic had no place: down there, pity for the downtrodden *did not exist*. But on that train we were still human and, it seemed to us, free: so we couldn't leave Vanda.'

4

Fossoli is a nondescript village at the heart of Italy's prosperous Modena province; in 1944 it was the main Nazi-Fascist internment camp for Jews. For German purposes, Fossoli was ideally placed for the railroads north through the Brenner Pass to the killing fields of Poland. The nearest town is Carpi, a Renaissance treasure in uneasy proximity then to the barbed wire five kilometres away. In 1955 a memorial was erected in Fossoli to the deported prisoners, but today the blockhouses are vandalised and abandoned, with detritus dropped among the collapsed masonry. Originally the Fascists had built the camp to hold Allied soldiers captured in North Africa; by the time Levi arrived most of the British and New Zealand POWs had been deported to Germany for forced labour, so Fossoli was now to be a holding camp for Jews. It was to remain in operation until July 1944. One of the last Jews to be deported from there was Franz Kafka's German lover Margarethe ('Grete') Bloch; having escaped to Italy in 1938 from Berlin, she had hoped that Mussolini's anti-Semitism would continue chaotically *all'italiana*. Fraulein Bloch perished in Auschwitz.

The Jewish prisoners were overwhelmingly Italian; arrested in the occupied zones, they had been transferred to Fossoli from the city jails of Milan or Turin. Initially eight of the camp's twenty-eight barracks were set aside for Jews. During Levi's internment, however, that number was to increase dramatically as the Nazi round-ups intensified. The remaining barracks housed Italian political prisoners and common criminals. Signs proclaiming a 'DANGEROUS ZONE' reminded locals that Fossoli was heavily guarded. Officially the camp was run by Italians; in reality it was a German collection-point from which Jews were shunted to their death.

Fossoli's superintendent, Commissar Domenico Avitabile, was a Naples-born ex-policeman on good terms with his prisoners. His outwardly warm manner helped to reassure them of their safety. Vanda Maestro was happy to be here after her month and a half of solitary confinement in Aosta. The camp's few remaining British POWs and Gentile Yugoslavs were an amiable distraction for her, she said. Vanda quickly regained weight and was content to start smoking again. In the evenings she played cards and read books. Levi's attraction to her seems to have been reciprocated, though not physically, and the affair began to flourish. On 4 February she wrote the first of several postcards to her Jewish cousin Nella 'Benedetto' (real surname: De Benedetti) in Milan:

> Dearest Nella,
>   The atmosphere here is *really* good . . . The Jewish company is most dull; the Aryan, excellent. If you do send me a parcel, I'd like if possible to have a pair (or two) of shoes and a couple of dresses. Old ones, that is, that you don't wear any more – they'd fit me nicely now that I've put on weight. Also, a towel and a table cloth . . . You absolutely mustn't worry about me. I've waited over a month to come here and I can assure you that I breathed a great sigh of relief on arrival. If you see Anna Maria (she's Primo's sister), tell her to write to me and that Primo is well . . . Urgent request: good toilet and laundry soap!

Visits were allowed. Under a false name, Vanda's brother Aldo was able to pass his sister smart new walking boots through the electrified fence. He never saw her again.

Though Commissar Avitabile was a corrupted and dubious personality, his willingness to bend the rules made the camp 'strangely human', recalled Nissim. 'For as long as I'm here,' he told the Jews in his care, 'you'll be all right.' If they had money, prisoners could obtain cigarettes or writing paper from him. In return for sexual favours some Jewish girls in his custody were allowed to visit the dentist or public baths in Carpi; a few even got their hair set in Modena further afield. Levi became so fond of Avitabile that after the war he tried to meet him again, unsuccessfully.

Each of the eight Jewish barracks was encouraged to appoint a spokesman – a *capobaracca* – to ensure that newcomers were welcomed and put at ease. Luciana Nissim was elected to represent her female barracks and she comforted the worried mothers and distressed children under her care. During daylight hours, men and women were not segregated; families had their own private quarters where they could stow belongings. Each internee was given a daily ration of pasta, rice, oil and lard, to be eaten communally in a large central hall. Money was pooled to buy extra food for the needy: wealthier inmates bought delicacies from the vendors who visited daily from Carpi. The neighbourly spirit was enhanced in many other ways. When Avitabile challenged a 'robust young friend' of Levi's to a boxing match, the encounter was billed as a 'friendly sporting event' and not the public humiliation it might have been under the SS. A school was set up with makeshift desks and report cards. Inmates could write to friends with special requests: Luciana Nissim was glad to see a suitcase arrive full of the clothes she had asked for and other necessities.

Prisoners tried to maintain a semblance of normality. Surrounded by family and friends, relationships carried on as usual. Nissim even sat her state medical finals within the camp (answering her exam questions by correspondence), while Levi wrote several cards (now lost) to his old physics professor Nicolò Dallaporta. Though the dormitories were heated, the winter of 1944 was unusually mild. Thus Vanda was able to write to her cousin Nella in Milan: 'There have been very few uncomfortable moments.' Avitabile's seeming agreeableness, and the easygoing atmosphere of his barracks, was a trap. Indeed, Fossoli was a microcosm of Fascist policy towards Italian Jews up to the Occupation, who had been lulled into a false security by Mussolini. The Duce had not been consistent in his discrimination against them; until the last moment they hoped for a reprieve, and now it was too late for them to leave.

Many of the Jews in Fossoli had been arrested as they tried to cross the hazardous mountain passes into Switzerland. A Turin doctor, Leonardo De Benedetti, had reached the camp with his wife Jolanda a month before Levi. Accompanied by relatives and a group of Yugoslav refugees, the De

Benedettis had set out from Milan one day in early December to reach the Swiss frontier high above Lake Lugano. 'We cut through the wires and descended into the woods,' recalled one of the party, Simone Fubini, who was thirteen at the time. 'It was terrible. Leonardo's mother was paralysed from the shoulders down and clearly dying.' The Swiss guards were in no mood for compassion. They declared that only refugees over the age of sixty-five, pregnant women, the sick and parents with children under twelve were to be allowed into neutral Switzerland. The rest were shown the path back to Occupied Italy. In later years Leonardo De Benedetti wished he had lied to the Swiss that his wife Jolanda was pregnant. Instead, he was forced to leave his mother, Fortunata De Benedetti, in Switzerland (in her eighties, she would never see her son again), while he and Jolanda returned to Italy. They had scarcely unpacked their bags in a hotel in Lanzo d'Intelvi when they were arrested by Italian Fascists.

Leonardo De Benedetti, in his forties, was a reserved and studious man with a dry sense of humour. His wife Jolanda came from a wealthy landed family near Turin and was distantly related to the first Italian Jew to achieve eminence in public affairs, Isaac Artom. Her parents had named her after Duchess Jolanda of Savoy, who had famously allowed Jews to dwell *ubi voluerint*: 'where they wanted'. Letters sent by the De Benedettis from Fossoli have survived. In faded red-brown ink they give a poignant picture of life in the camp and its myriad deceptions. Most of the correspondence was sent to a hotel in Alessandria province (Piedmont) where Jolanda's younger sister Elsa was hiding with her baby son. Occasionally, as an extra precaution, Jolanda used Hebrew code (*manordi* for 'money') to communicate more urgent needs; in this way she was sent cash, precious knitwear, fresh linen, tins of food.

A refined woman, Jolanda strove to maintain her dignity and sense of purpose in the camp. 'We've almost got used to this very simple life. Whenever possible we try to help each other. Everything is just fine. For the moment we don't want for anything.' In a hot and steaming kitchen she daily doled out meals to sixty inmates, while her doctor husband Leonardo swept the barracks and gathered firewood. To a trusted Catholic go-between, Signor Alocco, Leonardo wrote: 'There's no shortage of good company here and the days go by quickly and serenely enough.' The neighbourliness and intimacy of the camp only contributed to the false sense of security.

Friendships and family were the lifeblood of the camp. Early in her captivity Jolanda had met two Venetians who turned out to be first cousins (by marriage) to her aunt. The encounter so cheered her that she was able to write again to her sister: 'We don't feel lonely here. Almost everyone is a friend or knows some relative of ours.' Primo Levi was able to renew his acquaintance with Franco Sacerdoti, a young Neapolitan who had moved to Turin from Naples shortly after the racial laws in 1938. Franco had worked in Turin in his uncle's textile business and had met Levi briefly during the Jewish forced-labour scheme of 1942. Sacerdoti's story was as poignant as those of all the Jews in Fossoli. No one knows for sure how he was arrested. Today, relatives say he had ventured out of hiding to fetch his wife Nucci's fur coat from Turin, where the SS were waiting for him on a tip-off. His ten siblings, safely ensconced in Allied Naples, only learned of Franco's fate after the war. He had just got married in the previous year of 1942, and there is a photograph of him on honeymoon with his sixteen-year-old bride Nucci Treves; he is stylishly dressed in a fedora and turn-ups, Nucci in a floral dress and veiled *chapeau*. Now Franco was behind barbed wire; he did not dare write and tell Nucci.

The presence in the camp of so many children persuaded the Jews that their imprisonment could only be benign. Most Jews hoped they would remain imprisoned here for the duration of the war, assuming there was an Allied victory. It was not such a bad place: beyond the electric fences and observation towers stretched picturesque farmland and rice fields. Jolanda loved to play with five-year-old Emilia Levi, whose family had apparently been betrayed at the Swiss frontier. The child's happiness at Fossoli encouraged Jolanda to report to her sister Elsa that everything was going to be all right. There was really 'no reason to worry at all'.

5

Outwardly Commissar Avitabile's may have been a benign regime, but this was a concentration camp that gathered Jews fleeing Nazi-controlled areas of Europe. By early February – two weeks into Primo Levi's imprisonment – almost a quarter of the Jews at Fossoli were foreign. Some had come from as far afield as Tripoli in Fascist-conquered Libya. Ill-prepared for the Italian winter they shivered in their light clothes. German, Austrian or Yugoslav refugees, separated from their homes for as long as three, even four years, still wore the clothes they had been arrested in; they were unable to obtain linen or toiletries, and spoke almost no Italian. To the wealthier Italian Jews these transients presented a frightening image of desperation and abandonment. They were a warning of what lay ahead.

Throughout February the transports continued to arrive, so many that the camp could not physically hold them all. Barracks designed to house a maximum of 100 prisoners were soon crowded with twice that number. Anxiety began to spread among the inmates. In theory the Italian police controlled the camp, as Domenico Avitabile was answerable to the Fascist prefecture at Modena, and not the German SS. Yet Avitabile's orders regarding the Jews in his care were not very clear. If he was not directly complicit in the Nazi round-ups, he must have known that Fossoli would at some stage have to be emptied. From 1 February the camp had been designated in Nazi files as a *Polizei- und Durchgangslager* – a 'Police and Transit Camp'. That meant the Jews were in a halfway house to death.

In the early hours of 17 February 1944 a young Sarajevo mathematician, Silvio Barabas, arrived at Fossoli with yet another consignment of Jews. He was taken to Commissar Avitabile's office, where he was registered along with the new arrivals. The mood was friendly enough, and Avitabile greeted Barabas light-heartedly: 'Welcome to Fossoli, though I can't say I'm happy to see you here.' But then the camp's new German commander entered the room and Avitabile froze, his manner visibly altered. SS Sergeant Major Hans Haage politely stood to one side to watch the proceedings; as the prisoners progressed down the line Barabas heard a Jewish woman plead with Avitabile that she was half 'Aryan'. At this the German loudly interjected: 'It is not enough to *say* your mother is Aryan! You must *prove* it to me!' To Barabas and the other Jews it was now clear who was in charge.

Word of an imminent German takeover had percolated through Fossoli for days, and Vanda Maestro's letters of this time take on a darker tone. One of them, addressed as usual to her cousin Nella in Milan, is dated 15 February:

> Dearest Nella,
>   Maybe I've chosen a bad moment to write to you as my mood is getting worse. My loved ones are so far away and who knows if I shall ever see them again? The thought saddens me terribly. I dream of them constantly and they are always in my heart. What little news I have is always bad . . . I beg you not to think ill of me. I can't see how I'll give you much trouble in the future.

Vanda's earlier letters had been full of optimism; but as the stress and uncertainty of imprisonment took their toll, so her equilibrium disintegrated.

On 20 February, after four weeks at Fossoli, Levi saw his first Germans. Four or five SS were touring the camp on an inspection. One of them was heard to comment in poor Italian: '*Campo grande, legno niente!*', 'Big camp, no wood!' Levi took this to mean that extra firewood was to be allocated to the Jews. As the SS continued their inspection, Commissar Avitabile was loudly upbraided for the lamentable state of his kitchens and lack of medical supplies. All this was bluster: under German command, conditions in the camp deteriorated medievally. SS Haage was a '*Scheinmännisch*', a 'pseudo human being', Levi recalled, and with his arrival at Fossoli the school was closed down, families could no longer stay together and letters were intercepted. Avitabile, that soft touch, was effectively ousted from the camp's management. The new regime was instituted on the orders of Friedrich Bosshammer, SS chief of Jewish operations in Italy. A former lawyer from Wuppertal in Rhineland-Westphalia, Bosshammer's instructions were always precise. Based in his grand SS headquarters in Verona, he was one of the so-called *Schreibtischtäter* – the 'desk-murderers' – who condemned thousands to death at the stroke of a pen.

During these winter months of 1944 Bosshammer tightened his control over the Jews of northern Italy. When Levi had first arrived at Fossoli on 20 January the camp had held no more than 200 Jews. By early February that estimate had risen so steeply that a group of newcomers were forced to sleep on the floor. Ideally, if a transport was to be 'economically viable', it had to contain up to 1,000 Jews. Thus by mid-February Fossoli's initial figure of 200 Jewish internees had swollen to 700. Wasting no time, Bosshammer ordered SS Haage to prepare him a Fossoli *Transportliste* and send it to him marked 'urgent'. Today no trace remains of the collusion between the Italian State Railways and the SS, but Haage must have negotiated with Italy's rail chiefs to supply the correct number of freight cars for the imminent deportation. In turn, Fascist administration had to ensure that the level crossings, the shuntings and signals were all in good working order right up to the Austrian frontier.

6

On the morning of 21 February SS Haage announced to the prisoners that they would be leaving early the next morning for 'Reich territories'. He had given them as little time as possible to panic or plan an escape. The deportees were recommended to pack pullovers, blankets and fur coats for a cold destination. This advice was given in an impartial, even friendly way ('with a wink', recalled Leonardo De Benedetti). Prisoners should also take with them money or jewellery as this could prove 'useful' where they were being sent 'for work'. To the Jews formerly under his control, Commissar Avitabile could only repeat the lie that they were going to work in Germany. 'None of us ever thought that we were all, or most of us, going to die,' recalled an Italian prisoner, Dr Aldo Moscati. On the night of the 21st the camp's external guard was fortified and discipline stepped up: for every Jew who tried to escape it was announced that ten would be shot.

As news leaked out of the imminent deportation, friends and family tried to make contact with the internees one last time. A Catholic relative of Franco Sacerdoti, Ala Manerba, cycled fifty kilometres through the fog with provisions. Amelia Foà, sister of the detained Jewish poet Arturo Foà, made her way to the camp under an 'Aryan' alias carrying foodstuffs. Vanda Maestro dashed off a final letter to Milan:

> Dearest Nella,
>
> I haven't heard anything from you, so I'm anxious. Maybe some of your letters have got lost; if you had written something important, please repeat it to me. Should you send me a parcel please include a good supply of that calmative which Aunt Ida used to take (you can insert it in 2 tubes of *Veramon*). It's quite hard to find but I'd be so eternally grateful to you . . . There's really nothing more to say.

The calmative was actually a barbiturate with which Vanda's aunt had chosen to end her life after a horrific road accident. The drug could be disguised inside an innocuous *Veramon* aspirin container. Vanda never got the barbiturates; her last letter cleared the camp censors on 23 February, by which time she was in a cattle-wagon.

As the sun went down over Fossoli on 21 February, fear spread through the camp. A murmuring of psalms and a lamentation sounded as women washed their children's clothes and hung them up to dry. Guido Dalla Volta, a fifty-year-old pharmaceutics entrepreneur and *capobaracca*, was still dressed in his pinstripe businessman's suit. He summoned the prisoners in his care. 'Maybe as barracks-chief it should be my task to tell you something encouraging, but I wish to be frank with you: I have no hope.' At least four prisoners had their birthdays on this awful day. Born in Genoa on 21 February 1894, Arturo Valabrega had been captured at the Swiss–Italian frontier. Emma Vitta had been arrested by Fascist police in her native Venice, where she had been born exactly fifty-seven years before. Alberto Riccardo Spitz, taken on the shores of Lake Como, should also have been celebrating his fifty-seventh birthday. Eloisa Ravà, aged sixty-six that day, had been born nearby in Modena. Like the other three prisoners, she had just five days to live.

Aldo Moscati, the Jewish doctor, recalled a moaning that night of 'hopelessness' and of something animal. 'The barriers which women normally place before men fell away. Anything was possible between people now.' Luciana Nissim slept in the arms of Franco Sacerdoti, who was married. Franco was a 'beautiful man', she remembered, with blue eyes and a gentle manner. Though Nissim was herself engaged to marry another Franco (the Action Party activist Franco Momigliano), she was attracted to the tall Neapolitan. In many ways theirs was an unlikely affair – the apprentice tailor from Naples, the middle-class medical student from Turin – but Franco's uncomplicated generosity pleased Luciana rather better than the pretensions of her own circle. Afterwards, Nissim preferred not to speak of the deportation; some things she has never revealed until now. 'I've not said this before,' she told me in 1992, 'but that February 21st there were other intimacies. I mean Primo loved Vanda that night.' She added that Levi loved Vanda far more than Vanda loved him. There was no sexual intercourse, but Nissim insisted: 'Primo *loved* Vanda that night at Fossoli.' It is hardly surprising that that winter night would later mean so much to Levi. Fear of impending death intensified his intimacy with Vanda; in the face of the unknown, they found solace in each other's company. Today in Turin many claim that Vanda was Levi's *fidanzata* – 'fiancée' – and amorously entangled with him. Nobody in Fossoli wanted to spend that night alone, and they clung to partners or even strangers for comfort.

To ensure that SS Haage's transport met the required quota of Jews, raids had been conducted on Jewish nursing homes. At least eighty of those on the *Transportliste* came from the Venice old people's home, which had been emptied two months earlier in December 1943; Anna Jona, eighty-nine, was among the Venetians. Two ninety-year-old women had to be carried out of the Fossoli infirmary moribund; an old man had been stricken by a cerebral haemorrhage. The other deportees might have wondered how the old and ill could reasonably 'work' in Reich territories. But to SS Haage those old men and women were part of a despicable foe – Jews – and deserved to die. At barely two months, baby Leo Mariani was perhaps the youngest on SS Haage's list. He had been born in a Venice schoolroom where his mother was detained with other Jews. It was especially imperative that Jewish babies be eliminated, as they were potential future enemies of the millennial Reich. At least thirty-one of the deportees on the *Transportliste* were aged thirteen and under.

As the Nazi arrests continued throughout February, more East European Jews arrived at Fossoli. Moshe Liko Israel, thirty-two, had fought in the partisan war in Occupied Croatia and perhaps knew what 'departure' meant. At least thirty deportees had family roots in the Levant, predominantly

Salonika. Salonika had been the Greek capital of Sephardic Jewry for five centuries, but in the space of a few months in 1943 the Nazis had destroyed it. Moise Saltiel and his fifty-nine-year-old wife Olga may have fled Nazi-controlled Salonika across the Aegean Sea to the safety of neutral Turkey, and thence to Milan. Now they were awaiting deportation from Fossoli, soon to increase the figure of 37,386 Salonikan Jews already gassed.

7

On Tuesday 22 February, in the cold dawn mist, the loudspeakers barked instructions for the prisoners to assemble on the barracks-square for roll-call. With their packed belongings, they jostled into rows of two. Machine-guns were trained on them. 'We felt sordid and defiled from the night before,' recalled Aldo Moscati, 'what had we done wrong?' It took over an hour to call out each of the deportees' names. Clutching an adult's hand or arm, the children answered as distinctly as they could. At least thirty-seven Levis were called: uncles, aunts, cousins. When the roll call was complete, an SS corporal strode up to Sergeant Major Haage to report to him: '*Sechshundert und fünfzig Stück*', 'Six hundred and fifty pieces'. Levi's precise recollection of this figure is the only proof we have that 650 Jews were ever on that Fossoli transport. Only 489 of this human merchandise – 'pieces' – have ever been identified by name or nationality. The rest are officially classed as 'persons unknown' and have vanished without trace: nobody knows who they were, or where they came from.*

At gun-point the deportees loaded their possessions on to buses waiting at the perimeter fence. Escorted by policemen on motorcycles, a ten-minute journey took them to Carpi station; Levi's bus was among the first to leave Fossoli, reaching the railway platform a little after 10:00 am. An SS ordered him up on to the roof of the bus to pass down luggage. At first Levi did not understand, and was viciously hit by the guard, who repeated the order. Failure to understand German was dangerous.

Twelve cattle-wagons, with an escort car for the SS, were waiting at the station. The freight-doors had been left open and the floors were covered

*According to Liliana Picciotto Fargion's vital record, *Il libro della memoria: Gli ebrei deportati dall'Italia (1943–1945)*, of the 489 Jews accountable on Primo Levi's transport, an estimated 296 entered the various camps of Auschwitz alive. (That is, 151 men and 145 women.) The rest of the transport, a total of 193, were gassed immediately. Most of the 296 Jews who survived the first selection subsequently died through exhaustion and hunger. In all, only sixteen men and eight women that we know of returned alive to Italy: twenty-four Italian survivors.

with straw. The initials RSHA – 'Head Office for Reich Security of the SS' – were stencilled on each boxcar. As the buses continued to ferry the deportees in shifts from Fossoli to Carpi station, the numbers on the platform swelled. The potential for chaos in the growing crowd encouraged the SS to become increasingly violent. SS Haage's insistence that prisoners board the freight-cars alphabetically must only have aggravated the tension. Friends and relatives, fearing they would be separated, struggled to stay close to each other; children gave way to terror as, harassed by attack dogs, they ran along the platform in search of their parents. Levi was hit with a rifle butt and kicked; one of his companions was slammed against a cattle-truck, leaving a gash on his forehead. SS Haage's inexperience in 'transport organisation' presumably was to blame for these unusual scenes of chaos. No future convoy would attempt to leave Fossoli in alphabetical order.

One of the Italian police, visibly shaken by the spectacle of prayer and despair the night before, exchanged a few awkward words with Levi on the platform. Levi told him angrily: 'Remember what you've seen. And remember that you're complicit in this, and will bear the consequences.' Ashamed, the policeman walked off to obtain Levi some water from the platform's drinking fountain. 'But what can I do?' he came back. To which Levi replied with scorn: 'Become a thief – it's a lot more honest.' (This memory only returned to Levi in the mid-1980s shortly before he died.)

By 2:00 pm, four long hours after Levi had reached Carpi station, the twelve freight-cars were full. SS guards closed the doors and secured them from the outside. In darkness the deportees waited for the engine to start. They were to wait an unconscionable time. Despite the directives for alphabetical order, Primo Levi, Vanda Maestro, Luciana Nissim and Franco Sacerdoti had managed to stay together. The boxcar was wretchedly overcrowded with forty-five people. Out of the wagon's tiny high window someone saw a white board affixed to the train's far side with the destination: AUSCHWITZ. Even the Polish deportees were unlikely to know that 'Auschwitz' was German for the small Polish town of 'Oswiecim'. Israel Gruenbaum had been born sixty-one years ago in Oswiecim; now he was about to make a final and fatal journey back to his birthplace. Many of the Italians assumed that their destination was Austerlitz. 'So we're off to Bohemia.'

After an agonising eight-hour delay, at 6:00 pm the train inched out of the station. It stopped just outside Modena for another long wait, and did not move again for several hours. Outside it was misty and cold. A few isolated snowflakes (recalled Nissim) were floating down. Finally the train set off; the Italian engine driver, the only non-German member of the transport staff, maintained the convoy at a creeping 50km/h.

*

Later that Tuesday 22 February, some time after 6:00 pm, Ala Manerba arrived at Fossoli to find the camp empty. Franco Sacerdoti, her Neapolitan Jewish relative, had boarded the cattle-trucks just hours before. The few remaining prisoners were Libyan Jews marked for Bergen-Belsen and a handful of others designated 'half-Aryans': in all, seventy-four internees. The Jews of mixed race were to stay behind to work as camp administrators, and to prepare for future deportations. Amelia Foà, sister of the Piedmontese poet Arturo Foà, also returned home disappointed. News of Jolanda and Leonardo De Benedettis' deportation reached relatives two weeks later. The Catholic well-wisher, Signor Alocco, wrote to Jolanda's sister Elsa in Alessandria of their fate: 'Sadly I have to inform you of their removal to an unknown place which we understand to be very far away.' A subsequent communication from Alocco, dated 11 March 1944, added that Jolanda was bound to send her news, though the 'prospects are far from rosy.' By then Jolanda had been gassed.

8

From the start the cattle-trucks were fetid and soon the stench from the packed bodies was unbearable. 'If there was any solidarity on our transport,' Luciana Nissim recalled, 'it was between families: otherwise prisoners bickered interminably and fought to conquer a few extra centimetres of space.' The warmth and generosity that prisoners had shown each other hours earlier at Fossoli vanished. Nobody was going to make way for an old woman or baby now. The fundamental law of the Nazi camp – take care of yourself first – had set in. There was so much luggage – blankets, boxes, bags – that people could not stretch out their legs to sleep. *Take with you everything for a cold climate.* So SS Haage had advised. Levi sat crammed against Aurelio Peccei's valise; Vanda and Luciana had left most of their belongings behind at the camp. 'We were pretty certain we would die,' recalled Nissim, 'but the others in the cattle-truck, no.' Under a shared blanket Nissim lay next to Franco Sacerdoti. 'Without that *dolcezza* – sweetness – between us, the journey would have been far more brutal.' Though Nissim felt guilty about her fiancé in Turin, the need for human contact was overriding. Vanda Maestro sat pressed against Levi. In the shadows of the twelve freight-cars the elderly already resembled corpses. Anna Jona lay lifeless in her daughter Angiolina's arms. Leo Mariani, the two-month-old baby, cried inconsolably because his mother's milk had run dry. His screaming aggravated the tension inside the boxcar and the prisoners longed for the baby to shut up or die. It was just as the Nazis intended; these Jews should suffer a slow torture by thirst and attrition.

162

'Thirst was our first tormenting pain,' Levi remembered. At a station further down the line, deportees in an adjacent boxcar pleaded for water, but an SS soldier shot at them through the wooden freight-doors. Almost none of the prisoners had thought to bring water: water costs nothing, and it was naively assumed that the Germans would not stint in supplying it. For five days the captives fought to scrape the morning frost from the bolts that infiltrated the cracks of the freight-doors. With the temperature below zero, tongues were seared on to the frozen metal.

As for bodily needs, men and women had to crouch in front of each other, with no extra straw to cover the mess. It had not occurred to the former barracks-chief Guido Dalla Volta to enquire after sanitary facilities. Now he stood wretchedly in a corner of the cattle-truck with his son Alberto. The Fascist poet Arturo Foà, his Napoleon III beard still elegantly trimmed, stared dejectedly out of the darkness. The deportees regarded him with distaste and suspicion. He had the unfortunate reputation of the *mal occhio* – 'the evil-eye' – and Levi's family used to make the sign of the devil's horns when his name was mentioned. Arrested in Turin on 4 February 1944, the sixty-year-old Foà had tried to form a band of Fascist faithful in Fossoli; to the end, he clung to his belief that Mussolini was a good man. Today he is remembered (if at all) as a minor Italian littérateur, whose work Gramsci had famously dismissed as sub-pornographic 'marzipan'. In the 1900s his purple verse had been the toast of Piedmontese salons; he had even presented Mussolini with a signed copy of his *belle époque* rapture to eastern mysticism, *From the Ganges to the Po*. But Foà did not survive the journey, and today his relatives in Turin believe he was beaten to death in the boxcar. Forty years later, during an interview, Levi was seen to weep at Foà's memory; he never verified whether the poet had been killed in the transport.

One of the mothers had brought along a baby's potty, which it was agreed would be used by all the deportees in Levi's cattle-truck, the defecation thrown out of the freight-car's high barred window. The sense of lost human dignity – *Entwürdigung* – would be far worse where the prisoners were destined. The train ground on past Trento into the Alto Adige, where Levi had spent a Zionist skiing holiday in 1940. Through a crack in the boxcar he saw Italians on bicycles, in the sunshine and snow. Sometimes the civilians stopped to watch the train pass by with its unknown awful cargo. Luciana Nissim recollected: 'We were already, at this point, *outside* life. Normal existence – cars, fields, farms – seemed another country to us. It's like when you're condemned with cancer. *Inside* you're dying, but *outside*, life goes on. It was very galling for us to see those free people going about their ordinary lives. On the plains near Padua we saw girls on bicycles. The world outside the train was *there* – but it was not for us.'

As the convoy slowed down Levi shouted angrily from behind the sealed doors: 'This train! It's full of babies. There's a load of women, sick, old. *These* are the people the Nazis are deporting!' At Bolzano, close to the Austrian frontier, as the train slowed down again, Levi managed to push a note through the barred window. Addressed to his Catholic friend Bianca Guidetti Serra, it bore no stamp and had little chance of reaching her in Turin. On a folded piece of paper Levi wrote in large letters the hopeful Fascist slogan, 'WE WILL OVERCOME': he knew the post was more likely to arrive that way; and, alongside it, the words, 'PLEASE POST'. Dated 23 February, day two of the journey, it commented:

> Dear Bianca, we're all travelling in the classic style. Give our regards to everyone. Long may you carry the flame. So long, Bianca – we wish you well. Primo, Vanda, Luciana.

Incredibly, Bianca got the message. Other notes were pushed through the grilled window. Nissim addressed hers to a Protestant doctor friend, Franco Operti, in Turin. A railwayman must have found Nissim's piece of paper, copied her note in his own hand and sent it on to Operti:

> Bolzano 23–2–44
> Luciana wishes to let you know that she is being transferred to Germany with Vanda and Primo and 500 others – Let others know this.

By an extraordinary coincidence the note reached Operti in the Turin hospital where he had just operated on Nissim's fiancé Franco Momigliano (who had sustained a fractured leg after leaping from a balcony while fleeing Fascist arrest.) Levi's sister Anna Maria also happened to be at Franco's bedside when the note arrived. Its bleak message – Levi was being '*tradotta in Germania*' – 'transferred to the Greater German Reich' – was the first Anna Maria knew of her brother's fate. Once the train had crossed the Austrian frontier, however, Levi had effectively vanished from his loved ones: those messages were the last confirmation she had that he was alive.

Once a day, far from civilian witnesses, the convoy stopped in open countryside. From each freight-car the SS selected three prisoners to fetch bread, beet marmalade and salted cheese from the provisions van. No water was distributed. The deportees were allowed to descend to eat. The chaos and fear at the start of the journey returned each time the doors were closed after food-distribution, when the prisoners struggled once more to stay with their friends and families. Some managed to eat snow from the rails to slake their thirst; others squatted shame-faced by the track under the disgusted gaze of the SS, who took photographs of those passengers with their clothes lowered.

By day two of the journey, 23 February, a crude cubicle had been improvised in Levi's boxcar with nails, string and a blanket. The gesture was symbolic: we are not animals yet. The train moved on through the Brenner Pass and climbed steadily towards Innsbruck, where the Italian engine driver was replaced by a German one. Usually Nazi policy was to keep corpses on the convoys, as there had to be a precise body-count at the journey's end. However, a concession was made for the seventy-six-year-old Signor Max, chairman of the Italian tinned-food company Max & Vitale. At Vienna the SS pulled Max's corpse out of the boxcar and dumped it on the platform. Herr Max had been born in Vienna: let him go home there. In another cattle-truck the sisters Marianna and Regina Jona, aged sixty-eight and sixty-seven respectively, were also dead. At Vienna, for the first and last time, the deportees were given a little water.

By Friday 25 February, day four of the journey, the train had reached Czechoslovakia. Oak and linden forests lay under snow: this was the wintry landscape of Schubert's *Winterreise*. At dusk that Friday the Jews crossed their last frontier into Poland. Dark winter fields showed pastoral scenes: a horse pulling a plough, boats moored on the ice-fringed Wista. The Jewish Sabbath had begun. Saturday 26 February, the next day, would be the thirteenth birthday of one of the deportees, and should have been his Bar Mitzvah. Born on 26 February 1931 in Dresden in East Germany, Wolfgang Hochberger would not be going home. By now everything in the boxcar was sticky with marmalade: hands, blankets, luggage. One last halt in open country at nightfall, then the locomotive started again, rolling at a walking pace.

At some time between 9:00 pm and 10:30 pm, on Saturday 26 February, after a journey of five days and five nights, the train stopped. Through the grille Luciana Nissim saw lights and reflectors illuminating a vast barracks area encircled by barbed wire. This was Auschwitz civilian station. A few metres from the motionless train stood a line of waiting trucks, engines idling. Some were painted with a red cross; Nissim and Levi took courage: maybe it would not be so bad. Some children in the boxcar were asleep. Vanda, resting her head on Levi's shoulder, had cut her wrist with Piacenza's razor; blood seeped out under her ski jacket. Levi would say he was related to Vanda; Luciana and Franco would also claim to be relatives. The prisoners waited for something to happen.

After a silence rifles pounded against the freight-door and the SS

Death's-Heads were screaming, 'Everybody out!' Dobermanns on taut leashes barked as the doors opened. Strange faces cursed and clubbed the startled arrivals. 'Get out! Leave your baggage!' Blinded by the floodlights, the deportees tumbled down on to the ramp, stepping on each other, losing friends and family. Clothing, shaving brushes, children's toys spilled on to the platform. In minutes the boxcars were empty. A sickly odour hung in the air. Anna Jona and her daughter Angiolina, deceased, were deposited on top of their luggage. Nobody spoke; children clung to their parents. More dogs leaped at the arrivals, truncheons rained blows, officials hollered in unknown tongues. 'Get away from the train!' At a signal a dozen SS moved among the crowd to interrogate the Jews, now divided into two groups: men, and women and children. 'You, how old? Fit? Unfit?' In minutes the able-bodied were selected from those who were unable to work.

Huddled together, the men in Levi's group were appraised with a practised glance: the only criterion for survival now was an outward appearance of health. Levi consulted rapidly with an older Italian by his side, Paolo Levi of Padua. 'I'll say I'm fit for work,' but the Paduan had given up hope. 'Say what you like – it's all the same to me.' Healthy men aged between twenty and forty-five were put in one group; in the other, the condemned. Some healthy men, hoping to save themselves, told the SS: 'I'm not well.' And with these words they sealed their fate, carried off into the night with the old and economically useless Jews: the *Schmattes*, the 'rags'.

The separations proceeded frantically. All it took was a second to lose everything you possessed. Torn from her mother, five-year-old Mirna Grassini was goaded away with a dog whip. Leonardo De Benedetti reached out for his wife Jolanda, but an SS yanked her away; they would never see each other again. Parents had no time to say goodbye to their children, no time to caress their heads, because the guards kept yelling, 'Hurry! Hurry!' Vanda and Luciana found themselves wrenched from Primo and Franco.

The Nazi practice of extermination – *Vernichtungswissenschaft* – was now so refined that most of the condemned remained deceived until the door shut on them in the false shower rooms. In perhaps half an hour the Zyklon B crystals would suffocate the pregnant women, the babies, the old, the unfit. Luciana Nissim urged Vanda Maestro to go on a red cross lorry because of her bleeding wrist, but Vanda protested, 'We must stick together.' Her razor-wound was superficial but, if spotted, would have been enough to send her to the gas chamber. As instructed, the mothers and children, the elderly, climbed on to those deceiving red cross lorries. After the selections, the railway platform was swept clean. Soon there was no trace of the deportation, no abandoned luggage, nothing left at all of the transport that had left Fossoli five days earlier. Steam hissed from the cooling train; the work was done.

Primo Levi, with twenty-nine other men, was loaded on to a truck for a camp eight kilometres away. This time the journey lasted twenty minutes. A German guard politely enquired if anyone had watches, gold or jewellery to give him. Nervous laughter greeted his request: for Italian Jews, this show of venality came as a great surprise. At Fossoli the SS had been inflexible and cruel; perhaps here they were not so inhuman.

In a hut the men were ordered to undress. Clothing, letters, money, family photographs, anything that connected them to their past was to be surrendered. And take special care that your shoes are not stolen, an SS officer told them. '*Rubate?*' the Italians murmured in chorus. Stolen by whom? A sign above a single dripping tap warned in Gothic script '*WASSERTRINKEN VERBOTEN*'. Ignoring this, Levi bent his mouth to the tap but quickly spat out the foul, brackish water. Four Polish barbers in striped uniforms then entered. Beards, head and body hair fell away under the clippers and razors. Within a couple of hours all thirty deportees had been shaved entirely. Pushed now into an adjacent bath-house, the naked men were left for the remainder of the night standing in five centimetres of water. Beaten and naked, they were unrecognisable even to themselves. Silvio Barabas, the Sarajevo mathematician, described to me his shock at the sight of the former barracks-chief Guido Dalla Volta: 'He was unshaved with livid marks under his eyes from lack of sleep. I saw him looking at the other Italians in disbelief. And I felt such pain for him.'

Cold, exhausted and traumatised, the men could not even sit down to rest. They danced from foot to foot in the cold water. Levi could not suppress a feeling of disgust at the sight of the naked old men: 'Clothes are a mark of humanity,' he would later say. Everybody talked but no one listened. Engineer Aldo Levi of Milan kept asking after his wife and children. He was no longer a family man. Jolanda De Benedetti had also vanished into the crematoria; only her hair, perhaps, remained. Her husband Leonardo stood shivering in the bath-house.

At a camp 800 metres from Auschwitz civilian station, Vanda and Luciana were briskly tattooed on the left arm with a number. 'That was already a kind of death for us – the moment we first died,' Nissim commented later. The women's only possessions now were a handkerchief, a toothbrush, some cotton wool and a last piece of bread from the train. Fortunately Levi had taught Nissim the German words for 'I'm a doctor': doctors were the only valued professionals at Auschwitz (teachers and lawyers were worse than useless). In deference to Nissim's privileged status her head was cropped but not shaved; Vanda's hair was shorn entirely. Thus mutilated, the women had to select coarse jackets and trousers from a pile of ill-fitting clothes thrown on the floor in front of them. Vanda's new mountain boots – the ones her brother Aldo had brought to her at Fossoli – were quickly stolen by an old hand.

After five hours in the freezing bath-house, Levi was subjected to a Lysol disinfection. Then he was given a frayed and patched striped uniform. String or electric flex had to make do as a belt; mismatched clogs with wooden soles, the uppers made of cloth or a plastic material, provided 'discreet protection against the mud and cold', Levi remembered. These clogs were instruments of torture that chafed painfully and caused lesions. With his fair skin, Levi would bear the scars of prison-camp ulcers for the rest of his life. In Auschwitz the smallest wound to the foot could spell death through tetanus or septicaemia. His striped beret, also threadbare, was too big for his head. There was no jumper or vest. Underwear was often made from the Jewish prayer shawl (*tallit*), or from women's cast-offs.

Now Levi had no past and no present. He was a subhuman. A few centimetres above his left breast a red triangle superimposed on a yellow one created the Star of David; this same badge was stitched to his left trouser leg 'four fingers below the belt line', Levi specified later. In alphabetical order the prisoners were then electrically tattooed. Levi's identity was the blue-grey number punctured into his arm: *Häftling* – 'prisoner' – 174517. Tattooing is a sacrilege forbidden by Mosaic Law; this was another insult to Jewish observance. Stripped of his name, that cardinal sign of human uniqueness, Levi's former self was gone. The transformation had occurred in less than twenty-four hours from the Saturday of his arrival.

Until Sunday evening he remained in a vacant hut, every moment for him uncertain and more fearful. The Italian latecomers instinctively collected in a corner, against the walls, afraid of being caught unawares or beaten for nothing. Levi now had some dim notion of his whereabouts. He was in the *Judenlager* of Auschwitz IV, a hybrid death-and-labour camp containing between 10,000 and 12,000 Jews. Auschwitz was not a single *Lager* (camp); thirty-nine *Lagers* formed an entire malignant universe. The main camp at Auschwitz I was the administrative centre; Auschwitz II was the extermination centre of gassing chambers and crematory ovens (Birkenau); the satellite of Auschwitz III was familiarly known as Buna–Monovitz after its half-constructed synthetic-rubber ('Buna') plant and other fuel works; Levi's camp, Auschwitz IV, fed Buna–Monovitz with slave labour.

On their entry into Auschwitz IV, a census had been taken of able-bodied prisoners (age, profession, university), in which Levi had declared himself a chemist. Later this brought him advantages. For the next nine months, however, he was part of the anonymous mass of unskilled prisoners, the camp's *Lumpenproletariat*. Jews with a serviceable skill – plumbers, solderers, welders – could expect to live maybe a few months longer, before they too were eliminated from the labour process and ended up in the extermination centre of Auschwitz II.

As the sun set, Levi saw a mass of prisoners returning from the 'Buna' plant to their barrack huts. Lined up five by five, they shuffled in shambolic military step as a pyjama-dressed orchestra struck out 'Rosamunda'. This was a polka played in ballrooms across Europe, yet here it was played with quick precision like a macabre fairground waltz. Every morning and evening as the prisoners went to and from work, the Auschwitz orchestra played beerhall songs, melancholy *Lieder*, foxtrots, military-style waltzes, but mostly they played 'Rosamunda'. The Jews were a slave army, after all, 'and like any army they needed an orchestra to march them quickly and regularly to work', Levi commented later. In the prisoners' zebra-striped rags and broken bodies Levi must have seen a future image of himself. Later that Sunday he was assigned to Block 30, one of sixty wooden huts in the Auschwitz IV *Judenlager*; made of tarred wood, the huts were all alike and geometrically aligned in rows.

9

From the first day, labour was designed to exploit and then exterminate the slaves. Fresh batches of *Häftlinge* were constantly brought in to replace the gassed or dying prisoners. They were made to work at the murderous tempo known as the 'SS trot'. Each morning at 5:00 am came the harsh Polish reveille, '*Wstawàch!*' – 'Get up!' – followed by the Bed-Making Ritual. Levi's mattress had to be four-square and perfectly aligned, the blankets folded just so, his straw pillow dead-centre. Failure to do this resulted in a beating. The morning ration was a spoonful of margarine with a piece of salami, milk curd or marmalade. Then came the torture of morning roll call. If the head-count failed to tally precisely with the register-office numbers, the entire camp had to stand until the guilty party (often a corpse) was found. Atrocious pains ran down Levi's spine and legs as he tried not to fall down.

All hours of daylight were working hours: eight in winter, twelve in summer. In the driving sleet Levi shovelled earth and heaved sacks of hard-core. He shunted railway sleepers, shouldered iron pipes, crossbeams, rail tracks and girders. He dug telephone-cable trenches and dragged rails. He did every gruelling task necessary to build the *Buna-Werke* chemical products factory in Auschwitz III. The prisoners braced themselves under the weight until their hearts nearly burst; the *Kapo*, the overseer, beat them about the head with the handle of a shovel when they could not move forward. This place was designed to crush the human spirit and to humiliate. Newcomers were not provided with spoons, which had to be earned on the black market, and this was no trivial deprivation: without a spoon, prisoners had to lap the gruel like dogs, and eat with their hands.

The midday siren brought a brief respite as the prisoners queued for their single litre of watery potato gruel; Levi was always so hungry that the soup 'tasted good', even though it contained no nutritious fat or animal protein. The slavery resumed at 12:30 pm and in winter continued until dusk at 4:30 pm. Then the *Häftlinge* were marched back to their barracks in time to the brass band. A tortuous evening roll call was followed by a litre of soup made from Auschwitz turnips known as *Rutabaga* (Levi did not recognise them from Italy) and half a litre of sugarless coffee substitute. On Sundays, as a singular treat, ersatz sugar was added. The day's ordeal did not end there. Each evening Levi had to strip naked for *Läusekontrolle*, Lice Control: if just one prisoner was found to be lousy, he was beaten and everyone was sent for Lysol disinfection. Of course it was impossible for the camp to remain free of lice, especially with new prisoners entering constantly.

From his first day Levi was in constant dread of punishment. He feared beating (or, far worse, a denial of food) for having failed to make his bed adequately in the morning. His jacket always had to have five buttons. (If a button dropped off he had to spend hours in search of a needle and thread or even a replacement button.) His clogs had to shine but there was no shoe polish, so Levi had to scour the camp's black market for tar, fat, machine grease or other types of surrogate polish. That was not all. His face had to be clean-shaven, though it was forbidden to possess a razor or scissors. The camp's myriad, senseless prohibitions and obligations – its sheer irrational orderliness – ensured that the degraded prisoners could think only of trivia and had no energy for insurrection.

In a matter of days, the instinct for cleanliness vanished in Levi. It was virtually impossible for him to wash his clothes. Underwear was changed only after thirty, forty days of wear. His striped uniform, stained with blood, pus, oil and paint, had been steam-disinfected so many times it was tattered. Cleanliness seemed to Levi a waste of energy – a superfluous luxury – when every effort was needed to get to the end of the day alive. A

Hungarian Jewish ex-army sergeant, Eugenio Gluecksmann, had upbraided Levi early on for his slovenly appearance: 'You *must* have a clean jacket and shoes.' Born in 1890, thirty years before Levi, Gluecksmann was the embodiment of a kind of Jewish dignity and soldierly fortitude that the Nazis had not yet managed to destroy. 'Man might have *risen* from the apes,' the Hungarian told Levi, 'but he is not necessarily *of* them.' Levi ignored him. He had quickly got used to the stench of hundreds of ill-washed bodies sleeping in such an appallingly overcrowded barrack.

It was a miracle that Primo Levi had survived the first few days at Auschwitz. Death was most likely to occur during this dangerous early period when no allowances were made for newcomers who failed to understand orders. In this extreme and totalitarian place, violence was frequent and casual, and the camp's gangster elite were merciless. 'An order was given once, yelled, and that was it: afterwards came the beatings,' Levi recalled. Newcomers who infringed the camp's numerous rules were often killed. The majority of Italians deported with Levi from Fossoli, if they had not been gassed immediately, had died during the first week. Elia Baruch, a forty-six-year-old docker from Livorno, was beaten to death by three old-hands: he had made the fatal mistake of responding to his first blow with a punch. Everything at Auschwitz was hostile. And the violence was administered less out of hatred than out of routine, the way a man might beat his dog. Violence was the universal shorthand of this place, the language understood by all.

The higher-ranked inmates despised inept greenhorns like Levi, whose serial number of 174517 instantly betrayed his freshman status and put him at the bottom of the camp's pecking order. In his first week Levi had naively believed a Yiddish-speaking *Häftling* when he told him: 'You don't like what you do? Go peel potatoes, then.' Levi asked if he could join a 'Potato Peeling Work-Detail', and for his ignorance was viciously beaten by a *Kapo*, while the others stood by laughing. Levi knew that he would suffer here, but he had not counted on the lack of solidarity against the Germans. Newcomers had to fight their battle alone – not only against the camp's extreme brutality, but against fellow *Häftlinge*. 'Nothing was more demoralising than to have your bread stolen by a bunkmate,' Levi remembered.

The *Kapos* enjoyed unlimited freedom to degrade and humble their subordinates, and Levi had to deal with four different *Kapos* during his eleven months at Auschwitz. His first was Oscar, a German non-Jew who lost no opportunity to beat those who had once been his 'betters' – businessmen, lawyers, judges. Oscar's class-resentment spilled over into pure hatred for Jews like Levi with their university degrees. Number 174517 was a *Doktor der Chemie*, was he? Fortunately Levi was lucky not to wear glasses, as these were the fatal insignia of *Intelligenten* – 'intellectuals' – and automatically invited violence. The Marseilles chemist-prisoner Dr Cremieux had been literally trampled to death by Oscar. The *Kapo*'s green triangle marked him as a former criminal; reprieved of murder in Germany, Oscar had arrived at Auschwitz in his mid-twenties.

In Levi's view, the Italians were especially ill-equipped to weather the assault of Auschwitz. 'We were like eggs without a shell.' As assimilated middle-class Jews, they were unable to develop the protective leathery hide needed to withstand the camp's depredations. The majority of prisoners at Auschwitz were tough Ashkenazim – mainly lower-class East European Jews – whose spoken Yiddish the Italians could not understand. Isolated by their linguistic ignorance, the Italians were despised by the Ashkenazim as inept *Makkaroni* who had not suffered the Nazi ghettos set up in almost every Polish town. While orthodox East European Jews could convince themselves that Auschwitz was sent as a test for mankind – an intolerable but manifest mystery of His will – Levi believed he had been deported without reason: 'I could understand why political opponents were put in camps – but to punish a man simply because of his religious *difference* seemed to me the height of iniquity and unreason.' Nevertheless, these orthodox believers set an important example and lesson for Levi: not everyone sank under the camp's inhuman conditions. A diminutive Jew from Galicia, called Waschmann (first name unknown), was able to offer Levi these near-religious words of comfort: 'Now we shall march for half an hour, but then we shall have a roof over our heads, and this is good; and then at eight in the evening they will give us soup, and that too is good; and if tomorrow we must die, this is good also.' If the long-imprisoned *Ostjuden* could survive, so could Primo Levi; he needed to watch them and learn from them.

Though Italians made up less than one in ten of the Jews in the Auschwitz IV *Judenlager*, a trustworthy compatriot could help to stave off death, as cooperation brought solidarity, more food and hope. When the Italian doctor Aldo Moscati collapsed on the worksite from fatigue, Levi tried to find him lighter work in the *Arbeitsdienstbüro*, or Work Office. 'It might seem strange to you that there was this solidarity, but Primo and I were Italians together – we were not going to go under.' The Italians had agreed to meet each Sunday in a corner of the roll-call square. Among them were Franco Sacerdoti, Guido Dalla Volta, his son Alberto, and the doctors

Aldo Moscati and Leonardo De Benedetti. Yet the Sunday group was so tired and hungry after work that meetings soon became impossible. Anyway it was distressing for the Italians to have to count the ever-decreasing number in their group, and to see each other grow progressively more emaciated.

11

Primo Levi was a young bourgeois adrift in the most extreme evil of our time. Within twenty-four hours he had learned what the mind and body could do when it is a matter of self-preservation. The prime stimulus in this new life was to find food. Levi's daily 500-gram bread ration was not enough to survive on. Gaining a *Nachschlag* – a 'second-helping' – could make the difference between life and death. Levi's was a chronic hunger unknown to free men. Later he described the agonised hunt for food: 'Every beat of strength remaining in you is intended to get something – any way, in every possible way – something to eat, something more to eat.' At night in his dreams he conjured up succulent meats and fantasy menus. On entering Auschwitz Levi had weighed only 49 kilograms, therefore he needed fewer calories to survive than a heavier man. Yet nothing could still his gnawing hunger. Each day civilian trains passed the Buna construction site with mocking advertisements for Knorr soup: '*BESTE SUPPE KNORR SUPPE*', as if Levi could choose between one brand and another. These trains underlined just how far he had come from civilisation and the warmth of home. The average life expectancy in his camp was three months.

Levi could not remain faithful to the morality he had left behind in the free world if he was to live; in order to survive, he had to steal. 'Stealing from the Germans – blankets, oil, anything – was considered a matter of pride, especially if the prisoner was not caught.' These items Levi could then barter for more food. For their kleptomaniac ability the Greek Jews, most of them tough Salonika dockers, were known as *Klepsi Klepsi*. Levi would have been appalled by their thieving as a free man; here, it won his admiration. What to steal was also a problem. A few desperate inmates stole rotten turnips from kitchen rubbish, but then diarrhoea would explode at night on the plank-bed. Bowel infections from mouldy bread constantly undermined Levi's strength, but he would not have endangered himself by eating rotten food. Early on he had learned to classify the plants, animals and vegetable matter found at Auschwitz into foods that were safe or unsafe to eat. (According to this taxonomy, a worm was quite as nutritious as a piece of chicken.)

Levi could have died from any number of causes in this early period of captivity, but chief among them was dehumanisation. Fear of sinking into the subhuman stratum of prison society – the asocials, the losers – was the most powerful incentive for Levi to stay alive. Levi's hardest lesson was to show no pity to those in the *Mussulman* state.* Unable to withstand the first shock of entering the camp, these men had no hope of survival. Helping them would have been an indulgence and a waste of energy. Levi hated these husks of men: association with them was dangerous because they carried disease and their nihilism was contagious. Moreover, Levi was afraid of what they represented. Gyula Deutsch, seventeen, came from a rustic outpost near Transylvania; he had gone half crazy with hunger, and was covered in sores and truncheon bruises. At all costs Levi avoided the walking shadows of Auschwitz IV.

Auschwitz IV contained up to 30,000 foreign non-Jews, almost three times its number of Jews. Among them were British troops forced into heavy labour on the construction site. Each day at dusk 300–400 British POWs marched past the *Judenlager* on their way back from work. Levi noted the Tommies' stout khaki battle-dress, their well-shaved cheeks and brilliantined hair. With straight, proud backs they whistled 'It's a long way to Tipperary' and gave the V for Victory. Alfred Battams, an eighty-one-year-old east Londoner, who had lived in the London borough of Hackney, was captured by the Germans in North Africa and subsequently interned in Auschwitz as a military POW. He was able to observe the Nazi crimes at first hand, if at distance, and recalled the wretchedly degraded Jews of Levi's *Lager*:

> We'd pass these endless columns of Jews marching five-abreast in pyjama suits, only they weren't really marching, shuffling more like. Some of them seemed to be cuddling little soup bowls. They didn't look human. It was unbelievable, some of them had these rags on their feet where their clogs'd worn through – walking skeletons. I saw kiddies only so high being horse-whipped by the SS. They had these long bull-whips and they lashed at the children, and they had these Alsatian dogs. I don't want to talk about it [crying]. It was unbelievable that people could've sunk so low.

---

*The curious name given to the camp's weak and inept, perhaps because their backs were bent permanently as though in Muslim (*Muselmann*: German) prayer.

These Jews were too debilitated to resist; Auschwitz was not a suitable soil for resistance. Even if prisoners had managed to get past the watch-towers, they would have to contend with the dogs that prowled between the double barbed-wire fences. The prisoners' clumsy shoes impeded stealthy rapid walking.

If they were to survive, the *Häftlinge* needed something to hold on to: a religious faith, a friendship or some hope. 'Those of us who thought only of the next bowl of soup died in droves,' Levi explained. Luck had helped many Italians to survive the first month of Auschwitz, among them Leonardo De Benedetti. He had been saved from the gas by one of the non-Jewish political prisoners (identified by their red triangles), who had access to the lists drawn of those destined to be exterminated and could switch the registration numbers. In Levi's view, while luck had helped him to survive thus far, what had saved him above all was his fierce desire to observe and make sense of the authoritarian system. His vigilant intelligence – what elsewhere he called his habit of 'detached curiosity' – was a bastion against death and a sort of moral armour in a place where it was 'extremely easy to die spiritually'. Levi was only able to exercise his curiosity because of his fierce will to live. He was a young man with his life before him, he had no dependants who were suffering; and somewhere he must have found the belief that he could hold out to the war's end.

The few surviving members of the 22 February 1944 Fossoli transport understood by now that they were probably going to die, not in twenty or fifty years as in normal life, but in a few weeks. It was vital for them to get some bearing on the camp before it killed them. While Levi remained ignorant of the exact purpose and geographical location of Auschwitz III and IV, he had quickly worked out where the camp's clothing warehouse was situated, the punishment block, the British POW quarters, the kitchen gardens, blacksmiths and SS dormitories. The more he understood about the nature of his confinement, the greater his chance of surviving. He had to locate himself on a grid: to record, mentally itemise, and categorise. This was his way of creating certainty in a world now robbed of certainty. Though Levi was learning fast, he often learned the hard way. During that first dangerous week he had unwittingly trespassed by the brothel (Block 29) and an SS guard brutally struck him on the face. He memorised the camp layout as soon as he could.

He was quick to learn the essential rules of survival. Never queue first for soup as any nutritious pieces are at the bottom of the cauldron. Never drink the camp's water, which carried typhoid. Never drink the methanol distilled on the construction site – the Russian POWs abused it and went slowly blind, then died. Moreover, Levi had learned how to stop working without being beaten for 'laziness' by a *Kapo*. He had learned how to balance the energy he derived from his meagre food against the amount he could afford to expend in work. He had learned to lick his precious spoon first before lending it to someone, the way children leave their spittle-mark on cutlery. He kept his feet warm inside his clogs with brown paper scavenged from the worksite. He had learned the art of sleeping on top of his jacket wrapped round all his belongings, including his spoon (to buy back a stolen spoon would cost a life-saving bread ration). Another factor in Levi's survival up until now was his ability not to draw attention to himself. To remain inconspicuous was a prisoner's best means of staying alive, for he was less likely to catch a *Kapo*'s notice and be beaten.

After two months in Auschwitz, as the snows were melting in early spring, Levi was slaving on the worksite when an iron rail toppled on his foot and left him in excruciating pain. Now he had to enter the *Lager*'s infirmary (Block 23), where patients were granted an outstandingly generous two months maximum in which to recover, failing which they were gassed: a Jew unable to walk was a Jew unable to work. The infirmary was a centre of massive corruption. Doctors and male nurses filched spoons from the dead (or from patients soon to be 'selected' for the gas) to sell on the camp's black market. Levi had to be especially wary of the doctors Waitz of Strasbourg, Coenka of Salonika and Samuelidis of Athens, as they were in a privileged caste of Jewish physicians who betrayed patients to the SS in return for favours. Almost all careerists at Auschwitz collaborated with (and to a certain degree modelled themselves on) the SS, and the doctors' determination to survive made them everybody's enemy. By contrast, the patients helped one another. In Levi's adjoining bunk lay the middle-aged Dutch businessman Walter Bonn, who had been deported in September 1943 from Westerbork camp in the province of Drenthe. Though Bonn was an old-hand, he charitably gave Levi his spoon. (According to the camp records, he died shortly afterwards on 20 April 1944.)

German and Polish newspapers, such as the *Silesian Observer* and the *Cracow Journal*, circulated in the sick ward. These may have been the first newspapers Levi had seen for four months, his first contact with the outside world. From these he was able to get some idea of events back home. The Fascist philosopher Giovanni Gentile had been murdered by partisans. The Allies were close to Rome. Hitler's Germany might yet be overthrown, and then this place called Auschwitz, *anus mundi*, would be liberated.

ELEVEN

Auschwitz: The Laboratory
1944–5

I

Levi's immediate family were still alive. His sister Anna Maria had not given up the partisan struggle: she was fighting on Primo's behalf, as well as her deported boyfriend's. Today she plays down the significance of her role in the Resistance. It was, nonetheless, important and dangerous. As Action Party *agent de liaison* she was an indispensable link in the partisan chain of command in Piedmont. She went most places on foot, coolly walking past the Hotel Nazionale in Turin where the Gestapo were billeted, her green bag bulging with clandestine propaganda. Until the war's end Anna Maria remained very concerned for her mother's safety. Using Ada Gobetti's contacts, she managed to obtain Ester the alias 'Signora Lanza'. But where should Ester go? Turin was very unsafe; a wave of crime hit the city as platoons of *mutini* (young militia in the pay of the corrupt Fascist Party secretary Ettore Muti) robbed and looted. The surgeon Luigi Stropeni, who had operated on Levi's father in 1940, was beaten by masked gunmen and left for dead.

By early March 1944 Ester was in the hilltop hamlet of Torrazzo deep in the *Serra* massif. Her cousin Irma Della Torre was hiding there with her family under the rather obvious identity of 'Clevi' (Irma's husband Riccardo was the brother of the author Carlo Levi), which they later changed to 'Cardone'. The local priest was known to be anti-Nazi, and Communist brigades operated securely within the area; Ada Della Torre's fiancé, Silvio Ortona, was chief of staff commanding four of them. Ester was content to help the inhabitants of Torrazzo – the *torrazzesi* – collect firewood, cook and tend their wounded partisans. But she could not stay long there. Italian Jews, hunted and tracked down, had to keep moving. So Anna Maria installed her mother in Borgofranco nearby, where she remained until Italy was liberated from the Nazis in 1945. The rest of the

Levi family was dispersed throughout Piedmont. Grandma Adelina Luzzati was concealed in a big draughty house in Santhià near Turin; she pointedly avoided all talk of Primo's arrest whenever Anna Maria visited, as deportation was taboo. The rest of her time Anna Maria divided between Borgofranco and the Gobetti house in Turin, which miraculously still eluded Nazi-Fascist surveillance.

The weather was perfect that early spring in Italy. On 25 March Emanuele Artom was caught by Italian SS. He was scrambling in the mist down a hillside in the Waldensian valleys with other partisans, when in the distance amid the rocks he saw uniformed men. Enemies? They were Italian SS and in an instant they were on the partisans' trail. Emanuele, debilitated from three nights' intake of amphetamines (he had needed to stay awake for sentry duty), was barely able to stand. 'You go on.' The Fascists took him to a barracks in Luserna San Giovanni. Another of the captured partisans, seventeen-year-old Ruggero Levi (no relation), was never revealed as a Jew as he had Teutonically blond hair and blue eyes. But Artom's ordeal had only just begun.

A week later Sandro Delmastro was captured. On 4 April he had been on a mission to gather intelligence (or perhaps to fetch explosives) in Cuneo near Turin. His chief Action Party contact in Turin, Paolo Braccini, had advised Delmastro to flee the city. From Cuneo, he seems to have taken a train in the direction of France. The train had got as far as Borgo San Dalmazzo when Fascist police began to search the passengers. They put Delmastro on a lorry headed for the Fascist Youth headquarters in Cuneo for questioning; for a few minutes he managed to evade his captors by jumping off. The late Anna Revelli, wife of the partisan leader Nuto Revelli, witnessed Delmastro's last moments. 'It was a lovely spring morning – I was lying in bed when I heard gun-shots.' From her bedroom window she saw a young man running fast down Corso IV Novembre. There was a burst of machine-gun fire; 'then the man did a slow-motion pirouette, and fell.' A teenager with a gun approached to inspect the dead man who was lying facedown in the road. Presently he was joined by a group of older Blackshirts who complimented him on his marksmanship. This was cold-blooded murder. After twenty minutes a refuse van picked up Delmastro's corpse. 'Only a partisan would have been carted off in rubbish. It was a gesture of contempt,' judged Anna Revelli. At the war's end it was discovered that Delmastro's killer had belonged to the delinquent Muti Gang, whose juvenile members were notoriously keen to prove themselves. Delmastro's was an inglorious end; yet, as Ada Gobetti noted in her diary, it was possibly an apt one for the 'simple, modest' Sandro. Today in Cuneo on Corso IV Novembre a plaque commemorates the 'naval officer and partisan leader'

Alessandro (Sandro) Delmastro who 'fell fighting for justice and liberty' on 4 April 1944.

The Italian SS forced Emanuele Artom to consume large amounts of alcohol, and for five terrible days tortured him. In the post-war trial of his presumed chief torturer, Italian SS Captain Arturo Dal Dosso, it emerged that Artom had been flogged with a rubber hose and stabbed with bayonets. 'Needles were pushed under his fingernails; one of his ears was cut off; his hair and teeth were pulled out.' The German weekly *Der Adler* (The Eagle), distributed throughout northern Italy, carried a photograph of the unrecognisable Artom propped on a mule with a broomstick: 'Captured Jewish Bandit'. Artom was still just breathing when he was left naked on the street outside the Luserna San Giovanni barracks. Partially 'devoured by dogs', he was removed on 31 March to a jail in Turin. A week later, about the time that Delmastro was killed, he died. His remains were never found. Today Artom is remembered as a remarkable spirit murdered before his thirtieth birthday.

2

In mid-May, after twenty days in the infirmary, Levi was discharged. Now began a painful and complicated period of readjustment as he tried to re-establish himself in a new barrack hut, Block 45. He had to face a new *Kapo*, a new barracks, a new pecking order. Inability to communicate with German-speaking *Prominents* – the privileged prisoners – was the first among many reasons why so many Italians had already died. Aldo Moscati had not recognised his prison number when it was called out in German and by the time he got to the soup queue he was told with a smirk: 'Too late!' By contrast, the German-speaking Jewish prisoner Joseph Hollander gained favours from the camp's German commandant simply because he came from the same town as him (Breslau) and knew his favourite beerhalls. If Levi could find a trustworthy German-speaking *Häftling* who was prepared to teach him the camp's harsh, barrack-room German in exchange for bread, his chances of survival might increase.

By an extraordinary coincidence there was an Italian in Block 45 who spoke fluent German. Alberto Dalla Volta had travelled with Levi from Fossoli; a twenty-two-year-old with a cautious, taciturn manner, he came from Brescia near Milan and, like Levi, was a chemist. At home in Italy he had spoken German with his mother, who kept a library of Heine and Schiller. His German had given him a head start at Auschwitz and provided an incentive for Levi to stay close to him. Alberto was also superb at 'organising' – Auschwitz jargon for acquiring illegal food and other stuff – and in this dangerous period after his sickbed recovery Levi needed to profit by his compatriot's hustling. The two Italians became inseparable and before long had agreed to divide any extra food between them. Such a relationship was almost unheard of at Auschwitz, and it proved stronger than the guns and barbed wire of the Nazis. Alberto's pride and determination not to be crushed by the enemy indeed lifted him above the camp's sinkpool of corruption. He was admired as a man of some account in Block 45, one who had retained his integrity.

Without Alberto, Levi would probably not have survived. Yet he was at a loss to understand why Alberto tolerated his business inefficiency. 'Because you're lucky,' Alberto told him. He looked out for Levi as he had looked out for the younger brother he had left behind in Italy. It was only by a fluke that Paolo Dalla Volta had not joined Alberto at Auschwitz. When Italian police had raided the family house on 2 December 1943, they found Paolo bedridden with typhus. The police were reluctant to handcuff a moribund – they were frightened of catching typhus – and assumed Paolo would die anyway. In reality they were loath to arrest any of the Dalla Voltas as they were respected and well liked in Brescia. Paolo and his mother were placed under house arrest; Alberto and his father were politely escorted to jail. Militia were posted at exits to the flat but Paolo managed to escape with his mother down a lift-shaft into a neighbouring apartment block. From there he reached a hospital, where he spent fifteen days under the false name 'Mario Rossi'; he did survive, and later joined the partisans.

Ever since childhood, Levi's need for the security of friendship and human contact had been exceptionally strong, and now it was overwhelming. As the spring advanced he made friends with Jean Samuel, a gentle oval-faced Frenchman from German Alsace with whom he spoke in French. Samuel was the so-called 'Pikolo' of Block 45 (from the Italian *il piccolo*, 'little one', or, in this case, the 'youngest'). Each barrack had its 'Pikolo': half errand-boy, half mascot, he was not infrequently the *Kapo*'s sexual plaything. Samuel's cheerful manner and quiet resourcefulness made him a popular inmate, however. In March 1944 *la famille Samuel* had been betrayed to the Gestapo and deported to Auschwitz. At that time Samuel had been studying pharmacology at Toulouse University. In Auschwitz he tried to keep his mind alert by setting himself algebraic conundrums. It seemed 'sheer folly' to Levi that Samuel should barter his bread for a book on integral calculus that had miraculously found its way into the barracks. But, in the evenings, while other prisoners argued or repaired their clothes, Samuel preferred to discuss mathematics. His sparring partner was the thirty-two-year-old French-Polish mathematician Albert Joulty, who had survived Auschwitz for an astonishing ten months. A similar need to rediscover his old self would strike Levi only later, when he recited to Samuel lines from Dante's *Inferno*. Samuel used his intellect as a defence and a continuous mental gymnastics against dehumanisation. The Nazis could make his body shovel concrete, but not his mind.

Mature for his twenty-two years, Samuel took an instant liking to Levi. And in late May or early June 1944, during a threatened Allied air-attack, Levi found himself alone with the Alsatian in a bunker. There was no *Kapo* on the worksite that blue summer day, no SS or vicious *Volksdeutsche* – ethnic Polish-German – to goad them with a whip. For twenty minutes they spoke of their families, their shared interests and their lives as free men. Conversation at Auschwitz, when it was possible, was such an extraordinary freedom; and today Samuel says those few brief moments of shared humanity in the sun were 'a shining moment of hope'.

It was dangerous to get involved with more than one friend at Auschwitz. 'You put up a protective shell that excluded everything that did not personally help you to survive,' said Samuel. Yet by the late spring of 1944, Levi, Samuel and Dalla Volta had formed a sturdy triumvirate alliance. Levi took German lessons from the bilingual Samuel, while Samuel took Italian lessons from Dalla Volta. The three men were not always together in the camp, but they each knew that the others were there. And this helped tremendously to sustain their morale.

3

Luciana Nissim and Vanda Maestro were in Auschwitz II, Birkenau, six kilometres from Levi's camp. Life was brutal there: up to 90 per cent of every Birkenau transport was sent straight to the gas chambers. As a Birkenau doctor, Nissim was a prisoner of some importance, with better food and her own bed. The old-hands treated her respectfully; she might be useful to them. The Birkenau infirmary where Nissim worked, known as the *Revier*, was one of the most perverse and hellish parts of the camp. There were regular 'selections' for extermination, which Dr Mengele's red-haired assistant Dr König attended with his clipboard; if they were not gassed, the women were used for medical experiments, injected with phenol, petrol, chloroform or air, or sterilised in the interests of 'science'.

The Birkenau crematoria never stopped working and, from her doctor's quarters, Nissim saw that the sky above the tall towers was flame-red and black. To facilitate the extermination of Hungary's 800,000 Jews, a new branch line of the Auschwitz railway brought the cattle-trucks right to the crematoria. In the merest blink of historical time an entire culture was to be wiped out. Nissim heard the cries – 'Mamma! Mammina!' – as children were pulled from their parents. The air was thick and warped with furnace heat. Whenever a new transport arrived from Italy, Nissim was terrified that she might know someone on it. One day an Italian deportee brought the miraculous good news that Nissim's parents were safe in Switzerland. That was a turning-point for her, when she said to herself: 'I'm going to make it on my own.' She went to visit Vanda Maestro most nights. The loss of dignity and identity at Auschwitz was more terrible for the women. Starvation left them without breasts or hips; their menstrual cycles ceased. After four months in captivity the vitality had been drained from Vanda, her tremulous grace extinguished. Bruises showed blue on her face from the *Kapo*'s rubber truncheon. A harsh word from anybody made her cry. One day Maestro turned her eyes on Nissim, and said: 'If I die, promise to call your baby Vanda.' Nissim kept her promise.

In this spring of 1944 the barracks and work-squads of Levi's camp were inundated with Magyars, so that Hungarian, not Yiddish, became the *Lager*'s second language. Many of the Hungarian Jews were middle-class professionals, industrialists, bankers, the sort of men Levi's father had known in Budapest before the Great War. As newcomers they were the subject of derision and intolerance. Levi cursed the Hungarian pharmacist Endre Szanto, who was appointed his workmate; he had no idea how to steal, lie, dodge work or find influential friends. He urged the Hungarian to stint in his workload, carry fewer bricks, economise on breath and movement. Szanto eventually understood, and taught Levi an Hungarian folk song, which half a century later he could still recite word for word.

As the Hungarians overwhelmed the camp, the *Kapo* Oscar announced the formation of a chemical work-squad. Kommando 98, as the squad was to be known, had nothing to do with chemistry in the laboratory sense; it was a heavy-transport detail attached to a magnesium-chloride warehouse. Few of its fifty recruits were even chemists but were chosen seemingly at random. They were lawyers, railwaymen, tinkers and pharmacists. Among the squad's six chemists was Béla Fischer, who had helped the Nobel Laureate Albert Szent-Györgyi discover Vitamin C (in paprika) back in 1937. Levi got on well enough with Fischer, a thirty-five-year-old Hungarian, but he had to be on his guard with others in Kommando 98. Few of them had survived with their humanity intact. Most had become emotionally blunted or to some extent complicit in the degradation of others. One such was Paul Steinberg, a young half-Russian Jew born in Berlin. Unlike Levi, Steinberg moved in a circle of flatterers, protectors and parasites – the beneficiaries of *protekcja* (protection). Disguised as 'Henri' in *If This is a Man,* his method was to seek out the vulnerable point in a German – say, his homosexuality – and work on him to get what he wanted. Still others in the squad had stayed afloat through brute physical force. Elias Lindzin, a Herculean Polish dwarf, had been transferred to Auschwitz from Majdanek camp in Lublin. A tough old-timer, the tattoo on his brawny forearm – 12812 – showed an impressive seven-month survival in Auschwitz. Lindzin stole constantly and automatically, even from bunkmates, and Levi judged him 'probably clinically insane and the likely inmate of a mental asylum'.

From morning to evening, under the blows and abuse of the SS and their Polish-German foremen, Levi shouldered sackfuls of caustic Phenol beta-Naphthol. Loose powder stuck to his face and left it raw and vulnerable to infection. At least Kommando 98 was well suited for barter in stolen goods, as it was stationed near the British POW camp with its aggressive black market. From the Tommies, Levi was able to wangle the odd soap bar. The butts from Virginia roll-ups provided tobacco for crude cigarettes: *Mahorca,* as tobacco was known in the camp, was a valuable commodity. Sometimes the Tommies threw the prisoners Nestlé chocolate tablets over the electrified fence, or slipped them a soldier's ration of egg powder. The POWs trusted their fellows in a way that was not possible among the brutalised Jews, and Levi envied their *esprit de corps.*

4

Two important events occurred this summer. On around 6 June 1944 news came of the Allied landing in Normandy. Here at last was the second front that might crush Germany. Later that month Levi was seconded to a brick-laying Kommando, whose two chief masons turned out to be Italian. But there was more good news. One of them was born in Fossano near Levi's ancestral Bene Vagienna. His name was Lorenzo Perrone, and his thick Piedmontese accent filled Levi with a surge of compatriotic solidarity. Perrone worked for Beotti & Co, one of forty construction firms – foreign and German – that built the Auschwitz III synthetic-rubber and oil plants. Today the Auschwitz Museum archives has the minutes to a German industrialists' meeting on 15 February 1943: 'Rome. It was decided that the Italian companies Stoelkher, Colombo and Beotti would merge with the German firms Pitroff and Vertreter. The Italians say they can supply us with 1,100 specialists, among them bulldozer-drivers, welders, engine-drivers and masons.'

Lorenzo Perrone was one of those 'masons'. Officially he was a volunteer worker in the Third Reich. As such, he could receive food parcels from Italy, sleep in comfortable Italian billets and was fed adequately on a German guard's ration. But like many Italian civilians in Auschwitz, he brusquely refused cigarettes and other luxuries from Germans, whose discipline and cruelty he loathed. Middle-aged, faintly stooped with greying hair, Lorenzo was a 'born desponder', according to his brother Secondo, with a peevish personality. If a German foreman so much as criticised his masonry he left the worksite. Perrone had seen things at Auschwitz that offended his dignity. The poverty of his birthplace in Piedmont, where people ate bread soaked in wine, was terrible, but in the violent, degraded environment of Auschwitz there was starvation.

Each day for the next six months Perrone smuggled Levi an extra soup ration. No words were said as he left the mess-tin by the half-constructed brick wall. The soup might contain a sparrow's wings, prune stones, salami rind, even bits of *La Stampa* newsprint reduced to pulp. The scrag-ends provided Levi with an extra daily 500 calories, without which he certainly would not have survived. Levi repeatedly warned the providential mason of his crime in helping a Jew – but Perrone shrugged his shoulders. He helped Levi as a moral duty, and for as long as Levi was his brick-laying assistant the food arrived safely. One day, when there was a sudden risk of discovery, the ration was left at a new agreed-upon location – the corner of H-Strasse by Bau 930. Even then Perrone had to be careful as the nearby *Italienisches Syndikats-Büro*, or Italian Work Office, teemed with spies. Moreover, there was a risk that someone else might steal the ration.

Perrone helped Levi in one other crucial way. Virtually no Jew at Auschwitz was able to smuggle letters out, let alone receive post in return. The weekly hour when the red (political) triangles read their post was the saddest for Levi; then he felt painfully alienated and estranged from home. Letters meant more to prisoners than anything else: they gave a slender meaning to their lives and a sense of connection to the world they had lost. Thanks to Perrone, Levi was able to send letters out of the camp and even receive them from his family. The plan was for Perrone to transcribe Levi's messages in his own semi-literate hand, sign them with his name and dispatch them to Bianca Guidetti Serra's address in Turin. Bianca, a non-Jew, could be relied on to pass the news to Levi's mother.

In writing to his family, Levi did not think of the possible repercussions for them. His mother was not in neutral Switzerland, but in Nazi-occupied Italy. Gestapo spies could easily uncover his secret correspondence. 'I was completely irresponsible. I had no idea how dangerous it was to send letters home.' Levi's immediate problem was to devise a message that the addressee could understand but which would not arouse the suspicions of the Auschwitz censors. In mid-June he composed his first note to the outside world. Rubber-stamped '*ZENSOR*' (verified) on 25 June, the postcard reached Turin on 19 July. It had a Hitler postage stamp and was signed by Lorenzo Perrone, 'Italian *Facharbeiter*', 'Specialist Worker'. For two days the card lay undetected on Bianca's doormat at 15 Via Montebello. Levi's mother, in her Borgofranco hideout, had had no news of her son for seven months, and feared he was dead.

By chance, Ada Della Torre was staying with Levi's mother when the card reached Turin. On the night of 21–2 July she had a peculiar dream in which she was gazing up at the stars in Milan when Primo, in his didactic way, began to name the constellations for her. He was wearing striped pyjamas. On Saturday the 22nd Ada left Borgofranco to attend to partisan business in Turin. News of the botched attempt on Hitler's life (a bomb had exploded in the Führer's East Prussia GHQ) had put the Germans in a vengeful mood, and to Ada everything in Turin seemed hostile and intent on her destruction. At Porta Nuova station she telephoned Bianca to see if she was in. Instead the maid answered: 'Come quickly!' Ada hurried to the flat, where she was handed a postcard. With a jolt Ada rememembered her dream of the night before:

> Dearest Signorina Bianca,
>   I saw Primo yesterday. He is well and he is working and maybe he will write to you, he's got a bit thinner and looks forward to seeing you again or at least getting your news. There's nothing new to report from here . . . I am your friend Lorenzo Perrone. I hope to get a letter from you goodbye.

A month later Levi received the first of two postcards from 'Signora Lanza', his mother. He read her card in a foul-smelling cistern on the worksite away from the camp's *Spitzelsystem*, 'spy system'. For one exalted moment Levi was taken out of himself, and childhood memories came back to him with a sharpness he could taste: rooms, smells, a Crocetta street. Levi's reply to his mother, copied out by Lorenzo Perrone in his own untutored hand and again sent to Bianca Guidetti Serra, passed the Auschwitz censors on 21 August:

> I am keeping in excellent health in fact with the good weather I feel better and by now I get along very well in German which is a great advantage for work. A while ago I learned that Luciana

[Nissim] is working not far from here, I have had no news of Franco [Tedeschi: Anna Maria's boyfriend].

Then these falsely consoling words:

> Don't worry about me and try to send me everybody's news. Take great courage and great hope. Accept my best wishes and an affectionate embrace from the one who always remembers you, your Lorenzo.

Bianca received the postcard six weeks later (mid-September 1944) and arranged to hand it to Levi's mother in Turin. 'I'll never forget the look on Ester's face when she realised that Primo may still be alive.' But after the elation, Ester pointed out that the message was sent a full month and a half ago, in which time anything could have happened. Consumed by anxiety for her *primogenito*, Ester would not see Primo for another thirteen months.

With news of the Normandy landings the atmosphere in Levi's camp deteriorated as the *Kapos* searched for illegal radios and brutalised the prisoners in revenge. An SS guard shot dead a British POW: 'There *is* no Geneva Convention – *this* is my convention' – and he pulled out a Luger. Healthy child-soldiers in the Hitler Youth came to stare at the Jews on the Buna worksite, and an SS lectured them loudly on the degenerates beyond the barbed wire. Were they not worse than animals? Yes, it was right to dispose of the Jews. Meanwhile the slaves of the chemical Kommando 98 were living in a world of half-verified information, smuggled news and rumours. Hitler was dead. The Third Reich was finished. But despite pressure from the Allies at the Normandy beach-head, French Jews continued to be deported to Auschwitz. The crematoria furnaces became so hot that the firebricks cracked. Additional burning pits were dug; the flames, once started, were fuelled by the fat running off the burning Hungarians.

In early July, a rumour reached Levi that 'specialists' were required to work in the camp's synthetic-rubber and oil plants, which were now completed. These were so gigantic that they consumed as much electricity as all Berlin and were designed to produce 20,000 tonnes of 'Buna' rubber a year for tyres and tank tracks. Now Levi saw his chance of escaping the brick-laying and chemical Kommandos. If he became a Specialist within the Buna plant, he might yet be saved and freed from the random violence of the worksite. Auschwitz III was the property of the German chemical colossus I. G. Farben. Even by modern standards this was an exceptionally resourceful organisation: from its 334 factories in Occupied Europe flowed the strategic raw materials – synthetics of oil, rubber and nitrates – necessary for the German war machine. I. G. Farben's mephistophelean pact with Hitler produced a military-industrial partnership such as the world had never seen. It involved whole-scale enslavement, plunder of occupied countries and murder. Among the I. G. Farben firms operative in Auschwitz III were BASF, Siemens, Bayer, Agfa, Hoechst, AEG and Pelikan (which provided the ink to tattoo prisoners). For the past five years these subsidiaries had been busy exploiting Jewish slave labour at Auschwitz and other Nazi camps.

On 21 or 22 July Levi sat a 'chemical examination' to ascertain whether he would be eligible for Specialist status. And so prisoner 174517 was escorted to the Polymerisation Department – the *P-M-Abteilung* – for his exam. Out of eighty hopeful candidates, only three would be selected to enter the Buna lab. From university Levi knew that 'Buna' was short for *Bu*tadiene and *Na*trium ('natrium' being the Latin tag for sodium). Moreover his fourth-year German chemistry primer, Ludwig Gattermann's *Die Praxis des organischen Chemikers*, had given the formula for Buna synthesis and explained that 'Buna' was the generic German term for synthetic rubber. Levi's examiner, Herr Doktor Wilhelm Pannwitz, was a high-ranking BASF chemist and (according to the BASF archives now held in Ludwigshafen) had been born in 1907. That made him thirty-seven years old. In the German's immaculate office Levi was conscious of his eroded status; his heavy sweat-charged clothes must have smelled and looked dirty. Pannwitz, seated imposingly behind his desk, was Levi's professional near-equal. Yet he treated him with a thin-lipped, icy civility. One essential dislike, formidable in its simplicity, pervaded his soul: Jews.

Only later did Levi discover that Pannwitz was responsible for Auschwitz III's Home Guard, or *Volkssturm*, a fighting force made up of old men, Hitler Youth and other desperadoes. He was bound to be anti-Semitic. When Hitler came to power, I. G. Farben's chief executive Carl Bosch had been expelled for Jewish sympathies and the organisation ruthlessly purged of non-Aryan elements. If he was to keep his job, Pannwitz had to renounce his former Jewish 'colleagues' and become one of Hitler's *Ja Sager*, 'Yes men'.

Pannwitz wanted to know what Levi had done for his main university degree thesis. 'Measurements of dielectrical constants,' he answered Pannwitz, though this was in fact one of two sub-theses on chemical physics. Nevertheless it had involved tests on benzene – and benzene is a vital component of 'Buna' production. Levi's knowledge of physics, or rather physical chemistry, seemed to have impressed Pannwitz: physics, quite as much as chemistry, helped to save Levi's life at Auschwitz. After a perfunctory grilling to assess his capabilities, the interview was brought to a close. On Pannwitz's command, prisoner 174517 was returned to the *Kapo* Oscar. On his emergence from the *P-M-Abteilung*, Oscar contemptuously wiped some engine grease off his hand on to Levi's shoulder, using him as a convenient rag. Forty years later Levi said this was the 'greatest insult' of his life; it was typical of the writer in Levi to see the large offence in the apparently small act. Levi would have to wait an agonising four months before he knew the result of his exam. Until then he was another expendable I. G. Farben slave.

Levi did not know it, but there was a sinister contract between I. G. Farben and the SS. For each Jewish slave provided by the SS, I. G. Farben paid them between four and eight Reichsmarks. Obviously Levi got no wage: that would have been like 'remunerating an ox', he later acidly observed. Yet there was a conflict of interest between the two German organisations. The SS, in their overzealous dedication to the Final Solution, were concerned primarily to exterminate Jews; I. G. Farben, though they could not care less whether Jews lived or died, needed to preserve enough slave labour for the synthetic-rubber worksite. This would explain why the SS had ordered each Jew in Levi's camp to steal four bricks from the I. G. construction yard, hoping thereby to deprive German industry of a precious 40,000 bricks. I. G. Farben, for its part, turned a blind eye to the blankets that Levi stole from his barracks in order to sell on the *Buna-Werke*'s black market. Conversely, the SS encouraged Levi to filch light bulbs from the factory site and barter them in the camp. In this curious rivalry between two opposed exigencies – the one political, the other industrial – Levi was just a number: 174517.

Levi had now survived two months beyond his allotted three-month span, and the longer he managed to hold on, the greater his chances were of living. On 31 July it was his twenty-fifth birthday. Rain was falling in sheets on the worksite as Levi scrubbed out an underground cistern with a Polish Jew. Gifts of food were acts of extraordinary generosity (one might say foolishness) at Auschwitz, yet the Pole gave Levi half his apple – the first and last time he tasted fruit at Auschwitz.

August 1944 came, and with it another dangerous obstacle to Levi's survival. The bullying *Kapo* Oscar was replaced by a Dutch Jewish *Kapo* who was far more dangerous. In his previous incarnation Josef Lessing had been an Amsterdam café violinist. Now he had a place in the Auschwitz orchestra – an extremely privileged position – which corrupted him with power. Levi tried to keep on the right side of Lessing (150724), but his viciousness could strike unexpectedly, when he seemed most placid. Lessing's rubber truncheon was designed to curl round the kidneys, and he beat prisoners with a bestial insouciance. In the upside-down world of

Auschwitz a *Kapo* like Lessing, who had never killed before he was deported, could be twice as terrifying as a convicted murderer like Oscar. He did not hesitate to send men to their death: Jewish *Kapos* especially felt they had to prove their worth to the SS.

The summer heat settled over Auschwitz, and for many prisoners this was the final oppression. In their raging thirst a few risked the camp's tap water contaminated with typhus, and died. At the end of August, Luciana Nissim prepared to be transferred out of Auschwitz into another camp. For the last time she went to see Vanda, who was now sick in the Birkenau *Revier*. 'Go,' Vanda told her. Only now, after all that Nissim had been through at Auschwitz, could she abandon Vanda with an untroubled conscience. At Hessich Lichtenau camp in Germany Nissim continued her dreadful work as a doctor. Her job there was to compile lists of Jewish women who were too sick for work and would therefore be gassed. 'Even then I knew that my future would be full of shame,' Nissim recalled.

That fierce summer of 1944, life in Levi's camp was extremely perilous. On 20 August the Allies bombed the synthetic-rubber and oil plants. Levi was shifting sacks of chemicals in a warehouse when a 227-kilogram bomb fell on the roof. Luck, or perhaps some fault in the bomb, saved him: it failed to detonate. All summer the raids pounded the *Buna-Werke,* devastating I. G. Farben's already long-delayed production schedule. As the Red Army moved nearer to the German lines, more pressure was put on the plant to produce 'Buna'. Tank tracks, tyres for lorries and jeeps were desperately needed, but factory efficiency was woefully below par. The Soviet forces were approaching the eastern banks of the Vistula close to Auschwitz, but for every step forward they took a step back. In 'Aryan' Warsaw the anti-Nazi Resistance had been ruthlessly quelled after a sixty-three-day battle in which 160,000 Poles were killed. A Polish schoolmate of Levi's, Antonina ('Nina') Kozaryn, was deported to Lamsdorf camp for her part in the August 1944 Warsaw uprising. Today she lives in Florida.

By the autumn the Levi family apartment in Turin had been expropriated by Fascists. Armed with a clipboard and a steel tape, on 2 September an accountant, Natale Rovea, broke into 75 Corso Re Umberto. His job was to make an inventory of the flat's contents and ensure that no Jew was left hiding there. Rovea was employed by the sinister Fascist EGELI agency (*Ente di Gestione e Liquidazione Immobiliare*), set up to impound Jewish properties. Just one cog in a highly organised programme of expropriation, EGELI worked side by side with the financial and fiscal authorities of the occupying Germans, as well as the Italian banks and insurance agencies, the landlords and caretakers of the apartment buildings. On the Levis' doormat, Rovea found unpaid gas bills. Some furniture had been removed to Turin's Gestapo headquarters awaiting auction, and bomb damage was extensive in the empty property. Shattered glass and plaster lay on the floor between collapsed partition walls. A gilt-framed embroiderery of a 'female figure' (Rovea noted) and a nineteenth-century 'print of Florence' hinted at other decorative furnishings now absent. In the hall a wrought-iron lamp with a glass bowl hung intact over a ponderously ornate armoire. All was chalky with bomb dust, and little of value remained. A bathtub, abandoned after someone had seemingly tried to remove it, obstructed the entrance. Rovea moved on down the hallway, pausing to remark on a closet of 'wood and tooled glass', a collection of ceramic plates and a painting 'mounted in the English fashion'. In the maid's room he noted a jumble of children's games, a wicker shopping basket and two tennis rackets 'without strings'.

In the study hung a photograph taken in 1901 of graduate engineers. Cesare Levi's walnut desk still contained its rubber-stamp holder, 'two ink wells' and 'an ashtray'. The engineer's medicine cabinet lay broken on the floor next to a small bronze statue fractured in a bomb-blast. Glass crunching underfoot, accountant Rovea entered the white-tiled kitchen where, with inventorial precision, he noted: '1 cake mould, 1 grater'. The flat's scant remaining furniture he valued at a paltry 4,000 lire (£160 in today's terms). His job done, he chained and padlocked the apartment door, sealing it with wax apparently to deter thieves. (After finding Natale Rovea's report in the files of a Turin bank, I showed it to Anna Maria Levi: 'I have never seen this before,' she said, visibly disturbed by what she read. Much of Fascist history remains buried in Italy.) Other Jews whose homes had been barred, bolted or chained by EGELI operatives often had to break into their own homes to retrieve belongings. Under cover of dark, Bianca Guidetti Serra had climbed up the drainpipe to her Jewish boyfriend Alberto Salmoni's house to get some clothes.

It was insane for Jews to be seen out and about in Turin that summer. Recklessly Levi's cousin Giulia Colombo headed for the San Paolo bank, which brokered the sale of confiscated Jewish properties on EGELI's behalf. The manager, Signor Sanna, had been Cesare Levi's chess partner and was certainly no anti-Semite. His jaw dropped at Giulia's request that seals be put on 'The Saccarello'. Since when had Jews *asked* to be locked out of their home? Giulia explained that the villa was vulnerable to burglary without seals (she did not know it had already been burgled). Sanna promised to do what he could, and nervously ushered the girl out through the bank's back door. 'The Saccarello' was never sealed.

The Germans were now in a frenzied hurry to exterminate Jews in the face of the steady Soviet advance. In Levi's camp there had been urgent rumours, voices rising in panic, of an imminent *Selekcja,* or 'selection'. In fact, the weakest slave labourers were to be eliminated to make way for an influx of prisoners from Poznan. On the morning of 15 October 1944, a Sunday, all the inmates of Auschwitz IV were locked into their barracks. In Block 45 the prisoners were ordered to strip down to their shoes and were each given a card with their prison number, name, age, profession and nationality. So Levi found himself in a mass of 200 men anonymously condemned and uncertain whether he would live or die. Amid a fanfare of noise and barked orders, an SS subaltern arrived. He was not even a doctor, yet he was to take a brief glimpse to decide whether a man should be gassed. Inmates desperately tried to conceal their physical state; some attempted to hide an operation scar, or a *Kapo*'s bruising, beneath a bundle of clothes. Others briskly rubbed their faces to bring back colour to their flesh.

For Jean Samuel the selection was an instant of pure horror that has stayed vivid for half a century – 'the most terrifying day of my life, Judgement Day'. Comparatively healthy-looking prisoners – such as the huge Transylvanian peasant Sattler – had been slated for gassing. Had Sattler neglected to shave? A total of 850 Auschwitz IV *Häftlinge* were selected that autumn Sunday for death. The condemned prisoners were served a double soup ration, then picked up by lorries forty-eight hours later and driven naked to their fate. Eight Italians from Block 45 that we know of were gassed. One of them was Alberto Dalla Volta's father, Guido. Born in 1894, by Auschwitz standards the fifty-year-old Guido was ancient. Alberto was stunned by his father's abrupt removal. Until now he had not indulged in any consolatory untruths about Auschwitz: life here was a war of nerves and brute survival of the fittest. But confronted by his father's extinction, he fled the truth. 'Papa's gone to a convalescent camp. He wasn't ill, was he?' A 'convalescent camp' did exist near Auschwitz, in the coalfields of Jaworzno, but Guido Dalla Volta did not go there. With Alberto (to use the modern term) now in denial, Levi could no longer trust him as he had: he had become an unreliable ally. And in a matter of days Alberto's imperturbable optimism gave way to something bleak and withdrawn: a significant realignment was under way in their friendship.

Two weeks later, on 29 October, a group of Italian women returned exhausted to Birkenau camp after slaving on a road-construction site. The Polish guards jeered at them '*Juden! Juden!*' as they jostled to drink from an outdoor tap. Enrica Jona was plunging her head under the water when from the corner of her eye she saw an 'apparition' on the hospital steps. A woman wrapped in a white sheet had come out of the *Revier* looking frail as a ghost. 'She must have heard us talking Italian because she asked from which part of Italy we came. I said I was from Piedmont, and this *wraith* replied that she was from Turin.' Then something extraordinary happened. The woman said: 'My name is Vanda Maestro.' Jona froze. She had heard much about Vanda from her brother Lino, who had been friendly with the Artom brothers in Turin. Under the Polish guards' hostile gaze the women hurried to exchange news. 'And while this happened I stood staring at Vanda and, I swear to God, she was white as chalk. Then she said these awful words to me, which I can never forget: "I'm not coming home." Those words were said to me with absolutely certainty. "*Io non ritornerò*", and in fact I believe Vanda died soon after.' Vanda Maestro was gassed on Monday 30 October 1944. It was said that friends had procured her a tranquilliser so that she would not go conscious to the gas. After the war, Enrica Jona never told Levi that she had seen Vanda alive.

The day after Vanda was 'disinfected', the Birkenau gas chambers, together with the lists of eliminated prisoners, were destroyed. Not only the documents, but also the buildings of destruction were to disappear. With the Red Army steadily driving the Germans out of eastern Poland and most of Hungary, the Nazis were in a hurry to eradicate all evidence of their crime.

7

Winter was approaching, and beyond the camp's barbed wire the snow lay piled in white drifts, muting the sounds and movements of Auschwitz IV. Almost four months had passed since the July exam, and still Levi had no word of the result. This was the second winter of his captivity, and the pre-dawn march to work seemed doubly icy and cold. One thought alone gave Levi hope: he had seen his registration number (174517) on a list of prisoners outside the Polymerisation Department. He did not know what the list was for, but believed that it referred to the I. G. Farben laboratory. Levi was right; he was now among a privileged caste of specialist slaves who were destined to live a few months longer than their fellows.

In the meantime he was living by sheer force of will, along with Perrone's soup ration, and nothing much else. Alberto Dalla Volta was with Levi when a food parcel arrived from Italy addressed to Lorenzo Perrone and again sent by 'Signora Lanza'. Levi shared his windfall of biscuits, ersatz chocolate and powdered milk with Alberto, then wrote a third message home via Perrone. This time he was less guarded about his hopes and fears:

> Dearest,
>   Finally we've received what for so long we've been waiting for
> – you can imagine our joy. I'm still in reasonable health despite
> the first signs of winter. My morale is steady. I beg you to contact
> the dellavolta [*sic*] family in Brescia I beg you for ever for ever. I
> dream of you all for whole nights and of our house and of how life
> was, and of how I hope it will still be. May God provide that we
> find each other again before long. I beg you. Do whatever you can
> because I have so much faith in you. All good wishes from the one
> who continues to remember you, your most affectionate Lorenzo
> bye bye.

This communiqué – Levi's last home – cleared the Auschwitz censors on 1 November. By then the Dalla Voltas were nowhere to be found in their native Brescia. Guido's wife Emma (now, unknown to herself, a widow) had vanished into the Mantovan hills, while her son Paolo had joined the Communist Resistance. Guido's five brothers were likewise dispersed invisibly throughout Occupied Italy. They could not have guessed at the savagery inflicted on their kin. One of their cousins, Riccardo Dalla Volta, had been gassed at Auschwitz at the age of eighty-two; formerly he was rector of Pisa University.

In mid-November Levi heard the extraordinary news that he had been chosen to enter the laboratory. Out of eighty candidates only two other Jewish prisoners – Jean Kandel, Palptil Brackier – had been accepted to work there as chemists. Kandel, a French Jew of Romanian extraction, was thirty-eight years old. Of Brackier there is no trace today in the Auschwitz files, other than that he was a Polish-born Belgian. For nine months Levi had been a Jewish slave labourer – the lowest form of Auschwitz life – but now he had made a huge step up the ladder to greater privilege. His paltry food, clothes and footwear would not change; he still wore the same unwashed striped uniform, and in the evenings he was once again a common *Häftling* to be brutalised in the usual way. Yet working during the day with a roof over his head, he was sheltered from the harsh Polish winter and so his need for food would be less pressing. Moreover, he would have potentially useful contacts with civilian workers and was in a unique position to steal chemistry glassware, soap, petrol, alcohol, to sell on the camp's black market. Lorenzo Perrone's daily soup ration could be supplemented with edible oxidised paraffin, toasted cotton wool (which contained cellulose nutrient: only a chemist would know that) or sustaining fatty acids. Now that Levi had privilege, he was treated better by the *Lager*'s upper castes. And the better-off prisoner had more self-respect and more hope.

Levi entered the Polymerisation Department towards the end of November. This vast complex had six telephone lines and thirty civilian staff recruited from the cream of German industry. A triumvirate of chemists ran the *P-M-Abteilung*. These were Dr Pannwitz, Dr Hagen and Dr Otto Probst. Their names frequently crop up in Auschwitz IV survivor testimonies; Probst, a barrel-chested man, was thirty-four years old and, like Pannwitz and Hagen, worked for BASF, which was one of the I. G. Farben subsidiaries. The department was shrouded in dirty fog and pervaded by a coal-tar stench.

For the first time in nine months, Levi found himself in the company of women. While he had grown accustomed to the sight of Polish prostitutes promenading with SS officers outside the camp's brothel on Sundays, the women had seemed unreal to him, mannequins with rouged faces. Now in the laboratory Levi was in daily proximity with Polish, German and Ukrainian women, florid maidens with swastika badges. Leaning close together, they whispered of the slave-chemist Levi that he was a '*Stinkjuden*', and chattered of what they would do for Christmas. Just one girl, Sina Rasinko, was sympathetic to Levi. She was one of fifteen Ukrainian women trained by BASF at Ludwigshafen in synthetic-rubber production and intended for work in Auschwitz. The women had all made the long journey east from Ludwigshafen by train. Levi remembered Sina as the 'sweetest' and 'most capable' of the girls; the others 'despised us and disdained to approach us [Jews]'.

8

The laboratory kept Levi alive that winter: outside it was fifteen degrees below zero, but inside, Bunsen jets burned orange, and a Höppler thermostat bubbled on the tiles. The aromatic amber odour of styrene must have transported Levi back to organic chemistry lessons. ('Styrene may be found in the balsam of certain Asia Minor trees', Professor Ponzio had lectured); most of Levi's time was spent dismantling apparatus during the ever-more frequent air-raids, then reassembling it once the alarm had passed. He felt uneasy at colluding in the German war effort and began to sabotage production by muddling test tubes and botching samples, secret misdeeds which filled him with a small joy. And his glee was shared by other saboteurs. Leonardo De Benedetti had worked briefly in a gardening Kommando, where he delighted in uprooting SS cauliflowers. 'I thought I was helping to famish the Third Reich,' he recollected. More serious sabotage was practised daily by the British POWs. 'The big roof trusses we put up on the worksite kept falling down and smashing because we never tightened the bolts,' remembered Alfred Battams. 'You have to laugh – it's the good times you remember.'

A sense of fear returned to Levi in the lab, such as he had not experienced on the worksite, where he was so traumatised that he could think only of his immediate survival. When you are near death, death is the last thing on your mind. But the warm lab now provided the emotional respite for Levi to take stock and reflect on the horror outside. On a number of occasions he considered killing himself with a lethal chemical; suicide would be preferable to death at the hands of the Nazis. (Curiously, there were very few suicides in Auschwitz: suicide is the act of a sentient human being – 'animals don't commit suicide,' Levi remarked.)

He did not seriously contemplate suicide as he knew that his story would have to be told – if he managed to survive. So he secretly began to jot down random observations: names, faces, incidents. A notebook had been assigned to him for analytic chemistry, 'but the very act of writing was suspect and highly dangerous', recalled Levi. Yet as defeat for Germany now looked possible, so he took greater risks in his efforts to stay alive. He had to stay alive – for the next minute, the next day, the next week – in order to write of what he had seen. For Levi was now the bearer of memory, a witness. The risk of discovery inhibited his note-taking, however, and in fact the notes never amounted to more than 'twenty lines'. Soon after, he destroyed the jottings and began to commit them to memory. *If This is a Man* was born in the Auschwitz laboratory.

In the weeks before Christmas 1944, ice formed on the chemical bottles and the suction hoods were frozen solid. Synthetic rubber production, due to commence on 1 February 1945, was again put back by the Allied air attacks. Everything was going wrong for the Germans. One day a commotion ensued when it was discovered that there was no more cotton wool in a packet: Levi had eaten it. He was so nervous that he accidentally broke some glassware. A tall, serious-looking German, whom Levi did not recognise, came in to impose order. His name was Ferdinand Meyer and he looked at Levi with a certain curiosity. He did not scold him for the shattered glass, but tried instead to calm him. Meyer even asked Levi why he looked 'so scared'. Levi was bewildered, embarrassed, and still very frightened of reprisal. He was unshaven and covered with scabs, yet a man was speaking to him as if he were human. 'Your eyes seemed to plead' – Meyer reminded Levi half a century later – 'and I cannot forget what then appeared to be your hopeless dejection . . . From that day on I became attached to you.' Afterwards Meyer obtained Levi a voucher that allowed him to visit the barber twice a week and issued him with a pair of leather shoes to replace his wooden clogs. Levi asked himself: what sort of specimen was this? Using the polite *Sie*, the German had enquired after Levi's welfare.

No trace survives today of Ferdinand Meyer in the Auschwitz archives. His name does not appear in the camp's main catalogue, nor in an index based on survivor statements, nor even in the 400 files held in the Auschwitz Museum on I. G. Farben officials. Seemingly, Meyer has evaporated from his place of shame. The little we know of him comes from his daughter Cordula and still-extant correspondence. A devout Catholic, thirty-six years old, Meyer had graduated from Cologne University and had been married for five years by the time he was transferred to Auschwitz from BASF Ludwigshafen. On arrival at the *Lager*, Meyer had been installed in BASF's plush Accommodation Block and introduced to I. G. Farben's technical director, Dr Max Faust. Faust told Meyer what was expected of him: Jews were to be given 'nothing but the most menial tasks – no pity for them was to be tolerated'. Yet, if we are to believe his own account, Meyer instructed a German foreman to issue a group of Jews with sheepskin jackets because of the cold. (It seems incredible that such an order could have been carried out.) On the few occasions Levi saw Meyer, he detected an awkward humanity in him. He noticed Meyer's indulgence towards the Ukrainian girls in the lab (whose 'cheerful yet melancholy singing' Meyer said he loved) and suspected an emotional entanglement with Sina Rasinko.

Meanwhile, hope of a Russian victory infected the prisoners. At great risk to his life, Perrone continued to bring Levi his half-litre of potato-peel soup, but this charity was not to last much longer. Perrone feared the Russians and, perhaps half believing Nazi propaganda about the barbarous Asiatic hordes, at the end of December he fled Auschwitz. Accompanied by a fellow Italian, he set out to reach Piedmont on foot. They slept in haylofts by day, and walked westward by night, orientating themselves by the stars.

Now Allied planes came to shake the camp daily; Hitler was going to lose the war. And, in face of the Soviet offensive, an element of disorder crept into the Nazis' heel-clicking *Ordnung*. A German chemist asked Levi to mend her bicycle tyre, and she even said 'please'. Despite the ban on Jews entering air-raid shelters, the technician Herr Stawinoga flouted orders by leading Levi to a bunker during a bombardment. Stawinoga's was a serious infraction of the 'Aryan' code that regulated Jewish relationships with Germans. But, as the camp's pyramid structure of red, green and yellow triangles began to collapse, so the civilians grew more heedless of SS authority. A Dutch chemist, Meister Gröner, smuggled bread to a Jewish compatriot, but then Gröner vanished. A rumour reached Levi that he had been sent to the Russian front in punishment.

On Christmas Day 1944 the Polymerisation Department closed. Ferdinand Meyer took the night train back to Germany and within a brisk seven hours was at Heilbronn. Now at last he could see Hitler's Germany for what it was: a moral and material ruin. Heilbronn, 'the jewel of the Neckar Valley', had been flattened in a single air raid. Meyer and his pregnant wife Christina picked their way through the city's rubble accompanied by their four-year-old daughter Angelika. Families were camping out with their children, competing with the rats for food and shelter. After a wretched Christmas in Heidelberg, Meyer despaired: 'There is no place left for us in this world.' On Boxing Day he caught the last train back to Poland. His transport was strafed by Allied planes outside Stuttgart but arrived safely at Auschwitz on the 27th. At the civilian station he stopped off to buy bottles of red wine for the New Year.

On 1 January 1945 the Germans disbanded the British POW and Italian camps of Auschwitz IV, evacuating the prisoners westwards. The Russian front was now very close, perhaps sixty-five kilometres away. In a last-ditch measure 200 Hitler Youth were mobilised into the People's Army under Herr Doktor Wilhelm Pannwitz. This ragtag army was expected to hold back the Russians and hide the secret of Auschwitz from the world.

Meanwhile the harshest winter on record had settled on Turin. Snow lay banked against apartment walls in the Crocetta. The Fascists had divested the streets and squares of any Jewish, Savoyard or foreign connotations. (The House of Savoy was now held to be traitorous, having sided with the Allies.) Corso Francia became Corso Gabriele D'Annunzio. And Corso Re Umberto was now Corso Indipendenza. At Number 96 Levi's sister lived in poky digs with her partisan comrade Ada Della Torre. The hideout was an ice-box, and through the long winter Ada was reduced to making hats out of her underwear, a contingency that Anna Maria Levi found unseemly. Starvation and disease were predicted for the coming months. And in the record snowfall on 5 January the Crocetta's big beautiful chestnut trees were felled for firewood; families squabbled over the sawn branches.

TWELVE

Waiting for the Russians

1945

I

The last days of Auschwitz were closing in. Again luck enabled Levi to survive. On 11 January 1945 he was admitted to the *Infektionsabteilung* – 'Infectious Diseases Ward' – with scarlet fever. As a result, Levi would escape the imminent evacuation of the camp, when most prisoners died of the cold. The small isolation room was clean, with ten three-tiered bunks, a wardrobe, stools and a closet seat, everything squeezed in a space of three by five metres. Levi now weighed just under thirty-eight kilograms. A scarlet rash had spread across his limbs and trunk; he was drifting in and out of consciousness. 'I never thought Primo would live,' recalled the Italian doctor-prisoner Aldo Moscati who came to see him. 'He had a high temperature and a strawberry tongue.' When Levi was admitted he was the thirteenth patient in the room. Two had typhus, three diphtheria, another a facial erysipelas. The rest had scarlet fever or more than one illness.

Outside, the camp was in chaos. Armoured cars, Tiger tanks camouflaged in white, Germans on horseback, on bicycles, SS with rucksacks, riderless horses, the Ukrainian guards and their dogs, the I. G. Farben officials and the Polish women from the prostitutes' block: all were leaving. On 17 January, Levi's seventh day in the ward, a Greek barber came in to shave the patients one last time. Chaim Aschkenasi (or Ashkenazy), thirty-three, had survived three long years at Auschwitz. Now that the camp was to be evacuated he could not contain his excitement, and he gibbered to Levi in German that all patients able to walk had better get up and leave; orders from the Reich government in Berlin were to leave no witnesses behind. Two Hungarian Jews with scarlet fever climbed out of the window and were never seen again. The total number of sick in the ward, including Levi, was now eleven. Levi felt he had no more resources: 'With a 40° fever I was extremely feeble and could not even walk 1 km', he later wrote to Jean Samuel. Alone in his bunk, he waited to be eliminated by the SS.

Irregular muffled bangs in the distance indicated that the Russians had moved almost within firing range. Budapest and Warsaw had been overrun by the Red Army. A few Jews, learning of the order to evacuate, expected a subterfuge for their mass murder. Nobody really knew what was happening – only that everything was collapsing round the Germans' ears. Comrades came to say farewell to Levi before they left on foot in the snow. 'Come and live with me in Nagykanizsa,' the Hungarian Juri Kaufmann told him: he had less than four days to live. Then Alberto Dalla Volta visited. It was unthinkable that they should be separated in this way. Had Alberto not caught scarlet fever as a child he might well be in the ward now with Levi. He saluted Primo awkwardly – *'Arrivederci, buona fortuna'* – and walked out to his likely death.

The Germans began to burn the Auschwitz registers and clear out the last medicines from Auschwitz III and IV. They dismantled the operating theatre, taking with them surgical tables, electric stoves, aspirin, tweezers. Nothing was to be left to the Russians. The Greek doctor Salomon Samuelidis, born in Athens in 1906, was well equipped for the winter journey ahead. He wore thick trousers, a balaclava hat and carried a rucksack. Suspecting that Levi was going to die, as a cynical parting gift he threw him a French novel, Roger Vercel's 1935 *Tug-Boat*. 'Keep it, read it, Italian. Give it back when we meet again!' he said in a mood of reckless gaiety. Samuelidis was last heard of at Buchenwald camp, in the east of Germany.

2

Outside the snow fell thickly. In the bunk beneath Levi was a young Dutchman from Amsterdam, Manuel Lakmaker. In the bunk above was Charles Conreau, a tall, lugubrious-looking Frenchman. He was a thirty-two-year-old former schoolteacher and Resistance fighter, not Jewish. His high registration number – 200258 – indicated a newcomer with no useful experience and Levi found him irritatingly naive. Levi hid his mess-tin under the mattress and slipped a spoon down the bunk frame; the handle had been sharpened to a knife.

Four other Frenchmen in the ward – Arthur Ducarme, Jean Sertelet, Dilvo Cagnolati, Yves Dorget – had also been Resistance fighters, and were Catholics. Ducarme, fifty-five, had been a cashier. Cagnolati, born in 1923, was a blacksmith. Dorget, in his early thirties, is listed in the Auschwitz files as a 'manual worker'. Sertelet, just twenty-four, was a farmer. All these tough Frenchmen bore the high 200,000 serial number of new arrivals. Therefore they had some body weight and resilience. Isaac Towarowski and Jacques Alcalai, the two French Jews in the ward, were in poor shape. According to the records, Alcalai was a Toulouse merchant and, by Auschwitz standards, already old at fifty-seven. Of the remaining two patients we know nothing save that they were Jewish. These were the Slovak businessman Schenck and the Hungarian chemist Sómogyi. With these ten men, Levi would have to concentrate his thoughts on survival until the Russians arrived, assuming they were not murdered by the SS beforehand.

In the small hours of 18 January, eight days before the Red Army's arrival, the evacuation of the Auschwitz IV *Judenlager* began. The SS in their greatcoats carried rucksacks and stamped their feet to keep warm while they waited for the order to move. Their dogs seemed nervous, growling and leaping restlessly. In the gathering blizzard the Buna-Monovitz *Häftlinge* were lined up at the gates in groups of 1,000, and steadily the sound built up of some 10,000 slaves marching out of the camp in the snow. This was to be a terrifying *Todesmarsch*, 'death-march', of Jews to camps deep in the German interior. Among the evacuees was Levi's old Fossoli companion Franco Sacerdoti, whose close intimacy with Luciana Nissim had paralleled his own with Vanda Maestro. Levi had last seen Franco nine days earlier, on 9 January; after the amputation of a callused toe, he seemed in reasonable health and able to walk. However, Franco's impediment would prove fatal in this mass migration in which all stragglers were to be shot.

The packed snow at the roadside gleamed in the dark as the men trudged onwards just ahead of the Russians. Fifteen metres on either side of the milling column, the SS goaded the weak with sub-machine-guns. Jean Samuel did not dare leave the column for fear of a bullet in his neck, and dragged himself along in the snow. The SS, some of them not much older than sixteen, were shooting prisoners even as they stopped to urinate. Eugenio Gluecksmann, the Hungarian Jewish ex-army sergeant who had counselled Levi to keep smart and clean, died. Thousands like him now lay frozen in roadside ditches. To the sound of frequent rifle-shots, Jean Samuel gave his stumbling Uncle René a hand. Jacques Feldbau, a Toulouse mathematician, walked by Samuel's side all night discoursing feverishly on Fermat's last theorem. Feldbau did not survive: with its hourly yield of debilitation and death, the *Todesmarsch* continued the work of the Nazi extermination programme.

Shortly before dawn on 19 January, a Friday, the evacuees were herded into a disused brick factory on the outskirts of industrial Gleiwitz. Here

Samuel sank gratefully to the ground and slept for four hours – until 10:30 am when the order came to get up. Those unable to rise were dispatched with a bullet. By late evening the column had arrived at Gleiwitz city. More than half the evacuation had now perished. In Gleiwitz the estimated 4,000 survivors were herded into an abandoned camp designed to accommodate 600 people.

3

In Auschwitz, almost 100 kilometres away, authority had fractured, and hardly any SS remained. To Jean Samuel, Levi wrote later: 'Of us prisoners only 800–900 were left in the entire *Lager* – the sick and the worst of the *Mussulman* prisoners.' There was virtually no medicine. A few prisoner-nurses had been appointed at random by the SS. One of these was Dr Aldo Moscati; in his barrack he watched helplessly as the dying made their last feeble journey crawling or tottering off their pallets on to the floor. One by one the 200 men in his care died. In SS parlance they were *Krematoriumreif* – 'crematorium-ripe'. To Levi's knowledge, seven prisoners from the chemical Kommando 98 remained in the abandoned camp. Among them were the Hungarians Römer, Schneider and Béla Fischer, the Romanian engineer Zalman Matkowic (or Matkovits), aged twenty-nine, and Schmul Stern (whom Levi would meet again in Israel in 1967). He did not know that Leonardo De Benedetti was in a nearby barrack, unable to walk owing to a worksite injury.

Levi's scarlet fever had diminished, but now it looked as though the end had finally come. 'The Germans had every intention of killing us and were only waiting to execute orders. On 19 January they inspected the hospital Blocks and made a separate register of Jews and non-Jews': Jews to one side; Aryans to another: that was never a good sign at Auschwitz. As the Germans hesitated between murder and flight, Levi read *Tug-Boat*, in which a Greek steamer is salvaged by the brave barge *Cyclone*. His excitment at reading this, his first book in a year, must have been intense; for a brief few hours he was transported back to the paternal library of 75 Corso Re Umberto and the civilisation of the printed word.

On the night of 19–20 January the Russians unleashed a formidable aerial bombardment on Auschwitz. Three bombs fell on Levi's camp, 'completely destroying Blocks 7, 4, 1, as well as others; all the wooden buildings were badly burned'. Levi was again lucky: his block was not hit. Much of Auschwitz IV, however, was a defenceless ball of fire; the few solitary SS ran for cover in a *sauve qui peut* panic. Assuming that the camp had been razed utterly and the Jews killed, the last Germans now abandoned their uniforms and pulled out. Leonardo De Benedetti, amazed to be alive, found a pile of SS jackets and trousers.

Levi had to rally himself while he was still strong, and salvage what he needed to live from the detritus left by the Germans. On 20 January he ventured out amid the debris and saw that there were 'no more Boches'. He was in a no man's land where nothing much moved or seemed to happen. Corpses lay everywhere, excrement polluted the snow. Prisoners had smashed, soiled, burned, stolen and revenged themselves on their oppressors, burning down the *Kapos*' quarters and scattering belongings like a ransacked wardrobe. A new social order based on small tribal enclaves had evolved with groups of men hunched possessively over pans of boiling cabbages. 'We were free: but we had nothing to eat. We were ill: but we had no heating or clothes,' Levi continued to Jean Samuel. 'The civilian Poles were hidden nobody knew where. We didn't have the shoes – let alone strength! – to look for food. Fortunately we managed to relocate those big potato silos which the SS had dug near our *Lager*, and this saved us from death by starvation.' The potatoes, prised from the frozen earth with pickaxes, were a godsend. Levi, Conreau and Ducarme, the least debilitated of the eleven patients, crept gingerly beyond the perimeter wire in search of a wheelbarrow to transport the food.

His feet bandaged with a torn blanket, Levi staggered unsteadily in the snow. By now Conreau had managed to get a few French words out of him. He understood that Levi was a chemist; otherwise Levi was not forth-coming. It was up to Levi and the two Frenchmen to organize food and heating not only for themselves, but for the eight sick comrades they hoped to save. After a year of uselessly back-breaking labour under the Nazis, this was an awesome responsibility. He went off with Conreau and Ducarme in search of embers from the smouldering barracks on which to cook the potatoes. The salvaged glowing timber provided Levi with his first meal as a free man. He spoon-fed the eight patients who were too weak to feed themselves. Here was an immediate return to humanity. Such selflessness would have been unthinkable under the Germans, when Levi recognised only individual survival. Much later, in a British television documentary, he described how his new-found liberty rekindled a sense of individual responsibility: 'Suddenly your neighbour was no longer your adversary in the struggle for life but a human being who was entitled to be helped. This really was a sort of reawakening for us. Our sensitivity and willingness to help others was being born again in and around us.'

Levi now had sufficient food to survive. Yet he ignored the cries for food coming from the adjoining dysentery ward. 'You think that was cynical?' he asked me in 1986. 'But it was like this: we were boiling soup – a wonderful moment for us because it was the first time we'd invented anything for ourselves. How to make the soup. How to construct a stove. How to fetch water. And there was enough soup for eight people, but not for *three hundred*. And so we shut the door on those patients next door. If we'd shared the soup among the others we'd *all* have perished: as it was, we succeeded in saving a few lives in the dysentery ward.' One of those lives belonged to Lello (Raffaello) Perugia, a wily Roman Jew with a Brer Rabbit's instinct for survival. Levi had heard his cries for help and decided to assist: they had already known each other briefly in the camp. In bringing Perugia water and the remainder of the day's soup, Levi did not know that he was laying the basis for a lifelong friendship.

Conreau was astounded by Levi's ingenuity, and recognised a peer in savoir-faire. In the half-destroyed surgery Levi found a cupboard of chemical flasks and unstoppered them one by one. ' "Hmmm!" – he'd smell a substance – "that's not good, that's okay, that's bad," and so on. In this way Primo found a type of salt for our potatoes!' There was no electricity – the reflectors on the guard-towers had been extinguished in the Soviet raid – but with the aid of a disused lorry battery and an electric bulb, Levi rigged up lighting for his ward. This resourcefulness, the capacity to make things work, was a lesson he had learned from the technically-minded Uncle Corrado.

Meanwhile the Auschwitz III worksite, with its synthetic-rubber and oil plants, was in technological dereliction. Having acted in complicity with Nazism, I. G. Farben was about to abandon the worksite; it had not produced a single drop of 'Buna' rubber. On 21 January, a Sunday, the last train leaving for Germany carried I. G. Farben's female staff. The remaining staff ate what food was left in the kitchens and binged on the alcohol. Ferdinand Meyer, terrified of the vengeful Soviets, spent these last uncertain hours in a bunker with Wilhelm Pannwitz. He asked Pannwitz if legitimate exit passes would be issued by the military. Pannwitz said they would not; in reality he had taken care of himself and obtained his own exit pass to travel home safely to Germany. His colleague in the Polymerisation Department, Dr Hagen, also a Nazi, had done the same.

At midday the government order came from Berlin to shut down the *Buna-Werke* and evacuate the site. Under cover of dark, Meyer left the plant by bicycle. It was 11:00 pm when he arrived at Auschwitz civilian station. There he waited anxiously until a train bound for the zones behind the front pulled in. Meyer clambered aboard and, for half an hour, slept soundly. There was a jolt as Nazi Party guards stopped the train. In a lonely, deserted place close to

Auschwitz, Meyer was told to get off and fight the Red Army. He watched in anger as Pannwitz and Hagen flashed their special red passes to freedom. They had climbed back on the train and slunk off into the night free men.

Meyer's situation was now very dicey: nearby, the sky was red with the blasts and concussions of Soviet artillery. However, he managed to evade his captors and scramble on to a westward-bound train. During the eight-hour journey through Czechoslovakia passengers glanced over at the unshaven German in a mute and hostile way. Through the train window Meyer saw Russian tanks advancing rapidly across the snow. A freight train passed full of Jews in open boxcars exposed to the sleet. Meyer wondered how long they would live. After a week of hazardous rail travel, he reached Dresden towards the end of January. Under constant US air attack, he waded across the River Elbe and made his way north to Bayer's nitrogen plant in Wittenberg, where he had worked before the war. At all costs he had to avoid conscription into the last-ditch Nazi formation, 'The Werewolf'.

At Gleiwitz the SS brutality was fearsome. On 21 January any survivors of the *Todesmarsch* were loaded into open coal-cars for Buchenwald. Many tried to stay as far as possible from the loading point in the hope that they might stay behind and be freed by the Russians. Those prisoners unable to walk were herded into a forest and dispatched with flame-throwers. Among them, it was said, were Alberto Dalla Volta and Franco Sacerdoti. They could barely raise their arms in self-protection. After an atrocious five-day journey, the death-train arrived at Buchenwald. Jean Samuel was among the survivors, though not his uncle René, who was dead from exhaustion. On that day Jean's morale was at its lowest.

On 23 January, as Levi later wrote to Jean Samuel, 'Eighteen Frenchmen had settled in the SS quarters when a patrol of dispersed Death's-Heads entered to find them in the dining-room about to eat. The SS killed them all, lining up the corpses at the bend in the road just where we [the prisoners] were banking on making our exit. Nobody had the strength to bury the dead – they remained there until the Russians arrived.' Before the leather could freeze, Levi removed the dead Frenchmen's precious shoes.

Next day the prisoners from Block 14 raided the empty British POW camp to find the carbonised remains of food parcels and other miscellaneous debris, including Red Cross chocolate, tins of salmon and bacon, soya-bean flour, English cork-tipped cigarettes and bottles of the sweet *Dunkel* beer. Levi's months of underground barter in Auschwitz had brought out the hawk-eyed trader in him, and he devised a currency with which to buy the POW loot. He made candles from beeswax filched from the *Elektromagazin*, and sold them to the inmates of Block 14, who had no electric light.

Corpses lay everywhere – in the snow, in the beds. 'And in this disgusting filth almost everyone suffered from dysentery. The latrines had long since filled up; most of the survivors lay rigid in their beds as though paralysed by hunger and cold,' Levi reported to Samuel. The seventeen-year-old Dutch boy Manuel Lakmaker lay dying in a pool of his own waste. Jean Sertelet, a Frenchman from the Vosges, was also dying. His air-passages had become obstructed: the only way to save him was to open his trachea. Levi went in search of Béla Fischer, but when the Budapest doctor heard the word 'diphtheria' he started back in horror and gestured for Levi to keep his distance. Then Sómogyi died.

At midday on 27 January, nine days after the evacuation of Auschwitz, Levi was heaving Sómogyi's corpse to the common grave when four men in white camouflage approached the camp on horseback. It was a Saturday of bright winter sunshine and the snow-bound wilderness seemed to extend to the edge of Upper Silesia. The horseriders announced: '*Germania kaputt!*' and, dismounting, showed the red stars on their caps. '*Ruski! Ruski!*' Soon they looked embarrassed, even revolted, by what they saw. Maybe these Russians had seen victims of famine, but the men before them were the casualties of more than famine: they were the victims of cruelty. And they had the furtive gaze and gestures of hunted animals. Some of the Jews covered their heads for shame and wept: how could Levi cheer *Evviva –* Hurrah? Riven by pain and foreboding, he hobbled back to his bunk.

On 28 January, the day after Anna Maria Levi's twenty-first birthday, the Red Army mobilised Polish civilians and collaborators to bring food to the camp and remove the corpses. Now the Poles could see for themselves the horror that lay on their doorstep. A cow was sacrificed to the prisoners' hunger, the haunch hacked and bloody in the snow. Many who had survived months of German inhumanity now perished from Russian kindness as, intoxicated by the taste of animal fat, they gorged themselves and died, their livers unable to cope with the surfeit of sugars and unfamiliar proteins. Leonardo De Benedetti stood by helplessly as, unhinged by hunger, his Austrian friend Vaxman (formerly Walt Disney's legal representative in Rome) literally ate himself to death. A sixth sense told Levi to feed himself slowly: it requires energy to digest food, and it was dangerous to impose an unreasonable demand on a frail body. So he ate judiciously from a *pot-au-feu* concocted from goat and packet K-rations.

*

Though he was better, Levi had a relapse of scarlet fever, and for a month he recuperated in a makeshift Russian hospital at the central *Lager*, Auschwitz I. No one yet realised the full horror of the place; even Levi was unaware of the extent of the gassings at Birkenau nearby. More than 500,000 children had been gassed there; day and night human ashes had rained down over the outlying villages. Colonel Vasily Petrenko, who had led the Soviet troops into Birkenau, was not prepared for the tonnes of women's hair and children's shoes he found there (the little boots neatly arranged and numbered). No one yet knew that all Jewish culture from the *shtetls* of Lithuania to the salons of Vienna had been wiped off the face of Europe. Charles Conreau, amazed to have crawled out of this hell alive, came to say goodbye to Levi. They had shared together a drama of extremity and isolation, and had rescued lives. For Conreau, Levi had been '*un excellent camarade*'; the men would meet again.

At the Russian hospital a ragged cross-section of humanity languished in the dormitory with Levi. The children were looked after with sisterly devotion by Laura Austerlitz (the 'Frau Vita' of *The Truce*). Half Jewish, in March 1944 she had been deported to Auschwitz from the infamous converted rice mill in the suburb of San Sabba in Trieste, the only *Lager* in Italy with gas chambers. Austerlitz had survived nine months in Auschwitz. Levi watched as she tried to coax some speech from a three-year-old child, named 'Hurbinek' after a Czech children's puppet. He had not been gassed because a *Kapo* had adopted him as a mascot. All that emerged from the infant's inarticulateness was *matisklo*, perhaps Czech for 'meat'. Levi was subsequently astonished to recognise this wolf-child in a Soviet newsreel of the liberation of Auschwitz: on his stick-like forearm he could make out the tattooed serial number. From Laura Austerlitz he learned later of Hurbinek's fate: 'After a month of suffering the poor lad died; his real name was Heinrich Iwan.'

Prior to the Soviet rescue, only one of the eleven of the *Infektionsabteilung* had died. Now survivor mortality shot up: five of Levi's comrades perished in succession, having been exposed to viruses that may not have existed in the self-contained world of the camp. During the winter the Frenchman Isaac Towarowski died (12 February), followed by Yves Dorget (3 or 4 March). By the end of January 1945 Levi also had to confront the news that Vanda Maestro had been asphyxiated by gas. The sleeping tablets procured for her by a friend had not worked and she died fully conscious. Levi was not yet able, psychologically, to accommodate grief and his first reaction was one of pained surprise rather than despairing grief. 'Nevertheless I knew with extreme clarity that I would suffer later for her death.'

During the long weeks ahead Levi developed an extraordinary friendship with Leonardo De Benedetti. The Russians had appointed the forty-seven-year-old Piedmontese in charge of a surgery in another part of Auschwitz. Though he was tremendously proud to be practising again as a doctor, he could not believe he was alive. Life had become unreal, a queasy dream, and he compared himself to a man 'who has just regained consciousness after a tremendous blow to the head.' Moreover, the camp had been such a 'singular chapter' in De Benedetti's life that he doubted a return to normality. His survival was not easily explained. Born in 1898, by Auschwitz standards he should not have lived beyond a week of entering the camp.

When he was not working in the surgery, De Benedetti wrote several letters home to Turin. Though these are full of tender references to nieces and nephews, they show signs of the first bite of depression. De Benedetti began to fear death in a way he had not done in the camp. As a doctor, his job was to prevent death yet patients were dying all round him. And for the first time he felt the wretchedness of his state. 'My nerves are worse than ever before, which is strange. I'm a free man, and safe, and I should really feel uplifted. Is this the collapse that follows on from a great relief?' De Benedetti's insight into his psychological state was rare among survivors. Few shared his awareness of the disturbance – the neurotic aftermath – that lay ahead so soon after liberation. In 1945 the effect on the psyche of the Nazi camps was simply not known, but De Benedetti had intuited something: that the wound of Auschwitz would never fade, no matter how fortunate he might be afterwards. 'I'm like a beggar who has lost everything – except life.'

4

Levi was in the care of the Russians, but when he would be repatriated was uncertain. On 6 March he left the infirmary on a horse-cart bound for Katowice, where the Soviets had set up a transfer camp. The cart was loaded with other survivors. One of these was a hard-hustling Greek, Leon Levi ('Mordo Nahum' in *The Truce*). The two paired up and spent a week together in search of food and shelter. Polish trains were haphazard and only just beginning to run again and passengers fought for space on the buffers. On the crowded goods-truck the Poles seemed cowed and hostile. No other European country had suffered so much in Hitler's war, and the Poles were in no mood to pity Jews; Levi, in his zebra-striped rags, inspired disdain and fear. At Trzebinia station some peasants stood gawping at him from the platform. A Pole who spoke French advised Levi to conceal his Jewish identity from them: *'C'est mieux pour vous.'*

The train never reached Katowice. Instead the two Levis got off at the small town of Szczakowa, where a Red Cross field-kitchen had been set up by Polish nuns in the grounds of Saint Elizabeth church. The church, dank but welcoming, offered sausage and sauerkraut. Their bellies full, the men proceeded fifty kilometres east on foot to Cracow in search of a bed. Freight trains loaded with machines and crated goods rolled by, with Russian soldiers riding on the flatcars. In the frozen fields smouldered Panzer tanks; bombed buildings showed jagged against the sky. Having arrived at Cracow, they found the railway station noisy with the high-spirited din of Tchaikovsky's 1812 Overture. Its adrenalin-quickening booms and bangs issued from loudspeakers rigged up by the Soviets. Tchaikovsky had written the music in memory of the Russian victory against Napoleon in 1812. In later years, whenever Levi heard this rich, plenteous overture, he was reminded of his week of vagabondage and scavenging with the industrious Greek Leon Levi.

In their terrified retreat the Germans had blown up Cracow's Debnicki Bridge, but the city's castles and steeples remained intact. Szeroka Street crawled with merchants peddling second-hand kitchenware and fur stoles. In entranceways, anywhere out of the cold, poultry was for sale. In what used to be Adolf Hitlerplatz milled Russian uniforms. A Polish priest offered Leon and Primo Levi directions – in Latin – to Cracow Cathedral, where steaming cauldrons fed the destitute. From the Cathedral the duo traipsed on to the old Jewish quarter at Kazimierz, where the synagogue had been desecrated beyond recognition and tombstones broken up by the Nazis for road construction. The Jewish students' home at 3 Przemyska was a brothel. Unknown to Levi, the Italian doctor Aldo Moscati was now assistant medical professor at Cracow's Jagiellonian University, and was allowed to practise privately in town. Moscati had organised new clothes, a comfortable bed and a salary. 'If only I'd known you were in Cracow!' he later wrote to Leonardo De Benedetti in Turin. In post-war Poland, awash with refugees, displaced persons and other lost souls, friends were easily separated. In fact, Levi soon lost sight of Leon Levi. The Greek had been a bickering companion who indulged in high-handed manipulation of his junior partner, forcing him to run errands and carry his bag. He shocked Levi's genteel poise but in return, Leon's hustling and scuffling had taught him tricks in the art of survival.

Levi was in Soviet-controlled territory, but repatriation was continually delayed. He now spent four months at a Soviet assembly camp just outside Katowice. Levi would get to know Katowice so intimately that it became the third most important city in his life after Turin and Milan. Liberated by the Red Army on 27 January 1945 (and soon to be renamed Stalinogród), Katowice had served as the corridor for Nazi infiltration into Poland and the Slav east. Goering had made it one of the main Reich offices for processing confiscated Jewish property, so the city was rich in stolen goods. On the crowded pavements men and women hawked stolen furniture, silverware, cigarettes, old books. There was still spasmodic rifle-fire in the city from the retreating Germans, so Katowice was not entirely safe.

The assembly camp was situated due east of Katowice in the dowdy suburb of Bogucice, where everything was (still is) covered in a grey coal dust. At the top of Wróblewskiego Street stood the camp's twelve barracks for DPs (displaced persons). Only one of these survives today, overgrown with yellow weed and cluttered with rusted mining machinery. Rye fields sway in the breeze; there are oak and linden forests nearby. Formerly the camp had housed the Third Reich's Polish mine-slaves; by the time Levi arrived in March 1945 there were French, Dutch, Greek, Czech and Hungarian DPs occupying the barracks, as well as Polish-Jewish Socialist *Bund* Party members. The internees were sectioned off by nationality. The *Italianski Lager* contained a ragbag of thieves and card-sharps from Milan's San Vittore jail, whom the Germans had deported wholesale to Poland. There were also demobbed soldiers and prostitutes. Levi was billeted with 800 Italians, all desperate to repatriate.

He mingled cautiously with the *furbi* – the smart ones – of the *Italianski Lager*. Cesare Di Consiglio and Giacomo Pavoncello were Jewish card-sharps from Rome's tumbledown Trastevere district, adept at fleecing Soviet guards for zloty bills. They described themselves as the *ragazzi* – 'the boys' – and entertained Levi with their cynicism and wit. Di Consiglio had enough tattoos to cover a circus tent; in *The Truce* he would appear as 'The Velletrano'.

As Levi resigned himself to the life of a displaced person, more desperadoes arrived at Bogucice seeking sanctuary and a safe passage home. On 13 March Leonardo De Benedetti appeared. He and Levi were overjoyed to be reunited. In his mismatched pyjamas, laddered socks and odd shoes, De Benedetti looked dishevelled. His toothbrush moustache (cultivated as a symbolic return to civilian life), bushy blond eyebrows and high-pitched voice lent him a comic air. De Benedetti was a superb diagnostician and soon not only Italians, but Soviet soldiers and Poles were queuing up for his ministrations. He clung to the belief that his wife Jolanda might still be alive; he saw her likeness – the ghost of a smile, a mannerism – in any of his patients. But, deep down, he knew he was chasing a will-o'-the wisp.

Levi had learned at Auschwitz the importance of creating for oneself rank and privilege. He asked De Benedetti if he could provide him with a job in the infirmary. The doctor readily obliged, and at Easter appointed Levi his outpatient clerk. From the start he found Levi 'very bright and willing', as Primo gently ushered patients into the surgery and offered them cups of tea and words of encouragement. De Benedetti was a man of habit and schedules. And his old-fashioned morality and stolid approach to life made him a rock amid the Soviet chaos of the camp. A unique friendship was in the making – based on the special camaraderie of former inmates – and before long Levi was calling the older man 'Nardo'. As a medical sergeant in 1919 De Benedetti had been stationed in the Russian port of Murmansk as part of the Allies' ill-advised expedition against the 'foul buffoonery' (as Churchill then called it) of Bolshevism. After six months he had returned to Turin across the Gulf of Finland, his fellow passengers dying from the Spanish influenza. The Polar Circle had given him invaluable insight into the Russian psyche at Katowice camp.

As Nardo's assistant Levi lived like a king. He ate the standard Russian soldier's ration of soup, vegetable purée, a side plate of fatty meat and 700 grams of bread. He was filling out and regaining his former strength and health. On 25 March – Palm Sunday – an Italian family in the camp invited Nardo and Levi to a Homeric banquet of tagliatelle, roast chicken and fried potatoes dunked in cream. Levi had forgotten that such good things existed. On the whole he found life at Katowice new and interesting. Even the comic indignity of a collective shower each morning was bearable: sixty inmates at a time were hosed down with freezing or (depending on the plumbing) scalding water. The camp's vodka-swilling Soviet guards were a far cry from the precise Prussian order of Auschwitz. It seemed incredible to Levi that these fur-hatted Cossacks and Azerbaijani warriors had beaten Hitler's tenacious and disciplined armies.

6

Meanwhile the frustration of enforced containment bit keenly. The Russians promised departure one day, only to postpone it the next. Italian internment was likely to be prolonged further as the Soviets bombed railways, making travel through western Europe hazardous. Turin was still a Nazi outpost; Levi's sister had been shot at by vengeful Fascists during a partisan funeral, the bullets striking tombstones as she ran for cover. For all Primo knew, his mother might have been deported anywhere, without food, water or medicine, perhaps awaiting the Russians. As it was, Allied planes dropped *matériel* by night over her refuge in Borgofranco, parachutes swaying to the ground with wireless sets and explosives. The Allies had launched their last offensive against the German lines in Italy and were advancing rapidly towards Milan. The liberation of northern Italy was imminent.

With the Russians closing in on the Third Reich from the east, Ferdinand Meyer was on the run. During Easter week his train was attacked by low-flying aircraft as he tried to reach his family in Heidelberg. Escape westwards was his only option as the Red Army surrounded Wittenberg, where he had found shelter with the Bayer firm. On 15 April, as darkness fell, he waded over the River Muld, only to be caught by American GIs and interned in a Leipzig schoolyard with Polish conscripts and other 'low-life' (the word is Meyer's). That same day British troops entered Belsen. Now the Reich's worst secret was out: the piles of naked, decomposed corpses, evidence of humanity dismantled.

On 26 April the Germans were forced to abandon Turin to the partisans. Battles raged round the Fiat and Lancia factories as Fascist snipers picked off targets from the rooftops. Eventually Turin was taken over by the local Committee of National Liberation (CLN), of which Levi's sister was Action Party secretary. Three days later, on the 28th, Mussolini was executed by partisans on the shores of Lake Como. He was strung up by his feet in a Milan piazza with his mistress Clara Petacci. There followed nationwide savage acts of vendetta – what the Mafia call 'balancing of accounts'. Fascists were hunted down and killed; in Turin a high-ranking Party member was driven round the streets on a lorry until a suitable tree was found from which to hang him. On Corso Polonia women were found strung from lamp-posts, their heads shaved and daubed with the legend: 'FASCIST SPY'. Two former chemistry classmates of Levi's, one unrepentantly Fascist, the other violently anti-Fascist, were brought face-to-face in a field outside Turin; when Emilio Lagostena, the Fascist, refused to renounce his beliefs, Morandini Cotta, the anti-Fascist, put a bullet in his head. At university they had been the greatest of friends.

In Berlin, on 30 April, the first Soviet soldiers entered the ruins. Hitler had already killed himself with a pistol (fired by his own hand or someone else's); the city was rubble. On 8 May, with Germany's unconditional surrender, war ceased on the European front. The blitzkrieg was over, and all northern Italy was free, though not all Italians lived to see the Liberation. Grandma Adelina Luzzati died of pneumonia on 4 May, four days before Victory Day. She never witnessed the return of her adored grandson Primo, whom she had been told had spent the war safe in neutral Switzerland. In Turin the GIs drove down the boulevards in jeeps daubed *War Daddy* and

Lucky Strike. For most Italians, the sight of their American liberators was extraordinary. It was the first time many of them had set eyes on black soldiers. The cheering crowds threw them flowers.

The Americans loaded Ferdinand Meyer on to a lorry bound for Hersfeld transit camp. A German-speaking US officer ('whom I was convinced was Jewish') interrogated him. On discovering that Meyer had Auschwitz papers, the American asked what he had done at the camp. Had he manufactured soap or other grisly commerce? 'What I did at Auschwitz,' Meyer replied self-righteously, 'I can justify before God and all men at any time.' The American flung down Meyer's wallet and dismissed him. Meyer was reunited with his family in Heidelberg at the end of June 1945. For the first time he set eyes on his two-month-old daughter Cordula. He had arrived home a full sixteen weeks before Primo Levi.

In mid-May Lorenzo Perrone reached Turin. He had with him Levi's address and went to see his mother at 75 Corso Re Umberto. Ester was now living in a single dank room as bomb damage had left most of the flat uninhabitable. She was startled to encounter this friend of her son, the Po valley artisan who brought news of Primo. Shy and awkward, Perrone told Ester that her son was unlikely to return from Auschwitz. Afterwards he called on Levi's sister at the CLN headquarters on Via Maria Vittoria. Intimidated by the chandeliers and red plush, he nervously approached Anna Maria in her office. 'I was certainly not a very elegant girl, but Perrone looked *unbelievably* wretched. He was so inhibited by my presence that he could scarcely speak.' To Anna Maria he repeated his gloomy prediction that her brother was probably dead. Ester never let on to Anna Maria that Perrone had seen her first: if her son was dead, she preferred not to speak about it, not even to her daughter.

Perrone then walked almost 100 kilometres from Turin to his birthplace of Fossano, where his homecoming was joyless. On 15 May he was found half-dead from brandy and fatigue in a field. Secondo Perrone, the mason's brother, recalled: 'When I asked Lorenzo where the hell he'd been, he refused to say and lurched off with a drinking crony. He didn't want to talk about Auschwitz, what he'd seen there, to anyone.' For most deportees the return to normality was traumatic. Other Italians, however, saw the war's end as a bright new beginning. The Fascist racial laws had been nullified, so Catholics could marry Jews. On that same 15 May Bianca Guidetti Serra married Alberto Salmoni. The new Mayor of Turin, Ada Gobetti, solemnised the civil wedding.

Levi worked hard to wheedle valuable commerce – shoes, shirts, rationed canned goods – from the Poles in Katowice. There was something incongruous about a Turinese of his education and background turning street trader. However, he had found a superb business partner in the Roman Jew Lello Perugia. The two had met in the last days of Auschwitz in the dysentery ward when Levi had brought Lello food. Most of the Turinese at Katowice regarded Lello as an amusingly vulgar, coarse-tongued chancer. He was as un-Turinese a character as it is possible to imagine. Expert in what southern Italians call *l'arte di arrangiarsi* – 'the art of getting by' – Perugia had a gift for imaginative improvisation and was always scheming ways to earn a crust. To avoid arbitrary conscription into a Red Army artillery unit he had clamped a damp cigar under his armpit and produced such a raging fever that he was exempted from the ranks. Another of Perugia's tricks was to simulate dysentery by mixing excrement (his own) with anti-incendiary sand; it looked yellow.

Yet beneath Lello's bravado lay a proud morality. The Gestapo had come for him in the Abruzzo hills in the spring of 1944, and after ten days' brutal interrogation deported him to Auschwitz. Of his four missing brothers, only Angelo was still alive; the others had died under the Nazis. Today Perugia lives on the outskirts of Rome with his Polish-Venetian wife and their dog Ugo. His memories of Levi are not always reliable, though he has immense charm, with his rich Roman argot and meridional nous. At Katowice his nickname for Levi was *Lapè* – 'Rabbit' – because his de-portee's hair was short and downy. ('And rabbits are good, kind animals.') In *The Truce* Lello is thinly disguised as the adroit Roman slyboots 'Cesare', and in *If This is a Man* as 'Piero Sonnino'.

No one could bargain like Lello, and Levi was quick to accompany him on missions to Katowice to wangle food and clothes. Like most Romans, Lello used a variety of hand gestures to emphasise a point, insult a rival or generally put someone in their place. '*Lapè* loved to watch me talking to market women with my fingers, smiling winningly at the girls!' For an entire week the Roman gorged himself on free clotted cream by going from one market stall to the next and, with the air of an expert, dipping his spoon in barrels to sample the quality. Lello did not think much of the Turinese in the *Italianski Lager*: they had poor business sense. '*Lapè* wasn't the only lousy organiser. I had to hustle on behalf of *twenty* Turinese.' Lello had useful contacts with the fishmongers and shoeshine boys from Rome's Quadrato district, who had stockings, cigarettes and other luxury commodities to barter. He was concerned that the Auschwitz IV soup –

Bunasuppe – had been impregnated with bromide to make the prisoners impotent. One spring day he had encountered in Katowice a market girl who asked him temptingly: 'Macaroni? Meat?' The macaroni, Lello recalled, was 'mushy', but one thing led to another and 'we went to bed'. Afterwards he clapped a consoling hand on Levi: 'You too will get the urge again, *Lapè*.'

On 6 June 1945, after three months of prevarication, Levi gathered his thoughts for a long letter home. He still did not know if his family were alive. Bianca Guidetti Serra was the addressee:

> We're not too badly off here, and there's more than enough to eat (though Russian cuisine does require a special stomach). We sleep soundly, do little work and enjoy some limited freedom. With a bit of initiative we can roam about town and treat ourselves to the luxury of some extra food, a film, or a cut-price tourist tour of the city. There are now over one thousand of us Italians here, including POWs, political prisoners and *rastrellati* [non-Jewish victims of Nazi round-ups]. The local population is well disposed to us, as are the Russians.

Then came an abrupt change of tone:

> Don't believe a word of what I was able to write to you from Buna-Monovitz; my year under the SS was terrifyingly hard, owing to the cold and hunger, the beatings and perpetual danger of being *eliminated* if you were consistently unfit for work. I'll be coming home to Italy (I hope) with my matriculation number tattooed on my left arm; a proof of infamy.

There was an extraordinary PS:

> Maybe I'll come home shoeless, but in compensation for my ragged state I've learned German and a bit of Russian and Polish, I also know how to get out of many situations without losing my nerve, and how to withstand moral and physical suffering. To economise on the barber I'm sporting a beard. I know how to make a cauliflower or turnip soup, cook potatoes in a hundred different ways (all without seasoning). I know, too, how to assemble, light and clean stoves. And I've been through an incredible variety of careers: assistant bricklayer, navvy, sweep,

porter, grave-digger, interpreter, cyclist, tailor, thief, nurse, fence, stone-breaker. I've even been a chemist!

There is no mistaking Levi's pride. He had received unique instruction in the philosophy of endurance, and had learned many things about the world and the ways of man: the Primo Levi who eventually washed up in Turin was not a helpless innocent. He concluded with a reference to Lorenzo Perrone: 'Nobody knows how much I owe that man; I could never repay him.' On receipt of this letter, Levi's sister went to the Polish military command in Turin in the hope of obtaining further information about her brother's whereabouts. Officers from General Anders's Army, in their long blond moustaches and gold service stripes, noted her Jewish surname and were not disposed to help. Ever tenacious, Anna Maria tried the Soviet military command in Milan where she was reassured: 'My dear, *all* prisoners of the Soviet Union are treated well!'

8

Summer continued, and still no word of Levi's return. Filled with nostalgia, harassed by anxieties, he had made up his mind to leave Katowice, when at the end of June he was suddenly ill. De Benedetti diagnosed the telltale 'rub' of advanced pleurisy. In a week Levi's body weight had reduced so drastically that an Italian inmate mistook him for an 'emaciated sixty-year-old'. Though Nardo lacked the knowhow to become a *commerciante*, he was forced to bargain in Katowice for calcium injections, sulpha-pills and penicillin. With the help of a dermatologist, Adolf Einhorn (the inscrutable polyglot Jew 'Dr Gottlieb' of *The Truce*), Levi's pleurisy lifted. Illness had brought him still closer to Nardo, creating an unbreakable bond of mutual affection and respect; in later years Levi said that Nardo 'saved' his life.

On 30 June, not for the first time, the Russians began shouting '*Ripatriatsiya!*' This time apparently they meant it. The Italians were to be repatriated via Odessa. Amid tearful farewells Levi was given glowing written testimonials by a Russian medical captain, who praised his good work with the out-patients. Pleasingly well documented by Soviet officialdom, Levi boarded a troop-train destined for Odessa with a herd of jubilant Italians. Among them were Nardo and Lello. From Odessa it was to be a journey by ship across the Black Sea and the Aegean to Bari in southern Italy. That was the theory anyway. The train travelled at a snail's pace, stopping at every station. Whenever Levi asked the driver where they were headed, he was told infuriatingly: 'We'll go wherever we find a platform.' After six days the train ground to a halt 240 kilometres outside Odessa. Word went down the line that the camp there could take no more refugees. For many that was the last straw; on 8 July Adolf Einhorn got off the train and vanished (surfacing sixteen years later in Rome to give Lello Perugia a silver wedding plate). Later Levi suspected that the Russians planned to hold the Italians hostage in the event of hostilities with America. There was already talk of an atomic bomb and confrontation between the USSR and the West.

Instead of proceeding south-west in the direction of Italy, the convoy now rambled interminably northward into the heart of the steppe, away from the promised Black Sea. The disorder and confusion *à la russe* had begun to fray Levi's nerves. After a five-day stop at Minsk, the Italians were escorted on foot to a camp sixty-five kilometres south, Starye Dorogi, in the wilds of Russia. The camp had no barbed wire; the DPs could come and go as they pleased. For two months, plagued by uncertainty and discomforts, Levi stayed here with the other Italians. He regretted that he had not followed the example of his braver compatriots and left Katowice months earlier: some of them would be in Italy now. Yet Levi would look back fondly on his eight weeks at Starye Dorogi. During the white nights he could hear in the distance the Red Army's carousing. Teenage Russian conscripts were on their way home from the front; some were heading for the frozen immensity of Tartar territory. From the top of Nazi buses captured in Berlin they waved to Levi, singing 'Kalinka Kala'. At a nearby collectivised farm Levi bartered for foodstuffs; the canny Perugia sluiced old herrings in soap-water to mask their rank smell; in return for this doctored produce he got chicken, cheese and butter.

9

On 31 July it was Levi's twenty-sixth birthday, his second birthday away from home. His health continued to be troublesome as he suffered a flare-up of bronchitis. Now that Jews were no longer debarred from National Service in Italy, Levi received a summons to arms. An Italian recruiting officer stamped his conscription papers on 9 August: 'FAILED TO REGISTER'. Levi stood accused of being absent without leave. Good news came for his mother on 11 August when, after a long bureaucratic wrangle, she obtained legal repossession of her apartment.

Levi was beginning to fear a third bitter winter away from home when, in September, the Red Army's defence commissar, Marshal Timoshenko, promised immediate departure. He asked the Italians to sing him 'O Sole Mio', which they tearfully did, and on 15 September they finally left for home. The sky was a wonderful heady blue, and as the train crossed the great plain of East Europe, Levi reflected on the nights of sickness, the ludicrous deviations into Belorus and the continuous official lunacy of the Soviets, but also their great unregarding munificence. But now he was embarking on the greatest journey of all, a thirty-five-day railroad odyssey home to his birthplace.

Steaming westwards, the train slowed down over Bailey bridges and new tracks laid over shell-bursts. The first shop-signs glimpsed in Romanian looked tantalisingly like Italian; there were fields of flax and farm-carts full of hay. On 24 September the convoy was steaming towards Austria when it ground to another halt at Curtici in Romania. 'What now?' Seething with impatience, Lello Perugia struck out on his own. With his rough unshaven face and his cropped hair, not surprisingly he found it hard to earn the air fare to Italy. Eventually he got himself a seat, reaching Italy in the last week of December 1945. The RAF Transport Command carrier landed at the southern Italian port of Bari, the burial place of the original Father Christmas, St Nicholas.

In early October, having been rerouted, deviated and delayed, Levi's train was clanking rapidly across Hungary. On the 6th he reached Budapest. Two days later, outside Vienna, the locomotive stopped. In this stricken city Levi saw pedestrians picking their way through the Allies' rubble. They had pale faces and distended bellies, and they did not look at Levi. There was not merely defeat here, but debasement. Picking up speed now, the train moved west through St Pölten, Loosdorf, and finally to a transfer camp at St Valentin, where the Italians were sprayed with DDT and fed a mulch of cabbage and potato.

On 15 October Levi entered the catastrophically razed city of Munich. His prison tattoo burned on his arm as he moved among the sheepish, shame-faced Germans. Munich, the cradle of Nazism, was now part of the depopulated and ruined Deutschland. Jewish refugees sat huddled in the now-roofless waiting room of the Munich Hannover station. Outside Munich, a truckload of Zionists and other scattered remnants of European Jewry joined the Italians' repatriation train. If Levi's family turned out to be dead, he would consider following them to the Promised Land.

The train sped on through ravaged southern Germany, a zone of blackened forests and blown bridges. In the fading light Levi saw German labour gangs traipsing homeward, and the sight did not displease him. When the convoy crossed the Brenner Pass he knew that his journey's end was near. Yet Levi was sick with fear that his present suffering must be followed by more suffering. Of the 650 Jews who had left Fossoli on 22 February 1944, Levi was just one of twenty-four returning. Everything that had gone before – the Russian chaos, the black marketeering – was an irrelevancy now as he was poised to be released back into civilian life.

On 17 October Levi reached Verona, the first big Italian city he had seen in twenty-two months. There was no connection for Turin until the following day, so he travelled on to Milan. Before he returned home, he wanted to know if his family – his mother and sister – were alive. He headed for 31 Via Ariosto, a Milan address he knew well. Pia Astrologo lived there. She and her husband Italo had been hiding in the snow-bound heights of Aosta when Levi was arrested in 1943. The doorbell rang as Pia was boiling water for a cup of coffee before putting her baby to bed. She put the sleeping infant down carefully on the table and went to open the door. On seeing who it was, she was overcome. She had not seen Levi in almost two years. Levi did not say where he had been. 'And I don't think I asked. You see, Auschwitz was an unknown name then – I had no idea what Primo had gone through, or how awful his disorientation must have been.' Instinctively Pia understood that she needed to talk to Levi of ordinary things. She asked him to light the coal fire in her grate because it was chilly. Levi crouched by the fire and, looking back over his shoulder, began to ask Pia questions. 'He wanted to know who was still alive among us, if the house in Turin was still standing. I told him that his mother and sister had survived, and that Luciana Nissim was saved.'

As the room filled with warmth Levi cradled the sleeping Silvana, the first Italian baby he had held since V-Day. Nothing else of consequence passed that afternoon between him and Pia Astrologo. Levi never told his mother of his brief stay in Milan, or wrote of the episode, or spoke to anyone else in the family about it. Perhaps he felt a sadness, or guilt, that he had not gone directly to Turin to tell his mother he was alive.

On the morning of 19 October 1945, Levi reached Turin. It was a Friday. Making his way past sleeping figures on the station platform he walked towards the Crocetta. No one recognised Levi. With the defilement of Auschwitz deep within him, he wondered what reception awaited him at home. And with a tremor he stepped over the threshold of 75 Corso Re Umberto. The first to see Primo was the concierge Marina Bertone, who had known him since his teens. But she did not recognise this bearded, scrub-headed stranger, and brusquely asked him what business he had. There was a silence before she began shouting up the stairwell to Primo's mother. '*Madama Levi! Madama Levi!*'

THIRTEEN

Homecoming
1945–6

I AM ALIVE, AND WAS DEAD . . . WRITE THEREFORE THE
THINGS WHICH THOU HAST SEEN.

Revelation, I, vv. 18–19

I

A childhood friend of Levi's, Leo Avigdor, called at 75 Corso Re Umberto later that Friday morning in October 1945. Avigdor had fled to Switzerland during the racial persecutions and had just returned to Turin. Ignorant of Levi's fate under the Nazis, he dropped by hoping to see his old friend. In the kitchen he found what he took to be a stranger hunched over a bowl of soup. He had a scrawny beard and his eyes were red from tears. But the most shocking aspect of his appearance was the swollen face. Malnutrition oedema – swelling of the tissues caused by fluid retention from a low-protein diet – had left Levi's face tumid and bloated. He was wearing a Red Army uniform. Levi's mother offered Avigdor a morning coffee, but he demurred and quickly left. The encounter had lasted scarcely five minutes but Avigdor hurried to spread news of the exile's return; he had been among the first in Turin to see Levi back alive.

Within twenty minutes the flat was milling with well-wishers. There were so many visitors that Levi's mother had to keep the front door propped open. At first Levi had wanted only to hide; unable to put his emotion into words, all he could say to his friend Bianca was '*Ciao.*' Others who had not seen Levi for two years were greeted in the same awkward way. But gradually he relaxed. Livio Norzi rushed round to find him holding court to a disbelieving circle of friends, among them Giorgio Lattes and Alberto Salmoni. 'After we had all been resigned to Primo's loss, his sudden return seemed all the more astonishing,' Norzi said.

In the two years of his absence Levi had been transformed, and many did not recognise him. Before deportation he had been slim and pale with wavy hair; now he was florid, pouchy, with unaccountably straight hair. On the tram one day in Turin his university colleague Nereo Pezza looked straight through him. 'I had no idea it was Primo – his face looked like a big red football.' But, in spite of his swollen aspect, friends and family continued to exclaim: 'How strange! You haven't really changed.' Indeed, to judge by his fat-looking face, it was assumed he had eaten abundantly and well. Bianca Guidetti Serra shared everyone's alarm at Levi's changed appearance but saw no hint of his emotional disarray. If anything Levi appeared more mature, his senses sharpened.

Within days, however, the exhilaration of his homecoming had evaporated. Bianca and company seemed so proud of their anti-Fascist militancy: and this rankled with Levi. The Resistance had been their most exciting adventure – a triumph immune from judgment or regret – but there was no glory in having been an Auschwitz slave. The shame was indelible. Levi began to envy his friends' contented, well-ordered lives; he was in reasonable physical shape, but he felt alienated and angry.

2

More than 6,800 Italian Jews – one-fifth of the country's Jewish community – had perished in the Nazi camps. Virtually every Jewish family in Italy had lost a relative or friend to Auschwitz. Levi's immediate family had survived, at least, and his house had not been destroyed. Crucially, too, Levi was young – still only twenty-six – and did not have to suffer the loss of a wife or children. A much older survivor, Leonardo De Benedetti, was sunk in the most intense period of despair. Nardo could never forget his murdered wife Jolanda, and he haunted Turin's railway stations in the hope of glimpsing her return. Still he was determined to live: his suicide would only be Hitler's victory. Anyway Nardo was luckier than some. As his repatriation train had pulled into Turin he saw that his cousin's house on Corso Sommeiller was still standing. Welcomed there, Nardo became a surrogate father to a host of cousins, nephews and nieces who lovingly nurtured him back to life. And so his 'unspeakable grief', as he called it, was tempered.

Meanwhile Levi's mother and sister had difficulties of their own – 75 Corso Re Umberto was scarcely habitable after the bombardments. And much of the family furniture – chests of drawers, Persian carpets – had to be retrieved from the cellars of the ex-Gestapo headquarters at the Albergo

Nazionale off Via Roma. (The hotel had been requisitioned by the Germans and turned into torture chambers as well as a warehouse for all the loot stolen from the Jews of Turin.) Thirty per cent of housing in Turin was destroyed or damaged, and half the streets, roads, bridges and railways were rubble. Ester Levi was much concerned with finances for the year ahead; but her son, hurled into the unaccustomed role of head of the family, was too mentally distraught to look for work. He no longer had the same enthusiasm or believed in people the same way. How could he? Sandro Delmastro had been shot, Emanuele Artom tortured to death; Uncle Mario and his son Roberto had been drowned in a lake. These deaths intensified Levi's experience of loss in the camp. And he feared death in a way he never had at Auschwitz. There, talk of death had been considered indecent by the prisoners – 'like mentioning cancer at a dinner party' – but now death was on Levi's mind constantly.

Levi was in trauma, and was disturbed in a way that only Nardo could understand. After the nightmare intensity of the camp, everything seemed colourless, futile and false. 'I had the sensation that I was living,' Levi told me in 1986, 'but without being alive.' Memories of his persecution surfaced unexpectedly. It was enough for trains to whistle distantly outside the Crocetta flat and Levi was back at Auschwitz. The habit of civilisation seemed to be very fragile in him. A friend was shocked to see him attack a wild persimmon bush on a walk one day, chewing on the fruit. On the first night of his homecoming Levi had slept with an SS eiderdown purloined from the camp, a chunk of bread secreted under his pillow; his own soft bed seemed an impossibly civilised amenity after his months of incarceration and railway vagabondage.

Levi was reluctant to seek medical help for his unending bad nights. Miranda Avigdor, who had accompanied him on the railroad journey home from Poland, was now in a mental home in Turin. Yet, Levi knew that the qualities which had helped him survive the camp must also help him find his way back to normal life.

The dark moods lifted somewhat in the mountains. In retracing his old climbs, visiting the familiar alpine huts and highways, Levi was recovering his youthful happiness. In a way, too, he was going back over the dead Sandro Delmastro's tracks. This was not morbid sentimentality. Delmastro had taught Levi how to withstand the cold and fatigue of the camp. With his ice-pick and rope, Levi needed to show that he was still strong and capable. He climbed the Maritime Alps with Livio Norzi, who found a moral and spiritual edification in high places. Norzi provided much-needed relief to Levi's weighed-down heart. Together they visited the prehistoric cave paintings on the French border at Montebego. There, Levi compared the

Stone Age hunters to chemists: by encouraging manual agility and a keen sense of smell, he said, chemistry took us back to our remote mammal origins. This eccentric chemist-as-hunter conceit was a glimmer of the old Levi.

Like all exiles, Levi felt that he had come back to a different world. Everywhere he went, Italians spoke fearfully of Russia's atom bomb and asked how long it would be before there was a Red Square in Rome. New class wars were prophesied with a final catastrophic crumbling of Italy's post-war society. But Levi, having been rescued by the Red Army from the camp, was unable to share the establishment's anti-Communism: Soviet Russia was no democracy, he could see that, yet without Stalingrad the Nazis might have won the war and all Europe would now be a vast German colony. Levi's instinctive pro-Sovietism only added to his feeling of loneliness and alienation. To aggravate matters, suddenly it appeared that no Italian had ever been a Fascist. As if the word 'new' could expunge a newspaper's murky Blackshirt past, Turin's daily *La Stampa* was renamed *La Nuova Stampa*.

3

Meanwhile the deportees continued to return to Turin, and photographs of lost souls appeared on the city walls: HAVE YOU SEEN THESE MEN? As well as deportees, some 378,600 Italian POWs had yet to be accounted for, dead or alive. As autumn 1945 turned to winter, Levi steeled himself for the worst task of all: seeking out the relatives of those who had not survived. He felt morally obliged to help these kin as they searched desperately for some meaning to their shattered lives. That winter he arranged to visit Alberto Dalla Volta's mother in Brescia, where she was living with her son Paolo. Levi knew for certain that Alberto had not survived the evacuation of Auschwitz and that his father had been 'selected' for the gas chambers. How to tell Emma Dalla Volta the truth? According to the offical records, her husband and son were presumed dead or, as the Red Cross put it, 'dispersed.'

Levi arrived in an ill-fitting greatcoat that scuffed the floor. In a low monotone he began to speak of Auschwitz, but Signora Dalla Volta asked him to change the subject. Without any proof to the contrary, how could she believe that her husband and son were not still alive? On a subsequent visit she explained to Levi that Alberto had sent her a note (in green ink) to the effect that he had recuperated in a Soviet clinic and was now working for the Russians as an atomic chemist. Emma Dalla Volta was not alone in preferring comfort to the truth. Levi's aunt Emma Agostina Coen took five years to accept that her husband and son had been drowned by the SS in Lake Maggiore. Bodies of murdered Jews continued to float to the lake's surface until the late 1940s (one policeman claimed to have counted more than 200), yet no corpse of Mario or Roberto Levi was ever found.

A burning question now stalked Levi's recovery: *perché io e l'altro no?* Why me and not the others? Levi's survival when so many had died had become his shame. Lorenzo Perrone was another who had developed a survivor's guilt. In the Christmas weeks of 1945 Levi sought out the mason in Fossano where he lived. Morosely, Perrone evaded the subject of Auschwitz and, with a drunkard's truculence, told Levi to go away. The locals had begun to call him *Tacà* after the Italian *attaccabrighe,* 'quarrelsome person'. Once, he had been a youthful, broad-chested athlete in Italy's crack Bersagliere army corps; now he was a drinker, and Levi could smell it too, the cheap grape brandy on his breath. Perrone spent his last lire on brandy and he had taken to sleeping off his hangovers in hedgerows and icy ditches. Levi managed to find him a bricklayer's job in Turin, but his old profession was hateful to him now. All Perrone could look forward to was the village festival of St Anna (26 July) when there was forgetfulness and free drink. His continued alcoholism was a form of suicide, Levi believed; Perrone was not strictly a survivor, but he was slowly dying of the 'survivors' sickness'.

4

Hunger and disease were predicted for the deepening winter of 1945, and Levi had to find work. He dropped in at the Chemistry Institute hoping to be employed there, but traipsed unrecognised through the corridors, saddened to learn that Professor Ponzio had died the previous spring, a week before V-Day. Officially Levi had never left the Swiss pharmaceutical company A.Wander Ltd in Milan, where his wages had lain unclaimed since the Armistice. In the weeks before the New Year – 1946 – he collected the money, which helped his mother and sister a little. As he had no luck in Turin he began to look for work in Milan. Like Turin, Milan was a wounded city full of bomb damage, but life had revived, the newspapers were coming out, the theatres had reopened. And it was about now that Levi said he began to buttonhole passengers on the Milan–Turin express and tell them of his ordeal. Soon he was talking to strangers on the trams and buses that were beginning to run again, reporting his story to anyone who cared to listen. The compulsion to do so was 'as strong as hunger', Levi recalled. 'But unlike the Ancient Mariner,' said Anna Maria Levi, 'Primo never actually waylaid people in the street. My brother was far too reserved and modest for that,' she judged. Nevertheless, Primo saw himself as a storyteller returned from the edge of civilisation with urgent counsel for his listeners. ('I come from Odessa,' he told one startled friend.) He made no apology for his compulsive talkativeness. Talking was his way of finding both consolation and himself again: years later Levi said he felt 'renovated' and 'released' by it.

For the moment, the moral duty to bear witness to Auschwitz was secondary to Levi's instinctive, overwhelming desire to disburden himself of his story. On the crowded trains, surprisingly, no one told him to lower his voice. One commuter even politely asked Levi if he could speak up as he was hard of hearing. Another asked Levi's permission to eavesdrop on his conversation as it sounded, he said, so 'incredible'. These must have been amazing moments for Levi, suggesting that a huge potential audience – not just his circle of acquaintances – lay out there wanting to hear his account. Only once did a commuter, a priest, ask Levi why he had to address strangers with such a malignant-sounding story. Levi replied that he could not help himself. It was a sign perhaps that he was emerging from the depths.

At first Anna Maria could not bear to hear her brother's talk. Her boyfriend Franco Tedeschi had perished at Mauthausen camp. But gradually she too began to listen. Levi was a born storyteller. Mila Momigliano (Luciana Nissim's sister-in-law) was astonished by his mesmeric gift. Each day for a week in the last cold months of 1945 Levi visited her bedside in Via Digione, Turin, where she was recovering from bronchitis. During these visits Levi provided Mila with a detailed chronicle of his survival. As she told me: 'I'd lie in bed spellbound, without moving or uttering a word.' After Levi left, however, Mila had to force herself to play the piano in order to exorcise what she had heard. If she was shocked, Levi wanted it that way. What he had to say was 'horrible' in that archaic sense of the word (still valid in Italian) of inspiring awe. And, as he cast his narrative spell, he demanded silence from his audience and brooked no interruptions. When a friend jokingly enquired about the Auschwitz brothels, Levi turned away in disgust.

As he sat by Mila's bedside, Levi was creating blow-by-blow the book that was to become *If This is a Man*. With endless retellings he was refining the subtle plays of suspense and pacing that would hold a reader's attention on the page. Levi was literally talking his masterpiece into life. Yet many found his manner of narration oddly impersonal, even chilling. 'He seemed to be talking about someone else's life, not his own at all – almost as though he was making an official statement.' Momigliano wondered how he could sit there and tell his ghastly tale with such a tranquil heart. Yet Levi wept when he spoke to her of Vanda Maestro: their love, he said, had been chaste.

On the Jewish New Year of 1946, at a party in Turin, Levi confessed that he did not know how to dance. The Fascist racial laws had prevented him taking lessons when he came of age, as was the custom for bourgeois young men in those days. A schoolteacher's daughter offered to teach him. Levi had known Lucia Morpurgo slightly during the war when she was a sculptor's assistant in Turin. And here, wonderfully, was this Jewish girl close to his body in a waltz. The dance seems to have been the classic *coup de foudre*. As the weeks went by, in a decorous way, Levi began to court Lucia, whose name he liked to think of as a homonymous near-miss to *lucciola*, 'firefly'. Lucia was interested in music, painting, could happily recite Dante (and did). She came from Perugia, and was said by many to have a faint provincial air of prudishness and propriety. She could also be difficult and jealous. But if the twenty-six-year-old Primo was sexually innocent, so too was Lucia. 'I was her first man (and she my first woman).' With her aquiline nose and long pale neck, Lucia was beautiful. And, crucially, she listened to Levi at a time when he needed desperately to talk. Lucia was his counsellor and confidante. And she was able to listen longer than most because none of her immediate family had perished in the camps. Born in July 1920, Lucia was a year younger than Levi.

Significantly, this encounter coincided with a furious burst – Levi called it an 'attack' – of poetry. By March 1946 he had written fourteen poems, a considerable flurry amounting to one-fifth of his entire poetic output. While Levi mocked the tomfoolery of waiting for poetic inspiration, he did have a quaint faith in the *daimon* – 'the divine creative spark' – of the classical Greeks. The *daimon* visited Levi that winter of early 1946 and out slewed dark, angry verse full of corruscating invective. 'Buna' transforms the slaves of chemical Kommando 98 into sulphurous Dantesque phantoms and legions of the damned. The verse bristles with the influence of Dante as filtered through Levi's old Italian teacher, Azelia Arici. Under Arici's capable tuition the stupendous greatness of Dante had come alive in class. And the more poetry Levi wrote, the more lines he adapted from *The Divine Comedy* in order to communicate the spiritual no-man's land of Auschwitz. Then, on 9 January he wrote a love poem secretly addressed to Vanda Maestro:

> I would like to describe the intensity
> With which, already overwhelmed,
> We longed in those days to be able
> To walk together once again
> Free beneath the sun.

The poem was cryptically entitled '25 February 1944', the date of the last night Levi slept with Vanda in the cattle-truck bound for Auschwitz. At some level, Levi felt he should have died in Vanda's place, and this is an intensely private verse, with its downbeat, intimate tones. He tries also to rescue Vanda from the rhetoric of the Italian Resistance, for Vanda was not a 'Saint Joan of the Partisans', as one obituary at the time claimed; she died wretchedly in a gas chamber.

A new mood of despair must have come over Levi as the New Year progressed, for he now produced his bleakest and most angry poem, 'Psalm'. Subsequently retitled 'Shemà', the verse was written while the Nuremberg trials were unfolding and lays a curse on those who forget or fail to tell future generations what had happened in Occupied territories. 'I command these words to you,' Levi intones with Biblical authority, 'Repeat them to your children – or may your house crumble.' The malediction rises to a pitch of indignation as he calls down shame and disease on the forgetful. None of this poetry was intended for publication: it was a private ritual cleansing. Before Levi could chronicle the story of his persecution in prose, the rage had first to be excised in poetry. Far from being an afterthought to the cool analytic prose to come, the verse was a vital part of the book now incubating.

6

On 21 January 1946, after three months of unemployment, Levi began work at a paint factory north-east of Turin. A crucial new phase of his life had begun. The sixteen months he was to spend at Du Pont de Nemours & Company – DUCO – would bring lasting friendships. At 7,000 lire (£120 in today's terms) his monthly salary was not enough to support his mother and sister, but it was a reasonable amount in ruined post-war Italy. DUCO, a subsidiary of the Nobel-Montecatini paint and industrial explosives company headquartered in Milan, was the second biggest business of its kind in Italy.

Trains to the lakeside village of Avigliana, where DUCO was situated, were so infrequent that Levi slept the week at the factory. He was assigned a room in the firm's Bachelor House (Casa Scapoli) for single employees. With its red-painted walls the villa was sometimes known as the Casa Rossa. Hot evening meals were served in the Nobel canteen where the cook, Signor De Ambrosis, was a tall, solemn character thought to resemble the P. G. Wodehouse butler Jeeves. Levi's room was spartan with a view over the mountains and a stillness that must have been wonderful after the shriek and brutality of Auschwitz. The Bachelor House had been requisitioned by

1. (*Above*) The Levi family's proudest property – 'The Paradise'. It was stormed in 1888 by vengeful creditors.
2. (*Below*) Cesare Levi in middle age, c.1933. His childhood holidays were spent in 'The Paradise'.
3. (*Below right*) The stairwell of 75 Corso Re Umberto where Primo Levi died.

4. (*Above*) Ester Levi with her firstborn, Primo, c.1920.
(Note the amber beads for teething.)
5. (*Right*) Grandpa Luzzati and his wife Adelina, with their
grandchildren Anna Maria and Primo, c.1926.
6. (*Below*) 'Children's Warm-Up' – The Swedish Gym in
Turin, c.1925. From left to right: Roberto Levi (later killed
by the SS), Primo Levi, Giulia Colombo; far right, Anna
Maria Levi, Primo's sister.

7. (*Above*) From left to right, bottom row: Anna Borgogno, Levi's Gymnasium teacher, Fernanda Pivano; middle row, Franco Operti, Rodolfo Villa. Primo is top row, far right.

8. (*Right*) From left to right: Primo Levi, Giulia Colombo, Anna Maria Levi, c. 1929. (Note the difference in height between Primo and his younger sister.)

9. (*Below*) 1934, Bardonecchia, the eve of Primo's near-fatal mountain expedition. From left to right, Anna Maria Levi, Primo Levi, Giulia Colombo and her mother Ida Luzzati Colombo.

10. (*Left*) 1935. Primo Levi (top row, fourth from left) at the 'M.D'Azeglio' Lyceum. Bruno Foa (top row, sixth from left); Mario Piacenza (top row, third from right); Giorgio Lattes (middle row, third from right); Ennio Artom (bottom row, third from left); Mario Losano (bottom row, far right).

11. (*Middle left*) 1936. 'D'Azeglio in formaldehyde': the school magazine in which Levi made his literary debut. (The Marquis D'Azeglio of Piedmont is seen stoppered in embalming fluid.)

12. (*Middle right*) Cartoon of Primo Levi ('An Editor') by Giorgio Lattes.

13. (*Below left*) Far left, Emanuele Artom (later killed by Nazi-Fascists); Azelia Arici (fifth from left); don Lorenzo Coccolo, c.1936.

14. (*Below right*) Bardonecchia, Mimi and Pupi Kind, 'Greek gods', c.1935.

15. (*Left*) The Chemistry Institute, Turin, overlooking the Valentino Park. (Note the minaret-shaped ventilation tower.)
16. (*Below top right*) Professor Giacomo Ponzio.
17. (*Below bottom right*) 1941. Dr Nicolò Dallaporta.
18. (*Below left*) 1930. Gladys Melrose, Levi's English teacher.

19. (*Above*) 1940. Photo by Primo Levi of chemistry contemporaries. Second row from the front, left to right: Ester Valabrega, Vanna Rava, and Clara Moschino (far right); Emma Vita-Levi (third row, far left).
20. (*Below*) Two chemist girlfriends of Levi: Gabriella Garda and Edith Weisz.
21. (*Right*) 1941. Levi cycling along the Italian Lakes.

22. (*Above*) Sandro Delmastro and his dog, Flush, c.1940.
23. (*Below*) Primo Levi and Alberto Salmoni, c.1940.

24. (*Above*) Primo Levi flying to work in Milan with his ice-axe and chemical implements. (On his wings are the names of various baby foods and tinctures produced by Wander Ltd.)

25. (*Above right*) Ada Della Torre (far left) undergoing forced Jewish labour in the water-bottle shed.

26. (*Below*) Primo and Anna Maria Levi in the Piossasco villa garden, c.1941.

the SS during the war, and by occupying it now Levi felt in some measure vindicated for the offence done to him as a Jew. In their retreat from northern Italy the Germans had blown up the factory's ammonium-nitrate plant and, along with the American bombs, this had left much of DUCO a twisted wreck. Nevertheless, Levi thought he could write here, and it suited him that the Bachelor House stood in such a glorious panorama. Winter sunsets of delicate glowing pink and orange were visible right across the Susa Valley. And from his window Levi could make out the medieval fortress-abbey of San Michele, a view that had not changed since John Ruskin sketched it a century earlier.

With work and a new sense of purpose, Levi was more content, and on 28 January 1946, a week into his DUCO apprenticeship, he wrote the surprisingly up-beat poem, 'Another Monday'. Being crammed back-to-back on a Monday morning commuter train to DUCO inevitably recalled a more sinister journey. Yet how different this Monday was to that other Monday of 21 February 1944 when the Jews of Fossoli had learned of their fatal 'rail transfer'. At this time, Levi also wrote a whimsical science fantasy in which a researcher demonstrates uncanny, memory-stirring scents he has concocted. One glass bottle releases a flinty odour like mountain scree; another, a dusty schoolroom aroma. As Levi was poised to transpose his impressions of Auschwitz into literature, not surprisingly he was concerned about the efficacy of his memory ('The Mnemogogues', the title of the story, is a coinage with Greek roots, meaning the 'arousers of memories'). Levi knew that he would have to perform an astonishing feat of recollection if he was to write the book he had in mind. He only had his memory to go on – there were no other resources for him.

7

The job seemed to suit him very well, and for the first weeks he did little but investigate niggardly paint problems. One of these was bizarre enough. DUCO's fridge varnish Dulox (fraudulently based on the world-famous Dulux) kept on producing pin-prick pimples on drying – what in paint parlance they call 'seeding'. Investigations consumed all of early 1946 as Levi searched for clues to 'seeding' in such obscure technical publications as *Modern Organic Finishes*, and sat for hours over a microscope in DUCO's draughty cold lab. It made no difference if the bothersome Dulox was applied by spray or brush: the mottling persisted. Meanwhile unexpected worksite noises made Levi jump. The factory, with its concrete loading bays and the railway that shunted in chemicals, must have recalled the Auschwitz

Buna-Werke. Levi had the air, recalled one DUCO employee, of a 'whipped dog'. Interestingly he preferred not to mingle much with DUCO staff. The factory was full of its own war grief and Levi was careful not to offend sensibilities by inflicting his own story on people with whom he worked. Those DUCO staff who had survived the winter retreat from Russia had suffered a far worse deprivation, so they believed, than Primo Levi. It would be many years before the knowledge of Hitler's genocide emerged in all its peculiar horror; for the meantime Levi was considered just another mishap of everyday Nazi violence.

He missed Lucia greatly on the days he was unable to see her. Sometimes after work he cycled the thirty-two kilometres to Turin just to see his *lucciola*. Levi was certain now that Lucia was the woman he had been looking for. She was, he said later, an 'uncommon person', 'honest' and 'generous', with many rare gifts, not least a 'natural understanding of children'. Lucia's modesty, keen moral sensibility and strong practical bent were a boon to the unstable survivor. And Lucia, for her part, had begun to love Levi. To restore this man to life – an invalid to health – was her private mission. They decided to marry. Yet the relationship was haunted from the start by the presence of a third woman. And this was Vanda Maestro. Three weeks into his work at DUCO, Levi wrote a love-lyric, '11 February 1946', ostensibly addressed to his future wife. But, consciously or not, it echoes Levi's poem to Vanda of only a month earlier, entitled '25 February 1944'. Both poems describe a man and a woman walking under the sun and have a yearning, plangent tone. Lucia's own feelings about Levi's poem to her remain unknown, but the verse was pointedly omitted from the privately circulated edition of Primo Levi's poems in 1970, and again from the published version five years later. Vanda Maestro was dead but far from departed.

8

During these first chilly months of 1946, Levi began to identify with two legendary exiles. One was Homer's homesick voyager Ulysses or Odysseus (Ulysses being the Latin form of Odysseus), who longs to recount his tribulations and return to his native land. Another was the garrulous foot soldier in an elegy by the Roman poet Tibullus, who tells his story of war and survival 'over a drink, sketching the camp in wine on the table-top'. Levi said he would have suffered terribly if he had been denied the chance to sketch his own camp – Auschwitz – on the table-top. Yet he knew that the enormity of his experience was such that it could not simply be talked out. By mid-February Levi had begun to record, pell-mell, thoughts and events, conversations, things heard and seen at the camp, on the back of train tickets, scraps of paper, flattened cigarette packets – anything he could find. This frantic note-taking continued Levi's personal exorcism, but was in readiness for something extraordinary. 'Probably if I'd *not* written my book, I'd have remained one of the damned of the earth': it was Dante again, the state of souls after death.

In later life, Levi constructed a sort of legend round *If This is a Man*. He claimed the book was written in furious haste immediately on his return from exile. In fact, it was not properly begun until sixteen weeks after his homecoming. The product of a gradual maturation, the book involved many different phases of drafting, among them oral accounts, poems, science fiction, even a trial-run in a medical journal.

Some time in 1945 Leonardo De Benedetti had asked Levi to help him expand a medical report he had compiled at the request of the Moscow government on the 'Hygienic and Sanitary Conditions' of the Buna-Monovitz *Judenlager*. The friends' joint dossier appeared in the July-December 1946 edition of *Minerva Medica*, then Italy's equivalent of *The Lancet*. Levi had little difficulty in bringing to mind the facts required for the article. He had already devised a map of the Auschwitz worksite showing its underground petrol tank, the clothing warehouse, the punishment block, the SS dormitories. All the streets and buildings had been drafted to scale from memory. Levi had even listed the previous professions and birthplaces of his fellow prisoners, minutely entering their calling, age and, occasionally, family circumstances. The article, whatever its medical interest, contains in truncated form the first and last chapters of Levi's book.

9

The original draft of what was to become *If This is a Man* was a fourteen-page typescript dated February 1946 and entitled 'The Story of Ten Days'. Levi had begun to write his book backwards, starting with the last chapter. Unsurprisingly, his most recent memories of Auschwitz – the flight of the Germans and the arrival of the Red Army – were the most pressing. So he began with these. According to one witness, he had scarcely finished supper in the Nobel canteen when he would cycle back to the Bachelor House in a state of anticipation. Instead of sleeping Levi plunged headlong into writing, and for the next ten months worked with concentrated energy on the manuscript. And he wrote with extreme facility, the words pouring out of him 'like a flood which has been dammed and suddenly rushes forth'. Only once in *If This is a Man* would he confess to a failure of language before the incredibility of Auschwitz.

Levi later liked to say that *If This is a Man* was free from consciously polished, lettered prose, but it is in fact a teeming, intensely literary work of great complexity, and far more calculatedly bookish than Levi cared to admit. So the chapter now unfolding in the Bachelor House was full of allusions to Italian literature – the literature that Levi claimed to have studied so unwillingly at school. Alessandro Manzoni's nineteenth-century classic of famine and devastated lands, *The Betrothed,* is Italy's most important novel. For the schoolboy Levi, however, it had been an 'insufferably boring' costume romance. In fact, Manzoni was an Italian moralist in the school of Voltaire, who used reason to try and understand all that was unreasonable in man. The novel's most grandly orchestrated set-piece – the celebrated description of Milan's devastation by plague in the 1600s – must have come back powerfully to Levi, as 'The Story of Ten Days' strikingly echoes it. Devastated by German troops in the Hundred Years War, Milan is a wreck and surgeons have abandoned the hospitals. For Levi, on the eve of their rescue by the Red Army, the living dead of Auschwitz grub for food amid 'trailing bandages', and drag themselves along the ground like a Manzonian 'invasion of worms'.

In spite of its gruesome subject matter, 'The Story of Ten Days' has flashes of quiet humour, and its affirmation of human dignity instils a kind of joy in the reader. Levi does not dwell on the mechanics of mass murder, but on what remained of the human face in the camp. And he never loses sight of a future beyond Auschwitz. Accordingly the chapter ends, not with a finite conclusion, but with a hint of other narratives to come: 'We have exchanged long letters and I hope to see him [Charles Conreau] again one day.' The famous concluding words of André Gide's novel *Les Faux Monnayeurs* – 'I am very curious to meet Caloub' – were surely an influence. Levi could not bring himself to write 'Finis' because he was then too full of outward-turned curiosity: his book was to have a beginning, but no end.

Levi's nocturnal burst of writing had aroused suspicions at DUCO, as his typewriter had been heard tapping in the Bachelor House until 1:00 am. A rumour went round that he was a spy in league with the Red Army stragglers who were reputed to infest the Avigliana hills. While few staff took these rumours seriously, Levi was considered a loner. 'I was the night-owl who typed,' he remembered. Certainly no one at DUCO knew he was in love. 'He didn't talk to any of us of Lucia,' recalled one employee.

On the afternoon of Thursday 14 February, one week after completing 'The Story of Ten Days', Levi retrenched himself in his spartan room to write one of the greatest hymns to the human spirit. 'The Canto of Ulysses' was written almost entirely in a single lunch break, from 12:30 pm to 1:00 pm: half an hour of hectic unbroken work, or so Levi later claimed. That day Levi was seen to wolf down his lunch in ten minutes and dash off to the Bachelor House, still in his belted white lab-coat. No doubt Levi was giving shape to the disordered longhand notes he had been jotting down since his homecoming; nevertheless composition of this chapter, the eleventh in the definitive edition of *If This is a Man*, was astonishingly swift. Levi's immediate subject was the French prisoner Jean Samuel, who he feared had not survived the evacuation of Auschwitz. Levi cast his mind back to that summer's day in 1944 when he had accompanied Jean to collect the camp's soup ration. As they trudged through the *Buna-Werke*, the Ulysses canto from Dante's *Inferno* had come flooding back to Levi. He struggled to translate the verse into French for Jean while explaining its significance. Ulysses is addressing his ship's crew as they embark on their final voyage:

> Think of your breed; for brutish ignorance
> Your mettle was not made; you were made men,
> To follow after knowledge and excellence.

In the hell of Auschwitz, Ulysses's words shine out with a sublime humanist dignity: Levi and Jean Samuel are not beasts; they were 'made men' to pursue virtue and knowledge. Later, many would question whether Levi really had been overwhelmed at Auschwitz by Dante: the counterpoint of classic beauty in one of the world's vilest places suggests the artifice of afterthought. But in Levi's Italy, Dante never suffered the fate he has in the English-speaking world, where he is often seen as a dreary exponent of medieval theology. In Victorian England, civil servants, clergymen and other worthies all had a go at translating *The Divine Comedy*. In the process they turned Dante (the saddest and most serious of poets) into a paragon of moral sobriety and reduced his crystalline cantos to galumphing fustian. This was not so in Italy, where Dante has passed from generation to generation enriched. It is hardly surprising that Dante's Canto XXVI should have burned itself into Levi's memory. As a teenager he had taken part in 'Dante tournaments' where Crocetta boys showed off their knowledge of *The Inferno,* one contestant reciting a canto and his opponent scoring a point if he knew its continuation.

From the moment Levi completed 'The Canto of Ulysses' he was set to become one of the most classically influenced writers in post-war Italy, his prose fortified by the grand literary curriculum of the 'M. D'Azeglio'. Again it was Azelia Arici, that eminent *dantista,* who haunted the Bachelor House that February afternoon. Years later Levi told a journalist that if he had to rescue two Italian writers from a library fire, they would be 'Dante and Manzoni'. Only a classical student with an enduring humanist education could have said as much.

II

DUCO, mid-March 1946, and in the build-up to Easter came the wonderful news that Jean Samuel, commemorated a month earlier in 'The Canto of Ulysses', was alive after all. Charles Conreau, Levi's French companion in the last ten days of Auschwitz, had tracked Samuel down to a small town in Alsace. Samuel's story was atrocious. His father, three uncles, a younger brother and a cousin had all been killed by the Nazis. Only Samuel and his mother came back from Auschwitz. Following the camp's evacuation, Jean had been forced to excavate underground tunnels in a *Lager* high in Germany's bleak Iron Ore Mountains. The infernal detonation of explosives, and smog from lignite-burning infected his every dream and slender hope of survival: at night he had slept in a paper sack crawling with lice. As the sole surviving male of his family, Jean was now trying to rebuild his life in Wasselonne where his father had been the pharmacist. He wrote to Levi after Conreau had contacted him. And on the morning of Saturday 23 March, in flawless French, Levi wrote the first of several letters to Samuel:

> I've always thought that you would have a good chance of pulling through, as you were spirited, intelligent and both physically and morally well-preserved. And now here it is: your long letter before my very eyes!

Levi briefly gave his own story of survival. And, as he did so, he asked after the fate of his Auschwitz colleagues Szanto and Fischer. And the dwarf Lindzin? And what of the block commanders? The red triangles? Had any of these accompanied Samuel on the death-march? Levi was seeking to establish details for the book he was now busy writing. He went on:

> It's a miracle that I'm still alive and in good health, and reunited with my family. I've made a vow never to forget this, and I repeat

it to myself every day like a prayer. Not that I thank Providence:
if there had been Providence, Auschwitz and Birkenau would
never have existed.

Anger lay beneath that last remark. Professor Nicolò Dallaporta, the
physicist who had helped Levi at university, had rashly attributed his star
pupil's survival to Divine Providence. 'It's not by chance that you have
come home, Primo – you've been saved in order to write.' Dallaporta, with
his belief that survival was somehow evidence of superior character and
intellect, had touched a raw nerve in Levi; he emphatically refused to be
among the physicist's chosen elect. The cruelty of Auschwitz screamed out
against Providence, he said. Signing his letter '174517', Levi posted it to
Wasselonne.

12

At the end of March 1946 Levi began the chilling 'Chemical Examination'
chapter. By then, his pitiless German examiner Dr Wilhelm Pannwitz had
died, not quite forty, of a brain tumour. In this section Levi describes not
only the Polymerisation Department under Pannwitz, but all Auschwitz, as
a giant laboratory experiment designed to transform the substance of
mankind. Two literary influences were at work. The first was Jean Henri
Fabre, the French entomologist, and the second Aldous Huxley. In *Insect
Adventures,* a childhood favourite of Levi's, Fabre had described a termite
society quite as ruthless and varied as that of Auschwitz, with honest toilers,
free-booters, producers and parasite ants. Accordingly, the Germans in this
chapter are the 'grey machine' marching like Fabre's ants in mindless
mathematical rank. The prisoners are 'spiders', the *Kapo* is a 'hen', while
Pannwitz himself is a nameless 'zoological specimen'. Huxley's early novels
had also teemed with laboratory imagery and the English author's biological
approach to writing was of great use to Levi now as he began to classify
species for the camp's inhuman bestiary. As a boy, Levi had been tirelessly
absorbed in the minutiae of insect life, and 'Chemical Examination' is a
showcase for his interest in the miniature. *Maxima in minimis,* the smallest
facts are the most significant.

13

Meanwhile, all through the spring of 1946 Levi laboured to find out why
DUCO's fridge paint No. 104 was determined to remain 'seedy'. Frustrated
by the pimpling, he wondered if more rewarding chemistry work was to be

233

had elsewhere. He saw a possible future for himself (not that it was any more exciting) as a 'glycerol phthalic resin' expert, and for one moment considered moving with Lucia to Paris. Then one day he made a breakthrough discovery. DUCO was situated at the mouth of the Susa Valley, where the weather was notoriously changeable, and it was this that affected not only the paint's drying time, density and viscosity, but also its tendency to pimple. What action DUCO took as a result of Levi's discovery is not known. But, now in his tenth week at DUCO, Levi had established himself as a hard-working, self-disciplined and reliable chemist. Impressed by him, the lab chief Giunio Ruspino put Levi in charge of translating extracts from the German paint magazine *Farbe und Lacke*; to Levi's chagrin, the Germans still led the way in varnish manufacture.

Levi had been two months at DUCO when he developed an unlikely friendship. The paint technician Felice Fantino, a tall, blue-eyed Piedmontese, had no literary interests and was five years older than Levi: yet his dour but good-natured humour was immensely reassuring to him. The source for many of Levi's future short stories, Fantino was a trove of paint-trade gossip, half-heard tales and Piedmontese anecdotes. He told Levi how DUCO's lovelorn manager Dr Bianchi had once tried to kill himself and his secretary, but the bullets lodged harmlessly in a sofa. One of Levi's poems from this time, 'The Witch', was based on Fantino's tales of the *settimin-a* ('wise-woman') to be found in every Piedmontese village. She combined the trades of midwife, bone-setter and faith-healer, and stimulated Levi's long-held fascination with the world of spells and magic. It was largely thanks to Fantino that Levi settled at DUCO; his new companion coaxed out Levi's light-hearted side. A favourite joke of Levi's was to dispatch marmalade instead of paint to the unsuspecting Giunio Ruspino for lab analysis. Levi not only found loyalty, affection and an easy playfulness in the thirty-two-year-old Fantino, but the friends also shared the suffering brought about by war. In 1940 Fantino had almost frozen to death when his Italian platoon was stranded in alpine ice near France. 'If every Italian had done like me and got frozen on a mountain top, we'd have lost the war in no time.'

Up until now only Lucia had seen Levi's work-in-progress. But as the winter of 1946 turned to spring, Levi took the brave step of showing it to a few DUCO colleagues, among them the resident physicist Dr Binotto and Gastone Compagnucci, a minor Tuscan aristocrat who lived with him in the Bachelor House. Compagnucci was impressed by Levi's mastery of language and his complex yet transparent prose. 'Your sentences seem simple, Primo, but I think you've had to labour for their simplicity, the words wrested out of you.' Compagnucci was right. There had been off-days when Levi was able to write only *porcheria*, 'pigswill'; and days when his anger and hatred of what had been done to him exploded into unintelligible jottings.

As Levi continued with his book in the spring of 1946, encouragement came from another quarter. He had been in touch with Luciana Nissim, who had been liberated by the Americans in Leipzig at the end of April 1945. She had reached Italy on 20 July, three months before Levi. In her native Biella, near Turin, she had tried to begin life again as a paediatrician, but was tormented by feelings of guilt and worthlessness. Later she became a distinguished psychoanalyst. Now married, she had had a baby girl named Vanda, who died during labour. Nissim's chronicle of Auschwitz, *Memoir from the House of the Dead*, was published in Turin in April 1946. It was written reluctantly and in the face of physical breakdown; nevertheless it was the first book in Italy to document Auschwitz, and Nissim's sense of obligation to the dead pervades its every page. In this raw, disarmingly lyrical work she does not flinch from describing horror. With anger and disgust she wrote of the SS who jeered and photographed the Fossoli deportees as they crouched by the railway sidings. (Levi, by some puritan stringency, could not bring himself to write of such humiliating scenes; his innate 'pudency', as he called it – from *pudentia*, 'susceptibility to shame' – dictated that the more bestial aspects of the Nazi persecution be omitted.) Nissim's chronicle amply alluded to Vanda Maestro and this must have stirred troubled waters for Levi. At the same time her book spurred him to complete his own; in some ways he felt he was in competition with Nissim.

Another literary revelation that spring was a collection of aphorisms, fragments and reflections on Fascism, *Short Cuts and Very Short Stories*, by the great Triestino poet Umberto Saba. Saba's shock at hearing of the Nazi death camps was contained in two words: 'After Maidaneck [a notorious *Lager* to the east of Lublin] . . .', and the rest of the sentence fizzles out. This was the earliest instance perhaps of the wordless response which some critics would say is the writer's proper response to the Nazi genocide. Few Italian writers had been as quick as Saba to grasp the enormity of the crime, and in a letter to him, Levi later expressed his deep admiration for his 'courage' in confronting Italy's Nazi-Fascist past.

With Saba and Nissim providing literary impetus, Levi returned to the writing table to begin 'October 1944' of *If This is a Man*. The chapter was started on 5 April, the day Ada Della Torre married Silvio Ortona, and was completed three days later on Thursday the 8th. During that time Levi examined the Nazis' greatest crime: the assembly-line gassings of human beings. His Dantesque language (the 'naked, frightened' prisoners) suggests a state of vacuous horror. But Levi's modern view of hell is far more disturbing than the pitchforks and devilry of Dante's medieval theology. In the twentieth-century inferno of Auschwitz, hell is no longer a malign external punishment for sins committed: at Auschwitz the innocent are punished, and the capacity to do evil, and to create hell on earth, lies in us all.

One influence runs through this chapter like the black line in a lobster, and that is Charles Darwin. The Victorian evolutionist had very precisely defined the sensory realm (sight, sound, taste, touch, smell) beyond which it was immoral for the investigator to stray. Accordingly 'October 1944' is strictly an eye-witness report, containing nothing that Levi had not seen or heard himself. Yet the chapter's careful objectivity collapses when Levi recalls the Jewish prisoner who loudly thanked God for saving his life from the gas chambers; swaying to and fro on his bunk, Kuhn addresses his petition to the Almighty in a Talmudic singsong. He is a selfishly blind Amen-sayer. 'If I was God, I would spit at Kuhn's prayer.' Levi rarely raises his voice and is never hectoring, yet here is the anger of the outraged. For one to extol God's glory while his companions had less than two days to live was for Levi a blasphemy. What Levi does not admit is that he, too, had been tempted to pray during that 1944 'selection'; but, as soon as he realised that he was not going to die, he was deeply ashamed, he said in a late interview, and 'held back'.

FOURTEEN

Rebirth and Rejection
1946–8

I

Midway through the book's composition, Levi was embroiled in a court case. On Saturday 4 May 1946 Edilio Cagni, the Fascist *agent-provocateur* who had been Levi's nemesis during the Resistance, stood trial in Aosta. Cagni was a fearsome figure from the days of the Occupation whom Guido Bachi, Levi's former partisan leader, had identified the previous summer. Bachi had found him indifferent to the accusations of espionage, banditry and torture, any one of which could have cost the spy his neck. Here he was in front of a courtroom scribe, and presumably a priest, blaming everything on his co-spies De Ceglie and Bianchi, as well as on his Fascist paymaster Prefect Carnazzi of Aosta. It was a fine performance: Cagni stood impassively in the dock to receive his death sentence. His grief-stricken mother, Angela Cagni, pleaded with Guido Bachi to help her son. While Bachi was moved to feel sorry for her ('a mother is always a mother'), he had no compassion for Cagni.

The responsibility to testify at Cagni's trial put Levi in a withdrawn mood; memories of his bungled involvement in the Resistance came back in troubled, restless nights at the Bachelor House, and he was haunted by the memory of the two teenage partisans who had been executed on the eve of his arrest. (They were commemorated in his poem of 1952, 'Epitaph'.) The following month of June came distressing news that Cagni had been reprieved by the so-called 'Togliatti Amnesty'. In an attempt at national reconciliation, Italy's justice minister Palmiro Togliatti had drawn up a grotesque legal distinction between 'ordinary' tortures and those that were 'particularly serious'. Thus Cagni's use of a hammer on Giuseppe Barbesino's feet was pardoned because it had been for intimidatory purposes and was not prompted by 'bestial insensibility'. Issued one week before Cagni's thirtieth birthday (June 1946), the Togliatti Amnesty was the spy's salvation. (Captain Arturo Dal Dosso, the Italian SS who had brutally tortured Emanuele Artom, ended his days comfortably in the Brasilian city of São Paolo, having also been released by the 'amnesty'.) We next hear of Edilio Cagni at the Perugia Assizes when, in November 1946, his death sentence was commuted to thirty years in jail. He did not serve his full term; his last known address, dating from the early 1950s, was in the Sicilian capital of Palermo on Via Divisi. Today the only Cagni listed as resident in the city claimed not to be a relative.

2

While Cagni stood trial in Aosta, an event of great political significance took place in Italy. On 9 May 1946 the Italian king, Victor Emanuel III, abdicated. Italians now had to decide by referendum whether they were to remain a monarchy or become a republic. Levi reflected a good deal on the abdication crisis, both frightened and fascinated by it. To Jean Samuel he wrote: 'After the long paralysis of Fascism, we're about to be intoxicated by politics.' He hoped the crisis and its attendant hoopla might bring about a complete social transformation. On the night of 23–4 April, however, neo-Fascists had stolen Mussolini's corpse from its grave in Milan, and the dictator's unburied body became a potent symbol of totalitarian resurrection. Levi feared a Blackshirt revival as fierce exchanges flared in the street and the old guard shook their heads and whispered secret praise of the Duce. Meanwhile in a clamour of books, films and newspapers the Italians were exhorted to join the democratic world. These were to be their first free elections in more than twenty years.

Referendum Day was 2 June 1946, a Sunday. Raised under dictatorship, Levi had never seen a ballot box before. For the first time in Italian history women were to be enfranchised. Levi arrived early at the polls to help count the votes. In anticipation of violence, armoured cars stood outside the polling stations. However, there were no incidents. With every vote that Levi personally counted for the republic, it seemed that a new world was being created. The results came through three days later, on Wednesday 5 June. The country was fairly evenly split, but by twelve million to ten million the Italians had voted for a republic. Europe's oldest ruling royal family, the House of Savoy, was finished. To Levi and his friends the republican Constitution was the most wonderful political event of the age. Bianca Guidetti Serra reckoned it was *the* defining moment of her generation's glory. 'Honestly it seemed to us that the world was on the move again and this time nobody was going to stop us.' Ousting the royal family from Italy meant shedding the past and the nationalist myopia of Fascism, the Duce and his cohorts for good. Levi's hopes for a new Italy were boundless and, as he later recalled, 'almost mystical'.

As the republican spirit spread across Italy, Rita Hayworth's raunchy hit, 'Amado Mio', from the Hollywood blockbuster *Gilda*, was heard everywhere in bars and cafés, exuding a sense of post-war sexuality and exuberance. At times it seemed to Levi that his love for Lucia was crystallised by the Hayworth anthem, the intensity of his longing for Vanda Maestro fading gratefully into the past. This sense of elation – the refreshing feeling that something worthwhile lay ahead – was overwhelming. And in cinemas across the land Charlie Chaplin's *The Great Dictator*, which mocked Hitler and Mussolini, was shown to great huzzahs.

3

In the heady aftermath of the June referendum, Levi's thoughts turned again to his book. The optimism that he felt for Italy's busy public regeneration impacted significantly on the writing of *If This is a Man*. Here was a book which harmonised with the tenor of the times, and with the happiness Levi now felt about his new life and impending marriage to Lucia. It was an intense relationship between two rather different personalities, and it was this closeness that impressed their friends and relatives, and which left its mark on *If This is a Man*. Lucia was not the only joy in Levi's life at that time. There was also his correspondence with Jean Samuel. Levi was elated that they could correspond in the warmth of remembered camaraderie, and on the eve of the referendum he had written to Samuel:

> On reflection the friendship which binds us is something very astonishing and unique. We met each other in particular circumstances more or less in the most miserable conditions where a man could be demolished. And we were united, not only materially but above all spiritually in our struggle against the annihilation of the *Lager*.

Levi enclosed three of his poems and 'The Canto of Ulysses' chapter in typescript, with apologies for inexactitudes and 'anything that could shock you in any way'. With false modesty he let Samuel know that the chapter was not his best. 'I wrote it when I could never have imagined you were alive and I haven't altered a word.' Samuel was staggered that Dante had meant so much to Levi at Auschwitz; if anything, the Frenchman had been faintly bemused at the time by Levi's attempt to interest him in a 600-year-old medieval poem that culminates in the mystical revelation of God in Paradise. Instead, Samuel's enduring memory of Levi in the camp was of their half-hour conversation during an Allied air raid, when they had spoken of their mothers.

Italy had only been a republic for ten days when, on Saturday 15 June, Levi began the 'Ka-Be' (Auschwitz hospital) section of his book. It took five days to complete, and was probably typed at home in his father's library, now restored, at 75 Corso Re Umberto. Much of 'Ka-Be' pays homage to Jack London, the alcoholic son of an Irish astrologer, who had been urged on Primo by his father. London had admired the British evolutionist Herbert Spencer, who coined the term 'survival of the fittest,' and his Klondike saga *The Call of the Wild* seemed to chime uncannily with Levi's own Darwinist analysis of the camp. The progress of the book's canine hero, Buck, from domesticity to wildness foreshadowed the wolf manner of survival at Auschwitz. Thus the subhumans of 'Ka-Be' are compared to Jack London's Arctic dogs in their 'struggle of each one against all', which slave until the last breath and 'die on the track'. The nine-page typescript was ready by 20 June. Nine days later Levi's mother had her fifty-first birthday.

Two years had now passed since Levi's homecoming, and as work on the book progressed, so he began to understand his responsibility to bear witness. 'Whether we like it or not,' he wrote to Jean Samuel (in a now-vanished letter), 'we are witnesses and we bear the weight of it.' *If This is a Man* was not just a self-exorcism but a calling to account. And, as Levi wrote the book, his hardest task was to contain his anger. If he gave way to grief or moral outrage it would tarnish his credibility as a witness. Dostoevsky had set down the humiliations and torment of his Siberian imprisonment in *The House of the Dead* (echoed in the title of Luciana Nissim's *Memoir from the House of the Dead*) not to horrify the reader – though it does – but in order to testify. 'Let the reader be the judge,' the Russian had said. Likewise it was Levi's intention that the reader should be sole judge and jury of the crime he was describing.

After seven months of writing, Levi still had no working title, though the book was shaping into a marvel of luminous precision and poise. Its most wryly ironic chapter, 'This Side of Good and Evil', was begun on Sunday 1 September, and it provided a lethal analysis of the prisoners' fox-hole barter in breadcrumbs, tobacco, gold teeth. The SS openly connived in this commerce, which made a mockery of their vaunted moral and racial superiority. Nietzsche's *Beyond Good and Evil* is archly parodied in the chapter's title. The philosopher's assault on western morality and scorning of Judaeo-Christian compassion for the weak had foreshadowed a moment in the 1940s – Auschwitz – when humanity began to die. Nietzsche had lived in Turin, and Levi knew that Hitler had used his violent Social Darwinism as justification for the extermination of European Jewry.

The chapter, with its communiqué style of exposition, was modelled on one of the reports Levi was expected to produce each week at DUCO. Circulated among the factory staff, these were read by all the workers from the lab assistants up. One of them, 'The Flooding of Enamels', was published at this time in the Italian trade journal, *Paints and Varnishes*, and analyses the mixed pigments Prussian blue and chrome yellow. The report bears no obvious connection to 'This Side of Good and Evil' beyond a precision and lucidity in the writing, qualities that Levi believed were the 'sovereign politeness' of the writer. Clear prose anyway was his most effective antidote to the language anarchy – the *confusio linguarum* – of Auschwitz. The book's clean-cut narrative creates an extraordinary sense of communion and intimacy with the reader, and ensured that one day it would be read by thousands of Italians of all backgrounds.

4

By December 1946 the book was virtually completed. Exhausted by the effort, Levi was also immensely relieved, and to Jean Samuel he again wrote: 'I've worked on this book with love and rage.' So Levi's ghastly tale was told – burned out of him – and the effects of the catharsis were plain to see. After eleven months at DUCO his face had lost its unhealthy moon-like appearance; clean-shaven, his whole demeanour had improved. The book's last chapter, 'Die drei Leute vom Labor', was pencil-marked '22 December 1946', the date Levi finished it, and a landmark in the history of Italian literature.

The manuscript required considerable work, however. Viewed together, the chapters did not have a clear sense of direction, jumping backwards and forwards in time. The book, in short, was in textual disarray. But Lucia, with her combination of criticism and encouragement, transformed the work, and she was well suited to the task. Her father Giuseppe Morpurgo had written two pre-war novels, *Yom Ha-Kippurim* and *Beati misericordes*, which were among the first in Italy to treat of Jewish themes. Their D'Annunzian purple prose has not worn well, yet they have efficient and very logical narratives. Levi had begun to think of Lucia, romantically, as his muse. And she started to help him impose coherence on the pages by putting the sections in order. Lucia was able to improve the pacing of the manuscript by asking Levi to read sections out loud to her, and she was an exacting critic: every word had to be aware of its own etymology, intended and considered. Occasionally the prose was lightened by replacing, for example, the fusty Latinism '*sine die*' with the straightforward 'without time limit'. Other Latinisms were snipped out, among them the too-antique '*tergiversare*' ('to hesitate'), as these did not accord well with the book's modernity.

As soon as the work was ready, Levi wanted others to see it. First on his list was his former literature teacher Azelia Arici. In Arici's view, Classics students alone were the carriers of civilisation, and the superiority of Greek and Latin was beyond question. On reading the manuscript, Arici was nevertheless surprised by how well a scientist could write, and she apologised to Levi for having so 'impudently' dismissed scientists as ill-educated. Basking in Arici's high praise, Levi now showed the typescript to his old English tutor Gladys Melrose. She recognised the quality of the writing and began to praise the stark prose-poem at the Berlitz School where she still taught in Turin. Camillo Treves, the Communist whom Levi had known in wartime Milan, was astonished by the maturity of Levi's vision. In the space of just a few years the 'lad' whom he had first met in 1942 had matured intellectually, politically and spiritually. 'If any book had a claim to the universal,' Treves told me, 'it was this': all life seemed to be written in its burning pages. Though Levi claimed not to know if his book was 'mediocre, good or very good', secretly he knew he had written an exceptionally powerful work, and the praise must have been wonderful for him. *If This is a Man* was a book that had to be written and Levi wanted it to be read by others. He needed to find a publisher.

Levi had a cousin in Massachusetts, Anna Yona, a respected local radio journalist. Hoping to break into the American market, he sent her sample chapters of his book. Yona translated 'The Canto of Ulysses' into English and sent it to a junior editor, Adeline Lubell, at the Boston publisher Little, Brown. In her day Lubell was one of the most brilliant (if not most commercially successful) editors in Boston. Impressed by what she read, she asked to see more material. However, her superiors at Little, Brown were sceptical. In 1946 the subject of Europe's dismal recent past did not engage – indeed it repelled – American readers. Lubell then tried an august Jewish authority, Rabbi Joshua Loth Liebman, for his view. Well connected in literary circles, Liebman had the power to launch Levi in America. He was a reformed rabbi based in Massachusetts, whose self-help guide, *Peace of Mind*, was the American bestseller of 1946. However, the rabbi recommended Little, Brown not to publish Levi. He was scarcely a suitable judge; his bestseller, a farrago of high-flown rhetoric, called for 'world peace', but made no mention either of Auschwitz or the Nuremberg trials that had just ended. Living so far from Europe, Rabbi Liebman had perhaps been unable or unwilling to countenance the *tremendum* of Auschwitz. It is likely that Levi's chapters went to the wastepaper basket largely unread. The rabbi may also have disapproved of the book's absence of prophecy and despair. Where was the Hebraic anguish, the Old Testament fierceness, in this cool document? Levi's modest effort at description and understanding looked too tame for its subject. He would have to wait forty years until America took notice of him.

5

By the New Year of 1947 Levi had begun to take his manuscript round Italian publishers. His first choice was Einaudi of Turin. From its humble origins in 1933, Einaudi had become the most fashionable and commercially successful publisher in Italy. (Today no cultivated Italian home is without its collection of white-spined Einaudi paperbacks, the cultural equivalent of Picador.) Giulio Einaudi, the founder, was brimful of initiative and always in search of what he called '*novità*' – the 'latest' in literature. He enjoyed a close and controversial relationship with the Italian Communist Party and was very much a part of Italian anti-Fascist culture. Dubbed 'The Prince' by his circle, Einaudi had an imposingly aristocratic manner and a reputation for frivolity, but his staff were hand-picked for their stringent moral seriousness. Cesare Pavese, now an immensely famous writer, was managing director. Levi hoped his manuscript would not land on Pavese's slush-pile: a lugubrious character, he was famous for rejecting typescripts with lightning rapidity.

Instead Levi put his faith in Pavese's assistant, the novelist Natalia Ginzburg. Unconventionally stylish with her boyishly short hair, Ginzburg had published her first novel, *The Road to the City*, in 1944 under a non-Jewish pseudonym: it showed a flair for laconic exactitude. Ginzburg was born to an exemplary anti-Fascist family; her father was arrested in Turin in 1934 on a 'Justice and Liberty' subversion charge, while her husband Leone Ginzburg had been murdered by Germans in Rome in 1944. (A Russian from Odessa, Leone had been among the first in Italy to urge a national anti-Fascist resistance.) There is no doubt that Levi saw common ground in Natalia's wartime suffering, and it was with high hopes that he left his manuscript with her at the Einaudi offices at 5 Corso Re Umberto. A week later came a devastating verdict. Natalia did everything to soften the blow; the book was not 'right', she said, for Einaudi's list. Levi was hurt and angry: why was he being turned down? His book *was* good, surely? As Natalia was a family friend, Levi did not insist on explanations. He retrieved the manuscript in dignified silence. It says much for his sense of loyalty to Ginzburg that he remained her close friend. 'She is a nice person, a fine writer, but she is not a thinker,' was his verdict.

In fact Levi was devastated, his pride and young ambition badly dented: Ginzburg's rejection was like an intimation of the literary scrapheap, yet her reluctance to publish Levi was part of a larger, collective reluctance among Italians to face their brutal and regrettable past. In 1985 when I interviewed Ginzburg for the *London Magazine* she contritely acknowledged what she called her 'error': 'It must have been a bleak moment in Primo's life, but you know I was young and foolish then, and besides I was not solely responsible for the thumbs down.' Cesare Pavese had also judged, correctly as it turned out, that the time was not right to publish Levi. Italians had other things to worry about, such as finding work, building a better world for their children, than reading of the German death camps. Italians wanted to say, 'It's all over. *Basta!* Enough of this horror!'

There was another reason, perhaps, why Levi was turned down. The book's classical allusions to Dante, the rhythmical beauty and grace of the prose, were construed as a throwback to Fascism and the regime's harping on Roman antiquity. Levi's marmoreal sentences betrayed the influence of the 'art of beautiful speech' – *l'arte di parlare bene* – which had been a staple of Fascist school education. Moreover, the Latin origins of some of the phrase-making ('Dawn came on us like a betrayer'), the shards of Virgil and Cicero, gave the book an antique literary richness. Italy's new generation of writers wanted to disavow classical influences and embrace the gritty 'news-reel-school' of realism, which aimed at an unpolished immediacy off the streets. Exemplary among these new authors was Italo Calvino; though his early fiction had a fabulous Gothic undertow, it was influenced by Hemingway and the anti-rhetorical films of the Resistance, such as Rossellini's *Rome: Open City*. But Levi belonged to no literary coterie or salon. Oddly exiled from the centre of things at DUCO, he had ploughed his own literary furrow. His only concession to the fashion for documentary *verismo* occurs in the preface to his book, and even then it is half-ironic: 'It seems to me unnecessary to add that none of the facts are invented.'

Levi's book was rejected by five other Italian publishers, among them Edizioni di Comunità, owned by the Jewish-Protestant company Olivetti. (The book was 'quite interesting', judged the Comunità editor, Professor Doriguzzi, but the moment was not right to publish it.) An element of snobbishness may also have counted against Levi. Where was the lustre to

Primo Levi's name? Among the crown royalty of Italy's new literary talent – Pavese, Calvino, Elio Vittorini – Levi had no standing.

6

As a result of Natalia Ginzburg's rejection, Levi revised and polished his manuscript with a view to submitting an improved version. When exactly the amendments were made is not known, but each alteration was incorporated into the published work, and are significant. In the first draft Levi is overwhelmed by Dante's Ulysses 'like a gulp of hot wine'; this simile is changed to the magnificently rousing 'like the voice of God'. Other alterations reveal Levi's lingering fear of retribution from prisoners. The *Kapo* Oscar's name is safely altered to 'Alex', while the sly French prisoner Paul Steinberg is newly identified as 'Henri'. (These changes were no minor, passing scruple. For the German edition of *If This is a Man* Levi went to great lengths to disguise the pugnacious dwarf, Elias Lindzin, under the false name 'David Kram'. What if Lindzin got his lightning-quick hands on a copy of the book? It was better to change his name.) In the first draft Oscar had been an 'ugly, violent brute, and treacherous', but these avenging adjectives are now excised, so that the *Kapo* can be observed more nearly as a human being. Levi did not want to rail against his tormentors: hatred was a bestial emotion to be kept at bay. Thus the Italian word *odio*, 'hatred', appears just once in the published manuscript, and even then it is directed not at a person, but at I. G. Farben's hated Carbon Tower.

Other alterations were a finicky tinkering, yet they always improved the prose. Like a carpenter whittling a stick, Levi planed the text carefully. If his book was to unfold as a judicial enquiry – the material presented as painstakingly as in a lawyer's brief – there could be no factual or spelling errors. Edith Weisz, Levi's wartime chemistry colleague, was consulted on correct German usage, spelling and grammar. 'Primo even wanted to know where to place an umlaut correctly,' Weisz recalled. Her father's Viennese birth made her, through some territorial quirk of the Austro-Hungarian empire, a German-speaking Slovak Jew.

Levi wanted his book to appeal to all men at all times: our human condition, not just the Jewish condition, was to be his subject. In the first draft, Jean Samuel had been compared to the Old Testament's 'Joseph in Egypt', but this Judaeo-biblical simile was removed in order to strengthen the book's secular, universal spirit. Elsewhere in the original Levi had referred to himself as '*un ebreo*', 'a Jew'; this label, too, was excised, allowing the book to communicate a greater human tragedy. The first to be persecuted by the Nazis were German Communists, Social Democrats,

245

Liberals, not Jews. As Levi said: 'I know suffering and suffering is the same for us all.'

In the early months of 1947 Levi's sister took the revised manuscript to Alessandro Galante Garrone, a Turin magistrate and former partisan. To Garrone she explained her brother's bitter delusion after so many rejections. And with his accustomed generosity Garrone agreed to look at the typescript. Expecting little of it, he found he was compelled to read it all in one sitting. 'This is not a memoir,' he marvelled, 'it's a work of art,' and he hurried to show it to his anti-Fascist publisher friend, Franco Antonicelli. Handsome and trim for his forty-five years, Antonicelli was an altogether striking creature, rumoured to dab eau-de-cologne behind his ears (so his widow Renata told me). Beneath the foppish, sexually ambivalent exterior, however, was a serious man. Antonicelli had shown tremendous courage as chief of Piedmont's National Committee for Liberation, by standing firm as the Germans threatened to turn Turin into a second Warsaw. Unusually for a man of letters, he had no ambition to become a writer himself. His publishing house was named 'Francesco De Silva' after an obscure fifteenth century Piedmontese printer, and was unsupported by influential journals, political parties or coteries of the day. It was an amateur enthusiasm that operated on a shoestring. Levi had found his man.

The offices, situated in a disused antique shop off Piazza San Carlo, were perishingly cold and during the frequent post-war power cuts the editors had to work by candlelight. Nevertheless, exquisite editions of Madame de Staël, Goethe and Dickens were produced. Natalia Ginzburg's husband Leone had been a great friend, and Antonicelli's new imprint was called 'The Leone Ginzburg Library' in honour of him. Ironically, given Natalia's rejection of *If This is a Man*, this was the imprint under which Primo Levi's book would appear. Antonicelli was delighted to handle a manuscript that had been turned down by the mighty Einaudi (the two men did not get on). But what struck him most at this early reading was the book's morality. Antonicelli was steeped in a venerable Italian tradition of secular, moral literature, exemplified by the refined and civil voice of Manzoni, and Levi's chronicle was a moral treatise on man in the tradition of Manzoni. Not that Levi lectured sententiously from the pulpit: his voice spoke to the reader, not *at* him. Prestige and maybe pecuniary advantage awaited Antonicelli for 'discovering' this masterpiece. On the other hand there was nothing to lose if nobody bought it, as De Silva was virtually bankrupt anyway. Antonicelli accepted Levi's manuscript for publication.

With the Einaudi débâcle behind him, Levi threw himself into launching his book. And, as the typescript left his hands, his contact with Antonicelli increased. Behind a door marked DIRETTORE CULTURALE the publisher welcomed Levi in for a glass of Fernet as they discussed galleys and print runs. Though Antonicelli had the unfortunate reputation of not paying his authors on time (or not paying them at all), he honoured every lira of his contract with Levi, a measure of his respect both for the author and his book. Levi was pleased to discover that he knew personally three of Antonicelli's staff. Marisa Zini had coached him privately for secondary school entry. Anita Rho (then Italy's greatest German translator) was friendly with Levi's sister. And Maria Vittoria Malvano, the only Jew at De Silva, was studying history of art with Levi's fiancée, Lucia Morpurgo.

8

Levi's confidence was bolstered by Antonicelli's advocacy of his book, but then came unexpected advance publicity. A local Communist newspaper, *The People's Friend,* wanted to serialise his book before it was published. At this stage the work was provisionally entitled *Sul Fondo* (*In the Abyss,* the title of an H. G. Wells short story). Serialisation was to be in five instalments, the first of which appeared on 29 March 1947. Flagged in the usual way ('By kind permission of the author'), the extracts were ruthlessly cut to accommodate column space, and Levi's prose is the more austere for it. The paper was co-edited by his old friend Silvio Ortona (who, like most Italian Communists, was somewhat to the right of the old British Labour Party). The *People's Friend* was based in Vercelli, a rice-growing area near Turin, and had an impressive weekly circulation of 10,000 copies. Levi's first readers were not metropolitan sophisticates, then, but ordinary men and women in the Piedmont provinces. The fifth extract on 31 May ended with parentheses '(To be continued)', but, owing to the post-war paper shortage, nothing further appeared.

9

These early spring months of 1947 were marked by two other events: one judicial, the other industrial. The trial of Rudolf Höss, the former Auschwitz commandant, was under way in Poland. Held in snow-bound Warsaw, the court case made international news, and Levi was asked to testify. Unfortunately he could not get the time off work. He would have given much to attend the trial of the wretchedy servile Höss. His justificatory memoir, *Kommandant in Auschwitz,* written in the months before he was hanged by the Allies (at the age of forty-six) on 7th April 1947, was the work of a stunted moral imagination. Yet it was a key, Levi believed, to understanding the century's atrocity. With disturbing indifference, Höss relates his apprenticeship in Nazi obedience and the immense pride he took in the smooth running of the gas chambers. Lack of imagination (not sadism) made him cruel; Höss was a warning to us of the dangers of blind adherence to ideology. Enrica Jona, the last Italian to have seen Vanda Maestro alive at Auschwitz, attended the Warsaw trial, accompanied by Nardo De Benedetti and the Jewish director of Milan's Search Committee for Deported Jews, Colonel Vitale. Away from the trial, the three traipsed round Warsaw's apocalyptic destruction, hoping to find some documentary trace of relatives or loved ones. They found nothing.

Meanwhile at DUCO Levi encountered another industrial problem. The firm's most prized paint, 'Cromomarina,' had turned gelatinous in the tin, and 120 tonnes of the stuff gone to ruin. Why? After days of rootling through file cards, delivery chits and order forms, Levi exposed the problem as an excess of lead oxide in an order, which had led to the formation of a salt that congealed the paint. Levi found a way to reverse the process. This was his greatest professional triumph in his sixteen months at DUCO: he had saved the firm a small fortune. DUCO's manager, Paolo De Bove, promoted him from humble assistant to deputy lab chief. Yet on 30 June 1947 Levi abruptly left DUCO. He had grown to dislike the corporate politics involved in working for a subsidiary of the Nobel-Montecatini chemicals giant. Before he left, Levi wrote a rhyming satirical poem, 'The Last Will and Testament of the Deputy Laboratory Head', which he distributed among DUCO colleagues. It would appear that the general manager in Milan, Dr Zanardi, had broken some promise to Levi, as his name here is rhymed with the Italian for 'liers', '*bugiardi*'. The doggerel ends on a note of self-assurance. 'I'm leaving the old roads for the new – late, but not too late.' After a year and a half at DUCO, Levi was free, but out of a job.

10

Help was at hand with Levi's old university friend Alberto Salmoni. After the war Alberto made a mint re-treading bald tyres and with the proceeds had bought himself a much-envied Fiat Topolino (then the smallest car in Italy); it cost him all of 860,000 lire, about £10,000 today, and none of his friends had one. Freelancing with Alberto seemed more fun than factory work at DUCO, and Levi rashly agreed to be his business partner. They worked side-by-side in a makeshift laboratory at 42 Via Massena, where Alberto's parents lived. Cluttered with jam jars, bunsen burners and mustard-pots, the converted bedroom was messy, yet Levi wanted to be a sleuthing chemist. He had his own phone line installed and business cards printed. What could go wrong? Everything – Salmoni was a Jonah. First hydrochloric acid spilled on to a neighbour's balcony, and burned holes in a mattress left out to dry. Then, a demijohn of cyanide broke on the stairs, infusing the apartment building with a bitter almond smell. Alberto's long-suffering father smiled indulgently on these mishaps: his own business exploits in Egypt had been quite as madcap.

Nothing on earth would induce Levi to give up – he enjoyed himself – and the commissions rolled in. One was very peculiar. The fashion designer Vittorio Venturino wanted to patent a coloured evening varnish for women's teeth. Green teeth could be matched to a green handbag, let us say, or red teeth to red shoes. If they could manufacture the tooth dye, Messrs Levi and Salmoni stood to gain financially. At first they were enthusiastic. Using his DUCO contacts, Levi ordered cut-price guncotton explosives, whose ethyl alcohol could serve as a non-toxic solvent to *remove* the dye once it had been applied. (The last thing Levi wanted was a law suit for indelible tooth staining.) One day he walked into the lab sporting bright-green teeth. 'How do I look in these?' The effect was generally agreed to be repulsive, and Salmoni wrote to Venturino regretfully: 'I do wish we had better news for you. The main problem is how to find a pleasant-tasting but *non-poisonous* solvent.'

Business might have collapsed altogether, had Levi and Salmoni not remembered Mario Revagli, who had a mirror-making apparatus in a workshop behind Porta Nuova station. Revagli was willing to pay good money for stannochloride, an essential ingredient in mirror manufacture, which is made from dissolving tin in hydrochloric acid. Levi pestered food manufacturers for tin cans. In acid the tin gave off an appalling stench and yellowish fumes wafted out of the Via Massena lab into the Salmonis' sitting room: the walls, even Signora Salmoni's silver hair, turned yellow. Business picked up splendidly. Levi cycled round to the mirror-maker's with the stannochloride crystals sealed in plastic bags. Revagli's face had been disfigured by a sniper's bullet, and Levi's late science fiction, 'The Mirror Maker', was possibly inspired by the ex-partisan Revagli, whose face was so cruelly reflected back to him in the mirrors he made.

Before long Levi had made enough money from stannochloride to buy himself a Lambretta. That summer he scooted to the Italian Riviera, where he was emotionally reunited with Jean Samuel. Jean hardly recognised the well-fed man who came to greet him with a full head of hair and a bagful of oranges and chocolates. The survivors could not contain their joy at finding each other alive and for three hours they exchanged memories and hardships. Two weeks later, on 16 July 1947, in a fifth letter to Jean, Levi confirmed that his book was now at the printer's. He told Samuel that he was due to marry in September and that Lucia Morpurgo was to move into 75 Corso Re Umberto with Levi's mother and sister. ('We're three, but soon we'll be four.')

11

While Levi corrected his proofs, he began and finished *The Great Betrayal* by the French philosopher Julien Benda. (Virtually all his reading at this time was foreign, a reaction against the isolation and censorship imposed by Fascism.) For the first time Levi read Joseph Conrad, one of his most important literary discoveries. Conrad's terrified recognition of human solitude struck a chord with the Auschwitz survivor. When the murderous ivory trader in *Heart of Darkness* exclaims 'Exterminate all the brutes!', he might well have been referring to Levi's own century of genocide, not the Belgian Congo of the 1890s. And as Levi read these Edwardian shipboard dramas in English, grappling with their dense maritime terminology, so he planned to write a Conradian saga with Sandro Delmastro as hero. Only it would be set in the Alps instead of on the sea. Just as Conrad had measured himself against the ocean, so Delmastro had measured himself against the mountains.

In the meantime Levi's book had changed its title from *In the Abyss* to *The Drowned and the Saved*, and then to *If This is a Man*. Antonicelli took the definitive title from Levi's poem, 'Psalm' (later 'Shemà'); in describing the destruction of man at Auschwitz, the poem had asked the reader to 'Consider if this is a man'. Antonicelli's was a brilliantly ambivalent choice for the title, since the Nazis as well as their prisoners had been dehumanised by their work in the camp. And Levi, by including both victim and aggressor in the title, reinforced the book's objectivity and moral authority. The line carried an echo of Coleridge's astonished question to the Ancient Mariner, 'What manner of man art thou?' But a more intriguing source for the line in the poem may have been the season's most popular film, Jean Cocteau's *Beauty and the Beast*, which was shown to spellbound audiences in Turin; the monster says to himself sorrowfully: 'If only I was a man.'

Levi was soon to marry. As was the custom in those days, Lucia and Levi's engagement had lasted two years. Lucia Morpurgo was delighted by his proposal. Her father, Giuseppe Morpurgo, reportedly a conservative, rather humourless man, liked Levi and after reading *If This is a Man* in typescript, was cordial and admiring. If there was anxiety about the future it was not shown. Yet the Morpurgos must have questioned the wisdom of their daughter in marrying a concentration-camp survivor. Lucia could not have anticipated Levi's nervous breakdowns, his periods of depression and selfishness, though she knew he was a vulnerable man, still ravaged by the effects of Auschwitz. Anna Cases, a friend of Levi's in Milan, spoke of a 'shadow zone' in Primo which no one, not even Lucia, could understand. 'Primo was a psychological problem-case, we could see that from the start.' Like many in Levi's circle, Anna had responded with alarm to the news of the engagement; privately she doubted if Levi was ready to settle down and have children. She also worried about his compatibility with Lucia. Unlike Levi's outwardly warm personality and transparent need to be liked, Lucia's emotional self-sufficiency could appear as coolness towards others. Levi's friends, many of whom were biased against Lucia from the start, also considered her intellectually his inferior. But just how reliable is this view of Lucia? As neither Lucia nor any of her friends was available for comment, we cannot know. At any rate, Levi was very much in love with her. And, fortified by her admiration for him and his book, Lucia had no intention of proceeding at less than full sail. She hurried on with the wedding preparations.

Primo Levi and Lucia Morpurgo were married at 11:10 am on the morning of 8 September 1947 at the Town Hall in Turin. Neither of them wanted the expense and fuss of a big wedding, so it was kept small with invited guests only. Lucia's cousin Alberto Finzi flew in specially from America; otherwise no one came from much further afield than Milan. After the vows were exchanged, Levi was still only married 'from the waist up', as he told his friend Leo Gallico. Later that Monday there was a religious blessing at the Morpurgo family home at 39 Via Napione. There was no honeymoon to speak of.

Lucia's twin sister Gabriella had a small flat on Via Giovanni Lanza in the green hills above Turin, and here the couple enjoyed a few days on their own. 'It was supposed to be a sort of experiment in self-sufficiency,' explained Levi's cousin Giulia. Neither Primo nor Lucia was remotely domesticated, however, and the return to 75 Corso Re Umberto was certainly welcomed by Levi. As an overattached, devoted son, his concern for his mother was deep and genuine, and he knew that Ester would be unhappy without him. This was not meant to be a long-term solution: Levi had asked Lucia to regard his mother's flat as a makeshift until they could find somewhere better to live. Many married Italians stay with their parents until they can afford a flat of their own. But as time went by, and Levi's mother got older and more needy, so it became impossible for Levi to break from Ester, or for Lucia to move out of the flat. The first signs of domestic tension surprised no one. But as 1947 drew to a close, Levi appeared to be unconcerned by the disruption and domestic upsets he had caused. Lucia, a prickly personality at the best of times, now found herself in an impossible situation. She was not allowed to furnish the flat as she might have liked, or to decorate it. The situation inflicted on Lucia by her husband was intolerable. And it was Ester, not Lucia, who was still the secure centre of Primo's world. As the newcomer, Lucia felt threatened by her. All this would cause bitterness subsequently within the '*ménage*', as Levi liked to call the domestic triangle.

13

One month after Levi was married, on 11 October 1947, *If This is a Man* was published. On a pale background the words *Se questo è un uomo* stood out in red; beneath them was a Goya etching of a dead man prone on his stomach, arms outstretched in blood. It was a draft sketch for Goya's famous canvas 'The Execution of 3rd May'. In those days, books were expected to make their own way. There were no author interviews, no magazine profiles, no launch parties. And the book's cheap post-war paper was virtually newsprint. Yet Antonicelli had made an effort. Publicity photographs of the twenty-eight-year-old author were distributed in bookshops, his face in moody half-shadow. And to drum up nationwide interest, Antonicelli's sales director Luigi Ventre embarked on a two-week publicity tour of Lombardy, Emilia, the Veneto and Rome, the boot of his car crammed with flyers and review copies. Unfortunately, word had got round Turin of Einaudi's previous rejection and this was to influence sales negatively.

Between November 1947 and the following spring no more than twelve reviews of *If This is a Man* appeared in Italy. Most critics gave measured, very conventional assessments, praising Levi's 'morality' while being uncertain what sort of book they were dealing with. In a long and immensely detailed review, *Il Ponte* lamely welcomed the presence of a 'new writer', but no word was forthcoming from Italy's so-called *grandi firme* – 'big names' – such as Alberto Moravia or Elio Vittorini. Most galling were those critics who pigeonholed Levi as a 'witness'. This Italian word, *testimone*, would settle on Levi like an albatross, and he came to resent it thoroughly. It seemed to him the most backhanded praise: Levi thought of himself as a writer first, and a witness second.

Amid the indifferent reviews, two stood out. One was by the great Piedmontese critic Arrigo Cajumi, the other by Italo Calvino. It would take a maverick like Cajumi to recognise Levi's greatness. A caustic wit, Cajumi famously scorned Italy's cultural eminences, and his review of Levi, on the front page of *La Stampa* (no longer *La Nuova Stampa*) for 26 November 1947, was aimed partly at Italy's literati, most of whom were in thrall to party-politics or the Church. 'Ignoring political parties, Levi arrives naturally at art.' Alone among critics, Cajumi identified a Darwinist undertow in the narrative. Levi had written of the central event of his life (also the central event of the twentieth century) like a 'born writer'. No other review would give Levi such intense pleasure; Cajumi had salvaged his literary self-respect after the Einaudi rejection and launched him as the writer he wanted to be.

Calvino's review for Italy's Communist daily *L'Unità* (6 May 1948) hailed a 'magnificent new book'. Levi's portrayal of Dr Pannwitz alone was evidence of an extraordinary gift for characterisation and a 'genuine narrative power'. Four years younger than Levi, Calvino had just published his extrovert first novel *The Path to the Nest of Spiders*, born directly out of his experience as a partisan in the Maritime Alps. With its triumphalist message of partisan revolt, Calvino's was a different sort of book from Levi's. Yet Calvino was twinned with Levi, by critics, as a 'promising' new Italian writer.

Though saddened and frustrated by the poor sales of *If This is a Man*, Levi was thrilled to be published and sent copies to friends with suitable inscriptions. Marisa Zini's read: 'To my dear teacher, who taught me how to read and write.' And there was one for the Roman character Lello Perugia, '*All'amico Lello*'. By the year's end Levi had learned the sad truth that *If This is a Man* had scarcely been read outside Turin, and then only by a phalanx of middle-class intelligentsia: doctors, schoolteachers, Action Party diehards. The sales figures speak for themselves: 6,000 copies of Calvino's Resistance novel had sold immediately on publication, while Levi's book sold no more than 1,500 copies. The disappointing sales – by no means a catastrophe – amounted to little more than half the book's print run. Italians, in their rush to find a new national consciousness, had preferred Calvino's jaunty partisan fantasy, with its black-and-white world of victor and vanquished, to Levi's disturbing moral treatise. With such mediocre sales Levi believed there could be no sequel to *If This is a Man*, no second act. He had fulfilled his civic duty to testify, at least, and felt he could do no more. So in early 1948, with Lucia pregnant, he abandoned his plans to become a professional writer and returned full time to chemistry.

FIFTEEN

Factory Responsibilities
1948–53

I

Levi's married life, outwardly stable, brought a new happiness into 1948. He and Lucia were expecting their first child. Meanwhile Levi continued to work with Alberto Salmoni in the makeshift lab. There he distilled clove oil to produce vanillin – artificial vanilla flavouring – but returns from this were slight. Then Levi decided to synthesise lipstick from serpent droppings. Python waste was coveted by cosmetic companies for the chemical it contained, alloxan. Levi saw his opportunity to obtain alloxan when the Italian television personality and amateur zoologist Angelo Lombardi ('The Animals' Friend') came to Turin with a snake exhibition. But Lombardi refused to let Levi in among his caged serpents, so that was that. In the summer he travelled to Pisa on his Lambretta, his wife riding pillion on the scooter. Aldo Moscati was an Italian survivor who had returned to Pisa and whom Levi had not seen since the last days of Auschwitz. Levi and Lucia passed through countryside that had speedily recovered since the war and was dotted with cherry trees. With Lucia pregnant and Moscati the proud father of a baby girl, it seemed that the world was being reborn.

The mountains continued to draw Levi out of Turin. Natalia Ginzburg's chain-smoking, whisky-drinking older brother Alberto Levi was Primo's new climbing companion. Alberto had the family's lopsided smile, and his cheerful manner attracted Levi. He seemed to make the room 'grow brighter' by his sunny presence, Levi noted in a later short story. Alberto's wife Miranda had lost her family to the Nazis; yet, with her elegant wit, she dealt with the loss discreetly. Levi and Alberto liked to hike through Piedmont's northern quarter of the Val Tournanche, where they scaled Mont Blanc. Alberto was a doctor living in Turin and now the Levi family's GP.

These post-war years were a time of recovery and stock-taking for the

Levis. The family textile business, forcibly closed during the Occupation, had reopened under the uncles Corrado and Gustavo Luzzati, and was doing well. Having sold 'The Saccarello' (today the villa is an agricultural college, the 'Istituto Agrario Bonafus'), the Luzzatis once more had money. Levi's sister had completed a doctoral thesis on Modigliani, and was now secretary of the Historical Institute of the Resistance in Turin. There were several unpleasant revelations. The woman who used to sell the Levis dairy goods, known as '*Magna Toma*' (Auntie Cheese), turned out to have been a Nazi informer who had betrayed Jews for money. One day Levi's mother saw her Persian carpets airing on a neighbour's balcony; they had been stolen from 'The Saccarello'.

Ten years had elapsed since Italy's Jews were first assaulted by the Fascist race laws; the horror of the death-camps underlined the Fascist iniquity. Italian Catholics, understandably, wished to view themselves as a *brava gente*, a decent people, and preferred to blame Hitler for the catastrophe. Yet there was no evidence to suggest that Hitler had ever demanded an anti-Semitic campaign as a pre-condition for an alliance with Italy: Mussolini had imposed the racial laws at his own bidding. In his 1946 history, *The Tragic and Grotesque Saga of Fascist Racism*, Levi's cousin Eucardio Momigliano had argued that Mussolini was no monster on the scale of Hitler or Stalin, but had 'simply' wanted to remove Jews from the mainstream of Italian life.

While many Italians had abetted the Nazis, there had also been a widespread reluctance to do so. Nearly all the Italian Jews who had come through the conflict alive owed their survival to neighbours – sometimes strangers – who gave them shelter. It was a rare Italian village or city diocese that had not offered underground help to Jews. Levi's mother would not now be alive without the protection of Catholics. Luciana Nissim's parents had been smuggled to Switzerland from Brusson by a priest; the town mayor, Serafino Court, had gone to jail for protecting Jews. Emerico Vuillaermin, a hotelier in nearby Arcesaz, had been executed for the same 'crime'. These men had acted with a contempt for the rules that was perhaps uniquely Italian.

2

With Lucia's pregnancy advancing, Levi's need to become *sistemato*, as Italians say ('fixed for life'), was urgent. Without the security of long-term employment, it would not be easy to bring up a family. Consultancy work with Salmoni was increasingly haphazard, and in the spring of 1948 the friends decided to liquidate the business. As builders were helping them lower the ventilation apparatus out of the window, the pulley broke and the glassware contraption plunged to the courtyard below. 'Funny, I thought it would make more noise,' Salmoni commented on the shattered glass and porcelain. Once more, Levi was unemployed.

Fortunately a wealthy industrialist in Turin, Rico (Federico) Accati, was seeking a bright young chemist. Outwardly ebullient, and a self-made man, Accati was the incarnation of *furbizia* (cunning), a quality that Italians value highly. During the war he had played a foxy double game of supplying information to the Allies while keeping in with the Germans. With the help of his brothers Attilo and Mario, in 1946 Accati had rapidly expanded the family paint and construction business, securing lucrative public-sector contracts. By the time Levi met him, Accati's paint operation was registered as the 'Industrial Firm of Varnishes and Associated Products' (Società Industriale Vernici e Affini, or SIVA for short). It was based at 274 Corso Regina Margherita, an unlovely part of Turin that is today lined with pornographic theatres.

Little suspecting that SIVA would detain him for the next thirty years, Levi gladly took up Accati's offer of work. As a 'technical employee', his monthly salary was 100,000 lire (£950 today), a welcome security in those frustrated, penniless years. On the minus side, hours were long, the equipment antiquated and the work (which included stoking the lab's wood fire) not very enthralling. Accati, a veteran penny-pincher, had stinted on basic amenities: he came from a textile town near Turin, Biella, whose inhabitants have a reputation for tightfistedness. There was no company canteen to speak of and worker safety precautions were non-existent.

Yet from the day Levi started at SIVA on 8 April 1948 he showed real ability for the job, which involved forging important links abroad, guarding valuable formulae and seeing to contracts up and down Italy. Without exception the staff liked and respected Levi, and he enjoyed their trust and camaraderie. The firm's ten staff were all tied to the Accati clan. The sales manager, an ex-army colonel named Peroglio, was Accati's cousin, while the company secretary Rita Perret acted as accountant, telephonist and paint-packager. The three tough Selvestrel brothers – Egisto, Piero, Redento – had previously worked in Accati Construction and came from Italy's impoverished Veneto area in the north. Accati prized them as 'sloggers' or workers who could be relied on. The firm's chief paint-mixer, Piero Selvestrel, was Levi's favourite, and he would say of this stubborn character: 'He'd rather eat bread and onions than admit defeat.' Levi was happy in the firm's warm familial life. The distractions of factory work – card indexes, copy orders, book-keeping – helped him stave off blue moods.

He became friendly with the production assistant Pietro Cavallero, a carpenter's son who was active in the Communist Party. Cavallero was an amiable, unpretentious fellow who often turned up to work with a furled red banner after attending demonstrations. Italy was again in political upheaval as the Christian Democratic Party battled with the Communists for victory in the forthcoming spring elections. Fear of Communism had reached a peak and the wealthy were packing their bags for Switzerland. Cavallero remembered Levi as a 'kind and approachable' boss, who was discreet about his *bandiera rossa* street tussles. Levi was fond of Cavallero, and treated him with a quasi-paternal regard. He was shocked when, in the 1960s, he became Italy's most feared and pitiless criminal, dubbed *La Belva*, 'the wild beast', for his murders and bank robberies.

Though SIVA was a refuge from personal troubles, Auschwitz weighed on Levi constantly. During lunch breaks he tried to trace survivor comrades. In the hope of locating Leon Levi, the Greek namesake who had wandered with him through devastated post-war Poland, he wrote to what remained of Salonika's Jewish community. A Greek rabbi replied, saying that perhaps one thousand 'Levis' lived in Salonika, of which a good thirty were called 'Leon Levi'. Auschwitz affected Levi in other ways. Each time he met a new client, he would assess how that person might have fared in the camp. This instinctive evaluation of strangers was something Levi shared with many survivors; he liked to say he could get the measure of a man in a 'split second'.

3

The outcome of the elections of 18 April, which resulted in a landslide victory for the Christian Democrats, ushered in Italy's long post-war period of stagnation, and confined the Italian left to ineffectual opposition. The dubious nature of modern Italian politics was set. The Christian Democrats quickly emerged as a party of mobsters, corrupt politicians and larcenous power brokers. And as they took control of Italy, a unique opportunity for reform was lost. Levi was painfully aware that the so-called values of the Resistance – national unity, Liberalism – had been trampled upon in the elections and it took him many years to weather the disappointment. Uplifting news came a month later on 14 May when the new State of Israel was proclaimed. Levi was fired with romantic sympathy for the little state, but alarmed by the antagonisms that flared immediately between Jews and the Arab world. Here was a turning-point in the fortunes of the world, more terrible than anyone could know.

*

During his first two months at SIVA Levi had not taken on any significant industrial work. But then Pirelli asked him to investigate a sample of powder called polyvinyl-formal, or PVF in chemist's shorthand. The powder, an American patent, was used in copper wire insulation and looked like off-white semolina, sticky to the touch. PVF was not commercially available in Italy and Accati hoped to manufacture it himself, turning powder into money. A chemist who had known Primo at university, Giovanna Balzaretti, was drafted in as Levi's assistant. Levi was 'coolly in control' during the PVF trials, remembered Balzaretti, if at times a little bossy. After weeks of exacting investigative work she and Levi managed to crack the sample's molecular make-up. Accati poured champagne in celebration and declared that SIVA was now ready to branch into PVF production. The first few kilos of SIVA polyvinyl-formal were sold to Pirelli as insulation material for electrical cables. Levi became an authority not just on paints, but on the arcane technology of lacquer-coated insulation cables.

Production was hopelessly inefficient until Balzaretti devised an industrial blender, which spun out PVF impurities (acetic acid, benzedrin peroxide) centrifugally. Balzaretti's invention saved hours on production time, but Levi was not happy with it. Whether from a contrary whim or a stubborn streak, he ditched it for a Heath Robinson contraption of his own where water cascaded down a series of cranky wooden steps. The steps clogged up with sludge and the PVF yield virtually ceased. Accati, who was usually at pains to conceal his temper from Levi, furiously ordered him to break up the contraption for firewood and go back to Balzaretti's blender. To this day Balzaretti is at a loss to understand why Levi initially rejected her giant Moulinex. Perhaps he did not like to be trounced by a woman, or was uncomfortable with her ingenuity.

4

On 31 October 1948 Levi's first child was born. The girl was to be fair with dark brown eyes. Her mother named her Lisa, and her father added Lorenza, after the mason Lorenzo Perrone. She was delivered in Turin at 28 Via Marco Polo, presumably a clinic. After the disappointment of the April elections, his daughter filled Levi with vitality and nervous expectation for the future. He walked the baby about in his arms singing Waldensian lullabies, just as his mother had done. The child caused an immediate disruption, however, as there was no more room in 75 Corso Re Umberto. Primo was periodically irritable, his sister surly, Lucia weak and nursing.

Living under the watchful eye of her mother-in-law was an uncomfortable experience for Lucia, who felt inhibited by Ester's presence. And it was on Levi that she unleashed her grievances. A perpetual tension reigned, and it became difficult for Lucia to remain in the same room even as her sister-in-law.

Since childhood Levi had confided closely in his sister; the siblings were, as Italians say, 'two bodies but one soul'. Anna Maria resented Lucia's claim on her adored brother and often treated her as a guest on sufferance. Levi disliked his sister's jealousy; it belittled her. Tension and quarrels ensued as Levi's wife vented her own frustrations on Anna Maria. 'For many years she behaved in a very horrible way towards my sister,' said Levi. There was misunderstanding on all sides, but the breakdown of communication – the stubborn refusal of all three women to communicate directly with one another – told its own story of resentment. Even Levi had to acknowledge that the atmosphere was becoming insupportable; 75 Corso Re Umberto was now the source of much discontent.

Levi found distraction in literature. Though he had given up on his dream of becoming a professional writer, he had not stopped writing altogether. In his first four years at SIVA he produced a clutch of minor short stories – half a dozen or so – which feature in disguised form the factory's various staff. The concierge Luisa Fracas and her husband Sante were from Friuli, near Yugoslavia, and Levi was fascinated by their dialect, inflected with Slovenian words. While Luisa was a bossy, superstitious woman (her lodge was hung with the Bleeding Heart of Jesus and other devotional knick-knacks), Sante was phlegmatic and solemn, often to be found in a tavern hunched over a bottle of wine. His job was to conduct the night-time paint-boiling sessions in the fields behind SIVA. He used grapepip oil and other vegetable substitutes and sometimes, disgustingly, he lobbed fish bones into the brew, stirring the cauldron with a long pole. Neighbours complained of the stench when cod liver oil was added. After three hours, Sante would introduce onion slices on a skewer: when these began to fry, it was a sign that the paint was ready. This noxious-smelling sludge was the basis of SIVA's top-quality house paint, SIVALUX, by 1948 a household name in Italy.

Levi's story 'Night Shift' transforms Sante Fracas into the dour worker Lanza, while 'The Guests' tells how Sante's fierce-tempered wife Luisa had expelled a regiment of drunk Germans from her home in Friuli during the war. Another story, 'Mary and the Circle', embellished an anecdote Levi had heard at DUCO. The jovial Felice Fantino had been frustrated in his attempts to decorate a kitchen by the antics of a three-year-old girl, so he chalked a magic circle round her, which he warned it was dangerous to step out of. Thirty years later this fable became the basis of the 'Titanium' chapter in *The Periodic Table*; probably Levi conflated it with an alchemist's legend from *The Microbe Hunters*, a childhood favourite, which told how spiders could not scurry out of a ring of powdered unicorn horn.

These stories – bagatelles really – are able but undistinguished. The *daimon* had left Levi now, and it would be another fifteen years before he produced an enduring work of literature. In his darker moments he wondered if he would have ever become a writer at all, without the catalyst of Auschwitz. The concentration camp had imparted a sense of urgency to Levi's task of writing, and would remain his great theme, the place where the writer in him was born.

5

The 1940s gave way to the 1950s. And these were the halcyon years of expansion for SIVA, when paint and PVF production trebled. All Turin was poised for an industrial boom as fridges, televisions and plastic goods rolled out of the factories. The city's population, swollen by the first southern migrants, increased by 42 per cent. Excited by this boomtime, in 1950 Rico Accati set up a sister company, SCET, which was to coat copper and aluminium wires with PVF-based enamel. He doubled SIVA's staff to twenty-one, taking on a new sales representative, Francesco Proto, who was to become Levi's closest friend and confidant at work.

Though Proto had good references from DUCO, initially Accati was suspicious of him, as he was a southerner. All the alleged Mezzogiorno characteristics of wiliness, corruption and violent intrigue seemed to be embodied in Proto's birthplace of Amalfi (as in *The Duchess of Malfi*). Yet Proto proved to be such a fabulously efficient salesman that Accati was obliged to revise his low opinion of the *meridionali* and took Proto's Amalfi relatives for a ride in the back of his Rolls-Royce. As SIVA's only Jew, Levi was instinctively drawn to an outsider like Proto, whose easy, bantering humour made a change from Accati's frequent moody silences, and soon an intimacy developed. Throughout the 1950s Levi occasionally accompanied Proto on sales trips round Piedmont, cans of SIVALUX knocking in the boot. They sold resins and PVF to Italian electrical engineering firms with such sturdy acronyms as EFEL, ELVI and CERRUTI (not the fashion company: this one made refrigerator motors), and travelled as far afield as Vercelli or Casale to do so. Invariably they made a point of stopping for lunch over a bottle of rough wine in a countryside trattoria. Levi was very attached to the pleasures of eating and drinking. ('I do not think this is an effect of the concentration camp,' he told me.) He had a passion for simple food, and immense detours would be made in search of modest taverns that served the Piedmontese speciality of tripe and beans. When Levi found what he was looking for, he was the 'happiest of gourmands', recalled Proto. The men were tactful with each other, and Proto found a wisdom in Levi humbly borne. 'He knew how to touch the *anima umana* – the human soul – when speaking of his terrible past.' But what most impressed Proto about Levi was his natural courtesy, even when talking to the most menial SIVA workers. Accati, by contrast, had little time for such shopfloor niceties, and this would cause Levi problems in the future.

6

In August 1950 Levi was reunited for a second time with Jean Samuel. They met in the picturesque Germanasca Valley in Piedmont, where thirteen lakes shimmer on the valley floor. Samuel was pleased to meet Levi's wife and his one-year-old daughter. He was on honeymoon in Piedmont with his French wife, Claude. That August Levi joked and talked with such ease that he seemed to Samuel a different man. However, one conversation with Levi was particularly memorable, as well as disturbing. Levi referred to Auschwitz in a callously ironic fashion as his 'university'. The concentration camp, he explained to Samuel, had taught him 'lessons' that he could not have learned on the outside. Auschwitz was even an 'adventure' and a 'rite of passage'. The camp had coincided with Levi's youth, and it was for this, and the few friends he made in the camp, that Levi felt a certain 'nostalgia'. To Samuel, however, who was emotionally destroyed by survival, the idea that suffering was somehow ennobling must have been uncomfortable.

At the end of the summer, while Levi was on holiday with Samuel, news came from Turin that Cesare Pavese had committed suicide. On the evening of 26 August 1950, in solitude and despair, Pavese had swallowed sixteen sachets of barbiturate powder in a Turin hotel room. Italy's greatest living novelist was dead at the age of forty-two. Levi had last seen Pavese at a friend's house in Turin in early August. He found him prematurely lined and furrowed, but could not have imagined his imminent death.

That summer, at least, Levi seemed vitally on the side of life, and was even able to dissuade a fellow survivor from taking his life. Marcello Franceschi, a non-Jew, had been arrested by the Germans in September 1943 for refusing to fight on Hitler's side and had by the war's end survived no fewer than five Nazi camps. In the worst of them, Turnich-Bokausen, he had worked underground in a lignite mine, where for eleven months he saw no daylight. Unhinged by the darkness, he became a 'vengeful beast', and threatened to kill a fellow Italian for stealing his morsel of bread. 'All I could think of was how to satisfy my hunger before it devoured me.' On his return to Turin, Franceschi resumed his studies and managed to graduate in chemistry, but at night he would wake screaming at hallucinatory German guards. A sympathetic friend now arranged for Franceschi to meet the author of *If This is a Man*.

The meeting took place on a humid September evening in 1950. Anna Maria made Franceschi tea; Levi listened respectfully to him as he told of his wish to die, then said to him: 'Go back to life, and take heart.' These words have a biblical tone. Nothing, Levi went on, 'can take the place of human dignity' – it is irremovable – and in refusing to fight for the Germans Franceschi had shown an exemplary courage. This was to be the most important encounter of Franceschi's life. 'Primo might have been the viceroy of India for all I cared. What mattered to me is that he spoke sympathetically to me and with an acute moral sense of what was *right*. I thought this man must be a saint.' At this stage in his life Levi was not reluctant to be seen in such hallowed light; only later would he find it a burden. Franceschi left 75 Corso Re Umberto at one o'clock in the morning. Levi had signed him a copy of *If This is a Man*: 'To Marcello, the mine worker who survived Nazi slavery.' So began another of his non-literary friendships that was to last thirty years. However, it was based as much on professional grounds as on reciprocal suffering: Franceschi was later manager of a synthetic-rubber ('Buna') factory in Chivasso, which was to trade chemicals with SIVA.

7

For the rest of 1950 and 1951, Primo and Lucia continued to live in the Crocetta apartment with Ester, baby Lisa and Anna Maria. Levi had promised Lucia that they would move out as soon as their finances allowed, but it was still rather a hand-to-mouth existence: Levi's SIVA salary was not enough to keep the whole household solvent. On 29 October 1951 Levi failed (not that he minded) his army medical owing to an 'insufficient thorax'; he was pigeon-chested. And as the autumn became winter, he turned his attention to another suffering friend. In the six years since his homecoming from Auschwitz, Lorenzo Perrone had become self-destructively alcoholic. The parish priest of Fossano, don Carlo Lenta, watched him selling scrap metal in the snow without an overcoat, his face blue. The priest told me in 1993: 'In the end Lorenzo contrived his own abandonment, no one could save him – not even Primo Levi.' One night, fired with grape brandy, Lorenzo fell in with an ex-policeman named Araglia who was homeless and, it turned out, tubercular. Perrone invited him home for more drink and the policeman slept rough on the floor with Perrone's five brothers and sisters. Inevitably Perrone's alcoholism made him susceptible to the tuberculosis, and within weeks he had begun to cough blood. Levi managed to find him a bed in Savigliano Hospital not far from Fossano, where he knew a doctor. There he bought the mason wool jumpers, a new pair of winter trousers, and sat by his bed holding his hand. Perrone began to hallucinate rats and lions and, according to his brother Secondo, 'winged beasts'. Briefly, hospital had looked like his salvation, but Perrone kept running away in search of alcohol. After six months in and out of the ward they found him moribund in a ditch: his liver had shut down. Lorenzo Perrone died in Savigliano Hospital in the early hours of 30 April 1952. The official cause of his death was: 'Tuberculosis complicated by bronchial pneumonia.' A wake was held at 14 Via Michelini in Fossano where the mason was born, followed by obsequies in San Giorgio church. Half the old townspeople had come to pay their respects; Perrone was laid out as a *caro estinto*, a 'dear departed'. Levi told the congregation: 'I believe that it is really due to Lorenzo that I am alive today.'

Perrone had helped other prisoners at Auschwitz, though typically without telling anyone. His charity made no distinctions: it was incontestably a holy act. This was the charity of Italy's long-lost *cultura contadina*, a peasant culture that had always looked after its own. 'In Lorenzo's day the bricklayers and fishermen of Fossano went out of their way to help the weakest in the community,' Father don Lenta explained. 'Though Lorenzo said he could no longer believe in God after Auschwitz, he retained a sense of religion, a pity for the downtrodden.' The deceased's five siblings, Caterina, Giovanna, Giovanni, Michele and Secondo, stood in silence as Levi placed flowers by the open coffin. According to the Fossano parish registers, Perrone was born on 12 September 1904. He was not quite forty when Levi first encountered him at Auschwitz. For some months after his death Levi was drawn and pale, and grieving for his friend. On 28 November 1952 his adored Uncle Enrico also died, at Genoa, aged seventy-three. All three Levi brothers from Bene Vagienna – Cesare, Mario, Enrico – were now dead.

About this time, Einaudi's science publishing director, Paolo Boringhieri, rang up to ask Levi if he would consider reading and translating scientific texts for Giulio Einaudi. No one at the publishing house could match Levi for his knowledge of chemistry, and in a rash moment he agreed to translate the first two volumes of Henry Gilman's mammoth *Organic Chemistry (An*

Advanced Treatise). Levi thought it would be interesting: instead it was thankless work, which took up months of his free time and got on Lucia's nerves. However, Levi now had one foot in the Einaudi salon. *If This is a Man* had gone out of print three years earlier when De Silva was taken over by a Florentine publisher in 1949 and the unsold copies transferred to a warehouse on the River Arno. On 16 July 1952 Boringhieri brought up the book at an Einaudi editorial. Everyone was in favour of re-publication except Giulio Einaudi. Levi might have written a 'fine work,' the director objected, but it was not 'right' for his list. Einaudi was still interested chiefly in *gauchiste* literature and had just published Beatrice and Sidney Webb's naive apologia for 1930s Stalinism, *Soviet Communism: A New Civilization*. It was thought that if Beatrice Webb could waltz at the age of seventy-five in Moscow's Red Square (which she did), then a bright-red future surely lay ahead for Italy.

Levi was disappointed by Einaudi's verdict, the more so because Italo Calvino, with whom he had been twinned in 1947, was an enormously successful writer. In 1952 his surreal fantasy *The Cloven Viscount* was published. A fairy-tale for adults, the novel seemed a far cry from Calvino's earlier, ostensibly neo-realist fiction of the Resistance, *The Path to the Nest of Spiders*. The viscount-hero is cut in two by a cannonball somewhere in medieval Bohemia. One half is good; the other (which delights in collective hangings and orgies) is not good. In the end, the two halves fight a duel, after which they are sewn back together by a doctor. Was this a parable of the divisions of the Cold War? The impact on Levi of Calvino's allegorical caprice was instant and dazzling. Just when he feared the *daimon* would not return, Calvino's extravaganza helped to free him from his Auschwitz chronicle and gave him the courage to write science fiction.

As a scientist, Levi was well equipped to write futurist fables. And though his fantasies of the early 1950s relied somewhat on Calvino for their whimsy and sly allegorical humour, ultimately they are Levi's own and they sparkle with philosophic humour and pastiche. What gave his fables edge and distinction, and lent them potency and originality, was the shadow cast by Nazism. 'The Sleeping Beauty in the Fridge', begun in 1952, is a macabre allegory that unfolds in Space-Age Berlin where Germans are gathered at the annual 'defrosting' of a woman stored alive in a deep-freeze unit. A soulless clone of approved human type (good heart, excellent lungs and kidneys), she has been subjected to a battery of Nazi doctor-style tests. Indifferent to the inhumanity of their experiment, the Berliners chatter blithely over drinks as the refrigerated Beauty thaws out.

Terrible events had overtaken the Wellsian faith in technology. Not only Auschwitz, but the aerial destruction visited on Hiroshima and the dehumanising effect of Stalin's technocratic Russia had showed how far man could go in the destructive misuse of technology. What Levi shared with Wells, however, was a gift for prophecy. His Sleeping Beauty fantasia foresaw the future science of cryogenics. Four years after the story was written, *Scientific American* (to which Levi subscribed) reported in 'The Freezing of Living Cells' that a live hamster could be frozen entire for an hour, and thawed out none the worse for wear. Another of Levi's 1950s science fictions, 'Full Employment', anticipated the use of insects in micro-assembly technology. In 1986 Levi showed me a photograph Calvino had sent him of one of these worker ants bearing in its mandibles a microscopic magnet.

<h1 style="text-align:center">8</h1>

The next year – August 1953 – Levi was promoted to technical director of SIVA. The post did not suit him as he always happiest in the lab away from administrative chores. But after five years at SIVA, Levi was an employee whom Accati trusted. Whatever its drawbacks, promotion brought Levi better pay, better hours, as well as a spacious new office. A framed photograph of his daughter Lisa, now four, and his wife rested on his desk. And beneath the inevitable SIVA calendar were rows of the books and journals that no self-respecting industrial chemist could be without. Among them was the trade magazine *Chemistry and Industry,* soon to be sub-edited by the British writer J. G. Ballard.

Meanwhile SIVA had moved its premises out to the suburbs of Turin. Settimo Torinese, sixteen kilometres north-east of the city centre, was a forty-minute drive down the motorway. An ex-policeman with the unlikely name of Signor Scasso ('Mr Burglary') ferried staff there in a special SIVA bus, but Levi preferred to go by train, where he could snatch a quiet half hour to read or sleep. At that time the trains were old-fashioned steam locomotives with plank benches. Ironworks loomed large as the train entered Settimo, and a tang of nitric acid and metallic mercury hung in the air. In the wake of Turin's post-war growth, Settimo was badly polluted and virtually one-fifth covered in concrete development. It was a dormitory town of 12,000 inhabitants. Before the war it had been famous for its laundry industry, when the outlying fields were white with lavender-scented linen left out to dry. Chemical giants (not to mention washing machines) had put the *lavandaie* out of business, and now the town was dominated by pharmaceutical and paint firms. A few old men still trawled Settimo's streams for shrimps and crayfish, or worked in the local bone industry (making cigarette holders and billiard balls), but plastics had killed these trades. For miles around the only pleasant aroma was of coffee ground in the Lavazza factory. In these industrial boondocks Levi was to spend the next twenty-two years of his working life.

Accati had cleverly sited SIVA's new premises by the motorway exit to Milan, where it was conveniently located for business. 84 Via Leyni was no ordinary building. In an extravagant gesture Accati had demolished one of his properties in Turin and transplanted it brick-by-brick to Settimo. Reconstructed with its art-nouveau stairway, curved iron balcony and green-painted wooden shutters, the resurrected villa stood out in Settimo as a model of old-world grace and charm. A new staff canteen was installed, and so began a long tradition of choice factory lunches. Luisa Fracas, having been promoted from SIVA concierge to company cook, made pasta dishes seasoned with acacia flowers followed by *dolci di carnevale*, chocolate rolls, the perfumed cuisine of her native Friuli. Levi, who had a good palate, chose the canteen wines.

After lunch, the chemists dozed in armchairs until the 2:00 pm siren for work. A fug of domestic *toscani* cigar smoke enveloped them as they read *La Stampa* or took a nip of whisky (Ballantines was Levi's favourite). Sometimes they would experiment with a Tarot deck; Levi surprised them by his ability to read the cards. He enjoyed these two-hour lunch breaks with their high-spirited repartee and gossip. There were staff snowball fights in the winter, or bicycle tournaments in the summer. It was known that Levi was an Auschwitz survivor, and his colleagues were tolerant of his eccentricities. It was noted that he ate with a hand cupped under his mouth as if to catch every crumb. And he always wore a short-sleeved shirt with a suit, even in winter, so that his prison tattoo was exposed whenever he removed his jacket.

9

In 1952, Nardo De Benedetti took up residence in a flat at 61 Corso Re Umberto, a few doors from Levi. Everything about the two men's mutual solicitude, affection and trust lay in their deportation. So this move was highly significant for Levi. Number 61 belonged to a Jewish bachelor friend of Nardo's, Arrigo Vita, who lived in the flat with his spinster sisters Laura and Giulia. It was a huge and gloomy ground-floor property, with heavy upholstered furnishings, and an odour of naphthalene and things locked away. All three Vita siblings had rooms of their own, but they shared their lives fully with Nardo, who lived at one end of the corridor. Arrigo Vita, an opthalmologist, was busy translating Anne Frank's diary for Einaudi. For a middle-aged widower who did not want to live alone it seemed the ideal solution. Nardo paid no rent and found a ready companionship with his flatmates. There was even some suggestion of an affair with Laura Vita (Nardo liked to crank out Viennese waltzes for her on his gramophone), though not marriage. At Fossoli, Nardo and his wife Jolanda had vowed that should one of them die, the other would never remarry.

Most evenings Levi called on Nardo for a chat over zabaione mixed with brandy, Nardo's favourite. Owing to stomach ulcers, Nardo could manage only the most unobtrusive fare such as chicken in jelly, boiled courgettes or egg-noodles, which Levi found slippery and offputting. ('My dear Primo, I don't eat for pleasure but to survive,' Nardo told him.) Frequent guests and raised voices made 61 Corso Re Umberto a lively rendezvous. The Vitas kept an open house for visitors from abroad, among them Liko and Gonda Israel, who regularly flew in from Jerusalem. Liko had been deported to Auschwitz from Fossoli and was a former Yugoslav partisan. His wife Gonda tried to steer the conversation round to families and common acquaintances (inmates, sadly, of the camps). Interestingly, Lucia rarely attended these reunions. According to the Hungarian survivor and writer Edith Bruck, she was 'possessive' of Levi's suffering. ('It was as though Primo was the *only* person who had ever been in Auschwitz. All the others – myself included – had in Lucia's eyes not really been in the camp or were in the second rank of survivors.') Politics, too, were often discussed at Number 61. Nardo had witnessed Bolshevik misrule at firsthand in 1919 in Soviet Minsk as a medical officer, and he loved to bait what he called 'silly reds'. One of these was the Turin author and painter Carlo Levi, who was a first cousin of the Vitas. A vain man full of loud bonhomie, Carlo's raucous company intimidated Primo, though he did admire *Christ Stopped at Eboli*.

A frequent subject of discussion was the corporate evil of I. G. Farben. In a famous post-war trial the German chemical holding had been accused of carrying out bacterial and viral experiments on prisoners. The granular vaporising pesticide that asphyxiated prisoners, Zyklon B, was an I. G. Farben product. By the early 1950s most of the company's convicted officials were back in business. Nardo, dismayed by their speedy rehabilitation, banned all German medicines from his doctor's cabinet. By 1953, however, he had reason to be hopeful. The West German government in Bonn had declared that Jewish survivors of the Nazi camps had the right to claim damages from I. G. Farben, now in liquidation. Levi asked a German lawyer in Turin, Rudolf Loewenthal, to initiate legal proceedings. An imposing sixty-year-old, Loewenthal specialised in survivor claims. Of his family only a niece had survived the Nazis; his uncle, brother and sister-in-law had all been eliminated. Having read and admired *If This is a Man*, Loewenthal was happy to litigate on Levi's behalf as well as Nardo's. The law suit dragged on interminably as a total of 10,000 claimants had to be interviewed separately across Europe to certify their eligibility. Six long years after Levi filed his claim, the German courts awarded him damages of 122.70 deutschmarks (which at today's exchange rate amounts to £6,000). Loewenthal refused a lawyer's fee from either Levi or Nardo, but in gratitude they presented him with a sumptuous Vatican Museum catalogue of Renaissance paintings.

SIXTEEN

Journeys into Germany
1954–61

I

In January 1954 Europe was paralysed by a heavy snowfall; Turin lay under a white blanket. Vienna was a perishing minus sixteen degrees when an unidentified train emblazoned with a Soviet star pulled into the Ostbahnhof. Eighteen men descended with hunched shoulders and their coat-collars turned up. They were Italian POWs who had been repatriated after twelve years in Russian captivity, and they wept to learn that the Second World War was really over. Throughout 1954 Italian POWs continued to be released from Russia, and their stories took Levi back to his own post-war Soviet wanderings. One of the returnees, the Piedmont mechanic's son Ludovico Scagliotti, told *La Stampa* that he had been shunted round half the USSR on a variety of Red Army jobs, from bricklaying in Estonia to navvying in the Arctic Circle. Slowly the idea for a 'train' book took shape in Levi's mind; it would be informed by the journeying metaphor of Jewish history and would continue the Ulysses theme of exile. It was to be called *The Truce,* a sequel to *If This is a Man.*

While this project was simmering Levi was to confront his past in a more direct way. In the mid-1950s, as a result of business opportunities, he travelled to Germany for the first time since the war. Levi had stated in *If This is a Man* that there was no point in trying to understand the Germans. But, as memories were reawakened by the returning POWs, the SIVA business trips and thoughts of a new book, so Levi had to reassess his view of Germany and the German people. Unsurprisingly, a part of Levi wanted revenge upon his persecutors (otherwise he would have been hardly human). In Frankfurt he had watched excavators pull out a wartime family of skeletons from a half-destroyed tenement. These scenes from derelict Germany would find their way into his science fiction. 'Angelic Butterfly'

270

seethes with images of the bomb craters and fractured pipelines of Germany in the aftermath of its Zero Hour. (The 'quintessence of Germany', we read, is a compound of 'blood', 'cat piss', 'sauerkraut' and 'beer'.) At some level, however, Levi had to come to an accommodation with the Fatherland: it would be bad for SIVA business if he could not.

On his first trip to Germany, shortly after Stalin's death in 1953, Levi had displayed no obvious rancour. On the contrary, he seemed keen to practise his spoken German, and confidently requested assistance from waiters and maids in beer-halls and hotels. He even picnicked alongside Germans on a Cuxhaven beach. But more than anything he loved tearing down the *Autobahnen* with his boss Accati at the wheel of his Maserati, which few German cars could overtake. Accati had been astonished by Levi's outward serenity. Levi told him: 'the Nazi period is water under the bridge.' It was not so, however. In 1942, Levi had objected to a cartoon of a German soldier being roasted alive: 'One must *not* put Germans on the spit.' After the war he changed his mind, and wrote: 'Primo is no longer in disagreement.' Elsewhere he said he would happily have murdered a German at Auschwitz.

2

On 11 April 1954 Levi was again in Germany, though not on business. He travelled to Buchenwald in Weimar (Soviet zone) to mark the ninth anniversary of the camp's liberation from the Nazis. The specially reserved train from Turin was packed with Italian ex-deportees, and in the restaurant car Levi sat next to the Italian-born chemist Franco Schönheit, who had gone to Buchenwald with his father in August 1944. They were joined by Gabriella Poli, a briskly efficient journalist who was covering the commemoration for the Italian Socialist broadsheet *Avanti!* Poli was not Jewish, but as a journalist she was keen to understand the Nazi genocide and to catalogue survivor stories. As she spoke no German, Levi agreed to act as her interpreter. It was not for altruistic reasons that he agreed; his curiosity had been aroused.

Buchenwald was a sea of banners: 5,000 survivors from across Europe had come to honour the camp's dead. In Schönheit's photograph Levi appears in a raincoat, tense and drawn, flanked by Soviet guards and German Red Cross officials. For three days he stayed with the Italian delegation at Weimar as guests of the East German government. Poli remembered Levi as her untiring guide and interpreter. And as she interviewed the locals, all she and Levi encountered was their lethargy, defiance and self-pity. 'Everything was blamed on Hitler,' she recalled. 'It was *him*. The Germans felt no responsibility for the war at all.' Levi translated the Germans' carping replies in colourless, neutral tones, like a witness in court. It was the first time since the war that he had spoken at any length to German civilians; he must have despised their wounded denials.

References abound in *If This is a Man* to 'the curt, barbarous barking of Germans'. At one point the Germans are addressed aggressively in the vocative – 'You Germans, you have succeeded.' And there are collective condemnations, coloured by the author's rage. Any German who had shown Levi a scintilla of humanity at Auschwitz – and there were several – is pointedly not mentioned in the book. Herr Stawinoga had smuggled Levi into a shelter during an air raid. Where is he? And Ferdinand Meyer? To some extent these omissions were an artistic decision: in a judicial enquiry pervaded by indignation, minor acts of German charity would be a distraction. Yet the fact remains that there are no even halfway decent Germans in *If This is a Man*. Only in his later writing would Levi investigate the exceptions that defied the stereotype: the good German, the kind *Kapo*.

In July 1954, three months after his trip to Buchenwald, Levi was in Germany for a third time. He did not have to return so soon, and indeed his hastiness disturbed Rico Accati: 'If you don't feel like going, for heaven's sake tell me.' Levi had gone to buy chemical products from the ex-I. G. Farben firm of Bayer. The Bayer headquarters were in the industrial sumplands of Leverkusen, eighteen kilometres outside Cologne. Levi was in an antagonistic mood and wanted to encounter an ex-Nazi. This longed-for confrontation he later called 'the hour of colloquy'. Levi went out of his way to ruffle sensibilities at Bayer by introducing himself to former I. G. Farben industrialists, 'Levi, how do you do', articulating the words carefully, the Jewish surname first. That Jew-hatred could still exist in a country where virtually no Jews were left was a tribute, Levi knew, to Nazi indoctrination. More than once he glimpsed an unpleasant instinct lurking beneath the polite surface of post-war Germany. When a Bayer director observed that it was 'most unusual' for an Italian to speak German, Levi countered: 'My name is Levi. I am a Jew, and I learned your language at Auschwitz.' A stuttering apology was followed by a silence. As an Auschwitz survivor, Levi could hardly pretend that he was in a normal business relationship with the Germans.

His most confrontational exchange took place at Bayer's opulent guest house on Kaiser-Wilhelm-Allee, in Leverkusen. Levi was seated at the dining table in shirtsleeves making small talk when, apropos of nothing, Bayer's electrical-insulation expert, Dr Meckhbach, asked him about the tattoo on his exposed forearm. 'It's a memento of Auschwitz', Levi replied.

A silence fell. Rico Accati's eleven-year-old daughter Luisa was in Germany with her father to improve her German, and she recalled the scene: 'All one could hear was this polite clatter of forks on plates as ten Germans – all men – shifted awkwardly in their seats.' What most struck Luisa, from her child's perspective, was Levi's glacial calm. 'His reply was made all the more devastating because it was delivered in such a deadpan manner. I'm absolutely sure Primo relished the moment.' His provocative remark, though it was made in the heat of the moment, does not suggest an attempt on Levi's part to 'understand' the Germans, but rather to shame them.

But, as the 1950s progressed, gradually Levi was able to see the Gemans as individuals, and could make a reasonable distinction in his mind between them and the Nazis. One German in particular helped to bolster his confidence in post-war Germany and its people. Seven years older than Levi, and a chemistry graduate of Göttingen University, Dr Karl-Heinz Mielke was chief of Bayer's Plastics Technology Development unit. During the war he had kept a low profile as a dynamite technician in Troisdorf, where he had neither resisted nor supported Hitler. A courteous man with an open, smiling manner, Mielke got on with most people, and Levi grew to like him immensely. Unfailingly kind to Levi, he took the trouble to check the tiniest technical details for him. Levi was aware that Mielke's perfectionism had a grotesque mirror-image in the Nazis' *Ordnungsliebe* ('passion for order'). Indeed, he believed there was something innately disciplined, organised and efficient in the German character. But for as long as civilised Germans like Mielke were at the helm of Bayer, Levi could hope that a Fourth Reich would be impossible. Gradually, Mielke became Levi's idea of the Good German.

As Accati spoke no German, Levi interpreted for him during negoti-ations to buy 'Desmodur'. This Bayer product gave off a disgusting odour of methyl isocyanate and was analogous to the chemical that would devastate Bhopal in India in 1984. Nevertheless it was the basis for a new SIVA lacquer patented by Levi for use in fridge motors, 'Elvar 58'. To German eyes, Accati was a crafty man who required careful watching; he put on a show of incompetence for Mielke, believing this would deceive him into not reading the fine print. While Mielke considered these theatrical performances unbecoming to *deutsche Treue*, 'German uprightness', Levi was amused by Accati's air of bluster and braggadocio. When it came to making money, Levi said, nobody was more 'sly' or 'devilishly clever' than Accati. Mielke's deputy, Willi Dünwald, agreed: 'Accati! He was difficult to trust one hundred per cent – a sly dog.'

Yet, for all his entrepreneurial nous, Accati was a casebook of neuroses.

He was an anxious man, socially, and it was only after fifteen years that he felt comfortable enough to address Levi by the intimate *tu*. Like many autodidacts, Accati was ashamed of his lack of culture and tried to make up for it by collecting modern paintings. Levi was sympathetic to this awkward self-improvement. He had reached a sort of 'brutal friendship' with Accati, he said, and had learned not to be embarrassed by his boss's pungent aftershave and man-of-mode clothes. Accati has been described by his daughter Luisa as a 'sort of wild boar' to Levi's 'species of flamingo'. One day, in a fit of rage while trying to repair a resin-making machine, Accati had grabbed a hammer and dealt it such a blow that it began to work again. 'In future you have to bash here,' he told a startled worker. Levi adored that story. Temperamentally he and Accati were opposites, but together they made an effective working team: Accati the wheeler-dealer, Levi the straight-talking German interpreter. Indeed, without Accati Levi could not have gone so often or with such ease to Germany.

3

The year 1955 marked the tenth anniversary of the liberation of the Nazi camps. As part of the official commemorations a photographic exhibition on the Nazi *Lagers* was held in Turin at the Palazzo Madama. Levi agreed to talk at the April inauguration, but feared his reception. He lacked the confidence to make a good public speaker. There was another problem. Survivors who told their stories stood accused of 'self-pity', said Levi, or of 'doting gratuitously on the macabre'. At worst they were considered liars and unseemly attention-seekers. As matters turned out, Levi had nothing to worry about. In the Palazzo Madama he was greeted by a surprisingly young audience, whose enthusiasm to know more about the camps was so overwhelming that Levi found himself responding with an unexpected warmth. The reception could not have come at a better time. Levi was thirty-five and suspected that he was finished as a writer. Now it appeared he was a figure of some note among the young, and the subject of curiosity in the local press.

This surge of interest in Levi and his book coincided with the resurrection of his literary career. The distinguished Einaudi consultant Paolo Serini, one of the elder statesmen of Italian publishing, said it was a scandal that *If This is a Man* should be remaindered in a Florence warehouse. Serini's opinion carried weight with Giulio Einaudi (he was a philosophy professor at Turin University). And, finally, Einaudi was willing to listen. Natalia Ginzburg's sympathetic replacement at Einaudi,

Luciano Foà, had read Serini's glowing report on *If This is a Man* and needed no further persuading. Einaudi's decision to take up Levi was underpinned by shrewd entrepreneurial insight. The cultural climate of 1955, a turning-point year for Italy, was fervent, restless and full of promise. There was a desire to move beyond the Catholic and Marxist cultures then dominant in the established Italian publishing houses, and to try out new ideas, new books. Italians now had relative prosperity after the grim post-war years, and were more willing to reflect on their recent past. The younger generation, in its first taste of affluence, was reading widely.

Other books on the Nazi camps had emerged in Italy since *If This is a Man*, and had been reviewed enthusiastically. Robert Anteleme's *The Human Race*, one of the most poignant French books on the camps, was published by Einaudi in 1954 – the same year as Anne Frank's diary. However, no book made more of an impression on Italians than *The Scourge of the Swastika* by Lord Russell of Liverpool (no relation to Bertrand Russell, the philospher). In this brief history of Nazi war crimes, translated into Italian in 1954, Russell had asked how a nation that gave us Goethe and Beethoven, Schiller and Schubert, could also have given us Auschwitz, Belsen, Ravensbrück and Dachau. Interest in the camps had become so extensive by 1955 that it was difficult to find anyone in Turin who could happily ignore Levi's book.

In his rooms at 61 Corso Re Umberto, Nardo De Benedetti began to give occasional talks on Auschwitz. These were so well attended that he decided to upgrade them to informal weekly seminars. People he had never met would sit through slide shows and listen to Nardo describe the dehumanised world of the *Lager*. Until now his need to bear witness had been overwhelmed by the grief he felt for his murdered wife. But he found a release in talking, just as Levi had done ten years earlier. The young encouraged Nardo to disburden his memories, and it was gratifying for him to see the impact of his words. This was the way to bear witness: directly, and to the next generation.

Giulio Einaudi agreed to republish *If This is a Man*, and on 11 July 1955 Levi signed a contract for an advance fee of 200,000 lire (£1,700). He was unaware, however, that Einaudi was in grave financial crisis. Just how grave was not yet clear, but Einaudi – spendthrift at the best of times – would be forced to sell off his book list to the rival firm of Mondadori in Milan. With heavy debts, money was not forthcoming to relaunch *If This is a Man*, and to Levi's dismay his book would not now come out until 1958 – another three years. In spite of this disappointment, he stood by his new publisher, and even invested a quarter of his author fee in Einaudi shares.

Levi now had time to amend the Antonicelli edition. Einaudi may even have asked him to make changes; his pride would not have allowed him merely to reprint the Antonicelli text. Eight years had passed since Levi wrote *If This is a Man* and so he could now view Auschwitz more dispassionately. A master craftsman of tiny refinements, he made no alteration that might distort the book's overall shape. Nevertheless, for a writer whose instinct was to pare down rather than amplify, a number of significant new characters were added, as well as an entire new chapter, 'Initiation'. Levi was in a hurry to complete these revisions, as Lucia was pregnant again and the baby was due in the summer. His first amendment was the most obvious: a new opening sentence. In typescript *If This is a Man* had opened rather blandly: 'At Fossoli any talk of departure was considered extremely ill-mannered.' Ten years on, Levi inserted the more dramatic incipit: 'I was captured by the Fascist Militia on 13 December 1943,' which is virtually a copy of the pre-Risorgimento patriot, Silvio Pellico, who had opened his celebrated memoir, *My Prisons*: 'On Friday 13 October 1820 I was arrested at Milan.' Clearly Levi's revised text was to resonate within the tradition of Liberal Italian literature, which championed Enlightenment and humanist values, from Manzoni to Pellico.

Some Auschwitz dead had been left out of the Antonicelli edition, or had had their names changed, as Levi was wary of ruffling privacies. One of those omitted was the five-year-old Emilia Levi, gassed at Auschwitz with her brother, mother and father. Into the Einaudi edition Levi now incorporated this tender micro-portait: 'Emilia, daughter of Aldo Levi of Milan, was a curious, ambitious, cheerful, intelligent child' – four carefully-chosen adjectives which poignantly capture the girl's spirit, and what she might have been. The revised edition *If This is a Man* was to be a book of commemoration as well as a documentary: if the Nazi crime could not be reversed by the writer's pen, at least it could be chronicled and remembered. Moreover, narrating the Auschwitz dead was a way of bringing them back to life.

For many readers, the most remarkable figure in *If This is a Man* is the Jewish Hungarian army sergeant, Steinlauf, who upbraids Levi for neglecting to keep clean at Auschwitz. Steinlauf had not appeared in the Antonicelli original. His real name was Eugenio Gluecksmann, and in the Einaudi version Levi chose the word *Stein*, 'stone' in German, to suggest the sergeant's straight-backed Prussian discipline. Probably Levi had based something of Steinlauf on Anne Frank's father Otto, whom he had first seen at Auschwitz and then later, in 1952 or 1953, at Nardo De Benedetti's. Like

Sergeant Steinlauf, Lieutenant Frank was among the 100,000 Jews who had served in the German army during the Great War, a dignified soldier whose pro-German patriotism later made no difference to his persecutors. As it happened, the real-life Gluecksmann had died on the eve of the Red Army's liberation; *Glück,* a cruel epithet in the circumstances, is German for 'luck'.

In addition to Steinlauf, Levi added six new pages to his original portrait of Alberto Dalla Volta. This was the most significant addition and the most revealing, too. The new pages described the friends' barter in the camp's black market. In the Antonicelli text Levi had remarked of Alberto, untruthfully, that he was unable to speak German. For the Einaudi version Levi made no attempt to rectify the untruth. We are told that Alberto can communicate with his tormentors only 'with gestures' and then in Italian. In fact, Alberto spoke fluent German. So why did Levi misrepresent him in this way? While Levi was happy to credit Lorenzo Perrone with saving his life, he did not do the same for Alberto. Ignorance of German was fatal at Auschwitz. Was it pride on his part that he could not admit to Dalla Volta's superior knowledge of German; or was it guilt that he had survived Auschwitz in Alberto's place? Many survivors find some aspect of their survival intolerable and prefer to bury whatever had been necessary for them to survive. In Levi's case we cannot say what led him to describe Alberto Dalla Volta in this way.

5

Levi worked hard on the Einaudi revisions: months went by doing little else. However, he was back in Leverkusen on Bayer business in September, and during the next year he returned there twice, on 1 February and 12 July 1956. In November, after eight years at SIVA, Giovanna Balzaretti left the firm: Levi was to miss her competence and professionalism greatly. The following year opened on a low note when, on 24 April 1957, Alberto Salmoni's (Egyptian-born) father Augusto died. Levi was very fond of this eccentric, high-spirited man and was seen to cry at this funeral.

By now he had been married for almost ten years and his disaffection with married life and domesticity had begun to show. Frequently he would escape the house to visit Tina Rieser's salon on Corso Francia. Tina, née Pizzardo, was in her early fifties, dark, stylish and intrepid. She was just twenty-four when the Fascists had jailed her as a Communist, and she remained fiercely non-conformist. Levi had first met her in around 1937 when she was a mathematics graduate in Turin. She had an upper-class Piedmontese background and a Jesuit cardinal as an uncle. Cesare Pavese had famously fallen in love with Tina, but she rejected the poet for a Polish

Jew, Henek Rieser, whom she married in 1936. In a fit of jealousy Pavese challenged Henek to a duel, but later backed down.

Tina Rieser's regulars included Nicoletta Neri, whose brother Agostino Levi had known at university, and who had killed himself in Professor Ponzio's laboratory with poison. Five years older than Levi, Nicoletta was a maverick who had tried her hand at many things. She had taught English literature in Manchester and Los Angeles, was personally acquainted with G. K. Chesterton (whom she translated), and had worked for a famous anti-Mafia charity in Sicily. Above all, Levi responded to her love of animals. After Levi had met Ralph, her cocker-spaniel, he showered her with books on canine behaviour. In many ways theirs was an incongruous friendship, based on dogs, the delights of vegetarianism (which Levi did not share) and the Father Brown stories.

Two friends from Tina's salon would later take their lives. They were the poet Gigliola Venturi (wife of Italy's foremost historian of the Enlightenment, Franco Venturi), and the magistrate and ex-Resistance fighter Giuseppe Manfredini. The salon, however, continued to meet for years and Levi would visit Tina, off and on, until the day he died. She was a born socialiser, who graciously put people at their ease, even if her circle was rather snobbish. Anyone who lived north of Corso Regina Margherita or west of Corso Racconigi – in the scruffier parts of Turin, that is – was not made very welcome. Lucia Levi herself felt inadequate among Tina's friends, especially if they were intellectual women, whom she saw as a threat.

During this time Lucia was teaching literature and history of art at the Jewish School in Turin, where she was much loved. Still an attractive woman, she was entrancing to the children, who responded to her dedication. Lucia was an exacting teacher, however, and often interrupted her pupils as they read their compositions out in class, instructing them to remove an adjective here, or put in a full stop there. (A decade earlier Lucia had subjected her husband's manuscript to a similar rigour.) She continued to teach during her second pregnancy, but in the course of the summer term of 1957 her labour began. On Tuesday 2 July, reportedly a stiflingly hot day, she gave birth to a boy. Like his sister Lisa Lorenza, he was named Renzo in honour of the late Lorenzo Perrone. The boy's middle name was Cesare, after Levi's father. By coincidence, the universally affordable Fiat 500 was launched on Renzo's birthday, baptised by the press that day as Italy's *nuova piccola nata* ('little newborn'). Italians were captivated by the car's charming design; Italy was on the cusp of a new mass motoring age.

When Lucia had first come home with a new baby, nine years before, the flat was more crowded. Four years later, however, Anna Maria left Turin to begin a new life in Rome where she worked in publishing and in the art world. And, as Levi lost his former closeness with his sister, so Lucia became more sympathetic to her, giving Anna Maria 'sound domestic advice' on the telephone and, again according to Levi, she 'helped' her when she could.

6

In August 1957 the Levis were on holiday in the Waldensian Valleys. This was a nostalgic return for Primo, who wanted to introduce his daughter to the Protestant Piedmont of his childhood. They rented a cottage in Subiasco owned by the gruff Waldensian farmer couple, Ida and Carlo Cordin. The Cordins led a spartan life that appealed to Levi; in between milking the cows and cutting the hay, they read the Old Testament and sought to purify the faith of Popery. Though he visited them for the next four years, and gave them cans of SIVALUX to whitewash their farmhouse, the Cordins never discovered that he was a writer. Subiasco was a delight for Lisa Levi; the new-mown fields of hay and the vineyards in neat terraces were the nine-year-old's playground. She was a slight, dark-eyed child with an affinity for the natural world around her. Lisa's wondrous curiosity must have pleased her father; a story he wrote four years earlier, 'A Mutiny', described a fearless girl who 'held crickets and spiders in her hand, without revulsion and without harming them'. In a mysterious switch of affections the story was later dedicated to an Italian writer (Mario Rigoni Stern). Yet it glows with paternal love and devotion to Lisa, who is the 'Clotilde' of the story; indeed, Levi wrote it to mark the occasion of his daughter's fifth birthday, though he never told her.

Whenever he could, Levi took his daughter to Ada Gobetti's house in the hills above Turin. (Ada was the widow of the illustrious anti-Fascist Piero Gobetti.) Here, on most summer weekends, old friends from the Resistance gathered with their children. Ada was a generous host in her spacious house and loved to see the children run riot in her garden. Often they wore fancy dress and their parents came as troubadours or oriental queens. Bianca Guidetti Serra appeared as a fairy princess with a magic carpet; Italo Calvino read from his classic anthology of *Italian Folktales* (Italy's answer to the Brothers Grimm). These were special occasions for Levi, when he could see old friends and feel close to Lisa, while Lucia was busy with the newborn Renzo. Back in Subiasco, Lisa's friend Erica Scroppo was staying in a cottage nearby. Erica, lively and talkative, was not Jewish but she had an impeccable Protestant Waldensian pedigree, which counted for much among Jews. The Scroppos saw themselves as liberals in the prevailing

279

Catholic darkness, and sent Erica to Turin's Jewish Primary School with Lisa. Her father, the painter and writer Filippo Scroppo, was friendly with Calvino, whose exuberant hosanna to his mother's Waldensian-Jewish roots and the Dissenting tradition had just been published. *The Baron in the Trees* was the talk of cultivated Italy in 1957.

The days in Subiasco fell into a pattern. Reading in the morning; a midday nap; walking or reading till tea; an early supper, sometimes with friends from Turin; and after supper more reading. However, the summer's lethargy was disturbed by news of a Fascist revival. Mussolini's corpse, stolen eleven years before by neo-Fascists, had been given up for burial. His interment was the pretext for Fascist trinkets, gewgaws and other memorabilia to go on sale across Italy. In a further ominous development, Italian newspapers began to speak of the Fascist past as romantic adventure and not the shameful blunder it had been. Levi was unsure whether this revisionism was the song and dance of a minority, or something more widespread and sinister. Presently the Subiasco party was joined by his old university friend Guido Bonfiglioli, his wife and two daughters. An uneasy tension existed between Bonfiglioli, who disliked the pedantic severity of the Italian Communist Party, and Erica's leftist father Filippo Scroppo who had worked for Italy's Communist daily *L'Unità*. The Soviet Union's brutal suppression of the Hungarian revolt the previous autumn had resulted in an *annus horribilis* for Italian Communism. Levi and thousands of other liberal-minded Italians lost any lingering faith they might have had in the Soviet Union. Italo Calvino resigned from the Italian Communist Party in disgust. A new age had begun of Russian bogeys, spy trials and the trap-door disappearance of dissidents.

Levi was fond of children, and liked to entertain them with feats and clever tricks; he could float a ping-pong ball in the air, stand on his head, pull clownish faces. In Subiasco he made his daughter and Erica a toy cable car from tin-foil takeaway trays. The car ran on lengths of string from Erica's balcony to Lisa's opposite; at each end Levi fixed a tiny bell so that the girls could send and receive messages without disturbing the baby Renzo, or Levi's mother, who sat dozing under a tree. However, Levi was not entirely indulgent of the girls. 'There were things one did not do, did not wish to do, in his presence,' recalled Erica Scroppo. 'Levi had a kind of invisible authority.' When Lisa put on a simpleton's voice to ask for the salt, her father angrily rebuked her: it was unkind to poke fun at the disabled. Another of the children's games that was promptly banned by Levi involved the torture of imaginary monkeys. Levi surely overreacted to the children's thoughtlessness but, as a bullied schoolboy, he knew how people liked to pick on a weakness, and was sensitive to the slightest suggestion of cruelty, even a child's. 'The moment the defenceless are derided,' Levi liked to say, 'is the moment Nazism is born.'

Towards the end of the holidays, Erica Scroppo went for a walk with her family and the Levis in Subiasco's chestnut forest. As usual, Levi carried plasters, penknives and other emergency provisions, a Boy Scout's precaution that never left him. Suddenly Erica was stranded on the far side of a stream while the others went on ahead. She was about to jump to the other bank, when a helping hand was extended. This was a life-changing moment for her. As Levi stretched out his arm across the stream, she noticed a grey-blue number on his forearm. 'What's that?' she asked. And with a pained smile Levi explained that it was a 'souvenir' from another age. Erica demanded a proper explanation. Should a young girl be exposed to the truth? Levi reported the incident to Erica's mother who, after careful consideration, decided to read out loud to her daughter from *If This is a Man*. Otherwise, it was thought, Erica would never stop asking questions. Though the reading included cuts and censorship, Erica was severely disturbed at what she heard. So young, and already she knew of the century's atrocity. One might question the wisdom of subjecting an eight-year-old to such horror. But from then on, Erica was awed by Levi. 'Only now do I realise that so many of the opinions I hold today are not the fruit of study or of ripening political maturity, but spring from that summer's day in 1957 when I lost my innocence.' With her eager curiosity, Erica Scroppo represented the next generation of Primo Levi's readers.

7

Five years had passed since SIVA had moved to Settimo Torinese, and by 1958 the plant had grown vastly, occupying 33,000 square metres of real estate behind Via Leyni. Machines pumped off clouds of pollutants as vapour hissed from vats and tanks. The use of chemical weapons in the Korean War brought a rash of orders from abroad. Kegs of Bayer's 'Desmodur' were used to manufacture the flammable products now in demand. But due precautions were not being taken against static electricity generation and other hazards. One dry hot summer afternoon a solvent caught fire as it issued from the reservoir tap. The worker, Silvano Fecchio, fled in terror as a burning puddle of toluol formed in the factory yard and threatened to engulf production. Luckily the section chief was nearby and leaped over a wall to shut off the main tap. The solvent burned itself out harmlessly, but it was a warning. After that, Levi ordered the Shell anti-static additive 'ASA-3', which significantly reduced static electricity.

'Thank God for ASA-3!' became Levi's catchphrase in these stressful times.

In the late 1950s Rico Accati set up a third company in Turin, SICME, which manufactured specialist ovens for coating wire filaments. He devised a personal coat of arms for the expanded firm, 'Evil unto him who thinks evil', and increased SIVA's staff from twenty-one to 170. By now Levi was negotiating with the German electrical giants Siemens and Hoechst (both of which had operated at Auschwitz); he controlled all aspects of varnish production, exporting some 400 tonnes of PVF annually. At night his clothes smelled of vinegary acetic acid, or the burned toffee tang of phenol.

After ten years at SIVA Levi suspected he would spend the rest of his working life at the factory. At thirty-nine, the prospect did not greatly please him. Equipment or materials often failed to arrive on time, there was much tiresome paperwork, and he had begun to weary of the drive to Settimo Torinese. It was the same 40-minute drive twice a day. By 8:00 am he was on Corso Giulio Cesare, passing the Coca-Cola hoardings. Once over the Dora Riparia, a polluted tributary of the Po, he joined the lorries and oil tankers rumbling for the airport. At the *autostrada* exit for Settimo, Levi paid the toll before reaching SIVA. He drove badly, and in the company car park his was the only conspicuously scratched vehicle. All the same, he found the pace of change at SIVA exciting and he enjoyed showing foreign clients round the plant. Since his promotion, Levi was climbing the factory pay-scale; he had a smart new Fiat Giardinetta estate in which to visit Zanussi, Pirelli and other firms that had an interest in buying SIVA enamels. After each sales trip he had to compile a detailed business report. These *relazioni* give some flavour of the technical and negotiation skills that were required of Levi to oversee SIVA operations. Full of insider-jargon, they drily assess the shopfloor safety of rival companies, their air-pollution policies and filtration systems. His *relazioni* were considered by SIVA staff to be the best of any at the firm, judiciously worded and unfailingly precise.

Levi looked much younger than his years, his faintly boyish face and animated blue eyes were beguiling; he always wore a sober grey suit and was never seen without a tie. Somehow Levi brought out the maternal in women, and was not above a degree of flirtation. Orsolina Ferrero, SIVA's new cleaner, was a widow in her early forties. She had a reputation of being a psychic and claims she had a dream that foretold Levi's death. He was captivated by her warmth and gossipy good humour and loved to bring her back gifts from business trips. In the weeks before Christmas 1958 he even drove her to see the plastic icicles and winking stars on display in Piazza Castello. Orsolina, overwhelmed by the Yuletide kitsch, hugged Levi. She became a significant presence in his life, and colleagues noted how cheerful he seemed around her. He re-created an artificial snowstorm for her in the lab with pressurised carbon dioxide, the white flakes floating down to the floor. Orsolina was attracted to Levi and to what she called his 'enigmatic inward smile'.

Accati's secretary, Franca Tambini, declared that she was also charmed by him. After a meal one lunchtime she guiltily indicated to Levi that a half-drunk bottle of wine was under her desk, and would he care for a drop? To her surprise, Levi said, 'Thanks, I think I will', and took a mouthful before handing her back the bottle. Another time on the way to work he lightly touched her face to remove a mascara smudge. 'Franchina, your make-up's not right.' Franca Tambini told me: 'It's a wonder we didn't crash.'

8

In June 1958, the twentieth anniversary of Mussolini's race laws, Einaudi published *If This is a Man* again. The dustjacket was an eye-catching design for the times: abstract bars superimposed on vertical stripes of orange, red and blue. The book was to be included in the revered series 'Einaudi Essays', rubbing shoulders with Dostoevsky and Gide. This was a vindication for Levi. Yet the promotional budget for his book was negligible – it was not even flagged on the cover of the Einaudi News Letter distributed among sales reps. Einaudi was sceptical that Levi could develop further as a writer: after his Auschwitz documentary, what else could he possibly write? Levi was not obviously highbrow and certainly not high-society, and Einaudi was not going to spend money on marketing him. Nevertheless, he had lifted Levi from literary obscurity, and Primo was grateful. One after another the critics stood up. In his review for *La Stampa* Franco Antonicelli glowed with pride at his protégé's long-deserved recognition. The Communist daily *L'Unità* welcomed a 'great comeback', while the Hemingway expert Bruno Fonzi hailed Levi as a literary 'outsider' who wrote more exquisitely than any *letterato*. Most reviewers highlighted the 'grave injustice' of Levi's ten-year neglect, and marvelled at his ability to put precise words to a defining atrocity.

Republication of *If This is a Man* unfortunately coincided with the arrival in Turin of Einaudi's most esteemed foreign author, Aldous Huxley. The English writer was to promote the Italian translation of *Those Barren Leaves*, and demanded all his publisher's attention. Levi, thrilled to be able to see the literary hero of his youth, attended Huxley's sell-out lecture in Turin on 21 November 1958. Yet he was saddened to see that Huxley had lost much of his mordant brilliance since his Los Angeles exile, and was unimpressed by his psychedelic rapture, *The Doors of Perception* (now the Newest

Testament among Europe's beatniks). Levi had grown up with Huxley's wife in 75 Corso Re Umberto but had not seen Laura since she left Turin in 1937 for Los Angeles. And to his regret he failed to see her this time round. The next day *La Stampa* carried a photograph of the Huxleys, Laura a beautiful elf next to the lanky, elastic-framed Aldous.

9

By Christmas *If This is a Man* had sold out. Levi had found a significant new readership among Italian ex-deportees and POWs. One of these, the thirty-three-year-old Catholic schoolteacher Lidia Rolfi, had been arrested by the Gestapo in 1944 and sent to Ravensbrück camp outside Berlin, where she was set upon by dogs, starved and made to slave for Siemens. No one wanted to listen to Rolfi's story when she returned to Piedmont. Though they knew of each other, Levi and Rolfi did not meet until that Christmas, when Primo accompanied her to a survivors' conference in Turin. It was foggy and cold, and Rolfi recalled that the heating in Levi's car did not work. They arrived at the Teatro Carignano where Levi was due to speak. During his talk, Lidia noted that he studiously shunned rhetoric. In measured terms he explained how the prisoners' daily food ration had been fixed at 1,600 calories – half those required to survive – bringing about a slow death by malnutrition. Rather than dwell on the macabre, Levi illuminated the Nazi demolition project using scientific language. When Rolfi's turn came to speak, she chose to use the same careful tones as Levi: at last it seemed she had found a way to relate her Ravensbrück ordeal. As the 1950s drew to a close, Levi became the unofficial representative of Italian deportees, both Jewish and non-Jewish.

The republication of *If This is a Man* was a turning-point for Levi. He was becoming better known in Italy, and foreign translators were interested in his book. Yet Levi was wary of them. An Argentine edition of *If This is a Man*, published in Buenos Aires in 1956, was a disappointingly ragged version of the original. Levi complained: '*Traduttore traditore*', 'The translator is a traitor'. Stuart Woolf, a young Oxford historian with Polish Jewish ancestry, was in Turin on a research fellowship, and wanted to translate Levi. Levi was impressed by Woolf's academic credentials and no doubt it helped that his fiancée, Anna De Benedetti, was related to Nardo. Sponsored by the historian Hugh Trevor-Roper, the Englishman was researching Piedmont's pre-Risorgimento aristocracy. Woolf had been living in Turin since 1956; he believed passionately that *If This is a Man* should reach a readership beyond Italy, and he called on Levi twice a week with his work-in-progress. Like most educated Italians, Levi was an Anglophile, and Woolf's dry humour and owlish English reserve appealed to him. As for Woolf, he was awed by Levi and found his knowledge of English literature impressively wide-ranging. Moreover, it struck Woolf as curious that Levi's judgments of other writers could be so 'trenchant and haughty', in one seemingly so shy and modest. When he lent Levi a copy of the first volume of Tolkien's *The Lord of the Rings*, the book came back to him the next day unopened. 'I can see now that Tolkien must have stood for everything Primo despised: wilful obscurity, cod-mysticism.' In the evenings, after SIVA, Levi was impatient to resume work with Woolf. Knocking back his whisky 'like a Russian', Woolf recalled, Levi would return to the manuscript with renewed vigour. By excising any ambiguities or solecisms from Wolf's translation, Levi taught him to value the weight of words and to choose them meticulously. At the same time he tried to preserve the distinct flavour and marvellously taut cadence of Woolf's English. From this collaborative effort, rare in the history of modern translation, emerged a creative transformation.

Meanwhile an American publisher with a branch in Florence, the Orion Press, was shown Woolf's translation. They specialised in de-luxe editions of European classics exclusively bound in buckram, but Levi was a classic of sorts. The moving spirits behind the Orion Press were Howard S. Greenfeld, a one-time Random House editor, and Eugenio Cassin, formerly of the patrician Sansoni Editore of Florence. No discovery gave Greenfeld more pleasure than *If This is a Man*, 'and I'm still basking in the glory today'. He paid Levi a handsome (in those days) $1,000 advance and promised him a first print run of 3,000 copies for distribution in both Britain and the United States. Proofs were to be corrected ready for publication late in the following year, 1959.

All this while, Levi attended to his increasingly heavy workload at SIVA; varnishes had to be selected and developed, endless tests run, more trips made to Germany. In July 1959, shortly before his fortieth birthday, he was in the Rhineland sprawl of Ludwigshafen to buy 'Vinoflex', a type of plastic made by BASF. On his return to Turin he learned that a German publisher was interested in acquiring translation rights in *If This is a Man*. Understandably anxious, Levi wrote an 'insolent' letter to the editors warning them not to remove a single word of his book or tamper with its integrity in any way. When Levi learned that Samuel Fischer Verlag of Frankfurt was a venerable German Jewish firm, which had published Thomas Mann since 1897, he was reassured. He promptly found himself a literary agent, the redoubtable Erich Linder of Milan, to negotiate the

German contracts. Linder, a no-nonsense businessman of 'portentous intelligence', according to Levi, managed to obtain him a fee from Fischer of 145,537 lire (just under £1,000).

Later in the summer of 1959, while Levi was still at work on the Woolf translation, he was approached by *La Stampa* as a potential contributor. The paper was owned by Italy's biggest company, Fiat of Turin, and it promised to provide Levi with a platform to air his views on a variety of subjects, from the trial of Nazi war criminals to space exploration. His debut article of 18 July, 'Monument at Auschwitz', exuded the new-found confidence of a man who was about to be launched in America, Germany and Great Britain. Striking a prophetic tone, Levi warned that if we fail to master the past, the past may master us. And as edifying literature he commended the Auschwitz commandant Rudolf Höss's wretched memoir, *Kommandant in Auschwitz,* which had just been translated (with Levi's help) by the Sicilian writer Giuseppina ('Pucci') Panzieri.

10

Finally in August Levi was contacted by his German translator, Heinz Riedt. They had not corresponded before, but Levi had read some of Riedt's sample translations and had been impressed by his knowledge of Italian literature. Riedt was bilingual and his letter to Levi was written in flawless, if formal, Italian. He had been moved by *If This is a Man,* and Levi was assured of a sympathetic interpreter:

> The publication of your book in Germany seems to me *extremely* important and necessary. I hope with all my heart that its success here will not just be in terms of the numbers sold, but that your book might penetrate the human soul, and be an occasion for reflection.

However, it was Riedt's parting remark that startled Levi: 'When you were at Buna-Monovitz, I was a partisan in Padua, and my father-in-law was also imprisoned at Auschwitz. This singular coincidence I believe will bring us closer together . . .'

Excited, Levi replied to Riedt on 20 August:

> Your letter filled me with joy and gratitude. I had already gathered from your specimen translation that you were not, as it were, an establishment figure, but a living human being close to the things I hold dear. Now your letter confirms it. I would be

286

delighted to meet you: indeed, maybe you are the very person I have been hoping all these years to meet.

As instructed, Levi sent his letter to Riedt's father-in-law in the western zone of Berlin, where the Stasi secret police were less likely to intercept it. Riedt himself lived in the eastern (Communist) sector, and was sure he was under surveillance. So began an extraordinary exchange of letters, some twenty in all, over a period of ten months. In the course of the correspondence, Levi learned that Riedt had not only fought in the Italian Resistance, but had done so in a 'Justice and Liberty' formation just as he, Levi, had done. Riedt was even born on the same day and year as Levi: 31 July 1919. His father-in-law, Herr Saar, a non-Jew, had been an Auschwitz 'red triangle', or political prisoner.

Anxious to maintain control over the translation, Levi offered to help Riedt with any queries he might have. 'Better still, it would be a welcome opportunity for me to refresh my meagre German. If you could let me see the entire translation (if only in instalments), I would be grateful.' At that point Riedt did not realise to what scrutiny Levi would subject his efforts. Not one page was approved by Levi without its first being checked by a German speaker in Turin (probably the German lawyer Rudolf Loewenthal). Immensely curious about Riedt, Levi had rapidly pieced together his extraordinary background. During the Nazi era of 1933–45 his father had been the German consul in Palermo, the capital of Sicily. Riedt spent his teens there, and managed to exempt himself from the Wehrmacht by forging sick-leave papers. His involvement in the Italian Resistance began at Padua University, where he was studying political science. The university's rector, Concetto Marchesi (one of the architects of Italy's post-war constitution), introduced Riedt to Padua's anti-Fascist underground. Riedt had few qualms about fighting the occupying Germans as he did not really consider himself German. His family had Dutch and Franco-Rhenish blood. By day Riedt was a student, by night a counter-intelligence operative in *la resistenza*.

There was no Berlin Wall in 1959 but Riedt was increasingly nervous of entrapment. In the Soviet sector his translation of Levi's book was illegal, because East Berliners were not supposed to work for capitalist firms like S. Fischer of Frankfurt. On one occasion when Riedt telephoned a rabbi in West Berlin to clarify a point of Jewish liturgy in *If This is a Man*, he was aware that his line was tapped. The Stasi had copious files on Riedt and they were not impressed by his role in the Italian Resistance. Riedt may have helped fight the demon Nazism, but in taking up arms against fellow Germans he had betrayed his own country. His intellectual credentials were all that endeared him to Communist Berlin, where Bertolt Brecht, the author Luise Rinser and the actress Lotte Lenya counted among his friends. With his German wife, a professional Russian translator, Riedt made earnest Socialist-inspired documentary films; they had one child, aged nine.

Though Levi was pernickety, his thoroughness improved Riedt's translation. In the final chapter of *If This is a Man* the Hungarian prisoner Sómogyi dies while feverishly muttering Nazi commands. Where Levi had written, 'he had finished', Riedt substituted, 'he had ceased to exist'. Levi vigorously objected, and explained why: 'When I wrote "he had finished" I was referring to Sómogyi's slow, terrible death-struggle . . . Ever obedient, here was a man who would only allow himself to die once he "had finished" saying *Jawohl*.' Such scrupulousness was understandable in a man who was about to be launched in the country that had humiliated him; Levi had to be sure that his translated work said to the Germans exactly what he intended. To Riedt's immense irritation, Levi stubbornly insisted that he incorporate the vulgar barrack-room jargon he had picked up in Auschwitz. However, Riedt did not feel that this savage Third Reich *Lager*-jargon should be allowed to burden the translation: its meaning would be lost on the average German reader. Eventually Levi conceded defeat.

In November 1959, when the Levi-Riedt collaboration was halfway, the Orion Press released *If This is a Man* in the English-speaking world. The American reviews were rather mealy-mouthed. The *New York Times* described the book as 'worth preserving', while the *New York Herald Tribune* more generously extolled Levi as a 'man of enormous moral and physical courage' (a notice that so impressed Levi that he cut it out and translated it into Italian). The *Saturday Review* admitted that Levi had 'humanity' and a 'talent for terse statement', but of his literary gifts, not a word. In Britain, where the book was distributed first by André Deutsch and then by Anthony Blond, the reviews were better. David Caute of the *New Statesman* said he had never read a 'more remarkable document', while the *Times Literary Supplement* offered this eulogy: 'What gives the book greatness is that reading it one feels that it could not have been written in any other way. It has the inevitability of the true work of art.' With the exception of the London *Jewish Chronicle* (which conceded that Levi had 'the skilful pen of a mature writer'), Anglo-Jewry remained silent. Having survived the Hitlerite storm, British Jews did not want to be reminded of that brutal past. Consequently *If This is a Man* did not make much of an impact in Britain beyond a small circle of non-Jewish enthusiasts, among them the actor Anthony Quayle, who in 1961 starred in a BBC Home Service radio adaptation of the book.

Though *If This is a Man* was on sale in America and Britain, months passed before Levi received his author copies. He was irritated, and to his agent Erich Linder in Milan he wrote a cross letter: 'I *beg* you to do all you can to speed up delivery of the books.' Linder assured Levi that the books were on their way – but after two weeks there was still no package from New York. By now apoplectic, Levi wrote to Linder: 'Would you *please* be so kind as to tell me *when*, by what *means*, and to *whom* my copies have been sent?' When the American copies finally arrived Levi was not impressed: the text was littered with typographical errors.

11

In the New Year – 1960 – Levi wrote to Riedt of an 'economic miracle'. The *miracolo italiano* was stoked by a massive upsurge in automobile production and by an American-style consumerism. Chewing gum, jeans, Coca-Cola were in; a sell-out production in Turin of *West Side Story* was followed by an Andy Warhol silk-screen exhibition. And no Italian film captured so brilliantly the flash-bulb glitz and glitter of the country's amoral, frivolous party than Fellini's *La dolce vita*. The movie was the smash hit of 1960, and launched Marcello Mastroianni as a national heart-throb. Oréal perfumes opened a new factory behind SIVA; the launch party was attended by a French ambassador, a cardinal and 500 cocktail guests. When Rico Accati drew up in his new Mercedes 300 SL with upward-opening doors, the *settimesi* – the Settimo Torinese locals – looked on enviously.

In the south, the other Italy, people were starving. The Italian 'economic miracle' had not extended to them. They began to flood the north in search of a consumer idyll. Television images of excursions in the family Fiat, Vespas, portable radios, drew them above all to Turin. Having arrived in the Piedmont capital with their cardboard suitcases, however, the migrants faced xenophobic abuse and shabby accommodation. The wretchedness of these transplanted southerners was its own indictment of Italy's vaunted financial renewal. Levi was not immune from the prejudice that southerners were *terroni*, 'earth people', good only for digging up fields. By the mid-1960s Sicilians and Calabrians had become so numerous in Turin that if Levi heard Piedmontese dialect spoken on the street he turned round, delighted.

In a letter of 6 April, Heinz Riedt invited Levi to visit him in East Berlin ('My father-in-law would also be delighted'); Levi was tempted by the invitation, but said he was too exhausted for travel. For the last few days he had been returning home from SIVA after 8:00 pm, tired and hungry. 'All I have time for is varnishes.' Levi had patented a wire-coating varnish,

'Eposil', for use in lift and escalator components, and he needed to plan for its production. In addition, on Monday nights, he had begun to attend a series of lectures in Turin at the Teatro Alfieri.

Ten lectures were booked, to run between 11 April and 13 June 1960; each speaker was to concentrate on a different aspect of Mussolini's oppression. Held each Monday at 9:00 pm, the lectures would become a landmark in Italian post-war political debate, which instilled a greater awareness in the young of the hollow pieties and dangers of Fascism. The sixth speaker on stage was the writer and former partisan leader Nuto Revelli. Tall, dignified, Revelli had an unwavering passion for the truth as well as the courage to tell it. His lecture began, wholly unexpectedly, with a confession: 'I, too, was once a bold young Fascist.' But in Russia's sub-zero temperatures the myth of the great Fascist army had collapsed before Lieutenant Revelli's eyes. There he had witnessed the débâcle of the Italian retreat at first hand. When Revelli returned to his native Piedmont on 8 September 1943 – Armistice Day – he was contemptuous of the Fascist generals who still spoke of the nobility of war. And, with his face disfigured by frostbite, he burned his officer's uniform and entered the Resistance. Revelli's account of Italy's Russia campaign, *Never Again*, published in 1946, was a classic to rank with *All Quiet on the Western Front*. Levi had read it and after the lecture he approached Revelli to compliment him. They had not met before, but there was an instant rapport. Neither was a professional writer – circumstance had compelled them to write – and they both felt an instinctive antipathy towards the 'fine writing' branch of letters. They became lifelong confidants.

On 13 May 1960 Levi sent his most important letter to Heinz Riedt. A remarkable document, it would become the preface to the German edition of *If This is a Man*:

> So our work is ended, and I am glad of it, satisfied with the result, and grateful to you, but also a little sad. You see, this is the only book I have written, and now that we have finished translating it into German, I feel like a father whose son has grown up and leaves home, and who can no longer look after him . . . Maybe it is presumption: but here I am today, 174517, able by your intervention to speak to the German people and to remind them of what they have done, and to say to them: 'I am alive, and I would like to understand you in order to judge you.'
>
> I do not believe that the life of man necessarily has a purpose; if I think of my own life, and the aims which I have set myself up

to now, I recognise that only one of them is well defined and self-evident, and it is precisely this: to bear witness, to have my voice heard among the Germans, to 'answer' the SS for the truss [a Nazi guard's mockery of a Jew's hernia truss in *If This is a Man*], the *Kapo* who wiped his hand on my shoulder, Dr Pannwitz, all those who hanged the Last One ['I am the last one!' a prisoner yells as the SS hang him], and all their heirs.

I am certain that you have not misunderstood me. I have never harboured hatred for the German people, and if ever I did I would be cured of it now that I have got to know you. I do not comprehend – I cannot tolerate – that a man be judged not for what he is, but for the group to which he happens to belong. Ever since I came to appreciate Thomas Mann and learned a little German (which I learned in the camp!) I know that there is much of worth in Germany, that Germany, though dormant today, is fertile, is a breeding-ground, a hope as well as a danger for Europe.

And then:

Yet I cannot pretend to understand the Germans: and something which one is unable to understand becomes an aching void, is a constant provocation that demands satisfaction. Nevertheless I hope this book will find some echo in Germany, and I say this not simply out of personal ambition, but because the nature of this echo will allow me to understand the Germans perhaps a little better . . . But enough of these crude, vague thoughts. I thank you with all my heart for your work, and for the diligence and love with which you have done it.

Their 'perfect collaboration', as Riedt called it, was now over, and Levi would miss the intellectual stimulation Riedt's letters had brought. Working with Levi on *If This is a Man* had filled Riedt – so he said later – with a sense of 'vengeance' towards his own people. The investigations that Levi had begun in the early 1950s into Germany and the Germans had found some resolution with this correspondence. After his dialogue with Riedt he could not possibly treat all Germans as moral pariahs: the mentality that judges people collectively belonged to the Nazi past.

In August Levi was in the mountain hamlet of Corvara high in the Dolomites. The region's dizzy clifftops inspired him to write a work of elegiac summer fiction in homage to Sandro Delmastro. Modelled on Conrad's novella 'Youth', and based on Levi's own near-fatal experience on a mountain above Bardonecchia, 'Bear Meat' was the story of a group of foolish young men marooned on a mountaintop, who almost died of cold. In contrast to these greenhorns stood 'Carlo', Sandro Delmastro, an iron-like youth capable of subsisting in all weathers on a diet of bear meat. ('Bear meat' was Delmastro's imaginary sustenance in an alpine emergency: 'The worst than can happen to us is that we'll have to eat bear meat,' he used to tell Levi on the snow-bound heights.) A quarter of a century had passed since Delmastro had been killed, but Levi's grief for him was unappeased.

Levi interrupted writing 'Bear Meat' to join Jean Samuel on the Italian Riviera for a third emotional reunion. *J'étais un homme* (I Was a Man), was due out in France in early 1961 and Samuel had an advance copy. The title alone came close to inverting the sense of the book and the translation was a farrago of errors. Levi signed a copy for Jean 'With apologies for the quality of the translation' and then tried (but failed) to have the French edition withdrawn and all copies pulped. Levi's shoddy treatment in France was perhaps not surprising in a country that was still uncomfortable with its wartime deportation of 75,000 Jews and its collaboration with the Nazis. Jean was surprised, but not annoyed, by Levi's semi-fictional portrayal of him in 'The Canto of Ulysses'. He had never been to 'Liguria' in Italy (as Levi wrote) and neither had he travelled anywhere 'by sea'. Most writers implant new soul into material drawn from experience. And Levi knew that something is always lost by reducing life to the page: so Samuel was made more colourful than he really was.

By February 1961 *Ist das ein Mensch?* – a question mark appended unaccountably to its title – was in the German bookshops. With a 50,000 print-run Levi's Frankfurt publishers were hoping for runaway sales. On the cover was the tentative recommendation: '*Das gute Buch für jedermann*', 'A good book for everyone'. The timing of the launch was perfect. Adolf Eichmann was about to be tried in Jerusalem, and on Christmas Eve 1960 the Auschwitz commandant Richard Baer had been arrested in Bavaria. The trials of these two Nazis generated publicity for Primo Levi's book, and though the reviews came out in dribs and drabs, there were a healthy nineteen of them. A few were nervously jocular (*'Ist das ein Mensch? Ja!*

Primo Levi ist ein Mensch'); others were blandly non-committal. An Austrian women's magazine complimented 'Primo Levy [sic]' on his 'accusation'. Hamburg's liberal *Die Zeit* gave the best review; its thoughtful, if wordy, piece concluded favourably: 'No other eye-witness account published in Germany has succeeded so brilliantly in outlining the unimaginable pain and brutality inherent in the Nazi system.' Over 20,000 copies sold immediately. Günter Grass recalled in a letter the 'painful impression' – '*schmerzlich beeindruckt*' – that Levi's book made on him in 1961. Until Riedt's translation, Germans had not read such a lucid or moving account of the Nazi *Lager*. Publication of *If This is a Man* in Germany was a moment of tremendous importance in the cultural history of Europe.

For a while in the early 1960s Primo Levi was the writer who spoke most directly to Germany's young. Karl-Heinz Mielke's teenage daughter Brigitte was typical of Levi's new reader. The more Brigitte had wanted to know of her country's past, the more her parents had brushed aside her troubling questions. Finally her father had admitted that he had an Italian colleague, Primo Levi, who 'bears the trace of the *Konzentrazionlager* – the KZ – in his face'. Brigitte had been unclear what that meant until she read Levi's book: from then on she called Primo 'The KZ Man'. Hundreds of young Germans like her, sometimes whole classrooms, wrote to Levi to complain of inadequate history lessons at school. These were difficult times for the German conscience. A student in Munich sent Levi a 'highly intelligent' letter about post-war Germany, so Levi wrote back asking certain questions; by return post she sent a postcard promising to reply to his letter in full 'as soon as possible'. A month passed before Levi received a twenty-three-page screed from the girl, almost a thesis. 'I haven't had enough time to write to you all I wanted.' Here was the Germans' famed *Gründlichkeit* – their fundamentalism, the going to the very root of a problem – without which Levi believed Auschwitz would not have existed, just inefficiently run camps along the Russian lines. All of the German correspondents expressed admiration for *Ist das ein Mensch?* Only one of them sought to defend Hitler: Levi wrote a 'violent reply', but never sent it. He regularly destroyed part of his correspondence once it created a backlog, but he kept every one of his German letters. His plan was to publish them as a book one day. For a quarter of a century these letters remained high on a shelf in dark-green box-files; then a selection of them appeared in the 'Letters from Germans' chapter of *The Drowned and the Saved*, Levi's last published book.

On 20 August 1961, a black day for Europe, the Levis were staying in the Bavarian resort of Ettal, West Germany, as guests of Heinz Riedt and his mother. East German police had begun to seal the Berlin border and put up frontier demarcation wire; thousands in the Soviet zone tried to flee through loopholes, or leaped from upper-floor windows. Marooned in Bavaria, Riedt had to decide then and there whether he and his family would remain in the West with his mother or return to the 'new jackboot zone' (as he called it) of East Berlin. They opted to stay in the West. In spite of the shattering news, Riedt welcomed the Levis with courteous affection. 'It was *bellissimo,*' he recalled thirty years later, 'we were on the same wavelength and in buoyant high spirits.' As Riedt showed Levi the historical sites of Ettal, he loudly proclaimed his dislike of the town's famously anti-Semitic Passion Plays. Levi enjoyed the German's provocative company. However, he refused to speak to him in German (only Italian) as he was fearful of making mistakes. After their emotional rendezvous, they did not meet again. Riedt spent his last days on the island of Procida off the coast of Naples, where he said he felt more at home than in Germany. 'Germans obey orders too easily, but Italians have the virtue of *humanitas.*' He died on 2 January 1997, aged seventy-seven.

Back in Turin, Levi caught up with his German correspondence and began writing more science fiction. He was in a good mood and his new tales were a gallimaufry of the funny and the sombre, with some satire. A special target was Italy's unflinchingly conservative minister of the interior, Mario Scelba. On his return from Buchenwald in 1954, Levi's passport had been confiscated by Scelba's ministry on the grounds that he had trespassed into the Soviet zone without the proper papers. Levi satirised Scelba's reputation for state reprisals in the Orwellian fantasy 'Censorship in Bitinia'. (The minister's infamous *celere,* or motorised riot police, are transformed here into the 'Bitinian force'.) By the end of 1961 Levi had ready half a dozen science fictions for submission to Einaudi.

Italo Calvino, Einaudi's most influential editor, agreed to look at the manuscript bundle with a view to publication. To Calvino, Levi also submitted his Conradian homage to Sandro Delmastro, 'Bear Meat', as well as a clutch of Auschwitz tales. To judge by this varied offering Levi was still undecided where to go as a writer: science fiction? war testimony? Levi was often asked if he would have been a writer had it not been for Auschwitz. Yet, long before he was deported he had written poems, two allegorical fables that appeared as 'Lead' and 'Mercury' in *The Periodic Table*, as well as a 'mediocre arabesque' (now lost – apparently a Wellsian time-travel fantasy). Levi's own views as to the sort of writer he might have become without the 'incentive' of the camp remain confused and contradictory. Either he would have become an 'extremely average writer', even a 'failed writer', or he would have penned the odd scholarly article on PVF, say. Auschwitz gave Levi his material 'on a plate', he told me in 1986.

Calvino, a solitary questioning man, immensely admired Levi. The son of botanist researchers in Havana, he had studied agronomy at Turin University, before changing to literature. In an interview I conducted with Calvino in 1984 he referred to Levi as his 'twin brother and soulmate'; he said he envied Levi's scientific background. Nevertheless his verdict on Levi's new stories was negative. In a long letter to him of 22 November 1961 he wrote that the tales read too much like a preliminary sketch to be coloured-in later. Compared to the futurist *ficciones* of Jorge Luis Borges (published in Italy in 1955: a revelation), Levi's were a pale shadow. Still, Calvino was impressed by one or two of Levi's efforts. 'Your attempt at a Conradian epic of mountaineering has all my sympathy', while the fable 'Man's Friend', in which intestinal worms are seen to develop poems, was in Calvino's opinion a three-page miracle with the structural neatness of an Aesop fable. Yet the bundle would not make a book. 'Would you like to write me a children's story?'

Stung by Calvino's rejection, Levi rekindled his long-nurtured plan to write a sequel to *If This is a Man*. And at a winter party in 1961 he found the impetus he needed to proceed with the project. Alessandro Galante Garrone, the Turin magistrate and civil-rights campaigner, invited Levi to Christmas drinks with friends. He and Garrone had become close friends after Levi had unearthed evidence earlier that year that the German engineering firm who built the Auschwitz crematoria, Topf & Sons, were advertising a 'new' and 'improved' cremation method for use in civilian cemeteries. (The company had not even bothered to change its name.) Levi asked Garrone to write an article on the outrage for *La Stampa*, and in a masterly piece of campaign journalism Garrone brought the Topf injustice into the open. (Needless to say, Topf did not respond to his article; their main concern was still efficient body turnover.) As the wine flowed, Garrone urged Levi to tell the assembled guests the story of his picaresque repatriation. Levi had narrated the story so many times now – reshaping the best anecdotes – that it had been polished to a fictional sheen. After a faltering start he was into his stride and his dry humour soon had the room spellbound. *If This is a Man* had ended too abruptly, the guests pointed out, leaving the reader curious to know what had happened to the author. Levi protested that when an author's first book is well received, as a rule his second book ends up a failure. Anyway, even if he did have another book in him, he doubted if it could match his debut. Yet Garrone's encouragement (by Levi's own account) was decisive: *The Truce* was conceived that winter night in his flat opposite the Turin Prefecture.

SEVENTEEN

Literary Acclaim
1961–6

I

Levi had been preparing himself to write *The Truce* since 1947, but after grave authorial doubts he had abandoned the book. Only in early 1961 did he find sufficient free time and encouragement to start writing. Levi happened to write *The Truce* during one of the most serene periods of his life. Home was often unhappy, but he was surrounded by friends and admirers and, in Turin at least, his reputation seemed assured. Levi also began to make a number of important new friends in the literary world. He was not attracted to self-consciously 'creative' authors, but chose instead the company of those who had another profession. Levi liked to see himself as part of a group of craftsman-like storytellers set apart from the *letterati* and *letteratini,* the literary peacocks who floated round Italy's salons and media coteries.

Not that his factory work was without interest. At a conference on epoxy resins in Milan in early 1961 he met the editor of Italy's trade journal *Paints and Varnishes,* Anna Maria Zambrini. They became friends. And during a foggy November lunchtime, as they were driving in Zambrini's cramped Fiat 500 to a Milan restaurant, she teased Levi: 'Tell me the truth – is this your most traumatic experience after Auschwitz?' Far from being offended by this remark Levi smiled, and said to Zambrini: 'You're not far wrong.' He was in a quiet, cheerful mood, Zambrini recalled, and efficiently business-like. Levi still enjoyed the challenge of industrial chemistry. A client had requested a paint for radiators on transatlantic liners that would be resistant to the sea's saline atmosphere; Levi loved any work that involved solving a puzzle or a battle with *la materia,* stubborn matter. At the same time during the 1960s, he began to feel that the factory stood in the way of his ambitions as a writer; he was dissatisfied with life at SIVA and dreamed of early retirement: he wished he had time to do nothing but write.

Levi began *The Truce* in an olive-green school exercise book, noting composition dates for each chapter, and their word length. The sequel was to be the same length as its predecessor: seventeen chapters. But in this new book, Levi had left behind the filth, sadness and horror of Hell and charted his purgatory after the camp. He drew on his own experience, just as he had done fourteen years earlier in *If This is a Man*. But, no matter how closely the narrative may fit the facts, the fictional process has usually been at work in *The Truce*. Levi had gone some way towards this in *If This is a Man*, where 'Piero Sonnino' is the fictional representation of the Roman trickster Lello Perugia ('Sonnino' is found in the 'Ka-Be' chapter set in April 1944, two months before Perugia had even been deported to Auschwitz), and the real-life Gluecksmann is transposed into 'Sergeant Steinlauf'. But this second book was a more elaborately wrought and literary creation: it was the first work where Levi consciously turned the raw material of his experience into literature. *The Truce* was therefore a signpost in his development.

The book went far beyond a conventional documentary memoir. Into his story Levi assimilated elements of fiction, allegorical pilgrimage, the continental tradition of the moral essay and, above all, the Homeric model of the odyssey. From the start Levi wanted to chart a drifting homeward journey to Italy that would reverberate with mock-heroic misadventure. Homer's *The Odyssey* – the way it unfolds in a tangible world of rawhide sandals and pitchers of shining wine – colours the book's every page.

Much of *The Truce* was written in Cesare Levi's old study, which contained more than 2,000 books. During composition Levi often consulted these texts. One literary influence was striking: Lajos Zilahy's *Two Prisoners*. In this Hungarian novel of his childhood, Levi found vodka-swilling Cossacks, Jewish and Tartar traders, as well as German and Italian prison-camp internees. The Siberian transfer camp of the book, called 'The House of Misery', was to provide Levi with a model for the Katowice transfer camp in *The Truce*, with its own milling of international humanity.

2

After his ten-hour factory workday Levi found he was often too exhausted to write. He said he needed a good hour to change into his writer's 'skin' and leave the factory behind. Even then he had to 'chain' himself to the writing desk. Renzo, now five, and Lisa, thirteen, resented their father's long absences from the family and they missed him. Writing sometimes made

Levi feel like a stranger in his own home; he wrote on weekends and public holidays too: there is a price to be paid for being a writer and a family man. The distress Lucia had experienced on first moving into 75 Corso Re Umberto had eased, but relations were still strained with her mother-in-law. After fourteen years, Lucia was resigned to bringing up her children in Ester's home, but resentment must have lingered towards her husband, who appeared to have favoured his mother's needs over hers. This apparent betrayal by Levi no doubt ensured Lucia's continued suspicion of her husband's friends.

By early autumn 1962 *The Truce* was almost finished. It had taken between 'three and four hundred days' to write, said Levi, and he knew he had written something special. There is superb comedy, farce, travel, young love; there are the great Russian landscapes. Levi liked to say that while *If This is a Man* inhabits a monochrome world, *The Truce* gives the impression of a rainbow radiance, a world in Technicolor. (The distinction, which has more than neatness in its favour, was originally made by Natalia Ginzburg's brother, Alberto Levi.) Pleased with the result, Levi handed the manuscript to his new editor at Einaudi, Daniele Ponchiroli.

Ponchiroli, a serious man, was attentive to his authors and worked for the love of books alone. Born to a peasant family in Mantua, he was now an immensely powerful figure at Einaudi. However, he was conspicuously ill-at-ease in Turin and took the most extraordinary detours to avoid the city's spacious squares: he was an agoraphobic. Italo Calvino, in his novel *If on a Winter's Night a Traveller*, immortalised Ponchiroli as the dedicated publisher 'Signor Cavedagna'. Like Levi, Ponchiroli rejected the notion (still prevalent in Italy) that literature was a precious salon pastime. Under his editorship was a stable of doctors, engineers and biologists who led parallel lives as writers. One of these was the Turin pathologist Lorenzo Tomatis, whose diary-novel *The Laboratory* charted the triumphs and delusions of a tumour specialist in Chicago. For Levi, Tomatis was a 'singular' and even 'revolutionary' writer, whose book put a lot of 'literature' to shame.

Another of Ponchiroli's authors was the incomparable war documentarist Mario Rigoni Stern. He was not a writer by vocation but, like Levi, he had a life-story to tell. The account of his soldier's life in wartime Russia, *The Sergeant in the Snow*, was a modern Italian classic, which Calvino compared to the military histories of Xenophon. His new story collection, *The Grouse Forest*, equally impressed Levi: its terse, Jack London-like accounts of hunters and wild dogs made him keen to know Rigoni Stern's native land of Alto Asiago, a chilly upland region between the Alps and the Adriatic. On

21 September 1962 Levi sent Rigoni Stern a letter of admiration. He was not sure if Rigoni Stern knew his name, but he saw the unmet author as a kindred spirit:

> Your new book was a rare pleasure for me. I believe it is an important work that will come to fill a void in Italian literature, these days so deficient in life-stories and the spirit of the 'Call of the Wild'. I'm convinced that yours is the most honest and serious way to write; it conveys more with less words, and as a result is the more poetic.

In his reply, Rigoni Stern suggested that they go camping together in the Asiago mountains. Levi was thrilled by the invitation, and sent him a copy of 'Bear Meat' by way of thanks. He asked him not to pass judgment on the story: 'Just accept it in the spirit of a chat among friends round the camp fire.' This was Levi's most important literary friendship; it took root immediately and continued for a quarter of a century until his death. Levi was drawn to Rigoni Stern because he was a maverick who kept his distance from literary cliques and salons. He also admired his practical resourcefulness; a resilient man, Rigoni Stern could survive in the wilds, and in time Levi grew to 'really love' this man, said his sister. Here at last was another Delmastro, a reassuringly rock-like figure in Levi's life.

3

The Truce finished, Levi settled to answering his correspondence. By 1962 he was receiving letters from all corners of Europe and (like many of his generation) he was punctilious in answering them. Albrecht Goes, the anti-Nazi pastor, had sent Levi a copy of his novel *Das Brandopfer* (*The Burnt Offering* – the literal German translation of Shoah, or Holocaust). The book reaffirmed Levi's view that there are human experiences of such enormity that they can be narrated only by those who were 'actually involved' in them. Towards the end of the year Levi was sent from Rotterdam an extraordinary draft proposal for a book by an unknown author, Dr Ezra BenGershôm. BenGershôm was a biologist and, on reading *Ist das ein Mensch?* he had felt compelled to contact Levi. During the war in his native Berlin he had destroyed his Jewish identity papers and, wearing a Hitler Youth uniform, remained in the city using an Aryan alias. Eventually he stowed away on a Turkish boat bound for Palestine. Levi was intrigued by this Chaplinesque epic of survival, and he wrote BenGershôm a morale-boosting letter: 'I exhort you to write your story: success cannot *fail* to be yours.' Levi's aptitude for spotting good 'non-professional' writers was unerring, and BenGershôm was to be the first of many literary discoveries.

At an Einaudi editorial meeting in November 1962 Levi's book was praised by Daniele Ponchiroli: 'Even if it lacks the pathos and tension of his first work, this is lovely, and always human.' Yet, in order to convince his colleagues, Ponchiroli had to explain just what was meant by a 'non-professional' writer. Most Einaudi editors considered Levi insufficiently glamorous as a chemist. The book's title, *The Truce,* was chosen by Levi's engineer friend Giorgio Lattes ('Big George'), who ran a chromium-plating factory on the outskirts of Turin. It was an intentionally ambivalent title, suggesting that Levi's joyous repatriation was a brief parenthesis, a queasy truce before other future cruelties. The book was published in June 1963, a few months after the Beatles released their first No. 1 hit, 'Please Please Me'.

A handful of glowing reviews put Levi in the front rank of contemporary Italian writers. Some critics spoke of *The Truce* in the same breath as Solzhenitsyn's *One Day in the Life of Ivan Denisovich*, which Einaudi had just published. Others suspected a heavy tincture of fantasy, and they were right. Levi had inserted a story that he had heard on a recent SIVA business trip. In an old people's home in Frankfurt lived a woman who in 1938 had sent Hitler a letter in which she implored him to stop his warmongering. The story seemed such a marvellous paradigm of courage that Levi incorporated it in *The Truce*. He had not so much subtracted from the truth as added to it.

Italo Calvino compared *The Truce* to Pushkin and Gogol, and many other Italian critics and writers picked up on the book's Russian influences, Tolstoy and Isaac Babel among them. But, in spite of its approving portrait of Mother Russia, *The Truce* was not well received in the Soviet Union, and is still not translated into Russian. One Moscow critic, reviewing the Italian edition, grumbled that Levi had done nothing but describe the 'same old, unchanging Russia of Dostoevsky'. His vignettes of Mongolian guards and Astrakhan-furred Siberians were condescending and formulaic: 'Levi has made no attempt whatsoever to see the new Soviet Russia, he makes not the faintest *effort* to understand the history lesson taught to us by the glorious defeat of Fascism. The author's observations are purely of the traditional Russian character – of the *Russian-ness* of our people.' The reviewer had a point. The Russians in *The Truce,* born and bred to inveterate indolence, suffer from deep 'Oblomovitis' (after the chronically lazy anti-hero of Goncharov's novel, *Oblomov*). In general, Levi chronicled them with exasperated affection combined with condescension. In Communist

Bulgaria, on the other hand, *The Truce* was highly praised, the Sofia-based *Yevreiski Vesti* ('Jewish News') hailing it as a 'humane' work.

Italian sales of *The Truce* exceeded Levi's expectations; within the first month of publication, 40,000 copies had gone. There was a reason for this. Levi was one of the first Europeans to describe the post-war Soviet Union from the inside; Italians were curious to read about the chaotic Red Bear, its people and their indomitable spirit. More than any other Italian book at this time, *The Truce* helped to heal Cold War antagonisms and free the Italian public from the political divisions of the dark post-war years. Indeed, it was no sooner in the shops than the smiling Pope John XXIII published his famous encyclical *Pacem in Terris* ('Peace on Earth'), which opened up a dialogue between the Catholic and Marxist worlds. Europe was changing, and Levi's book caught the new mood.

4

In his mountain retreat in Asiago, Mario Rigoni Stern read *The Truce* in one sitting. The book's mesmeric story-telling and difference in kind from other Italian accounts of the war impressed him deeply. Most Italian war chronicles were acts of self-exculpation written by the army generals who had directed the catastrophe.

The two men had not managed to go camping, but instead arranged to meet in Turin. The urbane Italo Calvino introduced Rigoni Stein and Levi at the new Einaudi offices on Via Biancamano. After a preliminary chat they headed off to the Caffè Platti for drinks. In appearance, Rigoni Stern called to mind the sea captain on the Player's cigarette packets; a grizzled, whiskery man, he was lean, not especially tall. Two years younger than Levi, married, with no children, shy and somewhat gauche, he felt happiest in Asiago chopping wood or tending his beehives. In spite of their differences, the unaffected Roman Catholic and the cultivated Jew found they had much in common, not least a mistrust of writers who were 'all-author'.

To Levi it seemed 'a miracle' that Rigoni Stern was alive at all. Having survived the French, Albanian and Russian fronts, in 1943 he had been deported from his native Asiago to west Prussia, where he was brutalised by the Hungarian SS. Mistaken for a Fascist spy, later he was almost executed by the British. At the war's end, on 9 May 1945, Rigoni Stern returned to Italy frostbitten, spirit-broken and haunted by his dead comrades in Russia. Levi found Rigoni Stern very good company, with a capacity to make comic drama out of his wartime ordeal. Yet, while Levi could himself relive Auschwitz, Rigoni Stern noted, he was not forthcoming about his wife and children. This was due in part to Levi's natural reserve, but also to an inbred conviction – shared by many men of his generation – that their wives were not to be discussed among friends.

5

Levi, like most writers, made life seem more interesting than it is, and in his defence he quoted the Tuscan proverb: 'The tale is not beautiful if nothing is added to it.' Thus in *The Truce* Lello Perugia is transformed into the larger-than-life huckster 'Cesare', whose vainglorious sexual conquests are contrasted with Levi's own punctilious reserve and sexual timorousness. In many ways Lello is the Ulysses evoked by William Morris as 'the shifty', the hero of many wiles, who lives off his wits and is a sweet deceiver. Levi suspected that Lello would be hurt on encountering his fictional counterpart, and felt a little guilty at ruffling his friend's new-found domestic happiness. In Rome, Lello was now married and a successful accountant. On 10 June 1963 Levi plucked up the courage to write to him:

> Honestly, I'd been meaning to send you the book for some time, but I'd hesitated somewhat because one of the characters has got something to do with you. I feared you might be annoyed. You must be the judge of that. But please remember: (1), the words and adventures which I attribute to Cesare have been liberally recreated, interpreted, and, in part, invented; (2), in the opinion of all the readers I've spoken to, and all the critics in the newspapers up until now, this Cesare (who knows why?) ends up being quite a genial character.

As Levi expected, Lello was offended by *The Truce* and a breach ensued that lasted many years. Of course 'Cesare' was conceived in the spirit of light-hearted comedy – his absurdities sprang not from dreary realism, but from Levi's own story-telling creativity – but Lello did not see it that way. 'He was quite severe with me,' Levi recalled, 'he complained that *The Truce* would have been a "much more important" book if I'd got my facts right.' In a subsequent letter to Perugia (1980) Levi wrote: 'It's a fact that having a writer as a friend is a risky business.'

If Perugia was upset by *The Truce*, the French prisoner Paul Steinberg was mortified by what Levi had done to him. Steinberg, by his own admission, had survived the camp by having a cynical disregard for others. Yet his transformation into the low, creeping flatterer 'Henri' of *If This is a*

303

Man had been a very great shock to him. Was this the same man? Steinberg was scarcely seventeen when he entered the camp, but the semi-fictionalised 'Henri' is twenty-eight. Perhaps Levi thought that Steinberg's worldly cynicism would be more credible in an older man. He disparaged the Frenchman's sexuality by comparing him to the arrow-pierced 'San Sebastian' as painted in 1527 by Giovanni 'Sodoma' Bazzi: Sebastian, of course, being a favourite saint among homosexuals.

6

The first half of 1963 was enhanced for Levi by his book reviews and warm critical reception. In July he had scarcely settled back into SIVA's daily grind when wonderful news came that *The Truce* had been shortlisted for Italy's Strega Prize. Past winners of this coveted award had included Cesare Pavese and the Sicilian aristocrat-author Giuseppe di Lampedusa for *The Leopard*. The presentation was to be held in Rome on 4 July. Levi was staying with his sister in her flat on Rome's Campo dei Fiori. Anna Maria had left Turin some fifteen years earlier; and away from the cramped conditions of 75 Corso Re Umberto she had been transformed into a worldly, attractive woman, who liked to hold literary soirées for friends and artists. At his sister's Levi found that he was able to shed some of his inhibiting *torinesità* and relax among the outward-going Romans. Anna Maria introduced her brother to the extrovert Roman author and information technologist Roberto Vacca, a handsome man with a stentorian voice (he spoke fluent Chinese). The two got on very well: Vacca, like Levi, was interested in the new logic of our lives as created by the emergent mass-communications landscape.

Later on that evening, Levi was in Rome's lavish Villa Giulia to attend the Strega awards ceremony. At the table next to him sat the screen idol Marcello Mastroianni and his director Michelangelo Antonioni, and all the Roman beau monde. Amid this glitter Levi confessed he felt like a 'martian'. He was one of just three finalists. The others were the macabre fantasist Tommaso Landolfi, and Levi's old antagonist and friend Natalia Ginzburg. Ginzburg's semi-autobiography, *Family Sayings* – a book that Levi admired greatly – won. The famously grouchy Roman novelist Alberto Moravia commiserated with Levi. Fireworks followed by canonfire ushered in the night's round of receptions and gala buffets; Levi wanted to get back to his sister's. 'I can't bear all this hand-kissing,' he whispered to his trade unionist friend Vittorio Foa, 'let's go.' For all that Levi disliked these sort of prize-givings, the critics' reception and sales of *The Truce* marked the beginning of his fame in Italy. And, as the plaudits continued, he felt confident enough to resume other literary schemes that had been hatched so hopefully earlier on. Levi told journalists that he had finished writing on the camps ('Absolutely not another word') and that he planned instead to write a book about his scientific research and profession as a chemist. 'We all know about prostitutes [a dig at Alberto Moravia's Roman stories] and street kids [Pasolini's steamy tales of Roman low-life] but very little about chemists. Nobody has ever bothered with us.' Eleven years before it was published, *The Periodic Table* was germinating.

7

For the August holidays Levi went with his family to Denmark. In Copenhagen they called on the Flemming Boldts (friends of friends), and afterwards explored the harbour with its skyline of ships' masts. Young Renzo was as timid a schoolboy as Levi had once been ('excruciatingly shy', according to Mr Boldt), but the holiday seemed to have been a success. In Copenhagen Levi learned that *The Truce* had not only won Italy's Alpi Apuana Prize, but had been shortlisted for the all-important Campiello Prize. Fearing that acceptance of the one would jeopardise his chances of winning the other, he declined to accept the Alpi Apuana. The Campiello had been set up as an alternative to the ostentatious Strega Prize and was generating a good deal of media attention.

By late August, tanned and healthy, the family was back home. Levi was now the most talked-about Italian writer of the season, the literary 'outsider' who led a double life as writer and chemist. On 23 August Ezra BenGershôm visited from Rotterdam, bringing with him his autobiography in manuscript. Claudio Magris, the noted Triestino critic, had seen an earlier draft and agreed with Levi that it was a 'really unique and enthralling work'. The mild and scholarly BenGershôm found the atmosphere in 75 Corso Re Umberto 'relaxed' and 'fun'; he was impressed by the extraordinary sculptures of giant owls and butterflies that Levi had made out of industrial copper wire.

This was, above all, Primo Levi's autumn. His literary reputation much enhanced, on 3 September he left for Venice with high hopes of winning the Campiello. On the train from Turin he was joined by Einaudi's new press officer, Ernesto Ferrero. Levi joked that the judges could not possibly give second prize to a 'man called Primo'. He was beginning to warm to his role as literary 'outsider': during the journey he sat reading an Isaac Asimov fantasy, pens clipped neatly to his breast-pocket. His father's outdated gold watch lent him a distinguished air. They reached Venice late in the

305

afternoon. And in the evening, amid popping flashbulbs, it was announced that Primo Levi had won the Campiello. As he went up to collect the gold plaque he feebly remonstrated with the camera-clicking paparazzi: 'Can we have a bit of a truce, please?'

Levi's success was all the more extraordinary as 1963 was such an exceptional year for Italian literature. Calvino's *The Watcher*, Gadda's baroque experiment *Acquainted with Grief*, and Leonardo Sciascia's historical inquisition *The Council of Egypt*: all these books, now European classics, had been published by Einaudi that year. Yet it was *The Truce* that made inroads into the public imagination. One Italian journalist observed that if historians wished to understand the twisted side of the twentieth-century, they would do better to study Levi than the 'ultramodern texts' manufactured by 'our so-called innovative men of letters'. This was a clear jibe at Group 63, founded that autumn in Sicily by avant-garde writers and critics (the then unknown Umberto Eco among them), who rejected 'conservatism' in the arts. *The Truce*, with its raw proletarian characters, had a strong neo-realist tinge that made it irredeemably old-fashioned to Group 63. (In 1947 *If This is a Man* had not been considered neo-realist *enough*.) But if Levi was an anachronism for the 'anti-traditionalists' of Group 63, for ordinary Italian readers he was a refreshingly readable author. A fiction without a story, Levi knew, was not worth its weight in paper, and he found many 'ultramodern texts' prolix, pedantic, self-indulgent and patronising.

Not without a degree of smugness, indeed, Levi allied himself with Italy's non-professional 'Sunday authors' who pitted themselves against the avant-garde. In Venice that autumn he met the young Istrian novelist Fulvio Tomizza, who was as far removed from Italy's *bel mondo letterario* as it was possible to be. Istria now lies almost entirely within Croatia; it had been part of Italy until 1947, when it was ceded to Yugoslavia. Tomizza's debut novel of 1960, *Materada* (much praised by Pier Paolo Pasolini, whose brother Guido was killed by Marshal Tito's partisans), described the post-war Istrian refugee exodus into Italy after the Communist Yugoslavs had taken over. Though the novel was written in Italian, it was interwoven with the Croatian and Slav dialects of the author's native Istria. Culturally, the Roman Catholic Tomizza was Italian; but in his blood he was a Slav. He was just twenty-eight when he met Levi at the Campiello presentations in 1963: 'I was astonished that he had even heard of me – most so-called writers have not.' Afterwards Levi kept in touch with Tomizza and his Jewish wife, Laura Levi. Primo saw their respective outsider status as something positive. 'It's like having a spare wheel or an extra gear,' he said.

On his return to Turin, Levi found that a celebratory meal had been laid on for him at SIVA with dancing and champagne. The firm's new cook, Adriana Bruno, prepared a peppery southern Italian pasta dish that had Levi gasping for water.

8

Stuart Woolf had begun to translate *The Truce* in the autumn of 1963. By then he had left Turin to teach history at Pembroke College, Cambridge, and missed his close collaboration with Levi. Unfortunately, no English-language publisher seemed to be interested in Woolf's manuscript. The Orion Press had gone bankrupt and sold *If This is a Man* to Collier paperbacks in the US (who grossly retitled the book *Survival in Auschwitz*), so it could not bid for Woolf's translation. In London the manuscript had been turned down by Hamish Hamilton, André Deutsch and Victor Gollancz. By the end of 1963 it had landed at the offices of the Bodley Head. On 19 November a reader's report on *The Truce* was ready for the Bodley Head's director, J. B. Priestley:

> There is no maudlin pathos here, no bitterness, even: there is genuine warmth, a delightful sense of fun and of the ridiculous. Levi has also, to my mind, the Pasternak touch in describing not so much the landscape of Russia as what it feels like to see and to live in that landscape.

The report concluded: '*The Truce* is a book which ought to be published simply because it is far too good not to.' A back-up report came from the Italian poet Camillo Pennati, chief librarian at the Italian Cultural Institute in London. While Pennati conceded that German concentration-camp-chronicles did not 'deeply involve the English mind at large', nevertheless 'I personally warmly recommend this book.' J. B. Priestley, an omnivorous and deeply curious reader, was keen to publish. And Priestley's softly-spoken junior editor, Guido Waldman, a former American GI, used his U.S. contacts to place *The Truce* on the other side of the Atlantic.

At the Atlantic Monthly Press (a subsidiary of Little, Brown), Sylvia Plath's former editor, Peter Davison, was enthusiastic about *The Truce*. There was just one problem. Davison insisted on a new title, *The Reawakening*, which neither Waldman nor Levi liked. Waldman wrote to Davison: 'Our feeling is that Levi knew exactly what he was after when he chose *La Tregua* (The Truce) rather than *Il Risveglio* (The Reawakening).' Reluctantly, Levi accepted his book's dual-title status: *The Truce* for the

307

British, *The Reawakening* for the Americans. It was hardly to be expected that an unknown author would have much say in this matter: 'All editors and book [people] are alike – any attempt to intefere with their mysterious programme is hopeless,' Levi tetchily observed.

In June 1964, seven months prior to British publication of *The Truce*, Guido Waldman wrote to Levi in the hope of commissioning another book from him: 'How does a man like you, who has been dragged to death's door, return to the world of daily work and everyday pleasures?' Levi was impressed by Waldman's foresight, and three days later wrote to him:

> I definitely will have other stories to tell, and they'll be the very ones which you imagine – the return to daily work, daily work itself. Perhaps I'll start this summer? But, you see, daily work is the chief *obstacle* to my writing: work takes up a lot of my time, and makes me tired and anxious.

Slowly the life of the factory was draining Levi.

Peter Davison sent proof copies of *The Reawakening* to every eminent Jewish critic he could think of. Weeks passed, but he heard nothing from them. Alfred Kazin, a personal friend, remained silent. So did Hannah Arendt, and Irving Howe. The truth is, *The Reawakening* was not much liked in the United States then. The catastrophe of the war was still unpalatable during America's economic growth of the mid-1960s. As a result, sales were relatively small (well under 2,500). As Davison put it later: 'It was too early for Americans to understand Levi's joy, his irony, his capacity for combining opposite emotions and contradictions.' In Britain, where *The Truce* was published in early 1965, the critical reception was much better. The *Observer*'s chief reviewer Philip Toynbee saluted a 'wonderful tragi-comic pendant to the hell which Signor Levi sounded in his earlier book'. Emanuel Litvinoff, the marvellous chronicler of London's Jewish East End, reported in the *Guardian* that *The Truce* was 'beautiful all the way through'. In the British provincial press, too, Levi was well received. 'Like Dante before him,' cheered the *Glasgow Herald*, 'Mr Levi has brought gold back out of hell.' In the glossy magazine *Queen*, the poet Elizabeth Smart applauded a 'fantastic Italian' who had managed to make a work of art out of the horrors of the concentration camp: 'no lies, no cheating: a beautiful objectivity'. Elsewhere in Europe *The Truce* sold poorly. In Germany the book had been 'manhandled by a translator who *doesn't even know Italian*,' Levi complained to Einaudi; it sold a wretched 1,300 copies.

At the end of 1963 Levi was faced, quite suddenly, with a disabling illness. As the weeks went by, he found he was losing his zest for life, and sleeping badly. He frightened Lucia and the family with his brooding, introspective moods. After the publication of his book he was feeling depressed: that much he understood. His low mood did not last long, but it was a pattern that was to repeat itself, with increasingly ghastly consequences, for the rest of Levi's life. Many writers are dispirited after the completion of a hard task (and not only writers) but Levi was more depressed than most. He feared that once his fund of real-life stories was exhausted, he would face literary extinction. With *The Truce* he believed he had definitively plumbed the depths of his unique, tragic and (for him) precious experiences. There was nothing left to say, he thought, and his literary prospects looked dismal. Six-year-old Renzo was ill with bronchitis, and Lisa was in teenage rebellion against home and country. Already the *miracolo italiano*, the 'golden age' of Italy's post-war prosperity, was losing its lustre; social protests, with clashes in Rome between police and students, marked the era.

Amid this gloom, good news came that the Italian director Francesco Rosi was poised to buy film rights in *The Truce*. Rosi seemed ideally suited to adapt Levi's chronicle of homecoming as he had a famously inquisitorial, documentary eye. Early contact had been established with the Soviet Union, as Rosi wanted to shoot on location. 'But it wasn't easy – the red-tape, the Cold War suspicion – and in the end I had to give up,' Rosi said during an interview for the *Independent* in 1987. Levi's health was still much below par, but he kept busy with various film projects over the next two years. Several meetings took place in Rome with the Tuscan director Mario Monicelli, who took up where Rosi left off. To Monicelli's surprise Levi, unlike many writers, allowed him considerable leeway in adapting the book. Monicelli's idea was to make a grand epic film but without losing the book's lightness of touch. Levi was asked to write the script, which he found surprisingly easy. 'It's principally a question of linking together episodes,' he announced. Soon a draft treatment was ready, and by early 1964 the project was beginning to produce 'concrete fruits'; but then Monicelli's American backer disappeared and the project was dropped. When Rosi's version of *The Truce* finally appeared in 1997 it was quite disappointing.

Levi did not give up hope. For 250,000 lire (£1,300 today – a risible sum), Franca Films in Rome bought an option on *The Truce*. Alberto Sordi, then Italy's favourite screen comedian, was to play the part of the streetwise Cesare (Levi said he wanted Lello Perugia himself in the role). A script based on the earlier Monicelli treatment was fleshed out but, in spite of lavish promises, nothing came of this project either. Levi was quite prepared for failure when Sophia Loren's movie-mogul husband, Carlo Ponti, considered filming three of his science fiction stories. Ponti soon lost interest, however, and today has no recollection of the project whatsoever. ('Primo *who*?') With all these cinematic *faux-départs* Levi was now understandably wary of the movie industry. 'If you allow me to give you some advice,' he told Ezra BenGershôm (whose autobiography was up for movie treatment), 'be very careful in negotiating the contract.' Incidentally, BenGershôm's *Escape from the Nazi Dragnets*, published under the alias Joel König, has now sold over 100,000 copies throughout Europe, thanks to Levi.

Through the mid-1960s, a variety of radio and theatre projects required Levi's attention. These brought him some satisfaction, more frustrations, and a good deal of hard work. In early 1964 a tape reached him of the Canadian Broadcasting Corporation's radio version of *If This is a Man*. It was a revelation. The shouting, clanging hell of Auschwitz had been reproduced with disturbing authenticity, even to the extent of recording the opening and closing of cattle-car doors in the Toronto stockyards. Sixteen tongues, from Yiddish to Magyar, captured the camp's language babel. 'Primo Levi's Personal Account of Annihilation', running for two hours and twenty minutes, is still powerfully unsettling for the listener. Some of the cast-members were survivors, and the German Jews among them could play Nazis only with considerable difficulty. 'Yet they were able to re-create and vivify a tragedy which most of us could not otherwise even begin to imagine,' said the CBC producer John Reeves. The adaptation went out late on Sunday night, 24 January 1964, and provoked such a barrage of phone calls to CBC that it had to be repeated twice.

Hoping to repeat the Canadian success, Levi asked RAI radio in Turin if they would produce *If This is a Man* for domestic radio. Giorgio Bandini, the corporation's chief director, took on the task enthusiastically. Bandini was friendly with the British playwright Arnold Wesker and still is as an immensely important figure in Italian radio. As in the CBC version, authenticity was to be paramount, and one night in a field outside Turin, Levi and Bandini set fire to a wooden door to simulate the sound of crackling as the Germans abandoned the burning camp. In a village above Turin, Brozzolo, peasants in their wooden clogs were recorded for the prisoners' march. (Brozzolo was the only place in Piedmont where peasants still wore clogs; at regular intervals the recording had to be interrupted by rifle shot so that birdsong would not distort the sounds of Auschwitz.) In the manner of Italian neo-realism, Bandini recruited a number of non-professional actors from the street, among them Silesian friars and a

Yiddish-speaking Polish businessman. To Levi's surprise, he found the German actor chosen to play an SS officer antagonised him. 'He performed in such a realistic way, shouting and threatening in crude SS-jargon . . . that nobody doubted his professional competence.' Levi learned later that the German had been in the Wehrmacht and had fought Italian partisans on the outskirts of Turin. Sometimes he left rehearsals seemingly on the brink of tears. Bandini explained: 'Re-creating Auschwitz was more draining for Primo than any of us realised.' The radio version of *If This is a Man* mattered enormously to Levi, and later he would say that the hours spent in the RAI studio were among the happiest of his post-war literary career. When the programme went out, late one Friday evening in April 1964, the audience response was enthusiastic.

Yet Levi still worried about the future. 'I haven't the faintest idea what the next year will bring me,' he said. Industrial discontent was sweeping Turin. There was talk of 'recession'. Southern migrant workers beat up their factory bosses in protest at low pay and conditions. Pietro Cavallero, formerly a research chemist at SIVA, had begun to shoot and loot his way across the industrialised north of Italy with his band of *sinistrini*. Levi's work at the factory was suffering, he said, from the 'general Italian crisis', and was becoming every month more 'dull and enervating'. Levi had now worked at SIVA for sixteen years, and had to admit that his teenage dream of scientific distinction had come to naught. 'I had hoped to go very far,' he said ruefully, 'to the point of possessing the universe, to understanding the why of things. But now I know you can't.' In his mid-forties, Levi felt he was in a professional rut; yet he had to earn a living. As the Italian saying goes: you don't spit in the plate you eat from.

In 1964 Levi was tempted to resign from SIVA and write full time, but it was a risk. 'I do not know if I shall be able to go ahead with both professions [chemistry and writing]: but to shift one's way at the age of 45 is not without danger.' Friends began to notice an increasing moodiness in Levi, a dissatisfaction often close to self-pity. What did he want from life? He had earned a literary reputation based on two classics which were destined to remain in print. Yet Levi was not content with that. 'He had the *orgoglio* [arrogance] and *fierezza* [pride] of the true writer,' commented the Turin critic Lorenzo Mondo. 'He knew his books on the camp were important not just for what they said, but for the *way* they were written, for their literary style.' Levi had to prove himself as a writer of other, and better, books. There was no worse fate, he thought, than to be pigeon-holed as *un autore univoco*.

It was a cold winter in 1964, and the economic downturn resulted in unemployment and more worker protests in Turin. Christmas in the city might have been fun, but it rained a great deal, and Levi was still depressed. At about this time SIVA acquired an important new client, who specialised in structural adhesives. This was an unknown field for Levi, and he was excited by the unfamiliar. Keith Barnes was a tall, big-shouldered English engineer whose optimism and good humour Levi liked. On Barnes's initiative, Levi began to investigate the use of PVF in bonding aeroplane wings, ski parts and car brakes, so that SIVA could move into the aeronautical, sports and car industries.

Before long, thanks to Barnes, Levi turned SIVA into a significant European competitor in polyvinyl adhesives, and in gratitude he signed the English engineer a copy of *If This is a Man*: 'To Keith, with real friendship, untroubled by *adhesions*.' Barnes, for his part, had an unshakeable admiration for Levi's literary gifts, a deep sympathy for his terrible past, and over the years would become a generous and loyal companion. (He had been in a British army signal corps at the liberation of Bergen-Belsen.) In 1964 Levi introduced Barnes to mountain hiking. On Friday nights, as soon as Barnes arrived in Turin, they would set out for the snow-capped Monte Rosa, where they stayed in a hotel and drank each other's health in the local raspberry liqueur. They had tremendous times together, and it was to be a happy ten-year friendship.

Barnes, by his own admission, was not Levi's intellectual equal. He liked to hear Levi discourse on life and religion, but was a little surprised to hear him claim the Bible as his favourite book – 'But Keith, it's an early version of the Brothers Grimm.' For Levi their friendship was a measure of how well he adapted to different company, though there were some comic misunderstandings. Seated at a restaurant table, Levi solemnly informed Barnes that he was eating mice – 'mice cooked in milk'. Seeing Barnes's disbelief, he wrote the word down for him on a napkin: it was 'maize' (pronounced 'mice' by many Italians). As well as polenta, Levi had a passion for frogs. 'It wasn't just the legs – Primo chomped on the *heads*.' Frogs were not all that disconcerted Barnes about Levi. There was also his driving. 'Either Primo drove like a Formula One contender *manqué*, or very, very slowly.'

By the end of 1964 Levi was ready to take on a new literary project. When a young Piedmontese actor wanted him to adapt *If This is a Man* for the stage, however, Levi took some persuading. He feared he would be accused of making money out of Auschwitz: what had once dehumanised him he now offered for sale, in the theatre. But the actor, Pieralberto Marché, was adamant: *If This is a Man* would have such an effect on stage, he assured Levi, that the audience would be left 'reeling'. The thought repelled Levi as much as it attracted him. Finally he relented, appointing Marché as the script's co-author. Work began in November and continued for a year, an experience that Marché sometimes found disturbing. One day Levi snapped at him: 'No, you really haven't understood have you? I was *grateful* that the *Kapo* beat me almost to death. Because without that beating I'd have gone on committing the same error until one day he'd surely have killed me for it.' (After their collaboration Marché looked on Levi as a quasi-religious figure. 'I thought he had *la verità rivelata,* the truth was revealed to him.')

11

On 10 April 1965 Levi returned to Auschwitz. The Warsaw government had arranged wreath-laying ceremonies to mark the twentieth anniversary of the camp's liberation by the Red Army, and Levi was an invited guest. Naturally he was curious to see Auschwitz again. By Polish government decree the camp had been turned into a museum, the largest graveyard in human history, complete with shrines and cafeterias. Levi was accompanied by Nardo De Benedetti and Giuliana Tedeschi, an Auschwitz survivor and Classics teacher living in Turin, whose deportation testimony *This Poor Body* had been published in Italy in 1946. From Vienna a seven-hour train journey took them to Katowice and then on to Cracow, where they stayed the night in a 'very dirty hotel.' The next day, Sunday 11 April, they were in Auschwitz.

The camp, milling with 40,000 visitors, looked to Levi more like a 'fairground' than a place of sorrowful memories. The extermination of European Jewry had been minutely planned and gruesomely enacted on this soil, yet Levi felt no emotion – 'absolutely none' – on revisiting. Notices constantly reminded him: 'YOU ARE ENTERING A PLACE OF EXCEPTIONAL HORROR AND TRAGEDY', but Auschwitz I, the main camp, had a 'sterile', memorial atmosphere. Levi felt differently at the Birkenau (Auschwitz II) women's camp, which he had never seen before. In this wasteland of broken huts and human malevolence Levi must have thought of Vanda Maestro, who had died here. He could not face the scene for long, and slipped away to explore his old camp, Auschwitz IV, or Buna-Monovitz. Yet it was impossible for him to imagine the *Lager* as he had known it. After the war the barracks had been razed for jerry-built Polish workers' quarters; of Blocks 30 and 48, where Levi had been interned, only the charred foundations remained. 'That really hurt me,' he said in an interview.

However, the synthetic-rubber and oil plant built by Jewish slave labour under I. G. Farben was still in operation. The Poles had renamed it 'Zaklady Chemiczne' and it was (and still is) the largest synthetic-rubber factory in Europe. Polish army guards refused to let Levi inside, but he was afforded a good view of the worksite from a gantry bridge. The concrete air-raid shelters pocked by Allied shrapnel. The acetic acid tanks. The carbide tower. The butadiene-storage spheres. All were exactly as Levi remembered them. A railway ran, just as it had in Levi's day, directly from Auschwitz civilian station to the chemical plant. There was even a stop – Chelmek Fabr. – for the 7,000 present-day workers. Travelling with these workers to the factory today is an experience that leaves the visitor feeling disturbed and contaminated.

12

The play of *If This is a Man* was a patchwork of scenes from the book; several aspects of the script – for example, Pieralberto Marché's idea of a Greek tragedy-style chorus – still made Levi nervous. But by late October 1965 the script was finished, and Levi said he was pleased with the result. It had cost him a good year's work. 'And this work continues right now in the shape of an intense (and pretty exhausting) round of presentations and contacts with directors, theatres and troupes,' he wrote to Giulio Einaudi. The letter's slightly harassed tone was due in part to Levi's increasingly difficult home life. Levi's mother, now seventy, had been operated on for an eye complaint the previous winter and needed looking after. Ester Levi's many ailments would make life increasingly difficult for her son.

Other matters required his attention. Einaudi planned to publish a volume of his science fiction, and Levi had to make his selection. In Italy, science fiction had long been synonymous with the cheap *Urania* paperbacks (on sale at tobacconists and railway-station kiosks) with tales of robot takeovers and dinosaurs clomping round Manhattan. In 1959, however, Einaudi had published a classic anthology, *Wonders of the Possible*, which contained the best of Ray Bradbury, Isaac Asimov and other American futurists. With Einaudi's imprimatur, Italian intellectuals could now enjoy science fiction in the form of America's best hard-edged fantasists. Sales of the anthology supposedly benefited from the fact that one of the editors, Carlo Fruttero, resembled a martian.

Levi called his new book *Natural Histories*, a consciously ironic title. Einaudi's marketing supremo Roberto Cerati did not think it would be possible to market a 'Levi-*Truce*' alongside a 'Levi-SF', and advised Primo to publish under a pseudonym. Levi himself was squeamish about publishing science fiction using his own name: to offer a collection of playful *divertimenti* to his serious readership would have been disrespectful, he thought. He had no difficulty in choosing a pseudonym. Driving everyday to SIVA, he passed an electrical repair shop down Corso Giulio Cesare, Malabaila & Co. So Damiano Malabaila would be Levi's nom de plume. The surname was Piedmontese for 'bad' (*male*) 'wet nurse' (*balia*), and psychoanalyst friends (among them Luciana Nissim) found Levi's choice of pseudonym revealing. He must have had an unconscious memory of poor childhood nutrition, was their view. (Someone had tactlessly mentioned this to Levi's mother and the thought of it upset her terribly.) According to Levi, he just liked the sound of the shop's name.

The book's fifteen fantasies drew widely on chemistry, astrophysics and molecular biology: together they constituted a satire on man's potentially destructive misuse of technology. Levi had invented a new character for the book, the jovial Oklahoma salesman and information theorist Mr Simpson. A hybrid of the hard-selling Rico Accati and Keith Barnes, Simpson embodied the scientific astonishment and discovery of the late 1950s, when the first sputnik was lobbed into space and a new age dawned of Fiat 500s and gadgets and 'gracious living'. Levi subscribed to the computer and information technology journal *Civiltà delle macchine*, which kept him abreast of scientific progress.

Though a theatre script of *If This is a Man* was finished, as yet there was no director or producer. With numerous delays, the play would not go on stage for a further year. In the meantime Levi was approached by another actor-director, Massimo Scaglione, who ran Turin's experimental Teatro delle Dieci. Scaglione wondered if Levi had anything else suitable for the stage, science fiction perhaps? After consideration Levi gave Scaglione three futurist fables – 'The Sixth Day', 'The Versifier', 'The Sleeping Beauty in the Fridge' – from his forthcoming *Natural Histories*. 'See what you make of them.' These parables of Martian bureaucrats, computers and cryogenics seemed scarcely stageworthy, but Scaglione turned them into three one-act plays, and wrote the scripts. Taking time off SIVA, Levi joined Scaglione as consultant; rehearsals continued through the winter of 1966. Levi was terribly shy with the actors and turned his attention, instead, to the technicalities of Scaglione's direction: props, tapes, lighting, sound effects. 'Primo was like a child with new toys,' Scaglione recalled. Levi's infantile side has been remarked on by others, and it could be charming. One stage prop, an antique Olivetti typewriter, absorbed him all afternoon.

The premiere of the 'Natural Histories' trilogy by Primo Levi (not yet Damiano Malabaila) took place in the basement of the Romano Cinema on 16 February 1966, eight months before *Natural Histories* was published as a book. Possibly for the first time in Italy, science fiction was presented on stage; the set was appropriately modernist with giant building bricks that brought to mind wartime air-raid bunkers. Levi sat nervously on the edge of his seat but he had nothing to fear: his first work for the theatre had sold out, and the critics applauded it.

13

By the spring of 1966 there was still no word on the stage version of *If This is a Man*, and Levi longed to have the cast and director settled. Frustrated, he left Turin with his wife to visit Mario Rigoni Stern in his native Alto Asiago. The Levis put up at the inexpensive Hotel Europa, and were punctually met the next morning by Rigoni Stern and his wife Anna in reception. All four then drove up to the writer's mountain house amid alpine pastures. It was a place of seclusion and great natural beauty. For three centuries Stern's forebears had lived here, crossing and recrossing the mountain ranges as far as Padua to sell butter and cheese. Alto Asiago was (and still is) a rural peasant society without noblemen, castles or grand villas; prim windowboxes and green-tiled churches suggest an Italian Bavaria. The film director Ermanno Olmi, later famous for *The Tree of Wooden Clogs*, lived next door to Rigoni Stern, and Levi was amazed to see wild goats nibbling in Olmi's garden.

Levi enjoyed the visit. After a lunch of two-year-old Asiago cheese and home-distilled grappa, Rigoni Stern showed him his beehives. This prompted Levi to draw an analogy between bees fed on honey-impregnated alcohol, and human society. In a story he had heard, the bees had sacked their own hives and flew off in a drunken frenzy to destroy others. 'They behaved exactly like men,' he told Rigoni Stern. During a walk in the Val di Nos forest, Lucia and Anna followed a few steps behind while Rigoni Stern pointed out to Levi the silver birches and firs, as well as the Great War cemetery nearby full of British soldiers (it is still maintained by Her Majesty's government). Asiago had been settled in ancient times by Germanic tribes and Levi was fascinated by the German aspects of Asiago culture, including the local Cimbro dialect inflected with Germanic words. Levi loved investigating roots and origins, and Stern was delighted to be able to show off his knowledge of Cimbro.

*

By July 1966 the play of *If This is a Man* had at last found a director. Gianfranco De Bosio lived at 51 Corso Re Umberto and was on nodding terms with Levi. His chilling Resistance film, *The Terrorist*, had been the talk of the 1964 Venice film festival; De Bosio was artistic director of Turin's revered Teatro Stabile, where his handling of difficult plays was well known. His Jewish Hungarian wife, the *danseuse* Marta Egri, appointed herself the play's co-director. In rehearsals she encouraged the actors to writhe round the stage and howl. These strenuous sessions filled Levi with mild revulsion. ('What *is* this? The *Kama Sutra*?' he asked his co-author Pieralberto Marché.) Keith Barnes went along to one of these rehearsals and recalled Levi's extreme distaste: 'When something was a problem for Primo, it was an *intense* problem, and that rehearsal, let me tell you, was a very intense problem.'

From the start the production had a chaotic air. The play was due to open in Florence in the autumn, but by August the casting was still not settled. De Bosio had not bothered to turn up for the first eight days of rehearsals, and Marché himself was devastated when, on the 25th, his mother died. Unable to face much more of Marta Egri's primal gymnastics, Levi wrote an icy letter to the forty-two-year-old De Bosio: 'Given the international esteem and circulation which *If This is a Man* enjoys, I am sure you will understand my anxiety.' He went on to express his 'extreme concern' for the haphazard nature of the stage preparations. Privately Levi acknowledged his difficulty with thespian types ('I kept telling Primo that the theatre's a den of wolves,' remembered Marché), but he was concerned about his book's reputation. Fifty-three actors from seven countries had been auditioned for what was to be an international, large-scale production. Most of them were amateurs who often failed to turn up to rehearsals. The 'disastrous' and 'dreadful' nature of Levi's relationship with De Bosio, said Marché, depressed him and wore him down.

Levi wanted to be usefully involved in the play, though. Costume was of tantamount importance, he felt – verisimilitude vital. Accordingly, Levi sent the set designer Gianni Polidori an extraordinarily detailed series of sketches for the prisoners' clothing. 'Henri' (Paul Steinberg) was to wear a 'spotlessly clean striped uniform *without* patches'. Wilhelm Pannwitz had to have in his breast-pocket a 'pencil and slide-rule'. With dress rehearsals finally underway, Levi asked the great avant-garde composer Luigi Nono if he would write the play's score. Levi had conservative tastes in music, to say the least, and one cannot imagine that he cared much for Nono's atonal theatre cantatas in memory of condemned partisans and downtrodden factory workers. Yet Nono was Jewish (he was married to Arnold Schoenberg's daughter) and Levi would have been familiar with his choral work, *Remember What You Have Done in Auschwitz*. Besides, the time was opportune for Nono's brand of agitprop composition. Taboos were being challenged, hemlines rising and the old political order was under fire by the young.

Perhaps Nono sensed a looming catastrophe; he offered, and then withdrew, his promise of help. The production was a shambles. But just when it looked as though *If This is a Man* would fail, De Bosio was saved by a natural disaster. On 4 November 1966, a Friday, Florence was devastated by an historic flood. The Arno burst its banks; the Ponte Vecchio risked collapsing; families took to the rooftops as the river flowed uncontrolled through the Tuscan capital, drowning eighteen people and all the animals in the city zoo. The play's Hungarian cast lost their belongings as well as their cars, reported Levi; 600 unsold copies of Antonicelli's *If This is a Man* were swept out of a warehouse to join the medieval books and manuscripts lost from the inundated Uffizi. On 6 November the only vehicles on the few streets above water were ambulances and army jeeps. With two-thirds of Florence under water, the premiere of Levi's play had to be postponed and the production was transferred back to Turin, where De Bosio could play for time.

The premiere of *If This is a Man* was finally held in Turin on the night of Saturday 19 November; Levi dashed off a good-luck note to Umberto Ceriani, who played his alter ego 'Aldo': 'In the midst of the last few days' brouhaha I've not had a chance to talk to you properly. I do hope we can remedy this deficiency when the ship is finally launched and sailing.' The Teatro Carignano was packed, with a large number of deportees and young people in the foyer. Levi slipped into a private box in the circle with his wife and tried to keep well back in the shadows. He was so nervous, reportedly, that he sat 'curled up with his hands over his ears'. In the event the public liked the sinewy, stripped-down production. For the finale the actors advanced slowly towards the audience, reciting, 'You who live safely in your warm houses . . . consider if this is a man.' Then the lights dimmed and after a long silence there was applause followed by a standing ovation. To Levi's immense satisfaction, *If This is a Man* later travelled to most northern Italian cities and, by popular request, returned to be performed in Turin from 13 December to 4 January 1967.

More than fifteen reviews appeared in various newspapers and periodicals. Most of the critics were indifferent: on stage *If This is a Man* was a pale shadow of the book, the lines sounded alternately too 'false' or too 'horrific'. Einaudi published the script anyway, which was ignored by the critics. Only in the Soviet Union did the slim little volume pick up favourable notices. Levi had written an authentic *documentalnaya povest* –

'documentary account' – whose multi-national, multi-lingual cast would serve as a reminder of the 'international nature of anti-Fascism' (a typical Brezhnev-era observation, this).

The play had not been eulogised, however, and neither was Levi's third book. *Natural Histories* was 'frivolous', according to most Italian critics, who agreed that the author was a better memoirist than fantasist. One Einaudi editor (Carlo Fruttero) put it unkindly: 'It was as if after *Macbeth* Shakespeare had written only fantasy bagatelles, pleasurable little *pièces*.' Try as they might, the reviewers could not reconcile the two halves of Levi's literary output – the fabulist, the war chronicler – and concluded that there must be something of Jekyll and Hyde in him. In truth, Levi did all he could to encourage this image of himself as a dual personality. In the book's most exquisite fable, 'Quaestio de Centauris' ('An Official Investigation into the Centaurs'), he imagines himself as a 260-year-old half man, half horse. This equine whimsy marks the beginning of an enduring, even obsessive attempt on Levi's part to present himself as two halves or twin poles. Levi was not the only Italian literary figure engaged in two careers, but he alone tried to create a grand personal mythology out of this cloven state; in countless interviews he remarked on the tension in his life between the factory and the typewriter, writing and the family. (To my knowledge, the only other contemporary figure who compared himself to a centaur was Jacques Tati, the inventor of the screen comic Monsieur Hulot.) Interestingly, centaurs themselves have dual personalities: on the one hand, wise teachers; on the other, lustful, drunken womanisers. Perhaps Levi wished to identify with the side of the half man, half horse that he was not. Though *Natural Histories* was indifferently received, Levi could be proud of his achievement. In 1960s Italy most literature still was unashamedly *casalingo* – rooted in domestic concerns – but Levi's minimalist fantasies of biology and evolution were anything but parochial. He wrote them long before Italo Calvino's own very similar fables about the origins of Planet Earth, *Cosmicomics*. Thus Calvino signed a copy of that book to 'Primo Levi, who travelled down this path before me.'

EIGHTEEN

'On the other side of the barbed-wire fence'
1966–8

I

By the end of 1966 Levi had a new correspondent whom he longed to meet. Hety Schmitt-Maas was a middle-aged German woman who lived and worked in Wiesbaden. Her ex-husband had been a chemist for I. G. Farben. Schmitt-Maas's correspondence to Levi became a full one; most months she fired off a dozen or so missives to him, some very lengthy, all of which she typed with great speed and gusto. From the outset, she told Levi of her mission to 'understand' the Nazi past, and that she was prepared to move mountains to have *Ist das ein Mensch?* read widely in Germany. She called that book '*Pflichtlektüre*' – 'compulsory reading': every German home should have a copy. Many Germans, in their excessive self-flagellation, had turned national guilt into a virtue, but Schmitt-Maas was not like that. Her first letter to Levi, on 18 October 1966, radiated a terrific candour and intelligence. 'You will never really be able to understand the Germans, even we Germans do not understand ourselves.' This letter marked a new epoch for Levi – the start of an extraordinary sixteen-year correspondence – though he little suspected it when he replied on 5 November 1966:

> Yes, even today I find it hard to understand the Germans. *Ist das ein Mensch?* had the echo in Germany that I had hoped for, but I do believe it came from the very Germans who least needed to read it. The innocent, not the guilty, repent: it's absurd – it's so human.

Levi wanted to correspond in Italian, but the language defeated Schmitt-Maas, so he switched to German, then to English ('a wonderfully flexible language'); then to French, and back again to German. Their polyglot correspondence was 'a real mess!' declared Levi, though it was nothing of the sort. Schmitt-Maas's second letter to Levi began '*Sehr geehrter* [Most Honoured – a very formal greeting] Herr Dr Levi'. She seemed to want to unburden herself of guilt: 'The only consolation for those of us who were on the other side of the barbed-wire fence is to know that people like you were able to start new lives after all.' Hety's restless mission to understand Germany had been sparked, she told Levi, by the strange behaviour of Reinhard Heidebroek, an I. G. Farben colleague of her ex-husband. Had Heidebroek done something 'terrible', Schmitt-Maas wondered? In 1941 when he was transferred to Auschwitz (as a benzene synthesis expert), he did not know that a death-camp was situated there. 'No one had any idea of what happened in Auschwitz,' Schmitt-Maas explained to Levi. With his fiancée, Renata Mündel, he left for Poland: he was the son of the rector of Darmstadt university, she was the daughter of the *Bürgermeister* of Konstanz. This refined, patrician couple were to be devastated by Auschwitz, and on their return to Konstanz in the summer of 1943 they seemed to Hety Schmitt-Maas to be unusually quiet. Reinhard began to drink heavily and play Schubert sonatas incoherently on his Leipzig grand. Renata, a Red Cross nurse, said nothing to Schmitt-Maas of what she had seen 'down there'. After the war, when Schmitt-Maas again questioned Engineer Heidebroek about Auschwitz, he snapped at her: '*Auschwitz ist ein KZ!*' 'Auschwitz is a concentration camp!' Then he fell silent. And in Heidebroek's impotent silence Levi thought he could detect many of post-war Germany's problems. After the war Germans like Heidebroek, who had remained compliantly behind Hitler's government to the end, were unable to distance themselves from the Nazi era. In Italy it was different. Italians could put the memory of Mussolini's era behind them with a good conscience, as there had been widespread mobilisation in the Resistance; however, only 2 per cent of the adult German population had been active at any level in the anti-Nazi struggle. On 10 December Levi wrote to thank Schmitt-Maas for her information on Heidebroek:

> You wrote: 'No one had any idea of what happened in Auschwitz'; but that was only (or principally) the case because in the Nazi period countless 'Heidebroeks' saw, heard, found out and remained silent. One cannot demand heroic deeds from everyone, but not to tell a friend what evil, indeed what profoundly disturbing things one saw in the concentration camp or on the construction site, can, in my view, only be explained in one way: by a lack of courage of one's convictions that the Nazi terror certainly aggravated, but could not have created out of nothing.

Levi went on:

> You say that Reinhard Heidebroek still does not care for
> questions; I have visited Germany often since the war and met
> many Germans who have behaved like that. I think this indicates
> that the longing for purification and release from the Nazi
> inheritance is not very widespread in Germany.

Levi understood that his unseen correspondent was a decent, ordinary
German with moral struggles of her own. Yet she must have contacts in the
former I. G. Farben. With her help, perhaps he could track down the
Auschwitz chemists whom he had dreamed all these years of confronting.
He asked her:

> Would it be possible to find out from Heidebroek if he had known
> the following Buna experts, and what became of them: Dr
> Pannwitz, Dr Probst, Dr Hagen, Dr Engineer Mayer (or Meyer)?
> They were employed in the Polymerisation Dept. of Buna-
> Monovitz; I wrote about Dr Pannwitz in my book; the last-named
> [Meyer] behaved *particularly well* towards us, given the
> circumstances.

This brief letter turned out to be one of the most important of Levi's life.

2

Meanwhile, there were disagreeable matters to be faced at work. Rico Accati
had promoted Levi from SIVA technical director to general manager.
When Levi protested that he was happy where he was, Accati's secretary
Franca Tambini nudged him under the table. 'Bloody fool!' she thought.
'What about your pay rise?' Reluctantly Levi accepted his promotion,
though it was immediately apparent that he was not cut out for it. Day and
night at all hours he had to be near a telephone in case of emergencies. One
evening he was in a cinema in Turin when the projectionist interrupted the
film with the announcement: 'Is there a Dr Primo Levi here?' Water had
flooded SIVA's storage and pumping facilities, creating an electrocution
hazard. Now Levi knew the sense of inconvenience that goes with authority.
His responsibilities weighed down on him and he said he felt 'closer to
neurosis' than at any time after Auschwitz. Above all he hated dealing with
worker complaints: any talk of wages was especially distasteful to him.
Whenever Levi could, he asked his deputy, Francesco Cordero (himself a

meek, diminutive man), to liaise with the workers on such unsavoury matters. Levi's diffidence created a bad impression on the staff. As one middle manager commented to me: 'Levi had no get-up-and-go, no ambition whatever. All he cared for was his writing – the rest was poetry to him.' So began eight increasingly stressful years of bureaucratic and administrative grind. To top all this, Levi's son Renzo had had his tonsils out, and the tonsillectomy left the nine-year-old tearful at night. Then came sad news for Levi's wife Lucia. On 7 January 1967 her father Giuseppe Morpurgo died, not quite eighty.

Within a month Hety Schmitt-Maas had found the information Levi was looking for, and on 24 January 1967 she wrote to him from Wiesbaden:

> Dr Pannwitz is dead. Dr Probst disappeared (or at least nobody has heard of him since). Dr Hagen was a terrible Nazi (nobody knows what became of him). If you need to contact *Dr Engineer Meyer* I can get his address for you . . .

Levi quaked. The man was still alive. He could scarcely view Meyer as representative of the Auschwitz butchers, as he had issued him with leather shoes and shown him other kindnesses. Yet Meyer was also a German, one of *those* Germans. Should Levi seek him out? He expressed an interest in contacting Meyer. And by the end of February, with Hety's compliments, Meyer had a copy of *Ist das ein Mensch?* along with Levi's address in Turin.

Meanwhile Reinhard Heidebroek, alcoholic and lachrymose, having read *If This is a Man*, had the gall to defend Pannwitz's contemptuous treatment of Levi in the 'Chemical Examination' chapter. Apparently all I. G. Farben staff had been briefed that Auschwitz prisoners – Jews and non-alike Jews – had 'criminal records'. Therefore how could Pannwitz possibly have shown Levi respect? On hearing this exculpation Levi was furious and wrote to Hety:

> Pannwitz was neither inexperienced nor ignorant. He saw the Jewish star stitched to our shirt fronts, and he knew full well what it meant to be called 'Levi' . . . Anyway I don't look like a criminal (unless of course Pannwitz thought all Jews by definition are criminal).

In these first cold months of 1967 the exchange of letters between Levi and Hety Schmitt-Maas brought a special energy into Primo's life. Until now his attitude to post-war Germany had been one, he said, of 'mistrustful good will'. But his attitude changed as he got to know more of Hety's extraordinary background. A Catholic divorcee, she was born in 1918 to an exemplary anti-Nazi family: when Hitler came to power her liberal-minded father had lost his teaching post. Following his stern example, Hety refused to join the Nazi BDM (Association of German Girls) and was expelled from school. She could never forget the day her family's Jewish doctor, in despair at the Goebbels persecution, had committed suicide after *Kristallnacht*. When she settled in Wiesbaden in 1959 to work for the Ministry of Culture she began to investigate seriously what she called the entire '*Komplex*' of Nazism. But first she divorced her husband Bernhard Schmitt who, during the war, had forbidden Hety to bring her father food in Dachau prison as he did not want to imperil his career with I. G. Farben.

From her office in Wiesbaden, Hety put survivors in touch with each other, creating an ever-expanding network of correspondence among them. In this way she hoped to counter Himmler's cynical pledge that the destruction of European Jewry would be an 'unwritten page of glory'. Her letters were undisciplined and expansive, but were much treasured (and carefully collected) by those who received them, including, later, Albert Speer. By Hety's admission her need to write was overwhelming and she wrote as though she was thinking aloud, the spontaneous sentences flowing from her fingertips. She was aware of how trying her attentions could be, and right from the start she apologised to Levi for her '*permanente Korrespondenz*'. The Austrian survivor and historian of the camps, Hermann Langbein, had endured Hety's correspondence for an entire year now and yet 'he *still* answers me – I find this most heroic', said Hety.

3

While Levi waited anxiously for Ferdinand Meyer to contact him, his literary standing in Italy was consolidated when, against all expectations, *Natural Histories* won the envied Bagutta Prize. The award was dispensed amid great pomp in Milan's famous Ristorante Bagutta. Confused and stunned by the applause, Levi managed a few embarrassed words before well-wishers crowded his table to shake his hand. The accolades continued as the year advanced. After forty days on stage in Turin, *If This is a Man* was awarded the St Vincent Prize for 'best play' of 1966–7. Though Levi was happy for his work to be applauded, he kept a studiously low profile. SIVA's new telephonist, Carmen Franchi, took an entire year to realise who Levi was. Each day she had sat next to him in the factory canteen, but 'he never let on that he was *that* Primo Levi'.

Now a series of factory incidents undermined Levi's fragile confidence as manager. His attempt to synthesise trimelitic anyhydride (an AMOCO patent) went disastrously wrong when pressurised oxygen combusted and blew out the laboratory windows. Flames licked the workbench while the cleaner Orsolina Ferrero wailed fearfully 'like an ambulance'. Levi's calm was impressive as he shut the laboratory doors and unhooked the fire extinguisher. Perhaps it was the same calm that had helped him survive the camp. From that day on, Levi was extra-vigilant in the laboratory, though he was not always so calm. When Renato Portesi, a newcomer to SIVA, innocently dissolved aspirin in a beakerful of water, Levi ran over to him shouting: 'Don't do it, Portesi!' He was convinced that the easy-going Portesi was about to swallow poison.

Portesi, an economics postgraduate, had been working at SIVA since the spring of 1965 and was overwhelmed by Levi. He admired his ironic deadpan humour and loved to discuss literature with him. Levi said he agreed with those who held the view that Prince Fabrizio's deathbed scene in the Sicilian novel *The Leopard* is 'the best death in Italian literature'. They ate Piedmontese specialities (including tripe and frogs' legs) in 'Il Muletto' near the factory; and during these meals Portesi noted that Levi's hands 'trembled' when he started on the subject of Auschwitz, and sometimes he stared distractedly at his plate. Levi had grown very fond of Portesi, who was in his early thirties, and joshed him for his idealistic Communism. A reserved person, he suffered Levi's criticisms of the Soviet Union in silence. Portesi's relation to Levi in many ways recalled the friendships Primo had had earlier with adoring schoolfriends such as Mario Piacenza, where Levi was the instructor, and Piacenza the uninitiated pupil. Above all Portesi loved to watch Levi at work in the laboratory. 'Primo insisted on making his own glassware, bending the tubes over a Bunsen,' he recalled. This artisan craftsmanship was considered eccentric at a time when the most complex chemistry apparatus could be assembled ready-made from kits. But Levi was an 'odd duck', said Portesi, and did things his own way.

One day, Portesi made a joke about the Germans that Levi found distasteful but amusing. On the threshold of death a sinner has to choose between an Italian-run hell and a German-run hell. In both infernos he can expect the same treatment – nailed to a cross by devils, doused in boiling oil. After a moment's hesitation the sinner opts for the Italian hell. Why? 'Because the Italian devils often run out of nails, or the nails go missing, and the oil never arrives on time.' Levi said the joke was an advert for Italian incompetence as well as Italian humanity, and that the two were not always 'unconnected'. Not that Levi approved of all Portesi's jokes. When Portesi filled a whisky bottle with tea, and passed it round the SIVA boardroom,

Levi did not laugh at all. 'He didn't like humour at other people's expense,' Portesi recalled.

4

Ferdinand Meyer's first letter to Levi on 2 March 1967, carried an elegant Heidelberg letterhead and was written in plain unadorned German. Meyer began by thanking Levi for the 'trouble' he had taken in tracking him down after twenty long years. 'I have read your book with much sympathy and felt a little satisfaction that for you the days in the laboratory [with me] were a slight relief.' He went on:

> I was filled with joy that you escaped the hell of Auschwitz and, as if by a miracle, were able to return to your family. I believe that a meeting in person would be both useful and essential, for the purpose of overcoming the terrible past. I just want to say that I have often thought of you as well as of your companions in all that suffering. Where are the following laboratory prisoners: Herr Brackier, Herr Kandel, the physicist Dr Goldbaum of Breslau?

Levi was amazed first of all that Meyer had remembered the prisoners' names: so they were not just numbers. At the same time he was wary. The frequent admonishments in West Germany to 'mourn and master the past' and to do 'the labour of mourning' (*Trauerarbeit*) struck Levi as pietistic and hollow. Meyer, with his talk of Overcoming, was adopting platitudes. Levi replied to him in Italian (his subsequent correspondence was in French):

> It is very important, and also welcome, for me to be able to address you. First of all because (as I am sure Mrs Hety Schmitt-Maas has already told you or written to you) I have kept a good memory of you, etched against a background where good memories were rare; and second, because I too think that any civilised man must achieve a '*Bewältigung*' – an Overcoming – of the past. Yet I cannot pretend that I am writing to you with an easy conscience; this is the first time that I have been able to communicate with someone who was on the other side of the fence, even if he was there against his will, as I believe you were, or as it seems I should understand from your letter.

Levi agreed that an eventual meeting would be 'essential', but for the moment he preferred to ask Meyer three specific questions by letter. First,

326

was his description of Pannwitz in *If This is a Man* 'valid'? (Hety's ex-husband had judged it outrageously prejudicial: 'And the Jews complain that *we* are prejudiced against *them!*') Second, did Meyer know under what circumstances I. G. Farben had taken on Jewish slave labour at Auschwitz? Third, what – if anything – had Meyer known of the Birkenau crematoria? Levi added that their 'epistolary encounter' was an 'unexpected and extraordinary gift of destiny' and that 'only good' could come of it.

When Meyer's reply came three weeks later, on 5 April, it was eight pages long and overflowed with emotions that must have embarrassed Levi as much as they touched him:

> The object of your life, which has been shaped by Auschwitz, is to bear witness to the horror of the crimes of which men are capable. Outraged, you castigate the icy coldness of their hearts, the narrowness of their enslaved spirit, their wicked presumption in judging other men, races and peoples.

The verbal inflation continued:

> Your testimony is more than just a lament over the appalling extent of the sacrifice . . . You have proclaimed to the world for all time that there really were *Menschen* at the edge of darkness. I want to thank you most sincerely for this testimony, and I am sure that many people will feel the way I do.

This was a very cramped, buttoned-up man, whose emotions emerged in clumsy, far-fetched flattery. Meyer's life-story, as he went on here to relate it to Levi, was typical of many young Germans of the 1930s. 'Originally carried away by the general enthusiasm for the regime, after Hitler came to power in 1933 I joined the National Socialist students' association.' This group was absorbed into the Storm-Troopers or SA (the prototype SS), but Meyer managed to leave on his 'own application and by way of a personal discharge decree'. At the outbreak of war he served as a 'simple private' in an anti-aircraft unit in Duisburg. It was there that he experienced his first stirrings of 'shame and outrage' at the war's 'senseless destruction'. In May 1944 he was relieved to be seconded from active service to work in Auschwitz for BASF. Meyer had no 'inkling' then of where Auschwitz was situated, or of the 'terrible things' that went on there. Yet this would suppose a level of ignorance (or unworldliness) in him that is hard to credit. Renata Heidebroek, Reinhard Heidebroek's widow, told me in 1994: 'When my husband and I were transferred to Auschwitz for a second time – that is, in 1943 – all of us Germans knew there was a *Todeslager* [death-camp] out there in the east.'

Meyer did not comment to Levi on his depiction of Pannwitz, as Levi had asked, but wrote instead:

> I certainly do not want to play down his guilt. There is not just one 'marked man', Dr Pannwitz, but many . . . There are all those unscrupulous people who will say Yes, who unhesitatingly, coldly and without emotion carry out every order against their fellow men.

Meyer added that he had known nothing of Pannwitz's cruel 'state exam' to ascertain Levi's professional abilities in Auschwitz. Meyer claimed it was he who had chosen the Jewish prisoner-specialists Kandel, Brackier, Gold-baum and Levi to work in the warm life-saving laboratory. In consequence Meyer and Levi had had a relationship almost of 'friendship between equals', the German said. Meyer then recalled the episode when Levi had accidentally broken some glassware:

> I cannot forget what then appeared to be your hopeless dejection. When telling my wife and children about my time in Auschwitz I have often stressed that particular encounter with you. From that day on I became attached to you. I no longer remember what privileges I obtained for you, but that encounter with you made me appreciate that I had met a man who still had the strength to rise above the wretched and hopeless routine of that life. Time and again, when discussing scientific problems with you I realised what precious human values were being brutally destroyed by human beings, remorselessly, in cold blood and senselessly.

Neither did Meyer answer Levi's question about the Birkenau crematoria. Instead he offered this self-deceit: 'It was well known that there was medical attention at Birkenau, even an X-ray department, and that every effort had been made to keep alive the few inmates of the camp who were still fit for work.' Offensively, Meyer added: 'Today I think that the order to show no pity to the Jews was a camouflage [*eine Tarnung*]. At least during my short stay at Auschwitz I was not aware of any incident aimed at exterminating the Jews.' And with these delusions Meyer was able to draw a veil over the horrors of which he claimed he had been 'unaware'.

But there was a PS to this letter: 'As I have your picture on the back of *Ist das ein Mensch?* I am enclosing a picture of myself. When we met in

Auschwitz I was 36 years old.' A studio portrait showed a large, benign-looking man, ten years older than Levi, striking a consciously pensive pose. (Meyer had a philosophy as well as a chemistry degree from Cologne University.) Again he stressed to Levi how 'anxious' he was to meet him, 'either here in Germany or perhaps in the autumn in Italy'. Oddly, since he wanted Levi's sympathy, Meyer did not mention that he had grown up an orphan; his father had died when he was two, his mother when he was ten.

What Levi did not know, and never would know, was that Meyer had largely rehashed this letter from the 'Life Book' he had begun for his daughter Cordula in 1960. In more than thirty pages of spidery handwriting, Meyer poured out his wartime ordeal of hunger and defeat. The whole is padded with quotations from Kant and Thomas Aquinas and is decidedly verbose. Yet Meyer was genuinely troubled by what he called the Jews' 'sad fate' and is full of self-doubting despondency at the role he had played in Auschwitz as a chemist. From the age of five Cordula had to listen to her father's tortured self-reproaches, and in her late twenties she became very ill – as a result, she believed, of her father's talk. It was then that she married a German Jew, Lothar Blossfeld, who was related to Anne Frank. Cordula vouched for her father's high regard for Levi: 'He spoke to me constantly of Levi and all his life he hoped he was still alive.'

It was clear to Levi, from reading his letter, that Meyer had found something in *If This is a Man* that was not there: Christian forgiveness. 'It seems to me that you, Dr Levi, have achieved a leap of faith in *If This is a Man.*' Meaning? Meaning that Levi had travelled from Judaism to the Christian injunction to love one's enemies. Meyer was not the only one to misconstrue Levi in this way. In a letter to Hety Schmitt-Maas, the Austrian philosopher and Auschwitz survivor Jean Améry disapprovingly referred to Levi as 'a forgiver'. Améry explained what he meant: 'Unlike Levi, I have absolutely no sympathy for men like Meyer who were part of the I. G. Farben Auschwitz leading personnel [*Führungspersonal*].' Meyer and Améry were wrong about Levi. Though Levi wanted justice, and the guilty to be judged, he never forgave the crimes committed, or those who committed them.

5

Hety Schmitt-Maas declared that she been 'strangely touched' by Meyer's attempts to face his past and recover his spiritual bearing. She did not know that he was a member of the German 'Knights of the Holy Tomb of Jerusalem' Catholic charity, which indulged in good works in Israel. By building schools in the Promised Land they hoped to renovate themselves morally. 'And strange as it may seem,' Hety told Levi in her slightly bossy way, 'you may be the very person to help Meyer.' She advised him not to reply to his letter 'in full' until they had met. 'Surely it would be better to talk first?'

Levi appeared to agree with her: 'The ponderous and breath-taking enterprise of Overcoming and Coping with the Past can best be achieved verbally,' he wrote to Hety, 'and if possible in your presence. Indeed, I feel that you are the ideal interpreter for this uncommon sort of affair.' There is no doubt that Levi felt a measure of sympathy for Meyer. He was 'not particularly courageous' but at the same time he was 'substantially unspoiled by the Nazi plague', and therefore open to human contact and colloquy.

Nevertheless Levi took five long weeks to reply to his angst-ridden overseer. And when he did write to Meyer – 13 May 1967 – the tone was less mollient. 'I would like to help you come to terms with your past but I doubt that I am able.' Levi went on to suggest to Meyer, albeit tactfully, that he had shown no sign in his correspondence so far of contrition. But, as he did not want to hurt Meyer's feelings, he added:

> No, I did not know that you were responsible for securing my place in the Laboratory, and consequently, in some measure, for saving my life. It will hardly do that I 'thank' you for it; the word sounds rather foolish and rhetorical in the context.

A meeting was tentatively arranged for the autumn of 1967. 'It would certainly be more comfortable to pursue our discussion *viva voce*,' Levi agreed. Yet he did not want to meet Meyer: the encounter might only renew his old feelings of slavish abasement. Anyway the German might cause a scene, for Levi suspected that Meyer was looking for absolution, but that was an unreasonable Christian burden on Jewish shoulders, indeed on anyone's shoulders. Levi did not want the responsibility – did not feel it was his place – to grant Meyer forgiveness.

In June, Hety met Meyer for the first time. The historian Hermann Langbein had wanted to interview Meyer for a book he was writing, *Humankind in Auschwitz*, and Hety had asked to sit in on their conversation. Meyer made a favourable impression on her. He was 'a very sympathetic and soft-hearted man [*sympathischen und weichherzigen Menschen*]', though Langbein judged him a spineless grey creature. Hety reported her impressions to Levi, and on 17 June Levi wrote to thank her for them:

Your description [of Meyer] was very precise and amusing, and worthy of the potential writer that you are. He is honest, cordial, fundamentally good-hearted, and, after two World Wars and the menace of a third, still bound to the academic and rhetorical patterns of 40 years ago. In fact, this is precisely the man one recognises in the two letters he wrote to me. However, I think that Langbein was wrong: such a man is not to be expected to resist actively, nor to commit sabotage; after all, not everybody is born a hero. If everybody in the world was like Dr Meyer, life would be tolerable, though a little dull.

In a subsequent letter, Meyer tried to entice Levi to Germany with an invitation to visit BASF. He worked there as a condensation specialist in the laboratory where Carl Bosch (a known anti-Nazi) had famously synthesised ammonia. Meyer concluded his letter 'With friendly greetings and a sincere sense of obligation', but he followed this with an ungainly attempt to flatter Levi: 'I am not the only one who recognises your literary talent.'

6

Later that month Levi was staying in an old Savoy castle deep in the Piedmontese countryside. He loved it from the first. The property had been converted into a hotel, and the garden, with its high, unkempt hedges, was a good place to drink and chat. The genial, chain-smoking author Nuto Revelli had been coming to Verduno Castle for fifteen years with friends, and this summer he invited Levi to join them. Levi liked Verduno so much that he returned there every June for the rest of his life. The castle helped to take him out of his dejected moods and away from domestic worries. Piero Femore (who had lost an arm) was the owner of Turin's 'Campus' bookshop in Piazza Carlo Felice. Another regular was the tall, wiry wine merchant and ex-partisan Bartolo Mascarello. Mascarello still produces the finest Barolo red in Piedmont and he sold it to Fiat's Gianni Agnelli, Italo Calvino, and now to Levi, who liked to drink it with game. Though Levi could be prickly towards those he disliked, Mascarello's impression was one of dignified modesty and sparkling good humour: 'Primo was a sort of owl, you know, extremely intelligent and observant – but at the same time apparently quite ordinary. Primo had a kind face, laughing eyes, extraordinary eyes – penetrating and sagacious. He struck me then and much later as *un uomo allegro*, a happy man. He was very measured but not in an aristocratic way, in a *human* way.'

*

On 5 June, while Levi was in Verduno Castle, the Middle East was in turmoil when Israel declared war on the Arab world. Like most Jews at this dangerous hour, Levi was filled with anguish; he believed that his own people stood on the brink of a second catastrophe within a quarter-century. Later in the synagogue he defended Israel: 'This land of martyrs and survivors must not be destroyed.' Egypt's President Nasser, seeming to goad Israel to war, had moved his troops into Sinai on the Israeli border, and Israel had retaliated. Levi organised a fund-raising for Israel at SIVA and was photographed for *La Stampa* donating blood. Most civilised Italians – Jews and non-Jews alike – were on Israel's side at this stage. President Nasser had openly proclaimed the elimination of Jews (and Christians) as part of his ideology.

In six days (the famous Six Day War) Israel defeated three Arab armies, tripled the size of territory under its control and occupied the Gaza Strip. Levi had to confess to Hety that his dealings with Ferdinand Meyer (what he called 'these Auschwitz remnants and problems') had paled to insignificance beside the June War. Israel's triumph was wonderfully uplifting for him and the Jewish world. But Levi was sad to see the Jewish state decline from a model-nation into a country like any other, 'good at fighting and quarrelling, inclined to national pride'. Whatever its future, Israel was no longer the Promised Land of peace and honey he had once taken it to be:

> Perhaps such lands do not exist on earth: but Israel, from its beginning, had accustomed us to such miracles that we just hoped it could perform the greatest, the only real miracle, the one of establishing a permanent peace with its neighbours.

As the days went by, Levi was increasingly unhappy with Israel's aggression and national self-absorption. On 10 June, with twenty-two other Turin Jews, he signed a manifesto in the leftist journal *Il Ponte* calling for urgent dialogue between Jews and Arabs. The signatories deplored the rightward swing of the Jewish Diaspora (no doubt aggravated by the Kremlin's pro-Arab stance in the June conflict) and urged Jews to maintain their 'time-honoured' links to Socialism.

On 17 June Oscar Pinkus, a Polish-born Jewish engineer and author living in America, came to see Levi in Turin. In October 1945, at the Austrian frontier, Pinkus had stowed away on the same Italian repatriation train that Levi described at the end of *The Truce* (Pinkus had checked the dates). Struck by their 'near collision', Pinkus wrote to Levi care of Einaudi. Levi was intrigued by this man whose post-war wanderings seemed to parallel his own, and now at last the survivors met. They spent the day at 75 Corso Re Umberto talking, reminiscing and exchanging books. Of course there was talk of the Arab–Israeli conflict, which had then just ended; Levi agreed with Pinkus that Israel's destruction would have been a 'frightful tragedy', but he did not share Pinkus's pro-Israeli triumphalism or faith in Israeli–American relations. To show goodwill he made Pinkus a present of a delicate copper-wire leaf he had sculpted from SIVA wire.

7

In late July 1967, as thousands of Palestinian refugees fled to Jordan and the Lebanon, Turin suffered a ferocious heatwave. The banks of the Po were parched, the city was under a petrol-fume haze. To escape the stifling city Levi took his family into the cool mountains, though not his daughter Lisa, who stayed behind in Turin to celebrate passing her school-leaving exams. With a group of classmates she contributed to the intellectual magazine, *Lo Zibaldone* (The Hotchpotch, after the poet Leopardi's notebook of the same name), which upheld the wartime Resistance values of rebellion and dissent. With the barricades of 1968 less than a year away, to be the child of an ex-partisan had cachet. That summer Lisa protested with friends against the US bombing of Vietnam.

As the heat lifted, the Levis moved into their new holiday flat in Pietra Ligure on the Italian Riviera, not far from Monaco. Levi had bought it as an investment for his children rather than for himself. (He disliked the mass August holidays when the beaches filled with noisy bathers.) To pass the time he made copper sculptures, including one of a giant spider, which he attached to the flat's balcony, apparently to wean him from his arachnophobia. Two packages arrived at Pietra Ligure, both of them expected. The first was from Oscar Pinkus, and contained the typescript of his marvellous autobiography, *A Choice of Masks*. Levi read it with intense interest, as Pinkus had studied engineering in Turin in 1947; they had friends in common at the student digs on Corso Moncalieri, and probably Levi had passed him on the stairs. Levi was always receptive to first-hand accounts of the war by unknown authors. Captivated by the book's descriptions of post-war Turin, he wrote to thank Pinkus for his efforts on 'behalf of all us Turinese', and offered to try to place the manuscript with Einaudi.

The second package was from Hety Schmitt-Maas, and contained paperback editions of Günter Grass and a batch of magazine articles to help Levi with his German. He and Hety had been corresponding for ten months, and Levi found her letters invigorating. They gave him a sense of sharing in the intellectual life of post-war Germany, of being part of a broad community of like-minded writers and survivors, which gave him ideas for future books. Hety's first letters to Levi had been succinct and carefully worded but now they were often five pages long and contained personal disclosures about family and private life. Furious rows had erupted between Hety and her children, who did not want to listen to her talk of Nazism. Marianne Felsche, Hety's daughter, today speaks of a 'very difficult and obsessive woman' who would bring books on Treblinka and Auschwitz to children's parties in case she got bored. 'Some things were too important for my mother, to dance attendance on a nursery tea.'

Levi had asked Hety to correct his written German, which he called a 'strange, hyperborean language', but she went further than that. She began to send Levi so many German books and clippings that they piled up at his end unread. The news clippings, especially, were not always welcome: 'As you certainly know,' he wrote to Hety, 'it is laborious for a foreigner to understand them: they contain hints and quotations which are familiar to the native reader, but *real puzzles for an alien.*' Levi began to make his replies more skimpy ('Don't be cross with me'), but this did not abate Hety's postal barrage. One day she sent him a copy of Saint-Exupéry's *Le Petit Prince,* which Levi dutifully said he had enjoyed reading. ('I am glad that you liked it – actually I sent it for your daughter.') When Hety heard that Levi's daughter Lisa was learning German, she invited her to stay in Wiesbaden.

Hety could be exasperating, but she had come to fill a void in Levi's life. Since childhood, friends had been important to Levi, but in recent years, for various reasons, his social life had diminished. Some friends had become involved in 'late love-affairs' (in 1964 Italo Calvino had married the blue-eyed Argentine, Esther Singer), or else they had left Turin. Others still had 'atrophied' into middle age. Tina Rieser's salon, once so lively, had depleted now that many of its associates were dead. In Hety, however, Levi had found a potential soulmate; their correspondence provided him with a refuge, a safe place to inhabit, when his home life became unmanageable. There may have been an element, too, of flirtation, even if chaste.

In September 1967 Levi arranged to meet Hety while he was in Germany on business with Rico Accati. First, however, they called on Emil Davidovic, the 'modernist rabbi' Mendi of *If This is a Man.* Davidovic had survived the death-march and was now living in Dortmund with his wife Chaja and three teenage children. Over coffee Davidovic corrected certain 'errors' about himself in Levi's book. He was not a Slovak, but a Czech; neither had he been a partisan or a lawyer, but he had studied philosophy at

Brun (now Brno) in Czechoslovakia. Afterwards, the survivors discussed old times and the fate of *Lager* comrades. Driving south to Wiesbaden, the anticipation intensified for Levi as he approached the Klarenthal suburb where Hety lived with her mother. Hety was watching from the window of her flat when a car with Italian number plates pulled up. '*Guten Abend!*' Levi greeted her. During their correspondence they had not exchanged photographs, and Levi had expected Hety to look rather intense. Instead here was a plain, pale-faced woman in glasses. The meeting was a wild success. Accati was on his best behaviour and Hety did not find him in the least 'disagreeable', as Levi had warned she might. Instead Accati was an expansive, beaming '*Charmeur*', said Hety; she could not understand why Levi had snidely compared him to Donald Duck's irascible uncle, Scrooge McDuck, a red-faced, stick-wielding fellow. Scrooge McDuck? Hety's mother thought Accati resembled the handsome German movie star O. E. Hasse.

Levi was the real surprise for Hety. Instead of the 'tormented', 'worn-down' man whom Hety had expected from his photograph on *Ist das ein Mensch?* Levi was 'open', 'relaxed' and even 'blooming'. More, he seemed to emanate '*Strahlkraft*' – 'radiance' or 'charisma'. Hety was not one for niceties – she could be bullish – and on a whim during the visit she decided to telephone Ferdinand Meyer. Levi's anxiety must have been plain. What was said between him and Meyer on the phone that day is not known but afterwards Levi confessed to Hety a great fear of meeting his Auschwitz overseer: '*Ich habe wirklich Angst* [I'm really scared].' Others in Hety's circle were not in the least surprised by Levi's reluctance. Hety had circulated the Levi–Meyer correspondence among her contacts, one of whom was the Austrian-born philosopher Jean Améry. Meyer's letters to Levi, said Améry, were exercises in lachrymose 'soul striptease', and brimful of 'metaphysical *Schmus* – baby pap'.

With difficulty Levi put Meyer out of mind. Returning home to Turin on 12 or 13 September, he was startled to hear the German's voice on the phone again. This time it sounded laboured and agitated. Meyer did not tell Levi that he was dying, but now he made no attempt to conceal his urgent need to meet. After a moment's hesitation Levi said he was sorry, he was not ready to see him; their correspondence would first have to 'ripen'.

As Levi continued to correspond with Hety Schmitt-Maas through 1967, Lucia began to feel increasingly excluded. Initially Levi had shared with her the extraordinary news that Hety's letters had brought of Ferdinand Meyer. But his correspondence was secretive; and now it had a guilty edge. In the six days between 2–8 November Levi wrote Hety a long letter that

335

contained painful revelations. The parlous state of his marriage had been simmering for years, but now for some reason he needed to confess it. The letter, written at SIVA during the siesta hours and in English, is the most explicit record we have of Levi's domestic unhappiness and, at the same time, of his enduring affection for Lucia. In the voice of a hurt child he complained to Hety that Lucia 'almost never accompanies me to parties or on travels, and silently discourages me from them'. He wanted to travel and enjoy it – he was famous now in Italy – but Lucia held him back. Or did she? Levi was despondent when he wrote this letter, and much of what he had to say about his wife was tainted by the warped outlook caused by his mood. When Levi married her, he went on, Lucia had been a young innocent woman full of goodwill; over the years apparently she had turned into an overprotective, constraining spouse, an entrapment; and Lucia was fearful:

> She becomes nervous, diffident, in front of intellectuals, particularly if female: she generally judges them braggarts, hypocrites, selfish people; most typically, she interferes in my speaking with them, breaks up the conversations with aberrant, wild opinions (of which she is herself obviously ashamed), and contradicts me stubbornly in a sort of naive sabotage.

Lucia was frightened of the 'brilliant ones', Levi's cerebral women friends: Bianca Guidetti Serra, Ada Della Torre, Nicoletta Neri, Tina Rieser. Not that this tells us much about Lucia: many wives might dislike 'highbrow' women. Anyway Levi's wife was bound to feel excluded. As a survivor's spouse, she inevitably remained outside her husband's circle of Resistance and prison-camp companions. Yet at times Levi wondered if Lucia was able to be friendly with anyone at all. He had never managed to 'enter' into her 'confidence'; the only person with whom she was intimate was her mother. Lucia was not even close to her twin sister Gabriella. Levi admitted that his wife was 'only partly responsible' for this impasse. In fact, Lucia had reason to feel resentful. She had overseen the birth of *If This is a Man* and, to a lesser degree, *The Truce*, but who had acknowledged her contribution? The needy and dependent man she had married in 1947 had become a successful writer: Lucia was no longer useful to him in the way she had been. Her resentment was further aggravated by the feeling that Levi had imprisoned her in 75 Corso Re Umberto. By now this uncomfortable domestic arrangement, where mother, son, wife and children all lived in the same flat, had persisted for two decades. And the stress it caused was often acute. After twenty years of marriage – some of them happy – Levi had to admit that his relationship with Lucia had gone wrong. Yet he conceded that she

336

was still his 'good and valiant' ally; her common sense was invaluable to him – he needed it – and he shared many of her opinions and tastes. They lived side-by-side amicably enough, but their creeping estrangement brought sadness into 75 Corso Re Umberto.

As an afterthought Levi added: 'I am resolved not to change anything in my relations with you, and I should ask you to do the same.' In other words, he was determined to continue his correspondence with Hety: by doing so, he was asserting his independence from Lucia. Once this letter was posted, Hety came to play a curious (and for her, delicious) role as counsellor to Levi, advising him (and even on one occasion inopportunely advising Lucia) on how to cope with his increasingly frequent emotional crises.

Lucia anyway had problems of her own. She was a volunteer teacher at a workers' evening school and came home late and exhausted after 10:00 pm. Among her pupils were some of the 60,000 southern migrants who had arrived in Turin earlier in the year. Though Lucia commended their willingness to learn, she was frustrated at home by her husband's self-absorbed and difficult behaviour. She did not know what went on behind his bleak silences. But Levi's mental health continued to be precarious – moving in peaks and troughs – for the next seven years until 1974. And as matters turned out, the bleak moods did not get any better; they got worse.

8

In the weeks before Christmas Levi received the upsetting news that Ferdinand Meyer had died. He had collapsed from a heart attack in the garden of his Heidelberg home, on 13 December, four days short of his sixtieth birthday. In his hands his daughter Cordula had found a copy of Thomas Aquinas's *Summa Theologica*. They buried him in Ziegelhausen cemetery in the white-and-red robes of his religious charity. On his tombstone was hewn the Latin inscription, 'God Wishes It.' Meyer's widow sent Levi a photograph of the grave which Levi said he found in 'rather lugubrious' German taste. Meyer's death had come as a wholly unexpected blow to him, and he was filled with pain and guilt that he had not agreed to meet him. 'Now it is too late, all is gone, for ever.' While Meyer had shut off a part of his conscience, he could not be accused of having no conscience at all. The humanity he had shown Levi at Auschwitz had been awkward, insufficient, guilt-ridden, yet it was still humanity. If anything, Meyer was a typical *tüchtiger-Deutsch* – an 'efficient German' with a specialist's tunnel vision. Because he viewed Auschwitz chiefly in terms of his special competence (synthetic-rubber manufacture) he was able to ignore the moral consequences of his work. Really Meyer was less infamous than inadequate.

After Meyer's sudden death, the year of 1967 ended on another dramatic note. Early on the morning of 31 December SIVA's concierge telephoned Levi to say that a tanker had overturned on the road outside: thirty-six tonnes of petroleum threatened to leak into the factory. At 5:00 am Turin was deserted as Levi sped to Settimo Torinese. When he arrived at the factory he found to his alarm that the fire brigade was trying to winch the tanker upright using wire hausers and a crane: if sparks flew, a fireball would consume SIVA. Levi suggested that they transfer the petrol out of the tanker into a reservoir by means of a pump. This was done without mishap, and by 3.00 am the following morning, 1 January 1968, the situation was successfully under control. Levi toasted the New Year with the firemen over beakers of spumante, he wrote to Hety.

NINETEEN

Israel, USSR and Depression
1968–72

I

The Italian revolution of '68, born in the universities, was fought by the children of the bourgeoisie. Lisa Levi, now nineteen, was a biology student at Turin University. She had a strong civic conscience, and helped to set up 'counter-courses' on the Vietnam War or organised faculty sit-ins protesting against napalm attacks. In the Sorbonne students did the same, but in Italy the idea of revolution was intensified because of the nature of Christian Democratic power: corrupt, hidebound, repressive. On Lisa's bedroom desk, beneath the inevitable poster of Bob Dylan, was a framed photograph of Chairman Mao. Her father called Mao a 'dictator', and there was some tension between her and Levi. Soon Lisa would leave home to live with a leftist of whom her father disapproved. Moreover, Levi did not think Lisa had the '*physique du rôle*' for battles with the police and feared for her safety. (It was alarming for him to see his daughter bruised after baton charges.) But, on many issues – for instance, the reform of Italy's antiquated divorce laws – Levi was behind the young and on the whole he respected their right to disagree. What he did not support was the students' rejection of the family: far from being the bane of society, the family was its foundation. However, there was immense excitement in the air – the *White Album*, the Black Panthers, Stockhausen's *Hymnen* in the record shops – and Levi was moved by it: 'It is astonishing how the same problems are ripening everywhere in Europe!' he wrote to Hety.

While Lisa was proud of her father's anti-Fascist militancy, she was irritated by his amused tolerance of some of her *gauchiste* antics. During her first protest march in 1966, against the government oppression of the Milan school magazine *La Zanzara* (which had dared to discuss birth control), Levi had waved at Lisa from a passing tram. 'It was excruciating,' recalled her co-marcher Erica Scroppo. 'Lisa and I were carrying these placards and we must have looked absolutely awful, like two Cheltenham ladies trying to be tough. Primo said we looked "rather sweet". By 1968 of course Lisa and I were ready to *kill*.'

In these months of ardent hope, Levi visited Israel for the first and only time. His Middle Eastern adventure was to provide him with another opportunity to understand what had happened to him under the Nazis. (He had now visited Germany twenty times and there was little more light the country could shed on his past ordeal.) Without Hitler, Israel would not have been born in the way – and when – it was. Levi's rosy view of the Promised Land had been tarnished since the June War, but Israel was still the 'life-raft' of the Jewish people, he said, and a testament to their will to survive.

2

He flew to Israel from Rome on 17 March 1968. Sponsored by the Italian anti-Fascist monthly, *Resistenza*, the trip was made in the lively and amusing company of forty Italian ex-partisans, most of them non-Jews, who had been affiliated to the 'Justice and Liberty' Resistance movement. Like Levi, they were curious to see the country that nine months earlier had stood up to the Arab world. Lucia remained behind at home. At first Levi was thrilled to be in this ancient land of the Christian Gospel. From the Crusader capital of Acre the Italians headed inland by coach, across the desert into Syrian zones occupied by Israel. Here were the first signs of unease. The Golan Heights were aggressively fortified and captured Arab shops were nailed shut. The unaccustomed sight of Jews as fighters perturbed Levi. He spent that night with the other Italians in a kibbutz by Lake Tiberias, within range of Syrian attack; pushchairs and bicycles abounded.

Next day, the coach hugged the ceasefire-line south through cis-Jordanian Palestine taking them to Jerusalem. They passed through lush plains littered with blasted Jordanian tanks. In Jerusalem's Arab quarter the Italians stayed at the Hotel Intercontinental. That night, Israeli government officials came to talk to them of peace, but the atmosphere in the hotel remained edgy, with sandbags in reception and frightened Arab waiters. In the dining room, Levi met Isaac Garti, a Yugoslav-born Jew who had begun to translate his work. Garti recalled that Levi was 'very troubled' by the Arab refugee problem and that he was dismayed by the lack of interest shown in his work in Israel. In 1963, Ezra BenGershôm had tried without success to find Levi an Israeli publisher. In Garti's opinion, Levi was problematic for the Israeli public because his books did not recommend life in Israel or some other redemptive solution to the catastrophe of Nazism. By the time a Hebrew edition of *If This is a Man* came out in November 1988 Levi had been dead for nineteen months.

The following night the Italians were escorted by Israeli soldiers across the Negev desert. Armoured Israeli columns had been shelled close by, and the sky was crisscrossed with anti-aircraft tracer. In Gaza and the West Bank shattered houses indicated where the six-day fighting had been especially bitter. Here Arabs had been made homeless in their own land; the atmosphere on the coach was scarcely relaxed as the Israeli guide spoke disparagingly of them. The Italians hesitated to object in case they appeared anti-Semitic. Alliances were inevitably created within the group. Early on in the trip, Levi had fallen for one of the Italian women. Franca Mussa Ivaldi was flaxen-haired, blue-eyed, with a sharp intelligence. Levi had known her in Turin through her husband, Carlo, a local Resistance hero. Levi's own marital problems and hunger for human contact drove him each day closer to Franca. There was no physical involvement that we know of; Levi's preference always seems to have been for asexual relationships with women. But the other Italians expressed annoyance that Franca had captivated Levi. 'With Franca around it was impossible to get anywhere near Primo,' recalled Gastone Cottino, 'they chatted the *whole time* in the back of the coach.'

After a week in Israel, Levi had to admit it was not the country he had imagined. Far from being a corner of Europe in the Middle East, it was a desert land of bearded soldiers, veiled women, Arab music and baklava. Generally he had found Israeli culture 'rather provincial' and was disappointed to find so little trace in Israel of the polyglot culture of Europe's Jewry. Israel merely confirmed Levi's preference for Jews of the Diaspora who had not abandoned their pride of origin, who were closely bound together by a love of words and music and debate, but who were essentially supranational citizens of the world, not of Israel. Yet, for all Israel's new bellicose spirit, Levi found it a country of bright intellectual ferment and disputation.

He had one last appointment before he flew home to Italy. Even with the bustle of people in the Tel Aviv hotel lobby, he instantly picked out Schmul Stern. He had not seen the Hungarian since they were rescued twenty-five years before from Auschwitz. Schmul was now a prosperous merchant in the Tel Aviv suburb of Ramat Gan. He was interested in planting trees and raising babies. Talking to him, Levi was able to clarify his thoughts a little on Israel. He had never doubted that dispersed Jewry had to find a home after Auschwitz, and Schmul had prospered here. It was just such a catastrophe that, in the rush to establish a Jewish state after Hitler's barbarism, safeguarding Arab nationalism in the Holy Land had not been a pressing concern.

On his return to Turin, Levi found he was engulfed by a wave of lethargy – a 'sort of *general* tiredness'. Turin seemed suddenly colourless and drab after his week in Israel, and his home life even more enclosed. In fact Levi was depressed. He tried to find a way out of his wretchedness through writing, but the sight of the blank sheet of paper made him 'physically sick', he said. There were other problems. Turin's Jewish community had advised him to disassociate from Franca Mussa Ivaldi as it was 'bad for his image as a witness and family man'. It must have been galling for a grown man to be thus reprimanded by a group of religious elders; still, Levi took note of their caution, and the flirtation was quietly ended.

He wrote of his frustrations and bleak mood to Hety Schmitt-Maas: 'It will pass away, it *must* past away.' And with a tremendous effort he tried to exorcise it in a short story, 'Creative Work', in which a writer finds he is unable to write because he simply has nothing to write about. Levi was on a downward spiral, but he took a stoic approach to his mood-swings: mostly he suffered in silence. On 28 October, he was interviewed at home by the Yugoslav poet and critic, Mladen Machiedo, for the Zagbreb literary magazine *Republika*. Machiedo noted Levi's 'anxious' expression but otherwise saw no obvious sign of his depression: Levi was becoming adept at concealing his emotions.

However, that winter when a wayward Italian radio director mangled a play he had written, then broadcast it, Levi could not contain his rage. His dystopian radio play, *Factory Interview*, went out on RAI radio in November 1968, but it was not at all as Levi had written it. The director had twisted the work into a pseudo-Marxist essay on worker alienation. Clanking machinery recorded in a screw-bolt factory outside Turin made the words in Levi's thirty-page script inaudible; there was a barrage of dissonant Stockhausen bleeps and Luigi Nono sounds. The actor Marco Parodi recalled Levi's 'extremely violent' altercation with the director, Carlo Quartucci: 'After a terrible battle Levi disowned the play.' Though Levi genuinely disliked what he called 'gratuitous experimentalism', his depression made him take offence where none was intended. He had been upset by the death on 7 November of the Jewish lawyer Rudolf Loewenthal, who had processed his claim against I. G. Farben.

*

With no other project of his own in progress, Levi was no doubt pleased when the Nazi-hunter Simon Wiesenthal asked him to contribute to a book he was compiling, *The Sunflower*. The volume was to contain the reflections of thirty-six European writers and thinkers on the moral problem of forgiveness. Each had to comment on the same harrowing story. A Polish Jew (Wiesenthal himself) listens to the deathbed confession of an SS who had burned Jews alive. The SS begs for absolution, but the Jew walks away leaving him an unforgiven man. The ghost of Ferdinand Meyer rose before Levi as he replied to Wiesenthal on 30 December:

> You did well to refuse forgiveness for the dying man. What would your pardon have meant for the German or for you? Probably a great deal to the German (a purification which would have freed his religious conscience, all too tardily aroused, from the terror of eternal punishment). But for you I think it would have been meaningless – an empty formula – and consequently a lie.

This brief reply indicated that Primo Levi was not inclined to forgive – not after Auschwitz, and probably never.

3

By the New Year of 1969, after ten long months of untreated malaise, Levi was finally emerging from the gloom of depression. On 25 January he wrote a bruised letter to Hety: 'Unfortunately, I am not new to such episodes, both before and after Auschwitz, and it is not easy to assign them a definite cause.' The early months of 1969 unfolded amid general strikes and student picketing at factory gates. In Turin the unrest and struggle against capitalist directors, who allegedly exploited southern migrant workers, reached a peak. During these turbulent times there were terrorist bomb attacks in cities across Italy. Anarchist? Blackshirt? Nobody knew. Apart from the hospitals, there was no place safe from the risk of a little bomb (as the Fascists used to put it). Owing to the unstable political situation Levi had to cancel various projects. He was supposed to be in Poland to help with a Canadian television documentary on Auschwitz, but his participation was postponed. Hety had promised to visit Turin but thought better of it. She did not want to be in Italy at this time of strikes and student protest. The atmosphere was that of a last stand, an imminent cataclysm, and Levi was not alone in fearing a military *coup d'état*, as had happened two years earlier in Greece.

While the Christian Democrat government threatened to impose a State of Emergency, the first six months of the year were taken up by routine

SIVA commitments. In March Levi was in Cambridge to see the genial Keith Barnes. Talk was of adhesive prices, batch and keg size, and the use of PVF in bonding car drum-brakes. (Keith recommended Levi read the American monthly *Adhesives Age*.) In the summer he was on the Dalmatian and Istrian coasts of Yugoslavia with Lucia. Surrounded by woodland and 'panting in an African atmosphere' (said Levi), the couple seemed happier. Three days were spent walking and swimming in Umag, where Levi again met the Istrian-born writer Fulvio Tomizza. He drank wine on the beach, moderately, and began to feel rested. 'It is astonishing how quickly one becomes accustomed to doing nothing,' he told Hety.

For the August holidays the Levis were back in Pietra Ligure, where for a fortnight they were joined by Lisa. Their daughter had temporarily neglected the revolution to attend to her biology finals; Levi detected a new unhappiness in her. 'Poor thing – she feels divided between fighting the system and fitting into it.' The Movimento Studentesco had now lost much of its acrimony and bitterness and found a new practical seriousness. Because of his mood disorders (and no doubt those of many of his survivor friends), Levi applauded his daughter's efforts to reform the 'fearful situation' (as he called it) of Italy's mental-health care system. The head-restraints and straitjackets used in Italian asylums appalled Lisa and her *compagni*, who were fighting to restore respect and dignity to the mentally ill. If Levi had been slow to seek medical help for his last depression, Italy's parlous mental health provisions might have been the reason why.

The 'Hot Autumn' began in Turin at the end of August, when Fiat suspended 35,000 workers after a series of strikes. Industrial strife had spread across northern Italy but by December, Levi reported to Hety, the 'situation appears well under control'. He disapproved of arbitrary police arrests and raids on 'New Left' groups, but supported the workers, who 'refused every provocation and valiantly contributed to the return to order'. The storm of student protest had given Levi a taste for debating some of the public issues raised. And as 1969 drew to a close, he found that his presence was much requested by Italian schoolchildren, who wanted to discuss the nature of Nazism in relation to Vietnam and the current American civil-rights movement. Levi obligingly took part in a number of school panels and found that he was made very welcome, not least because *The Truce* was now a set text in Italian schools. (If there was one thing Levi was proud of, it was the way in which he reached the young with his writing; his books were passed on from children to their parents, and a whole new demand for them was being 'born from below'.) Talking to the young became Levi's 'third profession' effectively, after chemistry and writing. However, he was disappointed that Luciana Nissim would not join him in these school visits. Over the years she had tried to cut Auschwitz out of her life completely, even to the extent of refusing compensation from the German government for her ordeal. Married since 1946 to the famous Italian economist Franco Momigliano, she led an outwardly tranquil life as a psychoanalyst in Milan.

Instead, Levi was accompanied to the schools by Feruccio Maruffi, an Italian survivor of Mauthausen camp. Maruffi remembered that the questions and answers in schools were lively and often touching, in that Levi elicited comment from the quietest members of class. But what impressed him most about Levi was his humility. 'If a pupil was writing an essay on *If This is a Man,* Primo would invite him into his house to discuss it with him. Where today could you find such a readily *available* writer?'

Dialogue with teenagers was not always easy, however. Catholic pupils raised on the virtue of forgiveness could not accept Levi's refusal to 'pardon' his tormentors. Why such intransigence? Forgiveness had been exulted at thousands of school and church occasions, yet Levi maintained that Catholics, by interpreting the Nazi crime as a battle between good and evil, over-simplified the enormity of what had happened. One pupil had the temerity to ask Levi to sketch a map of Auschwitz on the blackboard, as he wanted to show him how to escape. Watched by the rest of the class, Levi obliged by chalking the watch-towers and barbed-wire fences. The pupil told him: 'Here, at night, slit the sentry's throat; put on his clothes and run over to that power station and cut off the electricity.' Escape as a moral duty was the fantasy of POW adventure movies, Levi explained. 'Even if we prisoners had managed to get beyond the electrically charged fences, our wooden clogs would have made stealthy walking impossible.'

4

The revolution was over, and the non-revolution in store for Italy in the 1970s was to unfold amid squalid state reprisals, molotovs, sawn-off shotgun Mafia violence. During this time Italy was plunged into a deep social and political crisis, the so-called 'strategy of tension' when neo-Fascists allegedly connived with cabinet ministers and secret-service chiefs to implicate the left in acts of terrorism. A series of bomb attacks was perpetrated by a ragbag of ex-paras, neo–Blackshirts, Cosa Nostra commando groups. And in the last days of 1969 a bomb had killed sixteen bystanders in Milan's Piazza Fontana. The intention was to create such fear and instability that Italians would clamour again for an authoritarian leader. 'Luckily no appropriate strong man is in sight,' Levi commented. On 14

March 1972 the disfigured body of the *gauchiste* publisher Giacomo Feltrinelli was found in wasteland outside Milan. Feltrinelli's death spawned a variety of hydra-headed conspiracy theories. The *dietrologisti*, literally the 'behindologists', insisted that cliques and shadowy cabals were behind the incident. Levi found the Feltrinelli affair so murky that it defied all 'interpretation'.

These years saw a dramatic rightward shift in the Italian government when a new cabinet was formed under the Christian Democrat head of state Giulio Andreotti (a Mafioso politician later suspected of involvement in the murder of an antagonistic journalist). As the 1970s unfolded, the neo-Fascists grew arrogant again and there were calls to 'bring in the Colonels'. The Mafia began to infiltrate parliament, together with the secret services and various branches of military intelligence. Levi felt the time had come again to fight Nazi-Fascism, rather than just talk about it.

The bleak national mood was overshadowed by bouts of worsening depression for him. These went far beyond anything he had experienced before, and brought him close to suicidal despair. The only person who understood him at this time was the loyal, ever-sagacious Nardo De Benedetti, whose Crocetta flat had become Levi's comfort as well as escape from conjugal infelicity. Bravely, Levi struggled to face up to other accumulated problems: an emotional life divided between family and a dwindling band of friends, increased tensions at SIVA, growing uncertainty about his writing. ('What do I write? Nothing worthwhile.') In this fallow period Levi managed to publish only a second volume of science fiction. Nevertheless he was pleased to be published in Japan; *The Truce* appeared in Tokyo bookshops at the end of 1969.

Unexpectedly, it was the Soviet Union that was to provide Levi with the raw material for future literary works. SIVA had been quick to profit from Russia's economic thaw during the early 1970s and Levi visited the country three times in these years. He found little had changed since the war. Soviet clients displayed an all too familiar 'impromptu time-keeping' and 'noisy cordiality'. Rico Accati, in spite of his professed loathing of Communism, was happy to trade with the USSR as money was to be made out of Soviet labour and materials. At Accati's sumptuous villa in the Turin hills (136 Strada del Fioccardo, nicknamed by Levi 'The Dacha') lavish dinners were laid on for Russian clients. There was much carousing and drinking. Levi, who could not keep up with the Russians' vodka consumption, filled his glass with water. Accati costed these Soviet banquets down to the last lira, though he was less penny-pinching now that he was a millionaire. In a fit of largesse he flew a group of Russian engineers to Milan, and stocked their opera box at La Scala with champagne courtesy of SIVA. The Russian visitors were overwhelmed.

Russian operations had begun five years earlier in 1965 when Accati struck a deal to deliver wire-enamelling ovens to the Urals. Specialists from a Soviet Cable Works were sent to Settimo Torinese for training under Levi in copper wire-enamel manufacture. As Levi spoke no Russian, an interpreter, Tullia Ami, was hired for the purpose. Ami, a shrewd, matter-of-fact Sardinian woman, accompanied Levi on his Soviet trips. In Moscow they invariably stayed at the dingy Hotel Leningrad thirty kilometres from the airport, where bills were totted up by abacus, the lavatories overflowed and the food was usually unpalatable. As emergency rations Levi brought along a suitcaseful of Turin *grissini*, or breadsticks. He never ceased to complain of the 'inefficient' Brezhnevite spooks. Though public-sector corruption in Brezhnev's Moscow was rife, even in Italy the kickback and bribery culture known as *la bustarella* ('the little envelope') offended Levi. In business he was a man of unbending rectitude, and he disappointed his patrons in Moscow's Soyuzchimexport (the foreign-trade organisation that dealt with SIVA) by refusing to accept bribes.

In April 1970 Levi was in Moscow for six days. A shipment of SIVA's 'Acrilux' rubber-based varnish, made on a Goodyear patent, had not met with the Russian client's specifications. One drum in five was found to be defective; if the foul-up was SIVA's fault, damages would have to be paid. Agonisingly protracted tests were conducted at the Microprovod Institute. Levi had only a few days before his passport-visa expired. To calm his nerves he walked round Moscow with Tullia Ami. Most of the city he found ugly, monotonous and sad, though he was amused by the china flea-traps on display in the Kremlin Museum. Muscovites he found were quite decently dressed, and the public transport ran with 'praiseworthy efficiency'. But ever since the 1967 June War, when the Kremlin had ludicrously condemned Israel as a 'Nazi state', Russia's Jews had been made to suffer. In the press, they were branded as 'cosmopolitans' and 'parasites'. 'All Russians are equal, but Russian Jews are a little less equal than others', Levi sardonically observed.

Gallingly for Levi, his war testimonies were banned in Russia. The Soviet Ministry of Culture had declared that if Russians were to be allowed to read *The Truce* or *If This is a Man,* there was a danger they might compare the Soviet Gulag to the Nazi *Lager*. To his credit, Levi was one of the few Italian writers to champion Solzhenitsyn. Most left-leaning Italian intellectuals saw him as a Slav reactionary and mystic. In 1968 when Levi had read Solzhenitsyn's *First Circle* he understood why certain searching questions had been put to him by Soviet officials at the Katowice transfer camp in 1945. They had wanted to know about Auschwitz food rations and sabotage prevention. 'I was naive enough to assume that my very courteous Russian inquisitors were collecting historical data rather than information on how to run the Stalinist camps.' Levi left Moscow without settling the 'Acrilux' problem.

5

Back in Turin, Levi was once again in factory difficulties. He had got involved in a quixotic plan to build a water decontamination tower. Assembled on its side from pre-fabricated parts, the tower had gone up effortlessly, like Lego, and it instantly became a local landmark visible from the Turin–Milan motorway. Then the tower began to gurgle, filled with fumes and leaked sulphuric acid; it had overpressurised. In a rage Accati threatened to sue the Milan design engineer for loss of production weeks. After an exchange of angry letters it was discovered that cheap porcelain rings had been fitted inside the tower, which had disintegrated. The tower continued to swallow Levi's time and energy as workers began to mix potent Pernod-like cocktails out of the tower's intoxicating waste products. 'So I have to remain on the spot for many extra hours as a sort of baby-sitter (a baby tower 25 metres tall and costing about one hundred million lire),' Levi made light of the burden to Hety.

After his six days in Moscow, Levi resumed his business trips and appointments at schools. In June 1970 he had a premonition, the first of many, that his memory was going. To Hety he said he could feel 'lots and lots of neurons shrinking and decaying at a tremendous rate'. He felt that his intellectual self-confidence was slipping, his fluency in German deteriorating. He feared he had Alzheimer's disease (Levi was fifty). Loss of memory would take away the one thing that sustained Levi, the act of writing. But his fears were groundless: this was a *maladie imaginaire*.

Other concerns weighed on Levi. Natalia Ginzburg's brother, Alberto Levi, was dying of a glandular tumour. For twenty years he had been Primo's intimate friend, his mountaineering companion and the family doctor. Alberto's courage was 'remarkable', said Levi, who wondered how he could live on borrowed time like this and still be so happy. Though his face had become bloated and disfigured, he continued to offer visitors whisky at his doctor's practice on Corso Marconi, and hoped he could go skiing again before long. Levi marvelled: 'He has lost not a bit of his good humour and taste for lively parties and conversation.' But suddenly in the summer it became physically impossible for Alberto to move. He died in the last days

348

of 1970. People who had not even known the doctor attended the funeral, as he was much loved. At the burial Levi met Natalia Ginzburg, for whom this was the second bereavement in a year: her husband had died from alcoholism. At the age of fifty-four Natalia was left to look after a hydrocephalic daughter who could barely walk, talk or eat. What Levi called these 'very painful' events would only aggravate his fears and low moods, and in a Christmas card to Mario Rigoni Stern, dated 13 December, he remarked that life in Turin was 'sad and shrouded in mist'.

The only outings in the New Year of 1971 – apart from picnics in the winter sun with Nardo – were to drive the seventy-five-year-old Ester round Turin to visit relatives. The house was running itself reasonably well with hired domestic help. In early summer, on 3 May, Levi appeared before a West Berlin investigating judge in Turin. He was required to give evidence against SS Friedrich Bosshammer, Adolf Eichmann's right-hand man in Italy. In faltering German he told the judge, Dietrich Hölzner, what he could remember of those far-off days in Fossoli. Levi could not swear to having seen Bosshammer, though he did recall an SS officer who spoke in loud pidgin-Italian to his Fascist subalterns. At the end of the interview Levi gave Hölzner a copy of *Ist das ein Mensch?*, which was now out of print.

6

In mid-May, Levi returned to the literary limelight. His new science fiction collection, *Structural Defect*, was published by Einaudi. It contained twenty stories, most of them written over a two-year period from 1968 to 1970, in between periods of depression and domestic strain. If they showed signs of hasty composition, it was because Levi was in a hurry to publish again. Six years had elapsed since the pseudonymous Damiano Malabaila had made his SF debut. This second volume was another attempt on Levi's part to slough off his reputation as a war memoirist. On the whole his fourth book makes a very sombre impression. Originally entitled *Disumanesimo* (Inhumanism), it flickers with newsreel images of race riots, B-28 jungle missions and piles of skeleton corpses. Levi had been influenced by his friend Roberto Vacca's fictions of industrial apocalypse and nuclear meltdown. He said Vacca was 'marvellous', and he praised what he called his jagged, percussive *rovinografia* – literally, 'ruinwriting'.

In sinewy, consciously metallic language Levi explores the 'uncertainty' and 'unsteadiness' of twentieth-century life, and provides a modern allegory of urban breakdown. As a chemist he understood better than most that the world's immense transformations are born in the laboratory: new forms of chemical and biological warfare, anthrax, nerve gas, new instruments of death. 'We live in a world that is preparing for war,' Levi said in an interview. Beneath its images of technological dereliction, the book provides an insight into Levi's fears and state of mind in the early 1970s. In the fantasy, 'It is Written on the Forehead', a couple agree to have advertising slogans branded on their foreheads in return for money; not only do the captions turn out to be indelible, but the couple's child is born with one of the captions tattooed on its forehead, like the mark of Auschwitz. There is often a dark fear among survivors that their children might be psychologically or in some way genetically harmed by their parent's experience: here, Levi vents that fear. But the most revealing statement in *Structural Defect* is 'Westward'. In this fear-ridden fable Levi presents suicide as a merciful release from suffering. A couple of scientists offer a South American tribe a chemical antidote against self-murder, but the tribe politely refuses the miracle medicament because (and presumably Levi agreed) they 'prefer freedom to drugs, and death to illusion'. The absence of any metaphysical conviction in this story (no belief in the afterlife, no suggestion that life even has a purpose) makes it among the bleakest that Levi wrote.

The despairing vision in *Structural Defect* surprised some reviewers. A quarter of a century after the end of Nazism it seemed that Levi was preparing for the final countdown – the third world war that had begun with the atomic flash over Hiroshima. Yet on the whole, the book's reception was lukewarm, and Levi was not altogether surprised. To his cousin Anna Yona in Boston he wrote of a 'disillusioned and disenchanted' work that made for uncomfortable reading. Therefore he was puzzled when Anna expressed an interest in adapting the tales for children. 'They could actually do them harm'. Levi published very little *fantascienza* after this book, and in later years he virtually disowned his science fiction, claiming that it had 'suffered the fate of all science fiction – which is to undergo a rapid ageing process'.

7

Like a lengthening shadow the next depression crept up steadily on Levi. In a now-familiar pattern he was dispirited after publication of a book, yet *Structural Defect* was a minor precipitating factor in the illness. Levi's malaise was more general – 'a cold inward deadness', he called it – and this time his bleakness was tinged with thoughts of suicide. By the summer of 1971 his health had altogether collapsed, and for four months he drew into himself, shuffling between 75 Corso Re Umberto and SIVA, 'shipwrecked', he told Hety.

Levi did not want to be seen by anyone and was ashamed of his 'feebleness'. Yet Hety Schmitt-Maas was due to visit, and Levi could scarcely turn her away now. At first Hety did not recognise the pale, inhibited creature who met her at the station. Four years earlier in Wiesbaden Levi had been 'relaxed' and 'tanned-looking'. Now a 'dark cloud' hung over their June encounter. When Levi introduced her to his wife and children, his German suddenly dried up. His '*Sprachprobleme*' ('speech-problems') as Hety called them, may have been connected to the guilt he felt at betraying his marital problems to her. His depressive inarticulacy was very striking. As a gift (probably also a peace offering) Hety presented Lucia with a cashmere shawl. Levi stood awkwardly to one side as the women exchanged pleasantries. Afterwards all three – Levi, Lucia, Hety – went out to supper. Hety had expected Lucia to be withdrawn and suspicious, what she called '*kontaktscheue*' ('contact-shy'); instead her company was that of a radiantly 'self-confident' woman. But as the meal continued Hety watched in embarrassment as Lucia seemed to 'shrink' from view across the table. Finally she was quite 'absent' from the conversation. Lucia spoke no German, and Levi had given up on his attempts to include her in the conversation.

The next day was even more excruciating for Hety. Levi, 'tongue-tied and morose', impatiently drove her round the sights of Turin. At midday he dropped her off at the station, and brusquely said goodbye. 'We were strangers to each other, and I don't know why,' Hety noted later in her diary. A week on, seemingly in a better mood, Levi wrote to Hety of his 'great joy' at seeing her in Turin. She seemed enviably 'serene and at peace with the world'. In awkward English Levi added: 'This is not the first time I have experienced such "shipwrecks", but every time [I have one] it seems to be final and definitive . . . Next time it will be better, I promise.'

It did not get better. In Pietra Ligure for the August holiday the sight of well-nourished bodies on the beach filled Levi with disgust. The morning papers alone were a source of torment to him with their news of neo-Fascist bombings and wildcat industrial strikes. His days unfolded unhappily: up at 8:30 am to help Lucia clean the flat; 11:00 am, down to the beach; a two-hour siesta after lunch (Levi harried by 'nightmares'); up again at 3:00 pm, stupefied and scared. As so often in depression, Levi's anxieties eased somewhat after sunset, when he was able to write the odd letter. At least he was finally on tranquillisers. Then nightfall, like an anaesthetic, soothed his pain. Such was the rhythm of his summer holiday. While the drab routine provided some comfort for Levi, his depression put a strain on the family.

On 13 August Levi steeled himself to write to Nardo in Turin. 'I'm so anxious to see you again. Your wise, tranquil words would do me a lot of good; I feel I can tell you things I would never be able to tell Lucia, and perhaps to no other friend.' This was followed by an almost flippant remark about Auschwitz: 'For me this seaside life is no better than a concentration camp'; Levi would never normally have belittled his ordeal in this way, but he was disturbed and not his usual self: 'I no longer recognise myself [*non mi riconosco più in me stesso*]. All I want is to go back to being the normal primolevi.' The lower-case letters seemed to say it all: Levi's self-esteem was so low that even the sight of his name was an anxiety to him. The time had come for practical solutions. With Nardo's help, maybe Levi could work out what he called a 'sensible and prudent rehabilitation programme'? The same day Levi wrote a long, perceptive letter to Hety Schmitt-Maas, in English, analysing his condition and courageously putting his life under the microscope. 'I am here among a throbbing mob of bathers, desperately alone . . . I need medical help.' These bathers were 'throbbing' with life, while Levi felt dead:

> I have lost all *Lebenslust* [joy in living]; I do not rejoice in speaking with people, in reading, or writing. My mind returns with appalling insistence to my work at the factory, which is not going very well, and which I intensively hate; I have lost all hope in a future as a writer, so what sort of life can I expect?

He added that Lucia did not really understand – indeed underestimated – his illness, attributing it alternately to his being 'spoiled' or to 'arbitrary' visitations of a chimerical disease:

> What I need is to search for the root, if there *is* a root. Auschwitz, perhaps? No, I do not think so, the camp belongs to a far too remote past, and moreover it has been exorcised by my books. The very root of my uneasiness lies in an atavismus. I belong, whether I like it or not, to the Jewish people, and Jews have always been concerned with their future.

This word 'atavismus' has a Lombrosian ring. In 1880s' Turin positivists spoke of a *Psychosis Judaica* whereby Jews supposedly display a higher incidence of depression and suicide than non-Jews. Levi's claim was not entirely far-fetched. In post-emancipation Europe, suicide among Jews had increased dramatically. (Where previously religion had put a check on suicide, in more secular times the 'check' had been removed, with conspicuous consequences.) Painfully Levi tried to describe to Hety just how he had come to this present awful pass:

> Immediately after my return from the KZ [Auschwitz], I found a shelter under the wings of Mr Accati, and a more or less quiet life in his factory. In this way, fortified by a fleeting literary success, I have lived for 24 years; but now the wave has subsided, I am 52 (too old to undertake something new, too young for retiring), and the shelter is fading away, and my [children] look at me with astonishment, fear, a mocking smile, and a total lack of comprehension.

Levi felt he was on the ebb-tide of his literary achievements. What was once a source of pride to him – his books – now seemed worthless. He had no reason to believe this: *If This is a Man* was selling between 20,000 and 30,000 copies a year, and had been translated into six languages including Finnish and Japanese. Italians from intellectuals to secondary-school children were reading Levi. (Goethe's observation that a book becomes a 'classic' only when it has been accepted by a vast public, followed by an intellectual elite, was never more pertinent.) Still Levi was dissatisfied (his wife would say 'spoiled') by his success. He ended his letter to Hety:

> I was not always like this, and I must and can and shall return to a normal way of living: but, to achieve that, I must speak or write to somebody. Write to me – you know a lot about the world and people!

Back in Turin, Levi's mother was sufficiently worried by her son to write to cousin Anna Yona in Boston: 'Primo looks low to me; fortunately his physical health is all right.' Ester attributed his depression to a combination of factors, among them the 'gloomy situation' in Italy, the signs of a neo-Fascist revival, the burden of his work at SIVA. Levi was sleeping a little better again, but Renzo was causing trouble. Following his sister's example he had given up stamp-collecting for a life of protest, and cultivated a straggle-haired Che Guevara look. 'The other day we managed to get him to the barber – one has to be grateful for these small victories,' Levi's mother told Anna Yona. Renzo Levi was fourteen.

8

As the autumn of 1971 advanced Levi seemed to get better. And on 19 October he was well enough to celebrate the twenty-sixth anniversary of his return home from Nazi captivity, a date that his mother had never allowed herself to forget. Relieved from his wretchedness, Levi began to find enjoyment again in conversation, books and public affairs. But in Wiesbaden, Hety Schmitt-Maas was sick with anxiety. Levi had not written to her since his miserable August holiday. It was now December and four of Hety's letters had gone unanswered. Unable to stand the anticipation any longer she wrote a nervous letter to Lucia. 'I have been waiting for months for a sign of life from your husband. I feel that something is wrong'. And, rather intrusively, Hety suggested a number of reasons for Levi's illness, among them the concentration camp, the weather and stress. She included some German articles on depression and begged Lucia at least to drop her a line to let her know how Levi was. Lucia replied that her husband was now 'perfectly cured' and indeed about to go abroad on business.

Just before Christmas, accompanied by SIVA's sales manager Maurilio Tambini, Levi travelled to Liverpool. Tambini had never flown before and was so relieved to land safely that he tried to kiss the runway, but was prevented by Levi. They were on a mission to buy enamelled conductors from the Merseyside electrical company, BICC Conollys. In spite of the city's Christmas cheer, Britain was a gloomy place. The *Liverpool Daily Post* reported pre-festive IRA bomb attacks ('Terror Blast Kills Children'), as well as John Lennon's support for Sinn Fein. Levi was astonished to see the homeless sleeping rough on the Cathedral steps and to find parts of Liverpool still damaged from wartime bombs, 'neither demolished nor rebuilt'. The weather was very mild for December, however, and in the unseasonable sunshine Levi felt less dejected. Merseysiders were queuing up to see Norman Wisdom in *Robinson Crusoe*, and Levi visited the Cavern where the Beatles had first played. On Gladstone Dock (according to Tambini) he watched the city's last transatlantic liner, the *Empress of Canada*, leave on her valedictory voyage to Tilbury; boats hooted mournfully on the Mersey as the scrapyard beckoned. Levi felt terribly remiss in having neglected to write to Hety, and from the Edwardian splendour of the Adelphi Hotel he wrote her a postcard ('Most cordial regards!') promising to send her a long letter soon.

A 'not very merry' Christmas was spent at home while Levi's mother recovered from a broken leg. She was seventy-seven and had stumbled over the kerb of Corso Re Umberto, breaking the 'tip of her malleolus', Levi explained precisely to Hety. All the same, Levi was feeling happier. And his mood was bolstered by good news from Romania. Doina Condrea Derer, an Italian scholar based in Bucharest, was translating *If This is a Man* into

Romanian. Delighted, Levi wrote to her on 23 December: 'I consider it very important that my book is published in your country.' He did not have to explain why. In the German-speaking regions of Romania, ex-Nazis still mourned Hitler's defeat, lamenting a lost Aryan idyll. Yet Levi could be very insensitive at times. He asked Derer for a copy of her translation in manuscript, along with an Italian-Romanian dictionary (which he could easily have procured in Turin), in order to 'verify' the accuracy and quality of her work. Derer was offended; only later did she understand Levi's need to safeguard the passage of his testimony to a wider world.

On Boxing Day Levi wrote his long-promised letter to Hety. It was an odd mixture of apology, guilt and humility: Levi had reread his *cri de coeur* to her of 13 August (hatched at the height of depression in Pietra Ligure) and wished he had exercised a little more self-control. 'Almost all I have told you seems to me extremely silly; not false, mind you, just silly and foolish.' After two bouts of serious depression – the first after Israel in 1968 – Levi now had some degree of insight into his mood disorders. That he had this insight at all suggests his depression was only moderate by this time. He tried to describe to Hety the sense of powerlessness felt by all depressives during an 'episode':

> We are not masters of our mood, of our reactions, of our very personality: a slight disturbance in one's hormonic [*sic*] balance, and you are turned into *somebody else*; and you are liable to revert to this obnoxious state again and again, and each time you will stubbornly be persuaded that *this* is your real and final condition, that you will have no future . . . that there is [nothing to do] but sit and weep.

In April 1972 Levi was elected a member of the Piedmont League of Chemists, proposed by his friend Ennio Mariotti (who was president) and seconded by Professor Guido Tappi of Turin University. His recovery was overshadowed by a tragic professional blow, however, when during the August break one of SIVA's managers, Giovanni Torrione, fell to his death from a ladder while decorating his parents' home. He was forty-three. Torrione had been responsible for the upkeep and acquisition of varnish-making machinery, and until a replacement was found Levi had to stand in for him. This created a 'very disagreeable' amount of extra work which, combined with news of the publisher Feltrinelli's murky death and more neo-Fascist bomb outrages, provoked another bout of depression that lasted four months until the end of the year.

355

The one thing that flourished in these bleak summer weeks was Levi's correspondence with the survivor Hermann Langbein, who had been working on his book *Humankind in Auschwitz* for the last twenty years. It is an extraordinary labour of devotion and scholarship. An Austrian, Langbein had been appointed clerk to an SS doctor in Auschwitz, a privileged position from which he could observe the camp's mechanism of terror. By interviewing hundreds of ordinary Germans complicit in Auschwitz, he hoped to show that the *Lager* was not the work of demons but of ordinary *Menschen* – men like Meyer and Heidebroek. Over the autumn of 1972, Levi read the German draft of Langbein's book with a 'slight sensation of uneasiness', however. The Austrian's eminently civilised analysis of Auschwitz seemed to Levi somehow out of place now – an irrelevancy, even – amid the bombings and political upheavals that afflicted Italy. This will strike many as extraordinary, in the light of Levi's lifelong pledge to bear witness to Auschwitz. However, in Italy at this time the fear of a far-right putsch was immediate and pressing.

9

In October 1972 Levi flew to Togliattigrad in the USSR, a Soviet-style Detroit on the banks of the River Volga. Togliattigrad had been built with Fiat's help and named after Italy's post-war Communist leader Palmiro Togliatti (who was Russia's ally). From the day it opened in 1962 the industrial complex was a fiasco. The 'efficiency, skill and capitalistic ruthlessness' of Fiat had been grafted unsuccessfully on to the 'lazy, peasant-like, post-revolutionary body of Holy Russia', said Levi. The plant looked very shabby now; assembly lines designed to produce 3,000 Zhiguli Fiat cars a day (according to a Fiat catalogue) were turning out fewer than 1,000 in a week. Some 400 Italians, mostly Piedmontese, worked for Fiat-Togliattigrad as instructors, managers and machine-fitters. They spoke their own company language – *fiatese* – which mingled mechanical jargon with the dialect of their Piedmont home towns. Many had married Russians and were homesick. A Fiat train left Turin for Togliattigrad each week with spaghetti, wine and, most importantly, condoms. (Soviet condoms, Levi overheard a worker say, felt like 'lorry tarpaulins'.)

Levi was on a mission to sell the Russians a SIVA adhesive that he had perfected, with the help of Keith Barnes, for use in car brakes. The adhesive bore the sternly scientific-sounding name 'Prioflex', and Levi hoped it would break Fiat's monopoly with the rival adhesive 'Permafuse'. He was not optimistic: Togliattigrad was just too inefficient and corrupt. (In the Hotel Volga he found the nonsensical notice: 'IT IS FORBIDDEN TO GO TO

Yet Levi's
frustrated business dealings in Togliattigrad yielded material – incidents,
Russian life-stories and images – for a book he had in mind on the
seriousness and joy of work. Two outline chapters of what would become,
six years later, *The Wrench*, emerged during this period. Needless to say,
Levi failed to sell any car-brake glue.

Back in Turin, Levi's depression had aggravated somewhat. He always
seemed happiest away from 75 Corso Re Umberto. However, two months
later, in a letter to Hety dated 28 December 1972, Levi remarked that his
depression had terminated with 'astonishing abruptness (in a matter of
hours! Is that not queer?)'. This sudden lifting of depression – what
psychiatrists call 'rapid cycling' – is commonplace among certain patients;
for no apparent reason, the black mood vanishes.

Levi had sufficiently emerged from his low state to take part in the now-
classic British television documentary, *The World at War*. The series
producer, Michael Darlow, was in Turin to interview Levi for episode six,
'Genocide'. Darlow was dazzled by Levi, and had never met a more
'remarkable man', he said, in all his years as a producer. Though Levi
was 'engagingly, *charmingly* shy', he attended to Darlow's questions
scrupulously.

Darlow's response to Levi was characteristic of many who met him for
the first time. It was a crisp winter afternoon on 9 December, Levi was in a
white shirt and tie, and the sun streamed into 75 Corso Re Umberto. It was
not merely Levi's face (remarkably youthful for a fifty-three-year-old's),
but his conversation and darting intelligence that captivated Darlow. Off-
camera Levi spoke of chemistry with a child-like wonder, 'like a boy putting
samples in jam jars', said Darlow. Inevitably the conversation turned to
Nazi war criminals. Friedrich Bosshammer, Adolf Eichmann's chief Jew-
hunter in Italy, had earlier that year been sentenced to life imprisonment
(12 April 1972) for his part in the atrocities in Italy, and Levi said he had
been 'justly sentenced – but he should not be shot'. Either way it made no
difference: nine days after *The World at War* interview Bosshammer died in
a West Berlin hospital of natural causes.

10

That year, Levi had had an awkward family duty to perform. On 2 July 1972
his son Renzo was fifteen; just as he had done when his daughter was that
age, Levi chose to speak to him of Auschwitz. Until then Renzo had shut his
ears to all talk of the camp. Aged three, he had asked his father about the

grey-blue numerals on his forearm, 174517, and asked him: 'Why have you been written on?' After a pause, Levi replied: 'I was a prisoner once – that's what they used to do to us.' From that day on, Renzo asked his father no more questions: he preferred not to know why the war had been so important in his life. When Levi had tried to talk to Lisa of his ordeal, she ran from the room in floods of tears. An abyss of misunderstanding separated him from his children. He suspected that Lisa had read *If This is a Man,* as she had asked him to sign copies for teachers and friends. Yet if Levi asked her what she thought of the book, she abruptly changed the subject. After thirty years of writing Levi had to admit that his work had reached everybody but his children. Now, to his dismay, Renzo's reaction was exactly the same as his sister's nine years earlier: he bolted from the room in tears.

Lucia blamed her husband: 75 Corso Re Umberto was saturated with literature on the Nazi persecution; Auschwitz was in the air the children breathed. They wanted a normal father, not a deportee father – still less a depressed one. 'Survivors can be troublesome and tedious,' Levi acknowledged, 'we want to relive our sufferings and inflict them on others.' Levi reflected that he had neighbourly, but not affectionate, relations with his children. And that was a great sadness to him.

TWENTY

Dreams of Retirement
1973–6

I

In 1973 Levi's appearance changed. At the age of fifty-three, he wanted to grow a beard of Ancient Mariner proportions, but settled instead for a snow-white *barbetta* that friends said resembled Lenin's. In a radio interview Levi said the beard was the result of competition with his son Renzo, who had tried but failed to cultivate a Che Guevara growth. Increased media attention anyway made him more image-conscious, and to many Levi appeared suddenly stylised. Keith Barnes was startled to see him at SIVA in an open-necked flowery shirt and bell-bottomed trousers. 'Primo had gone a bit flamboyant.' He was driving a silver-grey Lancia 'Fulvia' convertible, and seemed much preoccupied by the sense of ageing. 'I warn you, Lucia's hair is grey and my beard is *white*!' he wrote to a friend. His daughter, now twenty-four, was teaching maths in Settimo Torinese and had left home. Renzo dabbled in basketball, Leninism and photography. Levi looked on his son with a fond if competitive tenderness; Renzo was sixteen and taller than him.

After twenty-five years at SIVA, Levi was now heartily sick of the factory grind and longed to write full time. Office responsibilities weighed down on him and he missed the old 'hand-dirtying' of laboratory chemistry. The factory had expanded mightily through the 1960s and the new staff were not always congenial to Levi. The replacement security guard, Signor Papandrea, was nicknamed by Levi 'La Lupara' after the Sicilian shotgun used by the Mafia. At night, this fanatically vigilant man prowled SIVA with a rifle. He was believed to be an unrepentant Fascist, who welcomed the signs in 1970s Italy of a Fascist revival.

In spite of his discontent, in early 1973 Levi applied himself to the book that was to mark a turning-point in his career as a writer and establish him, at home and internationally some years later, as one of the best-loved authors of our time. *The Periodic Table* was to celebrate the fumes, stinks, bangs and fiascos, as well as the triumphs, of the chemist's vocation. Instead of writing a conventional memoir, Levi would structure his book round elements of the periodic table. This grid table of the elements is the chemist's stock-in-trade, and Levi saw a symmetric beauty in it. Certain elements in the table – iron, vanadium, say – seemed to him to evoke images of his past life. He could use these elements as aides-mémoire, drawing from potassium, say, or gold, a thread of reminiscence to weave his life-history. The result would be an eccentric master work, daring in conception, peculiar in construction. Levi's most vital experience was to be here, from his first risky experiments in the Crocetta lab through to his capture leading to Auschwitz, and on to his post-war recovery as a writer. Spanning thirty-two years of personal experience, 1935 to 1967, *The Periodic Table* was to be Levi's attempt to give his life meaning and justification.

Levi had first mooted the idea for *The Periodic Table* in 1963 when he argued, in an interview, that chemistry was not an 'arid' subject for literature at all. ('That's a colossal nonsense!') Material for this chemical *Autobiografia* had appeared in different form in a magazine as early as 1948 – the 'Titanium' chapter. And, as old material was expanded and rehabilitated, so *The Periodic Table* had grown steadily more ambitious in scope. The book was to gather up an extraordinary range of writing, from detective fiction to epic war narrative to learned scientific treatise. In prose of tight functional elegance, Levi's myriad voices and literary influences would be triumphantly absorbed and reconciled. The book is also very funny – for example in 'Nitrogen', where the author discusses the use of snake droppings in lipstick manufacture. 'Primo's humour was not an Italian-style humour (as in our lamentably awful comic Italian films), but an understated Anglo-Saxon sort of humour,' commented a writer friend.

The 'Carbon' chapter, a poetic fable about the infinitude of matter, dated back to 1943, Levi claimed. In Aosta jail, facing likely execution by Fascists, Levi had pondered the notion of a novel (as it was then to be) about a carbon atom's odyssey. It is certainly remarkable that he could reflect on the miracle of life born of carbon at a time when his own life was probably about to end. In fact, the story was rooted in Levi's schooldays. His classroom science primer, *Chemistry in Our Daily Life* (1913) by Dr Lassar-Cohn, had demonstrated carbon's presence in every substance connected with the existence of life, 'be it an apple seed, or an animal's skeleton'. Another schoolboy text that influenced 'Carbon' was the Roman poet Lucretius in his treatise *On the Nature of the Universe*. Lucretius wrote of how rivers, foliage and pastures are transformed into cattle and how these cattle are consumed by humans, who in turn provide sustenance for predators: 'So nature transforms all foods into living bodies.' Lucretius did not know it, but he was writing of the quintessential element of life, carbon.

Cesare Pavese had noted in his diary, *This Business of Living*, that success and failure are 'the twin experiences of adult life'. Chemistry seemed to Levi to offer similarly stark alternatives. It taught one to learn from one's mistakes and to acquire knowledge through trial and error. So it is no accident that the Italian verbs *misurarsi* ('to measure oneself') and *provarsi* ('to test oneself') punctuate the narrative.

2

By early July Levi had completed the tenth chapter of the book, 'Sulphur'. But his despairing comment on the unfolding chemical instalments, 'Some are dull, some amusing, none is memorable', was not a good sign. If Levi was to stave off depression it was vital that he continue with his opus: writing was a path to what Levi called 'personal stabilisation'. A brief July holiday in Sardinia helped to revivify him. Away from Turin, Levi and Lucia were always more well-disposed towards each other, and Sardinia's peculiar ancient loneliness concentrated their affection. Levi delighted in the island's 'lonely horizons' and its 'age-old rocks' eroded by the wind into Henry Moore sculptures.

On 31 July, Levi was fifty-four, and full of birthday cheer. About this time he decided to write a sequel to his periodic table, which would be inspired by organic chemistry. Apart from the 'Carbon' chapter, the book surveyed only the inorganic field. Now Levi wanted to celebrate the world of organic hydrocarbons. These twin books may have been intended to mirror his university professor Giacomo Ponzio's two-part student primer on 'Inorganic' and 'Organic' chemistry. During the summer composition of *The Periodic Table* Levi often consulted Ponzio's bipartite opus, and sometimes even took from it. This 'adapted' material was not quite plagiarism; rather, it was secret praise for the *gran capo* Ponzio, who formed the bedrock of Levi's mature knowledge of chemistry. Some might say these borrowings weaken Levi's claims as an original writer, but they also demonstrate his gift for assimilating and popularising a fantastic variety of arcane sources.

3

That summer of 1973, serious neo-Fascist violence broke out in Turin. Thugs with chains and knuckle-dusters menaced pupils at the school gates;

swastikas were daubed on the synagogue walls. Leftist teachers were beaten and verbally abused, and Levi's son Renzo was jostled outside the 'M. D'Azeglio' school where he was a pupil. In a letter to a Yugoslav acquaintance, Levi described the Italy of 1973 as 'cancerous and decrepit, and maybe already dead of old age and assorted vices, if not decomposed'. These were unusually intemperate words for him. In order to help combat the neo-Fascist thuggery, Levi and some friends set up the parents' association, COGIDAS, which was to monitor the violence and liaise with police (or those police who were not pro-Fascist). This sort of vigil duty was not new to Levi – he had kept sentinel outside Turin's Jewish school in 1940. But he was not capable of squalid hand-to-hand fighting with juveniles in the Italian Social Movement (MSI) founded immediately after the war by diehard Fascists. He hurried to a school on Via San Secondo, where pupils had been threatened by Blackshirts armed with rocks. Accompanied by Alberto Salmoni and Ada Della Torre, he was lucky to escape the fracas unscathed. 'When we said we were from COGIDAS they threatened us with knives and truncheons,' Levi reported. The youths gave the stiff-armed Roman salute, held up photographs of Mussolini and chanted Fascist anthems. On 26 October Levi had another narrow escape when he was called out to the 'L. Burgo' technical college on Via da Brescia. Armed with iron bars and broken bottles, six Blackshirts pulled up in a car; before the police could arrive, the *squadristi* threw a teacher to the ground and beat up one pupil so badly that he was in hospital for two weeks. The fear again was of a military coup. Italy's so-called 'silent majority' wanted the return of an authoritarian government, and prominent left-wing activists were advised to sleep away from home and to have a 'safe' address.

At SIVA, meanwhile, Levi's troubles multiplied. The factory was using ever-more toxic raw materials; staff risked being chemically poisoned, or even killed. Sante Fracas, one of Accati's longest-serving employees, had died in the early 1960s from pulmonary complications casued by paint-fume inhalation; if Levi was not careful, he could go to jail for managerial negligence. Workers had begun to complain of burning eyes and heart palpitations; they reported unaccountable explosions of rage and loss of appetite. With their ungloved hands they scooped up the carcinogenic powder di-amino di-phenyl methane. Levi had ordered vast quantities of B250 (as the chemical was known) from BASF in Germany; he did not have to wait long before the first worksite casualties. Two workers were cleaning the inside of an aluminium reservoir when a spark ignited trapped gas and they were violently flung out by the subsequent explosion. Fortunately neither man was killed, but Levi should have been accountable for their safety. Instead of rubber boots they were wearing spark-creating hobnails. A month later workers ran for cover as a six-metre geyser of caustic phenol shot in the air. A fireman tried to close the reservoir's inspection door, but the phenol gushed under his gloves and burned his skin. All afternoon the air was hazy with solvent droplets; cars passing on the motorway were said to have had their enamel removed (phenol is an efficient paint-stripper). By evening the SIVA buildings and car park was encrusted with 130 tonnes of solidified phenol; the damage was immense, and Primo took responsibility for it.

In the first weeks of summer the stress and anxiety of factory life swept over Levi; he was living a frantic existence, struggling with *The Periodic Table* in the evenings, and in the mornings either dealing with a SIVA disaster or worrying about the next one. He could not conceal his state of nerves: in areas of the plant where toxic chemicals were known to be stored, he was heard to shout at workers in exasperation: 'Christ! Where are your *gloves*?' Much of his time was taken up with accident prevention. He insisted that staff wear protective masks and overalls, and allocated each of them a personal locker for their equipment, which was periodically checked to ensure that nothing was missing and everything worked. Levi studied the intoxicating effects of solvents, the electrostatic hazards of storing them and the likelihood of their spontaneous combustion. From America he ordered specialised textbooks on incendiary prevention; he pored over catalogues of 'conductive footwear'.

The feeling at SIVA was that Levi was no longer fit to run the plant on a day-to-day basis. He seemed unable to discipline workers – even if it was for the worker's own good – or take a firm stand on hiring and firing. If a worker was in breach of safety regulations, Levi had to send him a warning letter, then give him daily suspensions and if the behaviour persisted, sack him. He did none of these, and Accati began to mutter that Levi's character was too 'soft' for the managerial role. His professional stock had fallen, and Levi knew it. But he was in a difficult situation: the more orders he gave at SIVA, the more he felt uncomfortably like an Auschwitz *Kapo*.

Levi wanted early retirement; if he did not retire soon he could not finish *The Periodic Table*. As it stood, the book's every page bore signs of a 'difficult and painful begetting'. What had begun well was progressing in fits and starts; writing had become a 'terrific battle' against tiredness. After long discussion with his wife Levi decided it was time he left SIVA as the factory was beginning to undermine his mental health. Accati knew how low-spirited Levi was at SIVA, and was receptive to a proposal that he made. Paola, Rico Accati's daughter, was married to an English chemist, Michael Tinker. The couple lived outside London in Barnet. What if they moved to Turin? Tinker, after due training, could become Levi's successor. Accati agreed to the plan, and in August 1973 Michael Tinker arrived at SIVA. His arrival was very welcome to Levi; with pleasure he noted that Tinker was 'reasonable, eager to learn, clever and full of goodwill'. Born in Chester in 1943, and twenty-four years younger than Levi, Tinker looked up to his mentor; Levi, in turn, kept an avuncular eye on his apprentice, coaching him in Italian, taking him for walks round Settimo Torinese and out to lunch at the 'Ostu Bacu' on Corso Vercelli for frogs and polenta.

4

At the end of 1973 Levi faced his most serious challenge yet at SIVA: the world oil crisis. Petrol-based raw materials, such as phenol and xylene, were needed to manufacture PVF. But with global refinery stocks so low, these materials were unavailable or else OPEC, the oil-producers' cartel, had made them prohibitively expensive. During this nerve-racking time Levi disburdened all cost-making decisions on to Rico Accati. If the oil situation did not improve, the eighty workers under Levi's control faced redundancy. 'Not since 1945 have I found myself in such a critical situation,' he said. Attacks of self-doubt alternated with mild depression as he struggled to keep on an even keel. Keith Barnes had never seen him so low. 'Primo was a born worrier', he said, a man who had to 'worry about everything'. Over a meal in Turin, Levi explained to Barnes that oil was the planet's 'life-blood' and that the end of western society was nigh. Barnes seemed unperturbed. 'How I wish I was like you, Keith, so very simple.' (This was said in English: the Italian *semplice* can also mean 'straightforward', which was presumably what Levi meant.) No doubt Levi envied Barnes his uncomplicated nature. As he wrote in a science fiction: 'The English are a practical people.'

A winter holiday in Sperlonga on the coast between Rome and Naples put Levi in a slightly better mood, and tranquilly enough, he explored the sandy ruins of Emperor Tiberius's villa. But real health had not returned and no serious work was being done on *The Periodic Table*. In this unproductive period, fearing worse depression, Levi agreed to take part in two television documentaries. The first was Dutch, the other Italian.

Rolf Orthel, 'very nice and civil', was recording a documentary on the Auschwitz SS physician Dr Eduard Wirths, who had supervised 'selections', but had also tried to save lives (and finally hanged himself in jail). Wirths, who could not reconcile the killings with his medical conscience, brought Levi to reflect on the evangelical warning 'Do not judge', but, Levi wondered, 'how can one live without judging?' No one who had lived through Auschwitz was likely to abstain from judgment: it was understanding that came hard. The transcript of Levi's interview with Orthel – running to seventeen closely typed pages – provides a fascinating insight into the corruption and moral ambiguity of the Nazi camps. Levi would investigate these themes in his last published book, *The Drowned and the Saved*, in particular the 'grey zone' of prisoners who were forced to collaborate in order to survive.

The Italian documentary, *The Profession of Storytelling*, was dedicated to *If This is a Man*. Excited, Levi asked the French survivors Jean Samuel and Charles Conreau if they would appear with him on-camera. Samuel agreed; Conreau, camera-shy, said no. Levi tried to persuade him. 'But we *have* to defend ourselves by telling our stories and bearing witness to what Fascism did to us.' Still Conreau said no; Levi could visit him '*sans caméra*'.

In early March 1974, accompanied by an Italian film crew, Levi left on his most exciting adventure for years. He went by train to Strasbourg, where he would be filmed with Samuel. Opposite Levi sat the film's director Gianfranco Albano, earnestly smoking a cigarette. To camera, Levi asked Albano in rapid Italian: 'Did the events in *If This is a Man* really happen? Sometimes I feel I must have written a novel.' Only by talking to Jean Samuel, he added, would he be able to 'verify' and 'recapture' the memory of his ordeal. Having arrived in Strasbourg, Levi felt some of his confidence and good humour return. He had not seen Samuel for eight years, and was filmed walking with him over the city's canals and past its German-style cafés. Jean, healthy-looking and relaxed, chatted animatedly to Levi in his well-appointed flat opposite the Strasbourg synagogue, while his wife Claude looked on. At one point during the filming, Levi grandly compared himself and Jean to Dante's Ulysses. Dante had condemned the Greek voyager to hell for his boldness in wanting to explore forbidden territories. Similarly the enslaved Samuel and Levi had 'dared' to try and understand the terror of their confinement in Auschwitz. 'It seemed to me (and maybe also to Jean Samuel) that our punishment under the Nazis was not at all gratuitous,' said Levi. 'We were being punished for challenging the monster of Nazism – and not just us, but all anti-Nazi Europe.' By his own admission, these sorts of literary aggrandisements were lost on Samuel, a far less complicated figure than Levi.

The next day, without the film crew, Levi travelled on to the Vosges where he found Conreau enjoying his life as a retired schoolteacher. After toasting each other in Calvados they went for a walk in the pine-scented forest; there, like men who had survived the horrors of the trenches in the Great War, they spoke lyrically of their last ten days at Auschwitz, days that had been a supreme experience of comradeship: 'our finest hour', Levi called them. After this French trip, with the world oil crisis at last receding as OPEC prices came down, some sort of calm settled over Levi.

5

Though Levi's retirement was set for Christmas 1974, Accati managed to persuade him to stay on a little longer as a part-time consultant. Levi had helped him build up his wire-enamel empire and made him a wealthy man. The only blot on Levi's new-found happiness was the complicated paperwork he had to wade through to obtain a pension; with Italian 'standards of inefficiency', he grumbled, it would take a good eighteen months to process the claim.

Some chapters of *The Periodic Table* – 'Hydrogen', 'Gold', 'Arsenic' – were now ready for publication. Levi used the summer break to complete the opus. Through the hot month of August he stayed on his own in the Pietra Ligure flat: Renzo was in southern Italy; Lisa was in Prague with her new boyfriend ('near-husband', Levi disapprovingly called him); Ester had been packed off with Lucia and other relatives to a hotel in the Valle d'Aosta. With everybody thus 'settled', Levi hoped for three peaceful weeks of writing. And before long he had twenty-one chapters, ranging across the periodic table from 'Argon' to 'Carbon'. Some evenings when he had finished work, as the sun went down over the Riviera, he dreamed of places to visit in retirement.

Italo Calvino was the first to read Levi's draft manuscript, and on 12 October he wrote to him from Paris to express his delight. The book was proceeding 'very well', Calvino said; in fact the entire 'apparatus' now seemed 'robust' enough for publication. Exalted by Calvino's praise, Levi was encouraged to entertain other literary projects, one of which was an Eric Ambler-style industrial thriller. (Nothing came of it.) Knowing that he was soon to retire, Levi made one final SIVA trip to Germany. In Leverkusen on 28 October he said goodbye to Karl-Heinz Mielke of Bayer; they had worked together for eighteen years.

Levi's retirement party was held at the SIVA head office in Settimo Torinese, at the end of November. It was snowing. Colleagues had put up a display of broken test tubes to signify unwanted laboratory explosions, and coils of copper wire to honour Levi's myriad varnish products. Rico Accati proposed a toast to Levi and his forthcoming book, *The Periodic Table*, which left the author moved. Afterwards, staff presented him with a gold plaque etched with all their signatures, but when cries went up of 'Speech! Speech!' Levi cringed, mock-embarrassed. The extent of his speech was this: 'I believe I have always tried not to get on anyone's nerves.' Renato Portesi, somewhat inebriated, read out a valedictory poem he had written for the occasion, while the dancing continued until midnight. Accati later gave Levi a gold watch engraved with the date of his retirement, '1 December 1974'. Levi was fifty-five.

6

'Reborn', 'serene', 'free': Levi even went so far as to say he was sporadically 'joyful' in semi-retirement. And in such a mood he wrote to Hety Schmitt-Maas:

> Some doctor friends had warned me of the dangers of precocious ['early'] retirement. Apparently, many people in my condition suffer from dyspepsia and other diseases. Well, I must confess that, on the contrary, this slowing down of my activity is agreeable and healthful, and, until now, devoid of any un-desirable after effects!

However, Levi was not free of Accati just yet: for the next three years, as agreed, he would act as SIVA's part-time consultant and card-index man, cataloguing the factory's chaotic patent files dating back to 1955 and putting contracts in order. (The work appealed to the list-maker in Levi.) Over time, he scaled down his contribution to SIVA. At first he worked for just half the day, clocking off at noon; then he was at SIVA just once a week, then once a month, until finally he cut all ties with the firm. In this initial stage of his semi-retirement, the happiest, Levi was under no great stress. The Italian national gas company, 'Italgas', asked him to sit on its board of directors; he politely declined.

In the afternoons Levi read a great many books and tried to keep in shape at the American Club on Turin's Corso Trapani, where he took swimming lessons. (He had not learned to swim at school.) Some of his free time was spent in the Chemistry Institute, where he sought out graduate friends. Vittorio Satta, a diminutive Sardinian whose brother Orazio had designed the famous Alfa Romeo chassis, was happy to be reunited with Levi. He, too, had just retired, but another coincidence pleased him even more. 'You know everything, Primo, but there's one thing you don't know': Satta shared Levi's year of birth, 1919, as well as his birthday, 31 July. A lively character with a sharp humour, Satta was one of many friends who helped to restore Levi's conviviality after the tensions of SIVA.

Another university colleague whom Levi saw much of in retirement was Nereo Pezza. The simplicity of Levi's tastes surprised Pezza (and many other friends who had not seen Levi for a long time). He often brought Pezza to a Piedmontese trattoria in the cobbled heart of Turin, the Tre Galline, where he ordered tangy goat's cheese and chickpea pancakes. Levi was feeling nostalgic in retirement. And as he slipped comfortably into his new life, he reapplied himself enthusiastically to the sort of laboratory-based chemistry he had missed at SIVA. In the immensely strange 'Belousov-Zhabotinskii' reaction, a colourless solution changes from bright green to purple, through red to blue and finally back to green again, in a cycle that repeats itself as punctually as a Swiss watch (no fewer than twenty times). Levi asked a chemist friend to demonstrate it for him, and timed the rainbow transformations on a stop-clock; he had the leisure to indulge these curiosities now. Livio Norzi, a Crocetta friend, was another whom Levi frequented in retirement. An effervescent raconteur (whose gift for exaggerated invention contrasted sharply with Levi's more measured story-telling), Norzi loved to discuss various chemical conundrums. One day Levi showed him a handful of steel ball-bearings which, by long use in a SIVA paint-mixing mill, had been transformed into perfectly symmetrical twelve-sided shapes. Why? At such times Levi was at his best, recalled Norzi, 'launching the most audacious bridges between ideas that were at first sight wildly disparate'. He and Norzi were peas from the same Jewish-Crocetta pod, and they were now inseparable.

To avoid boredom and aimlessness, and also to make a little extra money, Levi asked if there was any translation work he could take on. An English editor at Einaudi, Malcolm Skey, suggested *Natural Symbols* by the British anthropologist Mary Douglas. Levi was familiar with Douglas's work on cultural taboos, which had brought her a certain *réclame* in highbrow Einaudi circles, and he was quickly absorbed in the translation. But all was not well. 'Levi's version of Douglas was pretty poor – his English wasn't up to scratch,' recalled Skey. Francesco Remotti, an Italian anthropologist of great intellectual distinction, was asked to help Levi with the book's technical terms. In Remotti's view, Levi himself was an 'anthropologist – of the death-camps'. While he was translating Douglas, Levi was put on a retainer with *La Stampa*. Like most Italian papers, it had a culture page, and it was for this that Levi began to write light-hearted articles on diverse subjects ranging from butterflies and etymology to the devilish art of translation.

He also made some important new survivor friends. The most significant was Edith Bruck, née Steinschreiber. The daughter of poor Hungarian Jews, she had been a child in Auschwitz. Bruck's background was quite unlike Levi's. By a wretched series of post-war events, she had married three times before she was twenty. Auburn-haired, green-eyed and striking, by the time Levi met Bruck she had been a ballet dancer in Greece, a tailor's assistant in Budapest, a model, a restaurant chef and a beauty-salon manager, all this before finally settling in Rome in 1955. Thirteen years younger than Levi, and the author of several autobiographical books, Bruck had considerable wit, a capacity for terse put-downs and a gift for coquettish fun that both excited and alarmed Levi. 'More than anything, what Primo needed was to be *touched*, to feel that he was *alive*. If anyone was a repressed Piedmontese bourgeois, it was Primo,' judged Bruck. Levi seemed inhibited by her presence, and could not even bring himself to walk by her side. 'He always traipsed one step behind me, like Auschwitz prisoners in single file.' If Bruck tried to envelop Levi in her arms (she had the motherly tendency), he flinched away red-faced. Probably Bruck intimidated many men but Levi always preferred strictly asexual relationships with women. This was, supremely, an attraction of opposites: Bruck the Hungarian proletarian allied to one of Italy's most rarefied minds. Yet their antithetical qualities made for a more intimate union, and Levi's friendship with Bruck would endure until he died.

Even in this first happy flush of retirement, Levi investigated some dark themes. The case of the morally ambivalent SS doctor Wirths had re-ignited his interest in corruption and collaboration within the Nazi camps. Levi was looking for some way, he said, of breaking through the stereotype of brutal oppressor and victimised oppressed, the ruler and the ruled. Nazism did not sanctify its victims; it degraded and engulfed them, converted them to its methods. The subject of Chaim Rumkowski, another ordinary man degraded into collaboration, had tempted Levi for years, and only now had he the time to look into it. Rumkowski was a Polish Jewish industrialist who, with Nazi support, had set himself up as elder of the Lodz ghetto, exploiting and abusing fellow Jews, only to end his reign in the gas chambers.

Levi's unflinching absorption in what he called the 'alarming subject of Jewish collaboration' received further impetus when the Dutch television director Rolf Orthel sent him *The Night of the Girondists* by the Netherlands historian and author Jacob Presser. Levi was so struck by this semi-fictional account of moral bankruptcy in Occupied Holland that he decided to translate it from the Dutch (not so unlikely as it sounds: Dutch has similarities with German). If we are to understand the human situation and protect ourselves in the event of a 'similar trial', said Levi, we must recognise the sordid Rumkowskis of this world.

On 25 October 1975 Levi was in Rome at the inauguration of the exhibition 'A Minority's Contribution to the Struggle for Freedom', about the Jewish role in the Italian Resistance. The exhibition attracted a good deal of media attention and response. Among the guests were the rabbi of Rome, Elio Toaff, various representatives of the city's Jewish community and Levi's old Roman friend Lello Perugia. Levi gave a talk on the psychological consequences of deportation and touched briefly on his ill-fated career as a partisan. Lello embraced Levi like an old friend; he was now a plump civil servant, married with children. Later in the autumn Levi spoke to Waldensian schoolchildren on the nature of anti-Semitism. Their teacher, Pastor Giuseppe Platone, edited the Italian Protestant newspaper *La Luce*, for which Levi occasionally gave interviews. Platone was surprised to hear Levi define himself as *'una persona in ricerca'*, 'a man in search of a faith', since he assumed that Levi was atheist. In fact Levi envied believers – the more so, the older he got – and wished he could believe in God. 'To have a father, a judge, a teacher would be good, calming.'

Until retirement, Levi had blamed his scant participation in family life on the demands of the factory, but now he had time to call on relations. His mother's two surviving sisters, aunts Ida and Jole, had entered old age gracefully and were delighted to see more of their adored nephew. Aunt Ida was a widow in Turin and suffered from 'some sort of nervous disturbance' (said Levi). Aunt Jole, Levi's favourite, also lived alone in Turin, at 76 Corso Rosselli, and Levi confided many of his problems to her. He saw more of his uncles who, having sold the family textile shop in 1971, were in genteel, if contented, decline. Gustavo Luzzati, never very healthy, went on Mediterranean cruises with his wife Lea. She was famous for her purple poetry ('Why *does* Aunt Lea write such junk?' Levi asked – he could be quite cruel in his judgments of others, even of family), and in the winters she took Gustavo off to Rapallo where they sat under the palms, wrapped in blankets and sipping syrupy rosolio liqueur. Levi's main concern was for Uncle Corrado. After a mild heart attack, the seventy-five-year-old continued to hurtle round Turin in sports cars. Having grown up at a time when inventing and making were honoured pastimes, he could not now resist tinkering with glass valves, pliers, soldering irons and screwdrivers. Corrado had introduced Primo as a boy to the world of radio, film and gadgetry and, revisiting him now, Levi was returned to those happy, explorative days.

The tenor of Levi's life was happy throughout 1975, and occasionally he was enlivened. He saw much more of his sister Anna Maria. Still in Rome, she had married the American film critic and scriptwriter Julian Zimet, who during the war had served alongside John Cheever in Frank Capra's legendary film unit. (Caught up in America's post-war anti-Communist witch-hunt, Zimet left Hollywood to lie low in Mexico, before transplanting to Rome where he worked for Ciné Città.) He and Anna Maria had built a holiday house on the shores of Lago Bracciano near Rome, which Levi loved to visit. There, intoxicated by the lake's 'musky perfume' and 'ancient scent of burnt twigs', he listened to the gulls and wrote poetry.

Slowly, quietly, he was absorbed in his new life as a semi-retired industrialist. Crocetta neighbours became friends. One of these, a figure of sage-like status, was Turin's political philosopher Norberto Bobbio. A leading luminary of the political wing of the Italian Resistance (twice imprisoned by Mussolini), Bobbio was a staunch defender of human rights and utterly devoted to Levi. What he admired in him was the sober rigour and proportion of his prose – its 'human measure' – and from the earliest days had been one of Levi's most assiduous readers. Bobbio was ten years older than Levi, but fully shared his moral scruple, moderation of judgment and – above all – a sense of the complexity of things. Their friendship was strengthened by the fact that Bobbio was an old friend of Levi's first publisher Franco Antonicelli (who had sadly died in 1974). Most Saturdays they tramped in the Susa Valleys, and during these mountain excursions Levi liked to amuse Bobbio with examples of Talmudic hair-splitting, Jewish jokes and witticisms. Levi's wife was pointedly excluded from the walks. Instead, the men were joined by Bianca Guidetti Serra, who was now a renowned left-wing lawyer. During these alpine hikes Levi loved to point out marvels of the natural world. He showed Bianca a tiny ball of compacted twigs, feathers and minute bones. It was an owl's pellet. Another time, using a twig, he deviated a line of processionary ants across the mountain's path. 'Even though we were grown-up, these were the little things that amused us,' recalled Bianca.

For more eccentric diversion Levi frequented Ennio Mariotti, the chemist and bomb-disposal expert who had found him his job in the asbestos mine back in 1942. Until retirement, Levi's relations with Mariotti had been formal as he had visited him for chemistry advice, rather than as a friend. Now Levi called on Mariotti at least three times a week in his lab on Via San Secondo. Like the alchemists of old, Mariotti liked to weigh, calibrate and distil substances by hand. Above his door hung the cryptic axiom 'NATURE TO BE COMMANDED MUST BE OBEYED'. As well as being an old-fashioned chemist of the sort that Levi admired, Mariotti was a passionate gourmet; the pair would trawl the Turin markets for *fiaschi* (straw-covered bottles) of Barolo wine and the pungent white truffles of Alba. But literature was their main passion. One of Mariotti's current enthusiasms was for Isaac Asimov, whose mammoth hymn to biochemistry, *Building Blocks of the Future,* Levi agreed was a 'masterpiece'. Mariotti also introduced Levi to Turin's white-magician Gustavo Rol, the undisputed psychic star of 1970s Italy and a close friend of the film director Fellini. Rol reanimated the interest Levi had always had in the paranormal, and which his table-rapping father Cesare had first instilled in him. Mariotti had more bizarre interests, too. In his Crocetta bathroom he kept a live carp as well as a menagerie of porcupines, caged rats, tortoises, cats (and one swift). On the occasional Sunday Levi liked to accompany Mariotti to Turin's Porta Palazzo market to buy ducks (not to eat, but to keep as pets). In the 'Nickel' chapter of *The Periodic Table* Mariotti was immortalised as the blue-eyed 'Tuscan lieutenant'.

7

Now that he was semi-retired, Levi assumed he would have ample time to travel and write, but that was not to be. There were considerable domestic obstacles. His mother's presence at 75 Corso Re Umberto was especially burdensome to Levi now that he was spending so much time at home. Ester rarely went out on her own (she was eighty), so Levi would accompany her twice a day on her *passeggiate* round the block, stopping at her favourite ice cream parlour, the 'Gelateria Testa' on Corso Re Umberto, for a vanilla cone. Her doctor, Adriano Vitello (an old partisan comrade of Anna Maria), had recommended plenty of exercise. Levi adored his mother and valued her judgment; their only considerable separation had been Levi's twenty-two months in Auschwitz and after. While the true nature of Levi's relationship with his mother is unknowable, the bond was unusually deep. And by bringing his wife to live with his mother for a quarter of a century, Levi appeared to have condemned the two women to a perpetual competition for his attention. Or was it that it suited his personality to be needed by them both? Levi described the women to Hety as 'highly decent people, [both] timid and obstinate.' They rarely quarrelled; when they did, they never brought their quarrel to Primo – which would have obliged him to take sides. The *ménage* was a minefield, with Lucia a sort of second-class mother to Primo. Just what demands Levi's mother may have made intentionally, we cannot know; but she was an old woman burdened by ailments, and in the end – for Levi, too – the burden seems to have been intolerable. And now it was not only Ester who required constant assistance.

Lucia's mother, Beatrice Morpurgo, was virtually blind, and consequently Lucia was unable to spend time with her husband in retirement as she might have liked. Instead she was often detained in her mother's gloomy flat on Via Principe Tommaso.

In early 1975 a series of school reforms in Italy known as the *decreti delegati* were issued. These devolved power down from the teachers to the parents, and generated great media attention. In the spring Levi was voted president of a parent-run council at his son's school, the 'M. D'Azeglio', and soon found himself run off his feet. Levi said he considered it his 'civic duty' to help reform Italy's antiquated school system. The council had to allocate school funds and listen to parent and pupil grievances, as well as deal with the restless and sometimes violent neo-Fascists who taunted pupils in the street. These council meetings were frequently sabotaged by far-left pupils, who demanded to know why they had been denied council representation. When Renzo stormed a meeting accompanied by a group of *sinistrini*, he could not bring himself to shout his father down. (This was a typical scene of mid-1970s Italy.) For 30,000 lire – about £75 – Renzo had bought a second-hand motorbike and had grown, finally, a Che Guevara beard.

On the whole, Levi presided over the school council meetings in a manner that softened antipathies and fostered amiable relationships between otherwise warring factions. Most students saw him as their friend. He lobbied for the introduction of sex education and, not surprisingly, tried to improve the school's standards in science tuition. He even arranged for a course in diabetics to be taught within natural-history lessons (Levi's maternal grandfather had died of diabetes). The council meetings, though often rowdy, were a novelty for Levi, and he enjoyed being in the ferment of reform, despite often returning home from them exhausted and disgruntled.

8

Levi had taken early retirement chiefly in order to write. He had never abandoned the idea of publishing his poetry. Five years earlier, in 1970, he had circulated privately and at his own expense 300 verse pamphlets among friends. Like certain medicines, warned Levi, the pamphlets were for 'internal use only'. Afraid of making a fool of himself, he had preferred that his poetry should appear first in a vanity-published edition. It elicited an especially favourable response from an old schoolmate. Delfina Provenzali (the 'Provençal Dolphin'), was Catholic, but her parents had obligingly safeguarded the Levi family jewellery during the Occupation. Provenzali was a chemist by trade and extracted artichoke essence for the Italian aperitif company 'Cinar'. Born in the Sicilian capital of Palermo, she was a dark, small-boned woman of strange beauty, who had published poetry of her own. There is no doubt that Levi regarded his new-found friendship with Provenzali as something special. 'To be reunited with you after so many years, and to have you as my bright and diligent sponsor, is an unexpected gift of destiny,' he wrote to her.

Provenzali suggested that Levi send his poems to Ezra Pound's former Italian publisher, Scheiwiller & Son, in Milan. Vanni Scheiwiller, a forty-year-old cycling fanatic, was very willing to consider the submission. There were twenty-seven poems in all, some of them written at the same time as *If This is a Man*. 'For Adolf Eichmann' ('Oh son of death, we do not wish you death') was a stark curse on Eichmann. In a much later poem, 'The Black Stars', Levi considered the disquieting evidence of quasars (quasi-stellar objects) and black holes. This theme of a 'blind, violent' universe, first mooted to Levi in 1941 by his astrophysics professor Nicolò Dallaporta, was one to which he would return in his last years. It was Delfina Provenzali who suggested the title *The Bremen Beer-Hall* for Levi's collection, taken from a line in his Heinrich Heine-inspired poem 'Landing'.

Meanwhile on the other side of the Atlantic another devotee of Levi, Ruth Feldman, was busy translating his verse into English. Feldman was an Ohio-born minor poet and painter, very wealthy, who lived part-time in Rome. Her childhood had been 'darkly shadowed', she liked to say, by her father's nervous breakdown and her mother's early death. She lived in Boston, where her Italian teacher, Anna Yona, happened to be Levi's cousin. Knowing of Feldman's interest in Italian poetry, in 1972 Yona had given her a copy of Levi's privately printed verse. Feldman was so taken by the 'poignancy and stark spare musicality' of the verse that she decided to translate it, and make Primo Levi's poetry her life's business. Levi was happy to have Feldman as his translator as her credentials as an *italianista* were good, but she wanted to enlist the help of Brian Swann, another minor poet and critic resident in Massachusetts. Swann had a far less exalted opinion of Levi as a poet: 'His poetry was ornamental to his prose and might just as well have *been* prose.'

Levi and Feldman got on well enough by letter. Always punctilious, she sent him reams of translation queries which, with twinges of impatience, Levi politely answered. When necessary he called Feldman's attention to some significant errors in her translation and tactfully corrected her Italian grammar ('*rovescia* is not a verb, but an adjective'). Occasionally he observed that her choice of an English word lacked sonority, or had too few

374

syllables to make for a good rhythm. Yet Feldman did not like being criticised, not even by Primo Levi, and wrote him an angry letter refuting his criticisms of the Swann–Feldman collaboration: 'We are good poets . . . Can you not trust us?' On receipt of this letter Levi at once replied from Turin: 'I beg you to forgive me: I did not want to offend anyone.'

On 13 May 1975 Feldman was in Turin. She was surprised when Levi did not invite her into his home and rather miffed not to be addressed amicably as 'Ruth'. At any rate an 'extremely pleasant' evening (so Levi subsequently reminded Feldman) was spent in a Crocetta bar discussing poetry and other matters. In reality the visit was not that 'pleasant' for Levi, who wrote to his cousin Anna Yona in Boston on 22 August, three months after Feldman's return to Rome: 'She is not a very nice person. A while ago, when I ventured to make some modest and very courteous observations about her translation methods, she wrote back to me with arrogance. Maybe she's a bit mad?' Luckily no further arguments developed and Levi thanked Feldman (somewhat two-facedly, given his comments to cousin Yona) for her 'kind involvement' in his poetry and her laudatory remarks about his writing in general.

Feldman's plan at first was to publish her translations piecemeal in the American Jewish magazine *Moment,* which rejected them, as did the better-known journal *Commentary.* In England the owner of the London-based Menard Press, Anthony Rudolf, decided to bring out Feldman's translations in a small bilingual edition. Rudolf was now, in 1975, thirty-three years old, an energetic and enthusiastic poet and editor. Raised in Hampstead Garden suburb, he had wide-ranging literary tastes and a deep knowledge of European Jewish literature. Bravely he decided to take on all the financial responsibilities that went with publishing a virtually unknown foreign author. Levi gave Rudolf his full backing and declared himself 'extremely delighted' to be in his hands.

9

Publication of *The Periodic Table* in 1975 was a decisive moment in Primo Levi's life, and a clutch of reviews appeared before the book was in the shops. The first was Lorenzo Mondo's, in *La Stampa* for 24 May, which acknowledged the wit and compact expression of Levi's literary style. This prompted a slew of spring and summer notices. *Espresso's* literary critic Paolo Milano spoke of Levi's lapidary integration of science and literature. The book especially recommended itself to reviewers who had been disappointed by Levi's last two books of science fiction. Catholics found *The Periodic Table* to be a holy work full of reverence for the physical universe, while the left-wing *Rinascita* favourably placed Levi in the tradition of the Italian avant-garde. Avant-garde? While Levi had no time for self-reflexive preening, 'Carbon' (to choose one chapter, not quite at random) exploits its own literariness in a determinedly modernist way. Critics sensitive to Levi's mosaic-like borrowings had in fact noted the striking similarity between 'Carbon' and the closing pages of Italo Calvino's allegorical novel *The Baron in the Trees*. Levi's carbon atom comes to rest (via a glass of milk) in the brain of an Italian author, who is raising his pen to put the final full stop to a work called *The Periodic Table*. Calvino's fantasy, published eighteen years earlier, ends on a similarly self-conscious note, the author's pen putting a dot over the final 'i' of his creation. When Calvino read 'Carbon' in manuscript he exclaimed to his wife, 'Goodness, but that's Calvinoesque!'

On 30 May, buoyed by the good reviews, Levi attended a Turin University reunion. He had always been happy to go along to these banquets, held every five years, and enjoyed mixing with chemists who had no artistic pretensions or preconceptions about literature. This year the reunion was held in the 'Ristorante il Pavia' on Viale Thovez. Levi was gestured to sit as the honoured head of the table, for this was also, as one ex-student put it grandly, a *Déjeuner Système Périodique*. Also present were Gabriella Garda and Clara Moschino, sweethearts of Levi's youth. As the luncheon wore on, Levi was asked if he planned to write a sequel to *The Periodic Table*. He said he did, but he had no working title. After discussion the diners came up with *The Double Bond*. Levi loved the title, which he said reminded him of J. D. Watson's *The Double Helix*, about the discovery of DNA.

By the mid-1970s Levi was a literary legend in Italy. The increasingly conferred title of *scrittore* (which Levi so desperately craved), and the fact that caricatures of him began to appear in the papers, promised a new and more confident Primo Levi. More than 32,000 copies of *The Periodic Table* sold in 1975 alone. While the book was not a national bestseller, nevertheless to have read it was the mark of the well-informed and cultivated Italian. Levi had been reviewed widely and favourably, and gained devoted new readers. Almost every day he received letters or telephone calls from admiring readers: his place in the nation's literature was established.

However, the joy Levi took in publication was undermined by protests of fictional distortion. There is always a special risk, Levi now knew, when putting real-life people into books. Not all the friends who had recognised themselves in *The Truce* and (to a lesser degree) *If This is a Man* had appreciated their transformation, and some had been annoyed or disquieted to find themselves as characters in Primo Levi's private drama. Levi believed these complaints were inevitable, as the whole process of transposing life and fiction (or semi-fiction) was highly subjective. 'Each of us is three different people: the person we really are, the person we *believe* we are, and the person other people see us as.' If Sandro Delmastro had been fictionally transformed in the 'Iron' chapter, that did not detract from Levi's elegant homage to his mountaineer hero. Yet Delmastro's nephews were very offended by Levi's portrait, and in a 'decidedly unpleasant' phone call they demanded an apology. Levi's insinuation that Sandro had been a *contadino*, or 'peasant' (in Italian the word has connotations of 'serf'), seems to have been particularly hurtful. Though Levi was distressed and genuinely surprised, he was also irritated, because he found the family's objections to what he saw as the exigencies of art, trivial. When it became obvious that Levi would not alter a single word of 'Iron' the Delmastros co-opted Sandro's fiancée Ester Valabrega to put pressure on him to change his mind. Levi stood his ground: his refusal to alter 'Iron' was due as much to his belief in himself as a creative writer as it was to his insensitivity, perhaps, to the Delmastro family's hurt.

The complaints continued. Another friend, Gabriella Garda, found her transformation into the flirtatious 'Giulia Vineis' of the 'Phosphorus' chapter very disagreeable. Before publication, Levi had called on Gabriella with a copy of the chapter in typescript but it was apparent from her expression that she was displeased. Levi never learned of the Dalla Volta family's extreme displeasure with the 'Cerium' chapter, as they did not make it public. Here, Levi wrote that Alberto's mother had given substantial sums of money to an Italian confidence trickster in return for the comforting tales he brought of her son, whom he claimed was alive and well somewhere in east-central Europe. 'I cannot forgive Levi for this distortion,' Alberto's brother Paolo Dalla Volta told me, 'you might call it poetic licence, but that's something *poets* take, not writers like Levi who deal in the facts.'

Yet Levi did not deal in the facts; he telescoped, selected and transmuted the facts into fiction. In some ways *The Periodic Table* was the closest Levi came to being a novelist, and nowhere is he more of a novelist than in the 'Vanadium' chapter. Levi tells how he came to trace his Auschwitz overseer Ferdinand Meyer. He received a letter at SIVA (we read) from a 'Dr Lothar Müller' concerning a shipment of defective resin; with a jolt he noticed that Müller had misspelled the word *naphthenate*, just as his I. G. Farben boss (also called 'Müller') used to. Could this be one and the same man? As we know, this is a fabrication. What astonished Hety Schmitt–Maas about 'Vanadium' was Levi's 'unkind' transformation of Meyer's character. Far from being the decent German whom Levi acknowledged him to have been, Meyer–Müller is a slyly mendacious ex-Nazi who apparently feels no shame for his past. Wounded by Hety's insinuation of literary untruthfulness, Levi tried to explain to her that he thought it would be more effective, from a literary point of view, to 'play down' Meyer's redeeming points and turn him into a prototype bourgeois German, made morally spineless by the Hitler regime. Mario Piacenza was unperturbed by his crude misrepresentation in *The Periodic Table* as the workaday 'Enrico' (although Levi later apologised for describing him as the son of peasant fishermen). However, when the German weekly *Die Zeit* published 'Vanadium' in its entirety, the Meyer family was furious. 'Müller' was easily recognisable as Meyer, and his widow felt angry and betrayed. She wanted to sue for defamation, but her son Thomas persuaded her against it. So Levi was never made aware of the potential legal action against him. Levi's writing had moved progressively towards semi-fiction, and the conflict between the writer he was perceived to be, and the creative writer he wanted to be, was heightened. In writing *If This is a Man*, Levi had felt under a moral obligation to bear witness, while in his subsequent work he felt under no such obligation. Some of his readers resented this departure from documentary *verismo*.

10

The objections to *The Periodic Table* continued to disturb Levi through the summer of 1975 as other readers voiced their grievances. But his anxieties were overshadowed by news of a senseless family tragedy. Lucia's twin sister Gabriella Treves lost her daughter Sandra in a mountain accident. On 19 July she was on a weekend mountain excursion in Biella when she slipped on a path and fell down a crevasse. Sandra's four-year-old daughter Ada was the only witness, but she would not speak. Lucia's sister was devastated. And Levi too was in a deeper state of shock than he knew. All that consoled him was the astonishingly resilient child Ada, who scolded both him and Gabriella for weeping so much: '*I* try to forget, why can't you?'

For the next four months, Levi stayed put, struggling with *The Double Bond*. The book was not going well and Levi worried that it would not interest the layman. Then, disappointingly, his poems received only middling reviews. At the 'Athesia' bookshop on Corso Duca degli Abruzzi, where *The Bremen Beer-Hall* was launched at a wine-and-cheese party, hardly anyone turned up. 'Levi was devastated,' recalled the owner, Anna Maria Candura. Almost no critic, except someone who signed himself

Bernard Delmay (Levi's university contemporary, Oreste Caldini), picked up on the volume's occasional blistering invective, so evident in the verse to Adolf Eichmann. However, Delmay referred to Levi's '*poemetti*' – 'little poems', and the use of the diminutive indicated an undeniable truth: Levi's poetry was very slight beside his other work. And there was another disappointment. *The Periodic Table*, one of the most daring and original texts of post-war European literature, failed to win any of Italy's first-division literary prizes, scraping the worthy (if unheard-of) Pozzale Prize, and the equally unknown Prato Prize.

In the meantime in Britain *The Periodic Table* had been turned down by no fewer than twenty-seven publishers. Fortunately in the last cold days of 1975 Levi's hopes for an English-language publication received a fillip. Stella Humphries, Oxford-educated, had served during the war in the Ministry of Information as director of one of its foreign-languages units. Her cosmopolitan temperament owed much to her grandfather, a Russian immigrant and Hebrew scholar, who had taught himself English from the King James Bible, mastering it sufficiently to translate Milton's *Samson Agonistes* into Hebrew. Inspired herself to translate *The Periodic Table* by Natalia Ginzburg's enthusiastic review, Humphries contacted Levi's London publishers, the Bodley Head, where she found a sympathetic backer in Guido Waldman. Waldman would gladly have commissioned Humphries but his editorial colleagues were not interested, and vetoed publication. *The Periodic Table* was not an autobiography and it was not a chemistry text. What *was* it? Such peculiar merchandise would never sell, it was agreed. Instead Waldman directed Humphries to Penguin Books, but Penguin showed even less interest. *The Periodic Table* was ahead of its time: science has only now become, in publishing terms, popular and attractive. Levi would have to wait another ten years until his book found a British backer.

Two other British admirers, Mirna Risk (an Italian married to an Englishman) and Sylvia Hunter, also wished to translate *The Periodic Table*. For a while these Manchester-based women were in almost weekly communication with Levi, sending him samples of their joint work-in-progress. Levi worried that they had mis-translated the 'Arsenic' chapter. Keith Barnes was on a Lufthansa flight from Turin to Frankfurt awaiting take-off when a voice came over the tannoy: 'Is a Mr Barnes on board?' A steward then handed him an envelope marked 'J. K. Barnes from the Author': inside was a typescript of the 'Arsenic' translation. Levi wanted Barnes's immediate verdict. The degree of self-importance required to hold up an international flight for such a minor matter is extraordinary. 'Primo was quite the obsessional,' judged Barnes.

In recent months, and particularly during the autumn of 1975, there had been a lull in Levi's correspondence with Hety Schmitt-Maas as she had been ill. It was the first lapse on her part in their eight-year correspondence. But now the letter-writing was urgently resumed. On 12 November Hety had visited Albert Speer, the repentant former Nazi, in his home above Heidelberg Castle. She was under no illusions about this Faustian figure, but wanted to commend Levi's book to him. Afterwards she wrote excitedly to Levi that she had left a copy of *Ist das ein Mensch?* with the ex-Nazi: 'I said he absolutely *must* read it!' Levi's bewilderment may be imagined. Speer, who as Hitler's arms minister had been the principal Nazi exploiter of slave and Jewish forced labour, was about to read Primo Levi. 'It looks to me like an odd dream that this book of mine, born in the mud of Auschwitz, is going to sail upstream – to one of the very Almighties of that time!' At the same time Levi was unsettled by Hety's cosy audience with the enemy. 'Explain to me: what moved you to interview Speer? Curiosity? Sense of duty? "Mission"?' This was the only time Levi sounded a note of annoyance in his letters to Hety. Speer's blend of self-laceration and self-advertisement was demeaning to the murdered dead and he wished Speer would not cart his rotten conscience through the world's media.

Did Speer read *If This is a Man*? On New Year's Day 1976 he wrote to Hety that he had 'skimmed' part of the book. Two weeks later, on 16 January, he added that he did not want to 'disturb' Levi by reading his testimony. Meaning? To this puzzling utterance Hety, sounding more weary than annoyed, replied a full six months later: 'I find it a great pity that you have not yet read *If This is a Man;* if you did, the insanity and diabolicism of the Nazi system would finally be made clear to you.' Speer never replied: Hety's last known letter to him, 5 May 1981, went unanswered. And then Speer was dead. As for Levi, he was relieved not to have to correspond with Hitler's faithful former paladin (as Hety surely wanted him to do): 'I would have had some problems with writing to this ambiguous fellow,' Levi told me.

In the New Year of 1976, Levi's mother was suddenly very ill: attacks of giddiness, followed by liver pains. For the rest of January she had no appetite. Nurses tiptoed round 75 Corso Re Umberto as Levi meditated on his mother's likely death. To Hety Schmitt-Maas, with awful sincerity, he wrote: 'We fear the worst.' By February Ester showed signs of improvement, though Levi was still very frightened and wondered what other shocks the unlucky leap year of 1976 would bring. Though he was semi-retired, his dream of full retirement still seemed a long way off; the world petroleum crisis three years earlier had brought SIVA close to financial collapse and Levi felt he could not abandon Accati. That would be 'like the mouse fleeing from a sinking ship', he wrote to Hety in charming English.

Now Levi encountered *another* Primo Levi. A priest in southern Italy had had the 'awful idea' (said Levi) of reissuing a flowery travel book, *Abruzzo, Sweet and Gentle,* by the nineteenth-century Italian patriot Primo Levi. Though in his preface the priest had carefully distinguished between the two Levis, some of his parishioners had not, and they enquired after the latest book, *Abruzzo, Sweet and Gentle,* by the Auschwitz survivor Primo Levi, only to find its author had died in 1916. In a moment of pique, Levi objected to a friend that his Abruzzo namesake was not even a *family relation.* In more happy times, this 'local confusion', as Levi called it, would have been treated more light-heartedly by him.

On 9 September 1976 Chairman Mao died. Levi was disturbed by the dictator's death and rushed into the SIVA laboratory to break the news. 'My God, Portesi, have you heard?' Renato Portesi, the youthful Communist, was puzzled to hear Levi go on to describe Mao as the 'most important figure of the twentieth century', since he assumed Levi was a political moderate. On the day Mao died, Levi resigned from the 'M. D'Azeglio' parents' council. After nineteen months as president, his initial reformist zeal had been dampened rather by talk of overhead projectors and school repairs. Now that Renzo had left for university, his father was anyway no longer eligible to sit on the council. Renzo was a good-looking nineteen-year-old with a proficiency in science. Earlier that summer, as he was little disposed to find himself a holiday job, Levi had persuaded Accati to take him on part time at SIVA. At first Renzo's work had gone well, and Levi proudly reported to Hety on his son's progress: 'He is very serious and diligent, appreciates his work, and apparently learns more than at university' (where he was studying physics), but then it all went wrong.

The quarrel was the result of what seems, in retrospect, a typical fear of late 1970's Italy. These years were to witness some of the bloodiest outbursts of terrorism yet seen in a modern industrialised society. Factory bosses like Accati were in danger of being knee-capped or kidnapped by the Red Brigades and other subversives who preached class warfare. Potential victims rarely ventured out of doors without a tourniquet, in case they were shot in the legs. Renzo Levi was certainly not a *brigatista,* but he had theoretical links with the revolutionary Potere Operaio, the Sinistra Proletaria and the Lotta Continua: most left-leaning Italian students at this time did. In Accati's eyes, however, this was sufficient to turn Levi's son into an urban guerrilla. And as the weeks passed, he arranged for a series of petty altercations to arise with Renzo, preparatory to his dismissal. After Renzo had been sacked, Levi's relations with Accati took a downward turn.

In the winter of 1976, as the industrial north was terrorised by the Red Brigades, Levi rashly embarked on a five-day lecture tour of Switzerland organised by an Italo-Swiss cultural society. Much as Levi was pleased to be the centre of attention, he had not suspected how boring and laborious such author tours can be. For five days he had to give the same talk, night after night, on his 'Experiences as a Writer'. His first booking, on 9 November, was in Zurich; afterwards he attended a cocktail party in the Italian consulate, where he was reunited with Luigi ('Gigi') Ventre. In 1947 Ventre had been Antonicelli's publicity director for *If This is a Man*, but Levi had lost touch with him after 1958 when he moved to Switzerland. Ventre had with him a copy of the Antonicelli edition in which Levi now wrote the semi-humorous inscription: 'To Gigi, who was this book's midwife.'

The rest of the Swiss tour went easily enough. Full houses for the next four nights in St Gallen, Berne and Chur, then back to Turin on 13 November. Levi was no sooner home than he ill-advisedly agreed to take on another five-day lecture tour. During this fallow period, when his poetry was not selling and *The Double Bond* was stymied, Levi needed to keep busy; moreover, he found it hard to say no. This time the tour was organised by the Italian Cultural Association (ACI). The second lecture-circuit in Italy seems to have unsettled and exhausted Levi.

By the time Levi reached Bari, on 24 November, he was not well. A sumptuous buffet had been laid on for him by the Bari socialite Anna Cardinali, but Levi arrived late looking 'morose', she recalled, and 'down-at-heel'. He seemed unable to relax and chat; instead, he sat in a corner with 'permanently restless' hands, low-spirited if not depressed. Conversation was awkward until Cardinali mentioned the saintly Lorenzo Perrone. 'Ah, Lorenzo,' Levi brightened a little, 'I used to call him Antony', after St Antony, who had fed the starving. Levi warmed as the evening progressed, and when Cardinali asked him what he really thought of writers, he replied with a mock-ironic look: 'We're a bunch of frauds!'

On 25 November Levi returned to an uncertain future in Turin. Not for the first time, he felt he had nothing more to write, that he was finished as a writer. But what really concerned him, at this 'dangerous turn' in his career, was that fame and overexposure could be detrimental. Newspapers and magazines asked him to dredge from his desk unpublished ephemera. Their quality was not important: what mattered was the byline 'Primo Levi'.

TWENTY-ONE

Mapping the World of Work
1977-9

I

Levi spent Christmas and the new year of 1977 in Turin amid the cameras of a RAI television studio. Three of his science fictions were being filmed, but even with the author on hand for consultation, the shooting was marked by near disasters. The actor Giustino Durano, a friend of the playwright Dario Fo, refused to learn his lines. The RAI director Massimo Scaglione recounted: 'Durano had never met Levi before and I don't think even knew what he looked like. After struggling a while with the script he threw up his arms in despair. "I'll never be able to memorise this tosh! Who *is* the crazy man who wrote it?" Dead on cue, Primo came out of the shadows to introduce himself. "Congratulations, I'd never be able to memorise it myself."'

Meanwhile Levi was being fêted on all sides; his life in Turin took on a frantic pace as he answered post, met friends, attended book launches. In April Levi read his friend Fulvio Tomizza's new novel, *The Better Life*: it was a revelation. Tomizza had incorporated Italo-Slovene dialect words into the writing. At the age of eleven Levi had pestered his father for an etymological dictionary of Piedmontese dialect; dialect had fascinated him ever since. The success of Tomizza's novel, which sold more than 400,000 copies in Italy, encouraged Levi to abandon his ailing carbo-chemistry sequel, *The Double Bond*, and push on with another long-planned project. Five years earlier, in Togliattigrad, he had conceived the idea of a semi-fiction about a bumptious construction worker, Tino Faussone, that would be inflected with Piedmontese dialect words.

In search of material for this book, Levi began to trawl car-repair shops and tinker's yards in Borgo San Paolo and other Turin *banlieues* where mechanics spoke a semi-industrialised argot spiked with technical jargon.

One of these specialist locutions was *daje 'n taï* ('knock it into trim'); another was *date 'n-a regulà a le valvule* ('adjust your valves'). They reveal the Piedmontese mechanic's concern for perfection and precision: they are Faussone-speak.

Tino Faussone made his debut in Levi's short story, 'With Malice Aforethought', published in *La Stampa* on Sunday 13 March 1977. Faussone is tucking into a plate of roast beef in a workers' canteen somewhere on the Lower Volga, Russia, one of two Piedmontese on contract to a factory there. The other, the unnamed narrator, is a Turin chemist and concentration-camp survivor, who remains silent throughout Faussone's drawn-out tale of rigging and construction. The story was published during a weekend of exceptionally bloody neo-Fascist shoot-outs and bombings by the Red Brigades. With a few deft strokes, Levi had skilfully denominated the character of his new fictional hero. In his mid-thirties, tall, lean, prematurely bald, Tino Faussone is a gruff type with a bachelor's roving eye (his Christian name is a diminutive of 'libertine'). He speaks a demotically colourful Piedmontese and has travelled the world as an oil rig and pylon constructor. Though not well educated, he has a smart if didactic intelligence, and is lovable and irritating in equal measure.

2

As 1977 advanced, Levi's most important task, he felt, was to complete a chain of Faussone stories and shape them into a book. It would be called *La chiave a stella*, 'the star-shaped key', a polygonal socket-wrench resembling a spanner, which Faussone carries close to his hip. In Britain the book's title was to be *The Wrench*. Levi worked on the book intensively for a year and a half until the autumn of 1978. Rarely had he found writing so easy; he wrote directly on to his electric typewriter, correcting little at manuscript stage. The essence of *The Wrench*, interspersed between Faussone's blue-collar tales of construction, is Levi's elegant and often witty vindication of *il rusco*, 'everyday work'. Levi was determined to write a life-enhancing book that dignified Faussone's construction trade and put it on the literary map, in much the same way that *The Periodic Table* had done for chemistry. The book drew heavily on Levi's childhood understanding of the work ethic. Pride in a job well done – *il lavoro ben fatto* – was an intrinsic part of what it meant to be Turinese.

In many ways, *The Wrench* was to be one of the most personal books that Levi wrote, one revealing his most deeply held cultural beliefs. The picaresque trials of Tino Faussone were in fact rooted in Levi's Fascist schooldays. During Fascism the virtue of toil was eulogised on billboards, and Mussolini never ceased to praise bricklayers and navvies who worked with their hands. Primo's first reading primer, *My Pearls*, warned that 'the lazy person is harmful to society' and that mental instability, if not death would result from idleness. 'Woe betide loafers!' lectured another of the boy's primers, *The Worker's Book*. From an early age Levi had the greatest respect for people who took pride in their work. It can be no accident that the foulest, most unforgivable insult in Piedmontese is *strassoun*, 'good-for-nothing'.

Though Einaudi would market *The Wrench* as 'fiction', most of Faussone's stories were based on true-life adventures told to Levi by friends and work colleagues. Faussone's epic of pontoon-building in India, 'The Bridge', for example, drew on Nicoletta Neri's Kiplingesque accounts of life in Calcutta in the mid-1970s, when she had seen families living destitute inside cement pipes on the banks of the Hooghly. Levi always did his research, and throughout composition of *The Wrench* he relied heavily on help provided by his engineer friend Livio Norzi. Norzi assisted with the book's arcane details of crane towers and suspension cables, and lent Levi technical books and articles on construction. Levi was justly proud of his skill in stitching Norzi's technical information into Faussone's narrative. A lesser writer would find it hard to sustain an imaginative engagement with 'caisons' and 'pontoons'.

Levi consulted Giorgio Lattes on other technicalities and studious precisions. Lattes, 'Big George', was still the manager of a chromium-plating factory on Turin's outskirts and Levi often visited him at his Via Serrano offices. He went there to drink whisky, laugh and hear anecdotes that might serve for his work-in-progress. Luigi Tosini, Lattes's deputy, recalled that Levi made a point of talking to the most humble workers at the plant. In every way *The Wrench* would continue Levi's literary credo that the proper study of mankind is man.

3

While Levi was writing *The Wrench*, he stepped up contributions to *La Stampa*. In the next four years he was to write more than sixty articles for the Turin paper, becoming the broadsheet's star contributor. He showed himself a master in the art of *haute vulgarisation* – high-class popularisation – and with agreeable courtesy made science accessible to the layman. His articles exuded a polymath's enthusiasm and a wholly affecting modesty. Levi was given a free rein to write about what he liked and put his keen mind to parapsychological marvels, Aldous Huxley's predilection for cats, and the religious rites of Ashkenazic Judaism.

La Stampa's culture editor, Alberto Sinigaglia, was distantly related to

27. (*Above*) 1943. Primo Levi: photo for false ID papers.
28. (*Above right*) Vanda Maestro, c.1941.
29. (*Right*) Luciana Nissim in her thirties.
30. (*Below*) 1942. Franco Sacerdoti on honeymoon in Padua with Nucci Treves.
31. (*Below right*) Jolanda De Benedetti.

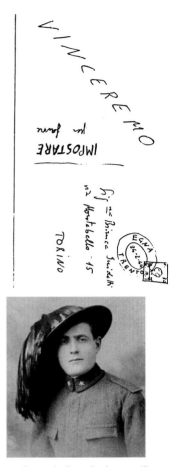

Bolzano, 23-2.

Cara Bianca, tutti in viaggio
alla maniera classica -
saluta tutti - a voi la
fiaccola. Ciao, Bianca,
ti vogliamo bene

Primo, Vanda,
Luciana

VINCEREMO

IMPOSTARE

33. Alberto Dalla Volta, late 1943, days before his arrest. 'A strong yet peace-loving man against whom the weapons of night are blunted.'

34. Lorenzo Perrone in 'Bersagliere' army uniform, c.1925. 'Nobody knows how much I owe that man.'

35. Jean Samuel, post-Auschwitz. He and Levi met during an air-raid alarm in the camp, when they spoke of their mothers.

36. Lello Perugia. May 1945, Katowice - five months after the liberation of Auschwitz. The 'Cesare' of The Truce, 'a child of the sun'.

Facing page
32. (*Above*) The note addressed to Bianca Guidetti Serra which Levi threw from the Auschwitz transport: 'Dear Bianca, we're all travelling in the classic style. Give our regards to everyone. Long may you carry the flame. So long, Bianca. We wish you well. Primo, Vanda, Luciana.'
This page
37. (*Above*) Franco Antonicelli, 1935.
38. (*Above right*) Cover of the first edition of *If This is a Man*, showing Goya etching chosen by Antonicelli.
39. (*Below*) 13 November 1952. Golden wedding anniversary of Augusto and Dora Salmoni. From bottom right: Primo Levi, unknown guest, Alberto Salmoni, Lucia Levi, Bruno Salmoni and Bianca Guidetti Serra.

40. (*Top*) April 1954. Primo Levi (sixth from right) at the Buchenwald concentration camp Memorial.

41. (*Right*) 1952, Vercelli. Left to right: Primo Levi, Ada Della Torre, Silvio Ortona.

42. (*Below left*) 1952. Primo Levi and Giovanna Balzaretti at SIVA.

43. (*Below right*) Federico ('Rico') Silla Accati, 'a very uncommon human specimen'.

44. (*Above*) 1963, at home in 75 Corso Re Umberto. From left to right: Lisa Levi, eighteen; Primo Levi; Renzo, six; Lucia Levi.
45. (*Right*) Author photo used for *The Truce* and *Ist das ein Mensch?*.
46. (*Below*) 1963, 'Strega Prize' presentations. From left to right: Italo Calvino, Giulio Einaudi and Natalia Ginzburg.

47. (*Top*) Leonardo ('Nardo') De Benedetti.
48. (*Top right*) Hety Schmitt-Maas.
49. (*Above*) Ferdinand Meyer, the 'Lothar Müller' of *The Periodic Table*. This is the photograph that Meyer sent Levi at the start of their correspondence.
50. (*Right*) Nuto Revelli at Verduno Castle.
51. (*Below*) Mario Rigoni Stern talking to school children.
52. (*Below right*) Edith Bruck.

53. (*Above left*) 8 June 1972. Orsolina Ferrero's birthday, SIVA. Primo Levi is standing on the left.
54. (*Above right*) Bianca Guidetti Serra deliberating in court.
55. (*Left*) Primo Levi (with new beard) and the SIVA company secretary Franca Tambini.
56. (*Below*) 30 May 1975. Chemistry students' reunion. Levi has just agreed to the title *The Double Bond* for his sequel to *The Periodic Table*. Giovanna Balzaretti is seated on the left of Levi.

57. (*Above*) 1980. Primo Levi explaining naturalist phenomena to Barbara Papuzzi.

58. (*Above right*) 31 July 1983, in the mountains above Cogne: Levi's sixty-fourth birthday.

59. (*Right*) 21 April 1986. Primo and Lucia Levi in Stockholm. Levi was entering a depressive episode.

60. (*Below*) September 1986, at home in 75 Corso Re Umberto. Primo Levi relaxes with Philip Roth in the room where he had been born sixty-seven years earlier.

Levi's maternal grandmother Adele Sinigaglia. A dapper man with a twinkling, understated humour, Sinigaglia was highly civilised, and Levi was quickly won over by his cordiality. In Sinigaglia's opinion, Levi was 'terribly irked' that his celebrity as an Auschwitz witness far outshone his reputation as a writer. Under Sinigaglia's gentle guidance, however, Levi was encouraged to write short stories for the weekend editions. He obliged with a series of 'Sunday' shorts, many of which had a dark autobiographical undertow. Uncle Corrado was very ill when Levi published 'At the Right Time', in which a death-haunted textile-shop assistant, Giuseppe, is visited by an angel of death. Giuseppe the fabric salesman is an aspect of Corrado Luzzati. In 'Self-Control' a hypochondriac bus-driver is unhinged by fears of liver disease and memory loss; when the story appeared in *La Stampa* in 1978, Levi's mother had just recovered from liver complications, and Ada Della Torre had been diagnosed with Alzheimer's disease. As increasingly happened with Levi, his deepest fears were displaced on to the more neutral ground of newspaper column space.

Levi also reviewed books. Lorenzo Mondo, *La Stampa*'s literary editor, was a physically overbearing, pipe-smoking Catholic, outwardly very different from Levi as an assimilated Jew and atheist. A relationship of trust and mutual respect was nevertheless established, and soon Levi was reviewing books on a variety of subjects, from gossip to philology to the environment. Whenever he was at *La Stampa* he also made a point of visiting Gabriella Poli, whose office was adjacent to Mondo's. Levi had got to know Poli in 1954 when she was covering the official visit to Buchenwald. She liked to serve him anchovy snacks and lemon tea, a ritual of *torinesità* that he adored. Poli belonged to a small circle of journalist friends to whom Levi routinely showed his works-in-progress before they were published.

But, for all the marvellous variety of his newspaper journalism, Levi could not escape his public role as commentator on the Nazi camps. In 1977 the normally temperate Levi published a caustic attack on films that he believed falsified the nature of Nazi violence. Tawdry box-office hits like *The Night Porter* or *Salon Kitty*, with their paraphernalia of whips and manacles, played on a fantasy of sexual relations between the SS and their prisoners. Worse, they reduced life in the Nazi camps to a stereotypical black-and-white contrast between oppressors and oppressed. These films were 1970s swastika chic, the stuff of *Penthouse* magazine, really.

4

On 1 September 1977 Levi finally cut all remaining ties with SIVA. The treadmill of factory life was over. 'After almost thirty years of forced labour,

I weighed anchor and said goodbye to everybody, especially to Mr Accati, who is by now more and more rich, busy and unhappy.' The autumn proved hectic. On 8 September Levi called for the resignation of the Christian Democrat minister for defence, Vito Lattanzio. Lattanzio had allowed SS Lieutenant Colonel Herbert Kappler to escape from a military hospital in Rome to Germany, from where he could not be extradited. The Nazi had been sentenced to life imprisonment in 1948 by the Italian courts for his role in the liquidation of the Rome ghetto and the massacre outside Rome of 335 men and boys in reprisal for a partisan action. Kappler was still technically an Italian prisoner and therefore minister Lattanzio's responsibility when he absconded from the cancer ward. The response to his escape was clamorous. Levi went on Turin radio with a locally famous anti-Fascist priest, Father Ruggero Cipolla, to discuss the issue of forgiveness of war criminals. He and the padre agreed that forgiveness was possible only for those who showed repentance. In the event, Lattanzio did resign (though not because of Levi), only to be offered two new key cabinet posts. 'Such are the ways of Christian Democracy,' Levi tartly observed. Ex-SS Kappler died peacefully at his birthplace in West Germany a year later in 1978, aged seventy.

On 22 October, in the midst of the Kappler affair, Levi was reunited in Aosta with his writer-friends Mario Rigoni Stern and Nuto Revelli. They were to talk to schoolchildren about their wartime traumas of detention, survival and resistance. Afterwards, the trio enjoyed a meal of polenta porridge and pork, and drank the strong local wine. Over the years this triumvirate friendship – what Levi called the 'three-leaved clover' – had intensified. All three met fairly often in Turin at book launches and survivor conferences, and they planned to visit the Great War battle grounds of Asiago, though the moment never seemed opportune. ('The unlucky washerwoman never finds the right stone' was the picturesque Piedmontese expression Levi used to describe the missed opportunities.) One crucial difference set Revelli apart from Levi and Rigoni Stern. The Resistance had been Revelli's triumph and liberation, while for Levi and Rigoni Stern the war had been a catastrophe. Yet Revelli remained more angry than either Levi or Rigoni Stern. A difficult, combative man, he had made it his life's work to record the unheard testimonies of Piedmont's war-wounded, the peasants who had survived the Russian retreat and not been listened to. After supper Rigoni Stern returned to his hotel, where he embraced Levi. 'We've been like brothers on holiday,' he said.

That autumn Levi worked on *The Wrench*, and in November he sent five chapters to his old Einaudi editor, Daniele Ponchiroli, who had retired to his native Padua: 'Let me know what you make of them.' *The Wrench* is Levi's most sunny book and Ponchiroli loved it. Written during the happy time of his early retirement, it confirms the author's gift for comedy that first surfaced in *The Truce*. Levi believed that Faussone was one of his finest creations, and in Piedmont *The Wrench* is held in great affection. Indeed Levi's portrayal of Faussone paid homage to a minor Piedmontese classic. The Marquis Massimo D'Azeglio's autobiography, *My Memories*, included the Piedmontese army captain Rubiera among its many grotesque and comic characters; Levi drew extensively on him for Faussone's gruff manner and improbable tales of globetrotting. However, Levi's principal model for Faussone was SIVA's electro-technician Felice Malgaroli. A solitary, self-educated man, like Faussone he had worked in forty-four countries incuding Iran and Venezuela. He was a global soul: displacement and uprootedness were what he knew best.

Faussone's fictional father was a compound of various men Levi had known, but his main source was the Turin coppersmith Signor Ciagne, who for thirty years had made boilers and alcohol stills for SIVA. Faussone's father is a copper artisan from Piedmont's Canavese region and, just as Ciagne had done with his own son Nanni, Faussone passes on to Tino a professional pride and integrity in his work. The Faussones are not Jewish, but Levi surely was thinking of the rabbinic injunction that a father must teach his son a trade. Ciagne died in 1960, but to forestall objections of fictional distortion, Levi sent Ciagne's son, Nanni, the 'Beating Copper' chapter in typescript; Levi was wary, for this was not a favour he granted everyone:

> I hope you will forgive the many liberties I have taken with your father: what you told me about him has served essentially as raw material and as a starting point. I trust that nothing I have written will upset you. If you don't mind (but if you do, let me know), I would like to mention you in the acknowledgments.

Though Nanni Ciagne corrected one or two technical terms, he had no quarrel with what he read; Levi had allowed his imagination to transform his father magnificently.

At the end of January 1978 Levi began to feel discomfort, sharp pains in his back, then a red rash with blisters broke out. Perhaps the skin trouble had been brought on by his handling of some virulent SIVA chemical? However, Nardo De Benedetti diagnosed shingles and noted that the condition would erupt every time Levi felt under pressure. For two weeks Levi underwent new treatments, always expecting to be able to return to writing the next week. He managed to drag himself to rehearsals in Turin for a radio version of *The Truce,* though 'The Bigs in Rome' (as Levi called his RAI producers) had been unhappy with his scripted treatment and asked him to rewrite it. The extra work had required a tremendous effort from Levi and he was glad to be shot of it. And he did not get on with the play's director, Edmo Fenoglio, an ex-mathematician with a taste in kitsch.

The shingles were very disruptive to Levi's life and work. Two weeks later they flared up again – badly – and Levi tried vitamins, country walks, rest. Nothing worked. Then he had an idea. The previous year, Nardo De Benedetti had been successfully treated for rheumatoid arthritis by a Chinese acupuncturist. (His hands had swollen so badly that he could not remove his wedding ring.) So for the next three weeks every Monday, Levi called on a Chinese doctor, more out of 'curiosity', he said, than in good faith. Dr Chan found Levi to be in reasonable general health, but detected certain weaknesses in kidneys and liver, which he treated with needles in the foot and knee. This went on for several weeks: Levi's health did not improve, and there followed eight months of dreadful neuralgic pain.

7

On 10 February 1978 Levi received notice that he was under investigation for causing involuntary 'personal injury' (*lesione colposo*) to workers under his care at SIVA. The notice was part of the inquisitorial Italian judicial process, and implied no guilt, merely that there were sufficient grounds for an inquiry. But Levi was potentially in very serious trouble: if the case reached the papers, the shock would be greatest for Levi's mother. As the author of *If This is a Man,* a book that upheld human dignity, Levi would be especially vulnerable to accusations of managerial inhumanity. He knew as well as anybody that a trial would be an unpleasant experience and that dirt of various kinds might be raked up.

Levi was indicted on two counts of 'personal injury.' The first dated back to 14 January 1977, when the worker Giuseppe Cordua was rushed to hospital with carbolic-acid poisoning. He survived (only to die of toxic complications eighteen years later in his native Santa Severina in Calabria). The second count was more vague and referred to a range of alleged worksite illnesses or injuries contracted by SIVA staff, or ex-staff, during Levi's directorship. In March 1977 Lorenzo Bagnasco was nearly blinded by a jet of xenol solvent; fortunately for Levi, he had not been present at the factory that day.

Levi would have had forewarning of the investigations. Three weeks before receipt of the legal notice, on 23 January, Turin's chief magistrate Raffaele Guariniello had descended on SIVA accompanied by government work inspectors and police officials. The team took photographs of the factory and randomly interviewed workers. On the basis of their findings, Guariniello felt he had no choice but to instigate legal proceedings. An extremely scrupulous and fair-minded investigator, Guariniello had many other Turin factories under his hawk-eyed surveillance, not just SIVA. He was one of Italy's *pretori d'assalto*, 'assault magistrates', so called for their raids on suspect toxic factories. For the Italian left, Guariniello, a Neapolitan tailor's son, was a crusader; for the right, a meddlesome do-gooder.

Three other SIVA bosses were arraigned with Levi on a 'personal injury' charge: Accati's son-in-law Michael Tinker, the firm's sales manager Maurilio Tambini, and Rico Accati himself. These three were also under investigation (unlike Levi) for 'contravention of work safety regulations'. Levi did all he could to distance himself from his fellow accused, and Accati was furious with him: Levi seemed out to save himself. Giovanni Lageard, a lawyer famous for his reactionary rough tactics, was to defend Accati, Tinker and Tambini; Levi was to be defended by Bianca Guidetti Serra. (It was the first time Bianca had defended a factory boss.) Levi's initial memorandum to her, dated 23 February 1978, stated that he had done his utmost to prescribe the use of gas- and dust-masks and other protective clothing. As the investigations progressed, seventy-eight workers were examined individually by medical experts. Evidence was found of hypertension, cerebral thrombosis, heart attacks, gum diseases (a telltale sign of lead poisoning), asthmatic disturbances, peptic and gastric ulcers and chronic bronchitis. Liver damage caused by di-amino di-phenyl methane (in 1964 the chemical had caused a jaundice epidemic in England's Epping Forest) was also found to be present. By any standards these were horrendous findings, which Levi wanted to put far behind him.

Above all Levi feared what he called a 'second IPCA'. IPCA was an artificial dyestuffs factory outside Turin, where numerous workers had died of bladder cancer caused by contact with beta-naphthylamine. The 'Cancer Factory' directors had all been jailed for manslaughter. But beneath this fear lay a deeper and more terrible one. At Auschwitz Levi had routinely handled beta-naphthylamine; it was used in synthetic-rubber manufacture. 'I'm not saying that Primo *believed* he had cancer,' said the Turin pathologist Benedetto Terracini, a friend, 'only that he was extremely concerned by the *possibility* of it.' The investigations dragged on, leaving a bitter taste for Levi that no amount of reassurance or support from friends like Professor Terracini could disguise.

Levi's second memorandum to Bianca Guidetti Serra, dated 3 February 1980, three years after the initial investigation, took issue with Professor Francesco Candura, an industrial-medicine expert at Pavia University, who had assessed each of SIVA's 600 chemical products for their toxicity. He described the professor's toxicological report as 'diligent, but hardly conclusive'. So Levi was not persuaded of his own guilt. By the time final sentence was pronounced three years later in Turin on 16 June 1983, the case had lost much of its horror for him. No evidence was ever found of intent to cause 'personal injury'; therefore Levi, Tinker, Tambini and Accati did not stand trial. For the secondary charge of 'work safety contravention' (for which Levi was not charged), Tambini, Accati and Tinker were absolved by amnesty. These *amnestie* are dispensed frequently in Italy; in their day they had allowed many Fascist war criminals to go free.

Michael Tinker was amazed by the outcome: 'If a trial *had* gone ahead there's no doubt in my mind that all four of us would have served a suspended prison term.' Initially Raffaele Guariniello, the investigating magistrate, had no idea of Primo Levi's connection to SIVA. 'I must say I was very shocked to find out. Here was a man who'd been through unimaginable deprivations at Auschwitz. But maybe because of what he'd been through, he was less inclined to attach due importance to other (albeit far less terrible) deprivations like worker safety and chemical contamination. In a strange way, Auschwitz had made Levi *undervalue* the gravity of the human situation at his factory. I'm afraid my impression was of a dangerously unprofessional man.' Levi had lacked the managerial will to see through reforms for worker safety: his employees, most of them, were kept in ignorance of the potential risks. The small family firm that Levi had joined in 1948 had changed beyond recognition. And at the time the incidents under investigation occurred, Levi had lost much of his affection for the firm.

As a coda to these legal upsets, in 1979 a young Italian chemist, Luciano Caglioti, approached Levi to write the preface for his book, *The Two Faces of Chemistry*, on the effect of chemicals on the environment. Sooner or later the human race, Caglioti wrote, would be forced to confront its own destructive tendencies. He was not unaware of the advances made by chemistry in medical and other fields, and the impartiality of his argument .

impressed Levi. Like most Italians Levi had ignored ecology; but, after magistrate Guariniello's investigations he was more alert to factory health scares, and he agreed to write the preface to Caglioti's book.

<h2 style="text-align:center">8</h2>

In tandem with Levi's personal drama at SIVA, a horrific national drama now occurred. On 16 March 1978 Italy's Christian Democrat leader Aldo Moro was kidnapped by the Red Brigades, and his five-man escort machine-gunned to death. For the forty-five days that Moro lay blindfolded in his 'people's prison', Italy was filled with anxiety, and Levi was as deeply shocked as any Italian. The distressing physical symptoms of his shingles were compounded by panic attacks brought on by Guariniello's investigations; almost every night he woke in fear, his panic increasing as he stared into the darkness. Levi's acute anxiety was complicated by the Moro affair, as well as by distressing news from West Germany that SS veterans were openly reuniting for parades and singsongs. Most were harmless men, but there were signs of younger support, and Levi was sufficiently worried by their activity to write about it for *La Stampa*. Hate had not died in the bunker with Hitler.

Two weeks into Moro's disappearance, Italians flocked to see Steven Spielberg's new escapist fantasia *Close Encounters of the Third Kind*. The veteran Turin novelist Mario Soldati reviewed the film favourably in *La Stampa*. Levi, in an open letter to Soldati ('Close Encounters with Tricks'), refuted the novelist's praise, but took the opportunity to reminisce about their meeting in Venice fifteen years earlier. They had met at the Campiello presentations when Levi won the prize for *The Truce*. Soldati, confessedly bisexual, was an immensely fascinating figure for Levi; educated by Jesuits, he wore hounds tooth tweed jackets and was famous for his trencherman's relish in fine foods, as well as his friendship with Graham Greene. In Venice in 1963 Levi's fame was no more than a distant rumour, yet literary recognition was thrillingly within reach. Now Levi was a celebrity and the trappings of fame were not only a constriction but, with an investigating magistrate on his trail, positively a danger. He wanted only to be back in Venice with Soldati, when life had been simple and uncomplicated.*

*

*In 1993 when I spoke to him, Soldati was suffering from 'nominal aphasia' (a form of memory loss). He inscribed a copy of his novel *The Capri Letters* to me: 'Why or when I met Primo Levi in Venice I can't remember. Venice means only one thing to me now: dear Graham.' Soldati had collaborated with Graham Greene in 1954 on a suspense-thriller movie set in Venice, *The Stranger's Hand*, starring Trevor Howard and co-scripted by the Italian Jewish novelist Giorgio Bassani.

On 9 May, nearly two months after his disappearance, Aldo Moro's bullet-riddled body was found in the boot of a car in Rome; he had been executed by the *brigatisti*. With so many years passed, it is difficult to appreciate the gravity of what the Red Brigades did: the kidnap and murder of Margaret Thatcher by the IRA might have been a comparable crime. Distressed by the event, Levi reflected a good deal on the institutions of modern Italy and the shameful inability of the police to locate Moro's cell (it has still not been found today). He condemned the terrorists in *La Stampa*, 'We All Know Who the Red Brigades Are', before reporting to Hety Schmitt-Maas:

> The Moro affair was felt by many of us as a sort of disease, superimposed on countless other diseases that infect this country and the world. The feat itself, the murder, has remained unexplained . . . Are the Red Brigades clever or stupid? Clever, since they planned (for more than one year, apparently) and carried out their crime with ruthless precision; stupid, as the crime itself led to no result, and merely contributed to the rehabilitation of Christian Democracy, helping to turn the unreliable and twisted Aldo Moro into a hero.

Levi was relieved when the renowned anti-Fascist Sandro Pertini was elected president of the Republic. 'It is the first time we have a really spotless man in Parliament,' he enthused. But his delight in Pertini's election was tempered by sad news in Turin. On Tuesday 4 July, at the age of eighty-three, his old literature teacher Azelia Arici died. Levi wrote her obituary for *La Stampa* and attended her cremation.

In Pietra Ligure between 1 and 18 August Levi worked hard to bring *The Wrench* to completion. His daughter was in Moscow, his son in Greece; his wife and mother were resting in Lurisia, a thermal resort nearby. Thus unhampered, Levi quickly finished his book. He sent the manuscript to Italo Calvino at Einaudi, who, happy with it, transmitted it to Nino Colombo for proofreading. For twenty years Colombo had taken a tooth-comb to Levi's typescripts but, in his long publishing relationship with Levi, rarely had to correct much. 'Levi was the most scrupulous author I'd ever known – his typescripts were unblemished.' Secretly, Levi resented the fact that his manuscripts were left more or less untouched by editors: he craved their comments and criticism, as any writer would. His circle of readers (Poli and other friends) had anyway done Colombo's work for him.

By the time Colombo went to work on *The Wrench*, news came that Bashevis Singer had won the Nobel Prize for Literature. Levi published a generous appreciation of the Jewish novelist in the 6 October edition of *La Stampa*. Singer was 'deservedly' the most popular Polish-American Yiddish novelist of our time: his fables of Ashkenazic village life were lit up by the 'spirit of Chagall and a rare honesty.' This newspaper praise, however, came from Levi's pen, not his heart: in private his opinion of Singer was very different. The Einaudi editor Luca Baranelli was taken aback by the vehemence of Levi's aversion. 'I don't like Singer *at all*,' he told Baranelli with emphasis: Singer lacked the 'backbone' to get into the first division of writers. Perhaps Levi was jealous of Singer's considerable popularity in Italy, but wanted to put on a show of magnaminity for *La Stampa*'s readers. This was not the first time that Levi's public persona would come into conflict with his private convictions, a dishonesty that was a consequence of fame.

9

After eight months of acupuncture under Dr Chan, Levi's shingles faded, though his skin was left curiously sensitive to the weather (which Levi said usefully enabled him to 'forecast storms'). For a week in October he and Lucia were in Campania, a southern volcanic land of plump red tomatoes and Roman amphitheatres. This was the second time the Levis had been to the Mezzogiorno; the first, in 1970, took them to the craggy limestone Gargano promontory. In Campania they visited Sophia Loren's birthplace – Pozzuoli – and the extinct Solfatara volcano with its pungent sulphur reek. At Pompeii nearby the victims petrified in volcanic debris fascinated Levi. A girl with her head buried in her mother's breast moved him to write the poem, 'The Girl-Child of Pompei'. The poignant ash-and-cinders child was compared to the Hiroshima schoolgirl whose silhouette was printed by the atomic flash on a wall.

Levi was not long in Pompeii when he read in the papers that the Austrian-born philosopher Jean Améry had committed suicide. On 17 October, in a Strasbourg hotel, he ended his life with poison. Reportedly Améry had been downcast by the resurgence of neo-Nazism in Germany and by fears of memory loss. Though Améry was well known in German literary circles, in Italy he was unheard of, and the journalistic tributes Levi read in Pompeii were scant. Améry had been born in Vienna under the name Hans Maier; though he was not strictly Jewish (his mother was of mixed Jewish and Christian descent), in Nazi eyes Améry was irrefutably so; captured and tortured by the Gestapo in Belgium, his long calvary of wretchedness and pain continued at Auschwitz. Levi was unable to share Améry's corrosive love-hate of Judaism ('For me, to be a Jew is quite a simple affair'), and disliked Amery's description of him as a 'forgiver'. Nevertheless on his return to Turin he began to translate the Austrian's book *At the Mind's Limits*. Published in Germany in 1966, the collection was an abrasive enquiry into the author's humiliation and self-loathing after Auschwitz. In the slim volume Levi said he found 'the lucid despair of a man wounded to the bone, dispossessed of his roots, who, having been tortured once (these are almost literally his words), is tortured for all life to come'. Though Levi was disconcerted by Améry's suicide, he was not surprised by it:

> Suicides are generally mysterious [he wrote in English to Hety]: Améry's was not. Faced by the hopeless clarity of his mind, faced by his death, I have felt how fortunate *I* have been, not only in recovering my family and my country, but also in succeeding to weave around me a 'painted veil' made of family affections, friendships, travel, writing, and even chemistry.

The day after Améry's death, on 18 November, there occurred an infamous mass-suicide. In his important article of this time, 'Jean Améry, the Suicidal Philosopher', Levi spoke of the Guyanese jungle massacre in which the Reverend Jim Jones ordered his flock to kill themselves by cyanide. What destructive genii had caused 911 people collectively to take their lives? Mind control? In comparison to Jonestown, said Levi, Améry's suicide was at least 'explicable'.

In November came further distressing news. At 2:00 pm on the afternoon of the 8th, there was a laboratory explosion in the Crocetta, which took off Ennio Mariotti's right hand and left him for dead. When firemen entered the blackened premises on Via San Secondo they found the chemist face-down in blood. Levi had just celebrated Ada Della Torre's sixty-fourth birthday when he heard news of the explosion. He rushed to the Turin hospital, where surgeons tried to save Mariotti's life. His easy-going friendliness and warm manner made him one of Levi's most valued male friends; and, miraculously, after five hours of surgery the sixty-four-year-old survived. After the blast Mariotti worked harder than before, pursuing his biochemical activities one-handed. His stoical and dignified recovery impressed Levi immensely.

10

At the end of 1978 Levi began to take German lessons at the Goethe Institut in Turin. He was the oldest in a class of seventeen women, whose company he enjoyed, and from the start he was a keen student. He had two teachers. The first, Jutta Pabst, found Levi dauntingly inquisitive and recalled his mania for wanting to know the precise etymology of German words: 'His hand was always going up in class: "Fräulein, excuse me, but what is the deeper – I mean the *true* – meaning of this word?" In some ways, *Levi* was the teacher, and *I* the student.' The other teacher, Hanns Dieter Engert, was the more important. Born in 1933 in the Rhineland city of Ulm, as a homosexual he believed, tragically as it turned out, that *amore* was less complicated and cheaper down south, and had left Germany twenty years previously in search of Mediterranean companionship. A shy, solitary forty-five-year-old, Engert was highly cultivated and spent time with Levi in the Goethe Institut library, consulting dictionaries, correcting his grammar. Unlike some men of his generation, Levi had no aversion to homosexual company and already had several gay acquaintances in Turin, among them the theatre director Pieralberto Marché, the radio director Giorgio Bandini and the bookseller Angelo Pezzana, whose cultural magazine *Sodoma* Levi was aware of. Levi responded eagerly to Engert's punctilious attention and welcomed his proposal to re-translate *Ist das ein Mensch?* (nothing came of it). Six months later, in vastly improved German, Levi wrote of his new teacher to Hety Schmitt-Maas:

> I must seem a very odd pupil to him, not just because of my age, but because my German is derived from so many different and ill-assorted sources, namely: the concentration camp, chemistry, business and a few books read at random – a mixture of classical and modern! [Engert] thinks that this is why my German is so colourful and funny; I often insert archaic or literary words into everyday speech and vice versa (as may well have happened in this letter).

Levi was clearly proud of his unorthodox German and he attended the Goethe Institut for three years to improve it. Always the first to sign on for a new term, he impressed his classmates by his studious dedication. Going back to school at the age of fifty-nine was fun, he said; he bought himself a pair of bifocals to see the blackboard better, which lent him an elderly, donnish air.

The class was joined by Anna Maria Savoini, a vivacious sixty-year-old. As the oldest pupils in the class, she and Levi sat next to each other and good-naturedly competed to impress Hanns Engert. Levi inscribed a copy of *The Truce* to Savoini 'with gratitude', for she had been sympathetic to his problems. 'Besides wishing to improve his German,' Savoini told me, 'Levi had another motive for attending the Goethe Institut – to escape his difficult situation at home.' In these early months of 1978 Levi was steadily more worried by his mother's health and the ever-more frequent demands he claimed she made on him. German lessons provided some small respite.

11

Publication of *The Wrench* was imminent. Levi had been with Einaudi for twenty-one years and the company had changed. Giulio Einaudi cynically played off editors against each other and liked sparks to fly at meetings. This made for an unhappy, chilly atmosphere, which Levi disliked. 'The company was like a fridgeful of frozen cod,' said one ex-consultant. One of Levi's few friends there was Oreste Molina, Einaudi's production manager, a slow-talking, incredibly precise man whom Levi had known since 1949. Taciturn but cordial, as a technician Molina was better suited than Giulio Einaudi to appreciate the chemist in Levi. Levi was often a guest at his farmhouse outside Turin ('La Mattutina') where he drank the effervescent Barbera wine of which Molina produced an impressive 1,500 litres a year. Slightly tipsy, they discussed book-binding, pagination and typesetting. Molina's unaffected, amusing conversation was a delight to Levi. Sometimes they were joined by Alan Nixon, a Scottish-born thriller writer who ran a translation agency on Corso Re Umberto. Like Molina, Nixon had a fine nose for Piedmont's wine and food.

To fill the void left by his editor Daniele Ponchiroli's departure to Padua, Levi discovered, at about this time, a new and equally genial comrade. Alberto Papuzzi excelled at mountaineering as well as journalism (today he is *La Stampa*'s cultural editor). By the time Levi met him, the thirty-six-year-old had published two important works of reportage; the first exposed the medieval abuses of a mental hospital outside Turin, the other was a study of Fiat's monopoly in Piedmont. Born in Bolzano in 1942, Papuzzi was a disillusioned former Communist with a restless, enquiring mind. He was Einaudi's new press officer and had the virtue, in such a snobbish environment, of being straightforward and plain-dealing. His attractive wife Luisa, born in Venice, made mouth-watering Venetian specialities, and was a lively spirit whom Levi liked. Papuzzi was now Levi's chief mountaineer companion. The two set out in his car for the Susa Valleys where, perched on the top of Mount Musiné, they would watch the gliders circle overhead and discuss all manner of subjects, from UFOs to the 1970s craze for Rubik cubes. One day when they came within sight of Monte Rosa dei Banchi, Levi remarked to Papuzzi: 'That's my all-time favourite mountain peak'; the mountain's pyramid-shaped crest was geometrical perfection for Levi.

The competitive aspect of mountaineering did not interest Levi: he never boasted about scaling a daunting peak. Instead, what mattered to him was the physical challenge and testing himself. Once, Levi calculated the kinetic energy that he and Papuzzi had expended after struggling up a punishing slope. However, climbing was not just about pulse rates and body temperature:

> One day [Papuzzi told me] we trudged for hours in the Val Champorcher at an altitude of maybe 3,000 metres, then slid down into a valley where we found a sequence of breathtakingly beautiful deserted lakes. On reaching the first of them, Primo said to me in a child-like voice: 'You know, I've never been to Canada before, but this is what I imagine Canada would look like.'

Another time, Papuzzi took his young daughter Barbara and son Davide into the mountains with Levi. It was late spring and there were traces of melting snow under a blue sky. Levi showed an extraordinary flair for pedagogy as he explained to the Papuzzi children why violet-coloured flowers grew in spots where the soil was less acidic. He showed them a hare's track in the mud caked by snow, and afterwards posed clownishly for their toy camera. Few people outside Levi's family had seen Primo play the fool. Papuzzi was surprised by it, while at the same time charmed by Levi's unabashed tutoring of his offspring.

12

Levi's sixth book, *The Wrench,* was published by Einaudi in November 1978 at a time of extreme national tension. The tumultuous 'years of lead' (so called after the Red Brigades' lead bullets) were drawing to a close amid nefarious Mafia operations and the election of an unknown pope, John Paul II, to St Peter's. In these uncertain times Levi's book aroused different responses. *The Wrench* was rightly seen as a contribution to the long tradition of Italian regional and dialect literature, and was favourably compared to Pier Paolo Pasolini's two dialect-rich Roman novels of the 1950s, *Ragazzi di vita* and *Una vita violenta*, which Levi admired. In Piedmontese dialect *faussone* can mean 'great falsifier'. The observation that Faussone (and, by extension, his creator) was a counterfeiter, a fib-mongerer, upset Levi greatly and he went to unusual lengths to defend his creation against the charge of tall story-telling. It is possible that Levi had named his 'great falsifier' after an industrial snoop and anti-Communist police informer at SIVA's sister company SICME. The man was nicknamed in Piedmontese *al faussun*, 'the false one'.

It was not long before Levi got his first hostile reviews. The fringe left-wing press had an almost unanimously adverse reaction to *The Wrench*. The book was seen as an attack on the revolutionary spirit of '68 and the view that work is punitive and alienating. This *gauchiste* image of assembly-line slaves and evil bosses had been infamously advocated by Nanni Balestrini in his avant-garde novel of 1971, *We Want it All*, in which work was described as a con devised by greedy Fiat capitalists to keep the workers down. Levi thought Balestrini's attitude was 'crass', even 'contemptible'. Certainly no writer since Joseph Conrad had offered quite so enthusiastic an exultation of work. Levi was seen as a reactionary who offered an out-of-date morality. The extreme left newspaper *Lotta Continua* published an angry reader's attack on *The Wrench*: 'I'd like to ask Levi why he doesn't write about one of the hundreds of workers injured on Agnelli's Fiat production line.' The controversy raged as critics took sides. When pressed, Levi acknowledged the 'sad and obvious' truth that not *all* work is pleasant, but he condemned as 'senseless' the left's wholesale dismissal of it. If work was rejected out of hand, we would all die of hunger. Only the Italian glossy magazine *Ciao 2001* had the sensitivity to note that *The Wrench* represented an exorcism of the cynical Nazi motto over Auschwitz: 'Work Makes You Free.' Levi had begun his literary career with a portrait of man the destroyer; he continued it with a vision of man the maker, *homo faber*. Suggestions that *The Wrench* was reactionary only increased publicity, and soon the book was making quite an impression.

This was Levi's first work to reach an appreciable non-bookish audience. At a book-signing near Turin a young man introduced himself to Levi in heavy Piedmontese, 'May I? I am Faussone. Guess what job I do?' And Levi replied, 'You must be a rigger.' He was: the Author had found his Character. When Levi heard that forty-six steel-riggers at Peyrani Construction had read *The Wrench* he asked the Turin firm to supply him with company brochures on which to base illustrations for a school edition of the book. 'Levi didn't want schoolchildren to form the wrong impression of what derricks and crane towers looked like,' said the company chairman Riccardo Peyrani.

13

The year 1979 opened with great misgivings for Levi as a rash of anti-Semitic prejudice was unleashed on Europe. It began in France. Darquier de Pellepoix, the former commissioner for Jewish affairs in the pro-Nazi Vichy government, claimed that the Nazi genocide was a 'Jewish hoax'. His obsessional little diatribe, published in *L'Express*, prompted another revisionist, the Lyons University professor Robert Faurisson, to claim in *Le Monde* that the gassings were indeed a pack of 'Jewish lies'. Levi felt morally obliged to contend the French falsifiers, but he refused to argue with Faurisson on Swiss television (the revisionist should not be provided with a platform for his monomania). He countered him elsewhere though. Levi's newspaper attack on Faurisson, the first of two, appeared on the front page of the 3 January edition of Milan's *Corriere della Sera*; printed alongside it was the Sicilian crime-writer Leonardo Sciascia's own demolition of the Lyons professor. Levi agreed with Sciascia that Faurisson's hypothesis was so extravagantly monstrous that it *had* to be refuted: 'If you deny the massacre . . . you must explain why the 17 million Jews alive in 1939 had been reduced to eleven million by 1945.'

The revisionist controversy could not have come at a worse time for Levi. With *The Wrench* he had hoped to slough off his role as a witness and ex-deportee, and explore the new semi-fictional ground opened up by the Faussone stories. Now he could see little ahead but newspaper articles on Auschwitz. The polemics and argument continued as Levi wrote one article after another protesting at pseudo-Nazi attempts to erase the past. The English 'historian' David Irving's disregard for verity and verification Levi saw as part of the larger revisionist movement, and therefore he refuted it. (Levi was not alive in 1997 to hear Irving dismiss *If This is a Man* as a 'novel' by a 'mentally unstable' Jew.) As the ranks of the pseudo-scholars swelled, Levi sadly had to admit that they were gaining the upper hand. It was not long before he was receiving hate-mail addressed to 'Filthy Jew'.

14

Levi spent the early months of 1979 in the seclusion of 75 Corso Re Umberto. As usually happened following publication of a book, he was disenchanted and unsure of himself after *The Wrench*, and his low moods came at intervals throughout the winter. He filled the hours reading Proust ('boring') and corresponding with the Italian psychoanalyst Silvano Arieti. Based in New York at the Psychoanalytic Institute, Arieti had fled his native Pisa during the Occupation; he was Jewish. Levi had admired Arieti's extraordinary account of the last days of Pisa's Jewish community elder, Giuseppe Pardo Roques, murdered by the Nazis. (Elder Roques was a phobic who rarely ventured out of doors for fear of encountering stray dogs; at the sight of his Nazi killers he had cried, 'Now I understand, the animals are *you*!' and the Germans were heard by neighbours to howl.) Levi was currently reading Arieti's books on schizophrenia and literary creativity. And though he found these 'fascinating', he told Arieti in a letter dated 21

February that he would probably not live long enough to 'tackle the subjects properly'. Rising sixty, Levi was already feeling the weight of his years. He sought the company of old friends.

One of his allies during this difficult time was the Paris-born sculptor Alessandro Lupano, who had a studio in Scandaluzzo not far from Turin. Lupano was lively, generous, proletarian and invariably hard-up; a rough-looking character, he sculpted impressionistically, lunging and chiselling at rocks and river flotsam: to Levi his art was 'dazzling' and 'brimful of poetry'. Despite their differences in appearance and background, the men had grown fond of each other. During the war Lupano had served in the Italian navy. He was captured by the Nazis in 1943 in Athens and deported to a munitions plant near Buchenwald. After the war in Turin, Lupano worked as a Michelin factory-hand and no doubt Levi saw something of Tino Faussone in this salty man. Though in Levi's case it sounds improbable, Lupano told me that he and Levi eyed up passing pretty girls on Via Po. This street, with its peeling stucco arcades and rusted balconies, was lined with plenty of cafés from which the men could do their ogling, as well as drink, smoke and joke (usually in French). Levi enjoyed going along with Lupano in these antics. One day at the traffic lights on Corso Re Umberto he told the sculptor, 'For God's sake drive on!' and tried to make himself invisible by sliding down his seat. *La Stampa*'s fashion editor, Lucia Sollazzo, was standing at the lights in a ludicrously large hat. She was a loud, excitable woman with literary pretensions, and Levi preferred to keep his distance. Lupano remembered this incident with great amusement.

15

Levi continued to visit schools round Piedmont, and on 21 March he and the Ravensbrück survivor Lidia Rolfi toured a number of them in the Lanzo area. Increasingly, Levi found these visits wearisome. He had visited at least 130 Italian schools by now, but for some time he had been discouraged by the pupils' dwindling interest in the camps; they had other fears and uncertainties to worry about: terrorism, the nuclear threat. Perhaps Levi's disillusionment was affected by a general low mood he could not lift. Whatever the reason, he welcomed the chance to leave Turin for the Italian port of Trieste. Accompanied by his wife, he was booked to talk about *The Wrench* on Monday 7 May at the city's Arts and Culture Club. There he met for the first time Trieste's legendary Jewish writer Giorgio Voghera. Voghera had certainly had his share of catastrophes (by his own account he was a 'born pessimist'), but even he was shocked when Levi told him in front of journalists that anyone who had been through Auschwitz 'cannot possibly have any faith in life or the improvability of mankind'. A mild depression most likely influenced Levi's comment; he was not usually quite so negative. Voghera sent me the following description of Levi which, interestingly, echoed an earlier account I had received from Levi's theatre director Massimo Scaglione:

> He was short, minutely built, but evenly proportioned, reserved and gentle, a man of pre-war courtesies. In spite of his white beard (dappled grey at the tip), he seemed to me to have an oddly infantile expression. My impression was of a child trapped in a man's body.

What some saw as vulnerable and endearingly boyish in Levi, others recognised as 'infantile'. After the talk Levi and Lucia again met the Istrian-born author Fulvio Tomizza, who had a small flat in Trieste. Proudly he showed them the city's old town, the Città Vecchia, with its crooked narrow ways and Slavic-Germanic-Italian cafés. Levi wanted to explore the Carso above Trieste, a forbidding outcrop plateau of the Giulian Alps. But Lucia was terrified of the *bora* wind that sweeps down the Carso, churning up the sea and rattling street railings. As Levi walked round Trieste with Tomizza, he confessed to him the anxiety he felt about his mother who was on her own in Turin. It seemed 'pathetic' to Tomizza that a sixty-year-old man could be so unsettled by his mother. Levi's guilt and anxiety about Ester would have been aggravated if, as seems likely, he was feeling low anyway.

Levi's days were long and increasingly bleak spent looking after his mother, and his weekly interventions in the papers on 'revisionism' left him morose. Over the spring of 1979 Levi, like thousands of others, stayed in at night to watch the Hollywood television soap opera, *Holocaust*. In retrospect this series was the media event of the 1970s, both for America and Europe. In West Germany it helped to break thirty-five years of near-silence surrounding Hitler's persecution. On the basis of its title alone, however, Levi was not disposed to like the series. He had always insisted that 'holocaust' was a sorry term. 'It seems to me inappropriate, it seems to me rhetorical, above all *mistaken*' (from the Greek, 'holocaust' means a sacrificial burnt offering to the gods: even by the barbarous standards of Antiquity, the Nazi genocide was not a ritual offering of victims). Then Levi feared the series would commercialise and cheapen the enormity of Auschwitz; when that happens, the process of forgetting has already begun. Yet Levi's verdict on *Holocaust*, published in the 20 May edition of *La Stampa*, was surprisingly favourable: the series was a 'well-intentioned', if glib, piece of pop that was pitched at just the right level to draw the ordinary viewer in. Elsewhere, Levi praised the documentary accuracy of the series, and compared it favourably to Erich Remarque's 'fabricated' prison-camp novel, *Spark of Life*, an egregious example of 'historical distortion'. In private, however, his view of *Holocaust* was quite different:

> I heartily disliked the series [he told Hety Schmitt-Maas]. It is superficial and untruthful; it lacks any historical explanation of the distant roots of Nazi barbarity and of anti-Semitism. And Frau Inga Weiss [played by Meryl Streep] is really too stupid! On the other hand the film *has* achieved its goal, both here and in Germany. People on the buses are talking about it, and also in the schools, which is good: it is, however, sad to think that in order to reach the man on the street, history has to be simplified and digested to such an extent.

Though Levi was once again inconsistent in his views ('It is the writer's privilege to be incoherent,' he told me), *Holocaust* was to benefit him in one unforeseen but immensely satisfying way. *Ist das ein Mensch?* had been out of print for eight years. But, thanks to the extraordinary response to *Holocaust*, his account was republished and on sale again in West Germany. He donated a copy to the Goethe Institut in Turin, with the amused dedication: 'From your oldest pupil.'

16

For weeks the salon gossip in Italy had touted *The Wrench* as the favourite to win the glamorous Strega Prize. Curiously, at least three other authors on the shortlist had other careers besides writing. One of these was Paolo Barbaro (born Ennio Gallo), a Venetian civil engineer whose novels charted the drilling and blasting of rock faces in Iran and elsewhere. Levi was, if not threatened by, certainly wary of Barbaro, who was treading on his patch with his novel *Footsteps of Man*. It investigated a theme dear to Levi: man's eternal struggle to dominate matter. At a buffet luncheon in Venice for publishers and their authors, the rivals finally met. Barbaro recalled that Levi kept looking at him in the chandelier-hung salon with sideways glances. When they approached each other cautiously to say hello, Levi said kindly to Barbaro: 'I hope you win a prize.'

In the end Levi took the Strega Prize. The winner was announced on 4 July 1979 at midnight by the novelist Giorgio Bassani, author of *The Garden of the Finzi-Continis*. (Levi did not much care for Bassani, a notorious snob.)

Cameras flashed as the society hostess Maria Bellonci hugged Levi theatrically. 'We should have given you the Strega sixteen years ago for *The Truce*!' she whispered in his ear. In his acceptance speech Levi made the uncharacteristically ungracious remark: 'The Strega's the only literary prize to have kept pace with inflation and so I'm delighted to have won it.'

The number of congratulatory messages awaiting Levi on his return to Turin was impressive, and he laboured diligently to answer them. To Anna Maria Zambrini, editor of *Paints and Varnishes,* he wrote:

> Of course I'm pleased with the Strega, but I'm also a bit bewildered by it. Deep down I'm still a paint and varnish man, and all these literary accolades (wonderful though they may be) seem to come from another planet.

Lucia gave her husband a miniature gold-plated wrench as a present. On 12 July it was Lucia's fifty-ninth birthday. Levi's sister came to stay briefly, but the flat was very cramped. Levi found a solution to the summer's overcrowding by decamping his relatives to Frabosa, not far from Turin. There, in the forlorn-looking Hotel Excelsior, aunts and uncles stayed for three weeks from 22 July to 10 August. For their amusement, the hotel manager Silvana Peano provided Monopoly and other board games.

Up in his room Levi continued to correspond with Hety Schmitt-Maas. He said he wanted to write a short story about the alcholic Auschwitz chemist Reinhard Heidebroek, though not from a 'judgemental point of view (I am no judge, I am no Wiesenthal, and Heidebroek is not a criminal)'. Could Hety put him in touch with Heidebroek? Levi undertook to mention no names in his story and 'no particular circumstances by which Heidebroek and his wife might be recognised'. But when 'The Quiet City' was published two years later in *La Stampa*, Heidebroek was quite recognisable in the wretchedly dipsomaniac 'Dr Mertens'. His widow Renata Heidebroek fortunately never read this story in which her husband (then recently deceased) was featured.

17

In the autumn, Levi was drawn into his first public dispute. Sponsored by the leftist newspaper *L'Unità*, the Italian Communist Party organised autumn fund-raising fairs across Italy. On 9 September Levi was invited to take part in the Festa dell'Unità in Milan. In between barbecues and children's games he was to talk on the vices and virtues of literary obscurity.

The novelist Paolo Volponi interviewed him. These men disagreed on just about every aspect of literature. Levi had never strayed from his belief that writing should be a public service that communicates clearly and directly to readers, while Volponi believed it was the writer's duty to reflect the disintegration and alienation of modern times (as he saw them) in narratives which themselves were fragmented, digressive, meandering. For Levi, Volponi's obscurantist aesthetic was an irritating vice of the times: we all *know* that the world is chaotic; describing it in a chaotic way helps nobody. Volponi was a romantic anti-capitalist.

The polemic had deep roots. Three years earlier, in 1976, Levi had published in *La Stampa* his now much-quoted credo in defence of literary clarity, 'On Obscure Writing'. This disparaged the modernist aesthetic of fragmentation and inaccessibility. Ezra Pound was lambasted, not for his anti-Semitism, but for the use he made in his cantos of Chinese, which apparently showed a contempt for the reader. This conservative anti-modernism of Levi's was one of his least attractive characteristics, and not surprisingly his article provoked a furore among Italy's 'front-page intellectuals'. The critic Giorgio Manganelli accused Levi of 'public welfare terrorism' for his preferment of 'sane' prose over 'mad' prose. Levi replied archly: 'Manganelli accuses me of being a "public welfare terrorist", which is a charming example of a contradiction in terms, and therefore of obscurity.' As far as Levi was concerned, when an idea is clear it automatically finds expression in clear language. Beneath his overwhelming need to communicate lay his experience of Auschwitz where communication was hazardous if not impossible. He condemned one of the greatest writers of the twentieth century, Samuel Beckett, for making a virtue (as Levi told me) of not-saying: 'Oh, Beckett annoys me terribly.'

At the end of September Mario Rigoni Stern was in Venice to collect the Campiello Prize for his glorious novella *The History of Tönle* ('Little Tony' in Cimbro dialect) about an Asiago-born Jack of all trades in Central Europe on the eve of the Great War. Einaudi's publicity director, Alberto Papuzzi, knowing how much Rigoni Stern disliked award ceremonies, arranged a private party for him at the Café Florian in Piazza San Marco. Levi was invited. And, 'laughing like a child' all evening, he drank champagne in Rigoni Stern's honour, pleased as punch to have escaped the prize-giving brouhaha. When the café orchestra struck up a sentimental Piedmontese ballad on Rigoni Stern's behalf, Levi began to cry. All his life he loved to listen to these melancholy tunes and he truly loved the one now being played, 'La Piemontesina Bella', a love song set in Turin. In many ways so controlled, Levi rather relished the notion of being overcome, and having drunk himself into a champagne melancholy, he 'could not stop the flood of tears', recalled Papuzzi.

On his return to Turin, Levi made the surprise announcement that he was working on a collection of essays on the Nazi camps. This would become *The Drowned and the Saved*, and he hoped to be free to write it over the winter. All sorts of distractions held up progress, though. The Italian bank robber Sante Notarnicola had been condemned to life imprisonment for murder. He was now active in the movement for prisoners' rights and had taken to writing poetry in jail. His lawyer, Bianca Guidetti Serra, did much to support his efforts to organise reading circles with other inmates. She sent him copies of *If This is a Man* to circulate in the cells, and urged him to write to Levi. Notarnicola sent Levi a sheaf of his poems with the unfortunate dedication: 'As you can see, the camps are coming back today.' Angrily, Levi replied that 10,000 people had died every day at Auschwitz: how did that compare to Notarnicola's jail? Over the years Levi had developed what he called an 'allergy' towards the sociology (so fashionable in late 1970s' Italy) that equated Italian prisons and factories with Nazi camps. Imprecise metaphors, debased coinages and graffiti of the sort 'FIAT=AUSCHWITZ' only degraded the survivors' experience. Today words like 'Holocaust', 'Fascist', 'Nazi' continue to be used in ways that Levi considered slipshod. Notarnicola apologised to Levi, and afterwards Levi became his patron, sending him books, taking an interest in his welfare (as well as that of his mother) and helping him out with publishing advice. By the end of the 1970s Notarnicola had made a discreet name for himself as a poet; unfortunately he has lost or destroyed his extensive prison correspondence with Levi.

18

Levi's last public appearance of 1979 was memorable. Under the rubric 'Turin-Encyclopedia', the city council organised a series of November lectures on subjects ranging from astrophysics to mountaineering. In a brilliant and highly allusive talk, 'Racial Intolerance', Levi developed a theme already evident in *If This is a Man*, that racial prejudice is animal and pre-human in origin. He quoted Konrad Lorenz, the father of modern ethology, on group hate in animals and spoke of the pecking order among hens and the horrific tribal aggression shown by rats (where the females bite through enemy rats' carotid arteries). These animal caste divisions and subjugations are also to be found among humans, said Levi: how much of the animal was there in the Nazis? At the lecture's end he touched on current affairs with a reference to Iran's slaughter of the Kurds following the Iranian revolution of 1979. In the light of this persecution Levi concluded that it would be 'imprudent' to be 'optimistic' about the human situation, for life is naturally terrible.

A dreary winter followed as Levi failed to settle to a clear writing plan. After 'sweating' over *The Drowned and the Saved* for six months, he had managed to produce only the preface and a draft of the book's contents. Levi was surely reluctant to dredge his painful memories of Auschwitz and re-examine them. Matters were not helped by Italy's increasingly dire political situation; Turin was now the 'capital of terror' as the Red Brigades pursued their strategy of annihilation. A journalist friend of Levi's, Carlo Casalegno, was executed on his doorstep at 25 Corso Re Umberto. Who next? The Levis endured a joyless Christmas. Lucia had recently retired from teaching and felt confused, directionless and a 'little depressed', said Levi. He made an odd choice of holiday reading in Erich Fromm's *Anatomy of Human Destructiveness*; its analysis of necrophilia, aggression and narcissism hardly brightened the festive period.

TWENTY-TWO

Reflections on the Resistance
1980–2

I

In the year following the publication of *The Wrench* in November 1978 Levi had not achieved any serious work. 'I'm resting on my laurels, but it's an uncomfortable mattress.' His concentration–camp essays would not flow. However, he had been tinkering with the idea of a novel about the Jewish Resistance to Hitler in Eastern Europe. This quixotic and ultimately ill-advised project – *If Not Now, When?* – was to be Levi's longest prose narrative yet and strikingly different from his previous works. A picaresque romance packed with speedy action, adventure, love and war, it would tell a story in grand old-fashioned epic style. Levi wanted to present to his readers an image of successful Jewish resistance: Jews had not gone to the slaughter like lambs.

If Not Now, When? had a characteristically long and hybrid genesis. At least since 1946, Levi had sought to familiarise himself with the lost world of *Yiddishkeit*. A poem of that year, 'Ostjuden', had described the brutalised world of East European Jewry – its derision, its sorrows and pogroms – in a brief haiku-like lament. Twenty years later, in 1966, writing on the Yiddish (from the German *Jüdisch* – Jewish) Warsaw poet Itzhak Katzeneslon, Levi had lamented Italian unawareness generally of Ashkenazi culture. At about this time he also read Oscar Pinkus's memoir of survival in Occupied Poland, *A Choice of Masks*. Levi had written to Pinkus: 'The history of the uprooting and extinction of East European Jewry is unknown and absolutely not understood in Italy.' To make up for his ignorance, Levi had read deeply into the literature of this dispersed people.

At Auschwitz, Levi had had to confront his antipathy towards the Ashkenazim, but later saw that he had more in common with the ragged Jews of Bukovina, Galicia and the Ukraine than he might have liked to think. *If Not Now, When?* was to be a gesture of belated solidarity and identification. The Ashkenazim's self-ironical humour and love of learning were characteristics that Levi saw in himself, and which gave him a sense of affinity and belonging. During business trips to the Soviet Union in the early 1970s, he had encountered the remnants of a *shtetl* culture that had survived the Hitlerian storm, and this too had confirmed a sense of belonging. Though in *The Periodic Table* Levi had claimed a Sephardic ancestry, his mother's maiden name, Luzzati, is distinctly East European. And many other Jewish surnames in Levi's extended family, such as Diena, Morpurgo and Tedeschi ('Germans'), are of Ashkenazic origin. If Levi had hesitated to acknowledge his Ashkenazic roots in *The Periodic Table,* it was because he was following the prejudices of his father, who had looked down on Eastern Jews as unlettered and uncouth.

Levi was impatient to begin *If Not Now, When?* but felt that his knowledge and experience of Ashkenazic culture was inadequate to the task. So there was a long period of research until the novel came into being. With his accustomed thoroughness he immersed himself in all the available Italian, Soviet and Allied documents on the little-known history of Jewish partisan activity in the Second World War. For eight months he was a regular presence at Turin's Jewish Library on Via Pio V (infuriatingly open only on Thursday afternoons), where he studied maps, language manuals, guides and borrowed Yiddish lexicons and popular reference works on Yiddish lore. Many felt that Levi was too meticulous for his own good. Edith Bruck, the Hungarian writer and survivor, suspected that he was to be fatally hampered by his dogged search for accuracy and authenticity. 'Right from the start I could see Primo was in danger of writing a stiff, starchy novel.'

Levi hoped to be the first Italian writer to describe the Yiddish world in all its rough glory. But, as the vast majority of Levi's readers in Italy were Catholic, there was a risk that such a determinedly ethnic novel would not be popular. During the course of his research, therefore, Levi found it amusing to circulate among his Catholic friends a selection of comically stern Talmudic dietary and sexual prohibitions. His friends' reactions to them would be a preliminary trial, he hoped, for the reception of his Yiddish adventure novel. The philosopher Norberto Bobbio was sent a startling transcription of rules regarding nudity, which absorbed him and his wife Valeria. The more extreme prohibitions regarding the Sabbath Levi took pleasure in reciting to Einaudi's brisk, business-like rights manager Agnese Incisa; he was tickled that Incisa had used a list of exacting food regulations as a guide for a kosher supper she cooked for orthodox Jewish friends in Turin. 'I hope your meal went well!'

For Levi, the great event of 1980 was a trip he made to Sicily, when for a few spring days he entered a world of deep-sea adventure, Sicilian orange groves and Greek temples. A national petroleum contractor, Saipem Italia SpA, wanted Levi to visit its futurist pipe-laying vessel *Beaver Six*, floating a few kilometres off the Sicilian coast. Levi could write up his visit for Saipem's in-house magazine, *Ecos*, and generate publicity. The chairman, Enrico Gandolfi, admired Levi's work and had distributed 2,000 copies of *The Wrench* among his staff at Christmas with the dedication: 'Faussone is one of you!'

On 22 March Levi was in the *Ecos* head office in Rome, where he was astonished to meet an editor, Luigi Valgimigli, whose uncle had worked as a tenant farmer for Cesare Levi's brother Enrico. It was a happy, if bizarre, coincidence that started the day well. Levi was then introduced to the *Ecos* staff writer Paolo Andreocci, a tall, genial Roman, who was to be his guide in Sicily. After breakfast he and Andreocci met the photo-reporter Andrea Nemiz, one of the original *paparazzi* of 1960s' Rome, who had photographed movie stars on the Via Veneto. All three men flew to Sicily. In its ragamuffin capital of Palermo the *dolce far niente*, sweet langour, with its Arabic tinge, overwhelmed Levi. To his northern eye the island looked more Moroccan than Italian, and he was impressed by the Saracen mosques with their pink-domed cupolas. Palermo's fire-blackened *palazzi*, which had not been restored since the Allied bombardments of 1943, reminded Levi, he said, of Liverpool's civic desolation. For lunch Andreocci recommended the Palermitan speciality of sardine pasta with fennel and pine-cone seeds, which Levi had never tried. Conversation was of travel, cooking and photography; Levi was curious about the petroleum industry and the countries Andreocci had visited for *Ecos*. Andreocci was fascinated to note that Levi spoke without hand gestures. 'He was an advert for *torinesità*, the opposite of an excitable southerner like me!'

The three men drove on towards the Sicilian port of Marsala, named after the Arab *Mars-al-Allah*, Harbour of God, and famous for its fortified wine. The Arab influence is strongest in western Sicily where the sirocco blows hot from Tunisia. Levi asked to visit the medieval fortress town of Erice, where his son Renzo had attended a biophysics course in 1977. The town was associated with the Sicilian nuclear physicist Ettore Majorana, who had disappeared in 1938 in murky circumstances and had not been seen since. (It was believed that Majorana had committed suicide because he feared the consequences of his research into atomic science.) From Erice's Norman castle Levi could see right the way across the Mediterranean to

Cape Bon in Tunisia. The photographer Nemiz was driving the hired Mercedes. They took a mule path down to the fantastic Greek ruins of Selinunte (from *selinon,* Greek for 'celery'). Here the fallen marble capitals and uprooted columns reminded Levi, he said, of a de Chirico canvas or a moonlit Borges fantasy. A pungent aroma of wild celery hung in the air. The pictures Nemiz took of Levi in Selinunte testify to his good mood that day; against the wine-dark sea he looks contented and relaxed in his tweed jacket. Later Levi spoke of '*un viaggio meraviglioso*', 'a marvellous journey'.

At Mazzara del Vallo, not far from Marsala, the three men registered at the Hopps Hotel and, recalled Andreocci, ate swordfish for supper. In the bay white fishing boats sailed into the hot breeze. Next day, 23 March, Levi was in the fly-blown Mafia port of Trapani, from where a Saipem company helicopter ferried him, Nemiz and Andreocci to the 42,000 tonne pipe-layer *Beaver Six*. From the chopper's window Levi could make out the lost Carthaginian island-city of Motya, floating in a shallow lagoon beneath him, and the Trapani salt-marshes with their Dutch-like windmills. In twenty minutes Levi was on the helideck of *Beaver Six* a 135-metre-long vessel that resembled an oil rig. Braving the downdraught, a girl came to whisk away Levi's luggage and for the next half-hour he worried where it had gone. The burly Tuscan captain, Pietro Costanzo, showed Levi to his cabin. The vessel had rooms for 330 people.

Levi was then introduced to a handful of engineers, whom he interviewed for his article. Soon he was entertaining them with humorous episodes from *The Truce*; they were held spell-bound. Levi showed a sympathetic interest in the loneliness experienced by the vessel's staff and their need for shore-leave. At one point a welder came up to say how much he had enjoyed *The Wrench*. Levi was delighted.

Later that night at Captain Costanzo's table, with half a dozen machinists and engineers, the diners craned closer to hear him talk again. It was clear that he had done his homework on *Beaver Six,* as he asked the most searching questions about deep-water pipe-laying. The wine flowing, Levi joked that if Saipem had contracted SIVA to paint *Beaver Six*, he would now be a millionaire. By the end of the meal, a little tipsy, Levi had renamed Pietro Costanzo 'Captain Nemo' after the submarine skipper of Verne's *Twenty Thousand Leagues Under the Sea*. Up on deck before going to bed, he spoke to the photographer Andrea Nemiz. The son of an Italian army officer in Ethiopia, Nemiz was forty, with piercing blue eyes. It was a moonless night and, looking up at sky, Levi pointed out to Nemiz the constellations. He said his secret passion ever since childhood had been to lose himself in just such a starlit stillness. 'Only then can we understand the insignificance of the world we inhabit,' he told Nemiz. For an hour the men gazed at the glows and silvery stripes; by midnight *Beaver Six* was moored near the jasmine-scented island of Pantelleria, on the verge of Africa. Then Levi and Nemiz retired to their berth. Levi took the lower bunk, Nemiz the top one. Embarrassed, they turned back-to-back to undress. Having rapidly climbed up the ladder to his bunk, Nemiz felt suddenly protective towards Levi. Later, Nemiz wrote to me:

> Without wanting to, my gaze fell on Levi as he turned to face the cabin wall to undress. He was folding, or pretending to fold, his trousers, and it was then I had the impression of a very frail man, terribly thin, with an adolescent's gawkiness. His legs were white and spindly. Ashamed to see this great man half-undressed, I averted my eyes. I don't remember who switched the lamp out finally.

After thirty hours on *Beaver Six* Levi was at Punta Raisi airport in Palermo bound for Turin. He signed Paolo Andreocci a copy of *The Wrench*: 'With friendship and real gratitude.' Always professional, back in Turin Levi typed up two accounts of his Sicilian adventure. The first, 'A Guest of Captain Nemo', appeared in the 6 April edition of *La Stampa*. The second, much longer piece for the May 1980 edition of *Ecos,* was circulated among engineers as far afield as Tunisia. From the control tower of *Beaver Six* Captain Costanzo telephoned Levi to express his delight at the articles and promised to send him a silver Saipem SpA medal with the 'compliments of Captain Nemo'. For weeks Levi was exalted by the memory of his Sicilian expedition; his sister found him in high spirits over Easter. They visited a baroque chapel on Turin's Via Garibaldi, normally closed to the public (a friend had a key), and signed the visitors' book 'with real admiration'.

3

Over the spring of 1980 Levi continued to research his Jewish partisan novel. His friend Giorgio Vaccarino, an historian in Turin, kept a remarkable archive of Resistance material, which provided Levi with useful documentation for the period. Once a week for a year, Levi called on Professor Vaccarino in his smart Corso Duca degli Abruzzi residence, often accompanied by his mother Ester. One of Vaccarino's volumes that Levi studied with special attention was *Les Partisans Soviétiques* (1945) by a Russian, Major-General Kovpak. To judge by his pencilled annotations Levi was particularly interested in the pitiless justice that led to the execution of drunk partisans or suspect informers. *If Not Now, When?* was to contain secret parallels with Levi's own partisan war. Just as Levi had been implicated in the execution of two renegade guerrillas in 1943, so in his novel a Russian partisan who had drunkenly revealed secrets to the enemy is unceremoniously shot. By patient sleuth-work Levi tracked down Moshe Kaganovic's 1947 eye-witness account, *The Participation of Jews in the Partisan Movement of Soviet Russia*, and then with infinite pains translated the entire book from Yiddish.

In April Levi began to work determinedly and with equal enthusiasm on another project. Count Giulio Bollati di St Pierre, one of Einaudi's several aristocratic editors, asked Levi to compile an anthology of his favourite writings. It could include extracts from botanical manuals or Flash Gordon strip-cartoons, said Count Bollati. Bollati's unswerving confidence in Levi was matched by Levi's faith in him as editor and guide. Bollati was of the old school: diligent, precise. As soon as he could, Levi ensconced himself in his father's old study to make his selections. He wanted to fly in the face of conventional wisdom about how literary anthologies should be compiled, and to enjoy it too. Of the thirty authors he eventually chose, seven were British, six Italian, four French, four Jewish, two German, one Austrian, one Latin (Lucretius), four American and one Greek (Homer); of these, eight were scientists and twenty-two were writers. If nothing else, the anthology was to reflect Levi's wide-ranging and cosmopolitan tastes.

Levi called the assemblage *The Search for Roots*, and he made some unlikely inclusions. Few can have got to the end of Thomas Mann's most soporific work *Joseph and his Brothers*. But the book's literary excellence was not the point for Levi. At a time when Hitler was persecuting the Jews, Mann had published a novel that portrayed Jews as the founding fathers of our modern morality. And there were other surprising choices. In spite of Levi's advocacy of classically measured prose, he included an extract from the Sicilian novelist Stefano D'Arrigo's sprawling opus *Horcynus Orca*. D'Arrigo's was an exuberant talent in the Rabelaisian vein (he had a bit-part in Pasolini's violent Roman underworld film, *Accattone*), and his novel was digressive and grotesque. Levi chose a darkly self-revealing excerpt in which armed Neapolitan urchins encircle a German tank-driver in the Second World War and skewer him with a bayonet. It is hard not to see in this choice Levi's continued anger.

Levi compiled most of *The Search for Roots* at home in Turin, with periodic interruptions when he needed to look after his mother. He took his selections and his textual commentary each week to Guido Davico Bonino, who was working freelance for Count Bollati in rented rooms off Corso Matteotti. Usually Levi called on Bonino in the early afternoons, worked for several hours cutting and reshaping the manuscript over menthol cigarettes, and then trudged back to the Crocetta after dark. Bonino found some of Levi's selections unsettling. One of these was the Romanian-poet Paul Celan's chilling poem 'Deathfugue', where the German lyric tradition seems to crash-land in the hellish landscape of genocide. 'I carry this poem inside me like a virus,' Levi told Bonino, 'it's pure despair.' Celan had committed suicide in 1970, and Levi had first read his nervy, pain-laden verse in Moshe Kahn's superb Italian translation of 1976. *The Search for Roots* was a 'night book', said Levi, where his other works were 'day books.' Bonino felt the number of scientific entries unfairly biased the book against the humanities. Did Levi really have to include a 'specification' paper on how to render an industrial varnish resistant to cockroach attack? Levi did: the dryly factual 'insect text' was associated in his mind with the writhing dung-beetle in Kafka's 'Metamorphosis'. Levi listened attentively to Bonino, but said those extracts that Bonino had singled out as too 'specialist' were the strongest, and he wanted them all to be published. After all, Levi's 'roots' were only part literary; he was a chemist. He got his way.

4

During the spring of 1980 two other matters took up some of Levi's time. Levi was not altogether satisfied with the translations that Ruth Feldman and Brian Swann had made of his poems, and wanted someone else to look at them. A medical student at Cambridge University, Miguel Hernandez-Bronchoud, had been at school with Renzo. Though Hernandez-Bronchoud had no publisher contract, Levi admired his polyglot abilities and offered him every encouragement and advice. His translation of Levi's verse won a Gonville and Caius College Prize and was later published in an Oxford University magazine. On 14 May Levi wrote to Hernandez-Bronchoud to congratulate him on his 'well-deserved' success.

On 28 May, with Levi's permission, his futurist fable 'To Be Born on Earth' was premiered in Turin. The play had a suitably Christian ring for the Easter period, but it was an unsettling work that investigated mind-control and an alien takeover of Planet Earth. Guido Davico Bonino, writing in *La Stampa*, reported warm applause and repeated calls for the author to appear on stage (which he did not do, presumably out of shyness). Levi dispensed free tickets to friends and never stopped thanking them for their attendance.

Meanwhile, Nardo De Benedetti was showing signs of depression, and his depression was slow to lift. He had lived alone in his cavernous, ground-floor flat for almost ten years since his flatmates had died, and he was vulnerable to burglary. Levi feared for his safety. As a doctor, Nardo was conscious of his own mood swings, observing them with professional detachment. He had become quite deaf, too, but Nardo refused to wear a hearing aid and shouted irritably as a result.

On 31 May, at the age of eighty-two, Nardo retired as a doctor. He was instantly happier and seemed much restored in health: he even grew a debonair moustache and tried his hand at writing short stories (on which Levi rather unkindly never returned a verdict). Since 1965 Nardo had been looked after by a railwayman's daughter, Anna Maralucci, tall with lustrous black hair and a pronounced meridional accent. She had migrated at the age of ten from southern Italy, and her love for Nardo was simple and unquestioning; she ironed his shirts, took his phone calls, opened the door to guests and served them at table. She devised a routine for Nardo that never varied; each evening she put his pre-prepared breakfast in the fridge, and for lunch she served him baked pears, bread and anchovies. In gratitude, Nardo made Anna a present of his Lancia coupé. However, a close daily intimacy between two people is never without problems. The one virtue that Nardo prized above all others was honesty, and he was apoplectic when he found out that Anna had lied that she was married. Nardo felt betrayed, and he tore into Anna, calling her a liar. When poor Anna eventually did marry, becoming Signora Anna Piersanti, she sacrificed her honeymoon just to be with Nardo.

In the summer of 1980 Nardo moved out of his Crocetta flat into Turin's Jewish Rest Home. A modest institution down the long, grey Via Bernardino Galliari, it was full of 'big old boys and big old girls', said Nardo. In an institution where people died frequently he was valued as a doctor, and the staff were very kind. Nardo had his own telephone to reach Levi and other friends, a radio to listen to his adored Viennese waltz music and a portable television for the late-night films. Fortunately the Rest Home was close to where Anna Piersanti lived on Corso de Gasperi and she visited Nardo daily. They had known each other for such a long time by now – fifteen years. On Sundays they ate ice creams together on Corso Vittorio, and fed the birds. On Thursdays they visited Via Madama Cristina market, where Nardo liked to buy fruit and exercise his legs. He found it too depressing to eat meals in the Rest Home and made sure he was invited out as often as possible to eat with relatives or friends.

At about this time Levi received a letter from an Italian ex-deportee, Elena Simion, who thought she had recognised Nardo De Benedetti in the

'Leonardo' of *The Truce*. Levi wrote back with Nardo's address in Turin: 'I think a letter from you would do him a lot of good.'

6 June 1980

Esteemed Dr De Benedetti,
    Perhaps you will remember me? We met at Katowice transfer camp shortly before Easter 1945. I'd been expecting a baby boy, which turned out to be a girl, Nadia. She was born on 25 May at Cracow hospital: you were the first Italian doctor she saw! Now I'm happy to tell you that my undernourished little newborn (who looked rather like a mouse) has grown into a healthy, beautiful woman with a baby girl of her own.

In the winter of 1944 Simion had been on a train that was stopped by Germans outside Venice. All the civilian passengers, regardless of age or race, were deported to Poland. Elena Simion was sent to Blekhammer camp (Upper Silesia) near Auschwitz, where she slaved for German industry. There she fell in love with a Scottish POW, Robert Hamilton, and was soon pregnant by him. In the confusion that followed the camp's liberation they lost sight of each other, and Nadia was born in Cracow. Robert Hamilton, her father, was last heard of in Woking, Surrey. Something of this wartime affair would surface in Levi's Yiddish partisan novel *If Not Now, When?*, which ends with the birth of a war child – a new life surviving, like Nadia Hamilton's, against the odds.

    Reunited with Nardo after thirty-five years, in 1980, Elena Simion was shocked to see how simply the doctor lived. Nardo ushered her into his drab room with its small *en suite* bathroom. The blinds were drawn (Nardo was sensitive to light), and the room was sparsely equipped with a small fridge and some shelves on which Nardo kept his current reading, mostly books on Napoleon. An original self-portrait sketch of Rembrandt and his wife Saskia, signed and dated '1696', was the room's sole ornament.

5

As always, the summer brought important birthdays for Levi to remember. On 29 June his mother was eighty-five; on 2 July, his son Renzo was twenty-three (almost the same age as Levi when he was arrested and sent to Auschwitz); Alberto Salmoni was sixty-two on 6 August; Alberto's ex-wife Bianca Guidetti Serra was sixty-one on the 19th. In the autumn, on 18 September, the trade unionist Vittorio Foa celebrated his seventieth birthday. Levi had known this affable man since childhood, when he had lived at 64 Corso Re Umberto. Foa had played a key role in Turin's 'Justice and Liberty', and his mother had been Ester Levi's first cousin. A large party was held in 'The Dacha' where SIVA used to entertain its Soviet clients. It was a cheerful, happy occasion with three generations of guests.

However the most important birthday celebration was on 12 July, when Levi's wife was sixty. To mark the occasion Levi wrote Lucia a birthday poem, which began tenderly, 'Have patience, my weary lady.' If Levi no longer leaned on Lucia as he had in the years post-Auschwitz, after thirty-three years of marriage he needed her still. The poem has an apologetic tone ('From the moment I fell to your lot'), in which Lucia is assigned the stronger role in the relationship. Levi tries to reach out to her with affection:

> It is no longer the time to live alone.
> Accept, to please me, these fourteen lines.
> They are my rough way of saying how dear you are,
> And that I wouldn't be in this world without you.

Levi was rarely so emotional in his writing. The last line refers either to the bleak post-war years when Levi was in despair but Lucia listened to him, or perhaps to more recent thoughts of suicide. We cannot know.

Levi and Lucia were in Frabosa for the summer holidays when, on 2 August, news reached them of a bomb outrage at Bologna station: eighty-six people killed, 200 injured. The first suspect was the far-right 'puppeteer' of Italian politics, Licio Gelli, alias the Venerable Wolf. During the Spanish Civil War Gelli had fought for Franco in a Blackshirt division and later in the Hermann Goering division of the SS. He was the grand master of Italy's outlawed P2 (Propaganda Two) masonic lodge, involved in acts of political espionage and terrorism. After the Bologna atrocity it looked as if Italy was poised to enter a period of neo-Fascist terrorism, after the earlier leftist terrorism of the Red Brigades. A few days of shocked silence followed before Levi wrote his blackest poem of 1980. 'Dark Band' ostensibly describes a stream of worker ants as they toil in the gutter of a busy Turin road. At first Levi's tone is jocular, then it turns abruptly nervous: 'I don't want to write about this band'; the black band recalls the ordered ranks of the SS, or perhaps the industrious legionnaires of Gelli's P2 as they streamed into Italy's political life. The Bologna bomb showed that Italy's long drawn-out Fascist trauma was far from over.

In October 1980 Levi began to write *If Not Now, When?* Jean Samuel, visiting Turin that autumn, found him in a state of great excitement. On Levi's study wall was a campaign map of Occupied Europe on which the notional route of the novel's Resistance fighters had been traced with a ruler. Later that day Samuel was to join Levi in a German television programme, *Industry and Terror*, about Hitler's slave labour. Samuel had not spoken German since the war, and it was with a sense of rising panic that he faced the camera. But speaking in the language of his tormentors again allowed Samuel to talk about his ordeal, first to his grandchildren, then to friends. The interview was the crucial event of his adult years, he said.

The year ended on a positive note for Levi when, on 18 November, Italian survivors of the Nazi camps were given the right to the same 'life-annuity' (*vitalizio*) as Italian ex-servicemen. Levi was now guaranteed free health care as well as a pension to supplement the one he already received from SIVA.

By the New Year of 1981 the writing was tumbling out of Levi. He seemed to be 'flying' and for the eleven months it took him to complete *If Not Now, When?* he led a 'blissful' life of contented work and intimacy with his partisan heroes. Inventing characters ex-nihilo, said Levi, was nothing short of 'wonderful'. Levi said he could feel the characters plucking at his elbow, telling him what to write, as though they had broken free of print. Naturally he borrowed from people he had known. The partisan leader Gedaleh Skidler is an Ariel-like spirit and intellectual *manqué* with a lovely singing voice, rather like Levi's university friend Alberto Salmoni. There is even a secret homage to Grandma Adele Sinigaglia in the Italian refugee assistant cryptically referred to as 'Signora Adele S'. And while it is clear that Levi put much of himself into the watchmaker Mendel, a peaceable, bookish, chess-loving man with a philosophic bent, Mendel becomes a strong and proficient partisan, unlike the ineffectual non-combatant Levi had been.

Yet these characters, many of them, seem to exist for the sake of what they have to say, their speech doctrinaire and sententious. Bianca Guidetti Serra, Levi's lawyer friend, was unimpressed by what she read of the work-in-progress, finding the characters wooden and the plot forced. 'I urged Primo to let the book mulch down for a while, but he went ahead anyway.' Much of what Levi was writing had a formulaic feel, in which elements of *Fiddler on the Roof* seemed to be crossed with Chagall-like flights of fancy. One of his less exalted influences was probably the television soap series *Holocaust*, in which Zionist partisans dynamite Wehrmacht depots behind the eastern frontlines before escaping to Palestine. Levi indulged in a crude rhetoric not found in his other work.

While in the afternoons Levi was working on his novel, mornings were dedicated to writing letters. In the winter he began to correspond with the Sicilian writer Leonardo Sciascia, whose essays and thrillers he had long revered for their caustic wit and civic morality. In 1979 Levi and Sciascia had launched a joint *j'accuse* against the French revisionist Faurisson; two years later, Sciascia sent Levi a copy of his recent book, *The Theatre of Memory*, a psychological mystery set in 1920s Turin. Levi wrote to thank the Sicilian writer, and took the opportunity to ask him about the word *'marsa!'*, with which, as a child, he used to call a truce in street games. Was this an Arabo-Sicilian term? After a week, Sciascia replied that he did not know; nor did his Sicilian friends. They hoped to pursue the matter in Palermo, where Sciascia lived among his collection of silver-topped walking canes, but this never happened. Levi reflected ruefully: 'Palermo is an awfully long way from Turin.' In 1985, Sciascia told me that Levi was the Italian writer he had 'most wanted to meet'.

The morning post brought regular requests for Levi to lecture. Boston University wanted him to attend a conference on 'Jewish Culture', which he had to decline. 'The main reason is my mother. It's not that she's unwell, but she's 86, and lives with us, so I can't leave her in my wife's care. My wife has to look after her *own* mother, who is 90 and blind.' In a poem from this time, 'Unfinished Business', Levi lamented these lost opportunities. Visits to faraway cities? Islands? 'You'll have to cross them off the programme.' He felt he could only accept invitations to lecture in Italy, preferably in Turin. At Turin's University of the Third Age he agreed to talk on the subject of food chemistry. Levi had been asked to write a history of the dehydration, smoking and salting of foodstuffs for a children's encyclopaedia to be published in Milan. He produced thirty (still unpublished) pages on 'The Preservation of Foods', in which he paid special attention to the German 'prince of chemists' Baron Justus von Liebig, inventor of long-life meat extract and founder of the famous Liebig (foods) group. The encyclopaedia came to nothing, but Levi decided to turn his article into a lecture. On 14 January 1981 his old friend Silvio Ortona introduced him to the audience. Levi spoke of Egyptian and Chinese food conservation methods, and finally emphasised the miracle of refrigeration. Not all the elderly audience had understood what Levi said, but most recognised that they had been in the presence of something unusual. Afterwards a woman asked Levi if 'synthetic sweeteners' were all they were cracked up to be. 'Probably not,' Levi laconically replied.

Levi regularly received much 'tiresome' correspondence from members of Italy's National Association of Ex-Deportees, or ANED. Many of these individuals were in need of money or psychiatric help: 'poor Christs', Levi called them. Some saw Levi as a public service to be importuned at any time. One ANED survivor telephoned him: 'You know who I am. I don't have long to live: write my book,' but Levi politely replied that he did not write for 'third parties'.

Midway through composition of *If Not Now, When?*, Levi received a long and immensely disturbed letter from the Catholic ex-partisan Teresa Azzali, also of ANED. On re-reading *The Truce*, Azzali had been 'unpleasantly reminded', she said, of what for her had been a nightmare odyssey home to Italy crammed in railway wagons. On 18 March Levi replied to Azzali:

> I'm sorry that *The Truce* was so painful for you to re-read. I'd have thought that in contrast to the months spent in the camp the memory of that crazy journey home would have been *happy* rather than sad. (At least that's how it was for me.)

In May *The Search for Roots* was published to good reviews. Italo Calvino in *La Repubblica* praised the anthology's 'hybridism' and its daring juxtapositions of Homer with Darwin, Conrad with a German chemistry text. Only one reviewer was unimpressed. Giorgio Di Rienzo, in the Catholic weekly *Famiglia Cristiana*, missed the point when he dismissed the book as 'culturally lazy'. Levi must own a 'very meagre library', Di Rienzo objected, if he had not bothered to include the Italian masters Dante and Manzoni and Leopardi. But, since these authors were part of the average Italian reader's library, Levi had left them out. For such an unclassifiable book, *The Search for Roots* did well, shifting 18,000 copies in the first few months; it filled the shop windows over the summer.

In June Levi took time off from his Jewish Resistance novel to attend an Einaudi editorial conference. It was no secret that he and Giulio Einaudi failed to see eye-to-eye; Einaudi preferred the company of more patrician or soigné authors: and while Levi was certainly cultured, he was not refined. (Einaudi was a looks and charm snob.) 'I never know what to say to him', Levi confessed to Alberto Papuzzi. However, now that Levi was an established and celebrated writer in Italy, Einaudi could no longer ignore him. Levi was invited to the annual 'Rhêmes meeting' in which thirty-odd Einaudi staff, writers and consultants came together in enchanting summer surroundings. These seven-day conferences were serious affairs during which participants were forbidden to bring wives or husbands. Everything was discussed, from dust-jackets to the latest literary theory emerging out of France; Levi was expected to advise on scientific texts. Proceedings were conducted sternly by Einaudi round a long wooden table. Rhêmes was chosen for its remoteness and, as usual, the three-star 'Granta Parey' ('Great Wall' in *valdostano* dialect) was booked for the conference; it resembled a Swiss chalet with its pine chairs and chequered linen tablecloths. The owner, Signora Guerrina, was solicitous beyond the call of duty, even to the point of bathing her guests' feet in hot water and juniper herbs. Her most important job was to prepare a huge picnic luncheon for the guests. Roast chicken, cheese, bottles of the delicious dark Dogliani wine were packed into wicker hampers and shouldered up to a beauty spot by Einaudi's chauffeur and errand-boys; it was an almost colonial spectacle.

The hotelier fondly referred to Levi as 'The Chamois' for the nimble, delicate steps he took up the mountain paths round her hotel. In the bar, Levi was joined by Natalia Ginzburg, smoking and smiling her crooked smile, and Calvino, who were neighbours in Rome's tiny Campo di Marzio. They sat sipping juniper liqueur, chatting contentedly. When the arch-fabulist Calvino claimed to have seen a wolf outside the hotel, nobody believed him. Calvino was busy revising an Italian translation of Raymond Queneau's crackpot account of the Creation, *A Small Portable Cosmogony*, but was defeated by the alchemical-scientific allusions. Could Levi make anything of them? Levi's help was an unexpected blessing; without it, Calvino could not have fathomed Queneau's mischievously dense, long poem. As the friends conferred, the hotel cat pawed the manuscript and mewed for milk. The poem was published by Einaudi the following year, with Calvino's acknowledgment to Levi.

On the whole, the week in Rhêmes passed swiftly and delightfully for Levi, and he was pleased to be with his friend Alberto Papuzzi again on the high peaks. On 28 June they scaled the ambitious Col Fenêtre which towered mistily above the 'Granta Parey', and returned exhausted in time for breakfast. Natalia Ginzburg was startled to see them tramp into the dining room with crampons and ropes. 'What? You've been up the *Col Fenêtre*?' 'Ah, that's nothing!' they chorused smugly.

8

Two dramatic events marked the rest of 1981. Levi's German teacher Hanns Engert committed suicide, and, in a highly bizarre episode, the mortal remains of the holy virgin and martyr St Lucy were stolen in Levi's name. This happened on the night of 7 November. A thief or thieves left an anonymous ransom note in the Venice church: 'St Lucy will be returned on condition that a page of *If This is a Man* be read each day in all secondary schools and lycées in the Veneto area.' A joke? To a reporter, Levi replied unhelpfully: 'I'd rather not speak about it.' Catholics prayed for the relics to be returned in time for the saint's feast day on 13 December, and they were. The police discovered the bones intact in a flat on the outskirts of Venice. A twenty-eight-year-old drifter, Gianfranco Tiozzo, already wanted for the murder of a restauranteur, admitted his guilt: 'It was just a hoax.'

Monday 24 November was the last day of a Yiddish Film Festival in Turin. It generated considerable interest locally in Levi's forthcoming Yiddish novel and brought a taste of ghetto wit and wisdom to the Piedmont capital. Early that day, in another part of Turin, Hanns Engert was found hanged. He had been due to appear that morning at the trial of his Tunisian lover, Ben Messud, who had threatened to 'expose' Engert as a homosexual and blackmailed him for money. The unpleasantness had continued with phone calls and extortion threats; in desperation Engert turned to the gay civil-rights activist Angelo Pezzana for help. Pezzana advised Engert to go to the police, which he did, and Messud was taken to trial. But on the night before the proceedings, in remorse it was said at having denounced his lover, Engert hanged himself: he was forty-eight. Levi was devastated by this abrupt calamity (which was reported in *La Stampa*) and there was widespread horror among Turin's homosexual community. Pezzana tried to persuade Levi to sign a declaration to the effect that Engert had been 'murdered', but Levi refused: 'Hanns killed himself – suicide is a right we all have.' As did the Stoics, Levi believed in the individual's right to choose the means and time of his death.

For a week after Engert's suicide Levi continued lessons at the Goethe Institut, but he disliked his new teacher. Lily-Maria von Hartmann was an abrasive, chain-smoking Berliner with an acidic sense of humour. Born in 1939, the year Hitler invaded Poland, she did not much care to know who Primo Levi was, or what he had suffered under the Germans. On their first day with her, pupils were asked to leave the classroom in pairs and come back with a brief description of each other in German. Levi was introduced by his elderly companion Anna Maria Savoini: 'This is Primo Levi, who needs no introduction. He was in Germany as a young man, but against his will.' Von Hartmann made no comment; instead, she passed round photographs of paintings by the half-demented Austrian artist Friedrich Schröder-Sonnestern. These were a nightmare of chattering skulls and lurid sexual couplings, but instead of provoking strong reactions in Levi, as von Hartmann had hoped, he feigned indifference. Then she did something tasteless. She set her class the essay theme 'Homosexuality and Suicide', presumably in reference to her predecessor. Levi vowed never to return to the Goethe Institut. But, so as not to hurt von Hartmann's feelings, he lied that the burdens and the demands of celebrity left him no time for her lessons. 'I've become famous for being famous,' he told her; there was some truth in that.

It was not long before Levi found a new German teacher. Hens Henrik Fischer was a German Balt who lived in the flat beneath Levi's Aunt Jole Luzzati. Born in 1941 of Estonian parents, the rosy-cheeked Fischer was very jovial but so nervous of meeting Levi, because of what had happened to the Jews in wartime, that he could hardly speak. Levi helped him to overcome his awkwardness by suggesting that they address each other by the informal *tu*, and that seemed to do the trick. The weekly conversation lessons were held in Fischer's flat on Corso Rosselli. To help with his grammar, one day Levi brought in his own translation of Heinrich Heine's bitterly ironic poem, 'Donna Clara', in which a woman dismisses Jews first as noxious insects, then as Christ-killers, and finally as persons whose blood will corrupt a nation. The poem had first been circulated in the Artom circle in the 1940s, and Levi's renewed interest in it was prompted by a renascent anti-Semitism. In 1981, in reaction to Israeli policy against the Palestinian Arabs, Italian synagogues were violated for the first time since the Second World War. In Rome a Jewish pupil, Paola Caviglia, was beaten and thrown down the stairwell of her school for the crime of playing Anne Frank in an end-of-term play.

In the last weeks of 1981 Levi published his third short-story collection, *Lilít*, made of Auschwitz fragments and science fiction disjecta. It was fairly well received, though the critics unanimously ignored the book's most intriguing aspect. Many have claimed that we lack the vocabulary to describe the enormity of Auschwitz. The concentration camp was unspeakable, inhuman, but Levi did not agree; he had recorded the human loss in everyday speech. Instead, he felt the inadequacy of language in other areas. In the thirteenth short story in *Lilít*, 'A Quiet Star', about an Arab astronomer, Levi lamented the limitations of our language to describe the scientific phenomena of the planets or the invisible world of the atom. These, Levi believed, were far more resistant to our everyday language than Auschwitz.

9

As the Old Year limped out, *La Stampa* asked Levi to make his forecasts for 1982. He obliged, and they were printed in the paper alongside those of the

British novelist J. G. Ballard. Levi's included the usual forebodings of robot assembly lines and computer takeovers. The year 1982 was to open on a sour note for Levi, when he was offended to learn that his journalist friend Alberto Sinigaglia had not chosen to include him in a book of interviews with Italian authors on the subject of the millennium: *Twenty Years until 2000*. The omission left a bitter taste, especially as Italo Calvino was interviewed. Levi could be touchy, but his touchiness was rarely at odds with an outwardly generous and courteous disposition. On 11 January 1982 he wrote the millennial poem '2000', and brought it to Sinigaglia for publication in *La Stampa*. 'It was Primo's quiet way of saying he'd forgiven me,' said Sinigaglia. The New Year did not pass altogether smoothly for some of Levi's friends. Ada Della Torre was dying of Alzheimer's, and Nardo had entered a wintry period of stock-taking. On that same 11 January he drew up his will: 'To my dearest fraternal friend Dr Primo Levi I leave my gold-plated money clip.' The clip had belonged to Nardo's adored cousins Nella and Ilda Segre and was engraved with their names; to his maid Anna Piersanti he left a chandelier, wardrobe and bedside table. Evidently Nardo had few worldly possessions (his Rembrandt sketch went to his family), but he had given Levi an item of jewellery that he had carried on his person for much of his life – an intimate bequest.

Winter turned to spring, and in April *If Not Now, When?* was published. The novel brought Levi more attention and applause than he had ever expected. Piles of the book were on display in Italian bookshops. Ironically Levi's weakest book got the best reviews. There was just one dissenting voice. Claudio Magris, in a respectful if finely shaded review for the *Corriere della Sera*, observed that Levi's prose did not quite catch fire. The problem was the fictional form Levi used. He was scarcely a master of it. Levi was not an imaginative genius like Joyce or Kafka. 'And this is the great paradox', observed the novelist Aharon Appelfeld. 'Levi's creativity was as a memoirist – he made of *narration* a creative act.' Levi wrote best from his experience. To publicise the book, he gave a string of interviews. His writer friend Roberto Vacca (his leg in a plaster at the time) travelled from Rome to tape-record Levi in Turin on 23 April. Levi confessed to Vacca that he was never much of a reader of modern fiction. 'With the exception of Conrad, I don't care for twentieth-century novelists. Novels bore me. Unless of course [Levi laughed] we're talking about my own.' The few novels Levi did read were mostly foreign (Italy does not have a tradition of the novel, rather of the short story and novella). An exception was Ippolito Nievo's Risorgimento romance, *Confessions of an Italian* (1867), which charted the rise of Italy's anti-Austrian resistance and, like *If Not Now*,

When?, was brocaded with high adventure. Discerning reviewers recognised other borrowings. One saw the book as derived from Beppe Fenoglio's classic Resistance saga of 1968, *Johnny the Partisan*. Fenoglio, a Piedmontese novelist and Oliver Cromwell fanatic, had narrated the Italian partisan war in grand style.

If Not Now, When? had no sooner shot to the top of the Italian bestseller list than the Russian-born artist Marc Chagall brought a lawsuit against Levi's publishers. Einaudi had neglected to ask Chagall's permission to reproduce part of one of his Jerusalem stained-glass windows on the cover of *Lilít*. On 4 May lawyers acting on the artist's behalf wrote to Levi via the Italian Society of Authors to complain of an illegal 'appropriation' and 'mutilation' of artistic property. The issue was not to be completely resolved until a year later, when it was settled out of court. Levi was made very unhappy by the threatened lawsuit, as he admired Chagall enormously. The artist had influenced his descriptions in *If Not Now, When?* of multi-coloured Polish sunsets and floating brides in white veils.

TWENTY-THREE

Strife in the Middle East
1982–3

I

If Not Now, When? was out, all the interviews and reviews were done, the party was over – and Levi felt numb. In spring 1982 he accepted a commission to translate Kafka. Giulio Einaudi planned to launch the new series 'Writers Translated by Writers', and with the centenary of Kafka's birth the following year, Levi was under pressure to complete the translation. At first he was enthusiastic; by translating *The Trial* he hoped to improve his German and stave off creative barrenness. Instead, Kafka involved Levi more terribly than he could have imagined. Kafka was not even one of his favourite authors; he found no 'joy' in *The Trial,* only darkness and a squeamish distaste for the physical world. If Levi had always tried in his writing to shed the light of reason on to things that are obscure and in ferment, Kafka was like a 'mole' who burrowed ever deeper into darkness. Levi's poem of 22 September 1982, 'Old Mole', is surely a veiled portrait of Kafka: 'I chose to live alone and in the dark,' the animal announces.

The deeper Levi became immersed in *The Trial*, the more he began to see his life mirrored in that of 'St Franz of Prague', as he called Kafka. The Czech had lived a life of quite exemplary tedium as an insurance clerk, rarely travelling beyond his home or parents. Levi's own life was just as hidebound, he thought. Moreover Kafka's three sisters, victims of the endlessly unravelling bureaucracy foretold by their brother in *The Trial,* had perished in Nazi camps. *The Trial,* with its presumption of guilt, seemed to foreshadow the Hitler terror in quite a frightening way. Kafka must have had an 'almost animalesque' sensibility, said Levi, to have been able to look so accurately into the future. Far from absorbing Levi in pleasurable work, Kafka revived his disquiet about Jews and Judaism.

427

And that summer Levi became more deeply involved in the Jewish situation than at any time since the war. He agreed to accompany a group of students, teachers and survivors to Auschwitz. Then on 6 June, Israel invaded Lebanon. Prime Minister Begin's mission to destroy the Palestinian resistance managed only to devastate large parts of south Lebanon and kill thousands of Arabs. At this terrible time Levi could not possibly remain indifferent to the Israeli war. *If Not Now, When?* was misconstrued by some left-wing Italians as a Zionist vindication of the Begin violence. Of course Levi had not intended it that way. None of the characters in the book is even a Zionist; they end up in Palestine not because of any ideology but because they have no homes to go back to. Still, it was unfortunate that a novel about Jewish partisans who find salvation in the New Jerusalem of Israel should now be a bestseller.

While Begin sent in Israeli tanks, Levi's attitude towards Israel and the Israeli government became ever more complicated; he told friends that for the first time since the June War of 1967 he found himself actively loathing the Israeli government. An Italian rabbi was irked when Levi asked him if he had been to 'Palestine'; the reference to Israel as 'Palestine' seemed to be an anti-Israeli provocation, and he tartly answered Levi: 'To Palestine, no; to Israel, yes.' What was unforgivable about Prime Minister Begin, in Levi's view, was that he used the mythology of victimisation by the Nazis to justify his militarism and victimisation of the Palestinians. Outraged, Levi applied himself to the task of launching a Begin Must Go campaign. On 7 June he contacted Moshe Kahn, one of the foremost progressive Jews in Italy, to decide what action to take. (Levi had first met the German-born Kahn in 1976 after reading his translation of Paul Celan's poems, which he admired.) Together they conceived the idea of publishing an open letter against Begin in the Italian press. Levi drew up the protest that same June evening, working on it with his Hungarian writer friend Edith Bruck until 2:00 am, and then he read the version out to Kahn on the telephone. Next day, 8 June, Kahn received the full text by teleprinter at *La Repubblica*'s office in Rome. Copies of the protest were then sent to Italy's principal Jewish intellectuals for signature. At first Natalia Ginzburg refused to sign, on the grounds that she was Catholic on her mother's side; yet as conservative Italian Jews closed ranks in support of Begin, so she felt she must sign. The 149 other signatories included such names as the Florentine historian Ugo Caffaz, the Roman psychoanalyst David Meghnagi and the Turinese biochemist Rita Levi Montalcini. Collecting so many signatures was bound to be slow, however, and the protest was not published until mid-June, by which time Levi had returned to Auschwitz.

*

On the eve of his departure for Poland, Levi found time to see a schoolboy who was writing an essay on 'Fascism and the Italian Jews'. Though Levi had vowed no longer to talk of this subject in classrooms, he continued to receive pupils individually at his home, about once a month. (One student even telephoned Levi about his school essay on *If This is a Man* which, it turned out, he had not yet read: 'I promise to read *all* your books soon,' he apologetically told Levi: Levi was politeness itself.) Antonio Samaritani called on Levi on the afternoon of 9 June, accompanied by his mother, who ran Turin's 'Athesia' bookshop. Levi welcomed them kindly and, as it was a scorching June day, offered them a selection of chilled fruit juices. The boy was eager to know what a real writer's apartment looked like, but he was disappointed: 75 Corso Re Umberto appeared to be the same as his parents' flat, and even smelled of cooking as their own home did. During the two-hour conversation, Levi avoided politics and said little about the Lebanon débâcle, feeling perhaps that it would go beyond a sixteen-year-old. He courteously answered Antonio's questions on Mussolini and the 1938 race laws; Antonio's schoolboy reminiscence, 'An Afternoon with Primo Levi', is an excellent piece of minor journalism. Meeting one's heroes is often a mixed blessing, but Levi had been a complete delight, and on leaving him Antonio felt elated.

2

On 14 June, a Monday, Levi and Lucia flew with LOT Polish Airlines to Warsaw. He had not been back to Auschwitz since 1965 and Lucia had never been before: Levi must have wondered how she would react. Next to Lucia sat Luciano Caro, chief rabbi of Florence, whom Lucia had taught history of art in the 1950s at the Jewish School in Turin. (Caro, in turn, had tutored Renzo Levi for his Bar Mitzvah.) The trip had been organised by the Florence town council; the Jewish RAI television programme, *Springs of Life*, was filming the occasion.

General Jaruzelski, in an attempt to outlaw the Solidarity trade union, had just proclaimed martial law and Poland was reported to be under curfew. At Warsaw airport the Italians were met by a Polish Ministry of Information guide. Her first words were to warn that any out-of-place informality could lead to arrest: the police were stern here. Yet she was solicitous of her charges and went to great lengths to procure Rabbi Caro and his wife the kosher food they required. Professor Baldassare Gullotta, the education minister for Florence who helped to organise the trip, later remembered Warsaw as an oppressed and frightened city: 'None of us could phone home to Italy. The lines were down. The shops were empty. There were bread and petrol queues (in the restaurants one was lucky to find a few bones described as chicken) and the Varsovians looked glum.' The Italians were advised not to dally at the bronze monument where the Nazis had burned the Warsaw ghetto to a cinder in 1943, as troops were patrolling the Muranów quarter of the ex-ghetto, visibly training their guns on people from the rooftops.

On the flight from Warsaw to Cracow anyone who wished to use the lavatory had first to ask permission of the armed Polish guards at the back of the plane. Predictably the Italians' hotel in Cracow (the Holiday Inn) was a black-market hive where prostitutes and money-changers worked the foyer; Levi was disturbed to share the lift with two drunken Poles who swore boorishly at each other, like *Kapos*. After breakfast the next day, a Tuesday, the group was driven to Auschwitz in a Polish travel agency (ORBIS) tour bus. On the bus, Levi again smelled the combination of odours that he remembered so well from the Polish winter of 1944. Toasted barley, burning coal. 'This is mining country, and for me at least, this is the smell of the Polish concentration camp,' he told the *Springs of Life* film crew. Levi's equanimity impressed the crew, and indeed everyone else on the coach. The film's producer, Daniel Toaff (whose father was the rabbi of Rome), asked Levi how he felt on seeing the Polish countryside again. 'Everything is different. I've travelled in these places as a lost, misplaced person, searching for a centre, for someone who would take me in, and truly it was then a desolate landscape.' The bus passed a railway station with closed goods wagons at the sidings, and at this point on the film Levi can be seen to flinch slightly. 'Even now the sight of those freight trucks has a violent effect on me.' Lucia was such a quiet and anonymous presence in her headscarf that she was not noticeable on the coach.

Levi was bothered by the Warsaw government's appropriation of Auschwitz as a place of Polish (rather than Jewish) 'martyrdom'. More than 90 per cent of the *Lager*'s victims were Jews. 'The fact is not exactly denied, but sort of bracketed off,' Levi observed. In protest, he had refused to attend the inauguration of the Italian block at Auschwitz two years earlier in April 1980, but had composed a few lines for the memorial, which can still be seen at the entrance to the Italians' Block 21:

Visitor, observe the remains of this camp and consider: whatever your nationality, you are not a foreigner here. Ensure that your journey was not in vain, that our own deaths have not been in vain. For you and for your children, may the ashes of Auschwitz serve as a warning. And may the dreadful fruit of hatred, whose

traces you have seen here, not grow again – not tomorrow, not
ever.

Nobody felt much like eating at lunchtime, and Levi commented on the macabre indecency of a cafeteria at Auschwitz. Daniel Toaff asked Levi if he thought the tendency was for people to forget Auschwitz. 'Signs do exist that this is taking place: forgetting or even denying it. This is significant: those who deny Auschwitz would be ready to remake it.'

On his last day in Poland Levi visited Cracow's Jewish quarter of Kazimierz. The few elderly worshippers in the synagogue-museum were too frightened to answer his queries about the Passover plates and sepia photographs on display: 'You'll have to ask at the Ministry,' they replied in Kafkan spirit.

Half the documentary footage taken of Levi by the *Springs of Life* crew was confiscated without explanation at airport customs. The missing footage had to be reshot in Turin against a faked-up Polish background. On the whole, however, Levi's impression of Poland and the Poles had been favourable. Later he wrote to a Polish friend in London of his 'positive and sympathetic image' of the Poles, quite different from the 'admittedly distorted one which I formed in the camp and which appears, here and there, in my books'. He added indignantly: 'It is not true that I "dislike the Poles". I disliked the Polish *political prisoners* I met in Auschwitz, most of them nationalists, anti-Semitic, violent and virtually Fascist; but I do not accept or approve of generalisations.'

3

While Levi was in Poland, the Arab–Israeli crisis had come to a head in Italy with publication in *La Repubblica* of the anti-Begin letter. It demanded an immediate withdrawal of Israeli troops from Lebanon and a stop to all further construction of Jewish settlements in the occupied territories. Italy's conservative Jews were furious with Levi. Who was Levi to judge? He was not acquainted with any of the distinguished Israelis in politics and his knowledge of Palestinian politics was non-existent. An icy contretemps developed between Levi and his pro-Israeli friends, among them Livio Norzi and Nardo De Benedetti, who objected to his outspoken expressions of dissent. After Lebanon, Levi's relationship with Nardo was never quite the same again. And he began to receive harrowing letters from friends in Israel. 'Are you blind?' they asked. 'Can't you see all the Israeli blood spilled in these years?' Levi was in moral torment, but he had no intention of changing his opinion of Begin. Instead, he resolved on further criticism of the Israeli Prime Minister. Disturbingly, the Lebanon invasion had made anti-Semitism respectable again. Cartoons of Jews, like those classically represented in the Nazi press, began to appear in the Italian newspapers. It was all too easy to identify Begin with the Jewish people as a whole. Thus the children's writer Roald Dahl (certainly not known for his philo-Semitism) wrote that 1982 was 'when we all started hating the Jews'.

Rita Levi Montalcini, one of the signatories of the anti-Begin letter, told Levi on the telephone that her only comfort in this time of war was to read *If This is a Man*. Levi answered her in bleak tones: 'You're lucky, that book gives me no solace any more. Sometimes I wonder if I belong to the Jewish people at all.' On the front page of *La Stampa* for 24 June Levi said he felt 'anguish and shame' at Israel's actions. News that *If Not Now, When?* had won the coveted Viareggio Prize only deepened his feeling of dejection. Levi suspected the prize had been awarded him less on grounds of literary merit, than out of sympathy for his embattled position as a Jew. Accordingly he asked the Viareggio chairman Leonida Rèpaci to withdraw his name as the winner. Rèpaci objected that the prize had never gone to a 'more distinguished' novel. He may or may not have been telling the truth.

At any rate, Levi was persuaded to accept the prize and on 26 June he was in Viareggio, Tuscany's largest and liveliest beach resort, to collect it. Alberto Papuzzi, Einaudi's press officer, and his wife Luisa, drove Levi there in their Renault. In the Grand Hotel Excelsior Levi bumped into Umberto Eco, one of the Viareggio judges, wearing his trademark tweed deerstalker. Eco, who was poised to make millions from his novel *The Name of the Rose*, later regretted that he had not spoken longer to Levi. Typically, the prize-giving banquet threatened to drag on until midnight; Levi managed to escape to a quiet sea-front restaurant, where (recalled Papuzzi) he enjoyed turbot and chips with the Jewish historian and ex-partisan Manlio Rossi-Doria. The next morning he wrote the poem 'Laid Up', a painterly vignette of Viareggio's mooring ropes and yachts. He was tentatively attracted to the water and managed to persuade Luisa Papuzzi to join him for a dip off the sands of Bocca di Magra nearby. Luisa was frightened of the waves (like Levi, she had only just learned to swim) but Levi insisted. He explained that immediately after Auschwitz he had attempted to learn to swim by watching ducks paddle on the water. Afterwards, still accompanied by the Papuzzis, Levi travelled a little way down the coast to the tiny resort of Sarzana, where at the local bookshop he was to help launch *Making Up for Lost Time*, an account of factory-life by the politician and ex-medical student Pietro Marcenaro. Marcenaro was well-connected in Italian left-wing literary circles: present at the launch were Natalia Ginzburg, her historian son

Carlo and the veteran trade unionists Vittorio Foa and Bruno Trentin (leader of the powerful metalworkers' labour union). Levi was in the company of friends, and Sarzana was a welcome diversion from the worries and upsets of Israel.

Meanwhile the Israeli controversy expanded like an oil slick, and reporters the length and breadth of Italy clamoured to interview Levi. He received a visit from *La Repubblica*'s Alberto Stabile, whose paper was known to be hostile to Israel and Jews in general. 'Are the Palestinians in the same position as the Jews under the Nazis?' Levi despised these pat analogies. 'There is *no* policy to exterminate the Palestinians.' By granting so many interviews to the Italian press, Edith Bruck thought Levi was putting personal advertisement ahead of the political issue. 'He didn't *have* to talk so much to the papers. Many of us preferred that he didn't. Primo had the writer's vice of narcissism.'

Levi's name was by now familiar to the millions of Italians who read a daily newspaper or glossy magazine, but not books. He had become a political celebrity figure, not just a literary figure. Unlike in Britain (where we positively disapprove of unprofessional involvement in politics), in Italy writers and university professors are expected to engage wholeheartedly in public affairs. Levi knew very well that his current celebrity was due entirely to his stance on Lebanon, and he kept up the attack. In the gossipy *Oggi* he even compared the Lebanon invasion to the Falklands War, which Britain had just fought. 'If the Argentines were wrong to invade the Falklands, Israel was wrong to invade Lebanon.' This was scarcely subtle political analysis.

On 11 July 1982 Italy won the World Cup; traffic was in a gridlock in Turin as football fans set up street parties. On this hot summer afternoon Levi observed for himself the political furore that *If Not Now, When?* was capable of rousing. Accompanied by the literary critic Cesare Cases and by Einaudi's sales director Roberto Cerati, he made his way to the working-class Lingotto area of the city, where he was to talk about his novel to Italian Communists. He was no sooner in the Party clubhouse, however, when a group of Palestinians verbally attacked him. Levi was seen as an emissary of Israeli officialdom and a supporter of Begin's militant Zionism. Above the racket Cases tried to explain that Levi's fictional partisans would never have shared Begin's arrogance and imperiousness: they were starry-eyed *intelligenty*, with roots in the October Revolution. But it was no good: the Palestinans raised such a clamour that Levi had to be bundled out of the clubhouse back door.

Once again, to escape the August dogdays, the Levis were cloistered with relatives in the Hotel Excelsior in Frabosa. Over the years Levi had become devoted to the Piedmont town, which was associated in his mind with tranquillity and family reunions. And in the hotel's monastic calm, though it cost him great mental effort, he tried to proceed with his version of *The Trial*. Translation should open a window to let in the light, Levi believed, and he sought to remove the knots and the occasional opaqueness in Kafka's German. But in the process of 'clarifying' Kafka he culpably misconstrued the original. Levi, who was so often angry with his own translators for their slipshod approximations, now took liberties with Kafka. (On publication, only Cesare Cases, at the best of times a waspish critic, grumbled that an alien 'optimism' had been grafted on to *The Trial*.)

Levi's last serious depression had disappeared after his bout of shingles in 1978, but as the summer progressed, Kafka seemed to revive it and send him into a by now familiar downward spiral of gloom and hopelessness. Levi felt 'contaminated' by Kafka's Joseph K and he began to see similarities not just between his life and Kafka's, but between *The Trial* and *If This is a Man*. Both books had narrated senseless events in a dispassionate tone – the voice of the courtroom testimonial – and both books had opened with an arbitrary and unjustified arrest. Moreover, Levi's short stories from this period offer some evidence of a Kafkan influence. In 'Birth Register', a foot-plodding clerk mechanically sifts through baptismal and death certificates in a registry that has something of the nightmare quality of Kafka's *The Castle*.

Levi's moods continued to fluctuate, but by early September he was well enough to fly to Venice to receive yet another literary prize. The Campiello, which Levi had won in 1963 for *The Truce*, was a far more important award than the Viareggio. Yet the presentation, held on the 4th, was largely a vanity. The Campiello's promoter, Mario Valeri Manera, was known to have Mafia connections with the Vatican banker Roberto Calvi, who had been found three months earlier hanging under Blackfriars Bridge in London. Calvi's gangland execution (as it certainly was) confirmed Levi's worst fears about the links between the Mafia, international finance and the far-right faction of the Christian Democratic Party to which Manera belonged. He did not care for Manera at all and would not be surprised when he tried to kill himself in 1986 following police investigations into his finances. But there was worse. The day before the awards the Mafia had executed one of the Campiello jury, General Alberto Dalla Chiesa. He and his wife were machine-gunned to death in the Sicilian capital of Palermo: it is not known what Dalla Chiesa made of *If Not Now, When?*, but he was a cultured man with broad literary tastes. He had been prefect in charge of Mafia investigations in Palermo for precisely 100 days.

Levi accepted his cheque from Manera in the floodlit forecourt of the Doge's Palace. A 'Gold Campiello' was awarded posthumously to the Italian novelist Ignazio Silone, whose Irish widow Darina received the prize, and she and Levi exchanged a few words. General Dalla Chiesa's murder cast a veil over the evening, though, and Levi was embarrassed by the uproar raised round his book and person. He turned to the Campiello jurist Sergio Grandini for advice on how to cope with the scores of interviews he had to give in Venice for radio and television. A Swiss-Italian industrialist, Grandini's calm and civilised air seems to have reassured Levi, who was vulnerable at this time. Later that evening, overwhelmed by the media attention, Levi gave Grandini a typescript of his unpublished story, 'Last Christmas of the War', with permission to publish it. He remembered that Mario Rigoni Stern had rated Grandini highly as a private publisher and art connoisseur. So began a friendship, mostly by letter and telephone, between Levi and the equally reserved Grandini.

At the opulent Hotel Danieli, meanwhile, a special banquet had been laid on in Levi's honour, but Levi knew it would be affected by a formality and sycophancy that he despised, especially as the hotel was owned by the (as it turned out) deeply corrupt P2 (Propaganda Two) affiliate Orazio Bagnasco. Levi flinched from individuals like Bagnasco and Manera, with their whiff of patronage and ill-gotten gains, and he wanted no part of their hospitality. Instead, he celebrated his victory privately with friends in a Venice bar. Emerging contented from the bar, he bumped into Italo Calvino and his Argentine wife Esther Singer, whom he had not met before. Calvino was on the jury of that year's Venice Film Festival. He did not have many years to live.

No matter how much Levi disliked the Campiello presentations, his fame in Italy was finally established and immense. Next day, 5 September, there were twenty articles on him in the newspapers, and the hundredth was published before the end of the month. By the year's end *If Not Now, When?* had gone through four editions and sold in excess of 110,000 copies.

Levi left Venice in dejection, and his mood darkened later that September with further news from the Middle East. In Israeli-occupied West Beirut, Maronite Christian militiamen, acting as Israel's client, massacred several hundred defenceless Palestinian civilians in the refugee camps of Sabra and Chatila. In a thirty-eight hour orgy of killing, men, women and children were shot and hacked to death, pregnant women eviscerated. While Begin seemed unmoved by the slaughter, the world stood horrified, and Levi condemned the 'bloody arrogance' of the Israeli president. On 24 September *La Repubblica* ran a second interview with Levi under the headline: 'I, Primo Levi, ask Begin to Resign.' The Beirut massacre had 'polluted' the image of Jews throughout the world, said Levi; it was to unleash the worst wave yet of anti-Semitism in post-war Italy. On 9 October unidentified terrorists bombed the synagogue in Rome, killing a child and wounding thirty-five worshippers. Then graffiti went up on the city walls: 'Jews! The ovens are waiting for you!' There was a new bitterness and violence in the language used by some Italian papers about the Jews. Italy's left-wing *Nuova Società* went so far as to superimpose Begin's face on a photograph of a Nuremberg rally. Levi was appalled, and the Jewish world was in ferment.

The Turin bookseller and gay-rights activist Angelo Pezzana, though he was not Jewish, prominently displayed copies of *If Not Now, When?* in his bookshop window as a gesture of solidarity with the city's Jews. He draped symbolic blue-and-white silk sheets – the colours of the Israeli flag – round a seven-branched candelabrum and made great pyramids from copies of Levi's novel. Levi was overwhelmed by the gesture and confided to Pezzana that the cover of *If Not Now, When?* concealed the Israeli flag. It showed a Russian winter scene (1904) by Igor Grabar of a snow-bound field dappled by a tree's blue shadow. 'Blue and white, you see!' Levi exclaimed to Pezzana. Naturally the jacket had been designed before the strife broke out in the Middle East.

5

In Turin the winter of 1982 was dark and severe, with snow from late November onwards, frozen puddles and black ice. On 15 November it was Nardo De Benedetti's eighty-fourth birthday; he celebrated on his own with a glass of Biellese *ratafià* liqueur (his current favourite). The rift between him and Levi over Israel had not healed, and a gloom had settled over the Jewish Crocetta. Levi's mother's health deteriorated; at eighty-seven, she was becoming senile and was often confused and feeling low. Levi's own health and moods had their ups and downs these winter months. A verruca on the sole of his foot, caught while swimming at the American Club, was burned out by cautery, but the site became infected, and to Alberto Papuzzi Levi said in exasperation: 'Now for the first time in my life I understand how a handicapped person must feel.' A depressed person typically would get things out of proportion. Nevertheless, Papuzzi was astonished that a trifling wart could bring an Auschwitz survivor so low. In fact, it was Auschwitz that made him so touchy: prisoners unable to walk were sent straight to the gas chambers: Levi still bore the scars of his primitive clogs. Meanwhile there was a continuing flux of people to see and forthcoming foreign editions to attend to. But Levi turned down invitations, and abandoned himself to black moods.

On 8 October he sent a telegram to the jury of the Sirmione Catullo Prize: 'Impossible to attend prize-giving owing to [verruca] surgery.' Levi was now quite indifferent to these literary awards – he had too many of them – and cared less and less for author junkets of any sort. The novelist Gian Luigi Piccioli was alarmed to receive a note from Levi, shortly after 5 November, that said: 'Unfortunately I can't attend the Pescara book festival because I can barely walk.' Walking was certainly laborious though not impossible for Levi: he managed a brief winter hike in the Susa Valleys with Papuzzi. Snow lay on their narrow path and Papuzzi trudged attentively behind Levi in case he fell. And he did fall – into a hole. Papuzzi rushed to help, but was brusquely elbowed aside. 'Primo didn't want to be thought of as invalid, he was determined not to be looked after by anyone.' After the war Levi had been willing to accept help, physical help, daily and un-remitting, from one woman, his wife Lucia. Now, according to a cousin, he quite intentionally eschewed even Lucia's assistance. In his deepening depression, Levi wanted to castigate himself.

By 12 November he seemed sufficiently recovered to attend a talk in Turin on supernovas (exploding stars). Margherita Hack was Italy's best loved astronomer; she edited L'Astronomia magazine for which Levi was an occasional contributor, and after her lecture he went up to talk to her – not about astronomy, as one might have thought, but about ageing. In his mid-sixties now, Levi was in that transitional age when men often feel that their life is over. He said how startled he was when, for the first time, someone had given him their seat on the tram. But, as he spoke to Hack, he seemed contented, and said he would not like to change places with a twenty-year-old. His organs, limbs and – most important – his memory seemed to be in working order.

Meanwhile Levi continued to give interviews, so long as they were not on the subject of Israel. On 27 November snow was falling thickly on Turin when the Tuscan literary journal, Firme nostre, sent along a reporter. She asked Levi if by chance he had ever 'identified' with the Italian Romantic poet Giacomo Leopardi. Levi replied in surprise: 'No one's ever asked me that before!' but it was clear that he was not happy to be compared with Leopardi. Famously pessimistic, Leopardi had a spinal disease and

437

defective eyesight which made reading difficult. 'Even if I *was* a skinny child, I wasn't deformed'! Levi protested. The truth is, he did increasingly identify with Leopardi, just as he had come to identify with Kafka. Leopardi's helpless capitulation to *noia* – accidie, existential dread – was not wholly uncongenial to Levi. In a short story of 1977, 'Conversation Between a Poet and a Doctor', Leopardi (not named, but easily recognisable) describes his vision of the world as a desert crossed by a despairing pilgrim, who longs for death as a release from wretchedness. The story suggests that life, even if it has its moments, is ultimately a misery. Yet when asked, Levi said he wavered most of the time between optimism and pessimism, 'depending on who I meet, what time of the year it is, what news I get', to which he might have added, 'or whether or not I'm depressed'. His article 'The Ugly Force', written in a later depressive episode, claimed that only in moments of 'clear-sightedness' are we able to sense the vanity and pointlessness that Leopardi believed lies just under the surface of all that we do. In these last years Levi turned more and more to Leopardi as a kind of negative solace.

And by December Levi was in a state bordering on despair. 'I'm going through my worst period since Auschwitz,' he told the Austrian historian Hermann Langbein. To top it all, his chemist friend Ennio Mariotti, who had survived a laboratory blast four years earlier, was dying. For two nights Levi sat by Mariotti's bedside in the Mauriziano Hospital in Turin. He felt helpless, unable to do anything either for Mariotti or his wife; in his last hours Mariotti lay in a coma, and the family knelt about the bed, praying. On 16 December the chemist's heart stopped. His body was taken to the Catholic cemetery in Turin, and Levi wept for his wife Maria and himself. He had known Mariotti for forty years; the loss went deep.

Now Levi was in financial difficulties. The poet and Philip Larkin translator Camillo Pennati would often see him hurrying down Corso Re Umberto on his way to the bank, 'like a quick-stepping ferret'. The spendthrift Giulio Einaudi was on the verge of bankruptcy and his publishing house about to go into receivership. Consequently Levi had not received a single lira in royalties for *If Not Now, When?* In bleak tones he told a friend: 'It appears unlikely that the Struzzo [Ostrich: the Einaudi colophon] will ever get up on its two feet again. It's like losing a piece of one's motherland'. Levi was certainly not facing penury, but the Einaudi crisis made life very uncomfortable for him as money was needed to pay the nurses for his mother's care. Unlike the wily Calvino (who was very knowing in the ways of publishing and celebrity), Levi lacked the mercenary streak to squeeze from

Einaudi all the moneys owed him. The best chance of shoring up his finances, he decided, was to invest in stocks and shares. He appealed to Sidney Calvi, an old chemist friend who was now a stockbroker at the Banca Commerciale d'Italia in Turin. Calvi delicately enquired into Levi's circumstances and decided that he should deposit shares in the bank. This proposal comforted Levi, whom Calvi had always believed had a 'poor head for figures'. Another form of assistance was also forthcoming. Francesco Proto, Levi's southern Italian colleague from SIVA, advised him to invest in gold sterling coins. This, too, was good advice, as the gold appreciated in value and Levi made a profit. By such expedients he stayed afloat.

6

At the end of 1982 Levi began to correspond with a Jungian analyst in London. Elegant and poised, but above all keenly intelligent and well read, Ruth Hoffman was three years younger than Levi. On the basis of her first letter to him, Levi seems to have been immediately attracted to Hoffman, and she to him. They would not set eyes on each other until three years later at a literary festival in London when, after a talk Levi gave, Hoffman wanted to introduce herself, but foreseeing embarrassment thought better of it. The correspondence was significant for them both. Hoffman's letters were a comfort to Levi, while she was thrilled to be in touch with a writer she had long admired. Fortifying herself with a glass of brandy (not something she normally did), in December 1982 she wrote to Levi asking if she might perhaps visit him in Turin. In his reply, Levi gave no indication of how depressed he was, but initiated a sort of postal flirtation:

> Did you really need to drink a fair amount of brandy to pluck up the courage to write to me and 'overcome your inhibitions'? Which inhibitions, if I am allowed to ask? Is an analytical psychologist entitled to have inhibitions? Perhaps they are connected with your Polish (and Jewish, I suppose) origins? ... I should be really glad to meet you; but please note that my spoken English is a bit worse than my written one.

Born in 1922 in a private clinic in Vienna, Hoffman came from a middle-class Central European Jewish background. She grew up in Bielsko–Biala, near what was to be Auschwitz. In October 1938 she fled to Scotland, where she first trained as a weaver (Woollen Technical College, Galashiels), and later graduated in medicine from Edinburgh University. Hoping to make a career for herself in psychiatry, after the war she enrolled at the London

439

Society of Analytical Psychology, where her reputation among fellow Jungians was (she said) for 'pricking bubbles'. Though we only have one side of the correspondence from which to judge, it is clear that Ruth Hoffman not only shared with Levi her love of books, but also a gift for wry self-deprecation. She was interested in Levi's mind, above all, and opened with interest the three long letters he sent her.

By the New Year – 1983 – Levi had begun to confide to Dr Hoffman the state of his mental health and traumas. He said he was ashamed of being so weak and 'shipwrecked'. Was there any hope of recovery, now that depression seemed to be the commanding side of his personality? Levi warned her not to call on him in Turin in April after all, as had previously been planned: 'I might be an ugly disappointment to you.' Shortly after 7 February, 'Dr R. Hoffman Analytical Psychologist' received this letter written in English:

> For some months I have not been well . . . I suffer from a depression which began insidiously after the wave of success with *If Not Now, When?* and was aggravated in December owing to my mother's illness. She is 88 and lives with my wife and I. Her illness has left her in need of every kind of help and above all she is seriously depressed herself. Her depression only adds to (or multiplies with!) my own, which is interwoven with a sense of guilt towards my wife, who is wonderful, expert, efficient and attentive, while I am inept, distracted, and useless in the house – except for shopping. At the moment I find myself totally incapable of writing (writing this letter has cost me a huge effort), and experience great difficulty in making even the smallest decisions. I am desperately [worried for] the future. Naturally I am following a cure, but I absolutely cannot predict how I will be (*who* I will be) in April. I don't know if I'll ever be in a fit state to meet you: I beg you to understand me as a doctor and to forgive me as a *Mensch*.

Years later, Dr Hoffman commented on the letter: 'Levi must have been really ill, yet he writes so *fluently*. Clearly there was a "healthy" part of his personality which enabled him to write this letter; the "unhealthy" part was in some close tie-up with his mother and see-saws with her state and mood.' The so-called 'see-saw' was almost certainly illusory, but it reflected Levi's deep identification with (and attachment to) his mother. Hoffman went on: 'In this particular case I can see how the wife comes off badly, with her expectations vanishing further and further as mother and son got more and more tightly tied.' In other words, by withdrawing temporarily from the world, Levi shared more deeply in Ester's sickness. Levi's letter prompted Dr Hoffman to look again at Jung's essays 'The Dual Mother' and 'The Battle for Deliverance from the Mother'. Whether his illness was compounded by Auschwitz, she could not say; she pointed out to me that suicide among women survivors was not nearly as common as among men.

TWENTY-FOUR

Recognition Abroad
1983–5

I

In 1983 Levi's fears multiplied. Translating Kafka had pitched him into depression. Now he felt guilty at his failure to cope at home. The symptoms of his depressive illness – typically, anxiety, tearfulness, insomnia, loss of appetite – made him despise himself as a malingerer and a burden on the family. Alvin Rosenfeld was an Indiana University professor whom Levi had met in Turin and liked. On 14 February Levi wrote to him in shaky English of his apprehension: 'I hope you never experience such an alteration of the soul; it is painful and thought-hampering, it prevents me not only to write but also to drive or to travel. Naturally I am under medical care, but I cannot tell how long it will last.' In desperation, Levi turned to self-help manuals that gave advice on depression. One of these was by his friend Roberto Vacca, and Levi wrote to thank him for it: 'Many people will find it useful, and perhaps I will too, for I'm living through an extremely difficult time . . . But to change oneself is much harder than you say.' With certain friends Levi chose to speak obliquely of his illness, because he was ashamed of it.

Ashamed to be seen so transparently wretched, in March 1983 Levi began a course of anti-depressants. This was a hard step for a man of his upbringing to take, especially so in middle-class Turin, where to use such drugs at all was considered a weakness. Revealingly, in 'Conversation Between a Poet and a Doctor', Levi's time-travel story of Leopardi, the nineteenth-century poet throws away his prescription anti-depressants in the gutter: he can do without those. Levi was prescribed Parmodalin;* he was sceptical that it could buffer his extremes of low and lethargic feelings,

---

*The English trademark equivalent is Parstelin; the drug contains an anti-depressant (tranylcypromine) as well as a tranquillizer (trifluoperazine).

yet in a very short while he was feeling better. A chemical delusion? In frank amazement he wrote to Dr Ruth Hoffman in London of his de-traumatised state:

> I'd just started a course of Parmodalin (without much hope) when in the space of two or three days the depression lifted. Whether my recovery was due to the drug (as well as to the psychiatrist who prescribed it), I don't know. This is not the first episode of this sort, and I know that it will not even be my last. It has caused me terrible suffering, and among other things deprived me of the pleasure of meeting you here in Turin. Once again, my apologies – though I think you will understand me, professionally.

This depression had lasted five months, from December 1982 to the end of May 1983, and was one of Levi's most acute and distressing episodes. Now the blissful sense of being in charge of his life returned. He began to help in the house again, was generally less frightened (and frightening to others). He had recovered from a most mysterious disease, and waited in dread for the next occurrence. All the same he was comforted by the knowledge that medication could help.

2

During the first half of 1983, his Kafka translation almost universally praised, Levi tried to generate interest in his work abroad. He was upset that an East German translation of *The Periodic Table* had been censored ('censorially deleted', he put it in English). And in the Polish edition of *If This is a Man,* all unflattering references to Polish anti-Semitism had been removed. Elsewhere Levi had fared better. The Finnish edition of *If This is a Man,* issued in Helsinki in 1962, was now republished with a preface by the twenty-six-year-old critic Dan Steinbock, widely acknowledged to be the most faithful defender of Levi's work in Finland. Levi asked his new Finnish translator, Pirkko Peltonen-Rognoni (who lived in Milan), to translate the preface for him, which she did. What Levi then read disturbed and impressed him greatly. Steinbock was the first critic anywhere to see Levi as a refraction of Kafka. 'Primo Levi *is* Josef K.' So Levi's fear that Kafka's spirit inhabited his life and writing returned.

Most striking was the lack of American interest in Levi's books. The significant Jewish market in the United States, one might have thought, should have endorsed Levi by now. His New York agent, Bobbe Siegel, had tried for almost twenty years to launch him across the Atlantic, but she was not exactly a 'ball of fire' (one insider recalled), and seemed to have little grasp of the Italian fiction market. Giulio Einaudi himself was at the best of times a lackadaisical salesman, with scant interest in the reception of his authors outside Italy. Hitherto, *If Not Now, When?* had been submitted to Random House, Knopf, Doubleday, Pantheon; none was interested. In Britain, too, Levi was still largely unread. Penguin had published *If This is a Man* and *The Truce* in one volume in 1979 (with a fine introduction by the novelist Paul Bailey); it was soon out of print. American negotiations moved ponderously until Levi's sister approached the doyen of Italian translators, William Weaver.

Anna Maria had met Weaver through her American husband Julian Zimet, and knew he could be relied on to give a nuanced and impeccable translation of *If Not Now, When?* Weaver had superbly rendered the polyglot braggadocio of Umberto Eco's medieval whodunnit *The Name of the Rose,* which had sold a freak five million copies worldwide. Not since *One Hundred Years of Solitude* had there been such a consensual success on the book market. It was hoped that Weaver's Midas touch could do the same for Levi. Weaver had first heard of Levi in 1949 when Fiori Pucci, the wife of the great Neapolitan novelist Raffaele La Capria, pressed him to read *If This is a Man.* Weaver demurred ('Not *another* memoir of the camps!') and did not read the book until nearly twenty years later. He was urged to do so by the celebrated Scots translator of Italian, Archibald Colquhoun. 'I could see immediately that this was a classic,' recalled Weaver.

Summit Books, a subsidiary of Simon & Schuster in New York, commissioned Weaver to translate *If Not Now, When?* According to Weaver, they were aiming to lure an ethnic Jewish readership with a 'Holocaust' novel. When it was discovered that Levi was an assimilated Jew with an anti-Israeli stance, publication was stalled and Weaver was not paid for months. From the start, Levi's irreligion did not endear him to some American Jews. Only after the noted Jewish critic Irving Howe had agreed to write the preface to *If Not Now, When?* did Weaver get his translator's fee.

There was no question that interest in Levi was growing in America. Schocken Books, a venerable Madison Avenue outfit, was keen to publish *The Periodic Table.* The editor Emile Capouya, a Pasolini translator and Italian literature expert, was initially wary when the book was put his way, as it had been turned down by no fewer than twenty American publishers. However, he completely trusted the judgment of Raymond Rosenthal, a freelance critic who had appointed himself the book's translator. In Rosenthal's view *The Periodic Table* was 'a masterpiece', and once Capouya had read it, he agreed. Capouya hurried to purchase American rights from Einaudi: they cost him $2,000.

Rosenthal had never solicited a blurb, much less a laudatory one, in his life, and was very surprised when his friend Saul Bellow sent Schocken Books this radiant praise:

> We are always looking for the book it is necessary to read next. After a few pages I immersed myself in THE PERIODIC TABLE gladly and gratefully. There is nothing superfluous here, everything this book contains is essential. It is wonderfully pure and beautifully translated.

Levi admired Bellow greatly and was overjoyed that the 1976 Nobel Prize-winner had condescended to praise *The Periodic Table*. Bellow's advocacy would set off an explosion of American interest in Levi: rarely has a puff had such a momentous effect.

3

Meanwhile in Turin, unaware that he was about to reach the public eye across the Atlantic, Levi continued to see old university friends: Alberto Salmoni, who ran a stationer's on Via Mazzini (and who was now a 'wise and tranquil man'); Vanna Rava, Giovanna Balzaretti and Clara Moschino (who had raised 'with heroic devotion' two haemophiliac sons). Mario Piacenza ('wealthy but not always healthy') sometimes visited from Peru, where he ran a paint factory. He and Levi spoke nostalgically of their schooldays in the run-down Crocetta laboratory. Levi also saw a good deal of his wartime comrade, Silvio Ortona. On 31 July it was Levi's sixty-fourth birthday and to celebrate he and Ortona climbed the snow-capped Pian delle Turnette near Cogne. It was a day of bright exalting sunlight and Levi looked healthy (to judge by the photographs) in his shirtsleeves. The friends shared the trials of family illness: Ortona's wife, Ada Della Torre, whom Levi had known in wartime Milan, was in the advanced stages of Alzheimer's; Levi's mother was showing signs of senile dementia.

Next day, 1 August, brought the unhappy news that Hety Schmitt-Maas had died. Levi felt a twinge of remorse that he had not written to her in two years, yet she had retained her verve to the end. 'You know, I've lived an interesting life,' she told her daughter Marianne, before dying suddenly and unexpectedly at the age of sixty-five. Her admiration for Levi (not always reciprocated) had been extraordinary, and Levi was always fond of her. Several pages in his books could not have been written without Hety. By the time she died she had written a total of fifty-seven letters to Levi, to match his forty-nine to her. Now that Hety was dead, Levi decided to use a section of her correspondence for *The Drowned and the Saved* ('Letters from Germans'), though he did not ask the family's permission. Hety's death seems to have caused Levi another bout of creative paralysis and black moods. He had corresponded with Hety for sixteen years; she had provided him with another of his safely unfulfilled flirtations with women as well as a lifeline out of 75 Corso Re Umberto. Now she was gone. Levi wrote to his friend Mario Rigoni Stern of a 'personal emptiness':

> Who knows what the future will bring? . . . If only I lived like you in the high plains, I wouldn't have all these problems. I'd just put on my skis and off I'd go cross-country. Here in Turin it's different. Cars are all over the place, stationary, in motion. You need a good hour's patience to fight your way out of the city. All my old friends are going through crises, from poor health or poor finances, or because their children have gone to the bad. Forgive this outburst, dearest Mario. One day I'll be able to stand on my own two feet again.

On 27 August, in an effort to dissipate his frustrations, Levi travelled to Milan to meet the survivor-statesman Elie Wiesel, who was due to promote an Italian translation of his Jewish folk-story collection. Levi was not very fond of Wiesel, or rather of what he stood for. Wiesel had cornered a sentimental middle-brow Jewish market and made a celebrity cult of his survivor status. Perhaps Levi was a little envious. He had never achieved – nor ever would achieve – the reverance bordering on idolatry lavished on Wiesel in America. Wiesel was published in Italy by the dubious 'psychoanalyst' Armando Verdiglione, who was said to be involved in fraud. A thirty-nine-year-old former Jesuit, Verdiglione had installed gold taps and four-poster beds in a wing of Milan's Villa Borromeo and, in a fit of Pharaonic grandeur, called it the Verdiglione Foundation. (He was sentenced in 1986 to five years in jail for extortion.)

At the Verdiglione Foundation Levi cautiously embraced Wiesel. Wiesel claimed to have had a great friendship with him in Auschwitz, though Levi had persistently denied it. ('We never met at Auschwitz, or if we did, I've forgotten.') If Levi envied Wiesel's success, a part of Wiesel surely envied Levi his higher literary standing and intellectual ballast. Before taking part in a public interview, the survivors were taken to lunch by Verdiglione at the Hotel Duomo opposite the Cathedral. Wiesel ate very little. And as the meal progressed, Verdiglione detected a certain *froideur* between the men. Indeed, Wiesel admonished Levi for his anti-Israeli stance and criticism of Prime Minister Begin's defence minister, Ariel Sharon, for his part in the

Lebanon invasion. In *La Repubblica* Levi had called Sharon a 'hard, unscrupulous soldier'.

Though it was a hot August weekend, the Verdiglione Foundation was packed with Italians who wanted to see the most prominent living witness of the genocide of European Jewry: not Primo Levi, Elie Wiesel. They were joined on the stage by *La Stampa*'s religious-affairs correspondent Sergio Quinzio, and the Communist intellectual Massimo Cacciari (later mayor of Venice). As the debate on Jews and Judaism unfolded, Verdiglione could see that Levi was not well. Earlier he had confessed to Verdiglione that he was on anti-depressants again, but that he continued to careen between good and bad moods. Once again, this was an unsettled time for Levi. As he had some problem with transport back to Turin that day, one of Verdiglione's disciples, Luciano Faioni, offered to drive him home. On the motorway Levi would not hear any talk of Wiesel. 'He seemed disturbed by the encounter – thoughtful and silent', Faioni recalled. Presumably Levi was also anxious to get back to his mother.

Next day, William Weaver dropped by. Levi called him the 'old wolf' for his business acumen and self-confident air. He retained an antique courtesy and charm from a childhood spent in Virginia, and was a youthful-looking sixty. Weaver had first glimpsed Italy in July 1943 as an ambulance driver for the American Field Service. Since then he had divided his time between New York and Tuscany. He had got to know Italian culture intimately, and was briefly Rome correspondent for the legendary *London Magazine*. Weaver had finished a tolerable first-draft translation of *If Not Now, When?* and, as was his custom, prepared a long list of queries for the author. Levi welcomed him cordially into 75 Corso Re Umberto. As the morning progressed, Weaver revealed to Levi the smattering of Yiddish he had picked up from Jewish New Yorker friends. Levi was always delighted when goys displayed an interest in Jewish culture. There was a lot of laughter, and at times a great deal of frustration, as the men searched in Leo Rosten's amusing *The Joys of Yiddish* for *le mot juste*. Weaver's impression then was that the Levis were not used to entertaining; for lunch Lucia served simple cold cuts. Afterwards Levi insisted on driving Weaver to his hotel in Piazza Castello, though it was within walking distance.

4

Just when Levi's mood seemed to be improving, on 16 October came devastating news that Nardo De Benedetti had died. The first to see the body was his maid, Anna Piersanti. Early that Sunday morning cries of 'Anna! Anna!' were heard to issue from Nardo's room in the Jewish Rest

Home: Anna was telephoned to come quickly, but Nardo was dead by the time she arrived. She found him in his armchair, bathed in sweat from what turned out to be a heart attack. A box of *marrons glacés* lay unopened by his side. Nardo had always wanted to die on his feet, and he almost made it as he struggled over from his bed to push the bell by his armchair. He was a month short of his eighty-fifth birthday. Levi was unrelieved in his grief. In spite of their differences over Israel, their friendship had seemed unbreakable: from Fossoli transit camp to Auschwitz and after, Levi had shared with Nardo all his life's darkest experience. Now Nardo was gone, and Levi's credentials changed: he became a lonely survivor. Jews are forbidden to burn their dead, but Nardo's will directed that he be cremated, and this was done. (He had wanted to follow his wife Jolanda into the fire and become ash.) At the cremation on 18 October the weather was muggy with rain. Anna Piersanti, Nardo's maid, whispered to her husband: 'Look at Levi – he's ruined.' After Nardo's death, Anna never again saw Levi smile. There are those who believe that he would not have died prematurely had Nardo been alive. Levi's moral support and consolation had been pulled from under him; he had reached a watershed in his life. Levi's depressions, his oppressive domestic situation, the recent deaths of Hety Schmitt-Maas and the chemist Ennio Mariotti, and now Nardo's, weighed down on him. It was Nardo he needed at this time more than anyone, but Nardo was dead.

In these last few months Levi had worked ineffectually on *The Drowned and the Saved*. A block, probably caused by depression, kept him from completing the prison-camp essays. But Nardo's death gave him the impetus to push on with the book. Levi felt he owed it to his friend. And on 29 October he gave a lecture in Turin, 'Memory and the Concentration Camp', which was effectively a dry run for the book's first chapter. Among Levi's anguished themes that day were the dangers of defective memory and defective understanding: he questioned the authenticity of some accounts of the Nazi camps, which had been contaminated by self-deceptions, falsehoods and stereotypes. Levi was now sixty-four years old and at that age one's memory, he said, 'deteriorates quite noticeably'. His new book was born, partly, out of an urgent concern not to let his memories disintegrate. Not that they were likely to do so. For forty years he had carried a musical motif in his head but was unable to identify it. Levi kept asking people if they knew what it was. Eventually someone recognised it as the first movement of Schumann's Piano Concerto in A minor (op. 54), and Levi had remembered it bar-for-bar. Other 'purposeless' bits of information, he observed humorously, cluttered his memory, including the number plate of his first car. In reality he did not want to forget anything.

On 17 December Levi made an important foray from his writing when the town council of Bardonecchia invited him to talk about his life and work. Traditionally a place of *villégiature* for wealthy Turinese, Bardonecchia held powerful childhood memories for Levi. He had spent his tennis-playing teens among fields, woods and houses that were still there. He was also keen to see his artist friend Eugenio Bolley, who worked in Bardonecchia. Bolley sculpted mechanical birds and clockwork pulley contraptions from discarded materials. He had first met Levi in 1971 in Turin, where he was a machine-fitter. Nobody could understand Levi's attraction to this man: bald, with a broad muscular frame and love of Japanese culture, Bolley was an eccentric. However, Levi was always drawn to outsiders.

Levi's train drew into Bardonecchia almost two hours late owing to snow on the line. He was carrying an old-fashioned overnight valise and wore a Russian fur hat. Bolley was waiting for Levi at the other end of the platform, accompanied by Maurizio Avato, an Italo-Albanian who worked in the Bardonecchia Town Hall. Avato's job was to arrange Levi's meals and hotel reservations, which he did with such military precision that Levi later called him 'my sweet executioner'. Avato took Levi's valise and checked him into the two-star Hotel Eurosport, where Levi unpacked his bag, lit a menthol cigarette and went out with his escorts on to Via Medail.

It was unexpectedly pleasant to see the town again. But Bardonecchia had changed, and Levi had changed too. In his childhood Via Medail had been a quiet street, now it was packed with space-invader bars. One of the oddest changes, Levi remarked, were the saplings he had seen planted, which were now eighteen metres high. At least the mountains were the same; looking up at them, Levi told the story of his teenage escapade on the freezing peak of Mount Melchior. It began to snow, and Levi asked to be left alone to explore his boyhood haunts. Some time later, when Avato was driving round Bardonecchia in his Fiat, he caught sight of Levi in the rear-view mirror; he was negotiating a slippery road uphill with difficulty. Avato did not want to intrude as Levi looked so purposeful and intent, but he saw the stooped figure pause to look at the sundial on the wall of a villa on Via Fiume: 'I, THE SHADOW, AM THE SUN'S DAUGHTER'. The past beckoned nostalgically to Levi; this was his family's old holiday villa. Crowds of schoolchildren came to hear Levi talk in the Town Hall; he found a bright and interested public, and was delighted afterwards to meet Elsa Begnis, one of the Bardonecchia girls who had haunted his troubled adolescence.

*

An exhibition of antique torture instruments was then travelling Italy, and had arrived in Turin. Levi visited it for *La Stampa*. Perhaps he also hoped to gather material for *The Drowned and the Saved*, in which he would quote Jean Améry's observation that 'Anyone who has been tortured remains tortured.' Inspecting the leg-locks and thumb-screws, all fetishistically displayed in Turin's Museum of Fine Art, Levi felt disgusted. His review of the exhibition, in *La Stampa* of 28 December, evinced a *saeva indignatio* worthy of Dickens. The curators were lambasted for their 'opportunist' intent to make the flesh creep; Levi also roundly chastised the European collectors who had loaned the instruments: what kind of men were these?

6

'*L'Anno Orwell*', as 1984 was inevitably baptised in Italy, opened glumly for Levi as his family affairs continued to disintegrate. His mother was now palsied and found walking difficult. As for Lucia's mother, Beatrice Morpurgo, she had been blind for thirteen years and could not be left on her own. Nurses were hard to find for the old women as the Italian health system, not for the first time, was *in crisi*. As Lucia was out of the flat much of the time, Levi was tied to his mother in a house that was fast becoming his prison. One of his own making, of course, but a prison nonetheless.

His children were adults and had left home. Lisa, thirty-six, worked in Turin's Natural History Museum; Renzo, twenty-seven, was in Atlanta, Georgia, where Levi was concerned for his happiness. He was working on a biophysics project at the Emory University School of Medicine and was reportedly quite unhappy. His tutor, Professor Louis J. De Felice, had tried to allay Levi's anxieties on the telephone by stressing that everyone at the Medical School liked Renzo and that he was an excellent researcher. However, Renzo had behaved strangely the moment he flew into Atlanta. At the airport he had insisted on calling home immediately and begged Professor De Felice and his wife to find him the change for the phone. Later, at home with the De Felices, after he had discovered that the professor and his wife had not heard of Primo Levi, Renzo looked relieved. He handed his hosts a British paperback copy of *If This is a Man* and *The Truce*, adding several times that the former was a 'classic'. He had more copies in his suitcase, should other people want them. There was a silence before Renzo confessed that he himself had never read Primo Levi. Why? 'It's too difficult,' he replied succinctly. De Felice thought that Renzo was relieved that he had never heard of Primo Levi, as it meant that he wanted

Renzo as a researcher for his own sake, and not because of who his father was. Renzo stayed in Atlanta for eighteen months.

Back in Turin, Primo Levi greatly enjoyed translating Claude Lévi-Strauss's *The Way of the Masks*. Beneath the book's punctilious descriptions of North American ceremonial masks and initiation rituals, Levi found a sceptical, enquiring intelligence not so different from his own. He declared the book 'charming'. Indeed, so charming that he decided to take on another Lévi-Strauss book, *The View From Afar*. On 17 January Levi addressed a long and impassioned letter to the *maître* at the Collège de France in Paris, where he was anthropology professor. Levi praised Lévi-Strauss as a 'modern myth-maker', and offered him this peculiar Italian gastronomic *trouvaille*:

> For Epiphany, *en famille*, we bake cakes out of a pastry mix containing two broad beans: one is white, the other black. The one who finds the white bean in his slice is supposed to have a happy year ahead; the one who finds the black bean will encounter only misfortune – unless he repents his sins there and then at the table. Incidentally, while we are on the subject of beans, *fava* [Italian for broad bean] is vulgar for 'tip of the penis'.

Lévi-Strauss's reply, when it came a week later, filled Levi with joy. The anthropologist said that nothing had pleased him more than *The Wrench*; this book, with its systematic mapping of man's relationship to work, was a 'marvellous anthropological creation', and Tino Faussone was a 'nomad for the machine age'. The Frenchman's letter fell on Levi like a benison in the midst of his family upsets.

7

Yet Levi seemed to have entered a happier phase. In early 1984 he took part in an Italian version of *Desert Island Discs*, recorded in five instalments in Turin over 1–17 February. Levi was on fine form as he responded to Paolo Terni, his interviewer. His choice in music proved conservative and included such stalwarts as Tchaikovsky's 6th Symphony (a favourite of his father's) and Bizet's *Carmen*. Levi said he could listen to *Carmen* a thousand times, exceeding even Nietzsche (who saw the opera fourteen times in Turin). He had been listening to the toothpaste and dandruff ads on the wireless as a child when the 'most beautiful music' began to play, which he thought was called *Carni*, Italian for 'Meats'. Though Levi considered

Wagner's music vulgar Teutonic chauvinism, nevertheless he chose *The Flying Dutchman*, an old favourite. Bach's *The St Matthew Passion* was his most dignified choice. This work of 'tender beauty', said Levi, was the counterpoint to the German marching tunes he had heard played each day at Auschwitz. His humour throughout the programme was curiously childish and, occasionally, appalling. Schubert's 'The Trout' was chosen because it reminded Levi of a Yiddish joke in which a hotel receptionist asks a visitor if he wants a room with 'running water'. The guest peevishly answers: 'What do you take me for? A trout?'

During the spring and summer of 1984 Levi's public life revolved round Resistance commemorations, and meetings with writers and foreign publishers. In this happier period he also took part in a series of conversations with the Turin physicist, Tullio Regge, which would later form the basis of a book. Levi made every effort to get out of the house; people began to see him in parks, bookshops, concert halls and cinemas. All the signs were that he had overcome the dejection of the previous months; he was no longer on anti-depressants, and it was quite a busy time for him. There was even a visitor to the flat for a few days over Easter. A Polish-born Jew living in Israel, Marek Herman had escaped Occupied Poland as a teenager, when he was found by some Italian soldiers who brought him home to Turin. He had operated a radio transmitter from a church belfry during the Italian Resistance; later he wrote about his exploits for his grandchildren. Levi, always a generous champion of authors whom he thought deserved recognition, went out of his way to find Herman an Italian publisher. (*Diary of a Jewish Boy* is now read in many schools in Italy.) Over drinks in 75 Corso Re Umberto, Levi and Herman discussed the Arab-Israeli conflict as well as Rabelais, Einstein and hang-gliding. There seemed to be almost nothing, recalled Herman, about which Levi could not be curious.

In April Levi presented a documentary film on the anti-Nazi Resistance in Piedmont. *The First Bands* was directed by Ada Gobetti's son Paolo, famous for his black bushy eyebrows and smiling goblin-face. During the Resistance Paolo had fought courageously alongside Sandro Delmastro and Alberto Salmoni. Sadly, Levi's presentation at the Chaplin Cinema in Turin was unrecorded, but not the effect it had on the audience. He was on 'marvellous form', recalled Gobetti. Levi had just come from the inauguration of a new recreation park in Turin, named in honour of his martyred partisan friend, Emanuele Artom.

The following month, on 2 May, Levi enjoyed the premiere in Turin of an extraordinary opera based on Rabelais's scatological sixteenth-century masterwork *Gargantua*. Levi had first read this burlesque adventure-novel in around 1940 in his father's Génie de France edition. Rabelais – monk, physician, philologist, traveller and humanist – was a true Renaissance man whose thirst for knowledge Levi liked to think he shared. The artist Emanuele ('Lele') Luzzati, a relative, had designed the opera sets. And the composer Azio Corghi had written the music, the atonal rawness of which did not interest Levi as much as the public response to the opera. Neo-Fascists in Turin vehemently objected to the libretto of *Gargantua*. Words like 'shittard' and 'turdous' offended public morality, they fumed. During the interval neo-Fascists thrust crude anti-Rabelais leaflets on to the audience and Levi felt a surge of rage. He was thrilled by the production and lauded the special effects by which Gargantua's urine-jet drenched the opera's cast of abbots, pie-bakers and dwarves. 'It's the most lively stage work I've ever seen – one great carnival!' he told a journalist, with all the fervour of a young avant-gardist. The prudes had lost the day; Levi felt vindicated, and zestfully invigorated.

Levi had six weeks in hand before he was due to begin work in June with the physicist Tullio Regge on *Conversations*. So when the Triestino writer Claudio Magris asked him to help launch the spring issue of the literary quarterly *Sigma*, Levi obliged. *Sigma* had published some of his poems in 1964 and he remained fond of the Turin-based magazine. Levi was a little envious of Magris's prolific output of plays, essays and travelogues. ('How on earth do you find the time to write such beautiful things and live at the same time?' he asked him.) Magris meanwhile had sent Levi the typescript of his novel, *Inferences from a Sabre*, about the bizarre Cossack presence in north-east Italy in 1944. Aware that a writer friend, Carlo Sgorlon, was working on a book on the same subject, Levi felt unable to enthuse much about Magris's. Sgorlon came from Italy's north-eastern province of Friuli, and his artless, plain-style novels of Friulian-speaking peasants immensely impressed Levi. (When they had first met in 1978 at the Strega awards in Rome they were both keen to escape the glad-handing and kissing for a quiet corner. Sgorlon saw Levi as 'an unromantic writer', a 'chemist on *loan* to literature'.)

The month of May ended happily for Levi when, on the 31st, *La Stampa* awarded him a silver medal for a lifetime's contribution to the 'culture and morality of Piedmont'. Levi sat for a few minutes in the Newspaper Club, head bowed with embarrassment, while the philosopher Norberto Bobbio gave a short speech in his honour.

Early in June Levi met his new German publisher, Michael Kruger, in a

Turin café. Lisa Levi, whose German was rather better than her father's, was on hand in case of misunderstandings. Levi was keen to be amusing; Kruger recalled his 'painful humour', as he kept interrupting him with comic tales of domestic woe. Levi complained that whenever he sat down to write, his mother would bang on the adjoining wall with her walking stick. Then he would have to go off and see what she wanted. Kruger found this 'excruciatingly pathetic'. He wanted to invite Levi to Munich for a publicity tour as he planned to republish all of his books in West Germany. After a moment's pause Levi politely declined the offer, though not – as Kruger had expected – because he had difficult relations with Germany and the Germans, but because of his mother and mother-in-law. These women, said Levi, prevented him from 'going anywhere'. It seems that Levi was becoming deluded, believing that two old women conspired against his liberty. His jerky, staccato gestures, 'like a Pinocchio puppet', recalled Kruger, suggested a man whose mind was elsewhere. Kruger returned to Munich frustrated by Levi's sense of duty to his mother.

8

On 14 June Levi was at Tullio Regge's in Turin. Regge is a very eminent physicist, who trained at Turin University, where he is currently Professor of Relativity. He is also a most extraordinary-looking character, his pale clown-like face topped by a mop of carrot-coloured hair. Though Levi was quite capable of following Regge on some of his more outré flights into science, it is hard to imagine two more contrasting types: Regge, ebullient, irrepressible; Levi, compact, reserved. They first met in 1970, when Levi had bizarrely announced halfway through dinner: 'By the way, during the war I was in a concentration camp.' In October 1980 Levi and Regge had met again at a computer-graphics animation demonstration in Turin, where a visiting mathematician from Rhode Island, Tom Banchoff, had attempted to visualise the fourth dimension using computers. (Levi was not at all sure that he had seen Banchoff's extra dimension.)

Their long, recorded conversation took place over two summer afternoons, punctuated by tea and whisky, in Regge's sitting room. It was hoped that what they had to say to each other would be interesting enough to make a book. There was no planned dialogue; it began as sprightly *badinage,* developed into a free-wheeling exchange of ideas, then settled into a remarkable mutual interview. Regge, who is not Jewish, began by mentioning his interest in Hebrew, then went on to discourse on computers, the Talmud and 'interstellar civilisations'. Though the dialogue seemed to be a collaboration between the two, and indeed was later published as such, primarily it was Regge's work. Levi's contribution was shorter, but his words are of greater interest to the general reader. As the second afternoon wore on, Levi grew uncharacteristically talkative, holding his own with the garrulous Regge, speaking of his father, his schoolteachers and the Fascist race persecutions. While the finished result, *Conversations*, was Levi's most extended reminiscence, it was not an exercise in self-analysis.

As the summer advanced, Levi was again embroiled in a potentially damaging argument over his writing. On 12 June *La Stampa* had published his short story, 'Guncotton Tights', in which a Nobel Explosives employee steals flammable wads of guncotton (cellulose nitrate) to make his girlfriend stockings. Predictably the girl catches fire wearing her combustible hosiery. The tale had been told to Levi in 1947 by the Nobel company doctor, Gino Crotto, himself a compulsive story-teller. But when Leonildo Carrà, the director of Piedmont Nobel Explosives, read Levi's article he was outraged. Levi's remark that all Nobel workers were similarly 'insane', 'desperate' and 'mutilated' was, in Carrà's view, a calumny. He was so incensed that he wrote to *La Stampa*'s chief editor, asking that Levi be sacked as a contributor and demanding an apology. Luckily for Levi, considering the expense that a court case might have involved, Carrà found out that 'Guncotton Tights' was in fact a fantasy and decided to drop the matter. He had assumed a stringent truth-telling on Levi's part which was in fact mere writerly elaboration. This was the last time that Levi would get into trouble for confounding fact with fiction.

On 14 July Levi received in the morning post William Weaver's translation of *If Not Now, When?* Having checked the proofs carefully, and finding them very satisfactory, 'both for the literary style and fidelity to the original', he gave Summit Books the go-ahead for publication. Later that day Levi scaled the Rocca Sella with Bianca Guidetti Serra, and from the mountain's summit he surveyed the beauty and lushness of the Piedmontese countryside. The summer idyll, however, was disturbed by a family death. Three days later, on 17 July, Uncle Corrado Luzzati died of a heart attack. The Levis were very fond of Corrado, but especially Primo, who had found in him an open-hearted and engaging companion. Corrado's brother Gustavo was to die later that year, on 10 December. Ester, Levi's mother, would have lost two brothers in five months.

9

Before the summer was out Levi bought himself a computer. Thus, at sixty-five, he became Italy's first well-known writer to endorse word-processors.

Renzo, who had returned to Turin at the end of June from Atlanta, advised his father to dispense with the Apple Mac instruction manual ('You need to learn by trial and error') and patiently showed him round the keyboard. Levi was soon rhapsodical about his hardware; Apple users are traditionally a committed group, and Levi was in danger of becoming a Mac bore. He sternly rebuked Ruth Hoffman for describing his Apple as merely a 'clever new typewriter'. 'It's a lot more than that! It's a memory prosthesis, an archive, an unprotesting secretary, a new game each day, as well as a designer, as you will see from the enclosed centipede picture.' Before long, Levi was comparing his computer to a drug, as he needed increasingly long hours at it, and 'now I've even started to peddle Apples to other people'. Shocked that William Weaver had no word-processor, Levi made him sit down and write on his Apple. The American managed to tap out: 'My name's Bill and I was born in Washington DC by mistake' (because he grew up in Virginia). Next day, Weaver bought himself an Apple.

Levi soon learned that word-processors can lead to prolixity. Therefore in the course of a day's writing he would often move over to the 'archaic side' (the north-facing side) of his desk to use his old Olivetti electric. Personal computers were still such a novelty in 1984 that, with certain people, Levi would not let on that he used one. The Swiss industrialist and art collector Sergio Grandini had apologised to Levi for writing to him by typewriter (instead of by hand, which he thought would have been more personal). Levi replied to Grandini: 'For heavens sake don't worry about typing! As you can see, I do it myself.'

At the summer's end, after thirty years of often indifferent translation of his own work, Levi was delighted to learn that the very capable Barbara Kleiner was to translate *If Not Now, When?* into German. 'I'm aware that there are translations and translations,' he wrote to her on 16 August, 'and I hope that this one has not caused you too much bother.' A fruitful nine-month correspondence ensued, in which Levi helped Kleiner with the rhyme and metre of Yiddish words and corrected errors in her typescript ('Sobibòr not Sobibov'). Not one of his letters to Kleiner was written on the Apple, perhaps because all of Kleiner's to him were type-written.

Renzo's American tutor, Professor De Felice, came to stay for a couple of days in October. Levi was very sociable during his visit, and introduced the biophysicist to his daughter, his wife and his mother (who, the professor noted, was confined to a 'back room'). Like many who visited the Levis at this time, De Felice was struck by how close the family seemed. Renzo lived next door; Lisa had a flat in the Crocetta nearby.

Drinks were served by Lucia on a silver tray. As the evening wore on, Levi told De Felice how much he liked his Apple chess program, and as he said this he cast an indulgent glance at his son. It was a mild October dusk. De Felice was enjoying supper when Levi got up from the head of the table and walked slowly to the French windows that opened three flights above Corso Re Umberto. In a letter to me, De Felice recollected what happened next:

> As he looked out through the open windows, his back to us, he rolled up his sleeves and placed his hands on his hips, elbows nearly touching behind him. I saw then the tattooed serial number on his forearm (I had seen one before only in newsreels). Levi looked liked a water bird standing there, his trim goateed face in quarter profile, looking out, thinking about what I cannot say. I have many times wondered if he was showing the tattoo to me, the only stranger in the room, in some ritual of transfer. As he turned back toward the table, he rolled the sleeves down.

In this unsettling scenario Levi seems to want to disconcert his guest by showing him the mark of Auschwitz. Was there a deliberate intent to draw De Felice into some unpleasantness or had De Felice misconstrued an innocent neutral event? Why *both* sleeves? It is impossible to fathom Levi's gesture. Levi had lived with his prison mark for forty years and must have often forgotten it was there.

10

In the winter Levi was disappointed when Einaudi declined to publish a new selection of his poems. Carlo Carena, the highly regarded classicist and Einaudi general secretary, had considered them 'insufficiently distinguished'. So Levi took them elsewhere. He submitted the manuscript to Livio Garzanti in Milan, Pasolini's publisher, a shy, prickly character with a reputation for being difficult. Partly at the instigation of his Piedmontese wife, the novelist Gina Lagorio, Garzanti agreed to publish the poems. Some sixty in all, they included verse that Vanni Scheiwiller had brought out nine years earlier in 1975, together with a clutch of new poems printed in *La Stampa*. Levi called the collection *At an Uncertain Hour,* after the Ancient Mariner whose ghastly tale returns to haunt him, says Coleridge, at 'an uncertain hour'. There were a number of verse translations, one of them of the seventeenth-century Scots vernacular, 'The Ballad of Sir Patrick Spens'. Why Levi translated this anonymous minstrel rhyme is a mystery.

However, it tells of a shipwreck; and 'shipwreck' – *naufragio*, in Italian – was the Crusoe-like metaphor Levi used to describe his depressions.

Gina Lagorio was acquainted with Levi through his books, but approached him for the first time at the Famija Turineisa cultural club on a Saturday evening, 17 November 1984. The Famija, a fusty establishment at 43 Via Po, was dedicated to preserving the 'noble and ancestral local traditions' of Piedmont. Levi's father had been an enthusiastic member and enjoyed its banquets and corny dialect plays until 1932 when the Fascists closed the club down. In the Turquoise Salon, Levi and Lagorio gave a joint talk on 'Piedmontese Literature and Identity'. Lagorio, a protective woman, found Levi 'extremely lovable' and the attraction was mutual: though sixty, Lagorio was photogenic and vivacious. In her presence Levi cast his eyes down like a bashful boy's. Lagorio was another of his curiously asexual flirtations with women. Just as Levi was attracted to protective and maternal women, so many women wanted to mother Levi, Gina Lagorio among them. Levi was fond of her first book, *Pollen*, with its short story 'The Jew', but was too shy to tell her. After the talk they were invited to drinks in the Famija's oak-panelled dining room. 'Come on,' Lagorio said, putting her arm round Levi, but Primo said he had to hurry home to his mother. Ester's dependence on her son was now absolute and, Lagorio said later, Levi was tormented by the thought of leaving her alone. 'He couldn't bear to fail in his filial duty to her.' Lagorio was among the first to suspect that Levi's domestic life was unhealthy.

11

In November *The Periodic Table* was published in America. The first review, by John Gross in the *New York Times*, was a glory. 'Mr Levi is a true writer, with a fine gift for narrative and a subtle insight into character.' In the *New York Review of Books* Neal Ascherson praised an 'enchanting, original' work. Glowing reviews also appeared in the national magazines, among them the *New Yorker* ('Every chapter is full of surprises'), *Newsweek* and *Time*. The book was brought to the attention of America's scientific community when *Science* magazine serialised it over the winter. The plaudits continued into the New Year of 1985. The *Los Angeles Times* gave as passionate a review as Levi could have wished for. Richard Eder, then a maker (and breaker) of LA literary reputations, outdid himself by comparing Levi to Melville, Wallace Stevens and (bizarrely) Trollope. Nevertheless it was a front-page notice and surely helped to introduce Levi to Los Angeles' sizeable Jewish community. Paul West in the *Washington Post*, featuring a publicity photo of Levi by his son Renzo, likened the author more than favourably to the scientific polymath Sir Thomas Browne, and his conclusion was rapturous. 'This is one of the most intelligent books to come along in years. Why have we had to wait 10 years to read it in English?' When the newly minted American editions of *The Periodic Table* arrived in Turin, Levi was thrilled, and he signed copies for friends and admirers. To Professor De Felice, on his second visit, he gave an autographed edition and, against his protests, jumped up to fetch him another copy. 'Who shall I dedicate it to?' Levi asked, excited as a child. By late December Schocken Books' initial 14,000 print run was exhausted.

The key factor in Levi's success was Schocken's publicity director Irene Williams, who was determined to put Levi on the American map. Aware that Levi had Italian admirers in the New York press who could be relied on for a kind word, she approached the *Corriere della Sera*'s Manhattan correspondent Ugo Stille, who agreed to obtain jacket quotes from distinguished Italian writers. In due course these came from, among others, Umberto Eco and Italo Calvino. Additional favourable notices were extracted from files at the Italian Cultural Institute in New York. Levi wrote to thank Irene Williams for her 'tireless efforts' and by 29 November she was able to reply to him: 'Your first book here in two decades is *news*.' In the United States Primo Levi's moment had come.

In many ways Levi's success was provident. Italian literature was now quite the vogue in bookish American circles. Readers had been alerted to the impending fashion by Gore Vidal, who since the late 1970s had championed Italo Calvino and Leonardo Sciascia in the *New York Review of Books*. More than anything, it was the triumph of *The Name of the Rose* that helped pave the way for Levi's transatlantic reception. By 1984 Eco was Italy's best-known literary export to America, and it is pleasing to think that two Piedmontese authors (Eco was born in Piedmont's Alessandria) had captured literary New York.

Summit Books, Levi's other American publisher, wanted to profit by the wave of interest in Levi, and wondered if he would undertake a lecture tour of America. *If Not Now, When?* was due out there in the spring of the following year, and Summit's youthful editor, Arthur Samuelson, believed the lectures would help promote the novel. At first Levi hesitated. Of course America has an Italian Jewish culture, but it was minuscule and had no single and famed exponent. As to lecturing, Levi was aware that he had no talent for oratory. And, like many Europeans born before 1945, Levi had a pronounced anti-American streak, which surfaced stridently in 1966 in a letter to the Italian writer and doctor Lorenzo Tomatis: 'We've given the Americans far too much space to talk about themselves, and they've filled up our heads with rubbish.'

It did not take Levi long to agree, though, as the offer was so good: the Italian Cultural Institute in New York would cover his expenses and share with him the cost of additional air fares to visit relatives in California. Having agreed to lecture, Levi proposed some topics which Arthur Samuelson tried out with the New York Jewish Lecture Bureau. After making a number of bookings, Samuelson wrote to Giorgio Colombo of the Italian Cultural Institute:

> The ideal time [for Levi to visit] appears to be the middle of April, as April 18 is the time that the Jewish community commemorates the Holocaust [actually Holocaust Memorial Day for 1985 was 21 April]. Thus there could be real demand for Levi.

Even from this brief memo, it is clear that Levi was to be paraded in America as a Jewish survivor first, and a writer second. (It had always been that way. When Indiana University Press offered to publish *The Periodic Table* in 1981, they stipulated that any chapters not pertinent to the 'Italian Jewish experience and the Holocaust' would have to go). What the Jewish Lecture Bureau wanted was a Mediterranean Elie Wiesel.

Though New York beckoned alluringly, 1984 ended on a bleak note for Levi: on 12 December he was at the funeral of his uncle Gustavo Luzzati. He had not been as fond of Gustavo as he had of Corrado, but still his death meant one Luzzati less, and that was especially painful for Levi's mother. His first letter of the New Year – 1985 – was to Charles Conreau, his companion of the last ten days of Auschwitz:

> How many years have passed since we last met? More than ten, and exactly forty since our first, memorable 'end of the night' [Céline's apocalyptic war novel, *Journey to the End of the Night*]. I often return in my memory to those ten incredibly intense days we lived together; and it seems to me that in spite of all the good that life has done us since, those were our *finest hour*.

Not for the first time, Levi felt that Auschwitz had been an emotional pinnacle from which he would never feel so intensely, or suffer and get so much from life, again.

Good news: Sergio Grandini, the Swiss industrialist whom Levi had met at the 1982 Campiello prize-giving, had privately published his short story 'Last Christmas of the War'. Levi was impressed. 'No other work of mine has ever looked so refined and elegant,' he wrote to Grandini (by hand, not computer). The story was printed on mould-made paper and sandwiched between marbled, chocolate-coloured card covers. Interestingly, Levi had charged Grandini a stiff 500,000 lire fee for permission to print the story. When it came to publication of his work, Levi had a mercantile side that served him well. He made sure he was well informed about his New York publisher contracts and took a keen professional interest in rights and royalties. Later, when the *New Yorker* expressed an interest in publishing 'Last Christmas of the War', Levi was careful to ask Grandini frst what percentage he wanted of the fee. Grandini replied that he had no interest in any sort of cut.

If Levi was triumphantly launched in America, in Britain he was still virtually unheard of. His first two books, *If This is a Man* and *The Truce*, had been published in Britain in 1959 and 1964 respectively, with a joint paperback publication in 1979, but these were long out of print. Henrietta Heald, a young editor at Michael Joseph, had nevertheless been monitoring Levi's American success with interest. Having noticed Saul Bellow's praise, she commissioned a reader's report of *The Periodic Table,* which came from Max Eilenberg on 21 January 1985: 'I'm amazed this hasn't already been bought. GET IT NOW – it's one of the finest things I've read in years.'

Heald was surprised when Michael Thomas of A. M. Heath, the literary agency that handled Levi's British rights, sold *The Periodic Table* to her for a mere £1,000. Thus a modern classic went for a song. In the meantime Michael Joseph's doughty publicity director, Sheila Murphy, agitated Penguin to republish its Modern Classic of *If This is a Man* and *The Truce.* It made sense for them to do this, as Michael Joseph was a subsidiary of Penguin. To Murphy's bewilderment, Penguin informed her that they had no intention of reprinting Levi's books: they had 119 copies in stock and wanted only to pulp them. For a pittance, Penguin eventually relinquished *If This is a Man* and *The Truce* to Sphere Books. Mike Petty, editorial director of Sphere's literary imprint, Abacus, not surprisingly then read the American edition of *The Periodic Table*. 'I knew immediately and instinctively that this was a book I wanted to publish.' He bought the paperback rights for £4,000 from Michael Joseph. Now Mike Petty and Henrietta Heald were the proud co-publishers – hardcover, softback – of *The Periodic Table.*

12

Levi prepared carefully for his American tour. Heavy coats made sense in the American if not the Italian spring climate; hats and gloves, too. He and

Lucia were to fly from New York to California, Indiana to Boston, and back again to Manhattan: a coast-to-coast two-week marathon. Levi said the undertaking 'terrified' him. With Renzo's help, he translated his lectures into English, as he did not want to perform without the safety-net of scripted preparation. Renzo made no comment on the content of the lectures, coolly jotting in the margin his amendments.

Levi needed this break. For too long he had led a sedentary life at home, tied to his mother. He loved trips and suspected he was a traveller by nature, but was always held back by the feelings of dependency, guilt and neglect that haunted his relationship with Ester. Anna Maria agreed to come up from Rome to look after Ester while her brother and Lucia were away. There was no question that Levi felt guilty at leaving his sister with full responsibility for their mother, but his relief at escaping Ester, if only for a couple of weeks, can be imagined. From her room at the end of the hall Ester had dominated her son's existence, waking him at 6:30 am, demanding breakfast by 7:00 am, calling out to him day and night. This was the first time that Anna Maria had had to look after her mother for any significant length of time.

Initially Lucia had been quite resistant to the tour, but pressure was put on her by Aunt Jole Luzzati, who never much cared for Primo's wife. 'You *must* let Primo go.' Levi anticipated problems with Lucia. She was shy and her English was not good. She had not travelled much outside Turin. Since Levi's retirement the strains in their relationship had eased: Levi was established as a writer in Italy now and was less eager for media attention. But in America Lucia would be an appendage to him. Accompanying her husband to parties in Manhattan, bookstore luncheons, watching him deal with autograph-collectors and admirers might be a strain for Lucia. But Lucia went; she could not leave her husband on his own in America. She would continue to support him as she always had done.

The Levis were set to leave when cousin Anna Yona in Boston wrote to ask Primo if he would consent to receive an honorary degree from Brandeis University, Massachusetts. Levi was flattered but felt he had no right to the honour as his written English was not up to it. Anyway his American lecture programme was 'megalomaniac' enough without having to worry about university honours:

> Honestly, if I was 20 or 30 years younger the prospect of a degree *ad honorem* would have me in seventh heaven, but these days I'm feeling burned out. I no longer care much for such glories . . . Lucia and I have decided to make this trip out of a sense of

curiosity, above all, but also so as not to waste what will probably
be a once-in-a-lifetime opportunity, and to free ourselves for just
15 days from the daily tread-mill.

Even in this letter, full of warmth towards his cousin and gratitude for the
Brandeis University proposal, Levi could not keep the burden of domestic
life from creeping in.

Meanwhile Levi learned that *If This is a Man* and *The Truce* were not, after
all, to be published in the German Democratic Republic. Plans to launch
Levi in Communist East Germany had been afoot since 1981, when most
publishers there had shaken their heads and declined. To the regime, Levi's
unflattering portrayal in *If This is a Man* of Communist and Social
Democrat prisoners as quasi-SS was tantamount to sacrilege. Levi had a
champion, however, in Joachim Meinert, at the East Berlin publisher
Aufbau Verlag. Meinert, a forty-year-old with a keen interest in Italian
literature, was certainly not a Party hard-liner. His enthusiasm for Levi had
the backing of two distinguished East German citizens. The first was the
Buchenwald survivor Fred Wander, whose concentration-camp memoir,
The Seventh Well, had been a surprise bestseller in Italy. Levi admired
Wander's book, and was delighted to receive from him a thirteen-page letter
expressing admiration for *If This is a Man.* The second was the film director
Konrad Wolf, whose brother was the East Berlin secret-service boss
Markus Wolf (the original for le Carré's *The Spy Who Came in from the
Cold*). Both Wolf and Wander wrote glowing appraisals of Levi, which
Meinert then submitted to the Ministry of Culture in East Berlin. Only if
the ministry gave the go-ahead could Meinert publish Levi.

The Ministry of Culture did not know what to make of Levi. Clearly his
books were problematic: should they be published? In a highly unusual step
they passed Levi's case on to the Committee of the Anti-Fascist Resistance.
This egregious body was composed of thirteen highly dogmatic men
('sclerotic' was Meinert's word) tainted by the Stalinist era. Their word was
final and they unanimously vetoed publication of *If This is a Man* and *The
Truce.* In their immensely detailed report these rigid ideologues attacked
Levi as an anti-egalitarian 'Zionist sympathiser' (for 'Zionist' read 'Jewish'),
whose prison accounts were an 'outrageous' slur on the anti-Nazi
Communist Resistance that had existed within Auschwitz. Levi would not
have been surprised by this report, which he never saw. The idea of
presenting the camps as a place of resistance was drearily propagandist and
false. 'All credit to those who did resist, but it was by no means the rule. The
rule was to give way, to be cut down,' said Levi. The Committee president,

Otto Funke, communicated his extreme disapproval of Levi to Meinert. Meinert then wrote a carefully worded letter to Levi, which stipulated that substantial cuts would have to be made to the two books if they were to be published in East Germany. Levi replied that he was prepared to authorise bowdlerised versions of *If This is a Man* and *The Truce* if that would help 'save' the books. Any excisions, however, would have to be 'authorised personally' by him. Levi heard nothing further from Meinert. Then, a year later, on 5 February 1985, he sent Levi the discouraging news that the cuts required by Otto Funke and company were greater than feared. Levi was about to leave for New York when Meinert's letter arrived; he wrote dejectedly to him: 'I can quite understand the reasons for the censorship.' If Levi had failed to write of the Communist resistance in Auschwitz, it was because he saw nothing of it.

TWENTY-FIVE

America is Waiting

1985

I

New York, wrote Levi, has an 'insolent, lyrical, cynical beauty', and when he and Lucia arrived there on Friday 12 April 1985, the city overwhelmed them. Manhattan was in the grip of a jogging and calorie-counting mania, and the sight of people running in Central Park (often with dogs in tow) was extraordinary. The Levis were met off the plane at JFK by Giorgio Colombo of the Italian Cultural Institute, who reassured Levi that *If Not Now, When?* would be a success and that its author was already hailed as the bright new Italian literary star. Levi was made nervous by this praise, but the diplomatic Colombo (who was distantly related to Levi's Bene Vagienna forebears) put him at ease. He took the Levis to the Doral Inn at 541 Lexington Avenue and 49th Street, opposite the Waldorf, where he had reserved them a room. After drinks he left them to rest for a few hours. Levi needed to lie down; his promotional schedule was to be heavy.

Later that evening the Levis were joined by Irene Williams of Schocken Books' publicity department. Pleasant-faced, with a reassuring manner, she made a favourable impression on the Italian couple. Though Levi seemed unusually reserved about his New York celebrity status, he did not object to the gruelling round of interviews Williams had arranged for him. He refused to go on television, though, as he feared making a 'fool' of himself. The interviews were planned for the following Monday and reporters were expected from all the main New York papers. Levi stressed that he preferred to speak to journalists in Italian, and warned Williams that his IQ 'went down by 30 points' whenever he spoke in English. Williams had never met a less egocentric writer, and was charmed by him.

She sat by Levi's side in the hotel reception jotting down notes in her publicity file. Levi began by asking her not to confuse him with Carlo Levi. (Einaudi himself had adopted the shorthand distinction, 'Levi Man' and

465

'Levi Christ'.) Less diplomatically, he warned Williams that he did not want to be pigeonholed in New York as a Jewish writer: 'I don't like labels – Germans do.' During their conversation Williams was impressed by how much Levi knew of the *New Yorker* cartoonist Saul Steinberg (creator of that much-reproduced view of the world as seen from 9th Avenue). Steinberg had been in Milan during the war studying architecture and Levi could remember his cartoons in the Milanese satirical magazine *Bertoldo*.

The Levis had the weekend to themselves and the next day, a Saturday, they explored the beautiful, jittery city. Just a few steps down Lexington Avenue was enough to dispel Primo's starry-eyed notions about New York. Here, in the middle of Steinberg's cultured Manhattan, were men scavenging for filth in trash cans. Later, Irene Williams recalled Levi's distress at the sight of beggars busking for alms outside a Manhattan cocktail lounge. The underside of New York frightened Levi; he was out of his depth.

On Monday morning, in the Doral Inn reception, Levi faced his first newspaper reporters. He was not prepared for how many there were, and they asked him silly questions. ('Do you speak fluent Yiddish?') Nor were the reporters prepared for Levi. Herbert Mitgang of the *New York Times* clearly had not read even a small part of his books, which immensely irritated Levi. A cloud of misrepresentation had preceded him to America, just as it had done Oscar Wilde and Charles Dickens before him. Some American newspapers, avid to see Levi, had offered advance descriptions based on photographs. With his expression of 'debonair sagacity', apparently Levi resembled a 'bearded version' of the English actor Michael Wilding. The *International Herald Tribune* labelled him the 'Jewish equivalent of a saint'. (As long ago as 1963 the Piedmontese paper *Il Popolo Fossanese* had described him as a 'saintly apostle'; Levi said he lacked the necessary 'charisma' and 'self-assurance' to be a fakir-like figure.)

Speaking in English to the journalists was a strain, and by the time National Public Radio came to interview Levi he felt that the morning's publicity had gone on too long. He then made what he called an 'ultimatum': he would not speak to any other journalist unless he or she had read at least one of his books. Thankfully one journalist, Alexander Stille, was more knowledgeable about Levi than the rest. A New Yorker of Italian Jewish descent, Stille was the son of the *Corriere della Sera*'s Ugo Stille, who had helped to launch Levi in America. Levi was immensely relieved that Stille spoke Italian: 'He greeted me like a friend from way back, like I was doing *him* the favour.' Levi's cordiality to Stille was characteristic of the warmth he showed those who had done their homework. Stille thought Levi seemed 'overwhelmed' and 'uncomfortable'. So far he had not come through the American trial very well.

The high point of Levi's stay in New York was his visit, later that Monday, to Columbia University's chemistry department. He went there on his own while Lucia stayed downtown shopping. Carlo Floriani, a visiting chemistry professor from Pisa, and his wife Rita welcomed Levi into their lab with open arms. Rita Floriani had read Levi's books avidly since 1958 at school in Italy, and as a lifelong admirer she was thrilled to meet him. Levi was relieved to escape the grind of publicity in the Doral Inn, and took a shine to the beaming, friendly Florianis. He agreed to pose in a chemist's apron for a *Newsweek* photographer, cradling the Florianis' hand-made Italian chemistry glassware. 'All I've ever held are beakers – I'm just a B-grade chemist!' he announced ironically.

Levi then asked to be shown round the chemistry department, a privilege that fell to Professor Leonard Fine, the director of undergraduate programmes. 'What really blew Levi out of the water,' Fine recalled, 'was our museum.' Here Levi marvelled at the dye collection, with its mauve samples donated by the Victorian chemist William Perkins. German dyestuffs from Bayer were also on display, along with shelves of galvanic batteries. Levi was impressed by the sixteen wooden display cabinets installed by Columbia's nineteenth-century chemist Charles Frederick Chandler. In the revamped Chandler Labs he was fitted with tinted perspex goggles and treated to a laser show. The lasers impressively picked out motes of New York soot, prompting Levi to comment in New Yorker Yiddish: 'Ah, *shmutz!*' One reason Levi liked New York was the opportunity it gave him to collect Jewish witticisms and gags. A favourite of his was, 'Okay, so we killed Christ. But only *for three days.*'

That evening Levi was to talk at the City University. Beforehand he and Lucia were taken to supper on West 42nd Street by Irving Howe and Yosef Yerushalmi, director of the Center for Israel and Jewish studies at Columbia University. Yerushalmi was unsettled to find Levi so nervous and discomposed, having imagined from reading his books a more poised presence. For most of the meal Levi sat in silence while Howe and Yerushalmi kept the conversation going. With a wan smile, Levi confessed that he had not travelled much outside Turin, and in New York he felt like a 'migrant off the Staten Island ferry'. He tried a few words of Hebrew which, according to Howe's Israeli-born widow Iliana, he could not pronounce properly. As neither Howe nor Yerushalmi spoke Italian, their exchanges with Levi were limited.

'An Evening with Primo Levi' was about to unfold in the City University auditorium. Levi kept to the back of the crowded hall, and seemed apprehensive. Yerushalmi was in the chair. Never shy of publicity, he began to dominate the evening. ('It was like *Yerushalmi* wanted to be the star, showing off with all this pompous highfalutin stuff that went over Levi's head,' reported Arthur Samuelson of Summit Books.) Raymond Rosenthal, the translator of *The Periodic Table*, arrived late to find a crowd clamouring round Levi to shake his hand or beg his autograph. 'It was impossible for me to get anywhere near him as Howe was literally chasing the audience away, screaming and throwing his weight round and yelling "Get back! Get back!" It was like Howe was acting as Levi's bodyguard.' Another such fiasco as the City University business and Levi might well have taken the next flight home to Italy. Rosenthal traipsed back to his brownstone, disappointed not to have met Levi.

Levi had been less than four days in New York and already the tour was having an adverse effect on him. And now he had to face a round of entertainments. In a brightly lit Manhattan apartment his other publisher, Summit Books, threw a cocktail party. On all sides Levi was besieged by garrulous New Yorkers, but Levi's awkward spoken English did nothing to ease his nerves. The din of excitable, raised voices intimidated him. Jim Silberman, Summit's genial old-school director, recalled that Levi spoke to him with grimaces and shy movements of the head. 'He didn't seem to know how to function socially. And this wasn't one of those Manhattan parties where half the guests wish for an author's downfall.' Yet the party did have a snobbish undertow, which Levi might have noticed. When Bobbe Siegel was introduced to Irving Howe as Levi's 'Manhattan agent', Howe turned his back on her. ('Howe was quite the snob,' Siegel recalled.) Instead Levi was very sweet with Siegel, as was Lucia, who seemed to Siegel the picture of a 'handsome, middle-class Italian matron in black and pearls'. But, as Lucia spoke only halting English, and Siegel's Italian was primitive, conversation dried up.

2

Levi began to survey his American cultural mission with a mixture of dismay and wonder. He asked Lucia if any non-Jews at all lived in New York; so far they had met mostly Jews. Afterwards, to friends at home, Levi described some of the most striking moments of his Manhattan tour. One of these occurred the following day, 16 April, when Arthur Samuelson picked him and Lucia up for lunch in a gleaming black limousine. Levi, with his sober standards, would have preferred a taxi; and the burly Samuelson could see straight away that Levi was a reluctant celebrity. In the back of the limo, his eyes darted nervously behind his thin-rimmed glasses. His humility had begun to clash with the demands of New York publishers, and the result was now painful to behold. 'Umberto Eco can handle publicity *no problem,*' thought Samuelson; but Eco was not an Auschwitz survivor, and for Levi there was something unsavoury in the notion of making fame and money out of one's survivor status. The limo stopped outside the River Café beneath Brooklyn Bridge, and this at least was an inspired choice for Levi. During the lunch he gazed awestruck up at the bridge's suspension cables and swaying walkway; here was an engineering feat out of *The Wrench*.

The courting of Primo Levi continued. Irene Williams of Schocken Books wanted to ensure that he and Lucia enjoyed their stay in New York: at no time should they feel neglected. That evening she took them out to supper at the 'Shun Lee' Chinese restaurant in the Lincoln Center. Here the waiters wore black uniforms and the tables were crowded with expense-account executives and chattering upper Westsiders. The Levis were not hungry after their lunch at the River Café and picked at their noodles. They would have preferred not to go out that evening, but they made an effort. Apropos of nothing Lucia said she was fond of English thrillers and had also enjoyed John Fowles's *The Magus*. New York must have been a terrific strain for Lucia; she understood little that was said to her in English, and her husband was too busy on the publicity whirlwind to help her. Afterwards Williams took the couple to a classical concert at Avery Fisher Hall, having promised to show them 'what Jews do in New York'.

Levi's first New York lecture, 'Jewish Contributions to Italian Culture', was at 12:00 am on 17 April in the Brooklyn College Student Center. Before-hand, Brooklyn's distinguished Dante expert, Bernard Toscani, took Levi on an enjoyable tour of New York's grimy Lower East Side. This was far from the rarefied air of the Upper West Side; a smell of burned meat was in the air, the manholes steamed and the windows were full of shiny red cooked duck. Levi was fascinated by the gradual Chinese takeover of Little Italy; his brother-in-law Julian Zimet was then teaching film courses near Peking. Levi asked Toscani to show him signs of lingering Italian life – pizzerias, delis – on Mulberry and Grand Street. Down Canal Street, once an open sewer, Levi was amused to be told about the neighbourhood's legendary women hoodlums, from Hell-Cat Maggie to Chinatown Gertie. The lovely Woolworth Building on Broadway delighted Levi, and as he gazed up at the green-and-gold mosaic ceiling he was 'lost in a New York dream of art deco', recalled Toscani.

The Brooklyn hall was so packed that some people were sitting on laps. As Levi took the podium the audience applauded politely. He was in reasonable spirits after his Chinatown tour and charmed everyone by his disarming humour: 'Look, normally when I speak in Italian I'm not a bore, but when I speak in English I'm in danger of being *extremely* boring.' Levi proceeded doggedly with his lecture, taking breaths, almost gulps (one can hear them on the tape-recording) as he read from his six pages of notes. It was a fumbling performance but Levi's attractively sweet voice, and the understated manner of his expression, won the room over. There was just one distraction; a woman in the front row sat winking and beaming at him. She had a corona of light brown hair and seemed somehow familiar.

After adjusting his microphone ('May I lower this gadget?') Levi fielded questions. 'Dr Levi, where would you locate the world centre of Jewry?' Levi replied in heavily accented English: 'After six days in New York I'd hesitate to locate it in Israel.' Laughter went up. At the lecture's end the woman in the front row appeared at the dais and introduced herself to Levi as Edith Weisz. It took Levi several apologising seconds to realise that this was the Edith of his university years. Hearing of Levi's lecture, she had come over specially from Norwalk, north-east of New York, where she lived. Levi was delighted, if a little disconcerted, by the surprise reunion. Newspaper cameras flashed as Professor Ponzio's old chemistry students embraced. The pleasantries over, Levi began to complain to Weisz of New York's 'acoustic inferno' and the demands of publicity: 'I'm being carried round like a prize zoo specimen.' Lucia, understandably, kept a suspicious distance throughout their conversation. The paperwork was accumulating unmanageably back home in Turin, Levi went on to say, what with all the contracts and royalties. Half-jokingly, Weisz volunteered to be his secretary. 'I thought it might help to take off the donkey work, but his wife gave me a withering, disdainful look.' However, it is just as likely that the look Lucia gave Weisz was a strained and nervous one. The New York publicity circus was as trying for Lucia as it was for her husband.

On Thursday 18 April the Levis arrived at Los Angeles. They were met at LAX airport by Lucia's first cousin Alberto Finzi, who had fled Fascist Italy to begin a new life under the palms on Pacific Palisades – a far cry from his native Ferrara. Lucia was happy at last to be with her relatives and away from shouting, clanging New York. Here in California she could speak for herself and be herself. A room was booked for the Levis in the Wilshire Plaza hotel on Wilshire Boulevard. Next morning they were met by Bernard Gordon, an old friend of Levi's brother-in-law Julian Zimet, who had found Levi a Hollywood film agent. Discussions were under way for a screen treatment of *If Not Now, When?* Harold Greene, Levi's agent, saw potential in the novel's moments of suspense and violence. The

French ex-fashion model Dominique Sanda was to star in the film if Levi had his way.

Gordon drove the Levis up into the desert chaparral and brushland of the Hollywood Hills. Laura Huxley, Aldous Huxley's widow, lived there in a villa below the first 'O' of the HOLLYWOOD sign, and had invited them to tea and pumpkin pie. Unfortunately they could not fit the invitation into their schedule. As they drove through the Hollywood heights, Levi reacted with lively interest to every LA sight and marvelled wide-eyed at the lawns and driveways of sun-filled Beverly Hills. Gordon had been worried that the display of wealth and materialism would displease Levi. Instead, Levi exclaimed with childish delight: 'Sunset Boulevard!' Typically he wanted to know the names of the trees that lined the Strip, but Gordon had no idea what any of them were. Naturally Levi saw no evidence of the murderous gunplay that defines the City of Angels but, odd as it may sound, he felt quite at home among the city's swimming pools and freeways. His enthusiastic curiosity about LA impressed Gordon deeply. 'It was akin to the honesty and open-mindedness that informed his writing about everything, Auschwitz included.'

Next day, the Levis were driven down the California coast through Ronald Reagan's Orange County constituency. At Laguna Beach they stopped for lunch in a restaurant on a Mississippi-style paddle steamer. Levi was not persuaded by Southern California's sun and surfing dream. After lunch he and Lucia reached the plush resort community of La Jolla-by-the-Sea. The sister of Lucia's mother Beatrice lived here. Though Maria Viterbi was ninety and deaf, she was sprightly and, as Lucia's aunt, welcomed the Levis cordially. She and her son Andrew Viterbi, an electronics businessman, were keen for Primo to meet a near neighbour of theirs, Professor H. Stuart Hughes. A California-based historian, Hughes had done much to introduce Levi to American universities. His book on Italian Jewry, *Prisoners of Hope*, contained a lengthy chapter on Primo Levi, and Levi was curious to meet his advocate. Hughes came round for Sunday tea, and it was a good-natured occasion. When Hughes asked Levi if he thought any ill effects had lingered from his Nazi internment, Levi told him decisively, 'No.' Conversation shifted to the more congenial subject of Californian wine.

It was Holocaust Memorial Day – 21 April – and Levi was to speak at the Claremont University Center in California. Upwards of 500 people came to hear him that Sunday. Like much in 1980s American culture, the 'Holocaust' had been subjected to the vulgarity of a public-relations exercise, and in California that evening Levi was venerated as a 'Survivor-Victim'. His subsequent violent death only confirmed the belief of many American Jews that the Jewish experience is torment and martyrdom.

('Can't you see that Levi was *sick*!' exclaimed a psychotherapist at a conference on Levi in New York in 1997.) Rabbi Ben Beliak of Claremont College introduced Levi to the audience. Beliak, the son of German survivors, had read *If This is a Man* in 1962 on the eve of his Bar Mitzvah in Phoenix, Arizona. Thanks to Levi's book, the unspoken story of his parents' ordeal was made dreadfully real to young Ben, and since then he had longed to meet the author. Levi opened the typescript of his lecture (which was to be the first chapter of *The Drowned and the Saved*) and spoke movingly of the concentration camp. Sara Adler, a Claremont professor of Italian, was called in to interpret for the question-and-answer session, but she was not up to the task and Levi had to correct her translations. This created some irritation in the hall. Afterwards Levi was awkwardly deferential to Rabbi Beliak. Though Levi was a secular, unbelieving Jew, he was respectful of a rabbi's status.

From California the Levis flew on to St Louis, Missouri, and then on to Indianapolis, where they landed late in the evening of 22 April. Levi had arranged from Turin to meet Indiana University's director of Jewish studies, Professor Alvin Rosenfeld, who was one of his staunchest American supporters. 'Holocaust' was a label that Levi was reluctant to use or have applied to himself, but he agreed to speak to Rosenfeld's 'Holocaust Literature' class: at least they had read his books. Later that evening at the university Levi delivered the lecture 'What it Means to be a Jewish Writer'. It went well and afterwards Levi asked Rosenfeld to join him on the podium for what he quaintly termed a 'duet' of question and answers. Levi was cornered by admirers, who wanted to prolong the discussion. And, as the American trip went on, he increasingly wearied of what he called the 'buttonholers'.

3

Manhattan, after a week-long absence, looked even more extraordinary to the Levis, its skyscrapers glinting at night 'like Dolomites of light'. They went up to the World Trade Center's City Lights Bar, and admired the view of sky and bay. On 25 April, Italy's Liberation Day from the Nazis, Levi addressed a record turnout at the Italian Cultural Institute on Park Avenue. Italian New Yorkers of all ages and backgrounds came to see him talk; the crush was extraordinary as people craned to see from the stairs and at the entrance. The Institute's director, Ivano Marchi, introduced Levi jovially: 'If Not Now, When *could* we invite him?' Raymond Rosenthal was overwhelmed finally to be sitting next to Levi; on the podium he helped him with audience questions. Levi knew that without Rosenthal his American success would not have been so extraordinary and unprecedented, and afterwards they chatted companionably. They were almost opposite temperaments, though: Levi delicately self-aware, Rosenthal a straight-talking New Yorker.

They got to know each other better the next day at a restaurant on Madison Avenue. At Levi's prompting, Rosenthal spoke of his life on the Italian island of Ischia after the war, where he had known W. H. Auden, and of the Silver Heart they awarded him for bravery during the Allied landings in southern Italy. Rosenthal was a curmudgeonly if lovable seventy-three-year-old, embittered by life, though – like many New Yorkers – warm, wistful and open-hearted. Levi then asked him to list the howlers he had made during his early days as a translator. One of these Levi particularly enjoyed: *selvaggina* ('wild game') rendered as 'little savage'. A German Jewish scholar, Nahum Glatzer, joined the men at the table. Glatzer had held the chair of religious studies at Frankfurt University in 1938 and was responsible, together with John Updike, for Schocken Books' Kafka Library. Rather detached from worldly concerns, Glatzer spoke in German to Levi. He was the one publisher whom Levi genuinely liked in America, and clearly Levi was awed by him. Rosenthal noticed that Levi had ordered prosciutto and melon, but left the ham untouched: he did not want to offend the religiously observant Glatzer.

4

As Levi's tour came to an end he gave one last lecture. This was scheduled for the Curtis Auditorium at Boston University on 26 April. Many students attended the talk, 'Beyond Survival', and again there was standing room only. Leslie Epstein (son of one of the Epstein brothers who famously wrote the *Casablanca* screenplay) recalled Levi's impact on the hall: 'His dapper, professorial appearance, understated humour and quiet, authoritative presence hushed us all. He was beaming, calm and palpably made of steel.' Despite Epstein's description, Levi was actually very nervous that Friday night. Pietro Frassica, a Princeton University professor and friend of the novelist Gina Lagorio, went up to speak to him, but found that Levi's mind was elsewhere. 'Where is he? Where on earth is he?' Levi was upset because someone had failed to turn up. This was Salvador Luria, winner of the Nobel Prize for medicine in 1969, and a native of Turin. Luria had arranged to meet Levi, but was held up at the Massachusetts Institute of Technology, where he lectured. Luria had very favourably reviewed *The Periodic Table* in *Science* magazine, but there was another reason why Levi was keen to meet him. In his autobiography, *A Slot Machine, a Broken Test Tube*, Luria

473

had spoken candidly of the beneficial effects of lithium (the third element in the periodic table) on his depression. He was anxious that other depressives should know of the medication, but now Levi would not be able to discuss this with him. Levi returned exhausted to the Howard Johnson hotel in Kenmore Square, Boston.

Later that evening, Levi went to stay with his cousin Anna Yona in Boston's leafy Cambridge. A remarkable woman whom Levi had always admired, Anna was a lively wit, whose struggle to survive as a radio journalist in post-war America had revealed an unsuspected resilience in her. Whenever Anna stayed in Turin, Levi visited her at the YWCA on Via San Secondo, which she made a point of patronising. To friends, Yona was · warm and generous; to enemies, unforgiving. (Levi's poetry translator Ruth Feldman had had several abrasive encounters with her.) Levi and Lucia arrived late at Anna's and she was not pleased that their supper had been ruined as a result. Levi seemed to Anna not only tired but 'fearful', and she was sure that his mood was connected to family worries. Indeed, now that Levi was in familiar company he let his feelings about his mother show. The next morning at breakfast Anna found him 'bewildered and brooding'. He brightened a little when she drove him round the sights of Boston, accompanied by Leslie Epstein.

Levi had written a newspaper article, 'Story of a Coin', that had borrowed heavily from Epstein's novel, *King of the Jews,* about the dictatorial Lodz ghetto president Chaim Rumkowski. But Epstein was not offended. On the steps of the Howard Johnson hotel he invited Levi to spend a few months with him at Boston University's creative-writing course in the summer. Levi appeared to ponder the offer, but graciously declined. 'He said he could never think of leaving his mother behind in Italy.' As usual that night the phone rang continuously in Levi and Lucia's room. There were offers for him to go on radio and television talk shows; offers of professorships and lectureships. Levi took the phone off the hook.

To the surprise of his family and friends in Turin, Levi stayed on in America for another week. On 1 May he returned to Columbia University, in New York, where he had agreed to present signed copies of *The Periodic Table* to the year's best chemistry pupils. Irene Williams had prepared the room with great care, laying on a kosher buffet luncheon and stationing piles of Levi's book near the door. In the presence of the university dean, Robert Pollack, Levi spoke briefly in English before autographing the books. He was positively captivated by the ceremony and seemed to be beaming. 'Study hard,' he told the students, 'you know that chemistry saved my life.' This was said with a gravitas that Williams had not seen in

Levi before. Afterwards at the buffet luncheon – smoked whitefish, bagels – Levi impishly confided to the Italian chemist Rita Floriani that what he really wanted now was 'a nice bit of salami'. The Columbia book-signing was the high point of Levi's American tour.

Later that day, Levi was at the Kenneth B. Smilen Book Awards. Smilen was a wealthy Manhattanite who each year gave prizes to the best Jewish book in ten categories: *The Periodic Table* won $1,500 for Autobiography. Levi arrived early for the presentations at 1109 Fifth Avenue, which turned out to be the Jewish Museum of New York. He was excited to be there, and went off on his own to explore. For the first time he was among a powerful Fifth Avenue Jewish contingent, people who showed *class*, in the 1980s' New York street sense of that term – verve, industry. Saul Bellow, who had done most to bring Levi to public notice in America, was also a recipient of the award, and understandably Levi was keen to meet him. But, with a 'frosty smile', recalled Irene Williams, Bellow snubbed Levi and hurried on to talk to other guests. In Bellow's novella *The Bellarosa Connection* an American Jew shuns the grateful European Jew he has rescued from Nazi-occupied Europe. 'One man's gratitude is poison to his benefactor,' writes Bellow. David Sidorsky, chairman of the Smilen Awards that year, insists that Bellow made a point of speaking to Levi, though he concedes that such a briskly paced event, 'with ten writers each receiving an award from a panel of three jurors', did not lend itself to conversation. Irene Williams is less forgiving of Bellow: 'He was very arrogant, cold and distant towards Levi. Primo's champion had cut him, and he was mortified.' And with this unpleasant memory he returned to Italy with Lucia. Lisa, her face 'keen and shining', recalled Levi, was waiting for her parents at Malpensa airport in Milan. 'I don't believe it was a useless trip', Levi commented later in a poem. Lisa drove her mother and father home to Turin.

It had been an extraordinary journey. In twenty days Levi had given six lectures and twenty-five interviews in six American cities. The critical acclaim that had eluded him for years in America was now his, and it frightened him. Levi had been overwhelmed by the crowds and deafened by the applause. He was puzzled by why the Americans had made such a song and dance of his Jewishness. He was a chemist as well as a writer; Judaism was just one of the many things that interested him. To friends in Turin he complained that the Americans had 'pinned a Star of David' on him. Yet in America, where people tend to segregate by ethnic group and background, it was inevitable that Levi's would be primarily a Jewish audience. Indeed, he was marketed as such. If there had been misunderstandings, it was because Levi represented an unfamiliar figure in the literature of the Nazi camps: a Mediterranean, rather than an East European, survivor. Still, if America had misunderstood Levi, he had been a welcome guest and people generally had liked him. 'Levi is the greatest hero I've ever known,' Irene Williams told me later. His immense international reputation stems from this American trip. And now that Levi was an unforgettable name in the States, he decided to write all his future books with an eye to their translation into English. His New York publishers were sure he would be back within the year.

TWENTY-SIX

The Prison of 75 Corso Re Umberto
1985

I

Levi returned to Turin in early May 1985. Back in his familiar world, he went swimming at the American Club, and took part in a RAI science television series, *Journey Inside the Atom*. He put his signature to his friend Bianca Guidetti Serra's candidacy for the *gauchiste* Democrazi Proletaria. It was to be another summer of domestic drudgery, hard work and correspondence. In June Levi went to receive a prize, the 1985 Aquileia Award, for his collection of newspaper articles, *Other People's Trades*. Levi was upset that, owing to Einaudi's financial crisis, the book had been published on poor quality paper. Nevertheless, at the ceremony he was pleased to meet the Friuli writer Carlo Sgorlon for the second time, and there was a good deal of affectionate talk. Sgorlon addressed his friend, 'My dear Primo', while Levi told him how much he admired his latest novel, *Army of the Lost Rivers*, about the Nazis and their Cossack allies in northern Italy. The book showed an admirable capacity for forgiveness towards the occupiers, said Levi. 'I don't think I'd know how to forgive,' he confessed to Sgorlon.

By the early summer Levi's British publishers had made plans to promote *The Periodic Table*. Sheila Murphy in Michael Joseph's publicity department wondered if Levi would agree to see journalists flown out specially to Turin. It would be cheaper than a promotional tour in Britain. On 13 June Levi replied to Murphy: 'Just please take care that the interviewer has read at least one of my books.' The irritations of America still needled Levi. In New York, meanwhile, the publisher Arthur Samuelson was in a great hurry to publish Levi's late prison-camp stories, translated by Ruth Feldman as *Moments of Reprieve*. Samuelson's initial disregard for these (admittedly minor) stories had bitterly upset Feldman, who had complained to Levi that Samuelson was uninterested in her efforts. Levi was unmoved by these complaints. Why did she continue to bombard Samuelson with her translations if he showed no interest in them? 'Don't distress yourself overly: there are worse things in the world,' Levi told her, before referring to the Palestinian hijackers who in October 1985 tipped an elderly Jewish tourist out of his wheelchair into the sea from the Italian cruise ship *Achille Lauro*.

2

On 25 June Levi took a short break in the Tuscan seaside resort of Viareggio. His friend Sandro Galante Garrone had won the Viareggio non-fiction prize for his essays, *My Mentors*, and Garrone's daughter Vanna, an enthusiastic folk singer, was also in Viareggio. Over the years Levi had grown fond of Vanna. As they dawdled along the beach front, Vanna persuaded him to go with her for a swim. The sea was chilly, but Levi luxuriated in his truancy from the prize-giving formalities. He swam like a beginner (which he was), but was suddenly worried that paparazzi might steal a photograph of him and Vanna semi-naked, or that some prankster might run off with their clothes. Older men who are attentive to younger women often have an *arrière-pensée*, but Levi was merely Vanna's devoted, uncomplicated admirer. They warmed up with a brisk sea-front jog. A few days after his return to Turin Levi celebrated his mother's ninetieth birthday, on 29 June.

Two disappointments marked the rest of the summer; the first was cinematic. Bernard Gordon, having found Levi a Hollywood agent, now had to inform him that *If Not Now, When?* was unlikely to reach the silver screen. Any work that 'attempts seriously to deal with the human condition is immediately suspect in these precincts', he tried to reassure Levi. Moreover, it was an 'honour' to be ignored by the Hollywood movie moguls. Levi was prepared for failure. Sophia Loren's husband Carlo Ponti ('the Pontifex Maximus of Ciné Città') had shown an interest in filming his work twenty years earlier, but despite lavish promises, nothing had materialised. Levi was also disappointed by the extremely poor American reviews of *If Not Now, When?* It was fortunate that these came out after Levi's homecoming, or they might have marred his American tour. Typical of the reviews was the one in the liberal Manhattan weekly, *New Leader*, which attacked a 'completely inauthentic' work, stiffly schematic and unsubtle. American critics, unlike their less rigorous Italian counterparts, recognised that the novel was a work of 'second-hand' *Yiddishkeit* by a Jew who was not an East European survivor, or a Hasidic Jew, or even a Jew influenced by Hasidism.

*

In July William Weaver called on Levi with a draft translation of *The Monkey's Wrench* (in Britain, *The Wrench*). Levi was pleased to see his translator again, but was disappointed by the American title for the book. To translate the Italian *La chiave a stella* literally as 'The Star-Shaped Key' might have been too poetic for Levi (or might have carried an unwanted sense of the Star of David), but it would have been preferable to Arthur Samuelson's insertion of 'monkey' into the title. 'I'm afraid they thought "monkey" would be cute,' Weaver tried to explain to Levi (but a 'monkey wrench', *una chiave inglese*, was not the wrench Levi was referring to). As Weaver got out of the lift, he saw a frail, bent woman shuffling down the hall. Levi introduced her as his mother. '*Io sono la madre*', she smiled uncomprehendingly up at the American. Weaver thought she was very sweet, and complimented Levi on having such a long-lived mother. Surely it boded well for his own longevity. Levi replied that it depends on *how* one ages.

In these summer months Ester was occasionally looked after by a young Israeli student, Amir Ishel, who had also helped at Uncle Corrado Luzzati's. Germaine Greer met Amir the day after Weaver's visit when she interviewed Levi for the London *Literary Review*. A young man (whom Greer assumed was southern Italian), 'muscles bursting out of his tight singlet and tighter jeans', very gently helped an ancient woman out of the lift. She took Greer's hand and gazed up into her face, wondering if she knew her, before shuffling past her into the flat. Everything about the woman, recalled Greer, bespoke the 'most loving care and attention'. Greer's conversation with Levi, interrupted by phone calls with enquiries after his mother's health, was revealing. Asked if he was frightened of dying, Levi replied that he could bear his own pain, but not that of others. Greer talked of the skeletal, degraded humanity she had just witnessed in famine-swept Ethiopia, which prompted Levi to confess to having 'Ethiopians' in the house – he meant his mother and mother-in-law. This rather aggressive remark referred to Ester and Beatrice's needy state. Levi went further. He compared the women to the 'drowned people', meaning those without hope, in the title of the book that was to become, in English, *The Drowned and the Saved*. This was not the last time that Levi would liken his mother to an Auschwitz prisoner.

3

Memories of Auschwitz continued into the autumn when, on 5 September, a Jewish couple arrived in Turin from England. Simone and Gerry Lakmaker were in their early sixties and hoped that Levi might shed some light on Gerry's missing brother Manuel. In 1943 the Lakmaker brothers had been deported from Occupied Amsterdam – Gerry to Belsen, Manuel to an unknown destination. After his rescue from Belsen in 1945, Gerry travelled to Israel in the hope of discovering some clue to his brother's whereabouts, but the records revealed only that Manuel had 'vanished in Central Europe'. Without a body or grave, Gerry could not grieve for his brother. At the war's end he left Holland to build a new life for himself in England, but Manuel's disappearance continued to haunt him, and he was often depressed. Family life was strained and, in despair, his wife Simone began to attend a Christian prayer group in Harrow, where she and Gerry lived. It was there that she met Brigid Pailthorpe, an Italian scholar who worked at Harrow School nearby. Pailthorpe was moved by the story of Gerry's survival at Belsen and the unresolved conflicts surrounding his brother; she and her Christian circle prayed that the dilemma might be resolved. Then, in 1984, Pailthorpe visited friends in Venice, where she picked up a paperback on their bookshelves. What the book was about, or who the author was, she had no idea. It was the Einaudi edition of *If This is a Man,* and, with her fluent Italian, she sat and read it to the end. In the final chapter Levi had described a Dutch boy, 'Lakmaker', who lay dying in the bunk beneath his at Auschwitz; 'Lakmaker' was seventeen, the same age as Gerry's vanished brother. The thought that Lakmaker could be a common Dutch name, like Smith or Jones, crossed Brigid Pailthorpe's mind. But causeless events did not really exist in her universe, and she believed that the coincidence was significant.

Back in Harrow, the revelation jolted and astonished Gerry Lakmaker, and in a state of agitation he wrote to Levi care of his publishers in Turin. Gerry could not have known that after the war Levi had himself tried to trace members of the Lakmaker family in Amsterdam (but the Jewish community there had drawn a blank). In his reply to Gerry Lakmaker, written in English, Levi was careful not to raise expectations:

> Unfortunately, after so many years, I am afraid that my memory of the young man has shrunk to the few phrases I had written in the book . . . He was tall, bony (but, there and then, everybody was bony), and, despite his suffering, of a very mild character. If it can mitigate your sorrow, he certainly did not die by gas: gassing was stopped at Auschwitz in the late autumn of 1944. He died of the consequences of his diseases after the liberation of the *Lager,* but I lost sight of him following the arrival of the Russians.

The Lakmakers arrived in Turin at 3:00 pm, tired after their day's drive through Switzerland. Though Levi was burdened by domestic problems he welcomed the couple. The introductions over, they showed him a photograph of Manuel: Levi was in no doubt, now, that this was Gerry's long-lost sibling. Even at a distance of half a century he instantly recognised the face. Before returning to Harrow, Simone Lakmaker felt she had to ask Levi if he believed in God. Like many people, she had found his presence 'oddly spiritual'. (Indeed, this perceived 'spirituality' was becoming part of Levi's personality. An electrical expert at Bayer, Hans Schlegel, had noted in 1974 that Levi's eyes were faintly almond-shaped and looked 'holy'.) In reply to Simone Lakmaker's question, Levi replied that he was an unbeliever. 'I believe in fellow man.' Though he was pleased to help solve the mystery of Manuel's disappearance, and assist Gerry in his life's quest, not for a moment did he believe that these extraordinary events were religiously ordained, or that he had a priestly role on earth to console the bereaved. The subject of Levi's humanist enquiry was man, and he urged Gerry to write down his memories of Belsen for the sake of posterity and as a human chronicle. Having returned to Harrow, Gerry Lakmaker lit Kaddish candles in Manuel's memory: finally the burden was lifting.

Two weeks after his audience with the Lakmakers, Levi received the awful news that, on 19 September, Italo Calvino had died. The writer had been rushed to hospital in Tuscany following a cerebral haemorrhage, but it was too late. Calvino was sixty-two. Umberto Eco's obituary in the *Corriere della Sera* took precedence over news of the Mexican earthquake. Shortly before he died Calvino had written to Levi asking for help with another Raymond Queneau translation, this time of the Frenchman's quirky homage to household plastics, *Le Chant du Styrène* (a pun on the 'The Siren's Song', *Le Chant du Sirène*). 'I don't know when you'll see this letter as I imagine you're away on holiday.' In fact Levi was at home (his mother kept him there) and he telephoned Calvino at once to correct a few technical errors in his translation. He found Calvino in good spirits, speaking of Queneau's French poem as 'quite impossible' to translate, but laughing about it. With Calvino's death, Levi had not only lost a friend, but he felt in some sense that the nation's modern literary life had ended. For days he could not concentrate – his attention span was easily broken – but whatever consternation he now felt, he suppressed it again with anti-depressants.

4

Autumn arrived in the middle of September, and the weather being unseasonably cold, Levi was ill with several bouts of 'flu. In an interval between bouts, on 6 or 7 October, he was recuperating at the sulphur baths of Albano, near Padua, when he was visited by Jean Samuel and his wife Claude. The French survivor found Levi very changed – drawn and strained, 'like a man with a great burden of unhappiness'. Levi's anxiety over his mother was plain, but there was another grievous concern: German revisionism. Unlike the earlier French falsifiers, such as Robert Faurisson, the revisionists under the historian Ernst Nolte in Berlin did not deny that the Nazi massacres had taken place, but argued instead that they were not unique to Germany. Rather, they were but one link in a chain that could be traced back to Stalin's class murders and on to Pol Pot's purging of two million in 1970s' Cambodia. In his present malaise, Levi saw Nolte's as a sinister move to diminish the Nazi crimes, and to Samuel he confessed his fear that all he had written on the camps would one day fall on deaf ears. It was the first time that Samuel had seen his friend in less than his usual breezy mood, and he returned to Strasbourg very concerned.

The revisionist disturbance was not the only cloud on Levi's horizon. An American review of his Jewish partisan novel, published in October, was to make him doubt his literary standing in the United States. Though Levi had been upset by the negative American reception of *If Not Now, When?*, nothing could prepare him for his mauling in the right-wing journal *Commentary*. The eight-page attack seemed to have been motivated chiefly by a desire to inflict damage on Levi's reputation as a liberal Diaspora Jew. Moreover, the combined accusation of assimilation with ignorance of East European Jewish culture justified Levi's suspicion that the magazine's pro-Begin and (according to the waspish Gore Vidal) anti-black and anti-gay editor Norman Podhoretz was behind the savaging. The author of Levi's demolition was Fernanda Eberstadt, a minor novelist and critic with fashionable New York connections, born in 1960. Until Eberstadt, no one had performed the outlandish act of attacking *If This is a Man*. The book was marred by 'pseudo-scientific prose' and 'hackneyed social psychology'. Levi was hit by these barbs, but what hurt him most was Eberstadt's implication, later in the essay, that his anti-Fascism had been an opportunistically belated development. According to Eberstadt, Levi had not found the will to resist Nazi-Fascism until the first signs of a decisive Allied victory. The suggestion that Levi had been watching the war bulletins carefully to see which way to jump was deeply offensive to him. Most writers at some stage have to face their savage critic, but Levi had come to the misfortune late in life, and he took it very badly. To his translator Raymond Rosenthal he wrote on 1 November:

> I too am astonished and saddened (though not too much) by the severity of Miss Eberstadt. I can't fathom the reasons for her

malevolence. Is is it because I'm an assimilated Jew? But we *all* are, in varying degrees; maybe more so in Italy than in America, but this is the result more of history than of individual choice. Or is it because I'm not religious? But here too, each individual has the right to make his or her own free choice!

Though Levi valiantly underplayed his hurt, that did nothing to diminish it: Fernanda Eberstadt bothered him a good deal. Just why his lack of religiosity should have so aggravated this twenty-five-year-old Manhattan neo-Conservative was all the more puzzling, as Eberstadt was Jewish only on her paternal grandfather's side, and therefore not really Jewish at all. When Levi found this out, he commented sourly to me (in English): 'It seems I was attacked by a rather anti-Semitist [*sic*] person!'

His reply to Eberstadt in the February 1986 edition of *Commentary* was urbane and even-tempered. Eberstadt's disapproval of Levi's assimilated status received the cursory attention it deserved. In putting his case, Levi had unexpected help from Alan Viterbi (Andrew Viterbi's son), who petulantly accused the adversary of being 'vicious and unforgiving'. Raymond Rosenthal also took up the cudgels. 'I know a hatchet job when I see it, and certainly Fernanda Eberstadt's article in your October issue qualifies for honors in the field.' In best Norman Mailer fighting-mode, he demanded an apology from the entire *Commentary* staff. (It was not forthcoming, and when I spoke to Rosenthal in 1994 he was still angry.)

Somewhere in this sorry business Levi was able to see comedy. That both his translator, Rosenthal, and his wife's nephew, Viterbi, had defended him in *Commentary* suggested a peculiarly Italian sort of *clientelismo* (favouritism and nepotism): 'And they say the Mafia doesn't exist!' Levi observed ironically. Eberstadt was an irritation, but she was just one of many negative experiences that preyed on Levi in these months. He concluded his letter to Rosenthal with the awful observation: 'It is not merely for this episode that I have lost my good humour and the will to live.' Shocking though it was for Levi to admit that he did not want to live, the announcement was made so matter-of-factly, without elaboration, and was followed by polite greetings to Rosenthal and his 'lovely' wife, that Rosenthal thought little of it at the time. Not knowing Levi well, he took his statement as a figure of speech. It is interesting that Levi should have slipped this information into a letter to a friend unconnected with his usual Turin circles. Even if Rosenthal were concerned, he could not have alerted anyone who mattered.

In the midst of this unpleasantness, finally, came some good news. *The Periodic Table* was selling well in Britain and in fact was at the top of the bestseller list along with Dick Francis. Sales of the book were bolstered by a forty-minute BBC television *Bookmark* documentary on Levi broadcast earlier that autumn. In the film, introduced by the late poet and critic Ian Hamilton, Levi is seen walking through the spring sunlight and shadow of the arcaded Via Po, and smoking cheap Nazionali cigarettes with Silvio Ortona in a café. In one marvellous scene, shot in Aunt Jole's flat on Corso Rosselli, a group of elderly women relatives share family gossip with Primo, who beams among them like the adored *primogenito* he had always been. It is impossible not to warm to Levi in the documentary and British viewers surely were charmed by this slight, softly-spoken Italian who had been to hell and back. Levi's first British review, appearing in the *Guardian* on 24 October, set the tone for what was to follow. Tim Radford hailed an 'extraordinary' work that seemed to be forged 'out of gold'. Paul Bailey in the *Observer* was pleased to praise an 'exceptional book', as he had long been Levi's admirer. Only Jonathan Miller (on BBC Radio 4's *Kaleidoscope*) was grudging: 'I just wish people would write books without laying claims to large schemes,' he grumbled. (In the margin of the BBC's copy of the radio transcript someone has written 'Silly man!') Nothing pleased Levi more than the favourable notices in specialist journals like *Chemical and Engineering News.* The Yorkshire chemist Sir Frederick Dainton, in *New Scientist,* commented on a 'triumphant book' of 'magical quality'. Levi was so delighted by this review that he wrote a long letter to Sir Frederick expressing his 'sincere gratefulness' for it.

Sheila Murphy, Levi's publicist in London, was delighted by his British reception, and on 4 November she wrote to him: 'We are so happy with the success of your book, and of course feel that it is no more than your due.' Would he come to England? Levi said he would, but 'may I ask you not to overburden my schedule?' Meanwhile Mike Petty of Sphere Books had picked up on rumours that Levi was under consideration for the Nobel Prize. 'Obviously it would be foolish to get too excited about this, but when you consider that we publish [the] paperback in October 1986, it does no harm to dream!'

One woman was a little miffed by Levi's delayed British success. Ten years earlier Stella Humphries had translated *The Periodic Table,* but no one was interested then in the book. She wrote to Levi on 30 October:

> You can hardly imagine what pleasure it gave us to see you on BBC television and to know that at long last your SISTEMA PERIODICO is available in English. We always look forward eagerly to any new publications of yours.

The letter was a little sore in tone, and in his reply Levi offered every commiseration:

> Your letter both moved and saddened me: I really regret that your prescient verdict on my TABLE went to waste, and that you moreover worked in vain to translate it. Please forgive me: indirectly I feel a bit guilty. But you must know that the destinies of books, like the destinies of men, are quite unforeseeable. After 10 years and the scant attention it received in Europe, my book's American success was a pleasurable surprise for me too, but also an unresolved mystery; or more likely, a question of pure good fortune.

5

As the winter drifted on, Levi grew silent and tight-lipped when people asked how *The Drowned and the Saved* was progressing. His 'unduly hasty' editor in New York, Arthur Samuelson, harried him with requests for material. And in a terse letter to Samuelson, Levi explained that his long-shelved sequel to *The Periodic Table* (still provisionally entitled *The Double Bond*) was 'for the moment a bare project'; he would tackle it as soon as *The Drowned and the Saved* was 'done away with'. These forceful words reflect Levi's growing impatience with a book he was committed to write, yet which was proving hard to finish. His mother, with her ailments and demands, kept him from completing the task, he complained. Stressed, Levi found that his thoughts turned to fantasies of flying and of weightlessness. The further you can rise above the earth, the better, they seemed to say. In a story from 1983, 'The Great Mutation', a girl sprouts wings and, like a figure in a Chagall canvas, sails gratefully through the air; the density of her body has become 'hateful' to her. (In 1963 Levi had chosen as the cover of *The Truce* a Chagall sketch of a man flying in a Russian night sky.) On 4 December 1985, *La Stampa* announced a 'Nongravity Competition' in which schoolchildren had to submit ideas for scientific experiments that could be carried out in zero-gravity conditions. Levi was too old to enter the competition, but in his newspaper article, 'The Man Who Flies', he admitted his desire to be weightless: breaking through the bonds of the Earth's gravity would be exhilarating. The general understanding is that dreams of weightlessness and flying – like those of swimming – are erotic in nature. Whether they were an expression of Levi's own sexual frustrations in marriage is fruitless speculation, but one is bound to wonder. Considering his deep, almost pathological relationship with his mother, Levi was unlikely to have been very fulfilled in marriage. Levi appears to have been a sexually troubled individual. The most intense period of his life was spent almost exclusively in the company of men: Auschwitz. And he was obviously threatened by his father's full-bloodied bonhomie. It is worth noting, too, that virtually all his flirtations with women were chaste. Instead he was infatuated by certain men, whom he surrounded with a mythic, heroic aura, beginning with the glamorous Kind brothers and moving on from Sandro Delmastro to Mario Rigoni Stern. From this one might deduce an ambivalent sexuality. Levi's desire to be released from the weight of his body continued until he died.

Levi had almost convinced himself that he would never finish *The Drowned and the Saved,* when a package arrived from Canada with a tape-recording of eighteenth-century Jewish liturgical music. The music originated from Casale Monferrato, east of Turin, where Levi had family roots, and it had been sent by the Toronto radio producer John Reeves. Levi wrote to Reeves of his enchantment on hearing the music: 'I listened to the Cantata with friends; and, in spite of my total incompetence in musical matters, I found it *extremely* beautiful.' He was able to enjoy the music because his depression was lifting. The loveliness of the unexpected gift helped shift his low spirits further and gave him the spur he needed to unleash his creativity. Five days later, on 12 December, after all the months of foot-dragging, Levi finished his book.

Feeling more confident now, Levi had a fairly sociable time for the rest of the year. On 13 December he was reunited with his friends, the writers Mario Rigoni Stern and Nuto Revelli at the 'Campus' bookshop in Turin. Rigoni Stern's war memoir, *The Year of Victory*, had just been published. Revelli brought along two bottles of Barolo wine to the celebration supper; reminiscing, the trio spoke of the pride they still took in remaining literary outsiders, operating on the periphery of the Italian establishment. Rigoni Stern and Revelli could not know that they would never see Levi again. Three days later Levi wrote a poem, 'To My Friends'. It was addressed to Rigoni Stern and Nuto Revelli and to all those who had been close to him, as well as to those who had lost the 'will to live'. The poem was tinged by an autumnal sense of loss, and suggested the self-examination of someone looking back on his life. Today Levi's friend Bianca Guidetti Serra says the verse was 'almost a farewell', and she can still recite it word for word:

> Now that time presses urgently,
> And the tasks are finished,
> To all of you the modest wish
> That the autumn may be long and mild.

When Levi's Aunt Jole read this, she knew that Primo was very low, and in a frightened state she telephoned her neighbour three flights below, Hens Fischer, who had taught Levi German. Jole told him bluntly: 'This poem is the work of a man who wants to kill himself.' As Levi did not want the verse to look like a *cri de coeur*, he sent a copy to the novelist Gina Lagorio with the mock-cheerful PS: 'Don't take it too tragically!'

TWENTY-SEVEN

In London
1986

I

Publication of *The Periodic Table* in America in 1984, followed by its appearance in England, should have given Levi the impetus he needed. He was sent copies of the American and British editions to give to friends and admirers, but Levi began to say, with ominous repetitiveness, that success no longer interested him. The news that Hollywood had taken out a six-figure option on *If Not Now, When?* only prompted fears of disappointment, which turned out justified. The optimistically named Neversink Productions appeared to have no money, and the film was never made. Though Levi had sensibly given up on Hollywood, this was one more bitter moment for him. At least he had his London tour to look forward to in the spring.

By the New Year – 1986 – Levi's exacerbations had intensified, and friends picked up on his dejection. Emma Vita-Levi sent him a letter full of praise and delight at rumours of the Nobel Prize, and invited him to stay at her lavish house on Lake Como. But Levi could speak only of his aches and anxieties. 'It's true that Como is near Turin, but, equally, Turin is very far from Como: family affairs have now deteriorated and become so complicated that travelling has become a virtual impossibility.' He added the plaintive-sounding PS: 'The Nobel is just a story – much more than that is needed!'

On 29 January he was in Milan for Italo Calvino's memorial. In his commemorative speech, 'Calvino, Queneau and Science', Levi celebrated their common scientific interests. He said he had always enjoyed Calvino's recurring theme of the labyrinth; Calvino's Monte Cristo tries to burrow his way out of captivity, only to encounter dead-end labyrinths. It would not be too much to say that Levi's incarceration in 75 Corso Re Umberto had attained this nightmare quality. Afterwards he greeted Calvino's widow Esther sadly, and said he could not stay for drinks, but had to return home to his mother. Before he left, their conversation touched briefly on the subject of literary executors and wills. When Calvino died, Esther told Levi, he had not made any provision for his books and manuscripts. Levi said that would not happen to him: only the other day he had instructed his wife what to do with his papers after his death. Esther Calvino commented to me later: 'Here was a man who no longer wished to live. Italo *never* spoke to me about his death, but Levi obviously had, to his wife.' But Levi had lived with the idea of his death for very much longer than had Calvino.

2

On 10 February the Mafia 'maxi-trial' opened. For the first time in Italian history the Cosa Nostra had been entrapped by the state. From the public gallery visitors could peer down at some of the 475 criminals in their cages. Like all Italians, Levi followed the Sicilian trials with rapt if appalled attention, and hoped they would drive a stake through the heart of the Honoured Society. 'The trial is the last chance the Italian Republic has to show that our institutions still work,' he told the Rome evening paper *Paese Sera*. The Italy of 1986 was a changed country and Levi did not like what he saw. Almost half a century had passed since the Italian Republic was founded in 1946 and since then Levi's hopes for a fairer, better Italy had largely evaporated. The roots of organised crime remained in Sicily, but *La Piovra* (The Octopus, as the Mafia is known colloquially) had spread its tentacles into northern Italy. Trafficking massively in heroin, by the mid-1980s they had begun to kill reporters, magistrates and police who obstructed them.

In his journalism of this time Levi alluded to these squalid developments. Italy may now have surpassed Britain to become the fifth industrial power of the Western world (*il sorpasso*, the Italians called it – 'the overtaking'), but behind the roseate flush of its new-found economic prosperity Levi knew there lay a deepening corruption. He revealed a conservative side when he called for tougher airport controls to stem the flood of North African immigrants into Turin. Like many Turin bourgeois, Levi suspected that the black prostitutes, known as *lucciole* (fireflies), who solicited round Porta Nuova station had caused an upswing in Turin's crime rates.

Levi found distasteful a new aspect of Italian politics: namely, politics-as-*spettacolo*. This commenced when the pornographic star Cicciolina ('Sweety Pie') campaigned for civil rights on behalf of Italy's Radical Party in early 1987. Cicciolina was symptomatic of the new, meretricious Italy and, to the Milan journalist Massimo Dini, Levi expressed his irritation with 1980s' politicians in general: 'It's their way of talking without

489

communicating that annoys me.' Italian politicians such as Giovanni Spadolini, who championed the Risorgimento ideals of national unity and public morality, won Levi's approval. And the respect was mutual. Spadolini asked Levi to contribute to the legendary cultural journal *Nuova Antologia*, which he then edited. Levi obliged, and his apocalyptic poem 'Memorandum Book' appeared in the spring 1986 edition; it contains images of plummeting comets, nuclear apocalypse and, again, that recurring image of wished-for zero-gravity:

> In such a night as this
> Someone stretches out next to a woman
> And feels he no longer has weight,
> His tomorrows no longer have weight.

Thoughts like these, of incorporeality and weightlessness, now came very frequently to Levi.

The unease he felt in these early months of 1986 increased in the spring when clouds of radioactive dust from Chernobyl spewed over the skies of Europe. Levi had been alarmed by Jonathan Schell's classic, awakening study, *The Fate of the Earth*. However, he was not a stern ecologist, and disliked what he saw as a pious and intolerant strain in Italy's anti-nuclear protestors. But, after Chernobyl, the nuclear Armageddon had a stronger claim on his imagination. At the time of the catastrophe in April he was reading an unpublished nuclear thriller by his physicist friend Guido Bonfiglioli, *Green Chili and Gamma Rays*. Levi told Bonfiglioli that no 'prudent publisher' could afford to let the book go. And he reflected that ours is an age of diminished human responsibility: the Chernobyl physicists felt no more morally responsible, personally, for the disaster than the US airmen had done for the atomic destruction of Hiroshima. Levi's earlier science fiction had made the point: in this technological age of ours division of labour can make the contribution of any single person seem unimportant; the Nazi death-camps had functioned on these lines.

3

In early spring Levi had to decide what to do about his ninety-one-year-old mother while he and Lucia were away in England. One plan was to install a nurse permanently in the flat; another was to have his sister come up again from Rome. But before they left for London, Levi received a letter from a Jewish family in England, the Zinobers, who claimed to have recognised their long-lost relative in *The Periodic Table*. The name 'Goldbaum' had leaped off the page in the *Sunday Times Magazine* extract of the 'Vanadium' chapter. Shaken by the coincidence, Vivienne Zinober wondered if this could be her uncle Gerhard Goldbaum, missing since the war's end. Goldbaum (Golden Tree) is an unusual German name and the details seemed to add up.

From Bristol where she was a doctor, Vivienne Zinober wrote to Levi saying that she was prepared to visit him in Turin. And she enclosed wartime photographs of her uncle for identification. A cultivated physicist, he had been born in Breslau in 1903. In 1934 Goldbaum settled in Amsterdam, where he later joined the Resistance. But the Gestapo caught up with him and, in 1943, he was deported to Auschwitz. Levi was startled by the photographs. He replied – in English – to Dr Zinober on 22 March 1986:

> The photographs you sent hit me like a blow on the face. There is not the slightest doubt: I recognised him [Gerhard Goldbaum] immediately . . . I preserve absurdly precise memories of that period, especially for human visages, and that was certainly the man who worked with me.

When she wrote to Levi, Vivienne Zinober had no idea of her uncle's fate, but Levi knew very well what had happened to him: he had died during the hurried evacuation of Auschwitz in January 1945. Jean Samuel had witnessed at first hand Goldbaum's 'ultimate destiny', and Levi advised Dr Zinober to contact the French survivor. (Levi had never liked to speak by proxy for witnesses.) For the time being Levi was able to reassure her that her uncle had not suffered 'extremities of hunger or exhaustion', at least not for the time they had worked alongside each other in the Auschwitz laboratory. 'I remember Goldbaum in a reasonably good nutrition state, as demonstrated by the fact that your photos coincide quite well with my visual memory.' Levi suggested that they meet in London during his imminent spring tour. There was a PS, in which Levi used a chemical analogy to describe the camp's genius for exposing the good and bad in man:

> One thing I can add to all that precedes. You see, the *Lager* was a terrific 'litmus paper' [test] to reveal hidden depths and weaknesses. I had not contracted a special friendship with Goldbaum, but he was at first sight an extremely respectable person, neatly outlined upon the degraded background of the environment.

Levi remembered that Goldbaum had 'ingratiated' himself with (perhaps he meant 'pandered to') the Dutch *Kapo* Josef Lessing who, in a perverse *esprit de nation,* dispensed special favours to Dutch co-nationals. Evidently since working in Amsterdam, Goldbaum had claimed to be half-Dutch. This was not the first time since Auschwitz that Levi had heard Goldbaum's name. It had surfaced in the course of his correspondence with his Auschwitz overseer Ferdinand Meyer. In a letter to Levi in 1967, Meyer claimed to have obtained 'Herr Dr Goldbaum' (as he fawningly called him) a privileged position within the lab and wondered what had become of this 'pleasant, devoted and conscientious man'.

Jean Samuel understandably felt at the time, though he did not tell Vivienne Zinober until much later, that what he had to say about her uncle was potentially disturbing. During the transfer march from Auschwitz, Goldbaum had been loaded at Gleiwitz station on to a 'death-truck' (a wagon for corpses): that much Samuel was prepared to tell her in his first letter. However, it was not until Samuel could talk face-to-face with her that he felt able to reveal the truth: Goldbaum was still breathing when they closed the freight-car doors on him in the corpse-laden wagon. When Dr Zinober learned the truth about her uncle she was nauseated but also, in a way, relieved finally to know the truth: 'Uncle Gerhard died in terrible death-throes, but I had to know.'

4

Levi and Lucia arrived in London on the morning of 12 April 1986, a Saturday of bright sunshine. They were full of good resolutions to enjoy themselves; in fact London was to be a glorious spring interlude for Levi, the last of his life. Giorgio Colombo of the Italian Cultural Institute was waiting for them at Heathrow airport. He had chaperoned the Levis round New York and they were delighted to see him again. Colombo checked them into the discreetly elegant Durrants Hotel in London's West End. On the Sunday after their arrival, the Levis were met by Sheila Murphy of Michael Joseph's publicity department. She noted at once the deference shown to Levi by the hotel staff. Though Levi was gentle and low-voiced – in every way *unobtrusive* – waiters and receptionists alike responded to his dignified presence. He looked more like a trustworthy family doctor, in his V-neck pullover and tweeds, than a cultural celebrity who commanded airtime and column space. Later that Sunday, Murphy accompanied Levi to Hendon in north-west London where a 'Festival of Italian Jewry' was about to open. The Egerton Gardens auditorium was packed with admirers, many of them Italian, who had come to hear Levi talk. Latecomers had to sit on the stage behind Levi for want of chairs. One of these, Rodolfo Goldbacher, was related to Franco Sacerdoti, the handsome young Neapolitan who had been deported with Levi, Nissim and Vanda Maestro to Auschwitz.

As usual Levi was afterwards besieged by autograph-hunters and admirers. Dr Ruth Hoffman, his Jungian analyst correspondent, wanted to introduce herself, but felt too shy, and went home saddened by the missed opportunity. Dr Vivenne Zinober waited a while before approaching Levi: 'Oh yes, I want to talk to you,' he said, and drew up a chair. But before they could talk Levi was engulfed again by admirers and Dr Zinober was squeezed out of the hall, frustrated and uncomprehending. Rodolfo Goldbacher then introduced himself. The Goldbachers were looking after Levi's niece, Ada Sacerdoti, in their East Finchley home; Ada's father was Aunt Jole Luzzati's son, and Levi felt a close family bond. 'Take care of Ada – we love her!' he raised his voice above the crowd as Goldbacher left the hall.

On the whole, Levi found his British interviewers better informed than his American ones. Tim Radford of the *Guardian* asked Levi if he still dreamed about Auschwitz. 'Very infrequently,' Levi replied. But in one occasional dream, he went on to tell Radford, he was being driven into the camp, but firmly protested: 'Gentlemen, I have already been here. It is not my turn.' Levi was received with immense respect wherever he went in London. On his third day in the city he was met by Sheila Murphy's publicity assistant, confusingly named Sarah Murphy. In Durrants Hotel she went through Levi's publicity schedule. Photographs had not prepared her for such an extraordinarily fastidious and delicate-mannered man. With infinite care Levi transcribed every detail of his appointments into a tiny notebook bought specially for the occasion. Later she noted in her diary:

> Levi is very neat, very small; both serious and amused by everything that goes on around him. He misses *nothing*, no nuance of expression or statement, and he responds with great thoughtfulness and patience to whoever addresses him.

When he had a mind to, Levi could speak English reasonably well. Yet each time he went into a London radio studio he made a point of warning the interviewer that he would raise his hand 'like so' if he felt the speed of the conversation to be running away from him. At BBC Bush House Sarah Murphy was taken aback by the number of people who approached Levi to express their delight and interest in his writing:

One lady, who did not announce herself, came over and shook Dr Levi's hand with such gratitude, quite overwhelmed by the chance to pay homage to such a great writer. Levi responded to her with enthusiasm, delighted at the opportunity to speak some Italian for a change, and even suggested that she come to the studio as an interpreter!

The London days passed quickly. Levi had supper with his friends at Michael Joseph, visited Harrods with Lucia, saw Buckingham Palace. On Tuesday he went to see Anthony Rudolf and his wife Audrey at their north London home. Rudolf had published Levi's poems in English in 1976 and was among his most loyal British supporters. The Rudolfs toasted Levi and his tour, but the evening was overshadowed by talk of the American attack on Tripoli earlier that day, 15 April, when US bombers had accidentally blown up the French embassy. Once again, Ronald Reagan's 'mad dog of the Middle East' Gaddafi had got away. In retaliation the Libyans launched missiles at the US radar base on Lampedusa island off Sicily: the projectiles fell harmlessly short of the beach. Levi confessed that he was no admirer of Gaddafi, but he could not see how shelling Tripoli would serve to combat world terrorism. He feared a calamitous outcome to the Middle Eastern tensions, a clash between Islam and the West.

5

On a morning off his schedule, Levi called on the Italian writer and journalist Gaia Servadio for lunch. They had met occasionally in Turin, when Servadio worked for *La Stampa*. But there was also a family connection. Servadio's father, Luxardo, was an industrial chemist whom Levi knew from SIVA. (His mother and grandmother had both perished at Auschwitz.) Gaia Servadio now lived in London, where she cut a figure in metropolitan society. From an early age she had proved a capable and fiercely independent reporter, and Levi had followed her career admiringly. He was attracted not just to her beauty, but to her witty and cultured company: it was impossible not to be charmed by her. Philip Roth was a frequent visitor at her Belgravia home, and Servadio had arranged for Levi to meet the American novelist later that Wednesday afternoon. Levi said he was intimidated by Roth's fabled wit and sarcasm. 'But I've only read *Portnoy's Complaint!*' he protested to Servadio. But Roth was Levi's devoted admirer and longed to meet him. Indeed, he was to have an un-expected influence in helping Levi consolidate his fame in America.

Lucia was present at the lunch, but Servadio, to her subsequent regret,

494

paid her little attention. The range of subjects was very wide. They discussed Pasolini's fondness for River Tiber *pissoirs* (Levi could not understand the attraction) and the joys of cycling round Piedmont. Levi said he had courted Lucia by bike and he seemed boyishly proud of his bicycle courtship. 'My impression was of a very tender relationship,' remembered Servadio. During the meal Levi often turned, smiling, to Lucia; here was a couple who had come through hard times together – and who were happier, as always, when away from 75 Corso Re Umberto.

Philip Roth was waiting for Levi at 39 Belgrave Square, the Italian Cultural Institute, where Primo was to talk later that evening. Passersby might have been struck by the contrast between the New Jersey-born Roth, tall and aristocratically thin, and the short and slight Levi. There were fifteen years between them; Roth, the droll recorder of American Jewishness, was in many ways an odd match for Levi. Levi was quite unprepared for what he found in Roth, who turned out to be an engagingly gentle man. Roth, for his part, found Levi unexpectedly accessible. 'With some people you just *unlock* – and Levi was one of them,' Roth told me in 1994. Levi could hardly have found a more willing listener, and for an hour inside the Institute they chatted enthusiastically. Roth was somehow able to break through Levi's customary guard, and as they said goodbye Levi said to the American author: 'You know, this has all come too late.' Only later did Roth detect a prophetic note in the remark. That Wednesday, after their meeting, Roth was exalted and took himself on a long walk with Gaia Servadio round Belgrave Square. 'Philip said how "wonderful" Levi was – I think he called him a "holy man" – and what a marvellous meeting it had been.'

At 6:30 pm at the Italian Cultural Institute Levi gave his talk 'From the Lab to the Writer's Desk'. No one there could forget the awful crush as people were turned back into Belgrave Square; under the fire regulations anyone standing had to be asked to leave. But no one did. Levi had requested that Servadio act as his interpreter and she was happy to oblige, even though her English was less exacting, she said, than Levi's. (Presumably Levi just liked to have her as a reassuringly familiar face.) The audience listened rapt as he spoke of science and literature. There was no incompatibility between the Two Cultures, he insisted, only 'mutual attraction'. Levi looked a little nervous, I remember, his manner hesitant, but when he had finished he momentarily regarded the packed room, then gave the most brilliant, charming smile. 'It was as if the sun had come out,' recalled one of the audience.

In the reception rooms upstairs drinks and canapés were served. Levi was manoeuvred into signing copies of *If Not Now, When?* and first in the queue

495

was the late British military historian Richard Lamb, who had been chief liaison officer between the 8th Army and the Italian partisans. Lamb remembered that Levi spoke a cultured, 'sort of donnish Italian' and that he looked somewhat 'careworn and anxious'. In fact, Levi was disappointed that Lord Dainton, the Yorkshire chemist, had failed to turn up as expected. Mike Petty, Levi's British paperback publisher, was keen to show Levi a proof of the cover of *The Periodic Table* and he hovered, clutching the sample jacket, before managing to introduce himself. Levi said he liked the design, but vigorously objected to the *Washington Post* quotation, which described his book as 'mystical'. He did not like the suggestion of 'irrational' in that word 'mystical' and asked Petty to remove it. While they spoke, Petty became aware of a knot of people at Levi's elbow. 'As I said my farewells and stepped aside, it was apparent that something rather extraordinary was happening: there were rapid bursts of Italian, and a distinct sense of heightened emotion.'

In fact they were the friends and family of Vivienne Zinober, among them her children Laurence and Tamara, her brother Alan, and her husband Chaim Joffe. The family were not Italians at all, but had roots in South Africa. They closed round Levi and for twenty minutes fired questions at him about their uncle Gerhard Goldbaum. Deafened by the cocktail-party chatter, Levi tried to give the family every recollection he could. They seemed distressed, especially Tamara, who refused to accept that an 'evil Nazi' like Ferdinand Meyer had in any way helped her uncle. Earnestly Levi tried to explain to her that Meyer was not a heinous Nazi but a typically 'ambiguous grey character'. If Tamara was upset, the fault was partly Levi's. One of the grating assumptions of 'Vanadium' is that Meyer (disguised in the chapter as 'Müller') was some sort of ex-Himmlerian concentration-camp jailor, when he was nothing of the sort. Vivienne Zinober managed to hand Levi a gift of a blue mohair scarf and a card thanking him for his time. But her state of mind on leaving the Belgravia salon was exceedingly disturbed, and she returned to Bristol with a host of unanswered questions.

Levi's lecture had been very much praised, and afterwards the Italian Cultural Institute's director, Dr Alessandro Vaciago, arranged for him and Lucia to dine at the Garrick. This London club, with its grandiose stairwell, was not quite to Levi's modest taste, but even more unfortunate was the company. Lady Powell, the flamboyant Italian wife of Margaret Thatcher's private secretary Charles Powell, was there. Another surprise guest was *La Repubblica*'s gossipy London correspondent Paolo Filo Della Torre. *La Repubblica*, with its pro-Arab slant and suspect anti-Semitism, was hardly Levi's favourite newspaper, and neither was the quasi-Fascist *Lo Specchio*, for which Della Torre had previously worked. These shiny Italians were exemplary of the 1980s Italy that Levi had come to dislike. In spite of the company, Levi was 'quite confident' at the dinner table, recalled Sheila Murphy, 'and even dominated the conversation from time to time'. Luckily he asked if he might bring Laura Lepschy along, and Dr Vaciago offered no objection. Lepschy was the daughter of the legendary Piedmont historian Arnaldo Momigliano. She taught at University College London and had Jewish relatives in Turin who knew Levi well. In the Garrick Levi was glad of her unpretentious company. And at the end of the dinner, when he said goodbye, he suggested that they meet again on his next visit to London. Sadly that visit never happened.

On Thursday Levi went on BBC *Woman's Hour*. Sue MacGregor, the presenter, paid him the highly unusual compliment of welcoming him personally at BBC reception. The ten-minute interview went well, and Levi responded gently to MacGregor's questions. Listening to the tape of the broadcast today, Levi's voice is beautiful: the fraction of a pause, the flowing answer. According to Sarah Murphy, he was tempted to relate yesterday's encounter with the Zinobers and the story of their uncle, but refrained in case the family might be listening to the radio and feel exploited. Instead (since this was *Woman's Hour*) he touched on the unique role played by women in the Soviet anti-Nazi Resistance. 'Women were chosen as pilots on account of their light weight.' Levi also gave radio interviews on the BBC World Service and Radio Two, and the most remarkable thing about this fairly heavy programme was his unhurried serenity. In London time passed quickly and enjoyably for him.

Next day, 18 April, Sheila Murphy picked the Levis up at Durrants Hotel. They spent the morning at the Institute of Contemporary Arts, where in a cramped upstairs room Levi was interviewed by the Channel Four editor Michael Kustow. The audience was appreciative and throughout the recorded dialogue Levi was amusing company and relaxed. Kustow's impression then was of a 'slightly effeminate, catlike' man, with something angelic about his appearance. Kustow admired, but did not like, *If Not Now, When?* Nevertheless Levi spoke engagingly about the novel. Only the other week he had been astonished to find aspects of it mirrored in a real-life partisan memoir, *A Voice From the Forest*. The author, Nahum Kohn, was a small-town Polish watchmaker, exactly like Levi's fictional partisan hero Mendel. 'Art imitating life!' exclaimed Kustow. 'Yes, yes!' laughed Levi. The rest of the conversation ranged over Levi's other books and preoccupations, including his friendship with the recently deceased Italo Calvino. What emerged was a fascinating dialogue, easily the most impressive of Levi's London dates. Levi was talking to a man who himself talked a good deal – and this record comes as near as anything to the way Levi talked with friends.

> KUSTOW: Your books grow out of the Jewish European experience of being the underdog
>
> LEVI: I was never an underdog.
>
> KUSTOW: But you were in Auschwitz . . .
>
> LEVI: The ones *below* me were the underdogs. I kept my human abilities. I never sank that far. Underdogs lost the capacity to speak, to articulate. An underdog would never be likely to write anything.
>
> KUSTOW: But you have the knowledge of what being an underdog means. Other writers don't.
>
> LEVI: Perhaps . . .

Philip Roth was expected to attend the ICA talk, but changed his mind at the last minute for fear of being recognised ('like the President of the United States,' joked Gaia Servadio). Instead, Roth's actress partner Claire Bloom came. According to Sheila Murphy, Bloom handed Levi a long letter from Roth, which astounded and delighted him. Having met Levi and read more of his work, Roth now said he wanted to interview him in Turin for the *New York Times*. Levi considered this letter most significant. An interview with Philip Roth might help to catapult him into literary fame beyond New York, and perhaps remedy the grievance caused him by *Commentary*. (Levi knew that Roth was deeply out of sympathy with *Commentary* and that his grievance had been sardonically vented in several of his novels.) Claire Bloom, who had not then read any of Levi's books, found that he had 'considerable charm'. In 1994 she told me:

> Most of all I remember his expressive and unforgettably beautiful eyes. Oddly, they reminded me of Charlie Chaplin's. Chaplin also had these incredibly beautiful childlike eyes. Levi's were clear and full of curiosity and life. Jean Rhys also had eyes like that – they're *childlike*, I say, and they remain with you until you die. Funnily enough Levi reminded me of Chaplin in other ways

498

– they were about the same height and build – but in Primo's case, there was also a deep wound, which I intuited from those *eyes*.

6

London had been far less of a whirlwind tour than America, and on the whole Levi enjoyed his seven days there. The city, he reported to Sheila Murphy, 'is endowed with all the gifts of an illustrious past combined with modern efficiency'. He had liked the red pillar boxes, the red buses and black cabs; its anonymity and reserve reminded him a little of Turin. Lucia, who had never been to London before, had found it a 'delicious' city, even under the April showers. The Institute of Contemporary Arts failed to impress her, but the Wallace Collection, with its French furniture, sculpture and objets d'art was a delight. To Murphy, Primo Levi wrote later:

> As I told you, it was the first time I had the opportunity to pay the town something more than a fleeting busy visit . . . We have found ourselves surrounded by sympathetic, intelligent, discreet people: starting of course with yourself, and with your so nice namesake [Sarah Murphy]. I feel thankful to everyone at Michael Joseph, and especially to you, for much of the pleasure we took in London has come from your personal engagement . . . Many, many thanks, and fondest wishes.

Levi's travels for that April were not quite over. On the 20th he and Lucia left London for Stockholm. Their flight was delayed and in the Heathrow departure lounge Sheila Murphy craved for a cigarette; previously she had refrained from smoking in case the Levis disapproved, but she could stand it no more. As she lit up the Levis chorused '*Finalmente!*' before taking out their own menthol 'Alaska' brand. Amid laughter, Lucia presented Murphy with a bottle of Miss Dior perfume, the Levis' parting gift to an engaging, warm-hearted woman.

The Levis arrived at Arlanda airport, Stockholm, late on Sunday night, exhausted and unhappy. The days of interviews in London and the stress of lecturing in English had taken their toll, and Levi was suddenly moody and irritable. Professor Mario Nati, director of Stockholm's Italian Cultural Institute, had arranged a two-night stay for the Levis in the city. Levi was now feeling acutely guilty at having abandoned his mother in Turin, and when Nati showed him and Lucia into their room at the Hotel Diplomat, Levi spoke of his '*madre malferma*'. An embarrassed silence fell as Nati did

499

not know what to say. Levi had surely begun to hate this ailing mother of his, who burdened him so. He wanted to flee Ester, and he was ashamed of himself for it.

Levi's reputation in Sweden was not high; only his Yiddish partisan novel had been translated there. Nevertheless much of literary Stockholm came to hear him talk at the Italian Cultural Institute on the evening of 21 April, and when Levi stepped on to the podium the applause was warm. Dressed smartly in a dark blue wool suit, he smiled weakly and then read from a prepared text, 'Beyond Survival'. Ingrid Börge, his Swedish translator, was in the audience and she could see immediately that something was wrong. Quite apart from Levi's 'tired' – even at times 'frightened' – expression, he was patently irritated with the efforts of his simultaneous translator, Tom Johanneson, whose Italian was not adequate to the task. So Levi read 'rapidly' and 'monotonously' from his manuscript, Börge recalled. 'But even before he started he had asked the director to tell the audience (remember the hall was full) that he would not answer any questions afterwards. Many of Levi's admirers were extremely disappointed. You got the feeling he wanted only to get it all done with as soon as possible. He came across as ungracious.' Levi was sinking into another depressive episode.

He was far from animated at dinner afterwards in Stockholm's fashionable Valentino restaurant. Indeed, he lacked concentration and seemed jittery; his hosts could see that the meal was not a success. Levi's Swedish publisher, Karl Otto Bonnier, Ingrid Börge and the writer Bengt Holmqvist all noticed his withdrawn, sad air. Next day Levi had little time to see 'fascinating but icy' Stockholm. Kaj Schueler hurriedly interviewed him for *Svenska Dagbladet* before he and Lucia visited Skansen Park with its grey rocks and silver birches. In the torrential rain they watched the royal guard change on the palace terrace. Levi liked what he saw of this well-scrubbed, northerly city, and later told Bonnier that he and Lucia 'hoped to come back again as tourists as soon as possible'.

7

The Levis were home on 22 April and the following week Levi received, as expected, a visit from his New York publisher Arthur Samuelson. The visit did not go as well as Samuelson would have liked. He had bought hardback rights to *Survival in Auschwitz* and the equally mistitled *The Reawakening*. Federal Trade Regulations had prevented him from restoring the books' original titles (*If This is a Man, The Truce*), but Levi's greatest disappointment was not over the titles. He had tried to convince Samuelson that the English translations of those books were in need of revision, but Samuelson had objected that it was cheaper to reproduce the old texts, and refused to alter so much as a comma. Levi did not want to argue with Samuelson as he was easily his most powerful American publisher. Over drinks, Samuelson asked about *The Double Bond*. The book sounded wonderful to him, and Levi said that writing it afforded him some 'solace' from domestic anxieties. Those anxieties were plain to Samuelson. 'Everything seemed too much to Levi, physically too much, every minute.' Levi was now a world figure in literature – ranking with the Ecos and Bellows who had championed him – and invitations poured in for him to attend conferences, seminars, launch parties. How to cope? Levi showed Samuelson the carefully drawn charts that he vainly hoped would keep track of his publishing endeavours round the world. During supper Samuelson tried to lure Levi back to America on a promotional tour of *The Monkey's Wrench*, but Levi had already given his answer: his place was at home, with his mother.

On 2 May Levi was settling back into a routine in Turin when Italy was put on a radiation alert. The Chernobyl cloud, travelling from the Ukraine, had reached Italian shores. Levi was feeling low anyway but the radiation threat prompted him to write an exceptionally bleak article for *La Stampa*, 'The Plague Has No Limit', about the danger of nuclear fallout. Levi's fear was real enough: 'Chernobyl has been not only a tragedy, but a terrifying message,' he wrote to Anthony Rudolf in London. And he went on Italian television to denounce in equal measure Soviet and Western coverage of the catastrophe: the Russians culpably underplayed the dangers, the West exaggerated them. Meanwhile Turin came under a torrent of rain, the sky turned lead-grey, as Levi translated for Anthony Rudolf apocalyptic verse by Leopardi: 'The Moon is very likely to crash one day in your field!'

During his withdrawn moods Levi found relief in playing chess on his Apple Mac and in the abstract pleasures of word games. At night he composed teasingly difficult palindromes – words or phrases that read the same backwards and forwards – as they helped with his insomnia. Calvino had introduced him to the riddles and associated verbal play of the quasi-Surrealist French literary group 'OuLiPo' and Levi derived much alphabetical fun and nonsense from their word games. On his computer he designed lexical and pictorial nonsense puzzles (rebuses) for publication in *La Stampa*. He did not want his name put to them – they were 'frivolous', he said – so the paper published them anonymously.

Giampaolo Dossena, one of *La Stampa*'s senior editors, encouraged Levi to submit other puzzles. He offered the sort of intellectual companionship that Levi had always enjoyed, unhampered by publisher's demands or rivalries. Dossena was amused to hear Levi say that he had always been unconsciously 'guilty' of wordplay. A student ('naturally a German') had written a doctoral thesis, 'Alliterations in the Works of Primo Levi', and sent him a copy for his enjoyment. After that, Levi said he had lost his 'unselfconscious innocence' as a writer. When Dossena called on Levi that spring he found him subdued, if healthy-looking, in a Lacoste sports shirt, smoking his usual menthols. Lucia came in with chocolates, more cigarettes and coffee. It was then that discussion came round to the rumours of the Nobel Prize that were still emanating from Stockholm. Levi joked that the award (worth £650,000) might help pay for the nurses who now looked after his mother twenty-four hours a day. Everything continued to revolve round Ester.

Another friend whom Levi saw at this difficult time was the legendary Tuscan-born publisher Bianca Tallone, whose printing press was the finest in all Piedmont, if not Europe. Levi liked to visit the press. To reach it he drove south through Turin's unlovely suburbs to Alpignano; in Tallone's huge garden were two antique steam locomotives, which Levi said reminded him of his post-war Soviet repatriation trains. Tallone's conduct with Levi was delightfully unpredictable; when the mood came on, she might suddenly offer him a glass of grappa or lemon syrup from Elba. Over the years Levi had become quite intimate with Tallone; aware of her interest in Dante, he liked to recite to her from the *Inferno*. Levi came chiefly to watch the compositors and pressmen at work and, typically, was fascinated by the artisanal mechanics of layout and letter-setting. As Tallone recalled: 'Primo took a chemist's relish in the plants and pigments we use to make our inks, and took a dim view of modern chemical-based inks which, Primo said, quickly lost their lustre.' Above all, Levi admired the typographic grace of Tallone publications and said of her *Pinocchio*: 'That's perfection!' He promptly bought a copy for 230,000 lire (about £150). Tallone thought Levi had changed greatly in this period and noted with concern his 'sad and tormented' look. She believed that her printing laboratory became a sanctuary for him in his depression.

8

During these weeks and into the summer, Levi, though often feeling low, did a little writing and continued to go on walks with friends. On 23 May he was in a warehouse on the outskirts of Turin to watch a stage version of *The Wrench*. Against all expectations he enjoyed it immensely. Previously he had not hesitated to tell the director Flavio Ambrosini his view that the Tino Faussone stories were not stageworthy. He had been so reluctant to help that one day Ambrosini had to extract him from the American Club, where he found Levi trying to lift weights. From the start, Ambrosini's intention had been to stage a Mel Brooks-style spectacular with minstrel jazz bands, *Cabaret* chanteuses, pantomime palm trees and monkeys. The actors were all amateur enthusiasts from the Italian equivalent of British Telecom, known as SIP. As soon as Levi arrived at the Corso Palermo warehouse he went to the box-office to buy himself a ticket. 'For heavens sake! You're the author!' an usher intervened, and led Levi to a front-row seat in the wings. But before the first act could begin, Levi had to come forward in response to the audience. With a shy bow he gratefully accepted a SIP company poster of the play and spread his arms out wide in a gesture of resignation. By the interval he was already feeling jubilant: a video-recording of the performance shows him craning forward on his seat and beaming boyishly. 'I can honestly tell you that Levi *cried* with happiness,' said Ambrosini.

Levi's wretchedness seemed to wear off briefly in the spring air, and on 26 May he went to collect a Turin Lions Club gold medal for having 'asserted and diffused in his books the rights and dignity of Man'. Levi was out of sympathy with these quasi-masonic rotary organisations with their ceremonial swords and silver trophy cups, but the Lions president-to-be, Guglielmo Lanza, was an old 'M. D'Azeglio' classmate and Levi did not want to disappoint him. On the morning of the presentation Lanza called on Levi to see how he was. Levi said he was worried about what to wear and had no 'black tie'. Lanza told him not to worry. As Levi got himself ready, there ensued a conversation about literary fame. Lanza, a pious, upright man, was shocked to hear Levi say he no longer cared for it. Pointing to the endless rows of his books in Romanian, Japanese, Finnish, he said: 'They mean nothing to me now.' Once, a new translation had been cause for celebration, but now it left him indifferent. In an effort to cheer Levi, Lanza took him to see the Lions Club president, Romolo Tosetto, a garrulous, well-meaning lawyer-friend who could be relied on to perk up the most downhearted. For half an hour Tosetto lavished Levi with unstinting praise and said he wished he could write as well as he. Levi thought Tosetto would never stop and, on leaving his house, said to Lanza in a deadpan voice: 'I don't know if your friend can write, but he certainly knows how to talk.' Later that day, more panegyrics issued from Tosetto as he hung a Lions Club gold medal on Levi in Turin's Lascaris Palace. To the assembled Lions and Lionesses, Levi said: 'I'm very lucky', then sat down again.

In June 1986 Levi's essay collection on the Nazi camps, *The Drowned and the Saved,* was published. This is the book in which Levi's memorial and moral obligations to the past are most thoroughly exercised, where the hardest questions are asked. In pained but lucid prose, Levi seeks to understand the nature of contemporary barbarism, and to explain to the world once more his mission to bear witness. At the book's terrible heart is a warning to those who deliver facile judgments of condemnation: only those who have survived the camps have the right to forgive or condemn, and even they are not properly fit to do so, for those who fathomed the depths of human degradation did not come back to tell the tale. For the cover, Levi chose a detail from Hans Memling's medieval altarpiece, *The Universal Judgement.* Here the damned, naked and howling in a Dantesque hell-pit, reveal the terror of the Christian revelation. Enrica Melossi of Einaudi's art department had never seen a more grave or gruesome cover, but Levi produced a book of Memling colour plates and said the Flemish *massa damnationis* was about the most frightening picture he had ever seen, and was perfect for the book. It certainly conveyed the awfulness of what he was writing about.

The book amplifies and deepens much of *If This is a Man* (a chapter in which was indeed 'The Drowned and the Saved'), but this time Levi writes of other people's experience of persecution, not his own. In the darkest and most painfully argued essay, 'The Grey Zone', he investigates the question of Jewish and non-Jewish prisoners who were forced to collaborate, to varying degrees, with the authorities in order to survive. In return for clothes and food, the Auschwitz Special Squads (*Sonderkommandos*) had to shepherd fellow Jews to the gas chambers. To implicate others in their corruption was, for Levi, the Nazis' unique moral crime. One may ask what drew Levi to this awful task of raking over his own torment and that of other survivors. It was not an 'obsession with evil' (as one Catholic Italian critic, Lorenzo Mondo, suggested) or some quasi-religious impulse towards disburdening a weight. The chief reason why Levi wrote *The Drowned and the Saved* was simply a need to 'know' and to 'understand'. Those two verbs, in Italian *conoscere* and *capire,* puncture the text regularly. And there was a another reason why Levi wrote the essays, one that goes to the heart of our moral history. He wanted to combat the tide of historical revisionism and to speak, for one last time, to the young. Memory, said Levi, is a gift, but also a duty.

The Drowned and the Saved is a more argumentative, tortured and sceptical book than its predecessor of 1947. *If This is a Man* had been written by a twenty-eight-year-old; these essays were by a man in his mid-sixties. Levi could no longer face up to things with the youthfulness and resilience of a newly married man in his late twenties. If the writing of *If This is a Man* had been regenerative – a journey from pain to consolation – *The Drowned and the Saved* had offered no such cathartic effect. Why? At the war's end Levi had been filled with a bright-eyed faith in history and the perfectibility of man. It seemed inconceivable to him, then, that humanity could commit a greater atrocity than Auschwitz. Germany had been punished and carved in two; Primo Levi was on the winner's side. Now he was not so sure. Almost half a century on, Nietzsche's 'festival of human cruelty' was far from over. The world that Levi once took to be so reformed after the war was in fact built on very shaky ground. In these essays Levi turns an appalled eye on the massacres in the Middle East and on Pol Pot's Cambodia, where one-third of the population had been exterminated for a fanatical ideal. While Levi never found an answer to the question of why the Nazi slaughter had occurred, he concluded that man essentially was brutal.

Italian critics spoke of a discomforting, tenebrous work that offered few consolations. Some marvelled at Levi's exacting and industrious memory and at how much he was able to withstand, and understand of the camps. Levi was sixty-six and had lived with Auschwitz for forty-two years, an amazingly long time. Yet the book occasioned surprisingly few reviews and hardly any interviews. Nor did it win any first-division literary prizes. Most reviewers saw the book merely as a supplement to Levi's primary accounts of the camps, and failed to appreciate its terrible importance. In fact, *The Drowned and the Saved* is the masterwork of late Primo Levi – in Piedmontese, his *caplavòr* – and stands as a great work of ethical meditation. For Levi was a moralist in a school where Montaigne and Manzoni were his fellows. As matters turned out, *The Drowned and the Saved* was to be Levi's last completed work, although he had planned to write a sequel that would investigate the German industries (BASF, Siemens, Bayer) involved in the Nazi camps.

It is not true that Levi turned to unprecedently bleak themes in *The Drowned and the Saved* or, as some romantic critics like to believe, that a wave of shame and pessimism had washed over him. Bianca Guidetti Serra first heard the words 'grey zone' from Levi in 1946. 'Right from the beginning,' she told me in 1992, 'there was always this problem of understanding what had happened and why men had behaved in the way they did. *The Drowned and the Saved* could just as easily have been Primo's first book as his last book.' A corrosive feeling of shame had accompanied Levi in varying degrees for most of his life; it had not suddenly overwhelmed him in his last years. As long ago as 1955, in his article 'Anniversary of the Deportees', he had confessed to his overwhelming *'vergogna'* – shame – at belonging to the same species that had built Auschwitz. A quarter of a century later, in 1980, Levi confessed to the Tuscan novelist Gian Luigi Piccioli his guilt that he had in some way collaborated with the Nazis, for they had 'pardoned' him by virtue of the fact that he was an industrial chemist. Levi's guilt that others had died in his place, that he was alive thanks to a privilege he had not earned, stayed with him. 'I know my guilt is quite unjustified,' he said to Piccioli, 'but I can't clear it from my conscience.'

Levi's unidentified antagonist in *The Drowned and the Saved* is Bruno Vasari, a large, dignified man, and chairman of the Turin branch of the National Association of Ex-Deportees (ANED). Vasari's chronicle of his survival in Mauthausen camp, *Bivouac of Death,* had been published in Italy in August 1945. Levi admired it, and he often called on Vasari in Turin. He was a courtly reminder of former times, dressed in dark suits that had been fashionable years ago. Vasari believed that ex-deportees had survived the Nazi camps not by cunning or brutality but by force of their virtue – *per belle virtù.* Those who survived – the 'saved' – were the best, according to Vasari. In *The Drowned and the Saved* Levi appears to claim the opposite. The good, 'the drowned', died; the bad, the 'saved', survived. And one feels the weight of this distinction – signalled by the book's Dantesque title – on every page. The belief that the 'best' died long ago is commonly heard among older Italians (with a sad shake of the head they say, *'Ah, i migliori sono quelli che muoiono'*). Levi extends this pitilessly to include all Auschwitz survivors.

Some Italian survivors felt they did not deserve this – they had suffered enough – but many others were glad of *The Drowned and the Saved.* The book was Levi's declaration of allegiance to the theme that mattered most to them: the Nazi camps. For forty years they had looked up to Levi as a guiding light and advocate of their cause, but he had written science fiction and (to them) other such frivolities. In 1969 Levi had written to the Italian survivor and Catholic poet Giorgio Chiesura that 'by now it is impossible to write anything further on the camps'. By abandoning the survivors' cause, it seemed to Chiesura that Levi had renounced his moral integrity, and in disgust he vowed never to read Levi again. So *The Drowned and the Saved* was like a peal of thunder for Chiesura – Levi had resumed his duty to bear witness to Nazism.

10

In June 1986, immediately after publication of *The Drowned and the Saved,* the Kurt Waldheim affair flared up. The senior Austrian politician was found to have lied about his wartime anti-Jewish activities. He was not a monster, but merely dubious. On 12 June Levi spoke at the launch of *The Drowned and the Saved* at the Einaudi Bookshop in Milan. Devotees had queued in the rain for the privilege of meeting him, but he was in a foul mood. Earlier that day in *La Repubblica* the famously truculent journalist, Giorgio Bocca, had tried to exonerate Waldheim by quoting from 'The Grey Zone' in the Austrian's defence. No love was lost between Levi and Bocca. The journalist, with his prize-fighter's face, was seen by many cultivated Turinese as a career antagonist. First he had been a Fascist, then a partisan, and now he was periodically accused of anti-Semitism. As far as Bocca was concerned, Levi was a totem of Turin's over-refined bourgeois elite and what he called the 'presumptuous intellectualism' of the Einaudi circle. 'I never found Levi very congenial – he was haughty and impatient of any kind of vulgarity or stupidity.' Perhaps there is some truth in Bocca's remark.

Survivors in the audience, angrily brandishing the day's *La Repubblica*, accused Levi of being ready to forgive ex-Wehrmacht Lieutenant Waldheim. 'Bocca has twisted my words,' Levi said, pale-faced and trembling. Teresa Azzali, a Catholic survivor, approached Levi in the Einaudi Bookshop: 'He seemed sort of glassy-eyed and stupefied – joyless.' Levi spoke to Azzali of the 'fatigue of living' and then said in a quiet voice: 'Who knows why I'm like this?' His mood that evening is confirmed by the novelist Oreste Del Buono, who was struck by Levi's severe and almost painful sensitivity to Bocca's article: 'Primo must have been low to react in the way he did.' As the bookshop emptied, Levi confessed to Del Buono his fear that he was 'losing his mind'. When a telephone call had come through from America the other day, Levi said, he found to his horror that he was unable to speak English. What he feared was not a simple loss of memory, but a loss of mind that might be irreversible, suggested Del Buono.

Later that evening in Milan, Levi had supper with Luciana Nissim at her flat in Via dei Chiostri. Nissim could see that Levi was overwrought by the to-do about Bocca, and made a point of soothing him. The situation was a little touchy, however, as Bocca was friendly with Nissim's husband, the economist Franco Momigliano. Nissim did her best to reassure Levi that Bocca had meant no harm.

TWENTY-EIGHT

The Downward Spiral
1986–7

I

The summer of 1986, which turned out to be Primo Levi's last, was marked by illness. He again suffered what he called in Italian 'St Anthony's Fire' (shingles), this time on his chest; then he developed ulcerations on his feet. What influence these painful conditions had on the months ahead we can only guess. Levi's neuroses seemed to be multiplying like germs, and he was often morbidly fascinated by them. He did not have Alzheimer's, as he had feared, but at the age of sixty-six neither was his memory what it once was. Other fears settled on Levi. *The Drowned and the Saved* was in the bookshops, but Levi was full of self-doubt about his abilities as a writer and uncertain what to work on next. He busied himself with a variety of distractions, agreed to judge a literary prize, and tried to get out of the house when he could. On 18 June he met his old physics professor, Nicolò Dallaporta, at a lecture in Turin entitled 'Hypothesis of a World Without Chemistry'. Polite greetings were exchanged as they spoke of their families and children. Levi confessed his sorrow that he might never be allowed to practise the 'art' of being a grandfather. With grandchildren, Levi might have felt he had more to live for. (His son Renzo is now a father.) When the sculptor Sandro Lupano became a grandfather the previous year, Levi had told him enviously: 'It must be hard work, Sandro, but such *lovely* hard work!'

Plans were adopted, then dropped. Levi had agreed to provide the voice-over for an Israeli documentary on Polish Jews under Hitler, *The Eighty-First Blow*. The recording equipment was set up in Turin, but at the last moment Levi withdrew. 'It's my mother,' he explained. Ester had difficulty walking and was often depressed herself, her moods seemingly alternating with those of her son.

Levi began to read Philip Roth's irreverent 'Zuckerman Trilogy', and looked forward to meeting Roth in Turin as planned. Roth's verbal fury and inventive energy were unlike anything Levi had encountered. The American's freedom in writing about sex excited and alarmed Levi; he admired his flouting of convention and broad literary tastes. Roth had long championed such undervalued writers of East Europe as Ivan Klima and Milan Kundera, and his attraction to Levi was part of this same wide-ranging curiosity for what lay beyond America. Levi instructed his New York publishers to send Roth galleys of *The Monkey's Wrench*. And in his letter to Roth of 1 June he made a great show of being swamped by work:

> I have been obliged to abandon temporarily Zuckerman because I am (for the last time in my life, I swear) in the jury of the Viareggio Prize, and am supposed to digest a novel plus a poetry collection per day for all the current month. This is a soul-destroying task, plugging all filters and poisoning all catalysts. Never more! Warmest regards to Claire [Bloom] and to you.

One of the most peculiar aspects of this summer was the devotion Levi showed not only to his readers but also to would-be writers. He always answered his fanmail and managed to be kind even to the tiresome. For example, on receiving from Massimo Cortini in Naples some complimentary remarks about his science fiction, he wrote: 'It's lovely to have letters like yours: they reassure me and give me hope that I have not written in vain.' Similarly when literary aspirants sent Levi their manuscripts, he usually read and commented on them. His chief effort now was on behalf of Mario Macagno, a Turin-born mechanic, amateur fossil-collector, ex-partisan and hopeful writer. Suspecting that Levi would be sympathetic to a literary underdog and outsider, Macagno asked him on the telephone if he would look at his poems. Something in Macagno's voice told Levi this was not the usual nuisance caller, and a few days later he sent him this morale-boosting letter:

> Dear Macagno,
>   Now let me explain to you why I hesitated when you offered to send me your poems. Each week I receive two or three helpings of verse, and most of it comes from deranged types (so many of them are young!) or is simply vacuous. Now, though your poems are very melancholy, I read them with relief. Here and there they'll need a few finishing touches, but they have real substance and, best of all, they are clearly not the work of a so-called

professional writer . . . I'm sure you'll have a lot more things to say, certainly you have the *means* to say it. Thank you for choosing me as your judge.

Levi's judgment proved sound, and Macagno was soon a published poet. As the summer advanced, Levi urged him to try his hand at short stories. 'If I say you can write it's because I *know* you're capable: remember that I'm more interested in *content* than form.' A month later Macagno left a sheaf of his stories with the concierge at 75 Corso Re Umberto; Levi was amazed by what he read. Macagno's prose had the guileless freshness of the amateur – and something of the awkwardness, too – yet this awkwardness was also endearing. On 30 June Levi sent him another encouraging letter: 'You have much to say about work, mountains, motor cars, women, and maybe about other things of which I know nothing.' There followed a series of commonsensical if rather patronising instructions: 'You *must* learn to distinguish between details which are necessary, or even merely curious, and ones which are superfluous.' If Levi was superior with Macagno, he was loyal to him, and noted with 'pleasure' that he had 'improved' his story-telling. At the same time he warned Macagno not to become too literary and to eschew belletristic politeness. The advice paid off: Macagno's short stories were published, though sadly five years after Levi died.

2

At the beginning of July Levi was in the Waldensian valleys, promoting *The Drowned and the Saved* in the small town of Pinerolo. The openness with which he answered questions from the audience in the Town Hall did not suggest depression: Levi was deft at hiding his state from others. Marino Revelli, a chemistry graduate whom he had not seen for forty years, turned up, and Levi's delight at seeing him was plain. Though he had never met Marino's wife Luisa, he signed them a copy of his book: 'To Luisa and Marino, with ancient and affectionate friendship.' The dedication was proof perhaps of Levi's warm good company that night. Afterwards he dined in Pinerolo with David Terracini, the son of the sculptor Roberto Terracini who had taught Anna Maria Levi to sculpt. Again, the spiritual malaise that had afflicted Levi in recent months was not apparent to Terracini; he testified to Levi's cheerfulness and wholehearted good company. As matters turned out, Pinerolo was to be Levi's last public appearance.

His mother was increasingly infirm and burdensome on him. Though Lucia had retired, much of her time was taken up caring for her own mother. Levi's daughter, Lisa, lived in another part of the Crocetta and reportedly saw little of her brother Renzo, or her parents. Renzo, now twenty-nine, was a biophysicist and busy with his career. He may have felt the need to get out from under his father's shadow; but, unlike Lisa, had managed only to move to a flat next door. It is unlikely that Levi was able to apply to him for much help, however, as Ester wanted only Primo. Even so, Renzo cannot have failed to feel family pressure, especially where his father's mental health was concerned.

As the summer advanced, Levi's home life turned more bleak. On 21 July he wrote an exceptionally dark letter to Paolo Andreocci, the journalist who had accompanied him to Sicily in 1980. Andreocci had praised the 'pricelessly valuable' *Drowned and the Saved*, but Levi was indifferent to his compliment, and told him so:

> I'm going through a very difficult period: family problems devour all my time. What you kindly refer to as 'pricelessly valuable' is for me no longer remotely valuable. I have no idea when – even *if* – I shall ever be able to write again. I can't make any promises. But if I don't write to you, it won't be because of a 'veil of silence', but because of a *non possumus*.

Levi was upset by the recent deaths of Emil Davidovic and Liko Israel, concentration-camp comrades, but his sorrow was not confined to them. News that the Sicilian writer Leonardo Sciascia had cancer of the bone marrow was a further blow. At the end of the summer, however, a personal disaster occurred that left Levi a permanently changed and bleaker man. On the morning of 27 July, after eight years of Alzheimer's disease, Ada Della Torre died; she was seventy-one. The part of her brain that still functioned said 'Why me?', but as Ada's self-control began to leave her, so she had become more aggressive and confused. In the end Ada could not even write her name. Levi had known her since 1942 and was devastated. The Sunday she died he published in *La Stampa* a short story, 'Force Majeure', which might have been an allegory of Auschwitz, or a story about the shame of being a victim, or just one man's despair at having to live at all. In this parable of gratuitous pain, an intellectual referred to in Kafka fashion as M ('Michele' was Levi's middle name) is waylaid in an alley by a thug and savagely beaten. Lying on his face trampled, M is dimly aware that he will 'never be the same man as before'. But the next day came a more terrible blow.

On the Monday morning of 28 July, three days short of Levi's sixty-seventh birthday, his mother collapsed at home from a stroke. The accident brought Levi to a crisis in his feelings about himself and his future; with his mother most likely to be paralysed, he feared being left stranded. Though he was a grown man, he was dependent on his mother's approval and his wife's help round the house. Levi's filial infantilism (as a psychiatrist might call it) now deepened. The slack summer season, when most Italians go on holiday, he and his wife would have to spend at home in Turin taking care of their mothers. Ester Levi was now ninety-one; Beatrice Morpurgo, ninety-five, was blind, and had trouble with her balance. A week before Ester's stroke, Levi had written this curiously prescient verse:

> Who stays in the city in August?
> Only the poor and the mad,
> Forgotten little old ladies.

Ester was in hospital for twenty days. The initial diagnosis – *ictus cerebrale* – showed that she was unlikely to regain full mobility and Levi wondered if she would even see home again. From his depressed point of view, Ester's ward seemed to be swarming with illness. During this time, Levi developed shingles. On 31 August, a month after his mother's stroke, he wrote the poem, 'The Fly', in which a bluebottle feeds on the plates of patients who 'can no longer eat'. As he had done so often in the past, Levi submitted the poem for publication in *La Stampa*, but this time with ill grace. 'Well, here's my contribution for August', he told the paper's poetry editor Giorgio Calcagno, tonelessly. By then it had been confirmed that Levi's mother had lost the use of her right arm and leg. Distraught, Levi visited her three times a day; she had difficulty speaking and her hopes of recovery, he said, were 'virtually nil'. To Alvin Rosenfeld of Indiana University he wrote: 'The future is completely obscure.' As matters turned out, Ester was to outlive her son by four years, dying on 21 December 1991, at the age of ninety-six.

While Levi despaired, Lucia devoted all her energies to nursing the old women. She had a genuine, caring purposefulness, and undoubtedly was good-hearted towards family members. But a part of her enjoyed the martyred sense of being put upon ('You who flay yourself a little every day,' Levi had written of Lucia in a poem). From the day they got married, Levi had made Lucia a prisoner in his own home: now she wanted her husband to know what a pass he had brought her to.

3

As his mother lay speechless in hospital, the ulcerations on Levi's feet broke out again. They were a long-term consequence of the chafing caused by primitive Auschwitz footwear. Levi sought medical help. His physiotherapist, Raffaella Pagani, was a grave, spiritually inclined thirty-year-old who liked to become involved in the lives of her patients. She had a melancholy attractiveness and wore her heavy brown hair cut short. By the time Levi came into her life, Pagani had been living in Turin for ten years (she was born in Stresa by Lake Maggiore.) Soon the gossips of Corso Re Umberto began to link Pagani's name to Levi's. Their affair was entirely platonic, though, and quite in keeping with Levi's many other asexual relations with women. Pagani lent a sympathetic ear to Levi's problems and brought all her instinctive and acquired knowledge of nursing to help him. Kneeling, she sponged his feet in water and passed an electric current through the ulcerations. While Levi disliked the role of saviour foisted on him by survivors, surely he luxuriated in Pagani's ministrations. No one else in these awful months allowed him to feel so special about himself. The sense of ministering not only to a concentration-camp survivor, but to a pillar of Italian letters, was not lost on Pagani. Levi had nine electrophoresis sessions with her; he never mentioned to her that he was married.

The treatment seemed to be successful, and as their friendship developed, Pagani spoke to Levi of her own depressions and suicide attempts as a teenager. Levi listened attentively. 'He neither condoned nor condemned suicide, but was non-committal,' she recalled. Emboldened, she began to show Levi her poems, which he admired, he said, for their confessionary tone and truthfulness. 'I was not really in love with Levi, but I will say this: Levi thought he'd found a daughter in me, and I thought I'd found a spiritual father in him. There was an edge of paternal tenderness to our relationship.' Levi, whose relations with his own daughter were often strained, was conducting a substitute father-daughter relationship outside the family. His old secretive nature was at work again.

The summer dragged on. Levi had no book in sight – his writing seemed hopelessly obstructed – and in July he told his old school sweetheart Lidia Carbonatto on the telephone: 'I've reached rock bottom'. In Britain at least his reputation was assured. In August he acquired a new editor at Michael Joseph. Susan Watt was formerly the fiancée of the KGB informer and *Daily Telegraph* Moscow correspondent Jeremy Wolfenden. Levi was intrigued by her, and on 20 August he replied to her queries about his mother and his difficult home life: 'No, unfortunately all is not well with us.'

4

By the autumn of 1986 Levi was again on anti-depressants, and was sleeping better; sleeping normally, he thought. During this brief period of relief, the first week of September, Philip Roth came to Turin with Claire Bloom. Roth immediately asked to be shown round Levi's old paint and varnish factory, and Levi was amused by the request, joking that SIVA was in fact the 'centre of Turin'. Paola Accati, Rico Accati's daughter, who was SIVA's new manager, chauffeured the well-known couple to the factory. Levi had preferred not to drive them there – 'I can't possibly drive and talk at the same time', he told Paola. He warned her not to mention *Portnoy's Complaint* to Roth, as the American was no longer so fond of his most famous novel. (Alexander Portnoy incidentally appears in Levi's short story 'In the Park' as a 'crass and whining' adolescent whom 'nobody could stand'.)

That Friday, 5 September, SIVA's staff were in holiday mood, and many of them had not seen Levi for years. Claire Bloom recalled that they were 'moved and delighted' by his presence. Levi was very high-spirited and entertaining as he showed his guests round the plant. In the laboratories he introduced Roth to Renato Portesi, and Portesi said how much he admired Roth's books. When Levi enquired which ones, Portesi blushingly admitted that he had not read any. An awkward silence followed before Levi hurried his guests on to the water decontamination tower. All this while, for his *New York Times* interview, Roth was writing down some of Levi's conversation, which amused him, especially when paint and literature was discussed. To Roth's knowledge, only two writers of importance had been managers of paint factories: Levi in Turin, Sherwood Anderson in Ohio. Levi, with an indulgent smile befitting his superior age, corrected him: 'I must add a third name, Italo Svevo, a converted Jew of Trieste.' (Svevo, who had been an English language pupil of James Joyce, specialised in anti-corrosive paints for ships' hulls.) Roth and Levi both being clever and eager to talk, a gentle rivalry developed in which Levi was pleased to teach and instruct the younger man.

Their wide-ranging conversation was resumed that evening at 75 Corso Re Umberto. The writers worked on the text of the interview together, later by questionnaire or by telephone, until it was tailored to fit the front page of the *New York Times Book Review*. A photographer came round to take their picture. Roth towered above the short-statured Levi, whom the American described as a 'little quicksilver woodland creature'. That evening Levi took Roth and his partner Bloom to a smart Turin restaurant where he was known to the owner. Roth noted that Levi declined to drink wine and correctly surmised that he was on anti-depressants (which can be harmful when taken with alcohol). 'Throughout the meal Levi was very charming – youthfully Pan-like, even perhaps a little girlish.' Roth's reference to effeminacy is characteristic: many others had noted Levi's delicate, slightly enervated side. It was in marked contrast to Roth's strong physical presence.

The writers had much to talk about, but when Roth asked Levi about his domestic situation, Levi suddenly looked small and frightened. His sense of entrapment and subservience to his mother disturbed Roth greatly. 'I've known some Jewish sons, but Levi's filial duty and devotion was stronger than anything I'd ever seen. There was a *pathetic* edge to it.' Levi made little effort to talk to Claire Bloom and when he did, he became so excruciatingly shy that his English, usually good, was tentative and stuttering: 'I'm sure Primo knew who I was,' said Bloom, 'but he asked me no questions about my acting career.' Of course Levi had done his homework (he always did) and knew that Bloom's first husband Rod Steiger had starred in the classic Italian thriller *Hands Over the City* by Francesco Rosi. While Levi talked to Roth, Lucia and Bloom looked on in virtual silence. Bloom explained to me why: 'When you're in the presence of two brilliant people, you don't want to open your mouth.' As for Lucia, she said almost nothing to Bloom, who had the impression that she was 'under some sort of cloud'. The meal ended early, as Levi said he had to get back to his mother.

Next day Levi showed his guests the Turin sights. They had been eating in the Caffè Fiorio off Via Po and afterwards walked to San Giovanni Cathedral to see the Holy Shroud; from there they turned east across Piazza Castello in the direction of the building where Nietzsche had completed *Ecco Homo* (and afterwards tearfully embraced a carthorse in the street: the German had syphilis). They proceeded to the Luxemburg Bookshop, whose owner Angelo Pezzana Levi had known since the early 1960s, when Pezzana's was the only outlet in Turin to stock English and American magazines, as well as gay literature. In readiness for the day's visit Pezzana had made a window display of audio books by Claire Bloom, among them her autobiography *Limelight and After*. In spite of his shyness with her, Levi clearly liked Bloom and after reading her autobiography he wrote to her admiringly: 'I really had no idea how much courage and belief in oneself are necessary to enter the world of the movies . . .'

Philip Roth was aware of an element of sadness – 'pathos', he called it – in Levi, but also found him tranquil. 'Not that Levi was the sort of person who emanates tranquillity and soothes you to sleep. The tranquillity I'm talking about was an *invigorating* tranquillity.' Unsurprisingly their parting in Turin, on Monday 8 September, was emotional; it had been a marvellous few days. And as the writers embraced they found themselves crying. In Roth's arms Levi said: 'I don't know which of us is the older brother, and which is the younger brother.' Levi had felt so close to Roth that he could speak of a blood tie. But he may also have had in mind worldly wisdom:

there were things that the younger Roth understood, which Levi did not know about, and the reverse was also true. Claire Bloom also cried at the parting. It was then that she recognised Levi as a 'candidate' (as she called it) for depression. In 1994 she told me:

> Something in the look of his eyes when he said goodbye will remain with me for the rest of my life. I don't exactly know what it was, but I *knew* something – and Primo *knew* I knew. A strange exchange, a sort of recognition of each other, had occurred, and it was very, very strong. Whether Primo knew something about himself, I don't know.

This is quite a theatrical recollection. Yet, clearly there was something about Levi that had the capacity to arouse special feelings in women. In Bloom he had evoked a maternal impulse, just as he had in so many women.

5

A fortnight after Roth's departure, Levi's condition plummeted. His descent into depression was first gradual, then precipitous: the last crushing episode. Accounts of Levi's final six months reveal a man snared by despair and sinking. But what was constant, say his most intimate friends, was an unrelieved greyness taking over. His hopelessness and overwhelming negativity about the future were warning signs of suicide, but few suspected that Levi was capable of taking his life. Like many depressives, he had learned to present a 'normal' face to family and friends – a face at variance with his mind. On 20 September, just as the disease began to take hold, he was at a lecture in Turin by the biochemist Rita Levi Montalcini. A bird-like woman with a delicate voice, Montalcini was herself a depressive, as Levi knew, for he had been treated by her psychiatrist in Rome in 1982. After the lecture he said to her: 'I didn't understand a word of what you said, but I liked it.' Though Levi seemed outwardly cheerful, Montalcini later said she could see that he was on the downward slope; she had a practised eye for these things.

In October Levi was advised by the family doctor to increase his anti-depressant dosage. The drug (Parmodalin/Parstelin) had worked for him four years earlier, and Levi noted a 'certain improvement'. His mental suffering remained unpalliated, though, and it was with immense difficulty that he wrote a newspaper article on the 13th congratulating Rita Levi Montalcini on winning the Nobel Prize for medicine ('Finally . . . a piece of good news!') He was tired, and everyone at home – his wife and his children – were tired of his moods. A few friends called round to visit, which brought some relief. On the morning of the 15th the Canadian radio producer John Reeves was in Turin. Levi had known Reeves since the early 1960s when he adapted *If This is a Man* for Toronto CBC radio. The men were fond of each other, and when Reeves's first wife died in 1970, Levi had a tree planted in her memory in Israel. They sat and reminisced in 75 Corso Re Umberto, speaking in French as they always did, before going out to lunch. The meal was proceeding enjoyably, but Reeves recalled the 'extreme anxiety' that came over Levi when he spoke of the burden of his mother and mother-in-law: 'Primo was depressed by not being able to see any light at the end of the tunnel: both these old women seemed likely to linger for years and extra nursing help was constantly needed.' Yet Levi made a splendid (and typical) effort to rise above his suffering in the presence of a visiting friend; later Reeves reflected how grateful he was to have seen Levi one last time before he died.

Philip Roth's interview in what Levi quaintly termed the 'ominous pages of the NYT" was flanked by a marvellous review of *The Monkey's Wrench* by Alfred Kazin. Levi had worried that the book's Piedmontese flavour would fatally limit its appeal in the United States. Instead, no: Levi was 'one of the most valuable writers of our time', said Kazin. After this approbation Levi's profile in America rose immeasurably; literary Manhattan was clamouring for his return. But the demands of a second US tour would have been too great; anyway, America had made Levi uncomfortable with its need to celebrate a survivor. 'I'm not in the mood for parties, conferences, festivities,' he said. By now most friends knew that Levi was not well.

Fernanda Pivano had been Levi's classmate at the 'M. D'Azeglio'. She was on the jury of the 1986 Ritz Paris Hemingway Award (set up to provide a rallying point for Italy's 'Americanisti') and she telephoned Levi to ask if she could nominate *The Monkey's Wrench* for the prize. 'Fine, but what have I got to do with Hemingway?' asked Levi. Jocular as he seemed, he quickly made Pivano privy to his state. He was prey to 'occurrences', he said, within his body, which he could 'not control'. (The meaning of these comments is obscure.) Unable to bring himself to write, all Levi could do was make copper-wire animal sculptures: at least that was therapy. Pivano tried to distract Levi with childhood memories of their teachers, but Levi spoke to her in a distanced tone, as if the affairs of the world no longer interested him. In the event, the Hemingway Award went to Marguerite Duras.

Levi tried to remain steadfast through his depression – his background required it of him – and on 20 October he put in an appearance at Turin's Historical Institute of the Resistance, of which he had been councillor since

1985. No functions were attached to the appointment and Levi's work there (taking minutes) was often dull. But, like many Turinese of his generation, he felt obliged to keep alive the memory of the partisan struggle. And as he was a 'personage' in Italian anti-Fascist circles, he could scarcely fail to attend a two-day conference in Turin on the Nazi deportations. This was held in the municipal Lascaris Palace on 21–2 November, and was sponsored by the Piedmont regional government. Apart from bringing survivors together, the conference was to launch a new government-funded publication, *Life Betrayed,* which was a compendium of 200 interviews with Piedmontese men and women, including Primo Levi, who had survived the Nazi camps. In Levi's preface he impugned the 'loathsome effort' of German and French revisionists who denied or underplayed the enormity of the genocide. Levi was depressed and disturbed by this move to 'diminish' (his word) what he saw as a unique instance of human infamy. For a man who rarely raised his voice, the preface sounded a clamorous note. During his interview for the book, Levi had surprised his interrogator by lambasting Bruno Bettelheim and his psychological enquiries into the Nazi camps, which he said were arid exercises in intellectualism. Levi was not normally so intemperate.

Levi had repeatedly made use of his mother's state of health to excuse himself from public functions and even dinner parties. Now, with the same explanation, he left the deportation conference early. Ester had been discharged from hospital and, confined to a wheelchair, she demanded all her son's attention. The assembled survivors considered Levi's sudden departure disrespectful, and they could not understand why their figure-head had so abruptly abandoned them. In fact, the crowds of survivors had provoked a depressive panic in Levi, that frightened him away. But there is another point to be made: Levi did not want to be a symbolic rallying point for other people's suffering; he had enough suffering of his own at 75 Corso Re Umberto.

Those who saw Levi in private this winter confirmed his low spirits. Raffaella Pagani accompanied him home after physiotherapy treatment and recalled the sad 'mausoleum-like' atmosphere of Levi's study and the darkness there. Levi could still speak engagingly to Pagani, but mostly repeating what he had said before, and always they sat in the darkness. Pagani wondered if the gloom somehow mirrored the way Levi felt inside. 'It was as if he'd closed the curtains on the day,' she said later. Levi's bleak and lonely moments had intensified with his mother now home again; paralysed, she was twice the responsibility and burden on Lucia, and on Levi.

*

Levi continued to make weekly visits to Einaudi, where he collected faxes and telexes from America. Two editors there helped him in these awful last months. Agnese Incisa was the daughter of the aristocratic racehorse owner Marquis Mario Incisa della Rocchetta. She has been described (by men) as a 'trooper' and a 'sergeant–major', who spoke her mind. Ernesto Ferrero, a dour, dry-humoured Piedmontese, had known Levi for a quarter of a century. Their lives were much affected by Levi's depression, and Levi was glad of their company. Incisa cosseted him and sometimes she was seized with pity, as he looked so wretchedly downcast. Levi began to complain to her that his mother 'took advantage' of him and made him 'do things' – run errands, mostly. Whether Levi's mother really battened on her son is impossible to say. A whining note had entered his remarks about Ester. When Incisa suggested tactfully that he put her in a home, Levi repeated in shocked tones: 'Put mother in a *home*?' To do so would have been loathsome to Levi: Ester had fed and looked after his children, when he and Lucia had worked; she had run the *'ménage'* (as Levi called it) and seen to domestic chores; and she was the legal owner of the flat. Levi was too good a son to think about ejecting his paralysed mother out of her own home. He had seen too much suffering, in another age, to inflict any of his own.

Nevertheless, Incisa was dismayed at a situation she felt could only end in disaster. She knew she had to put it starkly to Levi: 'Either you die or your mother dies.' At the end of November she was able to see for herself the alleged cause of Levi's misery, when Levi introduced her to his mother at 75 Corso Re Umberto. She was immobile in bed, but talkative. Incisa was unsettled by the flat's disconcerting tidiness. 'There were no newspapers on the floor, not even a Biro or anything to show that this home had ever been lived in by anybody.'

Ernesto Ferrero was sure that Levi's depression would pass – 'It could hardly have got worse,' he remembered – and he urged Levi to busy himself with concrete matters. One day he offered Levi the use of an office in the Einaudi building, where he could write unhampered by his mother's demands. After prevaricating, Levi moved into the room, only to abandon it two days later. He said he was worried about who would feed his mother at midday and in the evenings. This incident set the tone for many attempts that winter to help Levi. Agnese Incisa tried to chivvy him into taking the mountain air again, as he had done in better days. 'But Primo said Lucia would be "jealous" and anyway it was "unfair" to expect her to wash the picnic plates afterwards.' *Picnic plates?* What to a normal person might seem a minor inconvenience plunged Levi into feelings of panic, and this was surely a symptom of serious depression: Levi was getting things out of proportion because he was sick. Other absurdities continued in a sorry sequence. When Cesare Cases, the noted critic, called on Levi on 22 or 23 November, he found him so broken-down and 'nerve-wrung' that he later thought of him as 'an old ghetto Jew'.

6

Throughout the winter Levi's life continued at a retarded tempo. Occasionally he indulged in little trips round Turin, and one of them, on 10 December, brought him to the 'Campus' bookshop near the railway station. There he found Isabella Lattes Coifmann, a distinguished Italian naturalist, signing copies of her new book *Animal Intelligence*. Coifmann had never met Levi before and was delighted to be able to discuss with him the mysteries of the animal kingdom. A look of unease came over Levi as he confessed to Coifmann his fear of spiders. He said his old childhood terror had never really been scotched. And in the engulfing mental pain of his final months, indeed it had resurfaced. Levi's last published fiction was an 'Intimate Interview' between a journalist and a male-devouring female spider. Avowedly comic, it had a disturbing edge. Some of Levi's relatives have speculated that the story's 'Mrs Spider' was Lucia or Ester, devouring Primo alive in the web of 75 Corso Re Umberto. It is just as likely that this fable-like fantasy derived from the author's childhood memory of Uncle Enrico's copy of Dante, which had a Doré illustration of the mythical Greek weaver Arachne, transformed into a half spider and sprouting hairy legs from her back.

Christmas approached, and on 23 December Agnese Incisa again called at 75 Corso Re Umberto. Levi designed her a Christmas tree on his computer screen with the use of the mouse. 'It was the last time I saw him happy.' Shortly after, Levi received from Cincinnati in Ohio a Christmas card dated 22 December. On opening the envelope, he realised the card should have gone to Professor Raffaello Levi (no relation) at 26 Corso Re Umberto. Though Levi knew the professor, he accidentally re-directed the card to Number 25, from where it was returned to the sender in Cincinnati. When the envelope finally reached Raffaello Levi and his wife in Turin, they were shocked to find the hand-written note inside: 'Apologies – I opened this in error. Affectionate good wishes to you all from Primo Levi'. By this time Primo Levi was dead.

On 31 December he wrote to his southern Italian friend Francesco Proto of SIVA: 'I do my best to convince myself that the world is not going to the dogs. The New Year will bring serenity and prosperity (not to mention the joy of living!) to everyone.' Today these seem bitter, twisted words; Levi knew no 'joy' would come his way: the sense that his life was coming to an end was increasingly felt.

On New Year's Day – 1987 – Levi augmented his anti-depressant dosage from one tablet daily to two. He did this on his doctor's advice because his depression had intensified. The new dose only made him edgy and disagreeably anxious, however. It also – a potential side-effect of many psychotropic drugs – painfully blocked his bladder. A urologist diagnosed mild hypertrophy of the prostate. Though Levi was assured of a non-cancerous prostatism, he feared cancer: cancer had killed his father forty-five years earlier in 1942; moreover his ex-SIVA boss, Rico Accati, had had prostate cancer and would eventually die of a recurrence. By early January Levi was in an emotional pit or, as he put it to his friend Livio Norzi, in a 'sunken space'. As well as constant physical and mental pain, his work, mobility and leisure were all affected, as he was increasingly in the grip of the disease.

Levi's blankness and sinking feeling were made worse by his inability to complete his long-planned sequel to *The Periodic Table*. Conceived as long ago as 1975, *The Double Bond* was as yet little more than an outline. According to Ernesto Ferrero, it was to be an epistolary novel with an eighteenth-century cut. Through a series of love letters between an imaginary scientist and a Piedmontese noblewoman called Gisella, Levi would explore the chemical reactions that allow one to make mayonnaise, béchamel and vinaigrette. In this way the chemistry of cooking was to blend with the chemistry of love. The culinary-amorous experiment continued to occupy a little of Levi's time. From New York his publishers sent him Harold McGee's *On Food and Cooking: The Science and Law of the Kitchen*. Levi liked the positivist title, but more than McGee he admired Italy's own Mrs Beeton, Pellegrino Artusi, whose Risorgimento-era *Kitchen Science and the Art of Eating Well* is as much a recipe book as a culinary novel in its own right. However, no serious writing was being done. Reading round *The Double Bond* had taken the place of writing it, and soon even the amusement of research began to wear off. Friends began to wonder how serious the project was to Levi, though Silvio Ortona had been disturbed by the chapters he had read. 'The early ones read like a wonderful joke and were funny enough. But these ones frightened me: they were not written by the Primo I knew, they issued from some sort of nervous illness – *una malattia*. I told Primo for God's sake to shelve the project.' In a poem of 1981, 'Unfinished Business', Levi had spoken of a sadly uncompleted literary project: 'You'll find the outline in my drawer.' He was referring, most likely, to *The Double Bond*.

But if Levi's productive impulse was stalled, it had not entirely stopped. He had always been familiar with the analgesic properties of the creative act and, in spite of all, he managed to write three semi-jocose fantasies in which he imagined a journalist in conversation with a herring-gull, a mole, a giraffe and the aforementioned spider. These *jeux d'esprit* were hatched three months before Levi died, and they continued the tradition of the imaginary medieval bestiaries of Ariosto's *Orlando Furioso*. Typically for Levi, these 'Intimate Interviews' convey much teacherly information. We learn how the mole makes its perfectly cylindrical tunnels and why the giraffe sleeps on its feet. At the age of sixty-seven he had returned to the 'enquire within' world of *The Children's Encyclopaedia* and had begun to talk to the animals like Dr Dolittle. By composing these zoological frivolities Levi hoped to reassure himself that he was not losing his mind (or sense of humour), and that his creative powers remained intact.

As he endured the winter days of 1987 he was haunted by memories of the concentration camps. A schoolteacher in Padua sent him documentation proving the existence (long denied by the Italian authorities) of a Fascist camp known as Vo, just outside Padua. Forty-seven Jews had been sent from Vo to Auschwitz. What became of them? Levi wrote to thank Professor Francesco Selmin, the teacher, for his research: 'The rediscovery of Vo camp shows a rare diligence, competence and *pietas* in both you and your pupils.' January bought Levi another surprise from the Nazi past when the stub of a chewed-up pencil, salvaged as a keepsake from the wreckage of Auschwitz, arrived in the post. It belonged to the Italian survivor Liana Millu who, forty years earlier, had used it to begin her powerful chronicle, *Smoke Over Birkenau*, for which Levi had written the preface. Millu was not well; the short winter days gave her a sense that her end was near. Before she died she wanted Levi to have the pencil as a talisman of survival and resilience. Touched as Levi was by her gift, in his letter of thanks to Millu he admitted his own wintry sense that the end was approaching: 'For me too the days are getting shorter [*Anche per me i giorni si stanno facendo corti*].'

One of several concerned parties who tried to divert Levi at this time was the journalist Franco Pappalardo La Rosa. He recalled that Levi made enquiries at his bank as to the disposition of his finances in the 'event of sudden death'. Contemplating his end, Levi wanted to put his affairs in order. Actually his finances had been in a healthy state for some time. Between 1984 and 1986 his annual income from Einaudi averaged nearly 45,843,767 lire (about £22,000). This was not a bad showing, enough to keep his family afloat after he had gone.

During this same month of January, out of consideration for posterity, and almost as if he was making his will, Levi decided that a book about his life was in order. Giovanni Tesio, a critic in Turin, had broached the matter of a biography with Levi shortly before Christmas. And without saying so to Levi directly, he made it clear that his deep knowledge of Piedmontese culture made him the man for the job. After consideration, Levi appointed Tesio his official biographer. Tesio began his work enthusiastically on 12 January, and in the first of three winter meetings he talked with Levi and submitted questions to him. Tesio found that Levi was much preoccupied by the death of his Resistance companion, Vanda Maestro. Levi felt tremendous guilt for Vanda's capture; if he had not been in the Albergo Ristoro that fateful night, Vanda may not have been rounded up. Levi's guilt was doubtless exacerbated by his depression. Yet, as Tesio proceeded, he found that Levi was more reticent than cooperative, and not as available for candid discussion as Tesio would have liked. About his mother, for example, Levi refused to talk at all. And yet, he was more than ready to complain about her to other parties. His relationship with Ester was so bedevilled and tender and special that to have it pinned down between the pages of a biography would have been to besmirch it.

Other anxieties accumulated darkly round Levi. During his consultations with Tesio in the winter, he was unsettled by a public debate about the Final Solution that had opened in Germany and now spread to Italy. In the conservative *Frankfurter Allgemeine* the Berlin historian Ernst Nolte had argued for a supposed moral equivalence between Hitler's eradication of the Jews and the earlier Stalinist mass murder of the kulaks. Nolte is a serious historian, who regards *If This is a Man* as one the 'best accounts' of Auschwitz in any language. Yet he also believes it would be 'most misleading' to read Levi's book without first taking into account Solzhenitsyn's *The Gulag Archipelago*, for without the Gulag there would have been no Auschwitz. So he contends. No effort was needed to persuade Levi to take issue with what he called this 'sophistry'. His newspaper polemic, 'The Black Hole of Auschwitz', appeared in the 22 January edition of *La Stampa* and, given the mental state in which it was written, was a model of lucid argument. Levi's grievance was heartfelt and he argued it sharply: the industrial exploitation of the corpses and their ashes was a uniquely Hitlerian atrocity; never before had a government planned the annihilation of an entire people. Beneath the polite surface of Levi's prose, the granite was showing through painfully. Levi was as vigorous as ever when the subject of his past ordeal was touched on; it was only the effort to write creatively that was too much for him.

Levi had no sooner countered Nolte and other revisionists in *La Stampa* than he was obliged to confront a neo-Fascist bully in Turin. The meeting was just one more blow to Levi that contributed to his despair this winter. The Socialist journalist Carla Perotti had a wayward son, Emanuele Perotti, who was a pro-Mussolini provocateur. Having reviewed his works for theatre, Carla had got to know Levi well: she implored him to show some sense to her boy and, it was hoped, jolt him out of his moral deafness. Emanuele Perotti turned up at 75 Corso Re Umberto at the appointed time, armed with doctored photo-montages of Auschwitz which 'showed' that the gas chambers were false. 'Why dignify something with even a footnote that never happened?' he arrogantly asked Levi. Levi listened to Perotti in mounting sadness and disbelief. According to Levi's Hungarian friend Edith Bruck, 'A part of Primo came to believe that humanity did not deserve to know about Auschwitz. If a sixteen-year-old boy could deny the existence of the atrocity, the survivor has to remain silent, even if it's the worst thing he can do.' Eventually Levi asked Perotti to leave. In the sink of his depression he had allowed a spoiled, misguided youth to have a disproportionate influence over him: and from that day on Levi completely shuttered his heart to Italy's young – neo-Fascist or otherwise.*

On 27 January Levi celebrated his sister's sixty-sixth birthday. He had less than three months to live; it was the last family birthday he would mark. A few days earlier he had gone south to Naples to collect a minor literary prize (the Alberto Marotta) for *The Drowned and the Saved*. At the presentation in the lavish Villa Pignatelli he again met Isabella Lattes Coifmann, and again they spoke of spiders. Coifmann was intererested to know from where Levi got his information on spider thread. In an article of his, 'The Spider's Secret', Levi made the thread sound like a textile manufacturer's dream, stretchy and resilient. Levi promised to find Coifmann the *Nature* magazine article he had read on the secretion of spider silk, and on his return to Turin he looked in the library for the magazine. But he soon gave up. The most he could do was push his mother round the Crocetta in her wheelchair.

8

Levi was also suffering from intermittent prostatic pain which was so discomforting that he shelved all public commitments. He had been part of a government investigation into the German slaughter of 2,000 Italian troops in wartime Poland. Now he resigned from the commission. 'It's

*On 16 January 1994 Emanuele Perotti told me on the telephone that his meeting with Levi had been 'most unsatisfactory' and that he had never been a neo-Fascist.

tremendously late,' he told a reporter. Today those words – '*E'*
tremendamente tardi' – echo with a chill. Levi no longer found anything
interesting or enjoyable or worthwhile. Even his long-cherished plan to
accompany his friend Nuto Revelli to Fererre, a Piedmontese ghost village
depopulated by emigration, looked like a vapid, foolish enthusiasm. To the
Stresa-born artist Carlo Rap, who had wanted to sculpt Levi, he said: 'Some
other time'.

By February Levi's condition was so grave that he avoided friends and
retreated further into the dead-alive hole of 75 Corso Re Umberto. Against
the depression he had some unexpected support from an admirer in
England. David Mendel, a retired cardiologist, had first read Levi in 1986,
and his high regard for him was combined with a keen sense of
identification. ('If Primo played cricket for England, I played for Kent.')
They had met in Turin the previous autumn. One of Mendel's chief
interests then (though he did not tell Levi) was in writing his obituary for
the London *Times*. There was an element of sympathy as well as
discipleship in Mendel's attitude to Levi, and much as the Englishman
admired him, he could hardly disregard the wretchedness of his life. As
Levi had done five years earlier with Ruth Hoffman, he turned to Mendel
as a 'proper doctor' for help:

> I've fallen into a pretty serious state of depression; I've lost all
> interest in writing, as well as reading. I'm extremely dispirited
> and don't want to see anybody . . . For months I've been on
> Parmodalin, but without visible results. My fear is that this will
> never end. Everything I do, even if it is banal, costs me strength,
> including for example writing this letter. I feel I need help, but I
> don't know what sort.

In early February Levi was put on a different anti-depressant, Trittico
(British equivalent: Trazodone). This drug had the advantage of easing the
other pill's urological upsets; it also had a calming, sedative effect, which
suggests that Levi was not only depressed but also agitated and restless now.
All through February he waited anxiously for the drug to take effect.
Meanwhile even the most trivial actions – taking a bath, phoning a friend –
filled him with dread and a sense of unbearable effort. It seemed that
nothing could rid him of his malaise. On the morning of the 8th, Levi
telephoned his biographer Giovanni Tesio to postpone further interviews
with him until April, as he had to undergo a prostate operation. 'And don't
visit me in hospital. I'm very boring when I don't feel well.' Levi was to be
operated on for benign prostatic swelling; yet surgery (to excise part of the

gland) filled him with terror. He feared that anaesthetic would obliterate his memory and consequently damage his public image as the 'survivor who remembered'; any loss of intellectual powers, Levi knew, would show instantly in the quality of his work. Though his fears were quite realistic, they were compounded, partly, by the depression with its sinister hallmarks of confusion, failure of mental focus and feelings of foreboding. Behind this anxiety of memory loss also lay a fear of the Alzheimer's that had killed Ada Della Torre.

On 14 February, just before he submitted to surgery, Levi wrote to David Mendel that he could sleep only with the aid of an anti-psychotic, Neuleptil (British equivalent: Neulactil). He had a terror of the morning post, fearing it would bring him commitments he could not honour; he had no desire to talk unless it was about his depression, or his mother. The prospect of a book tour in Holland in the coming weeks terrified him: he would have to speak English and memorise new faces and names, be himself again. The most Levi could look forward to now was bedtime, when sleep at least would put an end to his fear. He had seen a '*neurologo*' (neurologist) who happened to be a friend, but he was not much help. Like many depressives, Levi believed in the absolute certainty of his bleak vision. To Mendel he explained:

> I know that this phase will pass, just as the others have done, but I'm aware of this only at the rational level; my overriding impression is that it will last for ever and that I will never find an exit out . . . In my waking hours I'm in a permanent state of unhappiness and anxiety. I seek refuge in sleep, even during the afternoon, with a couple of glasses of wine; otherwise the stress diminishes only in the evening, with the prospect of taking myself to bed.

While Levi's hopeless misery was a precursor of suicidal behaviour, not everyone afflicted by such hopelessness commits suicide. Yet Levi had reached that phase of the disease where all sense of hope had vanished, and with it any idea of a future. The day before surgery he was visited by Giovanni Tesio, who brought with him an anthology of Levi's writing that he had just edited. It included 'Arsenic' (from *The Periodic Table*), which, Levi tonelessly informed his biographer, had just been translated into Chinese. As Tesio stood by the door to say goodbye, Levi embraced him. That had never happened before; to Tesio it seemed unsettlingly out of character.

*

The operation for prostate hypertrophy was a success, so it seemed, and Levi made a good physical recovery in the Pinna Pintor clinic. While he was recuperating there, on 15 February, his article 'Adam's Clay' was published in *La Stampa*. Few readers could have guessed at the author's depressed state from the article, which looked at the origins of life and at the life-principle of carbon. In fact it had been written a full year earlier: *La Stampa* had asked Levi to scrape his desk drawer for material.

Shortly after Levi was discharged, he saw a psychotherapist, but broke off treatment when she tried to probe his feelings of aggression. Thus far, the lack of psychiatric expertise in Levi's case is striking. Perhaps Levi should have been in hospital: he had a potentially fatal psychiatric illness. However, it might have been difficult to have him admitted against his will – sectioned – because a professional consensus is required. It is impossible to know whether Levi would anyway have consented to be in hospital; for many mentally ill, however, hospital can provide longed-for relief from the daily struggle. Meanwhile Levi's family doctor prescribed a new type of psychiatric medication, Cantor.*

As Levi perceived it, the burden of his mother meanwhile grew, until it overwhelmed him. Concerned by rumours of his mental health, his Hungarian survivor friend Edith Bruck telephoned Levi from Rome. The only writing he could do now, Levi told her, was in the 'darkness' of his mother's room. There he filled a notebook with Ester's needs – cleaning, cooking, feeding – and all the drudgery she demanded of him from her invalid bed. In his depression, with all its attendant feelings of worthlessness and its delusions, Levi had turned his mother into a bully. He went on that his life was of no use to anyone and that he had lived a totally useless life. 'What are you *saying*?' Bruck countered. 'You talk a lot about your unhappiness, Primo, but what will you *do* about it?' Levi only replied: 'I can't write. What do I have to live for?' Later, Bruck confessed that she mistook Levi's despair for an extreme case of writer's block. She tried to console him with banalities such as, 'We survivors don't have the *right* to die. We should live a thousand years.' But Levi was at the frontline of despair, and on 19 February he wrote to his translator Ruth Feldman in Boston:

> I'm going through my worst time since Auschwitz: in certain respects it's even worse than Auschwitz, because I'm no longer

*Cantor had also proved effective in the treatment of 'senile dementia of the Alzheimer type', according to *The Lancet* (April 1985).

young and I have scant resilience. My wife is exhausted. I beg you to forgive this outburst, I know you'll understand . . . *de profundis*.

9

During these shattering spring days when Primo Levi was collapsing, he saw a few friends. They were unaware that it would be for the last time. On 9 March Levi was at an ex-partisan reunion in the Historical Institute of the Resistance in Turin. The city's anti-Fascist old guard were there, among them the philosopher Norberto Bobbio. People seldom notice despair in others, if those despairing make an effort to disguise their pain. So Bobbio would later remark: 'Until the day Primo died I was convinced he was the most tranquil and serene person in the world.' In spite of all, it was still Levi's habit to call on Bianca Guidetti Serra most Wednesdays after she had finished work in the law courts. In Bianca's elegant legal practice on Via San Dalmazzo he fell into gloomy talk of black holes and humanity's demise; he was filled with nihilism and was progressively delusional. It was only later that Bianca understood there was an anguish in Levi that she had 'failed to notice'. Her opinion then was that Levi was overworked, and she implored him to find a secretary to help with the paperwork, but Levi insisted that the scores of letters he sent each week had to be 'personal and personalised'. He seemed to be putting himself under the greatest possible strain, submitting to some morbid sackcloth-and-ashes oppression, as though he felt he 'deserved' the punishment. An American theologian in Switzerland wrote to say that he had read *If This is a Man* to his congregation in church; Levi replied to him: 'I am not worthy.'

As for family, Lisa Levi, now thirty-eight, was busy setting up Turin's new Natural History museum; Renzo was involved in various biophysics projects and Lucia was still detained for much of the time by her ailing mother. Whether his family was aware of the gravity of Levi's illness is impossible to know: they must have understood that he was deeply troubled, but his depression seemed so intensely private and unknowable that perhaps they did not want to intrude.

Apart from Agnese Incisa and Ernesto Ferrero, the only other Einaudi editor whom Levi saw with any frequency in these last weeks was Francesco Ciafaloni, a former petroleum engineer, moustachioed and outgoing. What endeared Ciafaloni to Levi, apart from his scientific background, was his genial Mezzogiorno temperament and his absence of snobbery. In his unpretentious company Lucia did not feel jealously excluded. According to Ciafaloni, the most overlooked factor in Levi's depression was the weight on

528

him of current affairs. Levi was unusually well informed about politics (certainly he read far more papers and magazines than most Italians), and in his last weeks he seemed appalled not only by his own suffering, but by the suffering of others. On one of these winter nights Bianca Guidetti Serra invited Levi and Ciafaloni to supper. Another guest, Gino Sacerdote, had just returned from Japan (where he had been teaching physics) by way of fundamentalist Tehran. As Bianca served drinks, Sacerdote cynically remarked that it would be 'wonderful' if the Iranians and Iraquis just 'killed each other off'. On hearing this, Levi blanched: it was said at the height of the 1980–8 Gulf War massacres, when half a million lives were already lost on both the Iranian and Iraqui sides. That an educated Jewish professor could make light of atrocity seemed to Levi to be a frightening return to barbarism. 'Primo felt strongly the coming of the bleak times ahead – the sense that the world was a brutally random, out-of-control place,' said Ciafaloni. For the rest of the meal Levi scarcely ate anything, overwhelmed, Ciafaloni thought, by anguish.

In this small city where everything was known, rumours began to circulate about Levi. Felice Fantino was at 75 Corso Re Umberto for supper. They had known each other since 1946 when they worked together at DUCO. As Fantino stayed until 11:30 pm, he asked Levi if he could phone for a taxi. This was done, and the friends said goodbye. Downstairs Fantino found not a taxi, but a police car waiting to take him home to nearby Avigliana. Fantino assumed that Levi had access to police protection (perhaps for his earlier outspoken views on Israel), but we cannot know the meaning of this police escort. Fantino never saw Levi again.

There were other peculiarities. Reportedly Levi lit candles in his dark study. 'They were for the dead or those about to die,' speculated a politician friend, Giorgio Ardito (possibly Levi was lighting Sabbath candles before sunset on Friday, or he was commemorating the anniversary of the death of a relative with Kaddish candles). Another story was that Levi discussed his impending death with Giorgio Lattes, the 'Big George' of his adolescence; once a tall, prepossessing man, Lattes was now paralysed from a series of strokes, and was thin and himself severely depressed. During their long, gloomy discussions the men wondered how they would feel, physically, before the final coming to rest. 'They were at their crossroads, debating whether to stay or drown,' commented Roberto Gentili, an engineer who knew both men well. Another mutual friend of theirs, the chemist Luigi Tosini, claimed he overheard Levi tell Lattes that he now wished he had 'died at Auschwitz'. In the race to end life Giorgio Lattes outlived Levi by four months, dying on 8 August 1987.

Just when it seemed things could get no worse, on the morning of 18 March, a Wednesday, Levi was re-admitted to the Pinna Pintor clinic. His bladder was blocked again. 'My hydraulic system's gone to pieces,' he confided to a friend. Further surgery was required. The anaesthetist, Roberto Pattono, visited Levi prior to the operation and recalls that his old fear of losing his memory under the knife had resurfaced. Pattono had been friendly with Levi since the mid-1950s and was aware that he might be a depressive. (Later he told an American journalist that he thought Levi was suicidal the first time he met him. 'Years ago, I said to myself: it is only a matter of time.') Pattono asked Levi the usual questions about past illnesses or allergies, and in answer Levi pulled back his sleeve to expose the Auschwitz tattoo: 'This is the worst illness I've had.'

In the evening, when Levi recovered consciousness, the surgery had been successful, and he remained at the Pinna Pintor until late the following week. On the Friday evening before he was discharged he was visited again by Professor Pattono. Levi asked his advice on post-operative exercises and Pattono assured him that his prospects for recovery were excellent; Levi seemed comforted by this knowledge. His last-known book dedication was a tribute in *The Drowned and the Saved*: 'To Professor Roberto Pattono, with infinite gratitude.' He seemed eager to get back to work, the anaesthetist remembered, and indeed was full of enthusiasm. In retrospect Pattono believes that Levi was 'suspiciously' spirited. 'Depressive patients can often seem calmer and "in better spirits" in the days prior to their self-destruction. Having resolved to die, Levi was at last relieved of the anxiety at having to live.'

At midday on 28 March Levi left his hospital bed. The next day, in what Professor Pattono now considers an 'ominous rise of enthusiasm', Levi was hard at his correspondence and responding to the flood of get-well cards. To many it seemed that he really was seeking to reassemble his life. Suicide is not at all uncommon towards the end of a depression when sufficient energy and resolve return to enable determined lethal action. And in a surge of good feeling Levi told the poet Delfina Provenzali, on 30 March, that he was about to start translating the poems of Gottfried Benn.

By the beginning of April Levi seemed cheerful enough to suggest meetings with friends for quiet dinners and conversation-filled evenings. Pietro Frassica, an Italian professor at Princeton, visited Levi on 1 April. For months Frassica had tried in vain to persuade Levi to take up his offer of a Princeton Fellowship; now Levi suddenly agreed to accept it. Frassica was delighted, but also baffled by this abrupt change of mind. About this time, Luciana Nissim called to see how the operation had gone, and found Levi 'fairly all right'. It was to be the survivors' last afternoon together. Nissim's impression of well-being was also reported by the secretary of Turin's Communist Party, Piero Fassino, who came round to persuade Levi to take up the honorary post of president of Einaudi. The publishing house, after four years of spiralling debts, had finally established a sound budget and sales, and was in the midst of a reorganisation. Fassino recalled that Levi was 'extremely flattered' by the offer. He said he would need a week to think it over, and asked Fassino to call him again on the morning of Saturday 11 April.

11

The abyss where Levi was blindly headed was the stairwell of the third-floor flat where he lived on Corso Re Umberto. Almost each day for the past sixty-seven years he had looked down this stairwell on leaving the flat. Indelibly imprinted on his mind, the stairwell (as I remember from my interview with Levi in 1986) gives a giddy sensation of a spiral void, and in all likelihood it had long exercised a fascination for Levi. This seems clear from the last chapter of *If This is a Man,* where he speculates that to contract diphtheria in Auschwitz would be 'more surely fatal than jumping off a third floor [*piú sicuramente mortale che saltare da un terzo piano*].'* The book was written forty years before, parts of it in the third-floor Corso Re Umberto flat. And perhaps – but we can only speculate – in some small closed corner within himself Levi had not forgotten the suicidal leap of his paternal grandfather Michele from a second-floor window in 1888. A suicidal tendency can be transmitted down the generations like a dangerous gene: was Levi lethally susceptible to his grandfather's example? Suicide methods, too, often run in families and the precise method chosen is very frequently the result of imitation. Thus the cause of death on Primo Levi's autopsy would be exactly the same as that on his grandfather's ninety-nine years earlier: '*precipitazione dall'alto*', a 'fall from a great height'. But there is more. The hospital where Michele Levi was pronounced a suicide in 1888 was described by his grandson Primo as 'imbued with the sufferings of generations'. Levi's remark may carry unconscious and prescient significance.

Grandpa Michele was not the only suicide in Levi's family. Uncle Enrico

*Stuart Woolf's translation of *If This is a Man* perplexingly refers to the 'fourth floor'; presumably the original American publisher (Orion) had insisted on American usage for '*terzo piano*', whereby the third floor becomes the fourth floor.

Sacerdote was the family black sheep; having married a morphine addict, in about 1970 he set fire to his mattress in the Jewish Rest Home and died asphyxiated by the fumes. Uncle Enrico's willed self-immolation is scarcely evidence of a genetic factor in Levi's death. Yet perhaps it is a fragment in the puzzle. Suicide is contagious not only among family members (Enrico was one of Corrado Luzzati's uncles), but also among acquaintances. Levi was personally acquainted with at least eleven suicides, among them his university chemistry colleague Agostino Neri, his German teacher Hanns Engert, his DUCO partner Gastone Compagnucci, the writer Cesare Pavese and the providential mason Lorenzo Perrone.

One suicide, above all others, haunted Levi. This was the suicide of the Austrian-born philosopher and survivor Jean Améry. Levi and Améry had rarely corresponded, as they were quite opposite characters. Améry was a splenetic individual who had made hatred (of the Germans) into his obsession; Levi declared himself 'physiologically incapable of hatred'. Still he was fascinated by Améry; his extraordinary account of growing old, *On Ageing,* had been a valuable philosophical companion to him during Ada Della Torre's decline from Alzheimer's. But it was Améry's sternly introspective defence of 'self-murder', *On Suicide,* that concentrated Levi's mind in his last days. No one knew all, or perhaps even most, of the motivations behind Améry's suicide in 1978, but his widow Maria ('Mops') Améry is sure of this: her husband chose suicide as a legitimate 'path to freedom'. And the comfort offered by Socrates – that death brings an end to pain – was surely the comfort that Levi sought.

Thoughts of suicide appear often enough in Levi's scattered writings, interviews and letters to signal at least an underlying concern with the possibility of self-destruction. In 1959 he had written to his German translator Heinz Riedt that suicide is 'an act of will, a free decision'. Nowhere in his writing did Levi disapprove of suicide as a selfish or shaming act. He was intermittently fascinated with violent, abrupt endings. The 'theatrical suicide' (as he called it) of Spandrell in Aldous Huxley's *Point Counter Point* had long intrigued him. Like the lid on a boiling saucepan, Spandrell holds down his self-destructive urges until one day he turns a gun on himself. Levi had often compared himself to a centaur (half man, half horse), his life split between the factory and the typewriter, between his family and friends. It is unlikely to be mere coincidence that the wretched centaur of his early science-fiction story, 'Quaestio de Centauris' ('An Official Investigation into the Centaurs'), kills himself out of a conviction that life is a vanity. (Indeed, Levi described the story to me as 'autobiographical'.) That is not all. Levi's late poetry displays a vandal's delight in destruction for its own sake. 'Give us something to destroy,' he implores in 'Give Us' (1981), 'Give us something that burns, offends, cuts, smashes, fouls.' After a lifetime of exemplary public conduct, Levi was tired of being the model survivor, the man who never lost control. Elsa Morante, the Italian novelist who took her life in 1985, was said to have kept a copy of 'Give Us' by her bedside as a sort of solace. If during his last days Levi saw a light at the end of the tunnel, it was the light of an oncoming train.

TWENTY-NINE

April 1987: The Last Six Days

These last days can be pieced together only sketchily; we are left with little other than final bits of conversation and guiltily remembered fragments. On 5 or 6 April 1987 Gaia Servadio telephoned Levi from London. 'I've tried everything,' Levi told her in a tone that suggested he saw no more to experience or discover in life. His feelings of hopelessness were such that no medication could help. Lucia had never seen her husband so wretchedly low, and could no longer endure the sight of his suffering. She implored Bianca Guidetti Serra to take Primo out of the flat, if only for an afternoon: a walk in the mild spring weather might do him good. On 7 April, if her calendar of events is accurate, Bianca telephoned Lucia to say she was on her way. It was just after 11:00 am when she reached 75 Corso Re Umberto. She managed to coax Levi out into the Valentino Park, and as they walked beneath the trees in their April blossom she tried to distract him with small talk. But Levi was not listening. Bianca asked him if it was Auschwitz that had returned to torment him so. Levi replied coherently: 'No, I survived, I was able to tell my story.' He said he felt 'at peace' with himself because he had borne witness.

The 8th, a Wednesday, was a dull rainy day. Neighbours saw Levi leave his flat for what was to be the last time. He stood with an umbrella on his arm at the main doors, then set out to post letters. We know that Levi wrote two letters at this time. One was to the Dutch film-maker Jeanne Wikler, the other to the Venetian novelist Ferdinando Camon. To Wikler, Levi said that he could not be interviewed by her until the summer, owing to ill health. He asked Camon to send him a copy of the article he had written on his life and work for the French paper *Libération*. The letter seemed so full of 'vitality and expectations', Camon said later, that he could not square it with a man who was about to take his life.

It would seem that Levi was again concealing his intentions behind a cheerful or improved behaviour. On the evening of that same Wednesday Giulio Einaudi found him 'quite vivacious'. Swift on the heels of Piero Fassino, Einaudi had come to persuade Levi to take up the honorary presidency of his publishing house. Levi seemed just the man for the position, both as an emblematic Turinese and as an old-fashioned humanitarian Socialist. So Einaudi made Levi the offer and was delighted when he accepted. Over drinks, Levi canvassed the wonders of his Apple Mac, and showed Einaudi the autobiographical dates he had stored on the computer for use in a forthcoming Einaudi *opera omnia* of his work. 'But how can I write a biography of myself when I'm still alive?' Levi semi-humorously asked. (When the Apple's hard disk was accessed after Levi's death, it was discovered that the chronology of dates stopped at 1975, the year his mother first fell seriously ill.) Einaudi left 75 Corso Re Umberto believing that his mission had been a success. But later that night, at the unexpected hour of midnight, his telephone rang. It was Levi: 'I can't do it.' He had decided not to take on the presidency after all; Einaudi assumed that pressure had been put on him to moderate his earlier eagerness, probably by his wife; Lucia wanted to protect Levi from any further burdens and responsibilities.

Two days before his death, on Thursday 9 April, Levi contacted the synagogue in Turin to ask if the unleavened bread – matzos – had arrived for the Jewish Passover. The Kaddish candles; the matzos: one might almost see evidence of an eleventh-hour religious revival in Levi, were he not a lifelong atheist. Levi spoke to Anna Bises Vitale, vice-president of the community, who had known him since 1963. 'Primo seemed cheerful enough – I'd never have thought he was on the threshold of taking his life.' But, just as Levi omitted much of his personal life from his books (elisions were part of his concealing art), so he could well have kept to himself any plan he may have formed to end his life. Ernesto Ferrero phoned later that Thursday, and as Levi sounded so low he tried to cheer him: 'One day you'll have to go to Stockholm to collect the Nobel Prize!' Levi made no enthusiastic reply. Next day, Friday 10 April, he told his biographer Giovanni Tesio in a happier voice that they should resume work together. As matters turned out, Tesio's biography was never to be written. Primo Levi was a man who believed himself to be finished and was about to prove it.

All the signs of improvement (if such they were) quickly passed. On this last Friday of his life Levi called cousin Giulia Colombo to ask if she was resting properly after some minor injury. 'Primo sounded strange – in a preoccupied frame of mind – though if he'd made up his mind by then or

535

not, who can say?' That same night, in another part of Turin, Orsolina Ferrero of SIVA had a premonitory dream. Levi appeared before her at the factory carrying a bundle of clothes under one arm like a pilgrim. 'Lina, I have to go away'. She begged him to take her with him. 'No, it's too early for you.' Then he stepped out of the laboratory window into the void.

To those already sick of the toils of life, waking up to a new day is often more than they can bear: 11 April was a crisp Saturday morning; Levi was in the flat with his wife, his mother and a nurse, Elena Giordanino, who had been in service with the family for nine months. At 8:00 am Giordanino gave Levi his habitual morning injection (of what, she does not say in her signed statement to the police). Then she left him and went to tend to his mother. Levi had asked the politician Piero Fassino to phone him on the 11th, and Fassino's call came through at about 9:00 am. Fassino did not know that Levi had already declined Einaudi's offer of the presidency, and was disappointed to hear Levi say, 'I don't feel up to it.'

Allegedly there was another call – made by Levi. Lucia had gone out shopping at 9:30 am; minutes afterwards Levi telephoned the chief rabbi of Rome, Elio Toaff, at his home. Levi had met Toaff on at least one occasion, but the circumstances surrounding this last call are very unclear. Levi was not a religious man, but still it seems odd that he should have disturbed a rabbi on a Saturday, the Jewish Sabbath. In a distressed voice Levi told him: 'I don't know how I can go on. My mother's ill with cancer – every time I look at her I remember the faces of those men stretched out on their plank-beds at Auschwitz.' After this call, Rabbi Toaff suffered many years of intense guilt and feelings of failure that he could not read 'the signs' of Levi's suffering.

At about 10:05 am Levi stepped out on to the third-floor landing and pitched himself over the railing of the marble staircase. His humiliations at last were at an end. Lucia, on returning from shopping at around 10:30 am, was heard to exclaim: 'No! He's done what he'd always said he'd do.'

A rope stretched across the main door of 75 Corso Re Umberto kept out the curious. They clustered open-mouthed on the pavement as an endless drill of photographers and newspapermen milled round the scene. Detectives had cordoned off the lift-area and were interviewing neighbours individually. In the first of her formal interviews to the police, Lucia could only repeat in tears that her husband had no longer wished to live. 'All it took was a moment's inattention.' Meanwhile Piero Fassino in another part of the city, having heard the news, marvelled to himself, 'But I only spoke to Levi a moment ago.' The apartment block where the suicide had occurred gave no external sign of mourning, the third-floor windows closed behind net curtains. There were no black funeral bands, no flowers. Journalists who rang the ground-floor intercom 'LEVI Primo' were rebuffed by a woman's voice: 'Please, there's nobody here.'

The writer Nuto Revelli was waiting for Levi that Saturday morning in a packed schoolroom in the Waldensian village of Angrogna. He and Levi were supposed to launch a book on the anti-Nazi Resistance by a local Protestant pastor, Jean-Louis Sappé. Levi did not turn up. At 11:00 am a telephone call came through for Revelli from Bologna. 'Bologna? Who do I know in Bologna?' Picking up the phone, he was informed by a journalist of Levi's suicide. The same journalist caught Mario Rigoni Stern at his home in Asiago. 'Primo dead? It's absurd!' Yet Rigoni Stern's first thought was: 'So this is it.' A few days earlier Levi had sent him a letter in which he confessed that he had 'lost the will to live' and that his home life had become intolerable.

Livio Norzi learned of his friend's death in a taxi. The driver had just heard the news on the radio. Norzi could not then help thinking impossible things, impossible *ifs*, and his agonised questioning went on for many years. News agencies everywhere treated the suicide as a matter of international literary concern. Though he had never met Levi, the Israeli novelist Aharon Appelfeld was overwhelmed by a sense of loss and remorse: 'I just wish I could have helped Levi. I should have got on a plane and knocked on his door.' The remorse and the 'if onlys' seemed to be endless. For friends and admirers of Levi, it was hard to reconcile the apparent calm reasonableness of his writing with so violent a death. Just by looking at Levi's handwriting, Appelfeld could not credit in him a will to blackness and self-destruction: 'It looked so ordered and neat and controlled!' Paola Accati of SIVA was shocked for another reason: 'One thing Primo taught me in our working life together was that there's never a problem without a solution.' She had never once seen Levi lose control in times of trial. 'But at the last moment I suppose his self-mastery fled him.'

In America there was some moral outrage at Levi's suicide. In the *New Yorker* it was reckoned that Levi had cheated his readers with a last and terrible act of denial. The belief remains as vulgar as it is short-sighted. Levi and his books are not one and the same. If anything, Levi's suicide reminds us that the life of the artist does not run parallel to his art. In one of his last interviews, Levi had warned his readers not to confuse the author with his books. 'In my work I have portrayed myself variously as courageous, cowardly, prophetic or naive, but always, I believe, well-balanced. However, I'm not well-balanced at all. I go through long periods of imbalance.' While Levi's family were engulfed in despair, friends sought to defend the suicide. 'Primo was a man like any other,' said Bianca Guidetti Serra, 'one should not judge his writing by whatever means he chose to die.' Luciana Nissim was in agreement. 'The suicide was Primo's own act. He had chosen to do it.' And by taking his life, he had in a sense gone to rest with Vanda Maestro, Nissim believed.

Some survivors were secretly disgusted, and saw Levi's suicide as a default of responsibility towards them. Jean Samuel said he was 'appalled' that Levi had chosen to end his life on the anniversary of his liberation from Buchenwald: 11 April 1945. Edith Bruck was incensed at the apparent selfish *uselessness* of the act: 'I couldn't forgive Primo.' But, as the realisation of the loss gradually set in, Bruck came to understand that Levi's suicide was his one true 'howl of freedom' in all his sixty-seven years. 'There are no howls in Primo's writing – all emotion is controlled – but Primo gave such a howl of freedom at his death.' For Bruck, Levi's suicide turned out to be an act, almost, of heroism: my life is mine and mine alone to take.

Others were shocked less by Levi's suicide than by the method he chose to die. As a chemist he could have ended his life discreetly, like Arthur Koestler, with a lethal drug. Instead, he chose to die like a character in a tabloid crime-sheet, down the stairwell. By this violent and theatrical death, it was pointed out, he had exposed his loved ones to a gruesome sight, which he would never have wanted them to see. And it is a fact that he had exposed others to the sight, too. But, as any proper doctor knows, suicidal depression does not tend to be a state of mind that is considerate of others. Levi had good reason to die the way he did. Jumping left little or no chance for detection or rescue by others. Neither did it allow, in its instant deadliness, for a last-minute change-of-heart. Levi was not worried about death – just getting there – and his flight down the stairwell was both swift and lethal.

Not since Pasolini was found murdered on the outskirts of Rome had there been such clamorous coverage in Italy of a writer's death. 'SAVED BUT DROWNED' and 'TURIN MOURNS THE MAESTRO', were the front-page headlines. Most of the Italian reports were grotesque, circumstantial. For two days Turin was ironically spared print coverage of the suicide as the city's newspaper, *La Stampa,* was on strike. Instead, all weekend the phones rang. 'Have you heard?' Turin, desolate and silent, was in mourning. Tributes and reminiscences flowed from the philosopher Norberto Bobbio and the writers Natalia Ginzburg, Fulvio Tomizza and Carlo Sgorlon. Levi had died at exactly the same age as Jean Améry: sixty-seven.

*

The autopsy was conducted hastily in the city mortuary on Via Chiabrera. Levi had to be buried before the week-long Jewish Passover began at sunset the following Monday, when funerals are not to be officiated. Though the family wished to keep the funeral private, thousands came to pay their respects, for Levi was loved by many people. All Monday morning the mourners filed in to sign the books of condolence: anonymous faces, neighbours. There were a number of survivors, both Catholic and Jewish, of the Nazi camps, as well as former 'Justice and Liberty' partisans. 'We've lost our guiding light, we're all of us orphans now,' one of them told the press.

At 2:10 pm on 13 April the chief rabbi of Turin, Emanuele Artom,* arrived at the mortuary. He had to raise his voice – '*Signori, permesso*' – to ask the crowds to move aside from the entrance. Standing over the coffin, he recited the Jewish mourner's prayer, the Kaddish. In Judaism, as in Islam, suicide is anathema. (Jews who commit suicide are denied the solemn seven days of mourning and – in the equally categoric interpretation – must be interred in a section of the cemetery reserved for the profane.) However, Rabbi Artom had made a theological exception for Levi. Levi was not a suicide exactly, but a victim of 'delayed homicide'. In Artom's view, anyone who has been interned in a Nazi camp and who then dies by his own hand is in a sense murdered – murdered by the Nazis. This was the exception.

The coffin left the mortuary at 2:30 pm. Under the pale April sun the crowds were silent. In this reserved city there were to be no burial speeches or noisy farewells. Levi's widow, in dark glasses and an ash-grey suit, walked behind the coffin, accompanied by Renzo, Lisa and Anna Maria Levi. Also attending were the editors Ernesto Ferrero, Agnese Incisa and Alberto Papuzzi, the lawyer Bianca Guidetti Serra and the physicist Tullio Regge. There were a number of wreaths, from Turin shopkeepers and total strangers, including one from his publishing friends: '*Amici Einaudiani*'. Levi's biographer, Giovanni Tesio, was also there, as was a grief-stricken Rico Accati, formerly of SIVA.

The hearse arrived at the cemetery on Corso Regio Parco at 3:10 pm. In this forlorn part of Turin the skyline is distinguished by smoke-stacks and gasometers, but the Jewish burial ground is signposted with uplifting words from Isaiah: 'Awake and sing, ye that dwell in dust.' Some 500 people joined the handful of relatives and friends who attended the interment. Rabbi

---

*The rabbi was distantly related to his more famous namesake, Emanuele Arton, murdered by Nazi-Fascists in 1944.

539

Artom again recited the Kaddish. Then he scattered graveyard soil on to the lowered coffin. Renzo, tense-faced, did the same, followed by his sister, and finally by Lucia, who 'accompanied her gesture with the tenderness of a last caress', said *La Stampa*. Within an hour it was over; five gravediggers came forward to cover the coffin in earth. Lucia was the last to leave. She watched as a grey marble plaque was sunk into the earth with the plain inscription: '1919–1987 PRIMO LEVI'. Later, Levi's concentration-camp number – 174517 – was added. Levi had said that he wanted as his epitaph the Greek words Homer used of his voyager Ulysses, *'pollà plankte'*. They mean 'much erring', or 'driven to wander far and wide'; in his homesick exile, separated from his friends and home, the long-enduring Ulysses was a kind of Everyman. And so was Primo Levi, which is why he still feels so close to us in the twenty-first century.

Epilogue

All suicides tend to generate false leads, false data, and Levi's was no exception. Experts' reports, inquiries, counter-inquiries: it was said that Levi suffered a persecution complex and had seen neo-Fascists aiming guns down at him the day he died. The most bizarre hypothesis was offered by the Sicilian novelist Gesualdo Bufalino: Levi had killed himself after watching Polanski's Grand Guignol film *The Tenant,* screened on late-night Italian television a 'few days before Levi's suicide'. In the film a Polish-French Jew named Trelkovsky leaps to his death from a third-floor flat in Paris. Levi's third-floor leap, according to Bufalino, was the result of an 'emotional contagion' with Polanski's film. Did Levi stay up to watch it? Bufalino's assertion is not to be entirely dismissed. The apartment block in *The Tenant* has an old-fashioned lift cage and a spiral marble stairway: in some ways it echoes the third floor of 75 Corso Re Umberto.

The romantic explanation for Levi's suicide, which is still the most enduring, is that Auschwitz claimed him. 'CRUSHED BY THE PHANTOM OF THE CAMP' blazoned the *Corriere della Sera.* Natalia Ginzburg concurred: 'It was the memory of those years which led him to his death.' Yet Ginzburg had little personal insight into Levi's last depression, as she had not seen him for three years when he died. The novelist Alberto Moravia likewise stated that Levi had died of 'the sickness of the camp which is incurable'. Yet Moravia had met Levi only once, and that briefly, in 1963. Levi's son Renzo appeared to collude in these Auschwitz theories when he retorted at journalists: 'Read the last page of *The Truce,* it's all written there.' There, Levi describes a recurring dream that he is back in Auschwitz and that 'nothing is true outside the *Lager*'. From the irritated tone of Renzo's remark, however, it is likely that he was telling the reporters what they wanted to hear in order to disperse them. 'Have a little respect!' he later told them as they jostled for the one comment that would explain everything.

Whether the depression that killed Levi was compounded by, or even had its roots in, his terrible past – the night he saw for the first time the sign *Arbeit Macht Frei* – we can only speculate. The Turin bookseller Angelo Pezzana perhaps came closest to the truth, when he said: 'Primo did not kill himself because of his mother or Auschwitz: it was something *deep* inside him.' Luciana Nissim, who survived Auschwitz with Levi, is frankly irritated by attempts to claim him as a posthumous victim of Hitler. In her analysis, Levi's suicide was the final outcome of the bad disease of depression. 'Primo was out of his mind with misery, no amount of love from other people could have saved him.' Levi's sister will not lay the blame on Auschwitz, either. 'It was nothing, absolutely *nothing*,' she said; as far as Anna Maria was concerned, her brother had been derailed by nothing more cataclysmic than a prostate operation. His death was that deeply ordinary.

For others, Levi was a casualty of his fame. Claire Bloom told me: 'Because of Primo's success in America, the world had opened up for him. But he was imprisoned by family circumstances, and somehow, that terrible act of throwing himself down the stairwell – in *that* place – was an act of violence and rebellion against the family.' That Levi took his life in 75 Corso Re Umberto at all is for his old friend Vittorio Foa the saddest fact. 'There was always a sense of family continuity at Number 75 – a sense that life would go on for ever. Now the family line is broken.'

The novelist Oreste Del Buono (a self-confessed hypochondriac) believes that Levi killed himself as a consequence of the wear and tear of age. 'The loss of resilience in muscles and bones, coupled with fear of memory-loss, was bleakly undermining for Primo. Let's call it an organic caving-in, *un cedimento organico*. In the end Primo had no strength left to resist his body's own cruel chemistry.' Others have speculated that Levi grievously missed his factory work at SIVA, which offered him a distraction.

There are always two suicides – the real one, and the one people think they know about. Over the years strident public claims have been made that Levi did not in fact kill himself. Underlying these attempts to exonerate him from 'self-murder' is the belief that a great and courageous man could not have done such a thing. But such men do, often enough. Some in the denial faction have said that if Levi was indeed brought to self-destruction, it was by a sudden, unpremeditated folly, a 'brainstorm'. While Levi's suicide was almost certainly impulsive (or due to an unknown event shortly before his fall), suicide is almost always an irrational act. Depression in most suicide cases probably *impairs* the capacity for rational thought. 'Just as one can throw a plate against a wall', commented Agnese Incisa, 'so Levi threw himself down the stairwell'. Others have tried to suggest that Levi, far from taking his life, was a victim of his anti-depressant medication. Or they have objected that he could not possibly have committed suicide because he left no suicide note. Yet very few suicide cases (perhaps one in four, according to a recent American study) do leave notes. To sit down and write a note – at *that* moment – would seem as futile as winding up one's watch. It is by no means certain, anyway, that Levi did not leave a note. Germaine Greer heard from her Italian publishers, Mondadori, that a suicide note was found. 'I still prefer not to believe that this is true,' she said. (Greer, like so many others, was so devoted to Levi that the idea of his suicide might have impaired her image of him as a writer, and as a man.)

In 1967 Levi had written of the Piedmontese poet Cesare Pavese: 'Nobody has yet been able to penetrate the reason and the roots of his suicide.' And the same must be said of Levi. His suicide was provoked by his clinical depression, which was compounded by a complex web of factors. His mother's illness, the prostate operations, the tide of historical revisionism, fears of mental incompetence: all these were provocations. But, however accommodating it is to see the concentration camp, or a domestic smothering, as the explanation, no one key will turn the lock. The real causes for suicide always remain fugitive, because the suffering of those who kill themselves is private and inaccessible. As Antonio Paccagnella, a carpenter who was rescued from Auschwitz with Levi, told me in 1989: '*Nessuno ha la verità in tasca*', 'Nobody has the truth in their pocket'.

Within months of his death Primo Levi was commemorated in the names of Italian squares, streets and schools. But his true memorials lie elsewhere, in his matchless books and in the memory of those who knew him. Livio Norzi, one of Levi's oldest friends, will have the last word: 'Now I begin to understand that there is a great consoling reality – Primo's everlasting work, a monument more durable than bronze.'

Acknowledgements

During the long period of research and writing of this book, many have helped me. But I owe my greatest debt to my wife, Laura Fleminger. She bore the brunt and supported me, drew up battle plans, discussed the work in progress, blue-pencilling and praising where needed. I frequently imposed on her time and patience, and her wise counsel helped to keep the frights at bay. The book has benefited enormously from her suggestions: without them, it would have been much less than it is. Throughout the long haul, the resilience of Maud, Sidney and Henry has been as extraordinary.

I was the first biographer to journey in Levi's tracks, and almost all the people I interviewed had not spoken at length about Levi before: dredging their memories, patiently reconstructing the past, was sometimes difficult and painful for them. Nevertheless, they granted me permission to quote material in their possession, and often sent me written recollections. I am very grateful to them all and feel privileged to have spent time in their company.

Among Levi's own close friends and family, I wish to single out for special thanks: his cousin, Giulia Colombo Diena, who provided important material and photographs, and endured my interrogations (all fourteen of them). I could not have re-created Levi's early years without her help. I would also like to thank Primo Levi's sister, Anna Maria Levi (to whom I spoke on six occasions), for her important insights and memories. I hope this book does not disappoint her. ('You already know too much,' she told me.) My immense gratitude also goes to Norberto Bobbio, Bianca Guidetti Serra, Alberto Salmoni and Silvio Ortona, who patiently withstood the fossicking of a literary detective. Luisa and Alberto Papuzzi were unfailingly generous with their hospitality and recollections: it is impossible to acknowledge adequately their help. Many other of Levi's friends were of great assistance to me: Leo Avigdor, Ezra BenGershôm, Alberto Cavaglion, Giorgio Diena, Laura Felici, Vittorio Foa, Guido Fubini, Alessandro Galante Garrone, Eugenio Gentili, Carla Gobetti, Sergio Grandini, Marco (Marek) Herman, Emilio Jona, Giuliana Lattes. I would also like to thank Andrea C. Levi and his brother Giovanni Levi, the artists Sandro Lupano and Emanuele ('Lele') Luzzati, Giorgio Luzzati, the late Frida Malan, Maria Vittoria Malvano, Elda Mancini, Bartolo Mascarelli (the legendary wine producer), Mila Momigliano and Luisa Monti. Many other of Levi's friends patiently tolerated my questioning: Nicoletta Neri, Mario Portigliatti, Vittorio Rieser, Gino Sacerdote, Ugo Sacerdote, Bruno Salmoni, Giorgio Segre, Bianca Tallone, Benedetto Terracini, Giorgio Vaccarino, Anna Bises Vitale, Rodolfo Weisz and Marisa Zini. I would especially like to thank William Weaver for his hospitality in New York and Tuscany.

I am sorry that Livio Norzi is no longer alive to see this book. In spite of his illness ('I'm a shadow of my old self'), he was willing to talk at length about his best friend Primo. Raymond Rosenthal, Lidia Rolfi, Guido Bachi and Luciana Nissim (to whom I owe a special debt of gratitude) are also sadly no longer with us; I feel fortunate to have spoken to them for this biography. Many of the following have also given me important help – interviews and/or correspondence – and I thank them all warmly. I list them according to themes in Levi's life.

School: Giovanni Agnelli, Elvira Barbera, Maria Borelli, Guido Filogamo, Franco Fini, Bruno Foa, Vera Gay, Barbara Gibellini, Camillo ('Mimi') Kind, Nina Kozaryn, Guglielmo Lanza, Enzo Levi, Vanna Nocerino, Franco Operti, Carla and Franca Ovazza, Lidia Carbonatto Palomba, Roberto Perdomi, Ada Pinardi, Fernanda Pivano (thank you for the meals in Milan), Giovanni Ramella, Sergio Valvassori. *University*: Giovanna Balzaretti, Guido Bonfiglioli, Sidney Calvi, Liborio Casale, Nicolò Dallaporta, Silvia Delleani, Bernard Delmay, Gaetano Di Modica, Leo Gallico, Carola Garelli, Franco Momigliano, the late Carla Moschino, Gabriele Pelli, Nereo Pezza, Mario Piacenza (for his correspondence from Peru), Vanna Rava, Marino Revelli, Guido Saini, Vittorio Satta, Ester Valabrega, Emma Vita-Levi. Special thanks to Edith Weisz (Godel) for her kindness in America and her marvellous letters. *The asbestos mine*: Tatiana Marchioli Fascilla, Maria Mariotti, Margherita Pasquotti, Libero Vernoli. *Wartime Milan*: Gabriella Garda (Aliverti), Anna Cases, Carla Consonni, Aldo Ribet, Camillo Treves. *Resistance*: Nini Agosti, Pia Astrologo, the late Gianni Dolino, Pier Paolo ('Poluccio') Favout, Vittorio Finzi, Mario Giovana, Gustavo Malan, Aldo Piacenza. *Fossoli and Auschwitz*: Teresa Azzali, Silvio Barabas (for his splendidly detailed letters from Canada), the late Alfred Battams, Paolo Dalla Volta, Chaja Davidovic, Marcello Franceschi, Rodolfo Goldbacher, Nadia Hamilton, Renata Heidebroek, Enrica Jona, Roman Jurczak, Gerry and Simone Lakmaker, the late Hermann Langbein, Father don Lenta, Ella Lingens-Reiner, Ala Manerba, Ferruccio Maruffi, Christina Meyer, Liana Millu, Aldo Moscati, the late Antonio Pacagnella, Secondo Perrone, Lello Perugia, Colonel Vasily Petrenko, Giuseppe Sacerdoti, Paola Sacerdoti, Renato Sacerdoti, Ulda Sacerdoti (Goldbacher), Jean Samuel, Giuliana Tedeschi, Piero Terracina, Italo Tibaldi, Bruno Vasari, Joe Van der Velde, Elio Vitale. *DUCO*: Bruno Barolo, Edoardo Camussi, the late Leonildo Carrà, Luciano Colombo (for his photographs and superb written testimony), the late Felice Fantino, Anna Pasio, Giunio Ruspino, Maria Tabasso. *SIVA*: Paola Accati, Keith Barnes, Luigi Bernardi, Nanni Ciagne, Francesco Cordero, Orsolina Ferrero, Carmen Franchi, Renzo Groff, Raffaele Guariniello, Felice Malgaroli, Carlo Molino, Virgilio Pecchio, Renato Portesi, Francesco Proto, Giorgio Schiavina, the brothers Selvestrel (Egisto, Piero and Redente), Maurilio and Franca Tambini, Marvi Targa, Michael Tinker, Luigi Tosini, Giuseppe Venezia. *SIVA trips to Germany*: Luisa Accati, Willi Dünwald, Brigitte (Wünsche) Mielke, Hans Schlegel. *Einaudi*: Luca Baranelli, the late Giulio Bollati, Guido Davico Bonino, Esther Calvino, the late Sergio Caprioglio, Carlo Carena, Roberto Cerati, Francesco Ciafaloni, the late Nino Colombo, Elena De Angeli, the late Giulio Einaudi, Ernesto Ferrero, Luciano Foà, the late Paolo Fossati, Carlo Fruttero, Agnese Incisa, Enrica Melossi, the late Oreste Molina, Alan Nixon, Nico Orengo, Ruggiero Romano, Malcolm Skey, Renato Solmi, Corrado Stajano, Corrado Vivanti. *Israel*: Gastone Cottino, Paola De Benedetti, Isaac Garti, Nina Harel, Gonda Israel, Franca Mussa Ivaldi, Avrom Kantor, Rina Klinov, Meir Michaelis. *La Stampa*: Piero Bianucci, Giorgio Calcagno, Oreste Del Buono, Giampaolo Dossena, Lorenzo Mondo, Gabriella Poli, Alberto Sinigaglia, the late Lucia Solazzo. *The 1970s and Levi's children*: Giorgio Ardito, Miguel Hernandez-Bronchoud, Marco Camoletto, Francesco d'Errico, Piero Fassino, Pietro Marcenaro, Sergio Parmentola. *Goethe Institut*: Hens Fischer, Lily-Maria von Hartmann, Jutta Pabst, Anna Maria Savoini, Carla Vernaschi. *Saipem trip to Sicily*: Paolo Andreocci, Pietro Costanzo, Andrea Nemiz, Gian Luigi Piccioli. *Return to Auschwitz 1982*: Emanuele Ascarelli, Ugo Caffaz, Luciano Caro, Baldassare Gulotta, Sandro Servi, Gisella Vita-Finzi, Emanuele Viterbo. *Visit to the United States of America*: Rabbi Ben Beliak, Emile Capouya, Furio Colombo, Giorgio Colombo, Leslie Epstein, Leonard Fine, Alberto Finzi, Rita Floriani, Pietro Frassica, Bernard Gordon, Roberta Heyman-Steppa, H. Stuart Hughes, Zella Luria, Lucian Marquis, Robert Pollack,

Alvin Rosenfeld, Raymond Rosenthal, John K. Roth, Arthur Samuelson, Bobbe Siegel, Jim Silberman, David Sidorsky, Sandro Stille, Michael Thomas (A. M. Heath), Bernard Toscani, Irene Williams, Andrew Viterbi and, above all, Anna Yona, for copies of the original typescript of *If This is a Man* and a memorable (if near-fatal) Chinese meal.

My thanks are also due to the following actors, directors, writers, historians, publishers, translators and journalists who knew or who felt close to Levi: Janusz Adamczyk, Flavio Ambrosini, Aharon Appelfeld, Maarten Asscher, Giorgio Bandini, Paolo Barbero, Peter Bedrick, Marina Berti, Claire Bloom, Anna Bravo, Edith Bruck, Cesare Cases, Guido Ceronetti, Saul Chapman, Giorgio Chiesura, Michael Darlow, Peter Davison, Gianfranco De Bosio, Frida De Matteis-Vogels, Doina Condrea Derer, Massimo Dini, Umberto Eco, Max Eilenberg, Ruth Feldman, Edmo Fenoglio, Peter Forbes, Alberto Gozzi, Günter Grass, Howard S. Greenfeld, Stella Humphries, Daniele Jalla, Marina Jarre, George Jochnowitz, Moshe Kahn, Barbara Kleiner, Michael Krüger, Michael Kustow, Gina Lagorio, Paul Lee, Laura Lepschy, Arrigo Levi, Guido Lopez, Mario Macagno, Mladen Machiedo, Claudio Magris, Pieralberto Marché, David Meghnagi, Joachim Meinert, Mario Monicelli, Sheila Murphy, Adeline (Lubell) Naiman, Sante Notarnicola, Giorgio Novara, Rolf Orthel (for his Dutch TV transcripts of Levi), Marco Parodi, Giuseppina ('Pucci') Panzieri, Pirko Peltonen, Camillo Penatti, Oscar Pinkus, Gillo Pontecorvo, Carlo Ponti, Delfina Provenzali, Tim Radford, John Reeves (for his generous Toronto correspondence), Max Reinhardt, Francesco Remotti, Nuto Revelli, the late Heinz Riedt, Luise Rinser, the late Lalla Romano, Netty Rosenfeld, Francesco Rosi, Philip Roth, Massimo Scaglione, Carlo Sgorlon, the late Mario Soldati, the late Stephen Spender, Mario Rigoni Stern, Vittorio Strada, Brian Swann, Lorenzo Tomatis, the late Fulvio Tomizza, Roberto Vacca, Giorgio Voghera, the late Paolo Volponi, Guido Waldman, Fred Wander, Matthias Wegner, Jeanne Wikler, Stuart Woolf, Aldo Zargani, Renzo Zorzi. I would also like to thank the scientists Corrado Böhm, Luciano Caglioti, Isabella Lattes Coifmann, Louis J. De Felice, Margherita Hack, Rita Levi Montalcini and Tullio Regge for their help and support.

Some people took on the onerous task of reading the typescript in its early draft, and I thank them: David Cesarani, Kerry Rankine, my literary agent Pat Kavanagh, and my parents John and Ingrid Thomson (my father heroically read the typescript three times, and helped to clarify numerous Latin and Greek terms). My parents-in-law, Drs Ruth and John Fleminger, offered insightful comments on Levi's depression and his relationship to his mother, for which I would dearly like to thank them. Gaia Servadio provided welcome encouragement for the work in progress. I also thank my copy-editor, Mandy Greenfield, whose skill and exactitude improved the book. Euan Cameron, my commissioning editor, made this biography possible; I am also grateful to my present editor, Tony Whittome, for putting up with this project for so long, and for his continual encouragement. I owe a debt of gratitude to all those who helped translate German texts for me, among them Lady Bramall, the late Dorothea Alexander, Iris Teichmann and Julie Deacon; but above all to Petra Wonnemann, who showed great patience and kindness going through the Hety Schmitt-Maas, Albert Speer and Jean Améry correspondence. My friend Cecilia Robustelli deciphered 1880s' Bene Vagienna legal documents, while Francesca Albini clarified (otherwise illegible) Italian trial papers from 1946. I am grateful to Zinovy Zinik for his help with Russian translations. My wife's aunt, Rita Brodie, put me in touch with Rabbi Toledano, chief of Britain's Sephardic congregation, for the clarification of Jewish terms. I thank them both.

Further thanks are due to the archivists and librarians at the following institutions for their material: Piotr Setkiewicz of the Auschwitz Museum (Muzeum Oswiecim); Lia Onesti, secretary of ANED in Turin (Associazione Nazionale Ex Deportati Politici nei Campi Nazisti); Colonel Umberto Mangia, Distretto Militare di Torino, Ufficio Documentazione e Matricola; F. Libertini of the Unione Culturale Franco Antonicelli, Turin; Paolo Momigliano of the Istituto Storico della Resistenza in Valle d'Aosta; the late Paolo Gobetti of the Istituto Storico della Resistenza in Turin; Bice Migliau of the Centro di Cultura Ebraica in Rome; Walter Barberis (Carteggio Einaudi); Pietro Crivellaro of the Centro Studi Teatro Stabile, Turin; Ilaria Cavallo of the Fondazione Istituto Piemontese Antonio Gramsci, Turin; Dr Lodi of the Births and Deaths Register in Turin (I could not have established vital dates without her help); Elia Vayra of the Archivio dello Stato, Cuneo; Nuria Schoenberg of the Archivio Luigi Nono; Elena Bruno Racca of the Associazione Culturale Italiana (ACI) in Turin; Liliana Picciotto Fargion and Gigliola Lopez of the Fondazione Centro di Documentazione Ebraica Contemporanea (CDEC) in Milan; Ingrid Kussmaul of the Schiller-Nationalmusuem Deutsches Literaturarchiv (which houses some of the Meyer–Levi–Schmitt-Maas correspondence); Aune Renk of the Stiftung Archiv Der Akademie der Künste, Berlin; C. S. Wichmann of the Wiener Library, London; Gillian Thomas (London) and Dr Meinzer (Ludwigshafen) of BASF public relations; Andrew Tait of Bayer public relations in Leverkusen.

My thanks are also due to: the Biblioteca Provincia and Biblioteca Civica of Turin; the Archivio dello Stato, Turin; the Central Science Reference

Library, London; the Imperial War Museum archives; the British Library; the London Library; the Bodley Head archive at Reading University; the Fondazione L. Einaudi in Turin; the Chemistry Institute archives, Turin University; the International Tracing Service, Geneva; the New York Psychoanalytic Institute (the Abraham A. Brill Library).

I am extremely grateful to the following for permission to quote from published and unpublished works, letters and diaries: Levi's writings in Italian, English and German are quoted by kind permission of the trustees of the Levi Estate, Giulio Einaudi editore, Faber & Faber and Carl Hanser Verlag; Carla Consonni, the late Heinz Riedt, Cordula (Meyer) Blossfeld, Marianne (Schmitt-Maas) Felsche and Carla Ponchiroli (for permission to quote from various unpublished letters); the Levi Estate (for the Zinober-Joffe, Schmitt-Maas, Meyer and Mendel correspondence); Vittorio Finzi, Leo Avigdor and Sarah Murphy (for their unpublished diaries); Vivienne Zinober, David Mendel, Jean Samuel, Enrico and Sandra Hirsch (for Jolanda and Leonardo De Benedetti's letters); Nadia Hamilton, Secondo Perrone, Dennis Linder, Charles Conreau, Simon Wiesenthal, Claude Lévi-Strauss, Jane Rye, Ruth Hoffman and Dr Pierre C. Schindel of the Jean Améry estate.

Finally, the following helped in all sorts of ways, and I salute them: Sion Segre Amar, the late Renata Antonicelli, Gloria Arbib, Maurizio Avato, J. G. Ballard, Mauro Barrera, Harold Baum, Marco Belpoliti (for his photocopied material), the late Isaiah Berlin, Denys Blakeway, Flemming Boldt, Ingrid Börge, Owen Bowcott, Lord Bullock, Ian Buruma, Anna Cardinali, the late Pietro Cavallero, Ida and Carlo Cordin, Azio Corghi, the late Lord Dainton, Franca De Benedetti, Eva Yona Deykin, Raffaella Di Giovanni, Luciano Faioni, Joe Farrell, Piero Femore, Michelangelo Fessia (for his unstinting help in Bene Vagienna), Laura Firpo, Dr Simon Fleminger, Guido Franzinetti, Diego Gambetta, Giovanna Galante Garrone, Anna Mila Giubertoni, Germaine Greer, my friend Louise Haines (who helped me more than I knew), James Hamilton-Paterson, Maurice Hatton, Christopher Hawtree, Henrietta Heald, Zöe Heller, Roald Hoffmann, Laura Huxley, Gabriel Josipovici, Mary Lawson (Sherborne School for Girls), Emanuel Litvinoff, Philip Lyons, Paola Mazzarelli (a very big thank you), Eva Menzio, Francis Miller, James Nagel, Mario Nati, Ernst Nolte, Paul O'Hanrahan, Riccardo Orizio (for the generous loan of his flat in Milan), Peppino Ortoleva, Raffaella Pagani, Brigid Pailthorpe, Roberto Pattono, Mike Petty, Angelo Pezzana, Jan Piggott, Lucy Plaskett, Pastor Giuseppe Platone, Robert Rayman (my Haitian comrade), the late, lamented Alan Ross, Monica Rovelli, Anthony Rudolf, Igor Sapožkov (for his Soviet reviews of Levi), Pastor Jean-Louis Sappé, Erica Scroppo (for your hospitality and recollections, along with broccoli and anchovy pasta), Mine Serefoglu, David Sexton, Darina Silone, Iain Sinclair, Risa Sodi, Norman Stone, Jane Streetly, Giorgio Sudario (*La Stampa*'s marvellous archivist), Vera Székàcs, Adrian Tahourdin of the *TLS*, David Terracini, Giovanni Tesio, Mark Thompson (for his Italian books and kind words), Laura Toscano (my best and truest Roman friend), Luigi ('Gigi') Ventre, Adriano Vitelli, Daniel Weil, Arnold Wesker, Robert Winder. This list of acknowledgements is inevitably a long one, yet I am certain to have missed some whom I should have thanked. I can only apologise to them.

I am very happy to acknowledge the Society of Authors, who generously allowed me a grant to complete this work.

REFERENCES

Where it is obvious from the text who is writing to whom, I have given the date only of letters (if known). I have listed in the Acknowledgements the libraries and institutions consulted, and to save space I have referred to them here as briefly as possible ('Distretto Militare', for example). The Archivio Centrale dello Stato, the Italian state archive (Turin), is referred to as ACS; the Archivio del Centro di Documentazione Ebraica Contemporanea in Milan is ACDEC; the Carteggio Primo Levi at Einaudi is CPLE; the Bodley Head archive at the University of Reading is BHUR.

Primo Levi is referred to throughout these notes by his initials: PL. My interview with him took place on 10 July 1986, and lasted approximately four hours. Wherever appropriate, I have used the many things Levi said to me, citing them thus: PL to author.

In January 1989 I interviewed several of Primo Levi's friends for an article that appeared in the *Sunday Times* (30 April 1989, 'Death of a survivor'). These interviews are identified below by *S. Times*. I have referred to my most-mentioned sources by their initials. These are:

PA: Pia Astrologo
GBC: Giovanna Balzaretti (Caccia)
EB: Ezra BenGershôm
GB: Guido Bonfiglioli
EBS: Edith Bruck (Steinschreiber)
GCD: Giulia Colombo Diena
CC: Carla Consonni
LDB: Leonardo De Benedetti
MD: Massimo Dini
GE: Giulio Einaudi

RF:	Ruth Feldman
EF:	Ernesto Ferrero
RH:	Ruth Hoffman
AML:	Anna Maria Levi
PM:	Pieralberto Marché
FM:	Ferdinand Meyer
AM:	Aldo Moscati
LNM:	Luciana Nissim (Momigliano)
LN:	Livio Norzi
AP:	Alberto Papuzzi
SP:	Secondo Perrone
LP:	Lello Perugia
MP:	Mario Piacenza
RP:	Renato Portesi
HR:	Heinz Riedt
RR:	Raymond Rosenthal
AS:	Alberto Salmoni
JS:	Jean Samuel
HS-M:	Hety Schmitt-Maas
BGS:	Bianca Guidetti Serra
MRS:	Mario Rigoni Stern
GT:	Giovanni Tesio
FT:	Fulvio Tomizza
SV:	Sergio Valvassori
WW:	William Weaver
EW:	Edith Weisz
AY:	Anna Yona

Other abbreviations are as follows:

SR:	*The Search for Roots*
VM:	*The Voice of Memory*
PL-TR:	Primo Levi and Tullio Regge: *Conversations*

For the purposes of accuracy and continuity, I have chosen to refer to the two Italian volumes of Primo Levi's work, *Opere I* and *II,* an edition published by Giulio Einaudi in 1997 and 1998. Though the edition does not include all of Levi's work (for example, his first published poem), it is reliable.

Preface

xiv   'total in intention …': VM, p.180.

1   'Corpse found in ...': quoted in police document (11.4.1987; H.15.00), Commissariato San Secondo Torino; signed Dr Carratta.

2   'I confirm that I perform ...': Processo verbale di sommarie informazioni testimoniali rese da GASPERI Jolanda (Commissariato San Secondo, Torino: 30.4.1987).

2   'Have you seen ...': Italian newspapers (12 April 1987) consulted for this chapter: *L'Unità*, *Il Mattino*, *Il Messagero*, *Corriere della Sera*, *La Repubblica*, *Il Giorno*, *Il Centro*, *Giornale di Sicilia;* also (13 April 1987) *Stampa Sera*.

3   'I confirm that I am a nurse ...': Processo verbale di sommarie informazioni testimoniali rese da GIORDANINO Elena (Commissariato San Secondo, Torino: 11.4.1987).

4   'Confirmed hereby ...': Servizio Sanitario Nazionale Regione Piemonte, U.S.L Torino 1-23 (Oggetto: const. decesso).

5   'Rigor present ...': Referto Medico: 13.4.1987. Università di Torino, Istituto di Medicina Legale.

5   'all papers relative ...': Atti relativi al suicidio di LEVI Primo. Tribunale di Torino: Ufficio Instruzione Penale (N.2078. Reg. Gen. Istr; N.1585/87 c P.M).

Chapter 2 : The Family Before Levi

7   'The locals would tut-tut ...': stories of the Levi family's ostentation were first told to me by Margherita De Santi (26 Feb. 1993), who now inhabits the Piazza Botero house. Documents relating to the Levi bank are in the State Archives of Cuneo (fondo del Tribunale di Mondovì, serie Sentenze Civili). The births and deaths of the Levi family are held in the Register Office, Bene Vagienna. Details of the fourteen properties owned by the Levis are in the Land Registry archives, Bene Vagienna. For an account of the Mondovì ghetto, see *Anni di prova* (1969), by the Italian historian and jurist Arturo Carlo Jemolo. Jemolo describes the ghetto during his mother's day in 1842, six years prior to the Jews' emancipation.

8   'My Dearest ...': a copy of Michele Levi's dissertation, 'Calcolo delle dimensioni d'una incavallatura Polonceau', is in the Biblioteca Civica, Turin.

8   '1 metre 67 ...': Michele Levi's military papers, State Archives, Cuneo.

8   '*benestante*': Register Office, Bene Vagienna. Adele Sinigaglia was

born either in 1855 or 1857 (her tomb in Turin says one date; the Turin city register, another).

8   'Signor Giuseppe Levi ...': State Archives, Cuneo (atti notarili). The document is stamped with the Savoy coat of arms: Victor Emanuel II was now king of a unified Italy. The record of the bishop of Mondovì's loan is also in the State Archives, Cuneo.

8   'The firm owned ...': *Gazzetta del Popolo*, Friday 3 Aug. 1888, under the headline: 'IL KRAK DELLA BANCA LEVI'. The firm's 500,000 lire (1886) = 2,443,729,400 lire (1966); calculation made by Banca d'Italia, London.

9   '*i Levi dei tulipani*': the 'tulip' epithet was told to me by the ninety-year old Olga Soardi (27 Feb. 1993), and substantiated by AML.

9   'Cedularius': the assault on the Levi house was first reported in the *Gazzetta del Popolo*, Friday 3 Aug. 1888.

10   '*precipitazione dall'alto*': Ospedale Maggiore di San Giovanni Battista: ufficio cartelle cliniche.

10   'a well-known Israelite ...': 'The Paradise' is described in the Bene Vagienna Land Registry archives as a '*vigne con casino*' (shooting lodge with vineyards). It was bought in 1876 from the Cavalier Augusto del Villar.

11   'anti-Jewish priest': Dr Cristofero ('Rino') Colombo to author, 29 May 1995.

11   'raving madness': *Gazzetta del Popolo*, 3 Aug. 1888.

11   'committee of inspection': Fascicolo del Fallimento del Giuseppe Levi. State Archives, Cuneo.

11   'ever more ruinous operations ...': ibid.

12   'To the dear memory of ...': the tombstone (in 3 Israel, quadro 4: fila 1, fossa 35) bears the inscription '*Alla cara memoria di/ Levi ing. Michele/ Rapito all' Affetto dei Suo/ Cari il 26 luglio 1888/ La moglie e figli pregano/ eterna pace*'.

12   'Honorary Health Inspector': *Guida di Torino*, 1920 (ed. Marzorati), under 'Beneficenza, Filantropia e Previdenza'. Rebaudengo saw to the health of 300 children in an orphanage on Via Gaudenzio Ferraris.

13   'Nobody wanted to stay ...': Augusto Monti, *Torino falsa magra*.

14   '*Salut, ingegné*!': GCD to author, 27 May 1992. Details of Cesare Levi's engineering course are in the Politecnico di Torino, Dipartimento di Ingegneria archives.

15   'Engineer Francesco ...': *La Stampa*, 8 Oct. 1918, p.3, under 'Stato Civile di Torino: Matrimoni'.

Chapter 3: A Blackshirt Childhood

17   'useful when it rains ...': PL to author.

17   'logical', 'spacious': ibid.

18   'one of twelve babies ...': *La Stampa*, 1 Aug. 1919, 'Stato Civile di Torino'.

18   'a Botticellian angel': Vittorio Foa to author, 22 Oct. 1992.

20   'it gave Laura nightmares ...': Laura Huxley to author, 1 Nov. 1993. (Parts of my interview with Laura Huxley appeared in the *Independent* Magazine, 'Seeing the Light', 30 April 1994.)

21   'a single kiss ...': PL to Rosella Fragola, *Piemonte Vivo*, June 1982.

23   'His arms were too long ...': AY to author, 20 March 1994.

23   'In order to accommodate ...': SR, p.4.

26   'She was a wise ...': AY to author, 20 March 1994.

27   'The Blackshirts had not ...': from transcript of unpublished interview with PL by Dutch TV journalist Rolf Orthel, 1974.

29   'My brother was fun ...': AML to author, 21 Oct. 1992.

30   'crystal clear ...': ibid.

30   'oppressively boring': PL to GT (unpublished interview); PL's words reported to author by GT, 15 Oct. 1995.

31   'my virginal mistress ...': *Opere II*, p.986.

32   'pretty stupid men': AML to author, 26 Oct. 1992.

32   'everybody's friend': SV to author, 25 Feb. 1993.

32   'industrious ant ...': Ignazio Filogamo to author, 15 Feb. 1996.

32   'expensive kit': Leo Avigdor to author (letter), 29 July 1995.

Chapter 4: An Anxious Boyhood

33   'five per cent Jewish ...': PL to author.

34   'I must be getting old ...': Luzzati's words reported to author by GCD, 27 May 1992.

34   'If I sin it's because the flesh is weak ...': PL to author.

35   'for days afterwards Primo enthused ...': GCD to author, 8 Sept. 1993.

35   'real dialogue did not exist ...': PL to author.

35   'At the age of five he had asked Cesare ...' PL interviewed by MD, 1984; unpublished transcript.

35   'planned to write a novel': PL's idea for this novel was told to me by Luisa Monti, 10 Feb. 1993.

36   'Trying to tell them about Schopenhauer ...': PL to GT, 'A

Proposito di una biografia mancata', *Primo Levi: Memoria e Invenzione*.

36   'I didn't like the way ...' PL interviewed by Paolo Terni, *'La musica e i dischi di Primo Levi'*, Italian radio interview, 14—17 Feb. 1984; unpublished transcript.

36   'Primo had been off sick ...': Archives, Felice Rignon School.

36   'splintered clean off': GCD to author, 11 June 1992.

38   'Primo felt he had to provide Ester ...': AY to author, 20 March 1994.

39   'On 17 April 1928': Register Office, Turin. Rebaudengo was cremated the day after at the age of seventy-six. (His urn is tersely inscribed: 'Al Dott. Felice Rebaudengo. Morto 17 Aprile 1928'.)

40   'trash and nonsense': AML to author, 30 March 1993.

41   'Out, idiot!': Bruno Foa to author, 1 July 1993.

41   *'crème de la crème* ...': Fernanda Pivano to author, 19 March 1992.

41   'a strange tiny animal': PL interviewed by MD, 1984; unpublished transcript.

42   'a plaque would go up': PL to GT (unpublished interview); Borgogno's words reported to author by GT, 21 Aug. 1995.

42   'mischievous, unconventional intelligence': Emma Andriani to author (letter), 18 July 1995.

42   'particularly stupid': PL interviewed by MD, 1984; unpublished transcript.

42   'in a late interview ...': ibid.

43   *'un israelita'*: 11 July 1998.

43   'my brainy maestro': MP to author, 9 July 1995.

43   'Giorgio undermined ...': Giuliana Lattes to author (letter), 30 Jan. 1998.

44   'like caged animals ...': 8 Feb. 1997.

44   '200 Hebrew words': PL interviewed by Risa Sodi, *Present Tense*, May–June 1988.

45   'fear of being judged ...': PL to author.

45   'magnificent philosophy ...': MP to author, 13 Oct. 1995.

45   'he is not someone ...': VM, p.276.

46   'The unofficial Fascist ...': details of *Il Tevere*'s anti-Semitism come from Renzo De Felice's *Storia degli ebrei italiani sotto il fascismo*.

47   'three cry-babies ...': PL interviewed by AP, *Rivista della montagna*, 61, March 1984.

49   'slovenly ...': Roberto Perdomi to author, 12 April 1995.

50   'He was extremely unpleasant ...': PL to GT (unpublished interview); PL's words reported to author by GT, 21 Aug. 1995.

50 'destroyer of every human value': Alberto Moravia to author, 14 Nov. 1984 (see also 'Alberto Moravia and Indifference', *London Magazine*, Nov. 1985).

50 *'pancia-sentito-o-no?'*: LN to author, 11 Nov. 1992.

50 'Once Primo finished the novel ...': AML to author, 30 March 1993.

50 *'Arroscice Primo!'*: Carla Ovazza to author, 10 May 1995.

52 'strongly disapproved ...': PL interviewed by MD, 1984; unpublished transcript.

Chapter 5: Chemistry and Adolescence

54 *'complessato'*: Fernando Camon, *Conversazione con Primo Levi*, p.70.

54 'I don't remember that he shined ...': Bruno Foa to author, 1 July 1993.

54 'scoundrels': PL to author.

55 'physical lightweight': Bruno Foa to author, 1 July 1993.

55 'Primo Levi! You never told me!': Lidia Carbonatto to author, 28 March 1995.

56 'first crush': PL interviewed by Rosella Fragola, *Piemonte Vivo*, June 1982.

56 'developed a pretty good ...': MP to author (letter), 28 July 1995.

56 'curious friendship': PL to MP (letter), 28 Nov. 1980.

57 'pages in a book': PL-TR, p.16.

58 'breaking my balls': PL to GT (unpublished interview); don Coccolo's words reported to author by GT, 21 Aug. 1995.

58 *'Gramaticus'*: ibid.

58 'A Classical education ...': Raymond Chandler to Hamish Hamilton (letter), 10 Nov. 1950.

59 *'Saltante-Tram-in-Corso'*: LN to author, 17 Feb. 1993.

59 'Pure affliction': PL to author.

59 'Practising pseudo-Olympics ...': SV to author, 25 June 1993.

60 'But I won't tell you their names ...': GB to author, 12 March 1993.

60 'stitch of clothing': ibid.

60 'All his life Primo was terrified ...': Laura Firpo to author, 5 June 1995.

62 'It's all over for us Jews': Artom's words reported to author by Enzo Levi, 2 June 1993.

62 'Can't you see we Jews ...': Diena's words reported to author by Guido Fubini, 11 April 1995.

63 'tremble': Franco Fini to author, 23 June 1993.

63 'The poem provides': at the end of the poem, in an archly misquoted

line from Petrarch ('*Povera e nuda vai, Filosofia*'), biology is banished as useless. 'BIOLOGY, GO AWAY POOR AND NAKED': PL is expressing his discontent with science teaching at school.

63 'great boredom': PL to author.

64 'jowly and masculine-looking': Gianni Agnelli to author, 15 Nov. 1994.

64 '*greco applicato*': LN to author, 11 Nov. 1992.

64 'ground her teeth': Carla Vernsaschi to author, 3 May 1995.

64 'diligent critical awareness ...': PL, 'Ricordo di Azelia Arici', *La Stampa*, 7 July 1978.

66 'intense feeling of dizziness': PL, *La Stampa*, 3 July 1981.

66 'Maybe my brother's name ...': AML to author, 26 Oct. 1992.

66 'I was certainly not ...': VM, p.49.

66 'high fever': AML to author, 21 Oct. 1992.

67 'We have the singular ...': in *La Stampa Sera*, 5 July 1937. For the rest of the day's exams, Levi had to comment in Latin on words by Cicero – 'Remember to keep an upright soul' – as well as translate into Latin speeches made by Mussolini in 1922.

67 'stunted and deranged': PL 'Fra Diavolo sul Po', *La Stampa*, 14 Dec. 1986.

67 'important people': GCD to author, 2 Feb. 1993.

67 'I'd never be such a fool': Fernanda Pivano to author, 7 June 1993.

67 'hash of my *maturità*': PL to author.

68 'It wasn't from what Cosmo ...': PL interviewed by S. Jacomuzzi, 19–21 Oct. 1979, San Salvatore Monferrato.

Chapter 6: University and Persecution

69 'bricks-and-mortar trade ...': my portrait of Professor Ponzio is based on the recollections of Giovanna Balzaretti, Liborio Casale, Leo Gallico, Carla Moschino, Vanna Rava and Edith Weisz.

70 'If something could be said ...': Bernard Delmay to author (letter), 10 March 1994.

72 'Physics goes much deeper ...': Persico's words reported to author by Professor Carola Garelli, 14 March 1992.

72 'services rendered ...': Ponzio to Rector (letter), 6 May 1935; in Chemistry Institute Archives.

74 'a shy small boy': EW to author, 24 March 1994.

75 'you couldn't ask him': Vittorio Satta to author, 30 March 1995.

75 'attentive and kind': Liborio Casale to author, 11 May 1995.

75 'harming sales ...': Sidney Calvi to author, 17 June 1993.

76 'Primo was a wonderful teacher': Nereo Pezza to author, 29 July 1993.

78 'hunted down like rats ...': Franco Operti to author, 1 Aug. 1993.

79 'funeral hearse': Elsa Morante, *History*.

79 'If the Fascist state ...': quoted in Renzo De Felice's *Storia degli ebrei italiani sotto il fascismo*, p.215.

79 'that Jew Pincherle': Alberto Moravia to author, 14 Nov. 1984.

80 'What? You don't ...': PL to author.

81 'Shame on Italy!': Azelia Arici's words reported to author by Guglielmo Lanza, 29 March 1995.

81 'Before the persecutions ...': GBC to author, 15 April 1993.

82 'A typical example ...': Anna Bises Vitale to author, 13 Oct. 1992

82 'simian degeneration': AML to author, 20 March 1993.

83 'I Too Am Disgusting': PL, 'Fra Diavolo sul Po', *La Stampa*, 14 Dec. 1986.

84 '*APPARTIENE ALLA RAZZA* ...': Distretto Militare.

84 'Since 1516': reported to author by Cesare Cases, 9 June 1992.

86 'to ascertain whether ...': the police information on Cristofero ('Rino') Colombo is in the 'Censimento Ebraica' (A. Statistica 1938) file at ACS.

87 'the Church and the Vatican ...': Cesare's words reported to author by PL, 10 July 1986.

87 'The catastrophe ...': PL quoted, *Lotta Continua*, 10 Nov. 1982.

88 'compassionate grounds': under 'List of Jews with Aryan servants', ACS.

88 'Who Never Gets Angry': see also VM, p.145.

89 'I think we should stop meeting ...': PL interviewed in *Gli ebrei e l'Italia durante la guerra 1940–45*, p.137.

89 'We never for one moment ...': Vanna Rava to author, 18 March 1993.

Chapter 7: University and War

91 '"Aryan" blood': Marisa Zini's personal file is at the ACS, under 'Accertamenti sulla razza' documents. Diana Reduzzi's file is also at the ACS (box no. 37).

92 'denounced': the record of Mario Levi's denunciation is at the ACS (box no. 34); so is Cesare Levi's.

92 'a shoulder to lean on ...': Clara Moschino to author, 19 May 1993.

93 'gentle sunset rambles ...': Ester Valabrega to author, 22 July 1992.

94 'Up there, when a rock falls ...' Sandro Delmastro to Franco

Momigliano (letter), summer 1941. In Istituto Storico della Resistenza in Piedmont, Turin.

94 '*Lo Sbatti–Uovo*': GCD to author, 11 June 1992.

95 '*physically* bound ...': AS to author, 14 Aug. 1992.

95 'Perhaps, in some obscure way ...': PL interviewed by AP, *Rivista della montagna*, March 1984.

95 'How do we get down?': ibid.

96 'I found him unpleasant ...': PL to Emma Vita-Levi (letter), 5 July 1984.

96 'felt offended ...': GB to author, 13 March 1993.

96 'Chemistry is superficial ...': PL's words reported to author by Vanna Rava, 27 March 1993.

97 'To most assimilated Jews ...': Giorgio Segre to author, 5 April 1993.

98 'the famous Primo Levi?': from transcript of BBC Radio 3 documentary on Primo Levi, 30 July 1987.

98 'Anti-Semitism in the Last Decade': unpublished interview with PL by Gloria Arbib, 8 June 1981.

100 'Gladys Snores': my portrait of Gladys Melrose is based on the recollections of Marina Berti, Livio Norzi and Anna Maria Levi.

101 'Not to Be Considered ...': Felice Archera's personal file is at the ACS.

103 'planet's imminent fall': PL to author.

104 'shone', 'superb': AML to author, 7 April 1993.

105 'Primo had a gift ...': BGS to author, *S. Times*.

105 'We're in Italy!': 'Tre Vite', Augusto Segre, *La Rassegna Mensile di Israel*, June 1954, p.228.

106 'It tasted really ...': AS to author, 12 Aug. 1992.

106 'We could have shaved ...': GB to author, 11 March 1993.

107 'notorious anti-Fascist', PL-TR, p.21.

107 'For me this was a clear ...': Emma Vita-Levi to author, 8 May 1995.

107 'Week of High Culture': Chemistry Institute Archives.

107 'If Primo was Jewish or Hindu ...': Nicolò Dallaporta to author, 22 Sept. 1993.

Chapter 8: Life During Wartime

111 'It was then I understood ...': Nuto Revelli to author, 1 July 1992.

111 'Jakub Trackan': ACS files, envelope 561.

112 'A Turin *Kristallnacht* ...': *Opere I*, p.1235.

113 'perfect gentleman ...': Libero Vernoli to author, 11 Sept. 1992.

113 'We all knew each other ...': ibid.

114 'charmer's smile': from transcript of unpublished interview with PL by Gloria Arbib, 8 June 1981.

115 'grey incessant ...': *La Stampa*, 24 March 1942, p.2.

115 'LEVI CESARE ...': *La Stampa*, 25 March, p.2.

116 'No. 253: Levi Primo ...': ACS files, envelope 561. Levi's uncles Mario Levi ('surgeon') and Corrado Luzzati ('merchant') are also on the list.

116 'Mestro Xanda'; '*scuttrice*': ACS. (PL's future wife, Lucia Morpurgo, is bizarrely listed as 'housewife'.)

117 'I told my boss ...': Gabriella Garda Aliverti to author, 3 Nov. 1992.

119 'blood from a turnip': ibid.

120 '*maliziosa*': ibid.

121 'jumped-up Jew': Ada Della Torre, *Ha Keillah*, June 1977, p.6.

121 'off to the concentration camps!': Ada Della Torre, *Messagio speciale*, p.15.

123 'WHEN YOU SEE ...': GCD to author, 2 Feb. 1993.

126 'whole groups of children': PL mentions these sources in his testimony against SS Bosshammer, 3 May 1971. A copy of Levi's testimony is at the ACDEC (AG.11.PPFB1, Berlin).

126 'Our ignorance ...': *Opere I*, p.851.

Chapter 9: Resistance and Betrayal

129 '*DUCE: ENTRAILS*': Camillo Treves to author, 15 May 1993.

130 'It was not a nice ...': unpublished interview with PL by Gloria Arbib, 8 June 1981.

131 'At two o'clock ...': Eugenio Gentili to author, 17 Sept. 1992.

131 'a stupid joy': PL to author.

132 'I was a young bourgeois ...': ibid.

133 'September was a month ...': AML to author, 21 Oct. 1992.

133 'what civilian ...': GCD to author, 8 Sept. 1993.

133 'The Germans are at the railway ...': ibid.

134 'Don't you know the danger ...': GB to author, 12 March 1993.

134 'After Salò ...': BGS to author, 3 July 1992.

135 'The Occupants of the Saccarello': letter in possession of GCD.

136 'Amay was a trap': GB to author, 12 March 1993.

136 'flock without a shepherd': PL to author.

137 'The machine-gunning ...': Aldo Piacenza to author, 19 June 1992.

138   'Free Italy': PL (Matricola N. 12999) in Distretto Militare.

138   'We more or less had to *invent* ...': PL quoted in *La Famiglia Cristiana*, 20 July 1975, p.43.

139   'the most obscure': PL to Paolo Momigliano (letter), 26 June 1980.

139   'We were foolish ...': Aldo Piacenza to author, 15 June 1992.

139   'How can I put this?': CC to author, 18 Sept. 1992.

139   'Get out of Brusson': Eugenio Gentili to author, 9 July 1993.

140   'Vanda was bright ...': LNM to author, 21 Sept. 1992.

140   'We had to sleep huddled ...': Aldo Piacenza to author, 19 Nov. 1992.

140   'If just *one* ...': Lia Segre to author, 30 March 1995. (The *Atto di matrimonio Fubini-Segre* is in the archives of the St Vincent Town Hall; LN's signature is also legible on it.)

141   'It was *so* false ...': PL to author.

141   'All we could hear ...': PA to author, 9 May 1995.

142   '*macchie nere* ...': unpublished interview with PL by Gloria Arbib, 8 June 1981.

142   'worthy imitator and disciple ...' police file on Cagni in Aosta Tribunal archives; signed 28 July 1945 by chief of police T. Ricciardi.

142   'most dangerous elements ...': Guido Bachi, minutes to the denunciation of Cagni (verbale di denunzia), 13 July 1945.

142   'If you want to join ...': transcription of Cagni's cross-examination (interrogatorio dell'arrestato), 18 Jan. 1946, Aosta Assizes.

143   'Bolshevik nature ...: from De Ceglie's report to the Prefettura Repubblicana of Aosta, 7 March 1944.

143   'from a distance of between ...': minutes to Aldo Piacenza's interrogation by Fascist Frontier Police (Milizia Confinaria) in Aosta, 11 Jan. 1944.

143   'Look, it was wartime ...': Aldo Piacenza to author, 15 June 1992.

144   'rather closed expression': Guido Bachi to author, 14 June 1992.

144   'penetrated very ably ...': Aldo Piacenza to author, 14 June 1992.

144   'Piacenza introduced me to ...': from De Ceglie's report to the Prefettura Repubblicana of Aosta, 7 March 1944.

144   'I referred and consigned ...': ibid.

145   'Maybe if Vanda had remained ...': PA to author, 9 May 1995.

145   'being a sensible man ...': unpublished interview with PL by Gloria Arbib, 8 June 1981.

145   'Primo was interested ...': LNM to author, 21 Sept. 1992.

145   'Call yourselves Italians!': ibid.

145   'I just hoped the damned ...': Aldo Piacenza to author, 14 June 1992.

147 'Ten feet ...': Aldo Piacenza to author, 14 June 1992.

147 'burned down': letter in Istituto Storico della Resistenza in Valle d'Aosta.

148 'Signor Ferrero': PL to author.

148 'Reich enemies': from transcript of Canadian Broadcasting Corporation radio adaptation of *If This is a Man*, 24 Jan. 1965.

148 'If you're a rebel': from transcript of Michael Darlow's interview with PL (9 Dec. 1972) for *World at War*, Thames television series. Imperial War Museum.

150 'Good morning ...': Aldo Maestro's words reported to author by his widow, CC, 18 Sept. 1992.

150 'Just say they're pharmaceutical ...': Ferro's words reported to author by LNM, 21 Sept. 1992.

151 'Unable to believe ...': LNM to author, 15 May 1995.

151 'That was the moment ...': PL interviewed by GT, *Nuovasocietà*, 167, March 1980.

151 'Under the Nazis ...': LNM to author, 21 Sept. 1992.

153 'Strangely human': ibid.

153 'friendly sporting ...': PL interviewed by Risa Sodi, *Present Tense*, May–June 1988.

154 'We cut through ...': Simone Fubini to author, 12 May 1995.

156 'Welcome to Fossoli ...': Avitabile's words reported to author by Silvio Barabas (letter), 7 March 1994.

156 '*Campo grande* ...': PL in his testimony against SS Bosshammer, 3 May 1971. Copy at the ACDEC.

157 '*Scheinmännisch*': PL interviewed by Nicola Garribba in *Karnenu*, March–April 1988.

157 'with a wink': LDB and PL, 'Rapporto sulla organizzazione igienico-sanitaria del campo di concentramento per ebrei di Monowitz': *Opere I*, p.1340.

157 'None of us ever thought ...': AM to author, 30 Oct. 1995.

158 'Maybe as barracks-chief ...': Dalla Volta's words reported to author by Silvio Barabas (letter), 7 March 1994.

159 'The barriers ...': AM to author, 30 Oct. 1995.

159 'beautiful man': LNM to author, 21 Sept. 1992.

160 'We felt sordid ...': AM to author, 30 Oct. 1995.

160 '*Sechshundert* ...': PL's testimony against SS Bosshammer (as above).

161 'Remember what ...': PL interviewed by MD, 1984; unpublished transcript.

162 'If there was any solidarity ...': LNM to author, 21 Sept. 1992.

162 'We were pretty certain ...': ibid.

163 'Thirst was our ...': from transcript of television interview broadcast by the RAI programme *Sorgente di vita* in April 1983 (in VM, p.208).

163 '*mal occhio*': GCD to author; Levi cried during an unpublished interview (May 1983) with Angelo D'Orsi.

163 'We were already ...': LNM to author, 21 Sept. 1992.

164 'This train!': *Donne contro il mostro*, p.21.

165 'Max & Vitale': from transcript of interview with LDB (30 Sept. 1982) by Anna Bravo and Daniele Jalla. Parts of the interview appeared in *La vita offesa*.

166 'I'll say I'm fit ...': PL to author.

167 'He was unshaved ...': Silvio Barabas to author (letter), 7 March 1994.

167 'Clothes are a mark ...': PL to author.

167 'That was already a kind ...': LNM to author, 15 May 1995.

168 'discreet protection ...': PL to set-designer Gianni Polidori (letter), 16 Aug. 1966. In archives of Teatro Stabile, Turin.

168 'four fingers ...': ibid.

169 'The Jews were a slave army ...': PL to author.

170 'tasted good': ibid.

171 'Man might have *risen* ...': Gluecksmann is 'the character that I rebaptised "Steinlauf" in the "Initiation" chapter of *If This is a Man*', PL to AY (letter), 25 Oct. 1973.

171 'An order was given ...': PL to author.

171 'Nothing was more ...': Ibid.

172 'We were like eggs ...': PL interviewed by Anna Bravo and Daniele Jalla, *Rassegna Mensile di Israel*, n. 2–3, May–Dec. 1987.

172 'Now we shall march ...': PL interviewed by Daniela Ámsallem, *Primo Levi*, Riga 13.

172 'It might seem strange to you ...': AM to author, 6 Nov. 1995.

173 'Every beat of strength ...': from transcript of *World at War*, Thames Television series, 9 Dec. 1972.

173 'Stealing from the Germans ...': PL to author.

174 'We'd pass these endless ...': Alfred Battams to author, 13 May 1992.

175 'Those of us who fought ...': PL to author.

175 'extremely easy to die ...': ibid.

178   'a lovely spring morning ...': Anna Revelli to author, 1 July 1992.

179   'Needles were pushed ...': testimony quoted by BGS in *Storie di giustizia, ingiustizia e galera*, p.20.

179   'devoured by dogs': Pier Paolo ('Poluccio') Favout to author, 8 April 1995.

181   'shining moment of hope': JS to author, 25 Jan. 1993.

181   'You put up a protective shell ...': ibid.

182   'I'm going to make it on my own': LNM interviewed by Annamaria Guadagni, *Diario* (*L'Unità* Magazine) 26 Feb.–4 March 1997.

182   'If I die ...': *Donne contro il mostro*, p.48.

183   'the likely inmate ...': PL to author.

183   'Rome. It was decided ...': Auschwitz Museum Archives (D-Aus.III – 4/2/ Nr inw. 151234).

184   'born desponder': SP to author, 7 Oct. 1992.

184   'I was completely ...': PL to author.

185   'Come quickly': Ada Della Torre, 'Un sogno', *Ha Keillah*, December 1978, p.9.

185   'Dearest Signorina Bianca': copies of Lorenzo Perrone's postcards from Auschwitz are in the ACDEC.

186   'I'll never forget the look ...': BGS to author, 27 July 1993.

186   'There *is* no Geneva ...': Alfred Battams to author, 13 May 1992.

188   'greatest insult': PL to author.

188   'remunerating an ox': ibid.

189   'Even then I knew ...': LNM to author, 21 Sept. 1992.

190   'female figure': EGELI documents in archives of Istituto Bancario San Paolo di Torino.

191   'Judgement Day': JS to author, 26 Jan. 1993.

191   'Papa's gone ...': from transcript of unpublished interview with PL by Dutch TV journalist Rolf Orthel, 1974.

192   'She must have heard ...': Enrica Jona to author, 24 April 1995.

194   'sweetest': PL to FM (letter), 13 May 1967.

195   'I thought I was ...': from transcript of interview with LDB (30 Sept. 1982) by Anna Bravo and Daniele Jalla.

195   'The big roof trusses ...': Alfred Battams to author, 13 May 1992.

195   'animals don't ...': PL to author.

195   'The very act of ...': PL to author.

196   'Your eyes seemed ...': FM to PL (letter), 5 April 1967.

196   'Jews were to be ...': ibid.

196   'cheerful yet melancholy ...': ibid.

197   'There is no place left …': '*Für uns war kein Platz mehr in dieser Welt*'. From the *Lebensbuch* (Life Book) which FM began to write for his daughter, Cordula, in 1960.

Chapter 12: Waiting for the Russians

198   'I never thought …': AM to author, 30 Oct. 1995.

199   'Come and live …': Kaufmann's words reported to author by PL.

201   'Of us prisoners …': PL to JS (letter), 23 March 1945. Except where obvious, all subsequent quotations are from this letter.

202   'no more Boches': ibid.

202   'Suddenly your neighbour …': from transcript of Michael Darlow's interview with PL (9 Dec. 1972) for *World at War*, Thames Television series.

203   'that's not good': Charles Conreau to author, 23 Oct. 1995.

205   '*Germania kaputt!*': Teresa Azzali to author, 20 May 1995.

206   '*excellent camarade*': Charles Conreau to author, 23 Oct. 1995.

206   'after a month …': Laura Austerlitz to PL (letter). Quoted in transcript of interview with PL by Dutch TV journalist Rolf Orthel, 1974.

206   'Nevertheless I knew …': this line was cut from the typescript of *The Truce. Opere I*, p.1420.

207   'regained consciousness …': LDB in a letter home ('Carissimi tutti'), 24 Feb. 1945.

207   'My nerves …': ibid, 7 March 1945.

207   'C'est mieux …': *The Truce, Opere I*, p.245.

208   'If only I'd known …': AM to LDB (letter), 24 Oct. 1945.

210   'very bright and willing': '*molto intelligente e volonteroso*'. LDB in a letter home, 28 April 1945.

210   'foul buffoonery': quoted in Martin Gilbert, *Churchill* (vol. IV).

211   'low-life': '*Gesinde*'. From FM's *Lebensbuch* (Life Book).

212   'whom I was convinced …': ibid.

212   'What I did at Auschwitz …': ibid.

212   'I was certainly not …': AML to author, 19 Oct. 1992.

212   'When I asked Lorenzo …': SP to author, 13 Oct. 1992.

213   'And rabbits …': LP to author, 7 Aug. 1992.

214   'You too will …': ibid.

214   'We're not too badly off …': PL's letter to BGS is in the ACDEC.

215   'My dear …': AML to author, 19 Oct. 1992.

215   'emaciated …': Teresa Azzali to author, 20 May 1995.

215   'We'll go wherever …': PL to author.

216   'FAILED TO REGISTER': '*DICHIARATO RENITENTE*'. Distretto Militare.

216   'O Sole Mio': Teresa Azzali to author, 20 May 1995.
218   'I don't think …': PA to author, 9 May 1995.
218   'He wanted to know …': ibid.
218   *Madama Levi!*': Words reported by Levi's aunt Jole Luzzati. BBC TV *Bookmark* documentary on PL, 1985.

Chapter 13: Homecoming

219   'After we had all …': LN to author, 17 Feb. 1993.
220   'I had no idea …': Nereo Pezza to author, 29 July 1993.
220   'unspeakable grief': '*indiscibile dolore*'. LDB in a letter to relatives, 14 May 1947.
221   'cancer at a dinner party': from transcript of Michael Darlow's interview with PL (9 Dec. 1972) for *World at War*, Thames Television series.
223   'quarrelsome person': SP to author, 13 Oct. 1992.
223   'survivor's sickness': *Opere II*, p.66.
223   'strong as hunger': PL to author.
223   'But unlike …': AML to author, 30 March 1993.
224   'incredible': from transcript of unpublished interview with PL by Dutch TV journalist Rolf Orthel, 1974.
224   'He seemed to be talking …': Mila Momigliano to author, 29 March 1995.
225   'firefly': *Opere II*, p.535.
225   'I was her first …': PL to HS-M (letter), 2–8 Nov. 1967.
226   'Saint Joan …': words of obituary reported to author by CC, 29 July 1993.
228   'whipped dog': Felice Fantino to author, 6 Feb. 1993.
228   'uncommon person': PL to HS-M (letter), 2–8 Nov. 1967.
229   'Probably if I'd *not* written …': PL to author.
229   'like a flood …': ibid.
230   'insufferably boring': ibid.
230   'night-owl …': ibid.
230   'He didn't talk …': Giunio Ruspino to author, 10 Feb. 1993.
232   'Dante and Manzoni': PL interviewed by Vanna Nocernio, *L'Ospite*, 1979, p.17.
234   'glycerol …': PL to JS (letter), 24 May 1946.
234   'If every Italian …': Felice Fantino to author, 6 Feb. 1993.
234   'Your sentences …': Compagnucci's words reported to author by Edoardo Camussi, 16 May 1993.
235   'pudency': PL quoted in *The Voice* (N.Y), March 1986.

235   'courage': PL's letter to Umberto Saba (10 Jan. 1949) in *La Repubblica*, 27 May 1989.

236   'held back': '*Mi sono censurato*'. PL interviewed by Paola Valabrega, *Primo Levi*, Riga 13.

Chapter 14: Rebirth and Rejection

237   'a mother is ...': Guido Bachi to author, 20 March 1998.

238   'After the long ...': 25 May 1946.

238   'Honestly it seemed ...': BGS to author, 7 April 1995.

239   'almost mystical': PL interviewed by Neliana Tersigni, *Paese Sera*, p.3, 2 June 1986.

239   'On reflection ...': PL to JS (letter), 24 May 1946.

241   'sovereign politeness': PL to author.

242   'If any book ...': Camillo Treves to author, 15 May 1993.

242   'mediocre, good ...': PL to JS (letter), 16 July 1947.

244   'She is a nice person ...' VM, p.32.

244   'It must have been a bleak ...': Natalia Ginzburg to author, 12 Jan. 1985. (Sections of my interview with Ginzburg appeared in the *London Magazine*, 'Familes and Friends', Aug.–Sept. 1985.)

244   'quite interesting': Doriguzzi's words reported to author by Giorgio Diena, 12 Sept. 1992.

245   'Primo even wanted ...': EW to author, 24 March 1994.

246   'I know suffering ...': VM, p.257.

246   'This is not a memoir': Alessandro Galante Garrone to author, 13 June 1993.

248   '*bugiardi*': *Opere I*, p.366.

249   'How do I look in these?': PL's words reported to author by Bruno Salmoni, 6 Nov. 1992.

249   'I do wish ...': AS to Vittorio Venturino (letter), 3 Dec. 1948.

250   'We're three ...': PL to JS (letter), 16 July 1947.

251   'shadow zone': Anna Cases to author, 14 Sept. 1992.

251   'from the waist up': Leo Gallico to author (letter), 6 July 1994.

251   'It was supposed ...': GCD to author, 22 June 1993.

Chapter 15: Factory Responsibilities

255   'grow brighter': *Opere I*, p.682.

257   'Funny, I thought ...': AS to author, 14 Aug. 1992.

257   'He'd rather eat bread ...': PL's words reported to author by RP, 9 Nov. 1992.

258 'kind and approachable': Pietro Cavallero to author (letter), 7 Sept. 1995.

259 'cooly in control': GBC to author, 15 April 1993.

260 'For many years ...': PL to HS-M (letter), 2–8 Nov. 1967.

262 'happiest of gourmands': Francesco Proto to author, 13 April 1993.

263 'Go back to life ...': PL's words reported to author by Marcello Franceschi, 23 April 1995.

263 'Primo might have been ...': ibid.

263 'insufficient thorax': '*torace insuff.*'. Distretto Militare.

263 'In the end Lorenzo': don Carlo Lenta to author, 7 Oct. 1993.

264 'winged beasts': SP to author, 13 Oct. 1993.

264 'Though Lorenzo told me ...': don Carlo Lenta to author, 7 Oct. 1993.

268 'My dear Primo ...': LDB's words reported to author by Enrico Hirsch, 21 May 1995.

268 'It was as though Primo ...': EBS to author, 5 Aug. 1992.

Chapter 16: Journeys into Germany

271 'the Nazi period ...': Accati's words reported to author by Orsolina Ferrero, 28 Sept. 1992.

271 'Everything was blamed ...': Gabriella Poli to author, 26 May 1992.

272 'If you don't feel ...': Rico Accati's words reported to author by Paola Accati, 13 July 1992.

272 'hour of colloquy': *Opere II*, p. 1125.

272 'My name is Levi ...': PL to author.

273 'All one could hear ...': Luisa Accati to author, 6 May 1995.

274 'brutal friendship': PL to HS-M (letter), 24 Sept. 1967.

274 'sort of wild boar': Luisa Accati to author, 6 May 1995.

274 'doting gratuitously': *Opere I*, p. 1113.

279 'sound domestic ...': PL to HS-M (letter), 2–8 Nov. 1967.

279 'the occasion of his daughter's': PL to author.

280 'There were things one ...': Erica Scroppo to author, 19 Nov. 1993.

281 'The moment the defenceless ...': PL's words reported to author by Laura Firpo, 5 June 1995.

281 'Only now do I realise ...': Erica Scroppo to author, 15 Jan. 1994.

282 'Thank God for ASA-3!': PL's words reported to author by Francesco Cordero, 13 Feb. 1993.

283 'enigmatic inward ...': Orsolina Ferrero to author, 28 Sept. 1992.

283 'Francina, your make-up ...': PL's words reported to author by Franca Tambini, 1 March 1993.

284 '*Traduttore* ...': PL to author.

285 'trenchant and haughty': Stuart Woolf to author, 1 April 1993.

285 'I can see now that Tolkien ...': ibid.

285 'I'm still basking ...': Howard S. Greenfeld to author (letter), 15 Nov. 1995.

285 'insolent': *Opere II*, p.1126.

286 'portentous intelligence': PL to RF (letter), 15 April 1983.

291 'perfect collaboration': HR to author, 31 July 1992.

291 'vengeance': ibid.

293 'painful impression': Günter Grass to author (letter), 27 April 1995.

293 'bears the trace ...: Karl-Heinz Mielke's words reported to author by Brigitte (Wünsche) Mielke, 8 Dec. 1995.

293 'highly intelligent': PL to author.

294 'jackboot zone': HR to author, 31 July 1992.

294 '*bellissimo*': ibid.

294 'Germans obey ...': ibid.

295 'twin brother': Italo Calvino to author, 4 April 1984.

295 'Your attempt at ...': Calvino, *I libri degli altri*, p.383.

Chapter 17: Literary Acclaim

297 'Tell me the truth': 'In ricordo di Primo Levi', Anna Maria Zambrini, *Pitture e Vernici*, p.17, May 1987.

298 'skin': PL to author.

299 'three and four hundred ...': PL interviewed by Gabriella D'Angeli, *Famiglia Cristiana*, p.28, 27 Nov. 1966.

299 'singular': *Opere I*, p.1139.

300 'Your new book': PL's letter to MRS, quoted in *Primo Levi: Le opere e i giorni*, p.199.

300 'really love': AML to author, 26 Oct. 1992.

300 'I exhort you ...': PL to EB (letter), 5 Feb. 1962.

301 'Even if it lacks ...': *Opere I*, p.1423.

301 'Levi has made no attempt ...': *Modern Foreign Fiction*, n.8, Moscow, Sept. 1964.

302 'humane': *Yevreiski Vesti*, 8 June 1963.

303 'Honestly, I'd been meaning ...': letter published in *Shalom*, n.5, April 1988.

303 'He was quite severe ...': PL to author.

304 'martian': PL interviewed by Adolfo Chiesa, *Paese Sera*, 12 July 1963.

305 'We all know ...': ibid.

305 'excruciatingly shy': Flemming Boldt to author (letter), 30 June 1995.

305 'really unique ...': Claudio Magris quoted by PL in a letter to EB, 21 Sept. 1963.

305 'relaxed', 'fun': EB to author (letter), 25 March 1996.

305 'man called Primo': EF to author, 21 May 1993.

306 'ultramodern texts': A. Todisco, *Corriere della Sera*, 1 March 1964.

306 'I was astonished ...': FT to author, 7 July 1992.

307 'There is no maudlin ...': report by Charles Bode, BHUR.

307 'deeply involve': report by Camillo Pennati (9 Dec. 1963), BHUR.

307 'Our feeling is that ...': Guido Waldman to Peter Davison (letter), 3 July 1964. BHUR.

308 'All editors ...': PL to EB (letter), 31 July 1964.

308 'How does a man ...': Guido Waldman to PL (letter), 22 June 1964, BHUR.

308 'I definitely will ...': PL's reply (25 June 1964) to Guido Waldman, BHUR.

308 'It was too early ...': Peter Davison to author (letter), 16 June 1994.

308 'manhandled by a translator ...': PL to GE (letter), 4 Nov. 1966, in CPLE.

309 'But it wasn't easy ...': Franceso Rosi to author, 10 June 1987. (Parts of my interview with Rosi appeared in the *Independent*, 'National Enquirer', 18 June 1987.)

309 'It's principally ...': PL to EB (letter), April 1967.

310 'Primo *who*?': Carlo Ponti to author, 23 May 1994.

310 'If you allow me ...': PL to EB (letter), 2 April 1967.

310 'Yet they were able ...': John Reeves to author (letter), 26 Jan. 1994.

311 'He performed in such ...': PL to EB (letter), 27 Jan. 1979.

311 'Re-creating Auschwitz ...': Giorgio Bandini to author, 23 May 1995.

311 'I haven't the faintest ...': PL to EB (letter), 31 July 1964.

311 'I had hoped to go ...': PL–TR, p.13.

311 'I do not know if I shall ...': PL to EB (letter), 31 July 1964.

311 'He had the *orgoglio* ...': Lorenzo Mondo to author, 1 June 1992.

312 'It wasn't just ...': Keith Barnes to author, 1 May 1992.

313 'fairground': PL to author.

313 'No, you really ...': PL's words reported to author by PM, 16 June 1992.

313 'very dirty': Giuliana Tedeschi to author, 17 June 1992.

314 'That really hurt me': PL interviewed by Antonio Monda in *Il Mattino*, 29 March 1988.

314 'And this work …': PL to GE (letter), 23 November 1965, in CPLE.

314 'Levi-*Truce*': Roberto Cerati in a letter to PL, 1 Aug. 1966, in CPLE.

315 'Primo was like a child …': Massimo Scaglione to author, 8 June 1992.

316 'They behaved exactly …': PL's words reported to author by MRS, 24 Oct. 1992.

317 'What *is* this?': PL's words reported to author by PM, 16 June 1992.

317 'When something was a problem …': Keith Barnes to author, 1 May 1992.

317 'I kept telling Primo …': PM to author, 16 June 1992.

317 'spotlessly clean …': PL to set-designer Gianni Polidori (letter), 16 Aug. 1966. In Teatro Stabile archives, Turin.

318 'In the midst …': PL to Umberto Ceriani (letter), 18 Nov. 1966. In Teatro Stabile archives, Turin.

318 'curled up with …': GBC to author, 15 April 1993.

318 '*documentalnaya povest*': *Modern Foreign Fiction*, n.2, Moscow, May 1968.

319 'It was as if after *Macbeth* …': Carlo Fruttero to author, 15 June 1992.

319 'Primo Levi, who travelled …': *Cosmicomics*, as shown to author by PL, 10 July 1986.

Chapter 18: 'On the Other Side of the Barbed-Wire Fence'

322 'Bloody fool': Franca Tambini to author, 8 March 1993.

322 'Is there a Dr Primo …?': PL to Michael Kustow, 18 April 1986.

322 'closer to neurosis …': PL to author.

323 'Levi had no get-up-and-go …': Maurilio Tambini to author, 18 April 1993.

324 'he never let on …': Carmen Franchi to author, 15 July 1992.

325 'like an ambulance …': RP to author, 9 Nov. 1992.

325 'Don't do it …': PL's words reported to author by Carmen Franchi, 15 July 1992.

325 'bending the tubes …': RP to author, 4 June 1993.

326 'He didn't like humour …': ibid.

327 'And the Jews complain …': HS-M to PL (letter), 14 March 1967.

327 'When my husband …': Renata Heidebroek to author, 11 Dec. 1995.

329 'He spoke to me constantly …': Cordula Blossfeld to author, 13 Dec. 1995.

329 'Unlike Levi, I have …': Jean Améry to HS-M, 28 Sept. 1967.

331 'a sort of owl …': Bartolo Mascarello to author, 29 April 1995.

332   'This land of martyrs ...': PL quoted in *Resistenza*, July 1967.

332   'Perhaps such lands ...': PL to HS-M, 17 June 1967.

333   'behalf of all ...': PL to Oscar Pinkus, 5 August 1967.

334   'very difficult and obsessive ...': Marianne Felsche to author, 16 May 1995.

335   'tormented': HS-M, diary.

335   'metaphysical *Schmus* ...': Jean Améry to HS-M, 28 Sept. 1967.

337   'rather lugubrious': PL to author.

Chapter 19: Israel, USSR and Depression

339   'It was excruciating ...': Erica Scroppo to author, 19 Nov. 1993

340   'life-raft': PL, quoted in Jewish Telegraphic Agency, 16 November 1990.

340   'very troubled': Isaac Garti to author (letter), 12 Nov. 1995.

341   'they chatted ...': Gastone Cottino to author, 24 Feb. 1993.

341   'rather provincial': PL to author.

342   '*general* tiredness': PL to HS-M (letter), 4 July 1968.

342   'bad for his image ...': Giorgio Vaccarino to author, 1 Feb. 1993.

342   'extremely violent': Marco Parodi to author, 13 June 1995.

344   'panting in an African ...': PL to HS-M (letter), 17 Aug. 1969.

344   'poor thing': PL to HS-M (letter), 14 July 1968.

344   'born from below', VM, p.165.

345   'If a pupil ...': Feruccio Maruffi to author, 13 June 1992.

345   'Even if we prisoners ...': PL to author.

346   'interpretation': PL to HS-M (letter), 28 Dec. 1972.

346   'impromptu time-keeping': PL to Charles Conreau (letter), 22 June 1972.

347   'praiseworthy efficiency': PL to HS-M, 13 June 1970.

347   'All Russians are equal ...': PL to Carlo Paladini, 5 May 1986, Teatro Rossini, Pesaro.

348   'I was naive ...': PL's words reported to author by Peppino Ortoleva (letter), 10 July 1995.

348   'He has lost not a bit ...': PL to HS-M (letter), 13 Dec. 1970.

349   'sad and shrouded ...': PL to MRS, 13 Dec. 1970.

350   'We live in a world ...': VM, p.70.

350   'disillusioned and disenchanted': PL to AY, 7 Sept. 1971.

350   'suffered the fate': PL to author.

350   'cold inward deadness': PL's words reported to author by LN, 17 Feb. 1993.

351   '*Sprachprobleme*': HS-M, diary.

353 'Primo looks ...': 7 Sept. 1971.

354 'perfectly cured': 21 Nov. 1971.

355 'very disagreeable': PL to HS–M (letter), 28 Dec. 1972.

356 'slight sensation ...': ibid.

356 'efficiency, skill ...': ibid, 26 Dec. 1971 (Levi returned again to Togliattigrad in 1972.)

356 'IT IS FORBIDDEN ...': Francesco Cordero to author, 13 Feb. 1993.

357 'charmingly shy': Michael Darlow to author, 2 Nov. 1994.

358 'Why have you been ...': PL to Milvia Spadi, Sept. 1986, Westdeutscher Rundfunk radio transcript.

358 'Survivors can be ...': PL quoted in Lotta Continua, 17–18 June 1979.

Chapter 20: Dreams of Retirement

359 'bit flamboyant': Keith Barnes to author, 1 May 1992.

359 'I warn you ...': PL to Charles Conreau (letter), 6 Jan. 1974.

360 'colossal nonsense!': PL in Settimo Giorno, 19 Oct. 1963.

360 'Primo's humour was not ...': Carlo Sgorlon to author (letter), 1 July 1993.

361 'Some are dull ...', 'personal stabilisation', 'lonely horizons': PL to HS–M (letter), 29 July 1973.

362 'cancerous and decrepit': PL to Mladen Machiedo (letter), 16 Nov. 1974.

362 'When we said ...': PL to COGIDAS, 29 May 1973 (letter in Gramsci Institute, Turin).

363 'difficult and painful ...': PL to EB (letter), 8 April 1973.

364 'reasonable, eager ...': PL to HS–M (letter), 29 July 1974.

364 'Not since 1945 ...': PL to Hermann Langbein, 10 Feb. 1974.

364 'born worrier': Keith Barnes to author, 1 May 1992.

364 'The English are a practical ...': Opere I, p.574.

364 'very nice and civil ...': PL to EB (letter), 27 Jan. 1979.

365 'But we have to defend ...': PL to Charles Conreau, 22 Nov. 1973.

365 'Did the events ...': from transcript of Il mestière di raccontare, RAI, 1974.

366 'standards of inefficiency': PL to HS–M (letter), 29 July 1974.

368 'launching the most audacious ...': LN, from transcript of BBC Radio 3 documentary on Primo Levi, 30 July 1987.

368 'Levi's version of Douglas ...': Malcolm Skey to author, 2 Aug. 1993.

368 'anthropologist – of the death-camps': Francesco Remotti to author

(letter), 28 Feb. 1994.

369 'More than anything ...': EBS to author, 5 Aug. 1992.

369 'alarming subject ...': PL to author.

370 '*una persona* ...': Giuseppe Platone to author (letter), 7 Jan. 1994.

370 'To have a father ...': VM, p.276.

370 'Some sort of nervous ...': PL to AY (letter), 29 March 1975.

371 'ancient scent ...': *Opere II*, p.547.

371 'Even though we ...': BGS to author, 18 June 1993.

372 'masterpiece': PL's words reported to author by Maria Mariotti, 6 April 1995.

372 'highly decent ...': PL to HS-M (letter), 2–8 Nov. 1967.

373 'civic duty': ibid, 27 April 1975.

374 'To be reunited ...': PL to Delfina Provenzali, 19 July 1975.

374 'darkly shadowed': RF to PL (letter), 12 March 1987.

374 'poignancy and stark ...': RF to author, 19 March 1994.

374 'His poetry was ornamental ....': Brian Swann to author (letter), 1 June 1994.

375 'extremely delighted': PL to Anthony Rudolf (letter), 13 Sept. 1974.

376 'Goodness, but that's ....': Esther Calvino to author, 9 June 1995.

377 'Each of us is ...': PL to author.

377 'I cannot forgive ...': Paolo Dalla Volta to author (tape recording), 1 April 1998.

378 '*I* try to forget ...': PL to HS-M (letter), 2 Dec. 1975.

378 'Levi was devastated ...': Anna Maria Candura to author, 8 May 1995.

379 '*poemetti*': Bernard Delmay, *Paragone*, Aug. 1976.

379 'Primo was quite the ...': Keith Barnes to author, 1 May 1992.

380 'It looks to me like an odd dream ...': PL to HSM (letter), 2 Dec. 1975.

381 'awful idea': PL to Gianfranco Moscati (letter), 22 May 1984.

382 'We're a bunch of frauds!': PL's words reported to author by Anna Cardinali (letter), 6 May 1996.

383 'dangerous turn': PL to HS-M (letter), 28 Dec. 1976.

Chapter 21: Mapping the World of Work

384 'Durano had never met ...': Massimo Scaglione to author, 8 June 1992.

387 'After almost forty years ...': PL to HS-M (letter), 13 Nov. 1977.

388 'The unlucky ...': PL to Daniele Ponchiroli (letter), 31 Dec. 1975.

389 'I hope you will forgive ...': PL to Nanni Ciagne (letter), 30 Sept.

1978.

390 'The Bigs in Rome': PL to HS-M (letter), 13 Nov. 1977.

392 'I am not saying …': Bendetto Terracini to author, 30 April 1995.

392 'If a trial *had* gone …': Michael Tinker to author, 11 June 1993.

392 'I was very shocked …': Raffaele Guariniello to author, 31 March
     1995.

394 'It is the first time we have …': PL to HSM (letter), 20 July 1978.

394 'Levi was the most scrupulous …': Nino Colombo to author (letter),
     12 July 1995.

395 'I don't like Singer's books …': PL's words reported to author by
     Luca Baranelli, 17 May 1993.

395 'forecast storms': PL to HS-M (letter), 22 Nov. 1978.

396 'lucid despair', 'Suicides are generally …': ibid.

397 'His hand was always …': Jutta Pabst to author, 1 July 1992.

397 'Besides wishing to improve …': Anna Maria Savoini to author, 6
     April 1995.

398 'fridgeful of frozen cod': Raniero Panzieri's words reported to
     author by Giuseppina Panzieri, 27 March 1995.

398 'That's my all-time …': PL's words reported to author by AP, 2
     Nov. 1992.

400 'I'd like to ask …': *Lotta Continua*, 14 Jan. 1979.

400 'Levi didn't want schoolchildren …': Riccardo Peyrani to author
     (letter), 20 May 1994.

401 'mentally unstable': David Irving quoted in *Independent on Sunday*,
     6 April 1997.

401 'boring': PL on Proust in *Paese Sera*, 21 Aug. 1981.

402 'dazzling': PL on a poster advertising Lupano's exhibition (Santo
     Stefano Belbo, 30 Aug.–7 Sept. 1986).

403 'He was short …': Giorgio Voghera to author (letter), 6 July 1992.

403 'It seems to me inappropriate …': VM, p.215.

404 'I hope you win …': PL's words reported to author by Paolo
     Barbero, 4 July 1993.

405 'Deep down …': 14 July 1979.

406 'Manganelli accuses me …': quoted in *Echi di una voce perduta*,
     p.108.

406 'laughing like a child', 'could not stop …': AP to author, 14 June
     1993.

407 'As you can see …': VM, p.128.

408 'little depressed': PL to HS-M (letter), 20 Dec. 1979.

409   'I'm resting on ...': PL to RF (letter), 2 March 1980.

409   'The history of the uprooting ...': 5 Aug. 1967.

410   'Right from the start ...': EBS to author, 5 Aug. 1992.

410   'I hope your meal ...': PL to Agnese Incisa (letter), 14 Dec. 1980.

411   'He was an advert ...': Paolo Andreocci to author (letter), January 1994.

412   '*un viaggio meraviglioso*': PL to Paolo Andreocci (letter), 21 July 1986.

413   'Without wanting to ...': Andrea Nemiz to author (letter), 10 June 1994.

413   'with real admiration': Cappella dei Mercanti, 29 April 1980.

415   'I carry this poem ...': PL's words reported to author by Guido Davico Bonino, 17 June 1993.

415   'night book': PL, introduction to SR, p.5.

416   'big old boys ...': LDB to Elena Simion (letter), 17 Nov. 1980.

420   'most wanted to meet': Leonardo Sciascia to author, 7 Dec. 1985. (My interview with Sciascia appeared in the *London Magazine*, April/May 1987.)

420   'The main reason is ...': PL to AY (letter), 8 May 1981.

420   'Probably not': from a tape of PL's talk, '*Conservazione degli alimenti*', 14 Jan. 1981.

421   'poor Christs': PL interviewed by MD, 1984; unpublished transcript.

422   'What? You've been up ...': PL's words reported to author by AP, 2 Nov. 1992.

423   'I'd rather not ...': PL quoted in *Il Giorno*, 24 Nov. 1981.

423   'Hanns killed himself ...': PL's words reported to author by Luca Baranelli, 17 May 1993.

425   'It was Primo's quiet ...': Alberto Sinigaglia to author, 14 June 1993.

425   'With the exception of ...': from a tape of PL's interview with Giorgio Vacca, 23 April 1982.

426   'mutilation': in CPLE.

Chapter 23: Strife in the Middle East

427   'St Franz of Prague': PL to author.

428   'To Palestine, no ...': Rabbi Luciano Caro to author, 1 Nov. 1995.

429   'I promise to read ...': from taped telephone conversation (1981) between PL and a pupil from the 'Marie Curie' scientific school, Grugliasco.

429 'None of us could phone ...': Baldassare Gullotta to author (letter), 17 May 1996.

430 'Everything is different ...', 'the fact is not ...': from transcript of television interview broadcast by the RAI programme *Sorgente di vita* in April 1983 (in VM, p.209).

431 'Signs do exist ...': ibid.

431 'You'll have to ask at the Ministry': Ugo Caffaz to author (letter), undated.

431 'positive and sympathetic': PL to RH (letter), 8 Dec. 1984.

432 'You're lucky ...': PL's words reported to author by Rita Levi Montalcini, 29 July 1992.

433 'He didn't *have* ...': EBS to author, 5 Aug. 1992.

433 'If the Argentines ...': PL quoted in *Oggi*, 14 July 1982.

436 'Blue and white ...': PL's words reported to author by Angelo Pezzana, 1 June 1995.

437 'Impossible to attend ...': copy of telegram in CPLE.

437 'Primo didn't want to be ...': AP to author, 14 June 1993.

438 'Even if I *was* a skinny ...': PL quoted in *Firme nostre*, Sept.–Dec. 1983.

438 'depending on who I meet ...': PL quoted in transcript of a talk to students in Pesaro, Teatro Rossini, 5 May 1986.

438 'I'm going through my worst ...': PL's words reported to author by Hermann Langbein, 5 Dec. 1994.

438 'quick-stepping ferret ...': Camillo Pennati to author (undated letter).

438 'It appears unlikely ...': PL to Emma Vita–Levi (letter), 5 July 1984.

439 'poor head': Sidney Calvi to author, 17 June 1993.

440 'Levi must have been really ill': RH to author (letter), 5 June 1994.

Chapter 24: Recognition Abroad

442 'Many people ...': 7 Feb. 1983.

443 'I'd just started a course ...': 8 Dec. 1984.

443 'censorially deleted': PL to author.

444 'ball of fire': Jim Silberman to author, 25 March 1994.

444 'I could see immediately ...': WW to author, 12 July 1993.

445 'wise and tranquil': PL to Emma Vita–Levi (letter), 5 July 1984.

446 'Who knows what ...': PL's letter quoted in *La Stampa*, 14 April 1984.

446 'We never met ...': PL to author.

447 'Hard, unscrupulous ...': VM, p.282.

447   'He seemed disturbed ...': Luciano Faioni to author, 1 Nov. 1995.

449   'My sweet executioner': Maurizio Avato to author, 6 June 1995.

451   'marvellous anthropological creation': Claude Lévi-Strauss to author (letter), 18 Dec. 1992.

452   'tender beauty': '*La musica e i dischi di Primo Levi*', 1984.

452   'marvellous form': Paolo Gobetti to author, 3 June 1995.

453   'It's the most lively ...': PL in *La Stampa,* 5 May 1984.

453   'How on earth ...': PL to Claudio Magris (letter), 10 May 1984.

453   'chemist on *loan* ...': Carlo Sgorlon to author (letter), 1 July 1993.

454   'excruciatingly pathetic': Michael Kruger to author, 7 Dec. 1995.

454   'By the way ...': PL quoted in PL-TR, p.viii.

455   'literary style ...': PL to Arthur Samuelson (letter), 14 July 1984, in CPLE.

456   'It's a lot more than ...': PL to RH (letter), 8 Dec. 1984.

456   'started to peddle Apples ...': PL's words reported to author by Piero Bianucci, 26 June 1993.

456   'My name's Bill ...': WW to author, 12 July 1993.

456   'For heaven's sake ...': 5 Dec. 1984.

457   'As he looked ...': 7 Oct. 1993.

457   'insufficiently distinguished': Carlo Carena to author, 10 June 1993.

458   'extremely lovable': Gina Lagorio to author, 4 May 1995.

459   'We've given the Americans ...': 27 Feb. 1966.

460   'The ideal time ...': 28 Nov. 1984.

460   'Italian Jewish experience ...': letter (9 Feb. 1981) to George Jochnowitz from Janet Rabinowith of Indiana University Press.

460   'How many years ...': 1 Jan. 1985.

461   'No other work ...': 5 Dec. 1984.

461   'I knew immediately ....': Mike Petty to author (letter), Jan. 1996.

462   'terrified': PL to RF (letter), 5 Feb. 1985.

462   'Honestly, if I was ...': PL to AY (letter), 16 Feb. 1985.

463   'sclerotic': Joachim Meinert to author, 20 Dec. 1994.

463   'Zionist sympathiser': Komitee der Antifaschistischen Widerstandskämpfer der DDR (declassified document), 24 Nov. 1981, addressed to Klaus Höpcke of the Ministerium für Kultur.

463   'All credit ...': VM, p.255.

464   'I can quite understand ...': 8 March 1985.

Chapter 25: America is Waiting

465   'insolent': *Opere II,* p.956.

465   'went down by 30 points': PL's words reported to author by Irene

Williams (letter), 19 July 1993.

466 'He greeted me like ...': Alexander Stille to author, 21 March 1994.

467 'All I've ever held ...': Rita Floriani to author (letter), 29 Aug. 1994.

467 'What really blew ...': Leonard Fine to author, 22 March 1994.

467 'migrant off the ...': PL's words reported to author by Iliana Howe, 23 March 1994.

468 'It was like Yerushalmi ...': Arthur Samuelson to author, 24 March 1994.

468 'It was impossible ...': RR to author, 30 March 1994.

468 'He didn't seem to know ...': Jim Silberman to author, 25 March 1994.

468 'handsome, middle-class ...': Bobbe Siegel to author (letter), 28 Jan. 1994.

469 'Umberto Eco ...': Arthur Samuelson to author, 24 March 1994.

469 'lost in a New York dream ...': Bernard Toscani to author, 22 March 1994.

470 'Look, normally ...': tape of PL's lecture at Brooklyn College, 17 April 1985.

470 'I'm being carried ...': PL's words reported to author by Edith Weisz (Godel), 24 March 1994.

471 'Sunset Boulevard!', 'It was kin ...': Bernard Gordon to author (letter), 3 Feb. 1994.

472 'Can't you see ...!' Jeremy R. Mack, April 1997 conference organised by Columbia University's Italian Academy of Advanced Studies.

472 'Dolomites of light': *Opere II*, p.956.

473 'His dapper, professorial ...': Leslie Epstein to author (letter), 17 Feb. 1994.

474 'bewildered and brooding': AY to author, 20 March 1994.

474 'He said he could ...': Leslie Epstein to author, 17 Feb. 1994.

475 'a nice bit ...': Rita Floriani to author (letter), 29 Aug. 1994.

475 'frosty smile': Irene Williams to author, 22 March 1994.

475 'with ten writers ...': David Sidorsky to author (letter), 5 July 1994.

475 'keen and shining', 'I don't believe ...': *Opere II*, p.619.

476 'Levi is the greatest ...': Irene Williams to author, 22 March 1994.

Chapter 26: The Prison of 75 Corso Re Umberto

477 'I don't think ...': PL's words reported to author by Carlo Sgorlon (letter), 1 July 1993.

478 'Don't distress ...': 21 Nov. 1985.

478   'attempts seriously': Bernard Gordon to PL (letter), 1 July 1985, in CPLE.

479   'Ethiopians', 'drowned people': from transcript of Germaine Greer's interview with PL in files at Carl Hanser Verlag, Munich.

480   'Unfortunately, after so many ...': PL to Gerry Lakmaker (letter), 20 Nov. 1984.

481   'oddly spiritual': Simone Lakmaker to author, 14 Feb. 1994.

481   'holy': Hans Schlegel to author (letter), 22 Feb. 1995.

481   'I don't know when ...': 10 Aug. 1985. Quoted in *La canzone del polistirene*, Libri Scheiwiller, 1985.

482   'drawn and strained': JS to author, 27 Jan. 1993.

483   'And they say the Mafia ...': PL to AY (letter), 25 Feb. 1986.

484   'sincere gratefulness': 29 April 1986.

484   'Obviously it would be ...': Sphere memo, 2 Dec. 1985.

485   'Your letter ...': 31 Oct. 1985.

485   'done away with': 9 Dec. 1985, in CPLE.

486   'I listened to the ...': 7 Dec. 1985.

486   'almost a farewell': *S. Times*.

487   'This poem ...': Aunt Jole's words reported to author by Carla Vernaschi (Fischer's wife), 24 April 1995.

Chapter 27: In London

488   'It's true that Como ...': 13 Jan. 1986.

489   'no longer wished to live ...': Esther Calvino to author, 9 June 1995.

489   'The trial is ...': PL in *Paese Sera*, 2 June 1986.

489   'It's their way of talking ...': PL interviewed by MD, 1984; unpublished transcript.

492   'Uncle Gerhard ...': Vivienne Zinober Joffe to author, 22 April 1993.

493   'Take care of Ada!': PL's words reported to author by Rodolfo Goldbacher, 5 Nov. 1995.

495   'My impression was ...': Gaia Servadio to author, 28 Jan. 1994.

495   'With some people ...': Philip Roth to author, 6 June 1994.

495   'Philip said how ...': Gaia Servadio to author, 6 Feb. 1994.

495   'It was as if the sun ...': Mike Petty to author (letter), Jan. 1996.

496   'sort of donnish Italian': Richard Lamb to author (letter), 1 June 1998.

496   'As I said my ...': Mike Petty to author (letter), Jan. 1996.

497   'quite confident': Sheila Murphy to author, 27 April 1993.

497   'slightly effeminate ...': Michael Kustow to author, 10 Aug. 1994.

498 'Most of all I remember …': Claire Bloom to author, 6 June 1994.

499 'is endowed with all …', 'As I told you …': 30 April 1986.

499 '*madre malferma*': Mario Nati to author (letter), 2 Feb. 1994.

500 'But even before …': Ingrid Börge to author (letter), 14 Feb. 1994.

500 'hoped to come back …': PL to Karl Otto Bonnier (letter), 2 May 1986.

501 'Everything seemed …': Arthur Samuelson to author, 24 March 1994.

501 'Chernobyl has been not only …': 20 May 1986.

501 'The Moon …': Leopardi's poem-play 'The Dream'.

502 ('naturally a German'): PL to Giampaolo Dossena (letter), 3 Feb. 1986.

502 'Primo took a chemist's …': Bianca Tallone to author, 28 May 1995.

503 'I can honestly …': Flavio Ambrosini to author, 9 May 1995.

503 'They mean nothing …': PL's words reported to author by Guglielmo Lanza, 29 March 1995.

503 'I'm very lucky …': PL's words reported to author by Feruccio Maruffi, 13 June 1992.

504 'obsession with evil': Lorenzo Mondo, *S. Times*.

505 'Right from the …': BGS, *S. Times*.

506 'I know my guilt …': PL's words reported to author by Gian Luigi Piccioli, 21 June 1994.

506 'impossible to write …': 7 June 1969.

507 'I never found Levi …': Giorgio Bocca to author, 9 May 1995.

507 'He seemed sort of glassy-eyed …': Teresa Azzali to author, 20 May 1995.

507 'Primo must have been …': Oreste Del Buono to author, 9 Oct. 1995.

Chapter 28: The Downward Spiral

508 'It must be hard work …': PL's words reported to author by Sandro Lupano, 23 May 1995.

508 'It's my mother': PL's words reported to author by Paolo Gobetti, 3 June 1995.

509 'It's lovely to have letters …': 19 June 1985.

509 'Now let me explain …': 25 Oct. 1995.

510 'You have much to say …': 30 June 1986.

511 'I'm going through a very …': 21 July 1986.

512 'virtually nil', 'The future …': 30 July 1986.

512 'Well, here's my contribution …': PL's words reported to author by Giorgio Calcagno, 7 Nov. 1992.

512   'You who flay ...': *Opere II*, p.556.

513   'He neither condoned ...': Raffaella Pagani to author, 22 April 1995.

513   'I've reached rock bottom': PL's words reported to author by Lidia Carbonatto, 28 March 1995.

514   'I can't possibly ...': Paola Accati, *S. Times*.

514   'moved and delighted': Claire Bloom to author, 6 June 1994.

514   'I must add ...', 'quicksilver woodland ...': the *New York Times Book Review*, 12 Oct. 1986.

514   'Throughout the meal ...': Philip Roth to author, 6 June 1994.

515   'I've known some Jewish sons ...': ibid.

515   'I'm sure Primo ...': Claire Bloom to author, 6 June 1994.

515   'I really had no idea ...': 7 Oct. 1986.

515   'Not that Levi was the sort ...': Philip Roth to author, 6 June 1994.

516   'Something in the look ...': Claire Bloom to author, 6 June 1994.

516   'I didn't understand ...': PL's words reported to author by Rita Levi-Montalcini, 29 July 1992.

516   'certain improvement': PL to David Mendel (letter), 14 Feb. 1987.

517   'extreme anxiety': John Reeves to author (letter), 26 Jan. 1994.

517   'I'm not in the mood ...': PL to RF (letter), 21 Oct. 1986.

517   'Fine, but what have ...': PL's words reported to author by Fernanda Pivano, 19 March 1992.

518   'mausoleum-like': Raffaella Pagani to author, 22 April 1995.

519   'There were no newspapers ...': Agnese Incisa to author, 20 July 1992.

519   'It could hardly ...': Ernesto Ferrero, *S. Times*.

519   'But Primo said Lucia ...': Agrese Incisa to author, 8 June 1993.

520   'old ghetto Jew': Cesare Cases's words reported to author by Anna Cases, 14 Sept. 1992.

520   'It was the last time ...': Agnes Incisa to author, 20 July 1992.

520   'Apologies – I opened ...': PL's words reported to author by Sra. Rafaello Levi, 25 Oct. 1995.

521   'sunken space': PL's words reported to author by Livio Norzi, 17 Feb. 1993.

521   'wonderful joke': Silvio Ortona, *S. Times*.

522   'The rediscovery ...': 4 Jan. 1987.

522   'For me too the days ...': 7 Jan. 1987.

523   'best accounts': Ernst Nolte to author (letter), 30 Nov. 1994.

524   'Why dignify ...': Emanuele Perotti's words reported to author by Giorgio Vaccarino, 25 March 1993.

524   'humanity did not deserve ...': EBS to author, 5 Aug. 1992.

525   'It's tremendously ...': PL quoted in *Il Messagero*, 12 April 1987.

525 'Some other time': PL's words reported to author by Lidia Carbonatto, 28 March 1995.

525 'If Primo played cricket ...': David Mendel to author, 6 Dec. 1992.

525 'I've fallen into ...': 7 Feb. 1987.

525 'And don't visit me ...': PL quoted in *Vanity Fair*, Jan. 1988.

526 'I know that this phase ...': 14 Feb. 1987.

527 'What are you *saying*?': EBS to author, 5 Aug. 1992.

528 'Until the day Primo ...': Norberto Bobbio quoted in *Panorama*, 26 April 1987.

528 'failed to notice': BGS, *S. Times*.

528 'I am not worthy': PL to author.

529 'killed each other off': Gino Sacerdote's words reported to author by Francesco Ciafaloni, 12 May 1993.

529 'Primo felt strongly ...': ibid.

529 'They were for the dead ...': Giorgio Ardito to author, 3 April 1995.

529 'They were at their crossroads ...': Roberto Gentili to author, 16 March 1995.

529 'died at Auschwitz': Luigi Tosini to author, 28 May 1995.

530 'My hydraulic ...': PL's words reported to author by Eugenio Bolley, 6 June 1995.

530 'Years ago, I said ...': PL quoted in *Vanity Fair*, Jan. 1988, 'The Survivor's Suicide' by James Atlas.

530 'Depressive patients ...': Roberto Pattono to author, 2 April 1995.

530 'ominous rise ...': ibid.

531 'fairly all right': LNM to author, 15 May 1995.

531 'extremely flattered': Piero Fassino to author, 30 Nov. 1995.

531 'imbued with the sufferings ...': *Opere II*, p.751.

532 'physiologically incapable ...': PL to author.

532 'path to freedom': Maria Améry quoted in HS–M's diary.

532 'an act of will ...': 28 Nov. 1959.

532 'theatrical suicide': *Opere II*, p.638.

Chapter 29: April 1987: The Last Six Days

534 'I've tried everything': PL's words reported to author by Gaia Servadio, 6 Feb. 1994.

534 'No, I survived ...': BGS, *S. Times*.

534 'vitality and expectations': Ferdinando Camon quoted in 'Primo Levi's Last Moments', *Boston Review*, Summer 1999, Diego Gambetta.

535 'quite vivacious', 'But how can I ... ?': Giulio Einaudi to author, 6

April 1995.

535 'Primo seemed cheerful ...': Anna Bises Vitale, *S. Times.*

536 'Lina, I have to go away': PL's words reported to author by Orsolina Ferrero, 28 Sept. 1992.

536 'I don't know ...': Rabbi Toaff quoted in *La Repubblica*, 14 April 1997.

537 'lost the will to live': PL's words reported to author by MRS, 5 May 1995.

537 'I just wish ...': Aharon Appelfeld to author, 25 Oct. 1994.

537 'One thing Primo ...': Paola Accati, *S. Times.*

537 'In my work I have ...': VM, p.173.

538 'I couldn't forgive ...': EBS to author, 5 Aug. 1992.

538 'one should not judge': BGS, *S. Times.*

538 'The suicide was Primo's ...': LNM to author, 21 Sept. 1992.

540 '*pollà plankte*': Levi quoted in transcript of radio interview by Alberto Gozzi, *Lo specchio del cielo* (RAI 2), 7 Jan.1985.

Epilogue

541 'emotional contagion': Gesualdo Bufalino, *Giornale della Sicilia*, 22 April 1987.

541 'Read the last ...': Renzo Levi quoted in *Panorama*, 26 April 1987.

542 'Primo didn't kill himself ...': Angelo Pezzana to author, 1 June 1995.

542 'Primo was out of his mind ...': LNM to author, 21 Sept. 1992.

542 'It was nothing ...': AML to author, 7 April 1993.

542 'Because of Primo's success ...': Claire Bloom to author, 6 June 1994.

542 'There was always a sense ...': Vittorio Foa to author, 22 Oct. 1992.

542 'The loss of resilience ...': Oreste Del Buono to author, 9 Oct. 1995.

542 'Just as one can throw ...': Agnese Incisa to author, 9 Oct. 1992.

543 'I still prefer ...': Germaine Greer to author (letter), 28 March 1994.

543 'Nobody has yet ...': PL to HS-M (letter), 30 April 1967.

543 '*Nessuno* ...': Antonio Paccagnella, *S. Times.*

543 'Now I begin to understand ...': Livio Norzi, from transcript of BBC Radio 3 documentary on Primo Levi, 30 July 1987.

BIBLIOGRAPHY

Publications by Primo Levi

It is impossible to acknowledge all the works by Primo Levi to which this biography owes a debt. The influence of some (for example, Levi's articles on lacquer-coated insulated cables) is minimal. Levi's most important works are published by Einaudi in the two-volume *Opere*. Mention should be made of the diligent bibliographic efforts of Marco Belpoliti, whom I (and many others) helped to compile the Einaudi *opera omnia*. Much of Levi's literary remains – testimonies, film and radio treatments, plays, poems and other works – were scattered after his death, buried in newspaper and publisher archives or otherwise forgotten. Belpoliti cleared the ground and built on it. Even so, there are many texts that have not been collected in the *Opere*. I have used them in my book and some of them are cited in the editions listed below.

Works in Italian and English, in chronological order of publication

'*Voi non sapete studiare!*' ('You Don't Know How to Study!'), in 'D'Azeglio Sotto Spirito', Turin: Tipograf. Eugenio Gili, 1936. A slightly different version of Levi's debut poem appeared in Franco Fini, *Il libro della memoria*, Bologna: Grafica Ragno, 1991

La puntinatura degli smalti Dulox (Relazione n. 32), 1946: unpublished article on paint 'seeding'. Deposited in the private archive of Giunio Ruspino

Se questo è un uomo, Turin: De Silva, 1947 (also: Turin, Einaudi, 1958); *If This is a Man* (trs. S. Woolf), London/New York: Orion Press, 1959

Deposizione del Dott. Primo Levi: testimony regarding the Resistance and deportation, made in Rome on 14 June 1960. Deposited in Yad Vashem archives, Jerusalem

La tregua, Turin: Einaudi, 1963; *The Truce* (trs. S. Woolf), London: Bodley Head, 1965

Se questo è un uomo, 1964: unpublished RAI radio script, deposited at RAI Sezione Drammatica, Turin

'Furono I deportati di Birkenau a distruggere i forni crematori': open letter by Primo Levi, Leonardo De Benedetti and Giuliana Tedeschi to *La Stampa* (19 Oct. 1965) on the subject of resistance in the Nazi camps

Se questo è un uomo, theatre adaptation (with Pieralberto Marché), Turin: Einaudi, 1966

Storie naturali ('*Natural Histories*'), Turin: Einaudi, 1966; selections in *The Sixth Day* (trs. R. Rosenthal), London: Michael Joseph, 1990

'Specchio dei tempi' in *La Stampa*: Levi replies to a reader's question on the subject of forgiveness, 1 September 1967

Intervista aziendale ('*Factory Interview*'), 1968: RAI radio script (with Carlo Quartucci), deposited at Biblioteca Nazionale, Rome

Deposizione Primo Levi: testimony against SS Friedrich Bosshammer, made in Turin on 3 May 1971. Deposited in Centro di Documentazione Ebraica Contemporanea, Milan

Vizio di forma ('*Structural Defect*'), Turin: Einaudi, 1971; selections in *The Sixth Day*

Il sistema periodico, Turin: Einaudi, 1975; *The Periodic Table* (trs R. Rosenthal), London: Michael Joseph, 1985

L'osteria di Brema ('*The Bremen Beer-Hall*'), Milan: Scheiwiller, 1975; *Shema: Collected Poems* (trs. R. Feldman and B. Swann), London: The Menard Press, 1976

La chiave a stella, Turin: Einaudi, 1978; *The Wrench* (trs. W. Weaver), London: Michael Joseph, 1987

Lilít e altri racconti, Turin: Einaudi, 1978; with variations as *Moments of Reprieve* (trs. R. Feldman), London: Michael Joseph, 1986

'The Preservation of Foods': unpublished encyclopaedia entry. Delivered as a lecture in Turin on 14 Jan. 1981. Tape deposited in the library of Università della Terza Età, Turin

La ricerca delle radici, Turin: Einaudi, 1981; *The Search for Roots* (trs. P. Forbes), London: Penguin, 2001

'Vediamo un po' quali cose si sono avverate': Primo Levi (with J. G. Ballard: 'Il futuro non c'è più') in 'Tuttolibri', *La Stampa*, 3 Jan. 1982

Ad ora incerta ('*At an Uncertain Hour*'), Milan: Garzanti, 1984; *Collected Poems*, London: Faber & Faber, 1988

'Beyond Survival', *Prooftexts* (vol. 4/1), Baltimore: Jan. 1984

Se non ora, quando?, Turin, Einaudi, 1984; *If Not Now, When?* (trs. W. Weaver), London: Michael Joseph, 1986

L'altrui mestiere, Turin: Einaudi, 1985; *Other People's Trades* (trs. R. Rosenthal), London: Michael Joseph, 1986

I sommersi e i salvati, Turin: Einaudi, 1986; *The Drowned and the Saved* (trs. R. Rosenthal) London: Michael Joseph, 1988

Racconti e saggi, Turin: La Stampa, 1986; selections as *The Mirror Maker* (trs. R. Rosenthal), London: Methuen, 1990

Primo Levi and Tullio Regge, *Conversations* (trs. R. Rosenthal), London: Penguin, 1992

'Ciò che può essere amore'; 'La nostra vita'; 'La prima volta': unpublished poems addressed to (or sent to) Gabriella Garda Aliverti, precise dates unknown

Publications about Primo Levi

Amsallem, Daniela, *Primo Levi: Au miroir de son oeuvre*, Lyons: Cosmogone, 2001

Belpoliti, Marco (ed.) *Primo Levi*, Riga 13, Milan: Marcos y Marcos, 1997
—— and Gordon, Robert (eds), *The Voice of Memory: Interviews 1961–87 Primo Levi* (trs. R. Gordon), Cambridge: Polity Press, 2001

Borri, Giancarlo, *Le divine impurità: Primo Levi tra scienza e letteratura*, Rimini: Luisè, 1992

Camon, Ferdinando, *Conversazione con Primo Levi*, Milan: Garzanti, 1991

Cavaglion, Alberto, *Primo Levi e Se questo è un uomo*, Turin: Loescher, 1993
—— (ed.) *Primo Levi: Il presente del passato*, proceedings of the Turin conference, 28–9 March 1988, Milan: Franco Angeli, 1991

Cicioni, Mirna, *Primo Levi: Bridges of Knowledge*, Oxford: Berg, 1995

Dini, Massimo and Jesurum, Stefano, *Primo Levi: Le opere e i giorni*, Milan: Rizzoli, 1992

Ferrero, Ernesto (ed.), *Primo Levi: Un'antologia della critica*, Turin: Einaudi, 1997

Frassica, Pietro (ed.), *Primo Levi as Witness*, proceedings of a symposium held at Princeton University, 30 April–2 May 1989, Fiesole: Casalini Libri, 1989

Grassano, Giuseppe, *Primo Levi*, Florence: La Nuova Italia, 1981

Ioli, Giovanna (ed.), *Primo Levi: memoria e invenzione*, proceedings of the San Salvatore Monferrato conference, 26–7–8 September 1991. SS. Monferrato: Tipograf. Barberis, 1995

Levi Della Torre, Stefano (ed.), *Scritti in memoria di Primo Levi*, special issue of *La Rassegna Mensile di Israel*, vol. LVI, n.2–3: Unione delle comunità israelitiche italiane, May–Dec. 1989

Nystedt, Jane, *Le opere di Primo Levi viste al computer*, Stockholm: Almqvist & Wiskell, 1993

Poli, Gabriella and Calcagno, Giorgio *Echi di una voce perduta* Milan: Mursia, 1992

Rudolf, Anthony, *At an Uncertain Hour: Primo Levi's War against Oblivion*, London: The Menard Press, 1990

Sodi, Risa B., *A Dante of Our Time: Primo Levi and Auschwitz*, New York: Peter Lang, 1990

Tarrow, Susan R. (ed.), *Reason and Light – Essays on Primo Levi*. Ithaca, New York: Center for International Studies, Cornell University, 1990

Toscani, Claudio, *Se questo è un uomo*, Milan: Mursia, 1990

Varchetta, Giuseppe, *Ascoltando Primo Levi*, Milan: Guerini, 1991

Vincenti, Fiora, *Primo Levi*, Milan: Mursia, 1981

Essays, articles and interviews consulted

Note: I have included journalism that, though not exclusively on Levi's life and work, relates partly or indirectly to them.

Arbib, Gloria, unpublished interview with Levi, 8 June 1981

Anonymous, 'The Talk of the Town', *New Yorker*, 11 May 1987

Atlas, James, 'The Survivor's Suicide', *Vanity Fair,* Jan. 1988

Bailey, Paul, 'Saving the Scaffolding', *New Statesman*, 20 Aug. 1971

Cases, Cesare, 'Ricordo di Primo Levi', in *Tre Narratori: Calvino, Primo Levi, Parise*, Gianfranco Folena (ed.), Padua: Liviana, 1989

—— 'L'ordine delle cose e l'ordine delle parole', *L'Indice*, Dec. 1987

Cherchi, Grazia, 'Il suicidio di Primo Levi', *L'inea d'ombra*, May 1987

Bruck, Edith, 'Ebreo fino a un certo punto', interview with Levi, *Il Messagero*, 9 Jan. 1976

Darlow, Michael, unpublished interview with Primo Levi, 9 Dec. 1972. Sections used in Thames Television series *World at War* (Part Four: 'Auschwitz: The Final Solution'). Deposited in Imperial War Museum archives

Eberstadt, Fernanda, 'Reading Primo Levi', *Commentary*, Oct. 1985

Fontana, Luca, 'Interview: Primo Levi', *City Limits*, 1–8 May 1986

Fortini, Franco, 'Lettere da lontano: a Primo Levi', *L'Espresso*, 1 March 1987

Gambetta, Diego, 'Primo Levi's Last Moments', *Boston Review*, Summer 1999

Getzler, Dvorah, 'Branded in Memory, interview with Primo Levi', *Jerusalem Post*, 29 Nov. 1986

Giubertoni, Anna, 'Le Ragioni di Levi', *Filosofia*, Jan–April 1987

Guadagni, Anna Maria, 'Primo Levi', *L'Unità*, 21 Feb. 1993

James, Clive, 'Last Will and Testament', *New Yorker*, 23 May 1988

Judt, Tony, 'The Courage of the Elementary', *New York Review of Books*, 20 May 1999

Mendel, David, 'Requiem for a quiet man of courage', *Sunday Telegraph*, 8 Sept. 1991

Miller, Karl, 'Levi's Oyster', review of *The Drowned and the Saved*, *London Review of Books*, 4 Aug. 1988

Motola, Gabriel, 'Primo Levi: His Life and Work', *European Judaism*, vol. 21, n. 2, 1988

Nocerino, Vanna, 'Ricordo di Primo Levi', unpublished reminiscence (read out in Turin synagogue, 9 Feb. 1988)

Norzi, Livio, 'Primo Levi: A Contribution', unpublished reminiscence (extracts used by Paul Bailey in BBC Radio 3 talk on Levi, 30 July 1987)

Orthel, Rolf, unpublished interview with Levi, 1974

Ozick, Cynthia, 'Primo Levi's Suicide Note', in *Metaphor and Memory*, New York: Alfred A. Knopf, 1989

Pivano, Fernanda, 'Il mio compagno Primo Levi e io rimandati a settembre', *Corriere della Sera*, 18 April 1987

Radford, Tim, 'Lifeline from Auschwitz', *Guardian*, 17 April 1986

Rosenfeld, Alvin H., 'Primo Levi: The Survivor as Victim', in *Perspectives on the Holocaust: Essays in Honour of Raul Hilberg*, James S. Pacy and Alan P. Wertheimer (eds), San Francisco: Westview Press, 1995

Sodi, Risa, 'A Last Talk with Primo Levi', *Present Tense,* May–June 1988

—— 'An Interview with Primo Levi', *Partisan Review* LIV, Summer 1987

Spriano, Paolo, 'L'avventura di Primo Levi', *L'Unità*, 14 July 1963

Székács, Vera, 'Conversation with Primo Levi', *Nagyvilág*, June 1987; extracts in 'Primo Levi: Il sorriso necessario', *La Stampa,* 5 June 1992

Thomson, Ian, 'In the Heat of the Moment: A conversation in Rome with Italo Calvino', *London Magazine*, Dec. 1984

—— 'Families and Friends: A conversation in Rome with Natalia Ginzburg', *London Magazine*, Aug–Sept. 1985

—— 'Alberto Moravia and Indifference', *London Magazine*, Nov. 1985

—— 'Primo Levi in conversation with Ian Thomson', *Poetry Nation Review*, 58 vol. 14/2, 1987

—— 'Sicilian Writers and the Mafia: A Conversation in Palermo with Leonardo Sciascia', *London Magazine,* April–May 1987

—— Primo Levi: Obituary, *Independent,* 13 April 1987

—— 'After Auschwitz', Interview with Primo Levi, *Independent,* 14 April 1987

—— 'Mapping the World of Work', review of *The Wrench*, *Times Literary Supplement*, 5 June 1987

—— 'National Enquirer', interview with Francesco Rosi, *Independent*, 18 June 1987

—— 'A Town Called Aliano', article on Carlo Levi, *Sunday Telegraph*, 6 Nov. 1988

—— 'Death of a Survivor', article on Primo Levi, *Sunday Times*, 30 April 1989

—— 'Primo Levi: literature in the crucible', review of *Other People's Trades*, *Independent*, 21 Oct. 1989

—— 'Seeing the Light', interview with Laura Archera Huxley, *Independent Magazine*, 30 April 1994

Translations by Primo Levi, in chronological order of publication

Houwink, Dr R. *Elasticity, Plasticity and Structure of Matter* (Levi translated the chapter 'Phthalic Resins', unpublished, 1946). Deposited in the private archive of Giunio Ruspino

Gilman, Henry, *Chimica organica superiore* (*Organic Chemistry: An Advanced Treatise*), vols 1 and 2 of four volumes, Turin: Einaudi, 1955

Jacob (Jacques) Presser, *La notte dei Girondini* (*The Night of the Girondists*), Milan: Adelphi, 1976

Douglas, Mary, *I simboli naturali* (*Natural Symbols*), Turin: Einaudi, 1979

Kafka, Franz, *Il Processo* (*The Trial*), Turin: Einaudi, 1983

Lévi-Strauss, Claude, *Lo sguardo da lontano* (*The View from Afar*), Turin: Einaudi, 1984

—— *La via delle maschere* (*The Way of the Masks*), Turin: Einaudi, 1985

Bibliography

Agnelli, Susanna, *We Always Wore Sailor Suits*, London: Weidenfeld & Nicolson, 1975

Agosti, Giorgio and Bianco, Livio, *Un'amicizia partigiana: lettere 1943–45*, Turin: Meynier, 1990

Ainsztein, Reuben, *Jewish Resistance in Nazi-Occupied Eastern Europe*, London: Paul Elek, 1974

Alexander, Edward, *The Resonance of Dust: Essays on Holocaust Literature and Jewish Fate*, Colombus: Ohio State University Press, 1979

593

Alvarez, A. *The Savage God*, London: Weidenfeld & Nicolson, 1971

Améry, Jean, *At the Mind's Limits*, London: Granta, 1999

—— *Levar la mano su di sé*, Turin: Bollati Boringhieri, 1990

—— *Rivolta e rassegnazione*, Turin, Bollati Boringhieri, 1988

Antelme, Robert, *La specie umana*, Turin: Einaudi, 1954

Antonicelli, Franco, *La pratica della libertà*, Turin: Einaudi, 1976

Arbib, Gloria, *Partecipazione di ebrei alla resistenza nella regione Piemonte*, Milan: University of Milan Political Science thesis, 1980

Ardagh, John, *Germany and the Germans*, London: Hamish Hamilton, 1987

Arendt, Hannah, *Eichmann in Jerusalem*, London: Penguin, 1977

Arieti, Silvano, *The Parnas*, Philadelphia: Paul Dry Books, 2000

Arlacchi, Pino, *Mafia Business: The Mafia Ethic and the Spirit of Capitalism*, London: Verso, 1986

Arnaldi, Roberto, *Immagini di un passato ebraico nel Monregalese*, Mondovì: L'Unione Monregalse, 1982

Arpino, Giovanni and Antonetto, Roberto, *Emilio Salgari: il padre degli eroi*, Milan: Mondadori, 1991

Artom, Emanuele, *Diari: gennaio 1940–febbraio 1944*, Milan: CDEC, 1946

Artusi, Pellegrino, *La scienza in cucina e l'arte di mangiar bene*, Turin: Einaudi, 1970

Assandria, Giuseppe, *Augusta Bagiennorum*, Bene Vagienna: F.Vissio, 1925

Baccino, Renzo, *Fossoli*, Modena: Comune di Carpi, 1961

Bagnasco, Arnaldo, *Torino: un profilo sociologico*, Turin: Einaudi, 1986

Balestrini, Nanni, *Vogliamo tutto*, Milan: Feltrinelli, 1971

Barbaro, Paolo, *Passi d'uomo*, Milan: Mondadori, 1978

—— *Giornale dei lavori*, Turin: Einaudi, 1966

Bassani, Giorgio, *The Garden of the Finzi-Continis*, London: Quartet, 1974

Batham, D., *A Reminiscence of Gideon Algernon Mantell, Esq.*, London: Simpkin, Marshall & Co, 1853

Bebb, R. L (ed.), *Synthetic Rubber*, London: Chapman & Hall, 1954

Bedarida, G., *Ebrei d'Italia*, Livorno: Tirrena, 1950

Bedford, Sybille, *Aldous Huxley: A Biography*, London: Chatto & Windus, 1973

Belli, Giuseppe Gioachino, *Sonetti*, Milan: Mondadori, 1978

Belloni, Emanuela (ed.), *Un'avventura internazionale: Torino e le arti, 1950–1970*, Milan: Charta, 1993

Belluci, Maria and Ciliberto, Michele, *La scuola e la pedagogia del fascismo*, Turin: Loescher, 1978

Bernstein, Jeremy, *Cranks, Quarks, and the Cosmos*, London: HarperCollins, 1993

Bertinetti, Giovanni, *Le Orecchie di Meo*, Turin: S. Lattes, 1908

Bertoldi, Silvio, *Dopoguerra*, Milan: Rizzoli, 1993

Bertolo, Giovanni (ed.), *Torino tra le due guerre*, Turin: Musei Civici, 1978

Bertone, Gianni, *I figli d'Italia si chiaman Balilla*, Rimini: Guaraldi, 1975

Bertone, Giorgio, *Italo Calvino: Il castello della scrittura*, Turin: Einaudi, 1994

Bettelheim, Bruno, *The Informed Heart*, London: Penguin, 1991

Bianco, Livio D., *Guerra partigiana*, Turin: Einaudi, 1954

Biancotti, Angiolo, *Arturo Foà: L'uomo e il poeta*, Turin: S.Lattes, 1936

Bobbio, Norberto, *Autobiografia*, Bari: Laterza, 1997

—— *Profilo ideologico del '900*, Milan: Garzanti, 1990

—— *Trent'anni di storia della cultura a Torino: 1920–1950*, Turin: Casa di Risparmio, 1977

Boccalatte, Luciano, De Luna, Giovanni and Maida, Bruno (eds), *Torino in guerra: 1940–1945*, Turin: Gribaudo, 1995

Boitani, Piero, *The Shadow of Ulysses: Figures of a Myth*, Oxford: Oxford University Press, 1994

Bollati, Giulio, *L'Italiano*, Turin: Einaudi, 1983

Borgogno, Anna, *La città perduta*, Milan: Pan Milano, 1981

Borkin, Joseph, *The Crime and Punishment of I. G. Farben*, New York: Pocket Books, 1978

Borowski, Tadeusz, 'This Way to the Gas, Ladies and Gentlemen', London: Jonathan Cape, 1967

Bragg, William, *Concerning the Nature of Things*, London: G. Bell, 1925

Bravo, Anna and Jalla, Daniele (eds), *La vita offesa: storia e memoria dei Lager nazisti nei racconti di duecento sopravvissuti*, Milan: Franco Angeli, 1986

Brendon, Piers, *The Dark Valley: A Panorama of the 1930s*, London: Pimlico, 2001

Bruck, Edith, *Due stanze vuote*, Padua: Marsilio, 1974

Bullock, Alan, *Hitler: A Study in Tyranny*, London: Penguin, 1990

Buruma, Ian, *The Wages of Guilt: Memories of War in Germany and Japan*, London: Jonathan Cape, 1994

Caffaz, Ugo, *L'antisemitismo italiano sotto il fascismo*, Florence: La Nuova Italia, 1975

Caglioti, Luciano, *I due volti della chimica*, Milan: Mondadori, 1979

Caleffi, Piero, *Si fa presto a dire fame*, Milan-Rome: Avanti!, 1955

Calvino, Italo, *Why Read the Classics?*, London: Jonathan Cape, 1999

—— *The Road to San Giovanni*, New York: Pantheon, 1993

—— *I libri degli altri*, Turin: Einaudi 1991

—— *The Path to the Nest of the Spiders*, New York: Ecco Press, 1976

—— *Tarocchi: Il mazzo visconteo di Bergamo e New York*, Parma: F. M. Ricci, 1969

—— *I nostri antenati*, Turin: Einaudi, 1960

Camerana, Oddone, *Contro la mia volontà*, Turin: Einaudi, 1993

Campagnoli, Ruggero and Hersant, Yves, *Oulipo. La letteratura potenziale (Creazioni Ri-creazioni Ricreazioni)*, Bologna: Clueb, 1985

Canestri, Giorgi and Ricuperati, Giuseppe, *La scuola in Italia dalla legge Casati ad oggi*, Turin: Loescher, 1976

Caracciolo Nicola, *Gli ebrei e l'Italia durante la guerra: 1940–45*, Rome: Bonacci, 1986

Carcano, Giancarlo, *Torino antifascista: 1922–1943*, Turin: Edizioni A.N.P.P.I.A, 1993

Carrel, Alexis, *Man the Unknown*, New York: Harper & Brothers, 1935

Castronovo, Valerio, *Torino*, Bari: Laterza, 1987

Cavaglion, Alberto (ed.), *La moralità armata: studi su Emanuele Artom 1915–1944*, Milan: Franco Angeli, 1993

—— *La scuola ebraica a Torino (1938–1943)*, Turin: Pluriverso, 1993

Centro Furio Jesi (eds), *La Menzogna della Razza: documenti e immagini del razzismo e dell'antisemitismo fascista*, Bologna: Grafis, 1994

Cereja, F. and Mantelli, B. (eds), *La deportazione nei campi di sterminio Nazisti*, Milan: Franco Angeli, 1986

Cesari, Severino, *Colloquio con Giulio Einaudi*, Rome-Naples: Theoria, 1991

Cesarani, David (ed.), *The Final Solution*, London: Routledge, 1993

Chamberlin, Lesley, *Nietzsche in Turin: The End of the Future*, London: Quartet, 1996

Chiambaretta, Sergio and Panei, Alessandro (eds), *La grande Torino*, Turin: Gribaudo, 1988

Chiesura, Giorgio, *Devozione*, Milan: Mondadori, 1990

—— *Light Without Motion*, New York: Owl Creek Press, 1989

Chiodi, Pietro, *Banditi*, Turin: Einaudi, 1961

Clerici, Luca and Falcetto, Bruno (eds), *Calvino & l'editoria*, Milan: Marcos y Marcos, 1993

Cohen, A., *Everyman's Talmud*, New York: Schocken Books, 1975

Coifmann, Isabella Lattes, *L'intelligenza degli animali*, Turin: La Stampa, 1986

Curwood, James, *The Glory of Living*, London: Hodder & Stoughton, 1928

Dallaporta-Xydias, N., *Cristianesimo e mondi tradizionali*, Abano Terme: Piovan, 1991

Dante, *Hell* (trans. Steve Ellis) London: Chatto & Windus, 1994

—— *The Divine Comedy* (trans. C. H. Sisson), London: Pan, 1981

Davì, Luigi, *L'aria che respiri*, Turin: Einaudi, 1964

Dawidowicz, Lucy S., *The War Against the Jews*, London: Penguin, 1990

D'Azeglio, Massimo, *I Miei Ricordi*, Turin: Einaudi, 1949

—— *Dell' emancipazione civile degli israeliti*, Florence: Le Monnier, 1848

Debenedetti, Giacomo, *16 ottobre 1943*, Palermo: Sellerio, 1993

De Felice, Renzo, *Storia degli ebrei italiani sotto il fascismo*, Turin: Einaudi, 1961

De Kruif, Paul, *The Microbe Hunters*, London: Jonathan Cape, 1927

Della Torre, Ada, *Messagio speciale*, Bologna: Zanichelli, 1968

Del Noce, Augusto, *Giovanni Gentile*, Bolgona: il Mulino, 1990

Desmond, Adrian, *Huxley: The Devil's Disciple*, London: Michael Joseph, 1994

Diena, Marisa, *Guerriglia e autogoverno: brigate Garibaldi nel Piemonte occidentale 1943–45*, Parma: Ugo Guanda, 1970

Dolza, Delfina, *Essere figlie di Lombroso*, Milan: Franco Angeli, 1990

Dossena, Giampaolo, *La zia assatanata*, Rome: Theoria, 1988

Duggan, Christopher, *Fascism and the Mafia*, London: Yale University Press, 1989

Eatwell, Roger, *Fascism: A History*, London: Chatto & Windus, 1995

Eco, Umberto, *How to Travel with a Salmon and Other Essays*, London: Secker & Warburg, 1994

Enzensberger, Hans Magnus, *Civil War*, London: Granta, 1990

Eustace, John Chetwode, *A Classical Tour Through Italy*, London: J. Mawman, 1815

Fabre, Abbé Augustin, *The Life of Jean Henri Fabre*, London: Hodder & Stoughton, 1921

Fabre, Jean Henri, *The Wonder Book of Chemistry*, New York: Century, 1922

Fargion, Liliana Picciotto, *Il libro della memoria: Gli ebrei deportati dall'Italia (1943–1945)*, Milan: Murisa, 1991

Faurisson, Robert, *Mémoire en défense (contre ceux qui m'accusent de falsifier l'Histoire)*, Paris: La Vieille Taupe, 1980

Feltrinelli, Carlo, *Senior Service*, London: Granta, 2001

Fenoglio, Beppe, *Il partigiano Johnny*, Turin: Einaudi, 1970

Firpo, Luigi, *Gente di Piemonte*, Milan: Mursia, 1983

Foà, Arturo, *L'Italie en marche* Turin: S.Lattes, 1931

—— *Per Benito Mussolini*, Turin: Alberto Giani, 1926

Foa, Vittorio, *Il Cavallo e la Torre*, Turin: Einaudi, 1991

Formiginni, Gina, *Stella d'Italia, stella di Davide*, Milan: Mursia, 1970

Fraccaroli, Arnaldo, *Ungheria Bolscevica: Note di uno che c'è stato*, Milan: Sonzongo, 1920

Frei, Matt, *Italy: The Unfinished Revolution*, London: Arrow, 1997

Friedlander, Albert H., *Riders Towards the Dawn*, London: Constable, 1993

Friedlander, Saul (ed.), *Probing the Limits of Representation: Nazism and the*

Final Solution, Cambridge: Harvard University Press, 1992

Fubini, Guido, *Lungo viaggio attraverso il pregiudizio*, Turin: Rosenberg & Sellier, 1996

—— *L'ultimo treno per Cuneo*, Turin: Meynier, 1991

Gallico, Giuseppe, *Torino di ieri*, Turin: Palatine, 1954

Garrone, Alessandro Galante, *I miei maggiori*, Milan: Garzanti, 1984

—— *Libertà Liberatrice*, Turin: La Stampa, 1992

—— *Amalek: Il dovere della memoria*, Milan: Rizzoli, 1989

Gattermann, Ludwig, *Chimica organica pratica*, Milan: Hoepli, 1957

Ghersi, Italo, *Matematica dilettevole e curiosa*, Milan: Hoepli, 1913

Gilbert, Martin, *The Holocaust: The Jewish Tragedy*, London: Collins, 1986

—— *Auschwitz and the Allies*, London: Michael Joseph, 1981

Gill, Anton, *An Honourable Defeat: A History of the Resistance to Hitler*, London: William Heinemann, 1994

—— *The Journey Back from Hell: Conversations with Concentration Camp Survivors*, London: Grafton, 1989

Ginsborg, Paul, *Italy and its Discontents: 1980–2001*, London: Allen Lane, 2002

—— *A History of Contemporary Italy: Society and Politics 1943–1988*, London: Penguin, 1990

Ginzburg, Natalia, *The Manzoni Family*, Manchester: Carcanet, 1987

—— *La strada che va in città*, Turin: Einaudi, 1984

—— *Le piccole virtú*, Turin: Einaudi, 1982

—— *Vita Immaginaria*, Milan: Mondadori, 1972

—— *Lessico familiare*, Turin: Einaudi, 1963

Glover, Jonathan, *Humanity: A Moral History of the Twentieth Century*, London: Jonathan Cape, 1999

Gobetti, Ada, *Diario partigiano*, Turin: Einaudi, 1956

Gobetti, Piero, *La rivoluzione liberale*, Turin: Einaudi, 1964

Gobbi, Romolo, *Il mito della resistenza*, Milan: Rizzoli, 1992

—— *Operai e resistenza*, Turin: Musolini, 1973

Goldhagen, Daniel, *Hitler's Willing Executioners*, London: Little, Brown, 1996

Gotta, Salvatore, *Il piccolo alpino*, Milan: Mondadori, 1926

Gould, Stephen Jay, *The Mismeasure of Man*, New York: Norton, 1981

Gramsci, Antonio, *La Città futura (1917–1918)*, Turin: Einaudi, 1982

Gratzer, Walter (ed.), *The Longman Literary Companion to Science*, London: Longman, 1989

Gravela, Enrico, *Giulio Bizzozero*, Turin: Umberto Allemandi, 1989

Gregor, James A., *The Ideology of Fascism*, New York: Free Press, 1969

Guariniello, Raffaele, *Se il lavoro uccide: Riflessioni di un magistrato*, Turin: Einaudi, 1985

Guglielminetti, Clelia, *I miei ricordi del liceo Massimo D'Azeglio*, Turin: Vincenzo Bona, 1968

Gunzberg, Lynn M., *Strangers at Home: Jews in the Italian Literary Imagination*, Berkeley, CA: University of California Press, 1992

Haycraft, John, *Italian Labyrinth*, London: Secker & Warburg, 1985

Hayes, Peter, *Industry and Ideology: I. G. Farben in the Nazi Era*, Cambridge: Cambridge University Press, 1987

Hayman, Ronald, *Thomas Mann*, London: Bloomsbury, 1996

Herman, Marco, *Diario di un ragazzo ebreo*, Cuneo: L'Arciere, 1984

Hilberg, Raul, *The Destruction of European Jews*, New York: Holmes & Meier, 1985

Hobsbawm, Eric, *Age of Extremes: The Short Twentieth Century 1914–1991*, London: Michael Joseph, 1994

Hughes, H. Stuart, *Prisoners of Hope: The Silver Age of the Italian Jews: 1924–1974*, Cambridge, MA: Harvard University Press, 1983

Huxley, Laura, *This Timeless Moment*, California: Celestial Arts, 1975

Jamison, Kay Redfield, *Night Falls Fast: Understanding Suicide*, London: Picador, 2000

—— *An Unquiet Mind*, London: Picador, 1996

Jaspers, Karl, *The Question of German Guilt*, New York: Dial Press, 1947

Jemolo, Arturo Carlo, *Anni di prova*, Vicenza: Neri Pozza, 1969

Jesurum, Stefano, *Essere ebrei in Italia*, Milan: Longanesi, 1987

Josipovici, Gabriel, *A Life*, London: London Magazine Editions, 2001

Kedourie, Elie (ed.), *Spain and the Jews*, London: Thames & Hudson, 1992

Kennedy, Joseph P. (ed.), *Polymer Chemistry of Synthetic Elastomers*, New York: John Wiley, 1968

Kertzer, I. David, *The Kidnapping of Edgardo Mortara*, London: Picador: 1997

Klemperer, Victor, *Lingua Tertii Imperii*, Berlin: Aufbau Verlag, 1949

Koestler, Arthur, *The Yogi and the Commissar*, London: Hutchinson, 1965

Kolitz, Zvi, *Yosl Rakover Talks to God*, London: Jonathan Cape, 1999

König, Joel, *Sfuggito alle reti del nazismo*, Milan: Mursia, 1973

Kovpak, S.A., *Les Partisans Soviétiques*, Paris: La Jeune Parque, 1945

Kustow, Michael, *One in Four*, London: Chatto & Windus, 1987

Lajolo, Davide, *Il 'Vizio Assurdo': Storia di Cesare Pavese*, Milan: Mondadori, 1972

Lamb, Richard, *Mussolini and the British*, London: John Murray, 1997

—— *War in Italy 1943–1945: A Brutal Story*, New York: Da Capo Press, 1996

Lammer, Eugen, *Fontana di giovinezza*, Milan: L'Eroica, 1933

Langbein, Hermann, *Against All Hope: Resistance in the Nazi Concentration Camps 1938–1945*, London: Constable, 1994

—— *Uomini ad Auschwitz*, Milan: Mursia, 1984

Lanzmann, Claude, *Shoah: The Complete Text of the Film*, New York: Da Capo Press, 1995

LaPalomba, Joseph, *Democracy, Italian Style*, London: Yale University Press, 1987

Laqueur, Walter, *The Terrible Secret: An Investigation into the Suppression of Information about Hitler's Final Solution*, London: Weidenfeld & Nicolson, 1980

Lassar-Cohn, Professor Von, *Chemistry in Daily Life*, London: H. Grevel & Co, 1913

Letts, Vanessa, *New York*, London: Cadogan, 1991

Levi, Carlo, *Il futuro ha un cuore antico*, Turin: Einaudi, 1956

—— *The Watch*, London: Cassell, 1952

Levi, Fabio, *L'identità imposta*, Turin: Zamorani, 1996

—— (ed.), *L'ebreo in oggetto*, Turin: Zamorani, 1991

Levi, Michele, *Calcolo delle dimensioni d'una incavallatura Polonceau*, Turin: G. Derossi, 1873

Levi Montalcini, Rita, *Elogio dell'imperfezione*, Milan: Garzanti, 1987

Levi, Primo, *Abruzzo forte e gentile*, Sulmona: Di Cioccio, 1976

Levi, Stefano Della Torre, *Mosaico*, Turin: Rosenberg & Sellier, 1994

Levi, Riccardo, *Ricordi politici di un ingegnere*, Milan: Vangelista, 1981

Liebman, Joshua Loth, *Peace of Mind*, London: Heinemann, 1946

Lingens-Reiner, Ella, *Prisoners of Fear*, London: Gollancz, 1948

Loewenthal, Elena, *Figli di Sara e Abramo*, Milan: Frassinelli, 1995

Lomax, Eric, *The Railway Man*, London: Jonathan Cape, 1995

Lombardo-Radice, Giuseppe, *Lezioni di didattica*, Palermo: Sandron, 1936

Lombroso, Cesare, *After Life, What?: Spiritist Phenomena and their Interpretation*, Boston: M. Smart, 1909

—— *L'antisemitismo e le scienze sociali*, Turin: Bocca, 1894

Lorenz, Konrad, *On Aggression*, London: Methuen, 1966

Luria, Salvador, *A Slot Machine, a Broken Test Tube*, New York: Harper & Row, 1984

Lyons, Philip, *Literary and Theological Responses to the Holocaust*, Bristol: University of Bristol thesis, 1988

Macagno, Mario, *Cucire un motore*, Pollone: Leone & Griffa, 1992

—— *Cinquantotto anni che contano per cento*, Turin: Italscambi, 1986

Magris, Claudio, *Lontano da dove: Joseph Roth e la tradizione ebraico-orientale*, Turin: Einaudi, 1989

Malaparte, Curzio, *Kaputt*, New York: E. P. Dutton, 1946

Malgaroli, Felice, *Domani chissà*, Cuneo: L'Arciere, 1992

Manaresi, Angelo, *Parole agli alpinisti*, Rome: Edizioni del C.A.I., 1932

Mann, Vivian B. (ed.), *Gardens and Ghettos: The Art of Jewish Life in Italy*, Berkeley, CA: University of California Press, 1989

Mantell, Gideon Algernon, *Thoughts on Animalcules; or, a glimpse of the Invisible World Revealed by the Microscope*, London: John Murray, 1846

Marcenaro, Pietro, *Riprendere tempo*, Turin: Einaudi, 1982

Marchis, Riccardo (ed.), *Diario di Carlo Chevallard 1942–1945*, Turin: Archivio Storico della Città di Torino, 1994

Mayda, Giuseppe, *Ebrei sotto Salò*, Milan: Feltrinelli, 1978

Michaelis, Meir, *Mussolini and the Jews: German-Italian Relations and the Jewish Question in Italy 1922–1945*, Oxford: Oxford University Press, 1978

Mila, Massimo, *Scritti civili*, Turin: Einaudi, 1995

—— *Scritti di montagna*, Turin: Einaudi, 1992

Millu, Liana, *Il fumo di Birkenau*, Florence: Giuntina, 1986 (reprint)

Modiano, Patrick, *The Search Warrant*, London: Harvill, 2000

Modigliani, Carlo, *Una croce e una stella*, Milan: Gastaldi, 1959

Mola, Aldo Alessandro, *Storia della massoneria italiana dall'unità alla Repubblica*, Milan: Bompiani, 1976

Molinari, Maurizio, *La sinistra e gli ebrei in Italia:1967–1993*, Milan: Corbaccio, 1995

Molnar Miklós, *From Béla Kun to János Kádár: Seventy Years of Hungarian Communism*, New York: Berg, 1990

Momigliano, Arnaldo, *Pagine ebraiche*, Turin: Einaudi, 1987

Momigliano, Eucardio, *Storia tragica e grottesca del razzismo italiano*, Milan: Mondadori, 1946

Montale, Eugenio, *Auto da fè. Cronache in due tempi*, Milan: Il Saggiatore, 1966

Monti, Augusto, *I sanssôssi*, Cuneo: Araba Fenice, 1993

—— *I miei conti con la scuola*, Turin: Einaudi, 1965

Monti, Faustino, *Bene Vagienna: Ricordi popolari*, Cuneo: A. Riba, 1877

Morante, Elsa, *History: A Novel*, London: Allen Lane, 1977

Moravia, Alberto, *The Time of Indifference*, New York: Farrar Strauss, 1953

Morpurgo, Giuseppe, *Beati misericordes*, Turin: S.Lattes, 1930

—— *Yom Ha-Kippurim*, Florence: Casa Editrice Israel, 1925

Morris, Jan, *Trieste and the Meaning of Nowhere*, London: Faber & Faber, 2001

Mosso, Angelo, *Mens sana in corpore sano*, Milan: Treves, 1903

—— *Fisiologia dell'uomo sulle Alpi*, Milan: Treves, 1897

—— *La paura*, Milan: Treves, 1884

Müller, Filip, *Auschwitz Inferno*, London: Routledge, 1979

Nicco, Roberto, *La resistenza in Valle d'Aosta*, Aosta: Musumeci, 1990

Nissim, Luciana, *Ricordi della casa dei morti*, in *Donne contro il mostro*, Turin: Vincenzo Ramella, 1946

Nyiszli, Miklos, *Auschwitz: A Doctor's Eye-Witness Account*, London: Granada, 1978

Olschki, Marcella, *Terza liceo 1939*, Palermo: Sellerio, 1993

Operti, Piero, *Lettera aperta a Benedetto Croce*, Turin: Edizioni Superga, 1946

Orano, Paolo, *Gli ebrei in Italia*, Rome: Pinciana, 1938

Paglieri, Marina, *Torino Belle Epoque*, Turin: Lindau, 1994

Pancaldi, Giuliano, *Darwin in Italy*, Indiana: Indiana University Press, 1991

Papuzzi, Alberto, *Il mondo contro*, Turin: La Stampa, 1996

—— *Portami su quello che canta*, Turin: Einaudi, 1977

—— *Il provocatore. Il caso Cavallo e le Fiat*, Turin: Einaudi, 1976

Pasolini, Pier Paolo, *Una vita violenta*, Turin: Einaudi, 1979

—— *Ragazzi di vita*, Milan: Garzanti, 1976

Passerini, Luisa, *Fascism in Popular Memory: The Cultural Experience of the Turin Working Class*, Cambridge: Cambridge University Press, 1987

Pavese, Cesare, *This Business of Living: Diaries 1935–1950*, London: Quartet, 1980

Pellegrino, Oreste, *Le mie perle: scelta di letture per la quarta elementare*, Lanciano: R. Carabba Editore, 1922

Pellico, Silvio, *Opere scelte*, Rome: Cremonese, 1956

Pinkus, Oscar, *A Choice of Masks*, Englewood Cliffs, N. J: Prentice-Hall, 1969

Piovene, Guido, *Viaggio in Italia*, Milan: Baldini & Castoldi, 1993

Pitkin, Walter, *A Short History of Human Stupidity*, London: George Allen, 1935

Pizzardi, Tina, *Senza pensarci due volte*, Bologna: il Mulino, 1996

Pollack, Martha, *Turin 1564–1680*, Chicago: University of Chicago Press, 1991

Ponchiroli, Daniele, *Le avventure di Barzamino*, Turin: Einaudi, 1965

Ponzio, Giacomo, *Chimica organica*, Turin: Unione Tipografico, 1938

—— *Chimica inorganica*, Turin: Unione Tipografico, 1937

Presser, Jacques, *The Night of the Girondists*, London: Harvill, 1992

Prolo, Maria Adriano, *Storia del cinema muto italiano*, Milan: Poligono, 1951

Provenzali, Delfina, *L'incisione dura*, Milan: Scheiwiller, 1977

Queneau, Raymond, *Piccola cosmogonia portatile*, Turin: Einaudi, 1988

—— *La canzone del polistirene*, Milan: Scheiwiller, 1985

Re, Luciano and Sessa, Giovanni, *Torino, Via Roma*, Turin: Lindau, 1992

Revelli, Nuto, *Il disperso di Marburg*, Turin: Einaudi, 1994

—— *La strada del davai*, Turin: Einaudi, 1966

—— *La guerra dei poveri*, Turin: Einaudi, 1962

—— *Mai Tardi: Diario di un alpino in Russia*, Cuneo: Panfilo, 1946

Reynolds-Ball, E.A., *Unknown Italy: Piedmont and the Piedmontese*, London: A. & C. Black, 1927

Richards, Charles, *The New Italians*, London: Michael Joseph, 1994

Ridley, Jasper, *Mussolini*, London: Constable, 1997

Ring, Jim, *How the English Made the Alps*, London: John Murray, 2000

Rolfi, Lidia Beccaria and Bruzzone, Anna Maria, *Le donne di Ravensbrück*, Turin: Einaudi, 1978

Romanelli, Guido, *Nell'Ungheria di Béla Kun*, Udine: Doretti, 1964

Rosenfeld, Alvin H., *A Double Dying: Reflections on Holocaust Literature*, Bloomington, IN: Indiana University Press, 1980

Ross, Alan, *Blindfold Games*, London: Collins Harvill, 1986

Rossi-Doria, Manilo, *La gioia tranquilla del ricordo*, Milan: il Mulino, 1991

Rosten, Leo, *The Joys of Yiddish*, London: W. H. Allen, 1970

Roth, Cecil, *The History of the Jews of Italy*, Philadelphia: Jewish Publication Society of America, 1946

Rousset, David, *L'univers concentrationnaire*, Paris: Pavois, 1946

Rusconi, Gian Enrico (ed.), *Germania: un passato che non passa*, Turin: Einaudi, 1987

Russell, Lord of Liverpool, *The Scourge of the Swastika*, London: Cassell, 1954

Saba, Umberto, *Scorciatoie e raccontini*, Milan: Mondadori, 1946

Sacchi, Filippo, *Diario 1943–1944*, Lugano: Casagrande, 1987

Sacco, Sergio and Richietto, Gigi, *Il dinamitificio nobel di Avigliana*, Susa: Piero Melli, 1991

Sartre, Jean-Paul, *Anti-Semite and Jew*, New York: Schocken Books, 1948

Schwarz-Bart, André, *The Last of the Just*, London: Secker & Warburg, 1961

Sciascia, Leonardo, *Il teatro della memoria*, Turin: Einaudi, 1981

Segre, Augusto, *Memorie di vita ebraica*, Rome: Bonacci, 1979

Segre, Dan Vittorio, *Memoirs of a Fortunate Jew*, London: Peter Halban, 1978

Segre, Emilio, *A Mind Always in Motion*, Berkeley, CA: University of California Press, 1993

Segre, Renata, *The Jews in Piedmont*, 3 vols, Jerusalem: Israel Academy of Sciences and Humanities and Tel Aviv University, 1986

Segre, Sion Amar, *Lettera al Duce*, Florence: Giuntina, 1994

Selmin, Francesco (ed.), *Da Este ad Auschwitz*, Este: Giordano Bruno, 1987

Sereny, Gitta, *The German Trauma: Experiences and Reflections 1938–2000*, London: Allen Lane, 2000

—— *Albert Speer: His Battle With Truth*, London: Picador, 1996

—— *Into That Darkness: From Mercy Killing to Mass Murder*, London: André Deutsch, 1974

Serra, Bianca Guidetti, *Storie di giustizia, ingiustizia e galera*, Milan: Linea D'Ombra, 1994

Servadio, Gaia, *Un'infanzia diversa*, Milan: Rizzoli, 1988

Sgorlon, Carlo, *Army of the Lost Rivers*, New York: Italica Press, 1998

Siciliano, Enzo, *Pasolini*, London: Bloomsbury, 1987

Sinigaglia, Alberto, *Vent'anni al Duemila*, Turin: Eri, 1982

Smith, Denis Mack, *Mussolini*, London: Weidenfeld & Nicolson, 1981

Soldati, Mario, *The Malacca Cane*, London: André Deutsch, 1973

Solmi, Sergio and Fruttero, Carlo (eds), *Le meraviglie del possibile*, Turin: Einaudi, 1959

Spriano, Paolo, *Le passioni di un decennio 1946–1956*, Milan: Garzanti, 1986

Squarotti, Giorgio Bárberi, *Le colline, i maestri, gli dei*, Treviso: Santi Quaranta, 1992

Steinberg, Jonathan, *All or Nothing: The Axis and the Holocaust 1941–1943*, London: Routledge, 1990

Steinberg, Paul, *Chroniques d'ailleurs*, Paris: Éditions Ramsay, 1996

Stern, Mario Rigoni, *Amore di confine*, Turin: Einaudi, 1986

—— *L'anno della vittoria*, Turin: Einaudi, 1985

—— *La storia di Tönle*, Turin: Einaudi, 1978

—— *Quota Albania*, Turin: Einaudi, 1971

—— *Il bosco degli urogalli*, Turin: Einaudi, 1970

—— *Il sergente nella neve*, Turin: Einaudi, 1953

Stille, Alexander, *Benevolence and Betrayal: Five Italian Jewish Families Under Fascism*, London: Jonathan Cape, 1992

Stone, Norman, *Hitler*, London: Hodder & Stoughton, 1980

Styron, William, *Darkness Visible*, London: Jonathan Cape, 1991

Svevo, Livia Veneziani, *Memoir of Italo Svevo*, London: Libris, 1989

Svoray, Yaron and Taylor, Nick, *In Hitler's Shadow*, London: Constable, 1995

Tamburini, Luciano, *I teatri di Torino*, Turin: Albero, 1966

Tannenbaum, Edward R., *Fascism in Italy: Society and Culture 1922–45*, New York: Basic Books, 1972

Tedesci, Giuliana, *Questo povero corpo*, Milan: Editrice Italiana, 1946

Terracini, Benedetto (ed.), *La fabbrica del cancro: L'IPCA di Ciriè*, Turin: Einaudi, 1976

Thomson, Ian, *Southern Italy*, London: Collins, 1989

Todorov, Tzvetan, *Facing the Extreme*, London: Weidenfeld & Nicolson, 1999

Tomasi, Tina, *Idealismo e Fascismo nella scuola italiana*, Florence: La Nuova Italia, 1969

Tomizza, Fulvio, *Destino di frontiera*, Genoa: Marietti, 1992

—— *La miglior vita*, Milan: Rizzoli, 1977

—— *Materada*, Milan: Mondadori, 1960

Turi, Gabriele, *Casa Einaudi: Libri uomini idee oltre il fascismo*, Milan: il Mulino, 1990

Vacca, Roberto, *Il medioevo prossimo venturo*, Milan: Mondadori, 1971

Vasari, Bruno, *Mauthausen bivacco della morte*, Florence: Giuntina, 1991 (reprint)

—— *A ciascuno il suo*, Rome: Quaderni della FIAP, 1987

Vassalli, Sebastiano, *Night of the Comet*, Manchester: Carcanet, 1989

Viallet, Jean-Pierre, *La chiesa valdese di fronte allo stato fascista*, Turin: Claudiana, 1985

Vidal-Naquet, Pierre, *Assassins of Memory*, New York: Columbia University Press, 1992

Viglongo, Andrea, *Conoscere il piemontese*, Turin: A.Viglongo, 1980

Vittorini, Elio, *Diario in pubblico*, Milan: Bompiani, 1957

Voghera, Giorgio, *Anni di Trieste*, Gorizia: Editrice Goriziana, 1989

Volponi, Paolo, *Le mosche del capitale*, Turin: Einaudi, 1989

Wheatcroft, Geoffrey, *The Controversy of Zion: How Zionism Tried to Resolve the Jewish Question*, London: Sinclair-Stevenson, 1996

Wiesenthal, Simon, *The Sunflower*, London: W. H. Allen, 1970

Wilhelm, Maria de Blasio, *The Other Italy: The Italian Resistance in World War II*, New York: W.W. Norton, 1988

Wilkinson, James D., *The Intellectual Resistance in Europe*, Harvard University Press, 1981

Woodhouse, John, *Gabriele D'Annunzio: Defiant Angel*, Oxford: Clarendon Press, 1998

Zargani, Aldo, *Per violino solo: La mia infanzia nell'Aldiqua 1938–1945*, Bologna: il Mulino, 1995

Zilahy, Lajos, *Two Prisoners*, London: William Heinemann, 1931

Zorzi, Renzo, *Gli anni dell'amicizia*, Vicenza: Neri Pozza, 1991

Zuccotti, Susan, *The Italians and the Holocaust: Persecution, Rescue and Survival*, London: Peter Halban, 1987

INDEX

607

625